Christopher Hale is an award-winning writer and producer who was educated at Sussex University and the Slade School of Fine Art. He has made numerous films about the sciences and arts for all the major broadcasters, including the BBC. He has filmed and travelled in unmapped regions of Mozambique and the Yemen in search of a 'lost tribe of Israel' – as well as in previously unexplored parts of Borneo and on one of the remotest islands in the Pacific. He lives in London and New York.

www.booksattransworld.co.uk

HIMMLER'S CRUSADE

THE TRUE STORY OF THE 1938 NAZI EXPEDITION INTO TIBET

CHRISTOPHER HALE

BANTAM BOOKS

LONDON • TORONTO • SYDNEY • AUCKLAND • JOHANNESBURG

HIMMLER'S CRUSADE
A BANTAM BOOK: 0 553 81445 1

Originally published in Great Britain by Bantam Press,
a division of Transworld Publishers

PRINTING HISTORY
Bantam Press edition published 2003
Bantam edition published 2004

1 3 5 7 9 10 8 6 4 2

Set in 11/13pt Ehrhardt by
Falcon Oast Graphic Art Ltd.

Bantam Books are published by Transworld Publishers,
61–63 Uxbridge Road, London W5 5SA,
a division of The Random House Group Ltd,
in Australia by Random House Australia (Pty) Ltd,
20 Alfred Street, Milsons Point, Sydney, NSW 2061, Australia,
in New Zealand by Random House New Zealand Ltd,
18 Poland Road, Glenfield, Auckland 10, New Zealand
and in South Africa by Random House (Pty) Ltd,
Endulini, 5a Jubilee Road, Parktown 2193, South Africa.

Printed and bound in Great Britain by
Cox & Wyman Ltd, Reading, Berkshire.

Papers used by Transworld Publishers are natural, recyclable products made from wood grown in sustainable forests. The manufacturing processes conform to the environmental regulations of the country of origin.

To Alice and Felix

CONTENTS

Acknowledgements 9
Photograph acknowledgements 13
Maps 18

Prelude: Appointment in Berlin 25
Introduction: Secret Tibet 35

PART 1: FOOTHILLS
1 Call of the Wild 69
2 Edge of the World 103
3 Grand Inquisitor 122
4 The People Hunter 141
5 Return to the Fatherland 172

PART 2: PEAKS
6 Confronting the Raj 203
7 Trapped 228
8 Breakout 274
9 On the Roof of the World 300
10 Weird Barbarity 338
11 The White Scarves 366
12 Escape from the Raj 408

PART 3: VALLEYS

13	The Devil's Scientist	431
14	The Castle	460
15	Race Warrior	484
16	The Savage Mind	501
17	Retribution	520
18	Aftermaths	529
	Notes	540
	Select Bibliography	560
	Index	573

ACKNOWLEDGEMENTS

Any book, and especially a first one, arrives loaded with a tremendous cargo of debt. Here is a brief summary of the main ones. I must begin by thanking Deborah West Denno who convinced me that I could write the book you hold in your hands and provided consistent and stimulating encouragement throughout its gestation. Professor Steve Jones generously introduced me to his – and now my – literary agent Peter Robinson who provided expert guidance and support. Adam Sisman was also a font of writing wisdom. Doug Young in London and Hana Lane in New York were attentive editors and enthusiastic publishers.

I also much to my former colleagues at the BBC, John Lynch and Bettina Lerner, despite some differences over the years. They commissioned a film about the 'myth of Atlantis' for the BBC's flagship *Horizon* programme and, in the course of researching this now notorious film with terrific colleagues Jacquelines Smith and Laughton and Julian Hudson, I first learnt about the SS Expedition to Tibet. At SOAS in London, Alex McKay was consistently generous with ideas and leads – and set me right on many points. Roger Croston, an exceptionally erudite enthusiast about all things Tibetan, had been corresponding with Bruno Beger, the last surviving European member of the Schäfer Expedition. Beger had been convicted by a Frankfurt court as an 'accomplice to murder' in 1971 for reasons that are explained in detail in the last part of this book. While I was researching the films for *Horizon*, I was unable to obtain an interview with Beger – but Mr Croston was able to secure a number of meetings on my behalf in the autumn of 2001. Dr Isrun Engelhardt, the foremost authority on Ernst Schäfer, the zoologist who led the expedition, provided me with extracts from her heroic decipherment of Schäfer's barely readable expedition Diaries. Peter Longerich discussed his current work on Heinrich Himmler. In Germany, Dr Helmut Starrach and Dr Heinz-Georg Klös talked to me about Ernst Schäfer as a friend and colleague – but chose not to discuss his experiences during the war.

In the United States, Andrew Zimmerman provided authoritative guidance on the history of German anthropology and answered my very frequent queries. In Philadelphia the staff in the library of the Academy of Natural Sciences was consistently supportive. In New York, Hope Cook, the former wife of the late Chogyal of Sikkim, provided wisdom and all kinds of contacts. Jacqueline Hiltz shared her knowledge of Sikkim and its history, pointed me towards the Sikkim National Archives in Gangtok and sent me her notes on the material held in the Archives concerning Schäfer's friend Kaiser Thapa. In Sikkim itself, I have to thank Anna Balikci, 'German' Akeh Bhutia, Taj Thapa, T. W. Barphungpa, Jigme Dorje Denjongpa, Keshab and Sailesh Pradhan, Kelsang Gyatso and the many others who guided me as I tried to follow Schäfer's route beyond Gangtok. Jai Shree Pradham assisted me in the Archives in Gangtok. In Tibet I am indebted above all to Gyurme Dorje while in London a number of people assisted me with different puzzles and conundrums including Thierry Dodin at the Tibet Information Network.

Anyone researching in this field will inevitably come to rely on the following authors: Karl Meyer and Shareen Brysac who provided advice and assistance, and whose book *Tournament of Shadows* is an enthralling account of the Great Game and has a chapter on Schäfer. Peter Hopkirk's several books on the same subject were essential reading as were Nicholas Goodrick-Clark's *The Occult Roots of Nazism* and *Black Sun*. Melvyn Goldstein answered some of my most obscure questions and no account of Tibet in the twentieth century can afford to ignore his *A History of Modern Tibet*. Alex McKay's *Tibet and the British Raj* and Patrick French's book about Sir Francis Younghusband were both equally important as reservoirs of ideas and information. Simon Winchester's book about the Yangtze *The River at the End of the World* allowed me to 'see' and better understand a part of the world I could not visit. Other important sources were Ian Kershaw's two-volume biography of Hitler and the magisterial books by Deborah Dwork and Robert Jan Van Pelt on the Holocaust. My debt to all these authors is considerable and I hope they will forgive me for not footnoting every reference.

The bibliography on Nazism, the Second World War and the Holocaust is, of course, vast in English and German. The Schäfer Expedition itself left behind a tremendous quantity of documentation which few had examined let alone translated. To tell the story that follows, I needed to work across a Himalaya of German documents – and I would like to thank, especially, Diana Jasmin Böhmer, who waded through Ernst Schäfer's rather turgid narratives and answered endless questions about the precise interpretation of numerous other documents with an unquenchable supply of good humour, intelligence and commitment. Sabine Pusch, Ingrid Büchner, Michael Kolodziej and, in particular, Ruth Mulandi provided invaluable help and advice with other materials.

In Germany, Wolf Gebhardt guided me through the labyrinth of the Bundesarchiv in Berlin and the dedicated and courteous staff of the extraordinary Instit für Zeitgesichte in Munich gave me access to parts of Bruno Beger's trial record. In Koblenz, Berit Pistora made the task of examining the many thousands of prints and negatives taken by expedition members a pleasure. The staff of the National Archives in Washington, DC introduced me to their remarkable collections of captured German documents. In the same city, academic staff at the Holocaust Museum provided me with important and disturbing information about the transports from Berlin to Auschwitz in the spring of 1943 and Madelaine Matz in the Library of Congress showed me the rushes of Schäfer's film *Geheimnis Tibet* which had been taken to Washington at the end of the Second World War. Lawrence Fleischer was an enthusiastic source of even the most obscure of references and sources.

I must acknowledge a special debt to the staff at the Oriental and India Office in the British Library – and the London Library was as ever inspirational. The Public Record Office in Kew provided superbly transparent access to its collections. The New York Public Library proved to be a magnificent – and free – resource. John Lundquist in the Oriental Division was exceptionally helpful. In London, the Library of the School of Oriental and African Studies has one of the world's great collections of which I made frequent use.

Dan Balado struggled with a very long text, and some last minute alterations, with tremendous skill and tolerance. Sheila Lee used the expedition photographs to help create a beautiful book.

I am grateful to all those cited above but I take full responsibility for my interpretation of the records and information they so generously shared. Any errors are mine and mine alone.

Finally, my children Felix and Alice saw very little of me during the time I was writing the book, and I dedicate it to both of them.

Christopher Hale
London, March 2003

PHOTOGRAPH ACKNOWLEDGEMENTS

[BK = Bundesarchiv Koblenz; BL = British Library]

First picture section
Schäfer with camera: (BK) 135/KB/14/082

Beger as student: courtesy Bruno Beger; Himmler in 1933: AKG; Himmler at Wewelsburg and view of Wewelsburg: from *Heinrich Himmler's Camelot* by Stephen Cook & Stuart Russell, 1999

Schäfer with panda: from E. Schäfer, *Berge, Buddhas und Bären*, 1933; with bears: from E. Schäfer, *Dach der Erde*, 1938; Wang and Brooke Dolan: from E. Schäfer, *Unbekannte Tibet*, 1937; King of Muli: from E. Schäfer, *Berge, Buddhas und Bären*, 1933; Panchen Lama: (BK)

Beger, March 1938: courtesy Bruno Beger; Krause: (BK) 616 15-57 B; Geer: (BK) 135/KB/14/100; Wienert: (BK) 135/KB/15/058; Weinert and Beger: (BK); arrival in Calcutta: (BK) 135/KA/01//035

Dekyilinka: by permission of the BL – photo 1043/312; Gould: by permission of the BL – photo 1043/329; Gould with Tibetan official: by permission of the BL – photo 1043/5

Second picture section
Expedition with Maharaja of Sikkim: (BK) 135/KA/01/051

Kaiser: (BK) Krause 16-38; Geer and Kraus: (BK) 135/S/05/02–36; expedition in the field: (BK) 135/S/04/08/18; Beger measuring: (BK) 135/KB/15-081 and 135/KB/15/083; camp in Sikkim: (BK)

Tering Raja and wife: by permission of the BL – photo 1043/5; minister of Tering: (BK) 135/KB/11/083; Schäfer in extremis: (BK) 135/Sch/N11/10/22; shapi hunt: (BK) 135/Sch.N8/9/13; sneezing in snow: (BK) 135/5/8/12/4; dead shapi: from E. Schäfer, *Geheimnis Tibet*, 1943.

Crossing the pass: (BK) 135/Sch./N7/7/33; around the fire: (BK) 135/KA/03/100; Kaiser riding: from E. Schäfer, *Geheimnis Tibet*, 1943; Wienert at work: (BK) Kr. 616/15/-18; Akeh: (BK) Sch.6-22-24; Dzongpon's wife: (BK) 135/S/11/15/15

Krause filming: (BK) 135/S/6.17/9A

Third picture section
The Regent: (BK)

Möndro: (BK) 135/S/13/02/14; Tsarong: (BK); 13th Dalai Lama: Pitt Rivers Museum, University of Oxford SC.T. 2. 626; 14th Dalai Lama: Pitt Rivers Museum, University of Oxford SC.T. 2.630; Beger tending sick: (BK) 135/S/12/06/35; expedition outside Lhasa: (BK)

Potala Palace; Phari; Tibetan aristocrat; border stones: all from *Geheimnis Tibet*

Expedition with Gould: © B. J. Gould archive; expedition at table with Tibetans: (BK) 135/KA/10/012; Regent with Beger: (BK) 135/-13-11-14A; dog: (BK) 135/Schäfer N15/U1/36; sky burial: (BK)

Yumbu Lagang: from *Geheimnis Tibet*

Fourth picture section
At Quedlinburg Cathedral, 1938: AKG; Wiligut: from *Heinrich Himmler's Camelot* by Stephen Cook & Stuart Russell, 1999; Schäfer and Krause: (BK) 146/2003/6/1A

Rascher experimenting: Ullsteinbild; Natzweiler-Struthof: Photos 12; Himmler visiting Dachau: AKG; Clauss: Ullsteinbild; Kramer: © Bettmann/CORBIS

Brooke Dolan: © National Geographic Society; Schäfer: author's collection; all other images by Christopher Hale.

Deeds white and black, for minds are clean and foul.
Is the mind clean? Then earth and sky are clean.
Is the mind foul? Then earth and sky are foul.
For it is upon the mind that all depends.

– Tibetan proverb, quoted by Charles Bell

'German science must become fighting science.'

– Gerd Tellenbach in *Der Führer*, 1936

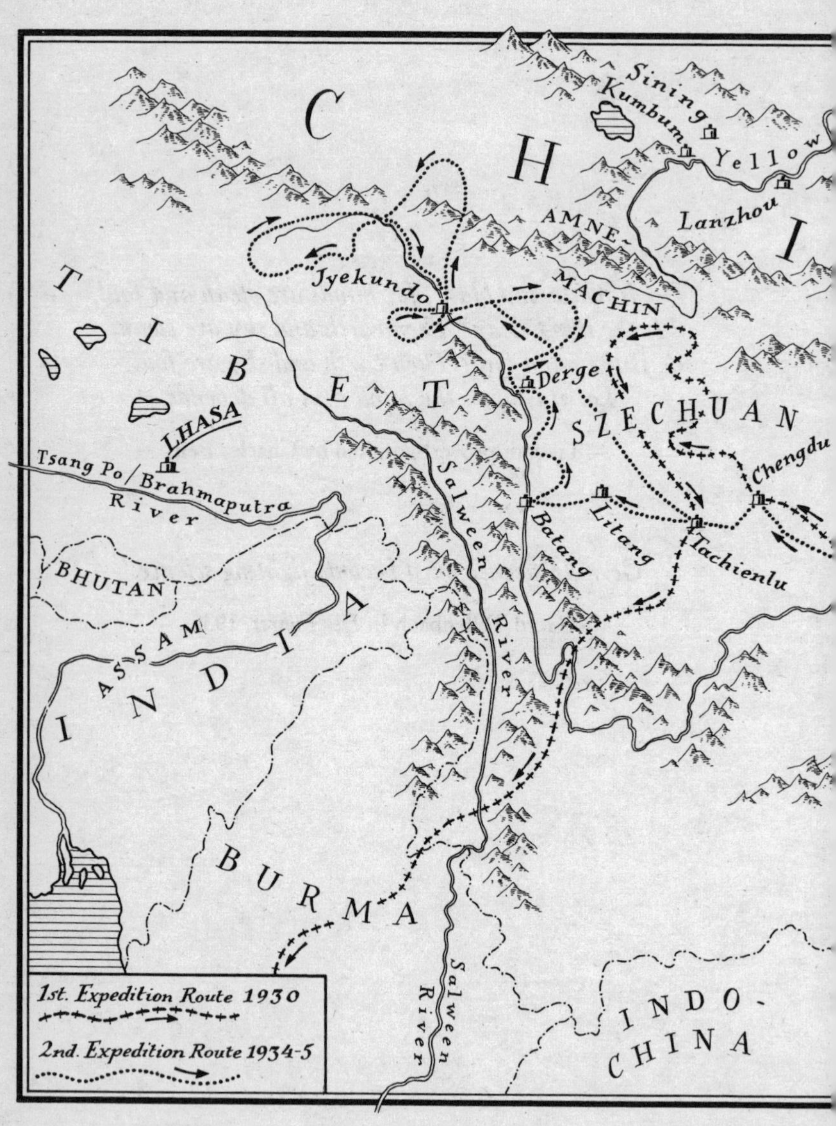

C H I
Sining
Kumbum
Yellow
Lanzhou
AMNE-
MACHIN
T I B E T
Jyekundo
Derge
SZECHUAN
Chengdu
LHASA
Tsang Po/Brahmaputra
River
Salween River
Batang
Litang
Tachienlu
BHUTAN
ASSAM
INDIA
BURMA
Salween River
INDO-
CHINA
1st. Expedition Route 1930
2nd. Expedition Route 1934-5

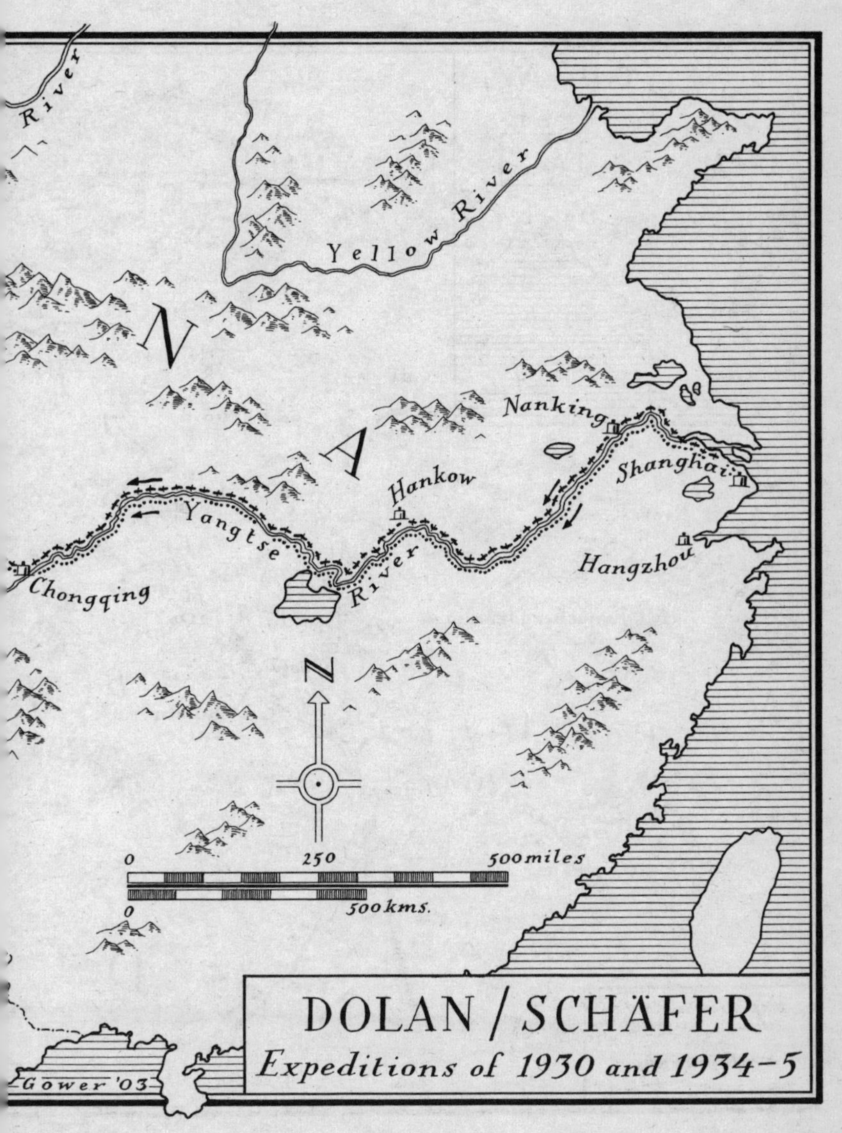
River
Yellow River
N
A
Nanking
Hankow
Shanghai
Yangtse
River
Chongqing
Hangzhou
N
0
250
500miles
0
500kms.
DOLAN / SCHÄFER
Expeditions of 1930 and 1934–5
Gower '03

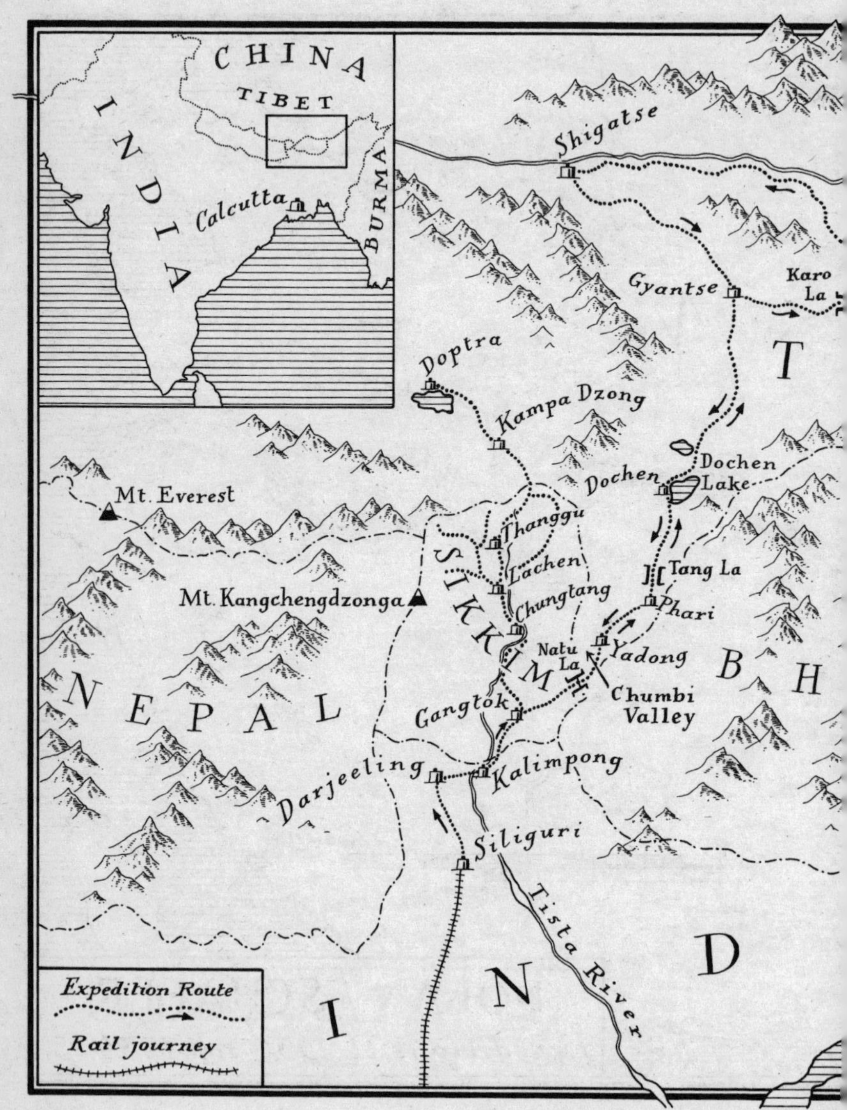

CHINA
TIBET
INDIA
BURMA
Calcutta
Shigatse
Gyantse
Karo La
Doptra
Kampa Dzong
Dochen
Dochen Lake
Mt. Everest
Thanggu
Lachen
Tang La
Mt. Kangchengdzonga
Chungtang
Phari
SIKKIM
Natu La
Yadong
Chumbi Valley
NEPAL
Gangtok
Darjeeling
Kalimpong
Siliguri
Tista River
Expedition Route
Rail journey
T
B
H
I
N
D

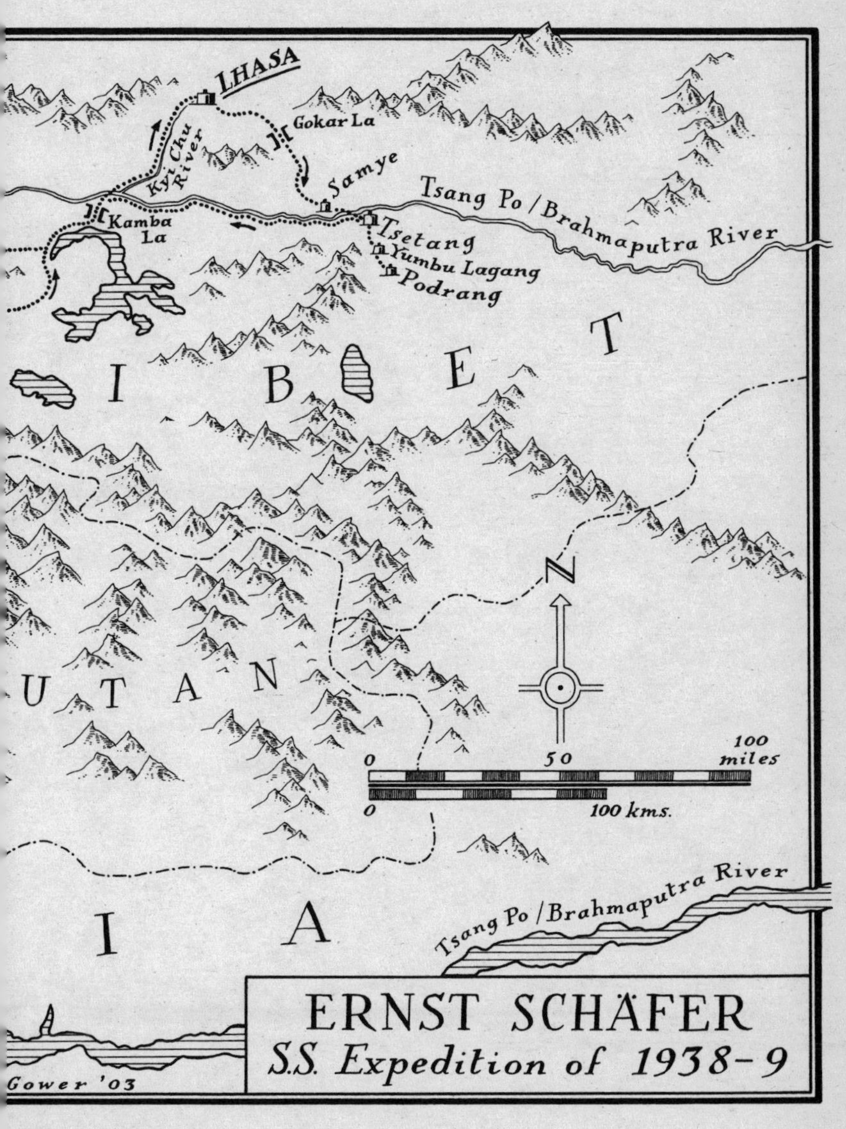

ERNST SCHÄFER
S.S. Expedition of 1938–9

HIMMLER'S CRUSADE

PRELUDE

APPOINTMENT IN BERLIN

'If the fate [of the Nazis] lay in my hands . . . I would have all the intellectuals strung up, and the professors three feet higher than the rest; they would be left hanging from the lamp-posts for as long as was compatible with hygiene.'

– German-Jewish diarist Victor Klemperer, writing in August 1936

At the beginning of 1939, Adolf Hitler unveiled his new Reichs Chancellery building in Berlin. It had been designed and built by the Führer's protégé Albert Speer with ruthless speed, and completed, as Hitler had demanded, in less than a year. Speer promised that the new building would last a millennium, at least. Hitler was very clear about what the Chancellery had to achieve. Anyone who stepped through its soaring marble portals and gazed along its gleaming, interminable marble corridors would understand instantly that they were in the presence of a Master Race destined to rule for a thousand years. Knowing that, Hitler said, they would 'shiver and shake'. A mere six years later, the Chancellery lay in ruins; Hitler's own charred remains smouldered nearby. Just as its millions of victims had, in Paul Celan's words, 'risen to the air as smoke', the Third Reich was rubble and ashes. The *Tausend-Jahr-Reich* had lasted a mere twelve years and three months.

At the beginning of another century, the leaden sky over Berlin is backdrop to a steel forest of cranes. Beneath their restlessly signalling arms, a new German capital is being conjured from concrete, marble, glass and steel. Glittering new façades ripple down Friedrichstrasse and Unter den Linden. Cherished monuments from better times before Hitler are lovingly restored, even rebuilt. The old, divided Berlin of the Cold War with its fractured topography is slowly and surely being smoothed and soothed away.

There are places in Berlin that stubbornly resist this crossing out, where memory still clings to walls and burrows beneath rubble or lurks in forgotten cellars. There is, for example, Tiergartenstrasse 4 where Hitler's *Schreibtischtäter* – 'desk-bound criminals' – deliberated on the killing of mental patients and other 'lives not worthy of life'. And hidden in trees behind Berlin's thronging lakeside pleasure beaches is Am Grossen Wannsee 56–58, the gracious villa where Adolf Eichmann and his SS bureaucrats discussed the practical details of how to murder six million people.

Another such place exists in the old heart of Berlin. It is a great slab of real estate ringed by wire fences. Inside is a pyramid of broken rubble and weeds. Acres of yellowing and ragged grass spread from its base. On the edge are trees, survivors from an old garden. Behind frayed trunks and dusty leaves are broken walls and cairns of charred masonry. This obstinate urban desert occupies an entire city block on Niederkirchnerstrasse, close to the looming granite hulk of Hermann Göring's old Luftwaffe headquarters. Berliners know this unlovely place as the 'Topography of Terror'. Before 1945, and the destruction of Hitler's Reich, Niederkirchnerstrasse had another name. Then it was called Prinz-Albrecht-Strasse, and number 8 was the most feared address in Nazi Germany.

Prinz-Albrecht-Strasse 8 was a magnificent baroque palace. Prussia's greatest architect, Karl Friedrich Schinkel, who believed that architecture should serve the cause of human reason, had designed its elegant interiors and sweeping cast-iron stairs. After 1933, Schinkel's resplendent palace had been appropriated for new purposes. In its offices and corridors, bureaucrats in perfectly tailored black uniforms adorned with silver death's-head insignia scurried from office to meeting and back again to do the bidding of the second most powerful man in the Nazi elite: the Reichsführer, Heinrich Himmler. All of these bright, well-turned-out young men were in the business of terror.

Himmler wanted his SS to be 'an aristocracy that never [grew] old'. They had to be 'the best physically, the most dependable, the most faithful men in the movement'. They were the new Teutonic Knights dedicated to *Herrenbewusstsein* (master consciousness) and *Elitebewusstsein* (elite consciousness). Every one of Himmler's Black Knights had been stringently vetted by white-coated laboratory technicians wielding callipers and measuring tape – and now they could work and act, above the law, to serve and protect the Aryan Master Race and crush its enemies.

One morning in the summer of 1936, a young SS Untersturmführer, Ernst Schäfer, emerged from the entrance of Hohenzollerndam 36 in Berlin's fashionable Wilmersdorf district, crossed the street and caught the S-Bahn to Potsdamerplatz. Outside the station he pushed his way through the surging crowds to the street. Here he waited impatiently for the famous traffic light to change, then strode across dodging the honking cars and swiftly moving through the knots of people clustered around the teeming intersection. Then Ernst Schäfer headed off past the Ethnological Museum towards Prinz-Albrecht-Strasse where he had an appointment with the Reichsführer.

Schäfer had been away from Germany a long time and Berlin still surprised him with its prosperity and optimism. Shops were full of most imaginable luxuries, and every night Berliners flocked in their thousands to cinemas, dance halls and theatres. Once feared and despised, Germany's dictator Adolf Hitler was riding a wave of adulation. In March, he had ordered his troops to reclaim the Rhineland for Germany, and many admired his daring. After the long-drawn-out humiliation of Versailles, Germans were rediscovering the thrill of national pride. Unemployment had fallen and there were abundant signs of prosperity. New organizations like 'Strength through Joy' sponsored holidays and cruises for the loyal and hard-working. Even liberal Germans had somehow been persuaded that vicious attacks on Jews and political opponents were becoming less ferocious. In an election held that year, the Nazis had won 98.9 per cent of the vote – which was not especially surprising since they were the only party permitted to stand.

It was all a sham, a mask to hide tyranny and murder. In the summer of 1936, as Ernst Schäfer marched towards Prinz-Albrecht-Strasse 8, it was very important that Germany looked its best. In August, Berlin would host the Olympic Games, and many thousands of visitors would be here – and taking a tough look at Hitler's New Order. All over the city there was a frenzy of building work and renovation. A new stadium had been thrown up in record time. Hemlines were higher. More than seven thousand prostitutes had been permitted to return to the streets. New lime trees were being planted in Unter den Linden. And with stunning cynicism, signs forbidding Jews to enter cities or public spaces had been hurriedly torn down and prisoners released from Himmler's concentration camps. It was a whitewash of monumental proportions, but it worked. It would have impressed an ambitious young man who had not seen the Fatherland for more than two years.

Although he was only twenty-six, Schäfer had already enjoyed a most unusual and plucky career. He was a fanatical hunter and naturalist and had taken part in two ambitious American-led expeditions to China and the perilous eastern borders of Tibet. He was a crack shot and had, in the name of science, cut a swathe of destruction through the fauna of these remote and hazardous regions. On his return to Germany, soon after the Nazi victory in 1933, Schäfer had eagerly joined Himmler's elite SS and had been rapidly promoted. Then he had left Germany again, this time for an even longer period. Despite – perhaps because of – his globetrotting, Schäfer had yet to complete his academic studies. He was now hard at work cataloguing his collection of Tibetan birds so that he could acquire his all-important *Doktortitel* (the equivalent of a Ph.D.). Hundreds of their skins littered his desk. Fiercely ambitious and energetic, Schäfer had, however, already started publishing. His first book, *Mountains, Buddhas and Bears*, was brewed from light science mixed with hunting yarns and wordy descriptions of a mysterious faraway world. Its success had already given him a taste of modest celebrity. Schäfer had certainly attracted the attention of the Nazi elite: he shared a passion for hunting with the Reichsmarschall, Hermann Göring. And now, he hoped, Heinrich Himmler was about to add more lustre to his career.

Schäfer paused for a moment to admire the baroque splendour of Prinz-Albrecht-Strasse 8. There were not many pedestrians lingering there, and it is unlikely that the few who passed quickly by would have recognized this dapper young man as the grizzled author of *Mountains, Buddhas and Bears*. In the wilds of the Tibetan badlands, Schäfer had looked every inch the fearless hunter – a German Teddy Roosevelt, his youth masked by a full beard, clasping the stock of his Mauser rifle with its lethal telescopic sight and proudly cradling beneath his arm a trophy culled from the thick bamboo forests of Kham: a dead panda, only the second to be shot in the wild. As he stood on the steps of the SS headquarters, Schäfer, bereft of beard and gun, seemed just another callow, eager youth. His features, under a shorn crop of dark hair, were not especially distinguished and his build not quite that of an Aryan warrior. More perceptive observers would have noted the obstinate gleam in his eyes and the pugnacity of his stance: Ernst Schäfer was very definitely used to getting his own way and knew what the *Führer prinzip* meant in practice. After a few moments' hesitation, he entered the SS headquarters and was escorted up Schinkel's elegant iron staircase. For Schäfer, what followed would be transforming.

Accounts of meetings with the Reichsführer have an unusual consistency. After passing the cordon of tall, blue-eyed, black-clad SS bodyguards, privileged visitors were ushered into Himmler's unexpectedly drab and poky offices. Few would be unaware that in cells excavated deep beneath them enemies of the Reich were being tortured on the orders of the modest, professorial man they were about to meet and few failed to comment on Himmler's unassuming physical attributes. 'To outward appearance', said one, he was 'a grotesque caricature of his own laws, norms and ideals'; to another he seemed 'mild-looking, mild-mannered, rather self effacing . . . His very indefinite features and his glasses make him look rather insignificant . . .' According to some he was the acme of charm and modesty; for others he radiated a warm, paternalist care.

It was an illusion, of course, a triumph of the will. Behind the pince-nez, usually held askance so that a gleaming reflection hid what lay behind, were eyes without mercy that could patiently examine, for hour after hour, lists of names or photographs of SS applicants, searching for any indication of racial inferiority. Henrich Himmler was fixated by secrets and plots, imagined and real, and would become the most implacable and lethal 'desk criminal' in the Third Reich.

The Reichsführer had by 1936 acquired colossal power. He was Hitler's '*treuer Heinrich*', the loyal and devoted chief of the German police, with complete mastery of every police department in the Reich. He and his loyal officers were rulers of a new empire of concentration camps which they ruthlessly filled and exploited. Himmler was also using his new powers to indulge some decidedly odd passions. He had recently founded the Ahnenerbe, meaning 'Ancestral Heritage', to promote the glory of the Aryan race. He shared at least one passion with Ernst Schäfer. Himmler had modelled the SS on a Hindu warrior caste and was fascinated by the East and its religions. He hated Christianity and carried a pocket book in which he had collected homilies from the Hindu *Bhagavadgītā* ('Song of the Lord'). To the unimpressive little man who sat inside the poisonous spider's web of the SS, Ernst Schäfer was an emissary from another mysterious and thrilling world.

The Reichsführer looked up as the man he had summoned to his lair was announced. He leant across his orderly, paper-strewn desk to shake his visitor's hand, and asked his adjutant to close the door.

There is no record of the conversation that took place between Heinrich Himmler and Ernst Schäfer that day in the Olympic summer of 1936, but what was said changed Schäfer's life for ever. We do know that this meeting began a close, frequently tense and sometimes argumentative friendship. There are other clues about what took place and what was discussed in documents held by the United States National

Archives in Washington. In the summer of 1945, Schäfer was captured in Munich by the Allies as they swept through Bavaria, the old Nazi stronghold. Because he was an officer in a 'criminal organization', the SS, he, like more than ten thousand other Germans, would now endure 'de-nazification'. Schäfer was interned for three long, uncomfortable years in Camp Moosburg (formerly POW Camp Stalag VII). He had to fight hard to get his *Persilschein*, the much-coveted certificate of exoneration. Now, for the benefit of his American interrogators, he had nothing but contempt for Himmler. When they met, Schäfer recalled, Himmler had disclosed a few of his more original convictions. The Aryan race, he believed, had descended directly and fully formed 'from heaven'. Races of giants had once roamed the earth. The universe had been formed from a cosmic battle between fire and ice. Schäfer told his interrogators that he had thought such ideas were absurd, laughable. It would have been impossible, he implied, for a hard-headed scientist such as himself to have admired a man like that.

Schäfer was, naturally, being disingenuous. For him, intellectual fastidiousness never hardened into rebellion. And there was a good reason. At some point during their conversation, Himmler must have asked Schäfer about his plans for the future. It must have been the opportunity Schäfer had hoped for. This, after all, was why he had come to the Reichsführer's sett. It is certain that Schäfer revealed his plan for a new expedition to Tibet, this time under the German flag with men of his own blood. He would have explained that, at this stage, there were a number of exciting possibilities. There was Amne Machin, the mysterious mountain in eastern Tibet that Schäfer had glimpsed on his last expedition which some said was as high as Everest and so far unconquered. Further south, Assam was largely unexplored, its wild and dangerous tribes unknown to science. And he is very likely to have reminded Himmler that Sven Hedin, the celebrated Swedish explorer who was a frequent and admiring visitor to Nazi Germany, had failed to reach Lhasa, the 'Forbidden City' of Tibet. Hedin had called it the city of his dreams. Lhasa, surely, could become much more than a dream – indeed, the jewel in the crown of German exploration. Schäfer was always persuasive, whether he was talking to a Chinese warlord, the Panchen Lama or the Reichsführer, and that morning in 1936 he must have thrilled Himmler with his stories about the icy world of the Himalayas and the secrets that lay beyond its frozen ramparts. It was an expert seduction, and Himmler eagerly proposed that Schäfer join forces with the Ahnenerbe, which was also planning expeditions to Afghanistan and Iceland. To be sure, a 'German Tibet Expedition' would have his blessing.

There is a photograph of Ernst Schäfer taken not long before he died in 1992. His eyes are withdrawn and hurt; his jaw juts defensively. To his persistent and well-informed interrogators at Camp Moosburg, Schäfer did his best to present himself as an unwilling recruit to the SS. He had even seriously considered exile in the United States. Like many others drawn into the world of the Reichsführer, Schäfer might indeed have experienced some moral discomfort. But by becoming one of Himmler's favourites – even if, as it would turn out, an unruly one – he had taken a decisive step. It was one that would make him a hero of the Reich – and then, when it was destroyed, an outcast.

In the wild, Schäfer had a favourite book. He read it night after night, under hissing kerosene lamps, in the freezing wilderness of Tibet. The book was Goethe's *Faust*. It is presumptuous to try to imagine Schäfer's thoughts as he walked away from Prinz-Albrecht-Strasse 8 and back into the sunlight and crowds to return to the dead birds strewn across his desk. But we can be certain that, like so many other scientists, doctors, lawyers and artists, Schäfer understood that Himmler had offered him something rare and precious. He could become part of an elite – and it promised him a great deal. He might have remembered the words Mephistopheles says to Faust: 'Sublime good fortune greets you now . . . The whole world lies in your embrace.' It is rather less likely that he would have reflected on the implications of Faust's speech a few pages later:

How logical and clear the daylight seems
Till the night weaves us in its web of dreams!
As we return from dewy fields, dusk falls
And birds of mischief croak their ominous calls.
All round us lurks this superstition's snare;
Some haunting, half-seen thing cries out Beware.[1]

INTRODUCTION

SECRET TIBET

'. . . it looked to Conway a delightfully favoured place, though if it were inhabited its community must be completely isolated by the lofty and sheerly unscalable ranges on the further side.'

– James Hilton, *Lost Horizon*, 1933

At the beginning of January 1939, five Europeans with a caravan of servants and muleteers approached Lhasa, the Holy City of Tibet. They had travelled across the Himalayas from Sikkim, a tiny kingdom in northern India, and would spend the next eight months in Tibet. They did research which mystified the Tibetans, and occasionally hunted. They took more than 60,000 photographs and exposed more than 120,000 feet of movie film. At a time when Tibet awaited the arrival of a new Dalai Lama, the five Europeans formed close, sometimes intimate friendships with Tibetan nobles and religious leaders, including the Regent. They clashed frequently with the British Mission officer stationed in Lhasa who had tried to prevent their journey and bitterly resented their presence in the 'Forbidden City'. In August 1939, the five men fled south to

Calcutta taking with them 120 volumes of the Tibetan 'Bible', the *Kangyur*, hundreds of precious artefacts and assorted rare animals. At the mouth of the Hoogli River, they boarded a sea-plane and began the long journey home – first to Baghdad, then to Berlin. Home for the five Europeans was Nazi Germany. When their aircraft touched down at Tempelhof Airport an ecstatic Heinrich Himmler was waiting on the runway. For the Reichsführer, the 'German Tibet Expedition' had been a triumph.

At the end of August, the SS stage-managed a series of provocations on the Polish border. On 1 September, Hitler ordered his generals to attack. Fifty German divisions smashed the Polish defences from three sides: the Second World War had begun. The five men who had returned in triumph from Tibet now became combatants in an imperialist and genocidal war. What could link an expedition to central Asia with the global catastrophe unleashed by Adolf Hitler in 1939? Few historians have even troubled to ask the question.[1] But the true story of this little expedition, told for the first time in this book, reveals that it was a summit of German imperial and racial fantasy.

From the middle of the nineteenth century, Tibet and its Holy City of Lhasa were closed to foreigners. Both the Tibetans and their powerful neighbour China feared, with good cause, imperial incursions. Despite this, an intrepid handful of explorers succeeded in penetrating the high, icy realm and even its mysterious capital – often in disguise and usually at considerable risk. They returned with astonishing tales which quickly transformed Tibet into the quintessence of the forbidden and exotic. By the 1930s, Tibet had become more accessible but the Himalayan passes remained strictly controlled by both the Tibetan government and the British – nervous masters of the Indian Raj to the south of the Himalayas.

The five Germans who arrived in Lhasa at the beginning of 1939 were rather different from the adventurers and diplomats who had embarked on pilgrimages over the Himalayas before. This would not have been evident, quite deliberately on their part, as they rode through the Barkokali Gate and looked up at the empty palace of the Dalai Lamas, but two days earlier, when the expedition was being ferried across the Tsang Po River, an observer might have glimpsed two rather unusual flags strapped to poles. One was a swastika, an ancient symbol of good fortune which represented the Wheel of Life in Tibet but since 1933 had been the national flag of Nazi Germany. The other showed double 'Sieg' runes: the pagan Germanic letter for victory, the unmistakable and chilling insignia of Heinrich Himmler's SS (from *Schutzstaffeln*, meaning 'protective squads'). Every one of the five German scientists was also an officer in the SS. They had journeyed from Hitler's Germany to the 'roof of the world' under the command of SS Hauptsturmführer Ernst Schäfer. They were the first official German expedition to enter Tibet and reach Lhasa, its holy city.

What were SS scientists sponsored by Heinrich Himmler doing in Tibet as Europe edged towards the precipice of war? Many different explanations have been offered and scores of conflicting stories told. Here are some of them: 'The German expedition to Tibet had as its mission the discovery of a connection between lost Atlantis and the first civilization of Central Asia'; 'Schäfer believed that Tibet was the cradle of mankind, the refuge of an "Aryan root race", where a caste of priests had created a mysterious empire of knowledge, called Shambhala, adorned with the Buddhist wheel of life, the swastika'; 'This small troop delivered to the Dalai Lama a radio transceiver to establish contacts between Lhasa and Berlin'; 'The SS men were magicians, who had forged alliances with the mystic Tibetan cities of Agarthi and Shambhala and had mastered the forces of the living universe'; 'They had mined a secret substance to prolong life and to be used as a superconductor for higher states of conscience'; 'In the ruins of Berlin, a thousand bodies with no identity papers were discovered by the Red Army. They were all Tibetans.'[2]

Every one of these statements is false; some are transparently foolish. In 1939, for instance, the 14th Dalai Lama had yet to be enthroned and Tibet was ruled by a regent. But like a clouded and broken mirror, these fantasies both mask and reflect the true story, which is altogether more remarkable. Its roots are buried deep in the nineteenth century but it unfolded in central Asia on the eve of a world war that was to consume the nations of Europe and the Far East. The final act was played out thousands of miles from the snow-shrouded peaks and plateaus of Tibet in the death camps ruled by the SS. It is, at its core, a story of vaunting ambition and ambivalent retribution.

Although Reichsführer Himmler made only a modest financial donation to its costs, the German Tibet Expedition was a pet project. Himmler has been called the 'Ignatius Loyola of the SS' and 'the architect of the Final Solution', the Nazi plan to make Germany 'Jew free'. His passionately held and deadly 'theories' about race were, in part, corrupted Darwin. As Himmler began a spectacular ascent through the ranks of the Nazi Party, he had tried to earn a living as a breeder of chickens. When in 1933 he and the Nazis took power, he began to apply the lessons of the hutch to the Fatherland itself. The *Herrenvolk*, or Master Race, he believed, must be protected from *minderwertigen*, inferior peoples who could contaminate their pure blood and its qualities: 'The German people, especially German youth, have learned once again to value people racially . . . to look at bodily forms and according to the value or non value of this our God-given body and our God-given blood . . .'[3] 'Bodily forms' were a preoccupation for one member of the German Tibet Expedition, its anthropologist Bruno Beger.

Himmler's racial fantasies were nourished by many malign currents of thought which he promoted through the SS. By 1937, he had become master of a security empire that reached into every part of the Third Reich. He had turned the SS into a national police force, an avaricious business empire and finally a murder machine. Himmler wanted even more. The SS would also be a university for Hitler's New Order. As he refined the instruments of terror and control, the Reichsführer was ever more in thrall to a bewildering multitude of peculiar intellectual hobbies and scientific fads. Himmler sent archaeologists to search for the remains of an ancient Germanic super race. He was fascinated by the lost kingdom of Atlantis and a cranky idea called the 'World Ice Theory'. (In one letter, written in 1940, he requested an urgent investigation: what might be the connections between the lineage of the biblical House of David and the 'records of the kings of Atlantis'? Could the biblical scribes have been mere plagiarists?[4] There is no record of a reply.) He used his empire of concentration camps to pursue experiments with homoeopathy and herbal medicine. He revered the ancient cultures of India and the East, or at least his own weird vision of them.

These were not private enthusiasms, and they were certainly not harmless. Cranky pseudoscience nourished Himmler's own murderous convictions about race and inspired ways of convincing others. At his SS stronghold, Wewelsburg Castle in Westphalia, refurbished by slave labourers procured from a concentration camp that had been specially built nearby, Himmler used ritual and myth to inculcate *Herrenbewusstsein* (master consciousness) in elite members of the SS. Some of these men were aristocrats; many more were academics, lawyers and doctors, the cream of Germany's professional classes. Like

Ernst Schäfer, they were young, impatient, pushy, cutting edge. When they had proved themselves, the Reichsführer sent them forth to do battle with the race enemies of the Reich and rob them of their wealth. The most ruthless would become the CEOs of the death camps. In this strange and terrible world, myths were the building blocks of genocide. They had this power because Himmler's passions were myths that masqueraded as science.

Himmler regarded himself not as the fantasist he was but as a patron of science. He believed that most conventional wisdom was bogus and that his power gave him a unique opportunity to promulgate new thinking. He founded the Ahnenerbe specifically to advance the study of the Aryan (or Nordic or Indo-German) race and its origins.[5] From the Ahnenerbe headquarters in the Berlin suburb of Dahlem, archaeologists were sent hither and yon to unearth the glories of Aryan prehistory. And woe betide them if they failed to uncover the potsherds and trinkets of the *Herrenvolk*. Scientists were set to work to prove that a cosmic battle between fire and ice had brought forth a race of supermen in the distant past. Anthropologists collected the skulls and skeletons of Aryans and made meticulous measurements in search of far-flung ancestors or cousins, and scientific expeditions were despatched to unearth the remnants of long-lost Aryan races, from whom all pure Germans descended. The German Tibet Exhibition was the most ambitious of these quests.

There was a logic behind the fantasy. One German cultural historian put it like this: 'the work of our ancestors . . . represents the great legal brief for territory'.[6] The activities of the Ahnenerbe, as well as legions of art historians, prepared the ground for conquest. With ancestors could come territory and the *Lebensraum* ('living space') that obsessed Hitler. If it could be proved that German blood had contributed to an apparently foreign culture or people, the Wehrmacht could follow. This is perhaps what Reichsmarschall Hermann Göring meant when he said, 'When I hear the word "culture", I cock my Browning' – in other words, culture justified conquest. Himmler's ancestor cult was the mainspring of aggression and scientific expeditions were one way of asserting future territorial rights. This was not a Nazi invention. During the First World War, such expeditions were frequently used as a cover for espionage by Germany.

Ernst Schäfer, who led the German Tibet Expedition, was described by one British diplomat as 'first and foremost always a Nazi and a politician – and almost a priest of Nazism'.[7] The British diplomat Hugh Richardson, who was in Lhasa in 1939, remembered Schäfer as 'an out and out Nazi'. But whatever his political convictions, Schäfer was no crank. He was a fastidious zoologist with a passion for Tibetan birds. The men he selected as fellow expeditionists were just as painstaking, their work equally as rooted in empirical observation. Ernst Krause was a botanist and entomologist; Karl Wienert was a geographer whose task was to measure variations in the earth's magnetic field in the Himalayas; and Bruno Beger was an anthropologist who would spend his time in Tibet measuring the heads and bodies of its people.

Here, then, is the first big puzzle: what did Himmler want from a zoologist, a geographer and an anthropologist? This leads to another, even more troubling mystery: what did *they* want from him? What was the function and value of these very diverse sciences in the Third Reich? I have used the story of Ernst Schäfer's expedition to try to answer these questions. But the journey should not be a blind one; we will need some working hypotheses.

First of all, the history of the SS shows that Himmler collected men like Schäfer to add prestige and glamour to the

SS. Some – and Schäfer is a good example – were genuine, even rather workaday scientists, but many were frauds and cranks. All of them, though, were opportunists who fluttered eagerly around the SS flame. From the point of view of Schäfer, who was highly driven, securing the admiration of Heinrich Himmler was, in the words of Shakespeare's Brutus, 'young ambition's ladder' to attain 'the upmost round'.[8] Hindsight judges men like these harshly, and with good reason. But simple disgust fails to come to grips with *why* intellectuals and scientists flocked to serve the Reich.

Imagine you are young and ambitious and waiting one foggy morning on a platform at Zoo Station in Berlin. When you think about the academic or professional world you work in, you see dead wood everywhere, old stick-in-the-mud professors or ambitious Jews blocking your way. Then, with a triumphant roar, a train pulls alongside. It is new, gleaming, powerful, and gives a definite impression it is going places. On the destination board you can see 'Professorships, Institutes, Laboratories – Last Stop: Glory'. Inside you can see sleek, well-nourished passengers who have boarded at other stops. They are, to be sure, a mixed bunch, perhaps even a little sinister. They wear black uniforms emblazoned with lightning bolts and death's heads. Stepping down from a carriage to greet you is a plump, smiling, rather professorial man. He wants to know if pure German blood runs in your veins, and you are certain that it does. It appears to be an innocuous enquiry. Satisfied with your *bona fides*, he invites you on board – and by now the train whistle is blowing insistently. Do you, as Ernst Schäfer did in the Olympic summer of 1936, get on board?

Sheer ambition will probably provide one answer, but perplexing ambiguities still attach to Schäfer's motivations and his response to the regime he served. Was he the 'priest of Nazism' described in the British records or an ambitious scientist, blind to everything but his work, who was handed irresistible research opportunities by a mass murderer? Was he both at once? How much did he know about what went on outside his laboratory? Frustratingly, while page after page of his diaries describe, at tedious length, birds and beasts, mountains and clouds, they give almost nothing away about his inner life. That was not his intention. We do have the record provided by his 'Interrogation Reports', but Schäfer, like many who served Himmler, was a complex, inscrutable man. He was both driven and tormented – and, as this story will show, he took moral as well as physical risks in pursuit of the treasures he hoped to find inside the 'Snowy Fortress' of Tibet.

The foremost authority on Schäfer's life and work, Dr Isrun Engelhardt, has concluded that the Schäfer Expedition was 'purely scientific'. It is only because of the historical context of Germany in the 1930s, she argues, that we view its goals as somehow sinister. Engelhardt's conclusions are based on meticulous and original scholarship. But while the idea of 'Nazi botany' or 'Nazi ornithology' is probably absurd, other sciences are not so innocent – and Schäfer's small expedition represented a cross-section of German science in the 1930s. And this has considerable significance.

It is now conclusively established that under the Third Reich anthropology and medicine were cold-bloodedly exploited to support and enact a murderous creed. One of Schäfer's colleagues demonstrates this all too well. Bruno Beger, the expedition's anthropologist, was a highly educated man who had studied at some of Germany's most prestigious universities. In the course of his lengthy education, he had absorbed from his professors ideas about race and the origin of the Germans that he hoped to prove in Tibet. Somewhere in central Asia, he was convinced, were the distant relations of the Aryan race itself.[9] Beger had seen photographs of the Tibetan nobility and suspected that their fine, elongated features provided evidence of a link to an older, founding race that came from northern Europe.

In June 1943 Beger undertook another journey in pursuit of Aryan ancestors who had proved to be rather elusive in Tibet. His destination was the Auschwitz concentration camp. Here he made a selection of more than a hundred Jews and prisoners from central Asia. He measured their skulls and bodies and had face masks made. When Beger left Auschwitz and returned to Berlin, every one of the men and women he had worked on were gassed. Their corpses were delivered to SS Dr August Hirt, an old friend of Beger, to become part of a university anatomical collection. By this time, Schäfer was the proud head of his own 'Institute for Central Asian Research', named after Swedish explorer Sven Hedin, headquartered in a castle near Salzburg. He was pleased when Beger, as instructed, sent him the data and face masks he had acquired in Auschwitz. One individual, Beger was pleased to report, had 'perfect Tibetan features'.

The five men who rode into Lhasa in January 1939 were not prophets. Like millions of other Germans they hoped, indeed expected, that a European war would be averted. It is unlikely that in 1939 they could have foreseen that their patron would promote the worst genocide in human history. But they were, by choice, SS officers and, in Schäfer's case, intimate with the man who would order millions to be annihilated. They had all boarded the train and could not alter its destination. It would take them to the Forbidden City of Tibet, but it did not stop there. It had other destinations, other purposes, as this book will show.

The German Tibet Expedition is also a story of Tibet. When Schäfer and his companions arrived in Lhasa this unique nation was at a crossroads. The 14th Dalai Lama, a three-year-old child, had recently been 'discovered' in a remote village close to the border with China and was about to be brought to Lhasa for his enthronement. Since the death of the 13th Dalai Lama in 1933, Tibet had been consumed by bitter rivalries and had seen violence that emulated any Jacobean tragedy. Its government, the Kashag, regarded both the Chinese and the British warily. They were vulnerable and divided. When he arrived in Lhasa, Schäfer learnt all he could about these tensions and fears – and exploited them.

In 1940 a secret warning was issued to German newspapers by Propaganda Minister Joseph Goebbels. It blocked any further reports about expeditions to Tibet: 'The Reich's Leader of the SS requests there be no further reports on his expedition to Tibet, until he himself gives the go-sign. The chief task of the Tibet expedition is of a political and military nature, and hasn't so much to do with the solution of scientific questions. Details may not be revealed.'[10] Records in the Bundesarchiv in Berlin show that, just months after his return to Germany, Schäfer hatched up a plot to return to Tibet, this time through the Soviet Union, which had become an ally of Nazi Germany. Schäfer would train bands of nomads and turn them into a fighting guerrilla army before unleashing them against the British. This is a matter of record. But did Schäfer begin laying plans for this hare-brained insurrection *before* his return to Germany and Hitler's invasion of Poland? I find it exceedingly odd that Schäfer, a passionate zoologist and hunter, should spend *close to three months* in Lhasa hobnobbing with Tibetan nobles and the Regent. Was Schäfer a scientist or a spy, or both at once?

These are some of the puzzles that attach to the German Tibet Expedition. There are others that will emerge in the course of the story that follows. The solutions, some of which must be conjectural, will link Beger's anthropology and even

Schäfer's birds and beasts with Himmler's fantasies about the origins of race. Above all, they reflect the strange and highly potent bond between European minds and central Asian peoples which, over the course of at least three centuries, alchemized Tibet into a realm of the imagination somewhere beyond the horizon.[11]

BETWEEN MYTH AND HISTORY

' "The gates are mine to open,
As the gates are mine to close,
And I set my house in order,"
Said our Lady of the Snows.'

– Rudyard Kipling, 'The Feet of Young Men', 1897[12]

Schäfer returned to Germany with many hundreds of reels of film shot by his cameraman and botanist, Ernst Krause. Over the next three years, with nagging interventions from the Reichsführer, they cut and re-cut, moulded and re-moulded the footage. In 1942, Schäfer eventually released a documentary entitled *Geheimnis Tibet*. It means 'Secret Tibet', although on the surface it shows little that had not been photographed by other travellers to Lhasa including the British: there are extended eulogies on the grandeur of the Himalayas – 'the icy peaks of savage mountain ranges'[13] – and seemingly interminable scenes of traditional dancing, 'the frenzied whirl of the folk dance'. Himmler had argued bitterly with Schäfer about the content. He insisted that the film attack the British as aggressively as possible. And, with breathtaking irony, Himmler ordered Schäfer to remove comments about Indians and Tibetans that he considered to be condescending. These dark-skinned people,

Himmler admonished, might one day be subjects of the Reich.

Geheimnis Tibet, when it was finally completed, was no mere travelogue. It is, viewed today, a dark and troubling work, a product of its time. Schäfer, as ordered, takes a few swipes at the British, who had 'forced alien forms of government and economy on India's ancient civilization', whereas Tibet remained 'the last retreat of traditional life' whose people live in 'strict isolation . . . in a forbidden land'. Just as egregious is that the British had used 'propaganda' and 'vicious calumnies' to tarnish Schäfer and his well-meaning German scientists and prevent their expedition reaching Lhasa. In other ways, *Geheimnis Tibet* is quite conventional and has many scenes in common with other films that were made about Tibet in the 1930s. To be sure, Schäfer and Krause were very fortunate to be able to film the New Year ceremonies and 'Great Prayer': here their film is rather special as an ethnographic record.

Much of *Geheimnis Tibet* was shot in northern Sikkim in the long frustrating period before Schäfer had been given permission to cross the border into Tibet. The tone changes when the expedition reaches Lhasa. Now the full intent of Schäfer, and presumably Himmler, stands out very clearly. Schäfer uses the film to tell his German audience about the history of Tibet, and he makes one point over and over again: Tibet, once a warrior nation, allowed itself to be corrupted and weakened by a religion, and that religion is, of course, Buddhism. But Schäfer uses a very particular word to describe this imported faith: he consistently refers not to Buddhism but to Lamaism, and he strongly implies that Lamaism was brought to Tibet by outsiders: 'Mongol lords defeated the worldly rulers of Tibet and so made way for the church state at the heart of Asia.'

Schäfer's choice of word was very significant. To describe Tibetan Buddhism as Lamaism, a word hated by Tibetans, is rather like referring to Roman Catholicism as Papism.[14] It is not complimentary: Lamaism implies superstition, fanaticism, something 'framed in imitation of the pontifical court'[15] – in brief, degenerate Buddhism. Disparaging Lamaism was a distinctly German prejudice. The word appears first in the writings of the German naturalist Peter Simon Pallas (1741–1811); Hegel dismissed Lamaism as 'revolting' and 'preposterous'; Johann Gottfried Herder called it 'monstrous and inconsistent'.[16] For Schäfer, it had an even more malevolent significance, just as it had had for the Nazi propagandist Joseph Strunk. Strunk published a book in 1938, the year Schäfer left for Asia, that linked Jews, Catholics and Tibetans in a conspiracy seeking world domination.[17] In *Geheimnis Tibet* Schäfer appears to agree with Strunk: 'the almighty Dalai Lamas still dream of *making their religion the universal religion* [my italics]'. *Geheimnis Tibet* was nothing less than a warning from history, and it was addressed to citizens of the Third Reich in 1942 just as the military fortunes of the Wehrmarcht were experiencing catastrophic reversals in the east.

According to Schäfer's film, Tibet had, centuries before, been a nation of warriors whose kings had founded and ruled an empire. When he shows the Yumbu Lagang, believed to be the oldest building in Tibet, he calls it 'the house of the first Tibetan'. 'Great kings', he tells us, 'ruled here over a brave warrior people.' At the end of the film, a 'medieval cavalcade' of horsemen 'in splendid array' and 'armed with glorious weapons, armour and the helmets of their victorious ancestors' provides a tantalizing glimpse of a long-vanished world: 'irresistible and sharp are its weapons . . . tenacious and swift the horses . . . brave and battle-scarred the warriors . . .' It is as if the old Teutonic Knights had ridden out of Germany and crossed the Himalayas, and these scenes at the end of Schäfer's film are made to resemble those phoney medieval pageants staged by the Nazis.

For Schäfer, the Lhasa cavalcade is mere theatre. The truth was that Lamaism had extinguished Tibet's glorious and imperial past. The narrator continues: 'Forgotten are the days of the kings. Triumphant Lamaism gives the land its character.' Schäfer bangs the drum against Lamaism in scene after scene. He shows a world ruled by lamas who fraudulently claim to have magical powers. Tibet's hardy, courageous people who have been tempered by their tough mountain world are cowed by sinister, freakish rituals and terrified by 'thousands upon thousands of gods and demons'. Schäfer shows 'gigantic monasteries the size of cities' crammed with 'filthy and degenerate monks'. All-powerful abbots 'oppress the people and grab what little wealth the country possesses'. Even worse, 'more than a third of the male population is lost to the nation and the workforce'. This would have been anathema to the rulers of Nazi Germany: Hitler and his cronies claimed that 'Work sets free'. By 1942, the Reich was dependent on the labour of tens of thousands of slaves procured by Himmler's SS.

Far from being a Shangri-La, Schäfer's Tibet had been sapped and ruined by religion. It had forgotten and neglected its warrior traditions. Its monasteries frittered away valuable labour power. It was at the mercy of imperialist powers like Britain and Russia – who were also Germany's bitter foes. Only at the New Year did the last representatives of Tibet's warrior past emerge 'like a vision from Asian history, like a scene from the age of heroes . . .' The 'age of heroes' was Himmler's fantasy, and with astonishing sleight of hand *Geheimnis Tibet* becomes a film about Germany. Tibet is the weakened, corrupted nation Germany could become if it too prostrated itself before the idols of religion and allowed its armour to rust. These were 'Iron Times' that needed 'Iron Brooms'. It was a message the Reichsführer must enthusiastically have endorsed, even insisted upon.[18] Himmler denounced the Church as 'an erotic, homosexual league', 'a plague' tainted by its Jewish roots. He revered the old pagan gods and a savage version of Hinduism. Besides, Nazism was a religion itself – a 'rape of the soul', as one Italian anti-fascist put it. The Nazi leaders aspired to be *Gottmenschen*.

It is true that Tibetan history bears some resemblance to Schäfer's account. Although its origins are veiled by myth, a Tibetan kingdom emerged in the sixth century in the Yarlung Valley east of Lhasa. As its kings became more powerful they united the clans and tribes and began to push the borders of their kingdom outwards. By the mid seventh century Tibet was a fierce and powerful empire whose soldiers were sent as far as Persia in the west and China in the east. Its kings practised a religion called Bön, which was, as far as historians can tell, founded on the burial cult of the Tibetan kings. According to Buddhist history, these early kings began to turn away from Bön. King Srongtsan Gampo married Buddhist princesses from China and Nepal, who began to build temples and shrines in Lhasa. He imported a written language from northern India, where Buddhism had its origins, and his successors commissioned translations of sacred Sanskrit texts. King Trisong Detsen sealed the religious future of Tibet by founding the Samye Monastery in AD 767 and making Buddhism the official state religion. Far from eroding Tibet's imperial ambitions, Buddhism became an important ingredient in statecraft. Bön continued to play a shadowy role, however, and even today some Tibetan nationalists refer to it as the 'true' religion of their country. Like Schäfer, they claim that the rise of Buddhism and the disappearance of Bön led to the decline of Tibet's military powers and eventually its destruction by China.

This was the secret Schäfer brought back from Tibet. But like so many others he had merely found what he and his patron already thought they knew. Schäfer's was just one more myth about Tibet, albeit a most unusual one. *Geheimnis Tibet* stands at the end of a long tradition.

THE GREAT MYSTIFIERS

'I have been in Tibet . . .'

– the mystic Madame Helena Blavatsky, who almost certainly had not

'I travelled for two years in Tibet . . . and amused myself by visiting Lhassa [sic] *and spending some days with the head lama . . .'*

– Sherlock Holmes in Arthur Conan Doyle's *The Adventure of the Empty House*, describing his activities after an apparently fatal encounter with Professor Moriarty at the Reichenbach Falls

The ground for these leaps of imagination[19] had been well prepared. For Indians, the Himalayas, the immense mountain barrier to the north, was the abode of the gods and of the Vidyadhara, a race of supermen blessed with occult knowledge and magical powers.

It was the Tibetans who first imagined Shambhala,[20] a land beyond the Himalayas shaped like a giant lotus, filled with sandalwood forests and white lotus lakes and ringed by mountains. Within the borders of Shambhala, it was said, were 960 million villages and a palace made of gold and silver, encrusted with mirrors. In the centre was the mandala of the Buddha. The kings of Shambhala ruled for a hundred years and were called the Holders of the Caste. The people of Shambhala were beautiful, rich and virtuous, but inside the giant lotus of Shambhala were some thirty-five million Brahmans all devoted to the ancient Hindu scriptures, the Veda, of India. Only when they converted and became Buddhist was Shambhala made completely perfect.

Shambhala fascinated the few Western travellers who managed to penetrate the closed Himalayan passes. The Hungarian scholar Alexander Csoma de Köros, writing in 1833, provided the first account of 'a fabulous country in the north . . . situated between 45° and 50° north latitude'. The Panchen Lamas, spiritual advisers to the Dalai Lamas, were believed to be incarnations of the rulers of Shambhala, and in 1915 the 9th Panchen Lama produced a guidebook, the *Shambhala Lamyig*, that contained precise directions for hopeful travellers and was widely translated.

Shambhala was quickly absorbed into Western mythologies. As with the myth of Atlantis, revived by the nineteenth-century fraudster Ignatius Donnelly, finding where Shambhala 'really was' became an obsession. Shambhalitis reached its feverish climax in 1926 when a party led by the Russian mystic and painter Nicholas Roerich attempted to enter Tibet. His expedition did not get very far; he and his party were detained and turned back by the British. Shambhala was left in peace.[21]

The idea of a hidden kingdom in the Himalayas, ruled by enlightened masters, has been remarkably pervasive and doggedly persistent.[22] Although it might seem to be merely romantic fantasy, the myth of Shambhala was not at all benign. It fed new and eventually dangerous notions, and it shaped the ideas Ernst Schäfer and Bruno Beger brought with them to Tibet in 1938, and to Auschwitz five years later. How could a rather attractive tale have any connection with the Nazi genocide? The suggestion appears downright outlandish, but there is a chain of connections whose first link is a most unusual nineteenth-century mystic, Madame Helena Blavatsky. How this 'hippopotamus of an old woman' (her description), this 'most interesting and unscrupulous impostor' (Kipling's), became the architect of Mysterious Tibet is one of the oddest of all stories of this period, but its impact cannot be overstated.[23]

Helena Andreyevna Blavatsky was born during the night, sick and premature, at the end of July in 1831. Her parents, Peter Alexeyeivich von Hahn and Helena Andreyevna, had the fragile infant hastily baptized but the newborn survived to grow into a highly strung and frequently ill child. Peter von Hahn was a professional soldier who made little time for his family. Bored by her husband and the drudgery of a military life, Helena's mother fled to pursue a writing career – an act of some daring in pre-Revolution Russia. She took her children to Astrakhan on the Caspian Sea at the mouth of the Volga. Hot and infested with gnats, Astrakhan was not a comfortable place to live. While its salons and theatres were full of the usual Russians and Germans, its rough streets teemed with people from all over the Orient. Here the young Helena saw Persians, Armenians and Indians. Most fascinating were a nomadic Tibetan people called the Kalmyck. Her grandfather had been appointed their trustee and Helena would always claim that the Kalmycks were her first vivid contact with the East. 'I was myself brought up with Buddhist Kalmycks,' she often said; she even suggested she might have inherited some Kalmyck blood.

Her grandfather maintained close relations with Kalmyck leaders, and one in particular. Prince Tumene had fought for the Tsar and lived in a fabulous palace on an island in the Volga. Inside the Tulene Palace was a Buddhist temple staffed by lamas, and its rituals and atmosphere permeated with incense and yak butter made an indelible impression on the young Helena. There were other influences, too. Her great grandfather had been a Rosicrucian Mason and had accumulated a large library of occult works. He had belonged to the Rite of Strict Observance, a German society which claimed to be in contact with 'Unknown Superiors'. Helena spent many hours studying in her grandfather's library and would later invent her own 'Superiors'. According to a childhood friend, she had a passion for 'everything unknown and mysterious, weird and fantastical' and a 'craving for independence and freedom of action'.[24]

That craving led Blavatsky to Paris, and then to New York in 1873, where she threw herself into the Spiritualist Movement. She quickly made a name for herself by manifesting more wondrous spirit guides than the usual clumps of congealed ectoplasm favoured by competitors. Her guides spoke French and Russian, and Blavatsky drew on her childhood memories of Astrakhan to add an exotic authenticity. Her unusual antics caught the eye of Henry Steel Olcott, a Civil War colonel who had turned to law then become a New York hack. Olcott specialized in sensational reports about East Coast séances. Madame Blavatsky fascinated him, and his articles for a New York rag called the *Daily Graphic* made her reputation. Soon they were the oddest, and to some the most fascinating, couple in New York. He was patriarchal, extravagantly bearded and austerely forbidding; she was unashamedly large, fond of extravagant gesture and with a razor-sharp, sometimes self-deprecating wit.

The 'two chums' had high ambitions. Olcott helped H.P.B., as Blavatsky now called herself, found an occult salon where she began to do much more than the usual tricks of ectoplasmic manifestation, table rapping and trumpet blowing. With Olcott's canny assistance, H.P.B. conjured up instead one of the great inventions of the nineteenth century – the guru. The elite of America's East Coast soon flocked to hear words of wisdom from this exotic female magus. Olcott and Blavatsky shrewdly issued shrill attacks on lesser mediums and eventually repudiated the movement altogether. At H.P.B.'s salons, there was little trickery. The mysteries of Egypt and Asia were fervently discussed and H.P.B. turned her spirit guides into Spiritual Masters who were teachers, sages, adepts and brothers rather than mere ghosts. Her home became known as the Lamasery.

Thus was born the Theosophical Movement. H.P.B. began writing and a turgid flood of mystical speculation gushed unceasingly from her pen. The first product of her industry was *Isis Unveiled* (1877). It was long, wordy and derivative but somehow managed to bolt together most of the occult fantasies of its time. It borrowed heavily from now forgotten authors. One was Edward Bulwer-Lytton, a writer of 'Rosicrucian fiction' who had described a secret fraternity, a brotherhood hidden behind 'the veil of Isis', where its members were introduced to Oriental rites by an Indian sage. Another was Louis Jacolliot who had been the French consul in Calcutta and had written a series of books about Indian occult sciences. He too proposed the existence of a secret brotherhood. He lived in a watchtower located somewhere in India that for millennia had observed the rise and fall of civilizations. From sources like these, Blavatsky invented a 'Great White Brotherhood' whose founders had originally been pupils of the Tibetan religious reformer Tsonkhapa. She spiced her recipe by claiming that *Isis Unveiled* had been dictated to her by a tall Hindu who came every day as she sat down to write. H.P.B. did not suffer from writer's block.

Like many charlatans, Blavatsky craved recognition as a scholar and her book was larded with gobbets of science. Science and spiritualism flirted throughout the nineteenth century. Phenomena were investigated and tested, and converts to the spirit world appeared among the scientific elite, men like William Crookes and even Alfred Russel Wallace, the co-discoverer of natural selection. Darwin himself, who had no interest in the occult, had a powerful impact on its development and was revered by Madame Blavatsky who claimed to have translated his works into Russian while in Africa. Not true, but Darwin's ideas, which had so dismayed the Church when they first appeared, were rapidly absorbed by occult thinkers.

By the time she had completed *Isis Unveiled*, H.P.B. – who had barely moved during the time she'd spent writing and now weighed 245 pounds – had become interested in India. She talked of 'going to Northeastern India, where the head of the order is and where I shall obey whatever orders they [her Masters] may give . . .'[25] At the end of 1878, H.P.B. and Olcott sailed for Bombay. Although she had flirted with 'Egyptian Mysteries', India was for her the source, and to the north were the Himalayas which, she believed, formed the 'veil of Isis' itself concealing the world of the Masters which lay in Tibet. In Bombay, the odd couple found supporters among the Anglo-Indian community as well as among Indian princes and nationalists. After all, the theosophists held Indian civilization in the highest regard, revering it even as they dissolved its reality in clouds of rhetorical incense. Her mahatmas, first dreamt up in New York, reached full maturity in India. She could now imagine their complete history – a history that began in Tibet, or at least the imaginary Tibet of her childhood. Now she called her Masters the 'Brotherhood of the Snowy Range', and Blavatsky always insisted that she had crossed the Himalayas to the Tashilunpo Monastery, near Shigatse, where she received instruction from one of her mahatmas called 'Koot Hoomi'.

Most historians have assumed Blavatsky was telling fibs, but the story may be rather more complicated. In an account written in 1881, she referred to a 'silly red cheeked Englishman' who pursued her across India until she was able to take leave of him 'with a thumb to my nose' and head off alone 'to the monastery of my lama friends'. The British certainly suspected

H.P.B. was a Russian spy and she was frequently shadowed by one Major Philip Henderson, chief of the Simla Police.[26] Recent research in Russian archives suggests that the British had cause to be concerned. In 1872, H.P.B. despatched a letter to the Russian secret service offering to use her gifts as a clairvoyant to 'discover people's hopes, plans and secrets'. In the same letter, perhaps to advertise her guile, she confessed that 'the spirits spoke and answered in my own words'. It was the closest H.P.B. ever came to a confession, and she must have been confident that Russian secret agents would not disclose her secret.

The truth may never be known. But a full year *after* she had made that claim, she took a well-documented journey as far as Darjeeling, the British hill station. This part of India had once been part of the kingdom of Sikkim, which had many ties to Tibet. She could at least see the Himalayas, and it is quite likely that, as she claimed, H.P.B. visited the Ghum Monastery and talked with an incarnate lama. She could not, of course, resist gilding the lotus and described spending 'hours in their library where no woman is allowed to enter – touching testimony to my beauty and my perfect innocence – and the Superior publicly recognized in me one of the feminine incarnations of the Bodhisattva, of which I am very proud'.[27]

It is really neither here nor there whether H.P.B. went to Tibet or not; it was important for *her* to give her disciples that impression and important for *them* that she claimed such an experience. There is firm evidence, however, that Olcott and Blavatsky had indirect access to Tibet through Sarat Chandra Das,[28] one of the 'pundits' trained by the British to travel secretly into Tibet, gather intelligence and make maps and surveys. Das visited the Tashilunpo Monastery where he met the Panchen Lama's prime minister Sengchen Tulku. In later writings, H.P.B. referred to one of her Masters as the 'Chohan

Lama of Rinch-Cha-Tze the Chief of the Archive Registrars of the Secret libraries of the Dalai Lama and Ta-shu-hlumpo Lamas Rimboche'. Olcott said that the Tashi (Panchen) Lama's master of ceremonies 'one of our own revered Mahatmas is'. This must be Das's Sengchen Tulku, the Panchen Lama's prime minister. He was fascinated by Western science, and in return for smallpox vaccine and a printing press had permitted Das to examine books in the library at Tashilunpo. It is likely that some of what Das reported was purloined for H.P.B.'s new books *The Stanzas of Dzyan* and *The Secret Doctrine*, and some scholars of her work have recognized in one of her citations allusions to the Tibetan *Kangyur*, a copy of which was presented to Schäfer's expedition in 1939. In *The Secret Doctrine*, Blavatsky refers to a Book of Secret Wisdom 'in the charge of the Teshu Lama' – in other words, the Panchen Lama.

There was no direct contact between Blavatsky and Sengchen Tulku, but he inadvertently fed Blavatsky's cult. It did him no good. For assisting Das, and, without knowing it, Madame Blavatsky, Tulku was arrested by the Tibetan government, beaten, flogged and thrown into the Tsang Po River with his hands tied behind his back. When his reincarnation duly appeared in a small boy, this innocent child was abandoned.[29]

All this shows very clearly that Blavatsky, like so many fantasists, spiced her stews with a seasoning of veracity. What came out the other side was pernicious drivel. While *Isis Unveiled* had drawn on Egyptian mystery and was a tirade against materialism, *The Secret Doctrine*, with its swastika-decorated cover, was a fifteen-hundred-page, two-volume account of human origin and destiny. It was a turbid cocktail of bogus Tibetan wisdom and evolutionary science, but its grand scheme of seven rounds, seven root races and seven sub-races had an enormous impact.

This, in brief, is the message Blavatsky brought back from her Great White Brotherhood. Humans had evolved through a series of evolutionary stages each of which had fashioned different races.[30] Several hundred million years ago, the first of these races inhabited the Imperishable Sacred Land. They were boneless, formless, spiritual essences called the Self-born – and were extinguished when their imperishable kingdom sank beneath the ocean. Next up were the Hyperboreans who, like their predecessors, had no bodily form and resided at the North Pole. Reproduction was a matter of spiritual rebirth. True sexual reproduction came much later with the appearance, eighteen million years ago, of the Third Race on a vast Pacific continent called Lemuria. The Lemurians are the villains in Blavatsky's yarn because they mated with lesser breeds, so Blavatsky has them destroyed in a cataclysm of fire and flood. Lemuria, too, sank beneath the waves. Eight hundred and fifty thousand years ago, the Fourth Race appeared on an island continent in the Atlantic Ocean. This was the fabled lost continent of Atlantis first described by Plato. The Atlanteans were, literally, giants. They were highly developed spiritually but also invented electrical power and powered flight. They built enormous temples and pyramids. Over time, however, they became immoral and misused their great size and skills. The Atlantic began to rise, submerging their kingdom. And so Atlantis joined the other lost continents on the now rather crowded ocean floor. All was not lost, however. An elite priesthood escaped the destruction of Atlantis, fled to the Gobi Desert and then into the Himalayas. Here they took refuge in the lost Tibetan kingdom of Shambhala. By now a new race had emerged in northern Asia – the Aryans. From their stronghold in Shambhala, the surviving Atlanteans passed on their wisdom to the Aryans, who began to spread south and west across the globe producing a Sixth Sub Race of Anglo-Saxon stock.

HERE COMES THE MASTER RACE

The Secret Doctrine made an especially powerful impression in Germany and Austria.[31] Olcott had even considered moving the Theosophical Society headquarters from India to Germany after the English Society for Psychical Research had exposed Madame Blavatsky as a fraud (she was caught out writing the letters which she claimed were 'precipitated' by her mahatmas). Some fifty years later, after 1933, theosophy would become even more popular as Germans were encouraged to turn away from Christianity and embrace faiths that were considered to be more Aryan. For many, *The Secret Doctrine* appeared to reconcile science and belief, nature and myth, and in Germany it catalysed a much older intellectual tradition.[32]

More than a century before Heinrich Himmler told Ernst Schäfer that the 'Aryans had come from heaven', German intellectuals and scientists had made race the cornerstone of their thinking. Quite deliberately, they set out to undermine the authority of the Bible and the status of its original language, Hebrew. Medieval and Renaissance philosophers by and large accepted the biblical story of the origins of man. The first humans were Adam and Eve, and the different races were simply descendants of the three sons of Noah. The first language was Hebrew, the father tongue. When European traders and explorers began to send back reports about a rich diversity of native peoples in the Americas and Africa, the biblical account began to look stretched. Shem, Ham and Japheth would surely not claim credit for native Americans, or native Australians. This Noachian or Jewish genealogy of mankind was quickly toppled from its pedestal. Human origins were now sought outside the Garden of Eden and Noah's family tree.

In France, Voltaire speculated about China; the Germans looked towards India. Johann Gottfried Herder, a Lutheran pastor, exhorted, 'Let us abandon these regions where our predecessors . . . sought the beginning of the world . . . The primitive mountains of Asia prepared the first abode of the human race', and the philosopher Immanuel Kant nominated Tibet: 'This is the highest country. No doubt it was inhabited before any other and could even have been the site of all creation and all science. The culture of the Indians, as is known, came from Tibet, just as all our arts like agriculture, numbers, the game of chess, etc., seem to have come from India.'

This German cult can be traced to the birth of comparative linguistics, and, ironically, to the insights of an English lawyer, Sir William Jones.[33] A precocious scholar, Jones came to India to take up a post as an assistant judge in the High Court of Bengal. Here he developed a passion for the cultures of India and, with some difficulty, began to study Sanskrit. He quickly recognized its close affinities with Latin and Greek, and came to a now celebrated conclusion: 'The Sanskrit language, whatever be its antiquity, is of a wonderful structure; more perfect than the Greek, more copious than the Latin, and more exquisitely refined than either, yet bearing to both of them a stronger affinity, both in the roots of verbs and the forms of grammar, than could possibly have been produced by accident; so strong indeed, that no philologer could examine them all three, without believing them to have sprung from some common source, which, perhaps, no longer exists . . .' Jones made this pronouncement in Calcutta in 1786 at the Royal Asiatic Society, which he had founded, and it set off an intellectual forest fire in Germany. Hebrew and the entire story of the Bible could at last be filed under myth. Real history started in Asia and used the language of India. This, however, was just the beginning.

At Jena University, where Bruno Beger would study anthropology a century later, Friedrich Schlegel was elated when he discovered Jones' insight. He too had studied Sanskrit and was convinced that India had produced the first civilizations. But Schlegel went much further than Jones. In *Über die Sprache und Weisheit der Inder* ('On the Language and Wisdom of the Indians'), published in 1808, Schlegel argued that Sanskrit was the language of elites and had first been spoken by a race of cultured warriors in northern India. Driven by the noblest of motives, these masterful northerners had conquered and civilized the world. They had founded colonies from Egypt, where they seeded the civilization of the Pharaohs, all the way to Scandinavia. The proof was in their words: Indian and European tongues had all 'sprung from some common source'. Schlegel gave a name to his masterful northerners: Aryans. Because of their association with the north, either in India or Europe they also came to be called Nordics. In Sanskrit the word means 'aristocrat' or 'noble', and Schlegel made a connection between Aryan and the German word *Ehre*, meaning honour.

The Aryan version of history blitzkrieged through German culture. In philosophy, folklore, geography and philology the Aryans made a triumphant entry, stomping down from the Himalayas and civilizing the world. They were the common ancestor of Indians, Persians, Greeks, Italians, Slavs, Scandinavians, Anglo-Saxons, and especially Germans. Aryans were soon being called Indo-Germans and given the status of Wagnerian heroes: they were youthful, tall, blond, generous, brave and creative.

The unstoppable march of the Aryans was powered by frustrated nationalism. Until 1871, Germany was a fragmented patchwork of states of different kinds and sizes, from kingdoms to duchies, which fluttered around the bigger national entities of Prussia and Austria. Prussians, Saxons, Bavarians and other semi-tribal groupings had their own centres of power; the

Prussians had their stronghold in Berlin, the Bavarians in Munich. The hopes and aspirations of nationalists – Pan Germans, as they were called – were continuously thwarted. Even Otto von Bismarck's 'Second German Reich', founded with blood and iron in 1871, was a disappointment since it excluded Austrians. But if nationhood could not be achieved in the real world then it could at least be imagined. Germans became a nation in their heads, and the world they saw there was aggressively exclusive. Jews, it seemed, were not part of the Aryan family tree. They were a rootless desert people who were only at home in the fluid, exploitative world of the city. The emancipation of Jews in the eighteenth century had, paradoxically, led to an intensification of anti-Semitism. As Jews sought to become Germans, breaking free from the ghetto and centuries of bondage, age-old hostilities were re-ignited. In Germany, as such enmities deepened, relations of blood took on mythic significance, and the idea of a German 'race' supplied the kind of blood unities politics could not.

In the 1870s, the tide of Aryanism was full. Richard Wagner had added the glamour of high art and had almost single-handedly sanctified German hatred of Jews. Then yet more ingredients had been added to the festering stew. In France, Count Arthur de Gobineau published a seminal work, *Essay on the Inequality of Human Races* (1853–4), which was widely read in Germany; it spawned Houston Stewart Chamberlain's massive *Die Grundlagen des neunzehnten Jahrhunderts* ('The Foundations of the Nineteenth Century'). Both men made race the foundation of culture. Great civilizations were inherited like a blood line. From England came Charles Darwin's theory of natural selection, filtered through the cult of Indo-German race theory and transformed by German biologists like Ernst Haeckel into a scientific justification of Indo-German superiority. Scientists denounced the horror of miscegenation.

If civilization was the gift of blood, then it followed that it could be poisoned by the blood of lesser races. The mingling of unequal blood lines was to be prevented at all costs. Haeckel, a respected scientist, founded the Monist League to campaign against mixed marriages.

Science had one other ingredient to add to the Aryan pot, and it is the one that will most concern us in this book. With the rise of imperialism and the conquest of Africa and the East, a new science emerged. Anthropology, the study of man, was from the beginning the science of 'other men', and the anthropologists followed the flags of imperial conquest. The diverse races they encountered in Africa and Asia became objects of exploitation, then subjects for study. German imperialism was late in coming, but it was founded on envy of other empires, and as a consequence was more ruthless. Its anthropologists acted with fervid aggression. Just as biologists believed they were defending the purity of their Indo-German blood line, so anthropologists would go out into the world to clarify and secure behind the ramparts of science the story of the Aryan conquest. And they would move steadily closer to the origins of that civilization – to the Himalayas and the Snowy Fortress of Tibet.

Madame Blavatsky, who had lied about trekking across the Himalayas to Tashilunpo, whose pathetic communications with mahatmas were so easily exposed, had nevertheless drawn together all these threads in *The Secret Doctrine*. All over Europe, and in India itself, theosophy became a cult. Its disciples were not the hungry masses who poured into spiritualist meetings and séances desperately seeking solace; they were intellectuals, diplomats, philosophers and even scientists. United under the Tibetan symbol of the swastika, they infested the salons and laboratories of Europe. As in *The Secret Doctrine* itself, science and occultism lay happily side by side in a fetid embrace. The German Theosophical Society had been founded in 1896 and soon had thriving centres in Leipzig and Berlin. Its success helped invigorate a rash of occultist societies that were fascinated by runes and swastikas, hated Jews and sought a new Pan German culture. Heinrich Himmler read their publications avidly and joined one of them, the Artamanen. According to these fantasists, the origin of Aryan man was somewhere in northern India, perhaps behind the icy bastions of the Himalayas. In 1933, Germany was overwhelmed by a political despotism whose leaders had absorbed many of the pseudoscientific ideas planted by their nineteenth-century forebears. Now they had the power to find the source of their culture and blood.

LHASA LO!

A final word about the origins of this book. In 1999, I made two films for the BBC's *Horizon* series testing claims made in favour of the existence of Atlantis or some comparable but nameless 'lost civilization'. These films were prompted by the popularity, on a global scale, of books and television series claiming that the emergence of civilization in ancient history could be explained by the alleged existence of a lost super-civilization that had flourished some twelve thousand years ago. The programmes concluded that such claims were pseudoscientific, bogus history.

I was also intrigued to learn about the birth and growth of such notions. It seemed that this new movement was fashioned from recycled flotsam and jetsam dredged up by the marginal and occult movements that had emerged in the nineteenth century. Lost civilizations, Atlantis, pyramids, the precession of the equinoxes, the Holy Grail, the Ark of the Covenant – such arcane ingredients, it seemed, were now being reformed and regurgitated. In the 1970s, an Austrian hotelier became a millionaire by adding spaceships to the brew. At the turn of the twenty-first century, 'theories' about a lost civilization in Antarctica and a travelling caste of white-skinned bringers of civilization have generated massive book sales.

These were the same 'theories' that had preoccupied leading figures in the Third Reich like Heinrich Himmler and Rudolf Hess. Both men had been involved in occult societies in the early 1920s and their memberships overlapped with those of the embryonic Nazi Party. Their interest in Social Darwinism and pseudoscientific ideas about lost polar civilizations seemed, at first sight, to be marginal to the realities of the Third Reich and the annihilation of European Jewry and gypsies. It became clear, however, that this bogus history of an Aryan Master Race had both energized and apparently ennobled the racial thinking that led to what historians have called the 'Racial State' of Nazi Germany.

Myth is never harmless.

PART ONE

FOOTHILLS

CHAPTER ONE

CALL OF THE WILD

'Do you know the long day's patience, belly down on frozen drift,
While the head of heads is feeding out of range?
It is there that I am going, where the boulders and the snow lie,
With a trusty, nimble tracker that I know . . .'

– Rudyard Kipling, 'The Feet of Young Men', 1897

It was an ideal place for an ambush. The expedition caravan had crossed the Chungtang Pass in eastern Tibet at 15,500 feet and arrived on a plateau hemmed in by mountains. Ahead of them lay another pass, and they needed to reach it before nightfall. Despite this, expedition leader Brooke Dolan blithely galloped off alone in pursuit of three gazelles he had spotted on a ridge to the south-east. He left his German companion Ernst Schäfer with their guide, the missionary Marion Duncan, to continue north. Both men were quite used to Dolan's mercurial changes of mind.

The caravan of yaks, horses and men proceeded noisily along a small river whose banks were littered with huge boulders, all of them at least as high as a man. This was bandit country, and

Duncan was nervous – as it turned out, rightly so. Just after noon bandits appeared, on the other side of the river, jumping with 'diabolical yells' from behind boulders and vaulting onto horses hidden behind some scrub. Then they galloped towards the caravan, whipping their mounts. When they reached the river, the bandits reined in their horses and stared fiercely at the intruders.

At the head of the caravan, Schäfer and Duncan sat high and tense in their saddles. Duncan had spent many years in this remote and lawless part of the world. It was border country, bitterly contested among fierce nomadic tribes like the Ngoloks. There was fighting, too, between a rag-tag Tibetan Army and the forces of Chiang Kai-shek, the Chinese nationalist leader. And Mao Tse-tung's Red Army was moving in from the south. The Tibetan border was not a relaxing place to go exploring.

Duncan had faced bandit tribes like this one scores of times. Staying cool was essential. One of his sherpas, a wiry old man called Tringleh, told him that the tribe were Lingkharshee and that he recognized one of them. The best plan was to parley or they could lose everything. After a brief discussion, Duncan sent Tringleh and two others to meet the bandits.

Duncan's companion fretted impatiently. Ernst Schäfer was twenty-four and, in Germany, a minor hero. He was also an officer in the SS, and there was little love lost between him and Duncan. The bandits surrounded the three sherpas, waving their swords and emitting high-pitched battle cries. Schäfer said, 'They will kill our men – I can pick them off.' Before Duncan could stop him, he had dismounted and knelt on the river's edge, bringing his Mauser up to his shoulder and aiming across the river. Duncan knew Schäfer was unlikely to miss and that a dead Chinese bandit would be a catastrophe. And besides, there would be others further up the river. So he spoke sharply: 'No, you must not. I know what I am doing.' He ordered

Schäfer to back away before he was spotted. Duncan recalled later that something in the 'calm and confident' tone of his voice did the trick and Schäfer did as he was told. But the glance he shot Duncan showed that he felt scolded and humiliated. By now, Tringleh had won over the bandits, who rode towards the caravan laughing and chattering. At the same time Dolan returned with two dead gazelles thrown over his saddle, disappointed that he had missed the drama.

For the rest of the day the bandits acted as guides, and by nightfall the caravan of men, yaks and horses had successfully crossed the pass and made camp. Beyond lay Tibet, the roof of the world. Duncan knew they had been lucky. Just ten years before he had lost an entire caravan in an ambush.

Schäfer brooded by the fire and read *Faust*, his favourite book in the wild. Through the flames he watched the two Americans Dolan and Duncan chatting and smoking. He had already made a decision to return to Tibet, but his new expedition would be a German one, led by himself and with men of his own blood.

From the beginning of his career as a naturalist and explorer, Schäfer had written voluminously about his adventures. In the 1930s, his books made him a celebrated, even glamorous figure in Germany. After 1945, he used his books to shake off the stigma of his past. In that, he never really succeeded, and he often complained bitterly about fellow Nazi travellers who had escaped the same reproach. Throughout his life, and it was a long one, Schäfer was always much more than those behind-the-scenes types who enjoy 'counting the hairs on the back legs of fleas'. His books make very clear that he lived to shoot. He was addicted to the hunt much more than to the science it yielded. Yet despite all the books and their flood of words, the man is elusive.

The same English diplomat who called him a 'priest of

Nazism' added an astonishing list of traits: Schäfer was, he reported, 'forceful, volatile, scholarly, vain to the point of childishness, disregardful of social convention or the feelings or the conveniences of others'. Schäfer was a divided and contrary man. A servant of the Reich, he also saw himself as a free spirit. He was, in short, a man who sought to realize vaunting ambitions under a murderous dictatorship. At first sight he appeared rather ordinary, even nondescript. But as his colleague Bruno Beger recalled, he 'commanded a room' with little effort. Beger also remembered Schäfer's volatile temper and prolonged sulks. But Schäfer was also a highly persuasive diplomat who more often than not got what he wanted. In an interview for German television filmed in the 1980s, he sits surrounded by animal skins. Rather daunting antlers protrude from the wall behind him. His energy is undimmed. He seems to push out of the screen as he describes a moment of crisis in Lhasa when his party was attacked by monks. His enthusiasm seems barely contained, even hysterical – another trait noted by that British diplomat. To the end of his life, inner peace was elusive.

In his books, Schäfer never discussed his experiences inside Himmler's SS. During his interrogations[1] he was at pains to present himself as a rebel. He was, he claimed, an unwilling recruit to the SS; he'd even been disciplined, on at least two occasions, by Himmler himself for insubordination. Schäfer's answers are self-serving and frequently deceitful, but there is other evidence that he *was* telling the truth, in part at least. In the Bundesarchiv in Berlin I unearthed a telling letter to Schäfer from Himmler himself: 'I am convinced that you will *now* behave according to my orders – and that you proceed with the requested task and last but not least accomplish your task: *with the unruly will that lies within you* [my italics].'[2] Schäfer instinctively resented anyone telling him what to do, even the Reichsführer. But he was never able to open the trap that Himmler had set for him.

For his part, it is clear that Himmler was fascinated by this forceful young adventurer who had risked his life in some of the most dangerous regions of central Asia. He saw the ambitious young scientist as a glorious youth who seemed to have burst, guns blazing, from the pages of a novel by Karl May, the best-selling German author of Westerns and Oriental adventures. In other ways, the two men had little in common. There is some fragmentary evidence that Schäfer was interested in the race theories that obsessed his colleague Bruno Beger, but his deepest passions were reserved for species of wild animal, not the races of man. Was Schäfer genuinely a 'priest of Nazism'?

Albert Speer was another young, impatient and driven 'expert', and a comparison between the two men is instructive. Schäfer's passion was animals, dead and stuffed; Speer's was architecture, building big. Hitler appealed to Speer's vanity; the Führer passed on small-scale projects, testing him, then gave him Berlin to rebuild on a colossal scale. Likewise, Himmler indulged Schäfer's passion for wild places, wild things, for killing the animals he loved and bringing his trophies back to the Fatherland. After his triumphant return from Tibet, Himmler flattered Schäfer's academic ambitions by giving him his own 'Institute for Central Asian Research'. Then he promised him another expedition, this time to the Caucasus and on a much bigger scale. The temptations became ever more alluring. The trap closed tighter.

Speer became much more than an architect. By the end of the war he was Hitler's Minister for Armaments and War Production. He wielded enormous power. In comparison, Schäfer was much smaller fry. He designed new winter clothing for the Waffen-SS and chased after a mythical 'Red Horse' that obsessed Himmler. But for both Speer and Schäfer, complicity was morally corrosive. As Hitler's Reich collapsed, both men sought salvation through confession: Speer in front of the world at Nuremberg, Schäfer at a de-nazification tribunal. Both were interned, Schäfer for three years, Speer for twenty years in Spandau Prison. In exile in Venezuela, Schäfer rarely discussed the war and seemed to find peace by conjuring up innocent escapades in the high mountains of Tibet. Speer, however, never stopped confessing; the struggle to shed his guilt never ended. Schäfer got on with his life, until his former colleague Bruno Beger walked into a Frankfurt courtroom in 1971 accused of murder.

The son of a wealthy businessman, Schäfer was born in Cologne in March 1910. The family was wealthy, and his father Hans was an imperious man with a passion for horses. His son was, according to his own account, born to hunt. At the age of three, he spent hours in a potato cellar with a catapult, picking off rats as they emerged from a hole in the wall. Years later in Tibet he would get round a ban on hunting by using a catapult fashioned from rubber insulation. The Schäfers moved to Hamburg where his father had become president of the local board of trade and industry. Young Ernst would disappear for much of the day on long expeditions out of the city. 'Of course I wasn't any good at school,' he wrote years later in Venezuela, 'my thoughts were in the woods where I would seek adventures every day. I had no need to read Karl May . . .' Schäfer turned his bedroom into a menagerie and experimented, cropping the tails of older mice to find out whether their offspring would inherit cropped tails. They didn't. His father, angered by poor school reports and by the tree frogs colonizing his study, tried to rein in his son: he was excluded from family Sunday walks, and when this proved insufficiently draconian he was sent – 'for taming' – to a boarding school in Heidelberg.

Here Schäfer was introduced to the occult power of the hunt. It would obsess him all his life. It would bring him glory, but heart-breaking tragedy as well. This is how, years later, Schäfer told the story of his induction. One May morning in 1922, the headmaster of his up-scale boot camp told him, 'Schäfer, get ready – we are going to hunt in the Odenwald.' It was warm when they drove deep into the dark green and brown forest, the very place where Siegfried had slain the dragon in Wagner's *Siegfried*. The headmaster, to whom Schäfer gave no name, stopped the car and retrieved his rifle from the boot. 'You will wait here,' he commanded. German schoolmasters were notoriously imperious and cruel. The boy waited; the minutes turned into hours and the forest darkened. Schäfer climbed into the car to sleep and the following morning, tortured by hunger, feasted voraciously on clover leaves. And then he waited all day until the evening, when the headmaster returned at last.

'Schäfer,' he asked, 'were you afraid?'

'No,' came the stout-hearted reply.

'Are you hungry?'

'Yes, Herr Direktor.'

Young Schäfer had answered appropriately and was rewarded with bacon, bread and Apfelwein. After his night in the woods, Herr Direktor would take him back to the forest every week. He was just twelve.

Two years later, a representative from IG Farben visited the Schäfer household and over dinner regaled them with stories about Wilhelm Filchner's expedition to Tibet. 'From this moment on I knew that I wanted to become a Tibet explorer,' Schäfer remembered. Filchner had explored the Antarctic as well as Asia and was rivalled in fame and prestige only by Sven Hedin, who would become another hero of Schäfer's. Filchner, a Bavarian, was more than a scientist and explorer; he was also a spy, as his book *Storm Over Asia* disclosed.[3]

After gaining his *Abitur* at a school in Mannheim, where he claimed in his SS application to have had difficulties with a communist teacher, Schäfer won a place at Göttingen

University to study zoology and geology. But he was restless, as many Germans were in the late 1920s, Heinrich Himmler and Bruno Beger included. The Schäfer family weathered the crash of 1929, but millions of others were ruined. They devoured the romantic adventure fiction churned out by writers like Karl May and dreamt of escape. On the streets of German cities, there was violence, tension and despair.

Many now turned to the increasingly powerful and vociferous Nazi Party. The Weimar Republic was battered and decaying, and for many democracy itself was spent and discredited. Hitler's NSDAP had been banned in 1927, but two years later the crash and fears of communist violence reversed Hitler's fortunes. In October 1929 the NSDAP candidates began to win bigger percentages of votes cast in local elections, and Hitler was able to demand two ministries in Thuringia. He prophesied that he would be able to seize power in Germany 'within two and a half to three years', and it would prove to be a precise calculation.[4] Schäfer claimed that his family were 'of the broadest democratic and international convictions'[5] and had little interest in Hitler and his party. He was probably telling the truth. Germany's upper middle classes despised – for now, at any rate – the 'little corporal' and could not imagine that this absurd demagogue would ever acquire power.

But at German universities like Göttingen, radicalized students flocked to the right in huge numbers. Student fraternities were virulently anti-Semitic and many openly supported Hitler. Violence against Jewish professors and students increased. Ernst Schäfer, unlike his future colleague Bruno Beger, was spared a prolonged exposure to this poisonous world. He joined a fraternity at Göttingen but disliked its activities and left very quickly. Then a chance encounter with an American explorer allowed him to escape Germany altogether.

Schäfer had much in common with Brooke Dolan, who would be his companion on two expeditions into the unknown. It was his adventures with this odd American that would make him famous, a German hero at the age of twenty-one. Dolan, too, was the indulged son of wealthy parents. His grandfather was a tycoon who had literally electrified Philadelphia and made a fortune. It meant that his grandson Brooke could be expensively educated, just as Schäfer had been. Dolan attended St Paul's School in Concord, New Hampshire, then Princeton, where he began studying zoology. But he quickly grew bored and dropped out. At Princeton, Dolan was already well on his way towards an alcohol dependency he would never shake off. He would die, perhaps a suicide, certainly mysteriously, in Chungking in 1945. At the beginning of the 1930s neither man could have imagined that they would be fighting on opposing sides in a world war ten years later, or that they would both enter the Forbidden City of Lhasa in very different circumstances, five years apart.

The two young, aspiring buccaneers met in Hanover in 1930.[6] Backed by the Academy of Natural Sciences in Philadelphia, Dolan was organizing an international expedition to Asia with American anthropologist Gordon Bowles and German zoologists and film-makers.[7] He'd come to Germany because he wanted to recruit the veteran explorer and panda hunter Hugo Weigold, who was director of the natural history department at the Hanover Museum. Weigold agreed to accompany the expedition, and he enthusiastically told Dolan about a remarkable young hunter and student naturalist called Ernst Schäfer.

According to the account of Schäfer's exploits in the SS journal *Das Schwarze Korps*,[8] Dolan began to hunt down the precocious young man – '*Wer ist Schäfer?*' The future explorer was still living at home in a room chock-full of birdcages and wild squirrels. The two men quickly hit it off, even though Dolan's uncouth manners appalled the Schäfer family. At dinner, he drained their wine cellar, put his muddy boots on their table linen, and when he finally went to bed he slept soundly with the boots still on.

The brassy, moneyed American lost no time in asking Schäfer to join him on an ambitious jaunt to the headwaters of the Yangtze where it crossed the Chinese border into the disputed Tibet provinces of Kham and Amdo. By 1930, explorers were beginning to experience difficulties when it came to finding the virginal 'white spaces' Sven Hedin and others had so brilliantly mapped. Western China on the borders of Tibet was the personal fiefdom of the Austrian-born American Joseph Rock, who travelled back and forth in style courtesy of the deep pockets of *National Geographic*. But this borderland between China and Tibet remained unstable and dangerous, its rugged, folded landscapes were perilous, and besides, Rock was a botanist. The fauna of Kham was not well known, and Philadelphia's Academy of Natural Sciences was enthusiastic about Dolan's plans to acquire specimens. Science was not the only motivation, though. Although Dolan had inherited money, he knew that a decent fortune could be made from rare animal skins.

Only just twenty, Schäfer was about to embark on a very big adventure indeed. He was over a year younger than the tough, hard-drinking American. 'Brooky' called his new German friend 'Junge', and there was no doubt that Dolan was in charge. Schäfer's accounts of these remarkable expeditions have never been translated into English, and Dolan's diaries gather dust in a vault in Philadelphia. Schäfer rarely discussed either his feelings for or his relationships with the men who accompanied him. Dolan is a shadowy figure who is only occasionally illuminated as if by a literary flashgun. But taken together, the books and diaries reveal an exotic and daunting world that would have been a revelation to Schäfer's readers. And they show, too, what made a young naturalist and explorer with apparently little interest in politics a favourite of one of the most powerful men in the Nazi regime.

According to myth, there is a long-haired wild yak of immense size living in the snowy recesses of Tibet. From its open mouth and long protruding red tongue comes a never-ending stream of water which, Tibetans say, is the source of the Dri Chu or Wild Yak River. To the rest of the world the Dri Chu is the Yangtze. This great four-thousand-mile-long river would be Dolan and Schäfer's road to glory.

Until the twentieth century Asia, rather than Africa, was believed to be the place of origin for numerous human and animal species. It was an idea that had led Eugene Dubois to search for the fossil remains of early man in Indonesia, where he triumphantly unearthed the skull of 'Java Man', and it was the lure for ambitious naturalists like Dolan and Schäfer who sought the founding, original species of the animal world on the desolate plains and in the high mountains of the Asian heartland, just as anthropologists would seek the origin of the Master Race. Tibet, the roof of the world, had a unique significance. Remote and inaccessible behind its mountain walls, this twelve-thousand-foot-high plateau was believed to be the lost refuge of scores of barely known animal species just waiting to be shot, named and collected. Dolan and Schäfer, like other naturalists of the early twentieth century, would use their rifles to harvest this cornucopia and bring their trophies back to the museums of Europe and the United States. Here they would be resurrected in spectacular dioramas which offered a pre-television age a simulacrum of an exotic natural world.

As a cub explorer, Schäfer had already found a model in Sven Hedin, whose achievements in the dangerous and unexplored regions straddling the Silk Road and in Tibet (he never got to Lhasa) made him famous, and an idol in Germany. Hedin was vainglorious and selfish. When he made unfounded claims about his discoveries at the Royal Geographical Society in London he was humiliated by other explorers who knew better and had the maps to prove he was mistaken.[9] Hedin came to loathe the British empire and revere Germany, and his passion grew even more fervent after 1933. He became a persistent and unrepentant apologist for the Third Reich – he opened the Berlin Olympic Games alongside Hitler in 1936 – even though his German great grandfather had been a rabbi.[10]

Hedin's many wordy books were very popular in Germany. He conjured up the romantic figure of a lone adventurer striding into the unknown, usually at tremendous personal risk. He was supremely arrogant. When he arrived at the source of the Indus, he wrote, 'Here I stood and wondered whether the Macedonian Alexander . . . had any notion where its source lay, and I revelled in the consciousness that, except for the Tibetans themselves, no human being but myself had penetrated to this spot.'[11] Hedin was also ruthless in his treatment of his native servants. Two unfortunates were left to die in the waterless dunes of the Takla Makan Desert in the course of one expedition. Hedin was Schäfer's model from the start, and he was determined to act the part.

Dolan's expedition was an international one. His colleague Gordon Bowles would investigate different strains of the 'Mongoloid Race' by taking skull and other body measurements and collecting cultural artefacts. Callipers, eye-colour charts and hair samples were standard equipment for many anthropologists in this period, but only American and German anthropologists relied so completely on anthropometric data. Both nations were preoccupied with race and with theories about race difference. Both shared a pseudoscientific language based on Aryan or Nordic superiority.[12] As a result, Bowles' work shared common ground with Bruno Beger's, as we shall see.

Bowles's doctoral thesis, written after the Dolan Expedition, can still be obtained, and it is revealing. In his introduction, he expresses 'sincerest thanks' to his tutor, Dr Ernest A. Hooton, who was a fervent eugenicist and disciple of the Italian criminologist Cesare Lombroso. Like his Italian mentor, Hooton believed that criminals had distinctive and measurable physical characteristics and were atavistic throwbacks to a 'ferocious and primitive' stage in human evolution. He disliked blacks and Jews and was fond of seedy jokes about Jewish colleagues. Hooton taught most American physical anthropologists in the 1920s and 1930s and his impact on Bowles' work in Asia is quite clear. I discovered one very striking example: Bowles claimed to have discovered 'an individual who harks back far into the past' with 'beetling brows . . . low cranial vault, [and] deep indented nasal depression'[13] – a clear echo of both Lombroso and Hooton.

Preparations began in the summer of 1930. Much of the equipment, as well as guns and ammunition, was acquired in Germany, 'only the tents, mountain saddles and some food' being provided by the Americans, according to Schäfer. Accompanying Dolan, Bowles, Schäfer and Weigold was a German cameraman and photographer, Otto Gneiser. The two Americans returned to Germany after Christmas, and the Dolan–Philadelphia Academy of Natural Sciences Zoological Expedition to West China was ready to depart by mid January 1931. On the 18th they set off from Berlin, travelling through Poland to Moscow. 'I remember the day we spent in Moscow', Schäfer wrote, 'as repelling and almost disgusting. Dirt and decay, ugly poor people, who all look the same. No laughter, but only dead-serious, pale Russian faces. In contrast to that those high-rise modern palatial industrial buildings, which appear to stand empty.' From Moscow they took the Trans-Siberian Railway to the Far East. 'We were', Schäfer continued, 'a "Young Man's Expedition" since it consisted, apart from Dr Weigold, only of young people. Bowles and Gneiser were in their mid 20s, Dolan was 22 and I was 20 years old. I explicitly mention this because I am deeply convinced that an expedition like ours, which made heavy demands on the physical toughness of each participant, can only be carried out with young people within such a short period of time. With little rest, we led the free and unattached life of nomads, full of vigour and enthusiasm . . .' This was a message to Germany, and to German youth in particular.

For many Germans, lands to the east had a powerful, even romantic appeal. Some had become convinced that Germany needed space for expansion. The Versailles Treaty had deprived Germany of her colonies in the Pacific and Africa, and after 1918 the demand for *Lebensraum* became ever more strident. The topic occupies many pages in Hitler's *Mein Kampf*; 'living space' was an answer to the psychological and economic plight of a nation still smarting from defeat. Schäfer made a quite deliberate appeal to this spirit. *Mountains, Buddhas and Bears* has a declamatory dedication to 'every real German "Junge" in whom *wanderlust* and energy are still alive . . . May they spread their wings to secure us colonies, a position in the world and a place in the sun again.' In his book, Schäfer flavours his call to arms with an apparently innocent romanticism. Although he was taking part in an international expedition led by an American, he frequently luxuriates in solitude and demonstrates lonely heroism in wild and challenging places. Many young men and women in Germany aspired to experiences like this at the beginning of the 1930s and the Nazi youth leaders did their utmost to exploit popular 'back to nature' movements like the 'Wandervogel'. In his diaries, Albert Speer wrote, 'We were always dreaming of solitude, of drives through quiet river valleys, of hiking to some high mountain pasture; we never felt the lure of Paris, London or Vienna . . .'[14]

After leaving the train in Teintsin, the expedition took a Japanese steamer across the South China Sea to Shanghai. A city of thirty-six nationalities, Shanghai was fractured by competing European powers who had arrogantly divided the city between them, and by stark barriers between the rich and the near destitute. Shanghai's other power brokers were gambling racketeers like the vicious 'Green Gang' who bribed Chinese and foreign police and beat up communists on behalf of the nationalists. Shanghai was wealthy and cosmopolitan, and it relished its talents for dissolution and sleaze. Its clubs, opium dens and brothels were infamous and promised to satisfy any vice. The white Russian girls who had been turfed out of Russia by the puritanical Bolsheviks were especially prized. While the poor died like flies – thirty thousand bodies were collected yearly from the streets[15] – the wealthier Europeans and Chinese made money and partied. Schäfer had little interest, it would seem, in the temptations of Shanghai. He visited the German Concordia Club, which was a rather tame affair compared to the Shanghai with its forty-seven-yard-long bar, and he went duck shooting with some gung-ho Americans.

Dolan was facing enormous difficulties. His destination was the 'Balkans of Central Asia', and in 1931 the border was in turmoil. Outside Shanghai, Chinese warlords were still a force to be reckoned with and were persistent thorns in the side of the Chinese nationalists, Chiang Kai-shek's Kuomintang. The Generalissimo himself, assisted by a German military expert, was more preoccupied with exterminating Chinese communists than with bringing order to his vast domains. The reality on the ground, as Dolan and Schäfer would discover, was that nationalist control of China did not extend very far outside the big cities. There was an ominous and growing threat from Japan, too, and posters began to appear in Shanghai, where there was a large Japanese community, declaring 'Kill all Japanese.'[16]

The situation on China's western borders was no better; it would cause Dolan no end of problems. The previous year, as he had been preparing to leave the United States, a local chief had seized the estates of a Tibetan monastery at Nyarong. The action had been supported by both the local warlord, General Liu Wen-hui, and officials of the Panchen Lama, who was in exile in China and stirring up trouble with Tibet's theocratic ruler, the 13th Dalai Lama. Monks from another monastery retook Nyarong, provoking the Chinese to seize control of the entire region. The monks appealed to Lhasa for assistance, and Tibetan troops marched east from the border town of Derge. The Dalai Lama, already furious with the Panchen Lama, asked Chiang Kai-shek to mediate even as his own ill-equipped troops were attacking the Generalissimo's army. Not surprisingly, his gesture failed to calm the situation, and by the spring of 1931 the Tibetan forces had pushed west as far as Tachienlu – Dolan's destination in Kham. The situation became even more hazardous when yet another Chinese warlord, the Muslim General Ma Pu-fang, opened a new front north-west of Chamdo. The situation was complicated and frequently baffling, and a recipe for trouble. Dolan would need all his powers and charm to persuade the Chinese authorities to issue permits for such a dangerous border.

Negotiations were tough and frustrating, and it was too long a wait for the impatient young Schäfer. He persuaded Dolan to let him push on ahead so long as he did not incur the wrath of the Chinese. By going ahead Schäfer would hire and train local taxidermists to join the expedition; they would be essential if the animal specimens were to get back safely to Philadelphia and Göttingen. Schäfer and Dolan arranged to meet again in Szechuan, and the young German travelled on alone heading for Chongqing, China's innermost treaty port, more than a thousand miles and twelve days' steaming away.

Schäfer soon found a steamer heading upriver, an armour-plated tub the SS *Ichang* whose captain was a somewhat decayed Englishman called Nichols. At dawn on a foggy morning, Captain Nichols weighed anchor and headed upstream across the Whangpo towards the wide, flat waters of the Yangtze. The river is ten to fifty miles wide at its mouth and has a sluggish, silt-surfeited current that builds treacherous mud banks just beneath the surface. Schäfer watched intently as they passed enormous junks with huge ragged and ribbed sails, heavy with wood-oil, tea and rice and steered, it seemed, by two intent eyes at the bow. Though Schäfer's writings rarely disclose details of an unmanly inner life, this journey up the Yangtze must have been an alarming experience for a young man who had never travelled far from a bedroom full of squirrels or the hills around Hamburg. He was now discovering that outside Germany there was chaos and the clashing of races and creeds.

Nichols travelled by day and anchored at night. The first stop was Zhenjiang, where the world's longest man-made waterway, the Grand Canal, joins the river. As they set off again, Nichols pointed out to the German zoologist the Yangtze dolphins riding the wake of the *Ichang*. As they steamed on past Nanking, Wuhu, Kiukiang and Kuling a savage world opened before Schäfer's eyes. At a stop downstream, he watched as 'seven wretches' were executed by sword in the open street. He saw 'screaming insane cripples, and mutilated beggars who slowly fade away in the excrement and dirt'. On board ship, he made friends with a Russian radio operator who took the prim explorer to cabarets in Hankow, an important junction on the Yangtze and often called China's Chicago. The British, French and Russians all had concessions here. There was even a small German *Bund*, or trade concession, but the Germans were late-comers and envied the power of their rivals. Hankow was the centre of the opium trade which had ensnared millions of Chinese in a prison of poverty and addiction. Brick tea, made from the dust of the tea factories, was sent from Hankow to Tibet, where it was mixed with yak butter and consumed in enormous quantities. Hankow had also been the condenser for nationalist passions that had overturned the Manchu emperors in 1912. Further downstream was Nanjing. Here, a century earlier, the English diplomat Sir Henry Pottinger had used his formidable negotiating powers to force the fading Manchu dynasty to allow their empire to be opened up for commerce and trade. Pottinger had also acquired the island of Hong Kong 'in perpetuity'. The Barbarians humiliated the Celestials, and the Yangtze became a pulsing artery for foreign commerce. Europeans and Americans steamed their way up and down the river building their *Bunds* and consulates and draining the wealth from one of the oldest empires on earth. There were fascinating lessons here for a German who envied the imperial triumphs of other nations.

Travelling on the Yangtze could be extremely hazardous, even though the foreign powers policed the river as best they could. After Hankow, Schäfer and the other passengers were provided with rifles, and American soldiers, bristling with machine guns, clambered on board. As the boat pushed back, it was almost immediately attacked by bandits – communists, according to Schäfer's account. As Captain Nichols called for full steam, there was a deafening roar of gunfire from the deck and cabin windows. Its ferocity took their attackers by surprise. They beat a hasty retreat and vanished upriver. The young

German was exhilarated. The rest of the journey was tense; only Schäfer and the marines were brave or reckless enough to stay on deck at night, smoking and sipping beer. As the *Ichang* steamed up the great dark river, Schäfer watched, mesmerized, burning villages with frantic human silhouettes criss-crossing the flames, and women and children huddled under the river bank. Miles away, on the hills above the river, other unexplained fires flickered menacingly. The *Ichang* steamed on through a great defile ripped out by the Yangtze known as the Three Gorges. At night, there were blood-curdling cries and the crackle of rifle fire.

After a nerve-racking journey, Schäfer arrived at Chongqing in Szechuan ('Four Rivers'). Here he stayed with a German family, the Dohrs, who were working for IG Farben and knew Schäfer's father. He found and hired a cook, who called himself August and had a smattering of German which he'd picked up as a galley hand on a German warship. With the Dohrs' help, he hired men he could train to work with the animals he and Dolan would acquire over the coming months.

Weeks later, the rest of the expedition caught up. Dolan and Weigold now had to spend several days organizing a caravan: finding horses and pack animals and hiring more than a hundred sherpas. They were delayed again by fighting between local warlords, much to Dolan's disgust. When the morning of departure finally arrived, Dolan and Bowles handed out Stars and Stripes flags to their sherpas. Unprepared for this, Schäfer dashed back and got the Dohrs to improvise a German flag. August held it proudly aloft. National differences were always just below the surface, and would emerge even more fiercely on Dolan's second expedition a few years later.

Schäfer and Dolan were about to embark on a journey deep into the Chinese and Tibetan past. From its headwaters in Tibet to its mouth in the East China Sea, where it dumps three hundred million tons of alluvium each year, the Yangtze travels nearly four thousand miles. In its lower reaches it is wide and flat, but travel higher and it becomes fast, turbulent and dangerous. On its long journey from a mountain pool in Tibet, at 18,750 feet, to its delta, the river falls nearly four miles. That's eight feet every mile, on average. To travel up the Yangtze means to ascend dizzyingly higher – and deeper into China's geological and human past.[17] Dolan and Schäfer were heading for that great crumple zone that was twisted and thrown up millions of years ago when India smashed into Asia. This stunning collision created an immense tangle of gnarled and craggy rock that buttresses the Tibetan plateau on all sides. This mass of rock and ancient ocean sediment is daily eviscerated by the relentless waters that cascade from Tibet's snow- and glacier-encrusted peaks. As well as the Yangtze, the Yellow, the Mekong and the Salween Rivers all drain from the great plateau that lay ahead of them.

Despite Joseph Rock's reports to *National Geographic*, west China and the Tibetan borders remained perplexing and mysterious to geographers. In old Chinese maps the headwaters of the river were always shown occluded by cloud and mist and the convention remained a valid metaphor even in 1931. Here, on the edge of Tibet, the Yangtze was the Dri Chu or 'Wild Yak River'. It is hard to imagine a more appropriate name, for at higher altitudes the yak is ubiquitous. These animals, which produce tamer breeds lower down towards China where they have mated with local cattle, are the mainstay of the nomads who still roam these high prairies. Yak-hair tents provide shelter and food; yak hair clothes the poor; yak-hair ropes tie yak-hair bags onto yaks; yak bones make glue; yak shoulder blades are used as surfaces on which to write prayers; yak horns make snuff boxes or whisky flasks; yak skin is used to make thongs, thimbles, snow goggles, sacks and slings; yak tails decorate horses; a yak's glands are used to cure many kinds of ailment. Boiled and roasted yak steaks are usually washed down with yak butter tea; hardened yak cheese and dried yak provide sustenance on the road. Schäfer and Dolan would need to like yak a great deal.

From Szechuan, Dolan led the expedition across the 'Red Basin', heading north-west towards Chengdu. As they rode or walked the hard, red ground, temperatures grew fearsomely hot as they approached the notorious 'Yangtze Furnaces'. Despite the roasting heat, they made good progress – as much as forty miles a day. At the furthest edge of the Red Basin, the land began to rise as they approached the foothills of faraway Tibetan ranges. Schäfer described the villages they passed through rather fastidiously: 'In one village, Dolan tries to clean excrement, which covers the street, from his shoes and steps onto a pile of straw by the side of the street. Immediately the straw comes to life and a leper beggar, who wanted to die in peace, looks at us from under the straw.' In Chengdu, which they reached after ten gruelling days travelling more than three hundred miles, the presence of Europeans had brought, Schäfer wrote, something resembling civilization. They found a university, parks, even a few cars. 'It is', Schäfer wrote, 'an oasis of higher civilization.'

Schäfer's attitudes to race are often contradictory. He appears to have absorbed the theories of his time and nation when, for example, he writes, 'The Tibetan women are very fertile and often give birth to about a dozen children. But due to a lack of hygiene the mortality rate of children is immense. As well as that, weak elements are eliminated [*ausmerzen*] by the harshness of the climate and they struggle for survival from an early stage so that the Tibetan people appear to be vigorous and healthy.' Struggle makes us strong. Such ideas were shared by Adolf Hitler in *Mein Kampf*, but they were also the mainstay of most German biologists and anthropologists. As he travelled deeper into Tibet he would come to see Buddhism, which he called Lamaism, as a force that weakened and corrupted this hardy people. But on other occasions Schäfer describes native peoples as 'children of nature'. They were less developed and lacked civilization but were more admirable. He liked to refer to himself as a kind of primitive, in harmony with the beasts he hunted. Many anthropolgists viewed native peoples in the same way and were convinced that they were destined to vanish as more developed peoples swept the world.

The expedition members now had very different needs. Bowles wanted to pursue his anthropological work in a place where he could find willing subjects in sufficiently large numbers; Dolan and Schäfer were itching to get into the mountains to hunt, shoot and collect. So Dolan, Schäfer and Weigold decided to part company with Bowles and Gneiser and travel north into the wilderness to hunt for the legendary 'Bambus-bear' – that is, the panda – then travel up the Min River into Tibet.

For the first leg of the journey, everyone took the narrow, paved path that led out of Chengdu and followed the tea caravans towards the city of Tachienlu – Dartsendo to the Tibetans – often called the doorway to Tibet. Tachienlu, whose name means 'horse tongue junction', is squeezed into a narrow gorge and appears set against sheer precipices. From a distance, its pagodas and temples seemed to float in the thin mountain air. It was a small place, just one or two dirty streets and a lamasery called Dorjedra ('Lightning Bolt Rock'), but it was a centre for the tea trade and for Bowles an ideal laboratory in which to study the peoples who teemed through its streets and thronged its markets. There were wild-looking Tibetans from Derge who bartered their musk and yak hides for silver with which they bought *tsampa* (barley flour), silk and sugar.

Keeping their distance from these ragged multitudes were the Chinese, who despised the sun-blackened Tibetans, and Muslims. The few Europeans were usually missionaries. Bowles and Gneiser stayed on in Tachienlu with a missionary family, the Cunninghams.

Dolan, Schäfer and Weigold pushed on with the rest of the caravan steadily upwards through the densely forested slopes of the Wuyaoling Mountains. Beyond they could see immense snowy peaks that glowed gold and pink and mauve in the setting sun. It was their first sight of Tibet. But progress was often slow. The Tibetan muleteers would not move on without consulting a local lama and the Europeans complained bitterly about the laziness of their men and their temperamental animals.

As they approached the border, they began to pass Tibetan peasants, their faces daubed black, Mongolians carrying salt from the Tsaidam Desert, merchants and elaborately attired nobles. Sometimes the entourage of an incarnate lama or rimpoche came clattering past. There were still numerous Chinese and Muslims on the road as well as nomadic Khamdos and even Lolos, whose isolated kingdom had recently been explored by Joseph Rock. They passed women with elaborately bejewelled head-dresses which rocked back and forth as they walked or rode. Small Buddhist monasteries clung to the sides of deep rocky valleys which amplified the throaty roar of the prayer horns and the tintinnabulation of bells. Many of the Chinese travellers, they discovered, were hopelessly addicted to opium. When the expedition halted at wayside inns they could always hear the incessant night-long sucking of opium pipes from adjoining rooms and smell its sweet resinous perfume. There were many elderly, emaciated addicts who simply lay down by the side of the road to die, their bodies drawing the attention only of vultures and other scavengers.

Schäfer was increasingly exhilarated by these experiences,

but he had, at first, mixed success with his hunting. On 18 April he spotted his first golden pheasant but was unable to bring one down. He managed to shoot a goral, a kind of goat-antelope, but then lost the corpse. Leopards failed to be tempted by a goat with a lamp strung around its neck, and everywhere Schäfer was persecuted by dogs whose favourite delicacy was human excrement; 'it's funny how these dogs always seem to know what you are about to do: they keep their eyes on you and follow you silently'.

The expedition set off again the following morning, now accompanied by a Chinese orphan boy called Bauze (or 'leopard') who had taken a fancy to Dolan, as well as five servants, eight hunters and many dogs. Despite his youth, Schäfer proved a hard taskmaster – the Hedin model – and tended to compensate by indulging a favourite. In Schäfer's case, it was a young Chinese man called Wang.

Here on the Tibetan borders, in the mountains of the Wassu, Schäfer and Dolan had one consuming obsession: the giant panda, *Aeluropus melanolueca*, known to local people as a *beishung*, or 'white bear'. Exquisitely adapted to the bamboo forests, the panda had until the twentieth century few enemies in the wild so they reproduced and matured slowly – and were unprepared for the arrival of Western hunters. The first panda to be shot in the wild was killed by two of the Roosevelt dynasty, its body returned in triumph to the Field Museum in Chicago. For Dolan and Schäfer, the panda was a holy grail and both men believed it was their sacred duty to hunt one down. But it had to be, or to seem to be, a solitary quest. Schäfer, impulsive as ever, headed alone with no water or food high into the mountains. He climbed higher and higher through often impenetrable fog, and at last entered the dense bamboo forests that covered the higher slopes. This at last was the realm of the giant panda. It was dark between the trees and Schäfer made slow progress. Every so often he stopped to listen, awed by the silence. No living creature stirred in the deep forest. Was he reminded of his ordeal in the Odenwald with Herr Direktor? The panda was, for now, elusive.

Schäfer took frightening risks with his porters and servants, just as Hedin had. At the beginning of May, he, Weigold and Dolan decided to explore and hunt separately, dividing up the landscape between them. Schäfer, Wang, young Bauze and an old Tsau Po hunter who had mysteriously appeared at the camp one evening struck up a steep rocky valley. Bauze was carrying seventy pounds of provisions and was quickly exhausted. After nine hours of fruitless marching – they saw few tracks and no animals worth a shot – the party made camp. As a chill, grey dawn broke the next day, Schäfer saw that he and his party faced a 'horrible descent'. Enormous boulders were strewn across the path down and the going proved to be exceptionally tough. It was hardest and most frightening for young Bauze, who had to negotiate a near vertical trail carrying his heavy load. Every step was perilous, and his eyes were wide with terror. Instead of relieving him of the packs he was carrying, Schäfer ordered him to follow as best he could. As the main party struggled over the tangled boulders, Bauze fell further and further behind. Soon they had lost him altogether, and with him all their supplies. As the light went, the rain came in torrents. Everyone was stumbling helplessly around in the dark when Dolan appeared out of nowhere with food to spare. There was still no sign of Bauze, but Schäfer recorded little anxiety. The next day, the exhausted lad eventually turned up with the food supplies still strapped to his back. For Schäfer this was good news: it meant he could stay away from the main camp another day and shoot.

His determination and ruthless tactics paid off. On 13 May 1931 he became the second white man to shoot a panda. In his book *Tibet ruft*, Schäfer had himself photographed after the hunt with a bird hanging from one hand and the dead panda nestled under his arm.

By the middle of June, Schäfer and Dolan were edging across the troubled border into Tibet itself. To be precise, they had entered 'Inner Tibet', so called because of its proximity to China and because here the Dalai Lama exercised little power. For centuries, the rulers of the Chinese empire had fretted over this murky border, their power waxing and waning, but always asserting their rights over the fragile nationhood of Tibet. Tibet is ringed by mountain ranges, but here in the east the rugged peaks and valleys are more vulnerable to human penetration than the mighty Himalayas or the Kunlun. This was Tibet's geographical Achilles heel. In 1904, the Ch'ing Empress sent a Manchurian magistrate, Chao Er-fang, and a Szechuan general, Ma Wei-ch'i, to terrorize the region, annihilate the Buddhist clergy and try to replace Tibetans with Chinese peasants. In 1910, the general marched on to Lhasa and forced the Dalai Lama to flee into exile. The roads Schäfer and Dolan now marched along would be used in 1951 by the armies of Mao Tse-tung to crush Tibetan independence. The world Schäfer observed twenty years before that catastrophe had been unstable and troubled for many centuries and was now a battlefield. In one village he found Tibetan prisoners, a hundred of them locked up in a shabby compound. Over the next weeks they passed through one smouldering Tibetan village after another, all razed by Chinese warlords or the forces of Chiang Kai-shek.

Despite this, signs of the Buddhist faith were everywhere Schäfer looked; at the summit of high passes were piles of prayer stones and wildly fluttering prayer flags. Pilgrims travelling to the sacred Lake Kokonor or the Kumbum Monastery prostrated themselves in the road on their infinitely slow progress to enlightenment. Almost everyone they encountered held prayer beads and incessantly turned prayer wheels. Everywhere they could hear the rhythmic chant of the Tibetan Buddhist prayer:

Om Mani Padme Hum,
Om Mani Padme Hum,
Om Mani Padme Hum.

By the time he had returned to Germany and written about his experiences, Schäfer appears to have begun to distrust 'Lamaism'. The Tibetans he viewed as 'hard and cruel like the land itself', but 'their whole life and work is dominated by their fanatical Lamaist religion. I know the Tibetans as a powerful, healthy people – but they suffer under the yoke of their religion, depriving them of any chance of development.' In 1939, Schäfer would tell the Regent that he was a devoted student of Buddhism, but the idea of a Lamaist dictatorship became ingrained.

As they travelled north and west, Schäfer described one very curious episode. After the moon had set one night, he and Wang slipped into a deserted cemetery and stole a skull from a grave. 'Tibetan skulls are almost unknown to science,' he wrote. The incident is an odd one. Most Tibetans are disposed of by sky burial: their bodily remains are dismembered and fed to vultures. Schäfer gives very few details. The grave might have been that of a Tibetan who had died in a Chinese village, been buried by villagers and the site marked by prayer stones or flags. Tibetan priests use human skulls in some rituals, but it is impossible to know this one's origins with any certainty. What the curious little story tells us, though, is that Schäfer was aware of the needs of anthropologists. Skulls were highly prized: his own university at Göttingen had its own fine collection. Perhaps this one ended up back there.

At dawn, Schäfer spotted an eagle riding the thermals above the camp, and shot it down. 'Should I scream for joy? Should I be sad?' he wrote disingenuously. A photograph shows the magnificent bird, its wings stretched wide by Schäfer's servants. Not content with that, he then joined Dolan on a gazelle hunt, although they were quickly separated. The pattern is characteristic: as a storyteller, Schäfer never shared out the derring-do, certainly not with an American. The following day Schäfer arrogantly shot a vulture – an especially holy bird in Tibet – and not for the last time had to placate a crowd of indignant Tibetans.

They passed through shabby 'degenerate' villages where people looked sick and begged the Europeans for medicines. Even the animals were in a poor condition. 'The women are ugly and small,' noted Schäfer. He observed that the swastika was a symbol of good fortune. The weather turned against the expedition again: it rained for two days and there were terrifying thunderstorms.

By now Dolan and Schäfer had cut a swathe through the fauna of west China and Tibet and their packs groaned under the weight of skins and other trophies. They began to head south and east back towards Tachienlu. After a difficult trek through a region of lush, tangled trees, they sheltered in a monastery which had been plundered by Chinese troops. There was still a forlorn group of 'Yellow Hat' monks in residence, 'sad and lonely in this Chinese environment'. The next day, the caravan set off again and descended further into China. There were feelings of regret: 'the romanticism of the unknown will lie far behind in the mountains, which no white man has stepped on before . . .' It was an exaggerated but, for his readers, a necessary claim.

Schäfer's mood changed quickly. In Tachienlu there would be mail waiting, and news from the Fatherland: 'I feel as if I have become a real human being again, because all my thoughts focus on this far away country called Germany.' It was 19 June 1931. They stayed at the mission Bowles and Gneiser had been using for anthropological and filming work. Schäfer and Dolan opened their mail, then took a bath, changed their clothes and soon 'looked like real gentlemen'. Plans now had to be made to return home. Dolan, Bowles and Gneiser would leave for Shanghai, where their collections would be sent on to Philadelphia and Hanover; Weigold and Schäfer decided to head south towards Burma. It would turn out to be an 'incomparable experience'. As they were about to part, Dolan commented to Schäfer, 'You know, Junge, I hate civilization and it might be true that I behave like a domestic dog . . .' It would turn out to be a prescient self-analysis.

Schäfer and Weigold, homeward bound, entered a long-vanished world of tiny isolated kingdoms and despotic rulers. The 'king' of Muli had once even tried to conquer the Tibetan capital Lhasa, and his defeat had turned him into an even greater autocrat at home, where he had absolute power over his subjects. He was also an incarnate lama and used religious superstition, spells and magical invocations to reinforce his power, spiced with a diet of frequent public executions. Schäfer had, naturally, begun to impose his own kind of power on the local wildlife, but hunting was forbidden in Muli and the king's guard accosted him and made him stop. 'Not being allowed to hunt in this wonderful stag country is hard for me . . .' he wrote in his diary.

By mid December Schäfer and Weigold had recrossed the Yangtze. Through stormy weather they headed towards the Likiang Mountains. On the 14th they stumbled on the camp of Joseph Rock himself, the great explorer.[18] The bedraggled Germans were amazed by what they found. Rock made sure he lived high on the hog. He had his favourite Austrian dishes prepared by his personal chef and served with the best wines from his homeland. He bathed in a folding tub from Abercrombie and Fitch. Porters carried him everywhere. The Germans were hairy, unkempt – and smelly. Rock witheringly told them, 'When someone is travelling like you in great haste and with little time, you have to do without hygiene and civilization if you want any success at all.' Schäfer would vigorously apply this lesson when he sailed for Tibet on behalf of the SS seven years later.

By 13 January 1932 it was all over. After a rapid journey through India, Schäfer realized he was back in civilization. He arranged for a car to take them to Calcutta. 'I have rarely hated – but I hate this car more than anything in the world,' he wrote. 'Nirvana [*sic*] is over – the jungle which only knows fighting but no hatred. The last thing I hear is the loud, happy screaming of the monkeys, the farewell song of the gibbons.'

Such were Ernst Schäfer's first youthful adventures, the serendipitous gift of an American friend. As he describes them in *Mountains, Buddhas and Bears*, his experiences have a freshness and simplicity, even an innocence, that must have appealed to men who had experienced the last bitter years of Weimar. Here in the thin, cold air of the Tibetan borderlands it was possible to forget the crushed hopes, the violence and fear that had begun to overwhelm Germany. But Schäfer's experience expressed much more than the pure bloom of innocence and high adventure. There is an insouciant brutality in his attention to the details of killing. He lived for the squeeze of the trigger, the dropping animal and the mastery of death. It was a ruthless passion that he shared with Hermann Göring and Heinrich Himmler, keen huntsmen both. Nature was not there to be experienced or enjoyed; it offered riches to be plundered and brought back to the treasure houses of Europe's museums. Here the proud representatives of nature would be stuffed and mounted. To collect was to control. Schäfer had also learnt that expeditions need ruthless leaders, and that he chafed at being led. He had discovered the *Führer prinzip* for himself.

Adventure was not enough, and he knew it. Although Schäfer's books contain little science – they are about collecting, not analysing – he knew that he faced a dead end if he did not return to university and finish his *Doktorarbeit*. So Schäfer accepted the inevitable and enrolled at Göttingen University.

Göttingen was a small German town in Lower Saxony famous chiefly for its university and its mathematicians. It had been founded in 1737 by George II, Elector of Hanover and King of England, and its elegant buildings were scattered throughout the town's narrow medieval streets and squares. In the Botanical Gardens statues commemorated illustrious scientists such as Carl Friedrich Gauss; Goethe and the Grimm Brothers had lived there, and the anthropologist J. F. Blumenbach had assembled a famous collection of skulls in the Anatomie. But for Schäfer, academic life proved to be as tedious as he had feared. He began to work towards his dissertation, and for month after dreary month 'counted and measured the hairs of deers'.

Outside the laboratory there was seismic change, and its impact would very soon be felt in Göttingen's tranquil streets and lecture halls. In May 1932, the German president von Hindenburg appointed a new chancellor – Franz von Papen, an aristocratic equestrian with a dubious record whom he hoped would fix the dizzying crisis. By now Nazi violence was impossible to avoid and SA stormtroopers fought daily pitched battles with communists on the streets of many German cities. The Nazi gangs sang '*Blut musst fliessen, Blut musst fliessen!*' ('Blood must flow, blood must flow!') and embarked on a campaign of brutal intimidation and murder. In the election that July, the Nazis dealt another blow to German democracy by winning 13.7 million votes and acquiring 230 seats in the Reichstag, making them the biggest party.

But then Hitler faltered. Many Germans who had voted for the Nazis were disgusted when Hermann Göring, Hitler's deputy, unleashed chaos in the Reichstag, and the murder of a young communist in front of his family in Upper Silesia repelled many more. New elections confirmed that the support for the NSDAP was indeed falling, but the party still had the upper hand in the Reichstag. But soon the stampede to disaster resumed.

On 4 January 1933, a right-wing banker called Kurt von Schröder invited the Nazi elite – Hitler, Himmler and Hess – to his villa and sent out signals that he and the former chancellor Franz von Papen would be prepared to support a Hitler chancellorship. At a series of meetings, many of them in the Dahlem home of Joachim von Ribbentrop, secret negotiations were opened between Hitler, President von Hindenburg and his ineffectual and opportunist son Oskar. On 30 January Hitler was made Chancellor of Germany. That year the rotten planks of Germany's broken democracy were swept away – the Nazi Revolution had begun. Hitler thanked one constituency in particular: the students and intellectuals who had voted for the NSDAP in their hundreds of thousands.

The brightest and the best were soon clamouring to join the ranks of Heinrich Himmler's elite SS. There is no record of Schäfer's thoughts and motivations in 1933, so he can be judged only by his actions. Urged by the Mayor of Göttingen, a friend of his father, he applied to join the SS. This might contradict Schäfer's claim that his family was a liberal and democratic one, but it was Ernst alone among his siblings who applied and underwent the obligatory ancestral investigations. The Reichsführer insisted on a clean Aryan record all the way back to the eighteenth century.

Walter Schellenberg, who became a leading SS officer,

remembered that the SS 'was already considered an elite organization. The black clad uniform of the Führer's special guard was dashing and elegant. In the SS one found "the better class of people" and membership of it brought considerable prestige and social advantages.'[19] Many of the young men, like Schäfer, who joined in 1933 hoped for brighter chances in the universities, which they viewed as moribund and decayed, offering minimal opportunity for promotion.

Himmler soon began to assault Germany's academia. After 1933, more than two thousand academics and intellectuals left Germany. Many were Jews or social democrats or communists sacked by thuggish former colleagues; others saw that mortal danger lay ahead and fled. For those who stayed there were new opportunities, and SS membership often ensured a glittering future. These young Turks might disdain the crass former corporal who had seized power, but a new world was taking shape. It needed doctors, lawyers and scientists, especially biologists. Join now or lose out for ever. And, quite suddenly, in the universities there were vacant chairs and fewer competitors. Change was happening quickly. Academic institutions have always been nests of vipers; who among the snakes would not have seized the new opportunities offered by simply filling in a form and checking who your great-great-great grandfather was?

The intellectuals who joined the SS were radicals. They believed in new ideas and new solutions. They valued expertise and professionalism. Many were lawyers, men like Dr Werner Best, Otto Ohlendorf, Reinhard Höhn and Franz Six who realized that they had much to gain if they were involved from the start in the legal revolution the Nazis had begun. Gunter d'Alquen was a journalist who became the chief editor of the slick SS journal *Das Schwarze Korps*. Himmler made sure that a doctor joining the SS would receive favourable treatment from funding bodies, and some at least were fascinated by the power over life and death implied by the 'death's-head' insignia.[20]

In that first year, the SS made little difference to Ernst Schäfer. He toiled away in Göttingen, then at Hanover University, and made the occasional trip to the Natural History Museum in South Kensington. Then Brooke Dolan re-entered his life.

CHAPTER TWO

EDGE OF THE WORLD

'On my earlier expeditions, which I conducted with Anglo-Saxons, I found a number of mistakes and shortcomings . . .'

– Ernst Schäfer, *Geheimnis Tibet*, 1943

On his return to the United States, Dolan had gone to Harvard intending to complete his zoological studies. But, once again, he was restless. He had to escape. So Brooky telegraphed 'Junge', cryptically: 'A quite large Tibet Expedition, do you want to come?' Schäfer responded to his friend 'with the blond tuft and blue eyes' with an unconditional 'yes'. Schäfer was not the only person Dolan had been wooing. In the spring of 1934, after a stormy engagement, he had married Emilie Gerhard and persuaded her to accompany his 'quite large' new expedition as far as Shanghai. But still Dolan was not happy.

Less than a week later, Schäfer spotted an American newspaper. Splashed across its front page was an astonishing headline: BOY EXPLORER GOES BERSERK! Seizing the paper, Schäfer read on with swelling dismay. 'Brooky', wildly drunk, had broken into a friend's house, demolished the furniture and hurled Ming dynasty ornaments to the floor. He had been pursued and quickly arrested. His orgy of destruction was estimated to have cost $50,000 and only the Dolan name and their expensive attorney saved him from a prison sentence. The Boy Dolan, with his 'wild Irish blood', was, as Schäfer knew, already a chronic drinker; he needed 'to take a long leave from high society in the wilderness to let grass grow over the thing . . .' Looking back from 1951 when Dolan had been dead for six years, Schäfer wrote with tut-tutting sanctimony: 'the second expedition wasn't the result of careful planning and calm scientific reflection but was the result of the crazy pranks of a young American who had too much money and was fed up with ordinary life and did not know how to use his surplus energy'. So Dolan escaped to Shanghai, leaving who knew what demons behind him in Philadelphia.

Dolan's 'quite large' expedition turned out to be somewhat small. He had asked Schäfer at the outset, 'Can I trust you?' and, not satisfied with the answer, had enlisted another and much more experienced American, Marion Duncan. So the new expedition comprised just three men. Duncan was a Christian missionary, a 'Disciple of Christ in Tibet and China' of twelve years' standing who described himself, with good reason, as a 'walking dictionary about [China]'. His correspondence reveals his practical expertise and knowledge. He was punctilious in all he did. In February 1934 he added a list of essential presents for the expedition: 'safety pins large sizes, pocket knives, mirrors, bottles about three or four ounce ones especially coloured ones useful for snuff, with corks to fit . . .'

The second expedition would turn out to be tougher than the first, and by the end friendships would be soured or broken. Schäfer is mentioned just three times in Duncan's account of the expedition[1] and always to his disadvantage. He is portrayed as impulsive and inexperienced, and Schäfer was by now enough of an *SS Mann* to anger the missionary with his beliefs – as Duncan's letters, sent to the Academy after the expedition returned, reveal.[2] Dolan appears to have enjoyed mayhem too much to select as companions people who would find each other agreeable.

By the time Dolan (with his new wife Emilie in tow) and Schäfer returned to Shanghai in 1934, Japanese aggression against China had entered a new and expansionist phase. In 1931, when Schäfer and Dolan were on their way home after their first expedition, a bomb had exploded under a Japanese train in Mukden (now Shen Yang) in Manchuria. The damage was minimal but the 'Mukden Incident' – organized, as it turned out, by Manchurian agents of the Japanese – was an engineered excuse to invade Manchuria, which the Japanese had long coveted. Because the armies of Chiang Kai-shek were tied down fighting the communists, Chinese forces were swiftly overwhelmed.

China, already broken by a bloody civil war, now plunged further into chaos. The communists were holed up in the Jiangxi 'Soviet' in the east. The nationalist armies – now commanded by a German, General Hans von Seekt, who had been sent to assist the Generalissimo by Hitler – repeatedly battered Mao's stronghold, squeezing the communists' territory by more than half and killing tens of thousands of Red Army soldiers and civilians. While Chiang Kai-shek routed the communists, the Japanese marched unopposed as far as the Great Wall and launched an assault on Shanghai itself. For the communists there was only one workable strategy – to retreat to the north and recoup. And so began, in the autumn of 1934, the Long March. The route the Red Army followed would take them west first of all, then north along the Tibet–China border, where Schäfer, Dolan and Duncan would shortly arrive.

When Schäfer disembarked in Shanghai he discovered Dolan at the quay wearing a uniform and waving a big revolver. It turned out he had joined what Schäfer calls a '*Hilfskorps*' – an aid organization set up to assist citizens of Shanghai after the Japanese attack on the city in 1932. Dolan used the revolver to shoot up glasses in Shanghai bars.

The expedition was stuck in Shanghai for two months negotiating permits, and Dolan and Schäfer used the time to practise what they called a 'Ngolok Cry'. 'We didn't care about civilization at all.' What Emilie Dolan made of all this is impossible to know since Schäfer and Dolan (in his diaries) very rarely refer to her presence. 'Sometimes Brooky's state of mind was really scary,' Schäfer remembered. 'He used to say, "I'm only going to Tibet to find the truth; if you help me with a scientific collection as well, even better."'

For his part, faced with the chaos to which Dolan seemed addicted, Schäfer probably began thinking ahead to his own German expedition. He decided to track down the Panchen Lama, and he had no intention of involving Dolan. He must have assumed that since the 'Great' 13th Dalai Lama had recently died and his incarnation was still being sought, the Panchen Lama would be able to open the door to Tibet and even Lhasa, the Forbidden City. But Schäfer was mistaken. The Panchen Lama had been a thorn in the side of the late Dalai Lama and was regarded with deep suspicion by the Kashag, the government in Lhasa, who suspected that he was being used by the Chinese. In this, they were correct. The Chinese were urging the timid, retiring Panchen Lama to return to Tibet accompanied by an 'escort' of ten thousand soldiers.

In June, still waiting for permissions to travel and with temperatures soaring in Shanghai, Schäfer decided to travel south to Hangzhou where he had heard that the Panchen Lama was staying in a mountain temple. He turned out to be a middle-aged man 'with a good-natured, but forceful facial expression and beautiful dark eyes'. In Schäfer's words, 'As he hears that I am German, his eyes become very lively. He asks how far away Germany is, if I have been attacked by robbers on that long journey and if my animals are well looked after. The Living Buddha asks me all these astonishing questions in a touchingly sympathetic manner, as he seems to believe that there are many travelling nomads in Germany and big robber bands that besiege the high passes, just like in the "land of eternal glaciers".' Although the Panchen Lama gave Schäfer letters of recommendation, they would prove to be completely worthless.

Marion Duncan joined them in July, and on a hot, torpid evening Schäfer and the Americans boarded the SS *Ichang* and began their journey. On board, Schäfer was delighted to discover the Russian radio operator who had been his companion during his solitary first voyage up the Yangtze in 1931, although there was no sign of Captain Nichols. The Russian did not return the compliment of recognition until Schäfer reminded him of 'the experiences we had together, the cabarets in Hankow, the shooting with the communists'. A melancholy smile then spread across the radio operator's face and he ponderously declared, 'I am pleased to meet you.' 'We shake hands. We don't have much to say to each other and so we gaze across the armour plates on to the wide, vast river . . .'

Nine days out of Shanghai, the temperatures grew searingly hot, the nights close and humid. 'Emmie acquired an atrocious sunburn on her legs,' Dolan wrote in his diary, 'simply by sitting at the rail and absorbing the glare from the water . . . but Schäfer and I spent a certain time each day on the sundeck roof. Most of the day we put in reading or writing or drinking beer.' The next day, they steamed into thick fog through which they could glimpse the conical and pyramidal peaks of the Tiger's

Tooth Gorge. On either side were precipices of gleaming yellow limestone. In the afternoon they reached the Ox-liver Horse-tongue Gorge where the *Ichang* stopped to view the 'Clown of the Yangtze' – a bizarre mass of twisted rocks resembling a cartoon-like human face. The following day the *Ichang* plunged into the ferocious Hsintan Rapids. From the deck, a steel cable was thrown out across the water and lashed to rocks by Chinese 'coolies' who inhabited squalid, moveable huts by the temperamental river and made a living guiding steamers through the seething torrent. The boat was then hauled through the rapids, 'squeaking in every plank', Duncan remembered, and 'seeming to stand still for awful moments'.

When they reached Chongqing, Emilie Dolan had had enough – of the heat and of her unpredictable husband and his *Boy's Own* adventures. And if she heard Schäfer and Dolan practising their 'Ngolok Cry' just one more time . . . So Emilie flew back to Shanghai. As her little plane shuddered into the thick air, Dolan could see rolling banks of cloud. The monsoon was coming.

For Schäfer, Dolan and Duncan – the odd trio of adventurer, missionary and SS officer – this marked the start of the expedition. Duncan hired a caravan from a 'coolie-jobber', and for 1,100 Mexican dollars they acquired the services of 110 barrel-chested porters who would carry their equipment the three hundred or so miles to Chengdu.[3] Schäfer and the two Americans followed behind, stopping at night in inns, whose tiny rooms were fragrant with opium. Dope sapped the strength of the coolies and Dolan seized the chance to replace them with two passenger lorries and a small touring car when they were just over halfway. By now the monsoon had arrived and the roads were 'in a shocking condition'. They crashed and jolted through deep, oozing trenches that threatened to shake them and the vehicle to pieces. Inside the car, everyone struggled to protect their rifles and a nautical chronometer. By the time they arrived in Chengdu two days later, tempers were frayed and they were 'bickering like infants'.

In Chengdu they had their first encounter with a Chinese warlord, Liu Hsiang, the 'General of Szechuan', who demanded to know if there were still 'wild people with long hair' in Tibet and if they would bring back some of them alive for him. Armed with his letters of introduction, the expedition left soon after, driving another car that was held together by wire, its depleted suspension bolstered with straw sandals. They set off at six in the morning and drove until noon, all the time passing an endless column of Kuomintang troops.

Now they were faced with long treks through sucking mud. Tensions between the three men, or rather between the two Americans and Schäfer, worsened: 'Our caravan looks like a stretched funeral procession,' Schäfer noted. 'The rickshaws crawl through the mud, the dogs are lame, we have got blisters on our feet, which burn like fire on the hot ground. I have to walk 40km today through the range of hills, while Dolan and Duncan are at least able to hire sedans. When I tried my luck with a bamboo sedan chair the coolies gave up after five minutes. "Master, you are so heavy," they say.' But he forced them to carry him, not wanting to be outdone by his colleagues. The weather reflected the dark moods of the three men. During the night the rain fell in torrents. Duncan described the thinly clad Chinese servants sheltering under rocks in their sodden clothing, their bodies quivering. The next morning, when they awoke after a sleepless night, the mists cleared to reveal a scene of liquid devastation. The Ya River had risen more than thirty-six feet during the night and there was flooding for hundreds of square yards. Dolan and his companions retreated to higher ground as the waters rapidly continued to rise. The water was waist deep in the cornfields, and waterfront villages were ripped away by the flood. Dolan watched an enormous tree trunk float past with a man calling from its twisting branches.

Duncan, in particular, knew what the endless downpour would do to the mountain paths, but there was no choice and they turned the caravan towards the mountains, which lay under a foggy blanket ahead. The rain had weakened the thin layers of soil and the path, which ran through deep forest, was frequently blocked by mudslides that cascaded, many feet deep, off the hills in torrents sweeping away everything that lay in their path. Dolan's horse became trapped in a viscous lake of mud and was only released after many hours of effort.

Six months after they had left Shanghai – it was now early 1935 – the expedition was on the brink of even more arduous months that would put enormous strain on the fragile relationship between Schäfer and the two Americans. They had arrived in a region near Batang which was racked by unrest and internecine conflict. Their goal was to get to Sining in the far north via Jyekundo. All along their intended route, robber bands harassed yak caravans and foreign expeditions alike; Tibetan and Chinese troops skirmished in the cities and mountain passes. Duncan had been through all this before, but he was now receiving reports of the 'red menace' sweeping up from the south. The Long March of the Red Army had reached the Tibetan border itself. It was a volatile, unsettled world that they were about to enter, and Dolan and Schäfer were quite unprepared for what lay ahead.

Their first encounter with 'real' Tibet was the sky burial of a high lama. Schäfer and Dolan watched fascinated as the dead man was wrapped in linen and laid out on a platform of stones. Prayer flags fluttered all around and priests burnt juniper wood. Men in white aprons, the *tomden* or *yogin*-butchers – members of Tibet's outcasts the *ragyapa* – wielding big whetted cleavers, approached and unwrapped the corpse, which they quickly and expertly sliced from head to toe, exposing flesh and bone. All the while, big restless vultures were gathering, their wings rattling as they flew down. They were kept at bay by men with long poles – but not for long, because they were important participants in the ritual. After the *tomden* had removed the corpse's viscera, he shouted, 'Shey! Shey!' ('Eat! Eat!') and the formidable birds, with their six and a half feet wing spans, descended on the corpse, covering it in a threshing mass of feathers. The *tomden* assisted their feasting by wading in to dismember the legs and arms. After just fifteen minutes, the vultures had completed their frenzied meal – or at least the main course. For the final dish, the *tomden* crushed the skull with a stone mallet, mixed the brain matter with *tsampa* flour and urged the huge birds to feast again. 'The ceremony would have been impressive', Dolan noted, 'but for the odour of the body which had evidently been buried for some time and exhumed on the appropriate day.'

They travelled as far as Litang. The fighting between different tribes, between the Tibetans and the Chinese, and between different combinations of all three had closed the roads to Batang and to the west. The northern route was also impassable. 'Now everything is over! Yes!' moaned Schäfer. Unwilling to give up, Dolan came up with a plan. They would send all their specimens back to Tachienlu and announce that they were retreating, but they would secretly break out northwards. Soon they were joined by anyone in Litang who wanted to leave town; altogether there were now some six hundred yaks, fifty horses and fifty armed men. One morning before dawn, Schäfer, Dolan and Duncan led the great procession out of Litang. It took until early afternoon for the last of the yaks to pass through the city gates onto the Batang Road.

After three days, they ran into a tribe called the Washi. There were ten thousand yaks and five hundred tents spread out on the grasslands, but everyone was in mourning for the Washi prince who had been killed in a raid. The tribe was now led by his princess, a beautiful forty-year-old woman of aristocratic appearance, Schäfer recalled. Although she was in mourning and thus prevented from having contact with any men including her sons – they were all at another encampment six hours away – she invited Schäfer and Dolan into her tent and tried to persuade them to stay. Schäfer took this as a rather demeaning insinuation that this *Vollblutweib* ('thoroughbred woman') did not view the bearded Europeans as men enough to compromise the laws of mourning!

The Tibetans in the caravan also offered their condolences to the Washi widows, but they had a more profane reason for doing so. Visitors were permitted to sleep with the tribe's women, and they took full advantage of this when they entered the tents of the 'suffering heroines'. On their last evening in the camp, the Washi princess prepared a lavish meal. Schäfer reciprocated by offering her a tin of sardines, but she recoiled in horror. Fish eat the corpses thrown into rivers, so to eat fish is to become a cannibal. The news of his *faux pas* spread and, when they travelled on, another Washi prince forbade him to fire a single shot in his territory. 'I could have blown up their whole camp!' said Schäfer.

The sardines were a turning point. Schäfer is unusually candid about the atmosphere in the camp the following evening. He had made a mistake, the expedition was increasingly stressful, and he was in a black mood. 'We have eaten our dinner silently. I didn't like it. Everybody is withdrawn and lost in thought. The few words that have been spoken sound hoarse and bitter. We are all sick and tired of each other . . . Such moods can easily degenerate into some kind of wilderness madness, an unproductive hatred against one's comrades.' In camp that night, Schäfer eventually withdrew from the camaraderie of the camp fire and nursed his dark thoughts alone.

In the archives of the Academy of Natural Sciences in Philadelphia are letters written by Marion Duncan in the late 1930s and 1940s to various staff members. They reveal exactly what Duncan thought of his fellow German expeditionist. 'Do you ever hear from Ernst Schafer [*sic*]?' reads one of them. 'Is he pushing up daisies on English soil or working up cases for the Gestapo in some foreign land? He had enough life to be an aviator or to do some daring work. Ernst had less conscience than I had or you would have more credit for this last expedition. I was always afraid he would take the bird skins back to Germany and get all the glory and possibly keep the birds besides.' Those bird skins bothered Duncan for many years: 'Sometimes I suspect that Ernst Schaffer [*sic*], one of Hitler's captains . . . Hitlerized Brooke and did not send back his report of the birds and his report of the new species . . .'[4]

The remainder of the journey to Batang was uneventful. Their arrival in the city at the head of such a big caravan turned into a triumphal progress. But more bad news awaited them, and although they did not realize it the expedition was approaching its bitter and divided climax. The road north from Batang to Dêgê led into the territory of the Seven Tribes (the Deshohdunpa), and like many of the scores of tribal peoples in the area they were on the warpath. The situation worsened when a party of Chinese soldiers – in fact Tibetans paid by the Chinese – captured a Seven Tribes raiding party and brought three of them back to Batang. The Chinese commander, General Ma Pu-fang, immediately signed their death warrant. Although Duncan ran to the general's compound to plead for their lives, he was too late. The young men, shaking violently, were stripped and their hands bound. They were then pushed onto their knees, 'their faces ashen grey', and beheaded.

Duncan knew the Seven Tribes would seek vengeance as soon as the news reached their yak-hair tents and that it would be foolish to take the road north. So they would travel east and then north, away from the Seven Tribes through the territory of the Lingkharshee. That night astrologers consulted the stars and hundreds of monks prayed for their safe departure.

The day of departure, 20 January 1935, dawned gloomy and depressing. The people of Batang bid farewell with wine and yak milk and some of the Tibetans drank so much that they could hardly stay upright on their horses. Schäfer called a halt after just one and a quarter miles to let them sober up. As they rode through Batang's east gate they passed the grotesque, naked bodies of the Seven Tribes men, their heads lying beside them, their blood spattering the road. All for a crime 'bred in the hatred of their conquerors'.[5]

The caravan followed the little Batang River and then threaded through a limestone canyon. To the east they could see the glinting peaks of Nehmdah and the Deer Mountain Pass they needed to cross. Temperatures plummeted as they climbed higher, and the canyon floor was slippery with ice.

The following days were spent fording the swift ice-cold rivers which tumble from the Nehmdah peaks, and crossing a frozen, deep-bluish lake in whose glassy depths were trapped shoals of carp and catfish. They camped on the lake's further shore, pitching their tents on a spongy carpet of dried yak dung left by many years of nomadic encampments. The next day they were taken by surprise when a raiding party of Lingkharshee galloped between their tents, German Mausers strapped to their backs, deftly picking up any loose object, including Schäfer's notebook (to him 'the sine qua non of any serious researcher'), which was soon lost 'within the cloak of a burly nomad'.[6] They had to send the wiry old Tringleh to retrieve it – for five rupees, the equivalent of five days' wages for a nomad.

The next day they rode down a barren, red, sandy valley and across a wooden bridge over a blue glacier to enter Dêgê. In 1935, more than half the people of Dêgê were monks who worshipped Padmasambhava, Guru Rimpoche, who had once exorcized the demons of Tibet. At the centre of the city was the palace of the Dêgê prince, which was shabby after long years of punitive Chinese taxation. The prince was a 'sad-faced young man of twenty-two' dressed in a dirty cloak, a costume he shared with his courtiers. Schäfer thought the city just as filthy, with dead horses rotting in the main street, dirty drinking water and women who entertained his men with, as he rather oddly put it, the morals of a 'dogs' nest'. No-one liked Dêgê, and Schäfer's mood seems to have become even darker. In a letter home to his father, he wrote, 'In order to endure a two-year stay in the wilderness without developing some mental defect, you have to be either a one-dimensional scientist or a phlegmatic. Without European "make up", the human is an ugly, stinking, obnoxious predator.'

Everyone was glad to leave the city behind. Their goal now was Jyekundo, 198 miles away, so they turned north, the caravan heaving up and down snub-nosed peaks. Icicles formed on the yaks and tinkled like glass rods. They were less than a hundred miles from the 'mountain of mountains', Amne Machin, meaning the 'old man of the plain' and called by Tibetans 'the gathering place of the world's gods'. The mountain had special significance for the Ngoloks, whose 'cry' Schäfer and Dolan had so assiduously practised in Shanghai and on their voyage up the Yangtze. The Ngoloks were reputed to be the most bloodthirsty of the nomadic tribes with a nasty habit of sewing their victims into yak coats and leaving them to roast in the midday sun. But if the expedition wanted to see Amne Machin, they needed to cross Ngolok country.

As they nervously rode north, Amne Machin remained

hidden by thick roiling cloud. Then one morning Schäfer awoke early. Opening his tent flap, he saw the mountain clearly for the first time: he felt 'close to Nirvana, the eternal nothing'. Duncan and Dolan joined him to gaze on the stupendous mass of ice and rock. That experience seemed to be enough for them. Duncan was increasingly fearful of Ngolok raiding parties so a decision was made to head straight for Jyekundo. Schäfer, however, made a resolution: he would return and conquer the Mountain of the Gods at the head of a *German* expedition: 'I want to conquer it for science with comrades of my own blood, with German men! That was like a vision.'

In 1935, Jyekundo, another city of tea, was a straggling line of houses on an onion-shaped bulge of land. It was plagued by sandstorms whipped up from the yellow clay of the region and swept through its narrow streets. The expedition, both men and animals, was exhausted and in poor physical shape. Schäfer exchanged his lame horse for a packet of cigarettes. But he was disgusted when his men turned to opium, wine and 'orgies with women' – 'and do everything to increase our debt'.

Everything now conspired to ratchet up the tension between the three men. Both Schäfer and Dolan wanted to push on towards Sining across the unexplored wilderness north of Jyekundo, but the local Chinese governor refused to let the expedition travel any further. Duncan was in an increasingly nervous state of mind and was getting reports of communist brigades approaching Tachienlu, which could block their escape to the south. Their Tibetan porters chose this moment to refuse to go any further into the land of the dreaded Ngoloks. There were unpleasant and heated arguments between the Europeans and running battles with the Tibetans. It seems as if the expedition was running low on money, too, and their porters could not be bought off, as they usually were in such situations.

After nineteen very tense days, the governor finally relented and Dolan persuaded Duncan and the Tibetans to agree to leave Jyekundo and head north. This hard-won agreement did not mean their troubles were over. Now they had to wait again until the Tibetans received approval from an astrologer. When that finally came, Dolan's caravan left Jyekundo. As it meandered out through the city gates it was watched, Duncan recalled, by cold and sullen eyes. The Dolan expedition now comprised thirteen yaks carrying *tsampa*, rice and flour, and horses and mules. It was not an impressive spectacle and everyone's spirits were low.

A mere three days after they departed, the governor changed his mind and sent a small armed detachment in pursuit. They caught up with the expedition and surrounded them. It was a menacing situation, and by now Dolan had had enough. He had always taken the brunt of negotiations with warlords and bureaucrats, was 'in a nervous strain' according to Schäfer and had obviously reached the final strands of his internal tether. Now he took drastic action – alone. They were camped in a smooth, grassy valley near Trindo when Dolan took Duncan and Schäfer to one side and outlined an escape plan. He would take two men and some mules and head for Sining alone and in disguise; in Sining he planned to enlist the support of the powerful Chinese warlord Ma Pu-fang, who would soon play a peculiar role in the discovery of the 14th Dalai Lama, and return as soon as possible for the others. 'He cannot be dissuaded from going on,' Schäfer wrote. 'Two hours later the tall American stands in front of us, evenly shaved and dressed as a Tibetan trader.' Dolan left that night, promising Schäfer, 'We'll meet in two months or in hell!' He hoped it would take just twelve days to travel more than four hundred miles, but it was a back-of-an-envelope calculation and hopelessly optimistic. Dolan and Schäfer would not meet again for eight months, and then in very bitter circumstances.

After Dolan had slipped away, Duncan and Schäfer made a 'dummy', arranged it in Dolan's tent and told the Chinese and Tibetans that the American was very sick and could not be disturbed. The missionary and the SS officer were now alone together. They turned back the way they had come and set up camp at the Drijyuh Monastery, a 'forlorn and dirty place'[7] on the banks of the Yalung. They spent a few days hunting, bagged very little and returned disconsolately to Jyekundo. On 1 May Schäfer wrote, 'Yes, these are miserable hours which make me realize that this life in the wilderness is only an intoxication – a delusion. In a melancholy way I am thinking of the *Heimat* [homeland] where people are celebrating today, where the trees are green and spring has already started. Here the blizzard is shaking our tent all night, and cold seeps through its gaps and cracks – somewhere Dolan is fighting for his life by himself.'

Dolan was indeed enduring the trek from hell. It took him thirty-five days to reach Sining across a terrain whose difficulties he had grossly underestimated. The weather conditions were often extreme, and supplies of *tsampa* ran out after a week. When they could, he and his companions lived on the raw meat of kiangs (wild Tibetan asses), gazelles and bears. The rest of the time they starved. Dolan's mules collapsed and were left for the wolves. He waded across rivers, the water up to his neck, with his cartridges in his mouth. When he got to Sining, he was barefoot, emaciated and very sick. And, after his month-long pilgrimage, Dolan could find no-one to help. His mission had failed. His journey had been heroic, remarkable – and finally ridiculous. After some days spent recovering he was able to hitch a lift on an aircraft – and flew out of the wilderness back to Shanghai. Here he rejoined his wife, recovered fully from his ordeal and lived it up as only he knew how. The memory of his companions slowly faded from his mind.

Schäfer, meanwhile, had set out on a series of hunting forays around Jyekundo, while Duncan headed south, with considerable trepidation, towards Tachienlu. He found the city more or less empty with the Red Army camped not far away across the river. In his telling of the story, Duncan repaid the expedition's debts and arranged to have the precious animal- and bird-skin collections – forty loads in all, including ten he had brought from Jyekundo – taken to Yaan and then floated down the Yangtze to Chongqing. Duncan then began the long journey back towards Jyekundo. This, at least, is what he claims in his book.

Schäfer has received a letter from Dolan explaining that his mission had failed in Sining, but it said nothing about returning to Shanghai. The German had every reason to believe that he would be seeing his friend within weeks. And unknown to him, as he stalked the wilderness north of Jyekundo, Duncan had come back then gone again. He'd had no idea where Schäfer was and, no doubt concerned about the communists, had not waited, taking everyone back to Tachienlu. There, 'in a scene never rivalled for heart-rending grief and controlled tears [*sic*], I bid goodbye, perhaps forever to the brave men who have followed me for almost a year . . .'[8] Duncan left Tachienlu and took a steamer down the Yangtze to Shanghai, then travelled north for a ten-day vacation in Beijing. He never saw Ernst Schäfer again.

Schäfer had added more rare beasts to his collection. Returning to Jyekundo, he found more letters from both Dolan and Duncan, many months old. He tore them open, eager for news of his companions, but – in his words – the 'earth moved under him'. Schäfer had been puzzled, troubled and angered by Dolan's silence; now he knew he had been betrayed. He took the road south from Jyekundo in the bitterest of moods. According to Schäfer's account, when he reached Tachienlu he discovered that Duncan had left behind a trail of debts and annoyance.

Schäfer paid off what he could, retrieved the collections that still remained in Tachienlu and headed back down the Yangtze, avoiding the route of Mao Tse-tung's Long March as best he could.

As he steamed down the Yangtze, Schäfer steeled himself for a showdown.

Hearing that Junge was on his way home, Dolan flew up from Shanghai and met Schäfer at a mission in Jachow on the edge of Szechuan. They had not seen each other for eight months. Schäfer prepared to punish his old friend. He bought several canisters of gasoline and had them delivered to the mission where Dolan was staying. As Dolan came to greet him, Schäfer stood his ground. His American friend looked well and rested, an ironic gleam in those disconcerting blue eyes which implied that there would be no apology, just an acceptance of fate.

As Dolan watched, puzzled, Schäfer silently made a pile of all the most precious skins the two adventurers had harvested from the ends of the earth. They included some of the most beautiful animals in the Himalayas, white stags, kiangs, and gazelles among them, destined for pride of place in German and American museums. Then he picked up a canister of gasoline and began pouring its contents slowly on the pyre. When he'd finished, he asked Dolan directly for an apology or he would burn every single thing. Dolan embraced his friend. 'In Sining I was an ill man,' he said. 'If I had come back I would have been another burden for you. When I knew I had failed, retreating was the best action I could take. I know it seemed like an ignominious betrayal – but I knew, Junge, that you could make it alone.' Schäfer was disarmed. The two men shook hands. But, Schäfer said, writing after Dolan's death, 'I admit frankly that I never understood Dolan's behaviour even though I tried hard afterwards.'

This second expedition under Dolan radicalized Schäfer. In

the book he wrote about his experiences between 1934 and 1936 he made his new thinking very clear. Although the trip had been sponsored by the Academy of Natural Sciences in Philadelphia, the book has the following dedication:

> It is true, the era of great geographical discoveries is over, and scientific expeditions have replaced adventurous journeys of discovery. But all those who are willing to be pioneers, who have the idealism to bear deprivations and who are proud to work for the Fatherland abroad and in the wilderness – all those will still be attracted to impetuously go to the 'white spaces on the map' for science and for Germany . . . it is essential now that our task is to make science a new vehicle for robust German manhood. Thus we do not only want to proclaim objective science, but be self-confident soldiers of the German spirit. For the German boy this book might be an incentive. I owe special thanks to: Reichsführer SS-Himmler, Berlin . . .

In Berlin, the Reichsführer had been reading with great interest about Ernst Schäfer's exploits in the East. He decided to meet this intriguing young man as soon as he returned to Germany.

CHAPTER THREE

GRAND INQUISITOR

'[Hitler] has set us the goal for our generation to be a new beginning – he wants us to return to the source of the blood, to root us again in the soil – he seeks again for strength from sources which have been buried for 2,000 years . . .'

– Heinrich Himmler, 1935[1]

'The Supreme Lord said: You grieve for those who are not worthy of grief, and yet speak the words of wisdom. The wise grieve neither for the living nor for the dead.'

– the *Bhagavadgītā*, 2.11

'His eyes', recalled his Scandinavian masseur Felix Kersten, 'were extraordinarily small, and the distance between them narrow, rodent like. If you spoke to him, those eyes would never leave your face; they would rove over your countenance, fix your eyes; and in them would be an expression of waiting, watching, stealth . . . His ways were the orphidian ways of the coward, weak, insincere and immeasurably cruel . . . Himmler's mind was not a twentieth-century mind. His character was medieval, feudalistic, machiavellian, evil.'[2]

Heinrich Himmler was the patron of Ernst Schäfer's third mission to Tibet, and Schäfer would be a troublesome favourite until 1945. Some German scholars have attempted to downgrade Himmler's involvement in the expedition,[3] but Schäfer's exploit would have been unimaginable without his patronage and support. After September 1939, all the men who had travelled with Schäfer to Tibet would be pulled deeper into Himmler's empire.

Himmler was the second most powerful man in the Nazi hierarchy. The historian Richard Breitman called him 'the architect of the Final Solution' – that is to say, he was the man who built, piece by piece and with a numbing attention to detail, the bureaucracy of genocide. Despite his education, Himmler became a virulent 'scientific racist' and used his power to sponsor pseudoscientific ideas about the purity of German blood. In his lifetime he attracted baffled contempt, even from his fellow Nazis. He was variously described as 'Hitler's evil spirit, cold, calculating and ambitious'; 'like a man from another planet'; 'he had a touch of the robot'; 'he was half crank, half schoolmaster'; 'What made him sinister was his capacity to concentrate on little things, his pettifogging conscientiousness . . .'[4] Himmler was a hobbyist. He dabbled in prehistoric Venus figures, telepathy, vegetables, trousers worn by Japanese peasants, reincarnation, fertilizers, sexual customs in Tibet, homoeopathy, 'Germanic astronomy', Hindu castes, runes, heraldry, the *Bhagavadgītā*, the 'World Ice Theory' and the lost kingdom of Atlantis. Always zealous and punctilious, he explained to his Gruppenführer in 1943, 'What about the women and children? I have decided to find an entirely clear solution here too. The fact is I did not feel entitled to exterminate the men . . . and to allow the avengers in the shape of their children to grow up for our sons and grandsons. It was carried out, without – as I believe I am able to say – our men and our leaders suffering injury to spirit and soul.'[5]

I began my search for Heinrich Himmler in the small German town of Wewelsburg in Westphalia. Perched above the lush valley of the Oder is the 'Order Castle' Himmler bought in the autumn of 1933. The 'SS School Haus Wewelsburg' was for the Reichsführer both monastery and fortress – an SS Vatican, the centre of the world. What really took place here remains a puzzle, but what can be deciphered from its strange history reveals much about this odd, prim and lethal little man.

The castle was built in the early seventeenth century for the Prince-Bishops of Paderborn. Sited on a tapering ridge overlooking the river, it is a narrow triangle in plan whose apex points due north. In 1933, Himmler had been immediately struck by this geometry and believed that it depicted the 'Spear of Destiny', an occult symbol. An immense round tower was built at the apex of the triangle, and inside it was Himmler's dark Camelot.

Today, there is little to be seen. Behind a locked iron door in the North Tower is a stone-lined room ringed by Romanesque arches. This was the *Gruppenführersaal* where, according to SS Brigadeführer Walter Schellenberg, higher-ranked SS officers assembled to 'practise spiritual training and meditation exercises'.[6] Embedded in the marble floor is a twelve-spoke *Sonnenrad*, a sun wheel which was once lined with gold and represented for Himmler the 'Centre of the New World'. Below this is an equally mysterious chamber. Its walls are exposed brick, making it resemble a torture chamber, and they bend upwards to a rounded dome. At its centre, Himmler's architect placed an elaborate swastika design set inside a concrete ring directly below the *Sonnenrad* in the chamber above. Beneath that was a sunken stone circle. It was approached by sweeping ceremonial steps and locked in place by three flat keystone blocks. Twelve stone pedestals ringed the walls. This was a place of the dead, a Valhalla where 'knights' of the SS were ceremonially honoured after death. The walls were once lined with the heraldic emblems of senior SS officers and decorated with runes, but today they are bare. Both chambers are reticent if not mute, as secretive as their designer.

Himmler had first stumbled on Wewelsburg when he was campaigning in Westphalia just weeks before the momentous election of January 1933. The castle was in a *Landberg* called the Land of Lipp, where the Nazis had achieved breakthrough results. Himmler was exhilarated. He was already fascinated by this region of Germany, where he felt close to some of the great figures of German prehistory. It had been the heart of the pagan empire of the Saxons and it was the ancestral home of Hermann, or Arminius, of the Cherusci, who had defeated the Roman legions in the Teutoberger Forest. According to Teutonic legend, the 'Battle of the Birch Tree' would be fought here some time in the future between an 'army from the West' and the forces of 'the East'. Just thirty miles away was Germany's 'Stonehenge', the mysterious Exsternsteine, a great cluster of misshapen rocks allegedly sculpted in antiquity which is still a place of pilgrimage for both New Agers and neo-Nazis. Himmler would send legions of archaeologists to the Exsternsteine and demand from them proof of its Aryan pedigree.

As he was driven through the fog-shrouded Teutoberger Forest in 1932, Himmler was in high spirits. After the Nazi electoral success, he looked forward to real power and he was incubating a vision of the SS. He would make it a noble order of warriors 'sworn to the Führer' and modelled on the Jesuits – with himself as Ignatius Loyola – and the Knights Templar. When he saw the North Tower of Wewelsburg Castle, Himmler knew he had found the perfect fortress for the SS, a Camelot where he could mould the hearts and minds of his officers.

In 1935, Himmler set about realizing his vision. Architectural plans were drawn up and models constructed. They reveal a vaunting, paranoiac ambition, intent on transforming not only the old castle but also the village of Wewelsburg, turning it into an SS city – according to Himmler, the centre of the world. Local villagers would be moved to a new 'model village' several miles away. The projected cost was 250 million Reichsmarks. Wewelsburg would be a pagan Vatican City where the SS elite would receive spiritual and *weltanschauliches* ('world view') training. Libraries would be assembled, astronomical observatories constructed, appropriate works of art acquired, special furniture made and decorated with arcane symbols and runes. Archaeological artefacts would be given pride of place.

To achieve this, prisoners were brought from Sachsenhausen, the concentration camp near Berlin, and a new camp was built in the Niederhagen Forest near Wewelsburg. The prisoners were forced to cut stone blocks from a local quarry and drag them to the castle. More than a thousand were worked to death. Wewelsburg was torn down and put back together again, then sumptuously decorated. Himmler called it an 'ancient Germanic cult centre' and brought in scientists and researchers who lived in cell-like rooms while investigating the 'foundations of Germanic culture'. These 'Reich Leaders' had to be 'free of any inclination to see science as an end in itself'; 'We need neither a fossilized scientist nor a dreamer.'

At Wewelsburg, pagan festivals were celebrated at the summer and winter solstices, and SS wives were admitted to the *Sippengemeinschaft* ('kinship') of Himmler's order. These ceremonies dispensed with the 'false altar trappings' of Christianity. The bride was forbidden to wear a veil and myrtle crown since these were 'oriental' customs. Instead, there were 'Sig runes' and swastikas, fir sprigs, holly and ivy. Ordination rites like these bound Himmler's officers and their families into a community dedicated to obedience and 'hardness'. According to Himmler, 'these inner feelings of the heart, of honour and of a feeling for the most real and profound world view are ultimately the things that give us strength . . .'[7]

Historians have, inevitably, looked to Himmler's childhood to find explanations for his deadly and puzzling use of power.[8] He was born on 7 October 1900 into an outwardly normal Bavarian middle-class family at 2 Hildegardstrasse in Munich. His father Gebhard could call himself a professor but was, by profession, a secondary school teacher and later deputy principal. According to the historian Klaus Fischer, he was 'an extremely rigid, pedantic and compulsively legalistic school teacher who exemplified the much dreaded authoritarian type that was so common in the German school system . . .'[9] Such a monster of a father might be sufficient explanation for the son, but other reports give a different picture: 'We felt that the refined aura which emanated from [Gebhard Himmler] was beneficent. He was supple, of medium build and kept his class's attention without a word of rebuke by the strict, but kind look in his eyes, behind his gold pince-nez. Stroking his small reddish beard, he was prepared to wait quietly until a pupil had found an answer.'[10] Whether or not Gebhard was a benign teacher, the German school system was authoritarian. Many teachers aggressively promoted German race values and the glories of war.[11]

We do know that the Himmlers revered the noble houses of Germany. Before taking up his school post, Gebhard had tutored Prince Heinrich of Wittelsbach, the youngest member of the royal family of Bavaria. This was a prestigious post, even at the turn of the century. In the years before the First World War, all the German states and principalities had a ruling family and the Bavarian royal household was especially renowned for its independence. The future Reichsführer was named after the prince, and Gebhard successfully petitioned that the prince be godfather to his new son. The Himmlers were just a generation away from the peasantry, and Heinrich's father worked hard to raise his social status. The family developed a finely tuned sense of rank, and Gebhard senior was described as 'laughably pushing and fawning towards the upper classes'.[12] Himmler would call the SS an aristocracy, but it was 'a nobility of privilege' he created himself.

Being named after a Bavarian prince must have given Heinrich, the middle son, some ascendancy inside the Himmler household. There were two brothers, and although Gebhard was older, Heinrich was always the family counsellor. To his younger brother, Ernst, he once wrote, 'Do not become unbalanced. Be a good, brave boy and do not vex Daddy and Mummy.' Years later, in 1923, when Gebhard became engaged to Paula Stölzle, a banker's daughter, Heinrich did not approve, suspecting her of immorality. He wrote to Paula, 'you will have to be ridden on a tight rein and with utmost severity'. He even paid a Munich detective agency to investigate and humiliate the hapless girl. Gebhard broke off the engagement.

As in many German families of the time, the Himmler children were strictly supervised; they had to be scrupulously clean, orderly and obedient. Both parents insisted on devout religious observance, including regular confession, and the young Heinrich developed a passion for the Jesuits. Gebhard closely supervised his sons' educational progress. At home, Heinrich and his brothers were required to keep diaries which their father checked daily, and corrected. Just after he became Reichsführer, Himmler travelled by train with the Hamburg Gauleiter Albert Krebs, who left an intriguing account of the six-hour journey: 'What concerned him were the "secret" conditions. Did the former Kapitänleutnant X really have a Jewish or half-Jewish wife? How did SA-leader Conn come by his remarkable name? Was it perhaps a camouflage for Cohn?'[13] Such meticulously enquiring habits of mind were laid down in childhood.

Another Himmler family passion was the past – at any rate, the German past. Gebhard junior recalled a room in the family home being transformed into a shrine 'for the ancestors'; it was known as an *Ahnenzimmer* and contained artefacts from prehistoric digs. From the beginning of the nineteenth century, Munich had been the home of the Society for the Study of Early German History and its daunting *Monumenta Germaniae Historica*, an ambitious publishing enterprise devoted to revealing the full history of German-*speaking* peoples. The italicization is the key: German history enfolded the Visigothic kings of Spain, the Lombard kings of northern Italy and the Merovingian and Carolingian rulers of what is now much of France, Belgium and the Netherlands. When this enormous history was published, 'Germany' was a mosaic of princely kingdoms (such as Prussia and Bavaria) which were unified only in 1871, and then in a way that disappointed nationalist aspirations by excluding Austria. Beyond the frontiers of Germany lay an archipelago of ethnic German communities allegedly left behind as a much older German empire shrank and decayed. Gebhard Himmler passed on to his son dreams of a German super nation, a shadow realm that extended from the Urals to the Atlantic.

Heinrich's father was also fascinated by the lands that lay far to the east of Germany's borders. Gebhard senior had once been taken on an expedition across Russia by Prince Heinrich. It gave him a glimpse of an exotic, far-away world and he was forever retelling the story to his pupils and his sons. Like many nineteenth-century German intellectuals, Gebhard believed that his deepest ancestral origins might lie in Asia. Such ideas, of course, came to fascinate his son. Germany had to be protected from Slavic *Untermenschen*, and had rights of conquest above all in the east.

As a youth, Heinrich's dreams of manly conquest were thwarted ones. According to a childhood friend, quoted by Peter Padfield in his biography of Himmler, he was 'downright podgy' with an 'uncommonly milk white complexion', and short-sighted. When he was Reichsführer, one of his personal staff commented, 'If I looked like Himmler I would not talk about race.' Heinrich Himmler was not a Nordic god, and it hurt him. In many ways a model pupil, his performance in gymnastics was pitiable. The same friend, Padfield tells us, recalled a humiliated Himmler looking at his mocking classmates 'with a strange expression of mixed anger and disdain'. In later life, Himmler would always admire fine Aryan specimens like his second-in-command Reinhard Heydrich or adventurers like Ernst Schäfer. He encouraged scientists to measure the physical attributes of lesser races and believed the results showed that they were 'life not worthy of life'. It was revenge for the gymnasium.

When the war began in 1914, Heinrich longed, too, for military glory – acutely so after his godfather, Prince Heinrich, was killed on the front. By 1917, his elder brother and a close school friend had left for training with the 2nd Bavarian Infantry. Heinrich pressured his father to let him join in this 'Holy War'. Gebhard realized that his son was not likely to be in much demand so he began a campaign on Heinrich's behalf by badgering the grieving royal family. When that failed, he applied to every regiment in Bavaria where he had contacts. Henrich was eventually accepted by the 11th Bavarian Infantry in January 1918. Then, for month after demeaning month, the podgy youth drilled and trained, hoping daily to get news of a posting to the front line. But, suddenly, the war was over. Overnight, Himmler became a *Fahnenjunker a.D.* – that is to say, a retired soldier. It was another personal humiliation. He had been denied the heroic struggle he had dreamt about for so long, which his decorated brother and friends had experienced, and now Germany itself, despite its proud history, had simply caved in and sued for peace. The Bavarian princely house collapsed; the Kaiser abdicated. A new social democrat government signed the Treaty of Versailles. Everything Himmler admired was brought low; those he despised had seized power.

National catastrophe wrought changes in the young Heinrich Himmler, churning over and recasting what had been laid down in childhood. An obsession with secrecy and order and with rank and hierarchy; a reverence for German history; a zealous devotion to pedagogic values; a sense of shame about his body and appearance – all these infantile traits moulded the adult Heinrich. It seems at first that there were few outward signs of change, for Himmler finished his education and began to cast around for a career. Sex repelled him, at least for now. It had too much to do with 'hot human beings' 'catching fire' and was 'a frightfully powerful natural drive'. Then, in 1919 he joined the Freikorps Landshut, to the dismay of his father. The Freikorps were private armies formed from the hordes of disgruntled ex-soldiers who now turned their weapons and training on communists and revolutionaries. In Munich, a force of thirty thousand Freikorps overturned the revolutionary government of Bavaria, killing at least six hundred people, but Himmler's brigade was never called into action and once more he missed the battle. Then came another break with his father when Heinrich opted to work on a farm for a year. It seems a surprising decision, but by turning to the land he was rejecting the academic values of his father and making a decisive shift towards *Völkisch* race politics.

Race was, to be sure, already part of the Himmlers' world view. The superior values of German history had been beaten into him from an early age, and there were few devout Catholics, as the Himmlers were, who did not espouse some distrust of Jews. Although German Jews were the most assimilated in Europe, anti-Semitism remained a powerful ingredient of nationalist thought – and a hatred of Jews, scapegoats for wartime privations, intensified after 1916.[14] Jews were blamed for the calamity of 1918, and the violent unrest that followed.

Himmler, like many radical conservatives after the war, turned to occultist groups like the Thule Society. There were many such sects and some had experienced a baleful renaissance fuelled by disillusionment and uncertainty. Inspired by Madame Blavatsky and other occult magi such as the Austrian Guido von List, these proliferating cults had emerged at the turn of the century. They celebrated a mythic German past and revived pagan ceremonies. They turned the swastika into a potent symbol of frustrated national pride and were all, without exception, anti-Semitic. Jews were, in the eyes of these occult nationalists, rootless predators who thrived only in the chaotic world of the modern city. Only the German peasants seemed free of the Jewish taint, and many saw them as blood banks of Nordic purity.

Getting back to the land would be Himmler's new crusade. In August 1919 he mounted his new motorbike and sped out of Landshut's medieval Altstadt and down the Munich road to a farming estate near Ingolstadt. Here he would turn himself into a peasant.

It was a disaster. Within a month he had come down with typhus and his farming idyll was over. He spent more than a month recuperating, then decided to forge a less arduous bond with the land at Munich's Technical High School, where he began to study agronomy. As Reichsführer, Himmler was fond of comparing politics to gardening. Gardens needed weeding, and Himmler became self-appointed gardener to the Reich, wrenching anyone unworthy of life from the soil and then throwing them into the flames.

Himmler now entered the city's student world. His letters and diaries reveal an immature youth anguished by sex and still obsessed with military glory. Academically, though, he did well. Like many German students, he joined a fraternity – the Apollo – and took up duelling, the supreme test of manhood. Scars were *de rigueur*, and Himmler made sure he acquired a manly quota of five. He was still consumed by fantasy, still something of a solitary drifter. In November 1921 he wrote in his diary, 'Today I cut an article about emigration to Peru out of the paper. Where will I be driven to go – Spain, Turkey, the Baltic, Russia, Peru? I often think about it. In two years I will no longer be in Germany, if God wills it, unless there is conflict and war again and I am a soldier.'[15]

By this time he was well on the way to absorbing the whole shebang of occultist thought and 'scientific racism', and had become involved in another cult, the Artamanen League.[16] Many future Nazis, like the man who coined the phrase '*Blut und Boden*' ('blood and soil') Walther Darré and the future commandant of Auschwitz Rudolf Höss, were members, and most of the League flocked to join the party in the late 1920s. Darré and his fellow Artamanens were utopians. Above all, they demanded that the German peasantry be sent to colonize the lands of the east and sweep away the lesser Asiatic and Jewish races. Out of blood and soil would spring a new German empire.

For Himmler there was a pantheon of new prophets to admire. He diligently waded through the race theories of Houston Stewart Chamberlain, the British-born admirer of

Wagner, and the early work of anthropologist Hans F. K. Günther. In 1931, Günther was appointed a professor at Jena University, where he inspired his student Bruno Beger to become an anthropologist. Günther's first book, *Ritter, Tod und Teufel* ('The Knight, the Death and the Devil'), was inspirational for many of the men who would become leading figures in the Nazi movement.

As he read the work of the man universally known as 'Rassen Günther' and other authors of the same ilk (all documented in his reading lists), Himmler's anti-Semitism became more rooted and more potent. Like many others, he was taken in by that faked blueprint for Jewish world conquest *The Protocols of the Elders of Zion*. Himmler added Freemasons and Jesuits to his growing list of villains, and astrology, hypnotism, spiritualism and telepathy to his enthusiasms. After discovering the novels of Herman Hesse, especially *Demian* and *Siddhartha*, he also became an enthusiast for Eastern philosophy, or at least his own Aryanized version of it.[17] Hesse led him to read the *Bhagavadgītā*, and he embraced its message of rebirth and karma. According to the memoirs of his Scandinavian masseur Felix Kersten, Himmler often quoted epigrams from the *Bhagavadgītā* and was fascinated by the caste system of elite Brahmans and warrior Kshatriyas.

Even more decisive was his reading of *Der Bolschewismus von Moses bis Lenin* by Dietrich Eckart. The book persuaded him to join the NSDAP – the Nazi Party. Eckart was a former law student who had become an enthusiast for pan-nationalism. He was a member of the Thule Society and editor of the anti-Semitic newspaper *Auf gut Deutsch*. *Der Bolschewismus* was a record of conversations between Eckart and a then little-known agitator called Adolf Hitler. The book was a long rant about the Jewish roots of Communism, and Himmler urged his *Völkisch* friends to read it. He had lost his religious faith. He now spoke of Christianity as merely another manifestation of Jewish superstition. Germany must rediscover the old pagan gods and rites that the Church had forced underground.

Politics now became the ideal arena for the battles he had craved for so long. He got a job researching manures in Schleissheim, a small town which happened to be a stronghold of extreme right-wing paramilitaries. Himmler enrolled in Ernst Rohm's Reichskriegsflagge ('National War Flag'), and then joined the Nazi Party itself. As the unit's standard bearer, he took part in Hitler's putsch in 1923: a photograph shows him behind a street barricade, earnest and bespectacled, proudly holding aloft the imperial war flag. Its defeat embittered him, filling him with new hatreds and fears. For months he believed he was being followed. He got a job campaigning for the anti-Semite Gregor Strasser, and while Hitler dictated *Mein Kampf* in his prison cell, Himmler proved himself to be an able and meticulous, if not pettifogging, propagandist. He was appointed, in rapid succession, Deputy Reichspropagandaminister then Deputy Reichsführer-SS in March 1927. Heinrich Himmler, half crank, half school teacher, was at last on the nursery slopes of power.

He had also married. His bride was Margarete Boden, a landowner's daughter and a nurse with a clinic in Berlin which was subsidized by her father and which specialized in natural remedies. She was seven years older than Himmler and already stout. All this was very appealing and he succumbed to Marga's charms. He was twenty-seven – 'about time', said a friend. Although the NSDAP paid Himmler a poverty wage, he resented his new wife's independence. Marga gave up the clinic and the couple bought a chicken farm in a Munich suburb. It proved to be a dreary hand-to-mouth existence and Himmler soon left the running of the farm, which would never be successful, to his wife. By now, politics was everything. Marga produced a daughter, Gudrun, but in every other way she was abandoned with the chickens.

As he sped off on his motorbike and the clucking of the hens faded away behind him, Himmler knew that he was ready for power.

The SS had started existence as a personal bodyguard for Nazi Party leader Adolf Hitler. Although Hitler had honoured the first SS Reichsführer, Joseph Berchtold, by presenting him with the famous 'Blood Banner', a hallowed souvenir from the beer-hall putsch, the SS had for some time performed somewhat menial duties. For the most part they had formed a black-uniformed screen around Hitler in order to fend off assailants and hecklers, and were overshadowed by the SA, the brown-shirted Nazi paramilitary organization led by Ernst Röhm.

Heinrich Himmler changed all that. In 1929, Hitler appointed him SS Reichsführer and he set about transforming an insignificant cadre into a new Aryan aristocracy. He enlisted Artamanen veteran Walther Darré to help him make the SS the vanguard of a new racial aristocracy, a blood carrier that would make history. Himmler abandoned his father's fawning to royal princes and their court; in the SS newspaper *Der Schwarze Korps*, one of his acolytes wrote, 'We have new standards, a new way of appraising. The little word "von" no longer means to us the same thing it once did . . . The best from all classes, that is the nobility of the Reich.'[18]

On the political front, too, Himmler began to make spectacular gains. Throughout 1933, as Hitler twisted and smashed the institutions of German democracy, Himmler expanded the boundaries of his empire until the SS became a 'state within a state'. In March 1933 he became police president of Munich, in April the political police commander of Bavaria.

In 1934, it was SS forces that destroyed Röhm's SA in the 'Night of the Long Knives'. Himmler organized for Hitler a coldly efficient coup against the brownshirts, and for this he was rewarded with complete control of the Gestapo. Just months later, Hitler handed all police powers to Himmler, including responsibility for the new concentration camps. Now this 'pudgy, short, unathletic, myopic and balding Bavarian'[19] stood at the pinnacle of a triangle of control and terror.

Himmler could now indulge his hobbyist passions and fantasies. Power liberated the newly appointed Reichsführer. He became convinced that he was the reincarnation of a revered German king, Heinrich I, also known as Henry the Fowler. When he remembered those tedious hours trapped in Himmler's company on a train in 1929, Albert Krebs, the Hamburg Gauleiter, felt he had to assume that Himmler 'lived among these conceptions, that they represented his world view, in face of which the real practical world, with its problems and tasks, fell into the background'.[20] SS Captain Dieter Wisleceny observed, 'The usual view of Himmler is that he was an ice-cold, cynical politician. This view is almost certainly wrong . . . Himmler was a mystic.'[21]

But unlike most enthusiasts for the occult, Himmler now had the power to do much more than bore his colleagues and friends. The SS would become an academy. A special rank, SS Ehrenführer ('honorary SS commander'), was created so that Himmler could admit scientists and diplomats – even Signora Ciana, the wife of the Italian foreign minister – into his elite corps, and in the summer of 1935 he created the Ahnenerbe.

To manage his new office, Himmler appointed the operatically bearded and saturnine Wolfram Sievers. Sievers had been a Nazi fellow traveller since the early 1930s; in 1945 he would try to escape the gallows at Nuremberg by making the preposterous claim that he was a leading secret agent in the

Nazi opposition. He would play a malevolent role in the lives of both Ernst Schäfer and Bruno Beger. Under Sievers' despotic rule, archaeologists, prehistorians, philologists and anthropologists would devote their minds to the past and future of the Aryan race. Its motto was deceptively benign: 'A people live happily in the present and the future so long as they are conscious of their past and the greatness of their ancestors.' They would find the facts, the 'thousands of mosaic pieces' as Himmler called them, that could prove his crackpot ideas. In the next few years, the Ahnenerbe would spread across fifty-one different areas of research. The costs were soon crippling, rising to nearly a million Reichsmarks a year. Money would, as Schäfer would soon discover, always be a problem for the Ahnenerbe.

To keep his enterprise afloat, Himmler hatched up a novel scheme to fund his pet department. SS Hauptsturmführer Anton Loibl had patented an illuminated disc which could be fixed to the wheels of bicycles to make them more visible at night. As the chief of police, Himmler could decree that all bicycles sold in Germany must be equipped with one of Loibl's discs. Loibl became a rich man as a result, but half of all his profits went into Himmler's coffers. Millions of ordinary Germans funded Himmler's fantasies with their feet. Himmler also set up – and again the language is a deception – a 'Circle of Friends', the Freundeskreis RFSS. Ernst Schäfer would soon become one of Himmler's *Freundes*.

Staffing the Ahnenerbe was a motley bunch of cranks and ambitious academics. Hermann Wirth, one of the earliest members, for example, was the author of an immense book called *The Rise of Mankind* published in 1928. In it, Wirth offered his readers a close examination of thousands of runic symbols from different northern European cultures. Inspired by the geological work of Alfred Wegener, who was the first to suggest the theory of continental drift, Wirth proposed a theory of 'polar shift' which implied that the icy north had once been the original homeland of the northern Aryan peoples. Shifting poles and wandering continents had done for Wirth's 'Arctic Race', although they had survived in isolated settlements like Atlantis. Wirth cited the findings of Knud Rasmussen, a Dane who had led an expedition to Greenland in 1906–7 and had claimed to have found 'mysterious' blond and bearded Eskimos. (Other explanations for this phenomenon did not, it seems, occur to Rasmussen.)

Himmler most admired a deranged former army officer called Karl Maria Wiligut, whose very odd biography Nicholas Goodrick-Clark has reconstructed. After the First World War, Wiligut became a celebrated magus-like figure for the *Völkisch* sects. He claimed to possess unique powers and to be the last descendant of a long line of German sages – the Uiligotis of the Asa-Uana-Sippe, no less – whose ancestry was allegedly rooted in prehistory. More than that, Wiligut was thought – or claimed – to have clairvoyant powers which gave him access to an ancestral memory enabling him to recall at will the experiences of his tribe over some three hundred thousand years, to a time when there were three suns in the sky and the earth was populated by giants, dwarves and other mythical beings. Wiligut's memory dredged up a remarkable tale involving millennia of tribal conflicts, lost cities, and a final reconciliation instigated by his own ancestors the Adler-Wiligoten. In 9600 BC – a favourite period for all alternative histories – a struggle began between the Irminist religion and the Wotanists (don't ask) which resulted in a long period of exile for the Irminists in Asia, where Wiligut believed they were persecuted by Jews and Freemasons. He founded his own anti-Semitic league and published a newspaper called *The Iron Broom* which viciously excoriated his ancestral enemies.

But in 1924, Wiligut was involuntarily committed to the

Salzburg insane asylum. There he stayed until 1927. In the report on his condition held by the hospital Wiligut was described as having 'a history of megalomania and schizophrenia'; he was violent to his family (his wife had failed to bear him a son) and had a 'history of grandiosity and eccentricity'. In 1932, he fled to Munich where an old friend, now an SS officer, introduced Wiligut to his chief, Heinrich Himmler. For Himmler, Wiligut's 'ancestral memory' promised to open a door into German prehistory. Wiligut joined the SS under the pseudonym Karl Maria Weisthor and was appointed head of the Department for Pre- and Early History within Darré's Race and Settlement Main Office. Relations between the Reichsführer and the old mystic were warm. It was Wiligut who designed the death's-head ring worn by members of the SS. He also worked on developing Wewelsburg as the SS Order Castle, and stage-managed the ceremonies and rituals which sustained the SS as an Order, bestowing on it an aura of fake tradition on elitism, racial purity and territorial conquest.

Historians have often viewed Himmler's occult obsessions as exotic marginalia in a life otherwise dedicated to efficient policing and ruthless genocide. The truth is that Himmler's enthusiasms about lost civilizations, prehistoric archaeology, the Holy Grail and, especially, the origins of the 'Indo-Germanic' races were intricately interwoven with the racial 'theories' that demanded the elimination of the unfit.

This was the man who watched Ernst Schäfer's career as an explorer and zoologist with such interest. He could, he believed, offer Schäfer a great deal. In return, he would expect Schäfer to bestow any glory he earned on the SS. He would need to be a loyal knight to sit at the round table. And slaving away in an SS office in Berlin was a keen young anthropology student who had studied with Rassen Günther, who was so much admired by Himmler. His name was Bruno Beger.

CHAPTER FOUR

THE PEOPLE HUNTER

'It is a rare and special good fortune for a theoretical science to flourish at a time when the prevailing ideology welcomes it, and its findings can immediately serve the policy of the state . . .'

– Professor Eugen Fischer, March 1943[1]

'To Reich Security Headquarters IVB4.
Attention: SS-Obersturmführer Eichmann.
Re: Skeleton collection.
With reference to your letter of September 25, 1942, and the consultations held since then regarding the above-mentioned matter, we wish to inform you that Dr. Bruno Beger, our staff member charged with the above-mentioned special mission, terminated his work in the Auschwitz concentration camp on June 15, 1943, because of the danger of an epidemic. In all, 115 persons, 79 male Jews, 2 Poles, 4 Central Asians, and 30 Jewesses, were processed.'

It is just two minutes before 12.45, our appointed arrival time, and Bruno Beger, the last European survivor of the German Tibet Expedition, is already waiting on his balcony, watching us approach and shielding his eyes from the sun. He lives in a modest block of flats in a small town outside Frankfurt. Clearly, he is a stickler for punctuality. Satisfied we will be on time, Beger waves and disappears behind a curtain.

It is a remarkable and in some ways chilling moment. For years, I have heard only that Beger is inaccessible and fiercely hostile to any discussion of his past. 'You won't get him to talk to you' is a warning I had heard many times, and I was to hear it again, ironically, just a day after this first meeting. At the beginning of the 1960s, German courts belatedly began to prosecute individuals who had been involved with the Nazi genocide. One of them was Bruno Beger, who had been living quietly in Frankfurt. After that his family had built an impenetrable wall around him. Yet there he was, waving from the balcony of a bland apartment block in a bland, affluent German town. I had not met a man before who had participated in the Nazi Final Solution and I had divided feelings about doing so now. By agreement, questions at this first meeting could be asked only about the Schäfer Expedition. It would take another meeting and many letters to persuade Beger to discuss 'other matters'.

As he opens the door, Bruno Beger is immediately recognizable. At ninety-two he is still the tall, aquiline-featured man who invariably rises above everyone else in the photographs taken by expedition members. He visits a gym once a week. Today he is dressed in dapper grey trousers, a crisp white shirt and rather elegant braces. His two daughters take up positions like sentinels on either side of their father. Beger's gaze is frank and challenging. He has strikingly large hands.

On the wall outside his apartment there are rather touristy photographs of purple-clad Tibetan lamas, but above his desk there are black-and-white pictures of the Schäfer party in Tibet. There is also a portrait of Sven Hedin, the Swedish explorer who inspired Schäfer and was an admirer of Hitler.

There are many books about Tibet, too. On a shelf above the door I can see his most remarkable treasure: a collection of face masks made on the cold, high plateau of Tibet. One of them, which his daughter lifts down for us, is of Ernst Schäfer's Sikkimese assistant 'German' Akeh Bhutia who, unknown to me at the time of this first meeting with Beger, was still alive. The room, I realize, is a kind of memorial; these frozen Tibetan heads from long ago and very far away speak of a different life. Tibet is Beger's Shangri-la, a land of lost content, a place he was privileged to experience before he chose to become involved with other plans of Heinrich Himmler's and took a train to Auschwitz one morning in June 1943.

I interviewed Beger on two occasions. Because he had published his Tibet diaries, I concentrated at first on his upbringing and education. I wanted to find out why he had devoted his science to the SS. I hoped that he might disclose how the noble quest for knowledge could become so profoundly contaminated. Beger, quite naturally, was not going to tell me that story directly and he was often canny about why I was asking particular questions. But when I listened to the tapes afterwards, I was surprised by how much he *had* revealed about the making of an SS anthropologist.

It is Beger's work that connects Schäfer's expedition with the occult science of race and the quest for the origins of the Aryan Master Race, the people Beger called 'Europids'. By the time he was born, in 1911, many of the ideas that would become excuses for murder had been laid down, layer after layer, at the highest levels of German academia, in universities, laboratories and museums. Here they simmered and fermented, warmed by nationalist passion and the frustration of military defeat. Himmler's SS did not originate ideas about the superiority of the Nordic race, but they acted upon what the science appeared to imply.

In the nineteenth century, science followed the flag. As the European nations conquered the world, it was realized that the new colonies offered a unique scientific opportunity. They would be transformed into vast laboratories of human types, and of different races. Indigenous peoples could be measured, photographed, even collected. Out from the homeland would go colonists, farmers, administrators, and behind them came anthropologists, the people hunters. They brought with them their callipers and cameras to measure and record. And while the colonists sent back the material bounty of their new kingdoms, the scientists returned to their museums bearing cases packed with trophy animals and sometimes trophy people. Between them, the markets and museums of Europe reaped a wealthy harvest from the colonial world.

No one nation had a monopoly on such scientific brutality. American anthropologists like Samuel Morton acquired skulls of Native Americans in their thousands, and usually by the most unscrupulous means. It is frequently pointed out that British anthropologists preyed on Australian aborigines both living and dead; but this was more akin to grave robbing and was never sanctioned by any scientific or government body. Francis Galton, the British inventor of eugenics, on the other hand, was without a doubt a pioneer of anthropometry. He had a passion for numbers and statistical comparisons. In the 1850s, Galton joined a scientific expedition to south-west Africa where he met an extraordinary woman, a striking African he called the 'Hottentot Venus'. Galton wooed her with mathematics. He made her stand against a tree and, as he put it, lacking the standard equipment, used a sextant to make precise measurements of her proportions. 'I took a series of observations upon her figure in every direction, up and down, crossways, diagonally and so forth,' he wrote. 'I worked out the results by trigonometry and logarithms.' But Galton was exceptional and,

Ernst Schäfer, 1938.

OPPOSITE TOP
A uniformed Bruno Beger as a student at Jena University, 1931.

OPPOSITE MIDDLE
Heinrich Himmler in 1933, SS Reichsführer.

OPPOSITE BOTTOM
Himmler visiting his SS 'Order Castle' at Wewelsburg in 1935.

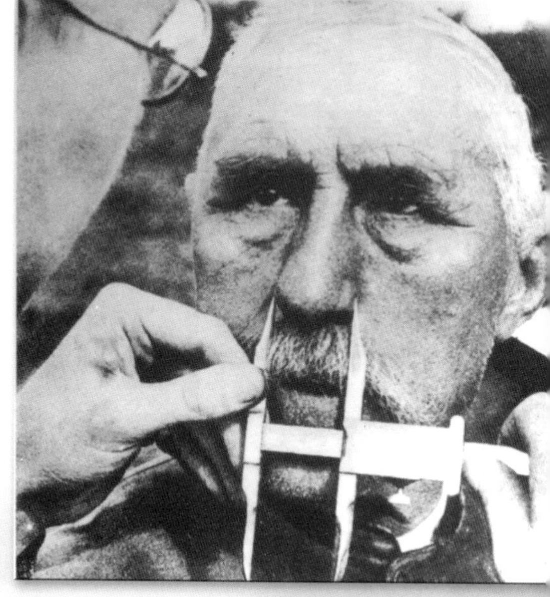

RIGHT
Anthropology Nazi-style, mid 1930s.

BELOW
Wewelsburg, Himmler's 'Centre of the World', in 1939.

OPPOSITE
The 9th Panchen Lama, whom Schäfer met in 1934 when the Lama was exiled near Shanghai. Schäfer hoped he would provide access to Tibet.

FAR LEFT AND ABOVE
Ernst Schäfer the hunter on his first expedition.

LEFT
Schäfer's loyal and long-suffering companion Wang.

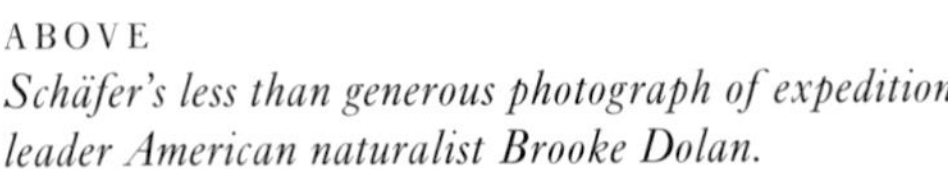

ABOVE
Schäfer's less than generous photograph of expedition leader American naturalist Brooke Dolan.

RIGHT
The ruler of the tiny kingdom of Muli, who held Schäfer captive.

Bruno Beger, expedition anthropologist, leaving for India in March 1938 with his wife and daughter.

FROM LEFT TO RIGHT
Ernst Krause, who was both expedition entomologist, with a passion for wasps, and cameraman. At thirty-eight, Krause was the oldest member of the expedition.

Edmund Geer, Schäfer's loyal expedition manager.

Karl Wienert, expedition geographer.

RIGHT
Horseplay in Calcutta. Wienert (top) and Beger.

BELOW
The German Tibet Expedition shortly after arriving in Calcutta, April 1938. From left: Karl Wienert, Ernst Schäfer, Bruno Beger, Ernst Krause, Edmund Geer.

ABOVE
Dekyilinka, the British Mission in Lhasa from 1936. Hugh Richardson is standing on the left. The British considered this ramshackle and draughty building to be 'incompatible with dignity'.

MIDDLE LEFT
Hugh Richardson, the British Mission officer in Lhasa after 1936 and Schäfer's implacable foe.

MIDDLE RIGHT
Sir Basil Gould, the political officer in Gangtok, Sikkim, dressed in full diplomatic splendour.

LEFT
Gould taking tea with a Tibetan official.

apart from the 'Hottentot Venus', there is no evidence at all that he exploited anyone or stole their bodies.

The measuring mania soon withered among English anthropologists, but it was a very different story in Germany. Germany came late to the imperial scramble for colonies and was a jealous and belligerent participant.[2] The German nationalist movements were fervent advocates of expansion overseas, to the east and into Africa. Bismarck, the architect of national unification, embraced the colonial movement after 1871: a new nation needed an empire. The search for a 'German India' became a consuming passion at every level of German society. Impoverished farmers dreamt of a new life under African skies, while soldiers, diplomats and businessmen greedily pursued the riches of colonial conquest. German academics, too, played a significant part in stoking the fires of expansion. *Lebensraum*, the notion that Germany was overcrowded and needed to expand to survive, had been coined and expounded by a geography professor in Munich called Karl Haushofer. In his highly influential books and lectures Haushofer did not simply argue that Germans needed more space; he believed that the health of the Indo-German peoples depended on territorial expansion. Thus, race theory became fused with that seemingly most mundane of sciences, geography. Among Haushofer's students was a wild-eyed new convert to Nazism called Rudolf Hess, who infected his friend Adolf Hitler with this new enthusiasm when they were both imprisoned after the beer-hall putsch. After 1933, Haushofer became a special adviser to the Nazi elite. 'Germany will either be a world power or there will be no Germany,' Hitler wrote, 'and for world power she needs that magnitude which will give her the position she needs in the present period, and life to her citizens . . . We [National Socialists] turn our gaze towards the land in the east . . .'

Long before Hitler, anthropology was enriched by

Germany's colonial empire.[3] The career of Felix von Luschan (1854–1924) shows this clearly. Von Luschan was educated in Paris and Vienna and became the most powerful and influential curator at the Ethnology Museum in Berlin. Here, in the wake of German colonial acquisition, he built up two new sections devoted to Africa and Oceania. He assiduously cultivated the colonial administrators and military officers who controlled the new territories so that he could do research or acquire artefacts, including human skeletal material. For their part, the administrators found their ideas reflected in anthropology. Both assumed the superiority of the German male animal.

In his books, Schäfer often referred to Tibetans as *Naturvölker* – 'natural people', or even 'children of nature'. It was an idea with a long ancestry. From the beginning of the nineteenth century German philosophers and historians had founded their thinking on a distinction between *Naturvölker* and *Kulturvölker*, people of nature and people of culture. Germans were the progressive bearers of culture, at the zenith of a long historical development; Africans and Pacific Islanders, the people now administered by German colonists, had neither culture nor history. They were part of nature, but as *Naturvölker* had no history, the historical sciences were not appropriate for their study. An entirely new science was demanded, and a new kind of scholar. So anthropology emerged as a science devoted to the study of the colonized, the *Naturvölker* now ruled by German colonists. Although they had no history, Africans and Polynesians had the distinction of being pristine: humans in the raw, untrammelled by civilization. For the anthropologists, *Naturvölker* offered a unique chance to study an authentic human nature.

To do this, anthropologists looked for ways to rid their new science of any kind of subjectivity. They viewed history as an impossibly soft science contaminated by interpretation. The proper study of *Naturvölker*, according to anthropologists like Adolf Bastian, demanded that they put aside the tricks of the historians which could 'never escape subjectivity, neither in its subject matter, nor in relation to the historian himself . . .'[4] Anthropologists had to adopt a position of 'pure objective observation, sharply distinguished from history. German anthropologists would seek out only the 'physical properties of humans'. Like Galton with his sextant and his logarithms, they would measure the bodies and above all the skulls of *Naturvölker*.

So, as anthropologists began to exploit the new German colonies in Africa and the Pacific for science, they were faced with a daunting task. A new technology of observation and measurement needed to be developed to turn these people, apparently without history, into objects fit for scientific scrutiny. Anthropologists turned to the camera, the calliper and the face mask. They photographed, measured and sculpted.

These techniques – and Bruno Beger would use them all in Tibet – led to discomforting encounters between scientists and their subjects. Being measured was not comfortable, and the arrival of anthropologists brandishing callipers came to be feared. Flesh is a problem for the anthropologist. He is interested in the bone beneath the skin, the pure objectivity of the skeleton; what lies on top – whether his subject is fat or thin – is the result of individual habit and experience. So the callipers needed to be wielded without mercy. Flesh had to be squeezed and pinched to get down to the bone. Being measured became a kind of torture. Rumours of approaching scientific visitors could empty a village in Africa or Polynesia.

In the 1870s the German explorer and amateur student anthropologist Hermann von Schlagintweit added a new technique to the anthropologists' armoury. This was the face mask, made from gypsum plaster and cast on the spot from the subject. Anthropologists like von Luschan seized on the new technique, and it became a vital part of an anthropologist's education. Making masks from visiting 'natives' became an entertaining ritual in German classrooms.

The anthropological face mask – and there are rows of them in collections all over the world – is often an object of great beauty, but it dehumanized. It turned its subject into an object – a clay cast. Beger's Tibetan face masks, the ones proudly displayed in his living room, are strikingly beautiful but they also resemble death masks or even decapitated heads. This was intentional. Von Schlagintweit's invention offered the facility of detachment. Once the cast had been made, it could be taken back to the museum and studied at leisure. The face mask is mute; it cannot protest. But like those fearsome callipers, the face mask could be a form of torture. Imagine, if you can, the experience of having your face covered in slowly hardening clay with only tiny vents or lengths of straw jammed into the nostrils to breathe through. The process lasted a minimum of forty minutes. Even pure gypsum plaster can cause unpleasant skin irritation; if contaminated, it can burn the skin. When Beger made his first mask of a Tibetan, his subject had convulsions.

Anthropologists could also use the dead, and it was often more convenient to do so. Corpses did not argue, fight back or run away. They did not feel pain. Rudolf Virchow, who became one of Germany's most high-profile anthropologists, also cultivated colonial administrators and knowledgeable travellers, persuading them to send back, in alcohol-filled zinc containers, fresh severed heads acquired from native burials. Like a collector of fine art, Virchow indicated that he would be interested in any skin samples, hands and feet that might be acquired at executions or from battlefields and hospitals.

There was worse to come. When German colonists arrived in

Namibia in south-west Africa, the dominant tribal society was the Herero who had for many centuries been cattle herders. The new arrivals were farmers, however, and they rapidly came to regard the Herero as an obstacle. In 1897, plague swept through native herds. Many Herero lost everything. The catastrophe offered the German colonists an opportunity they were quick to seize. Thousands of starving Herero were offered jobs on the ever-expanding European farms and many, close to starvation, accepted. With their cattle herds decimated and wage labour replacing traditional ways of life, Herero society began to collapse. These once proud herders were now virtual slaves. By 1904, the Herero had had enough and began to fight back. At first they had some success, so the colonists appealed to Berlin. The Kaiser called in General Lothar von Trotha, who had a reputation for ruthlessness, and ordered him to crush the uprising by 'any means necessary'. 'It was and is my policy', von Trotha said, 'to use force with terrorism and even brutality.'

He was true to his word, and launched a war without mercy against the Herero. Their ill-equipped forces were smashed. Then thousands were driven into the desert and corralled miles from any water source. Anyone who tried to escape was shot. By the end of the conflict in 1907, more than sixty thousand Herero had been exterminated. Von Trotha then attacked another tribe, called the Nama – usually referred to as 'Hottentots' – and killed more than half of them. Survivors were rounded up and incarcerated in camps, where thousands more died from typhus and other diseases. One German soldier recalled 'the death rattle of the dying and the shrieks of the mad . . . they echo in the sublime stillness of infinity.'[5]

Anthropologists back in Berlin followed these events with keen interest. War meant bodies; bodies meant bigger collections; collections led to knowledge, academic papers and prestige. Felix von Luschan had a contact in one of the German camps in Namibia and he was able to make appropriate arrangements. Whenever a Herero died, the women were ordered to strip the flesh from the corpse using shards of glass, then the skeletons and skulls were shipped to Berlin. Military doctors, too, were especially active when it came to collecting Herero body parts and 'fresh native corpses' then despatching them, expertly preserved, to the Fatherland. Even though its methods were brutal and anti-humanist, German anthropology was meticulous.

Bruno Beger was born not long after these grisly events, in April 1911. His first memory is of being taken by his father to the Nuerupinner See, a lake near Heidelberg. Friedrich Beger left his son alone for a few moments, reappeared in a bathing suit and walked to the end of a diving board. He was a tall, athletic man – the perfect German. He waved at his son, then turned towards the water and dived in a perfect arc. He was underwater for a long time. The boy stifled tears. Perhaps 'Vati' had gone for ever. Then, more than fifty yards from the lake edge, his father's glistening head burst above the water. He lifted his arm and waved slowly. The boy waved back. Beger also recalls a photograph of his father performing handstands on the edge of the kitchen table. Sports, the perfect body – Bruno Beger would become an ardent admirer of both.

The Begers were, before the catastrophe of war and defeat, moneyed and educated. After receiving his *Doktorarbeit*, Friedrich had become a forestry scientist. Bruno's mother Gertrud was an accomplished singer of concert *Lieder*. Friedrich was also a staunch nationalist, and at the turn of the century he left his trees behind and joined the Wehrmacht. After 1871, warrior myths had proliferated in Germany. Otto von Bismarck's Second Reich was heralded as a new incarnation of the First founded in the twelfth century by Friedrich Barbarossa who, according to legend, was still slumbering beneath Kyffhauser Castle in Thuringia awaiting the rebirth of the Reich. In the same region of Germany where Beger grew up, a gigantic monument commemorating Arminius, the Cherusci leader who smashed the legions of Quintilius Varus in AD 9, was erected in the Teutoberger Forest. The new Reich wanted living heroes, and Friedrich (like Himmler) must have been desperate to become one of the elect. At home, the atmosphere was fervently nationalist, but scholastic too. Bruno's uncles were practical scientists: Karl was a chemistry professor and Max an engineer. The Begers valued academic achievement and admired tough, empirical science dedicated to the service of the Fatherland.

Friedrich Beger was offered a chance for glory just months after the family celebrated Bruno's third birthday in 1914. According to *Mein Kampf*, Adolf Hitler felt 'constant anxiety' in the early months of that year and sensed an 'aura that lay on the chests of men like a heavy nightmare, sultry as feverish tropical heat'.[6] In June, Archduke Ferdinand travelled to Sarajevo, the capital of Bosnia-Herzegovina, which had been annexed by Austria, and was assassinated by the nationalist Gavrilo Princip, who feared that Austria had plans to grab Serbia. When the Austrians delivered an ultimatum to the Serbian government, Russia mobilized in support of Serbia. Germany pledged its support to Austria and began planning a strike against Russia's ally France. The first consequence of this catastrophic cascade of allegiances and aggression came on 1 August when Germany declared war on Russia and invaded France. Britain was an ally of France and soon made its own declaration of war against Germany. The world conflict that followed has been described as 'frightful and unnatural', an 'endless monotony of misery, broken by poignant tragedies'.

In the first months of war, many Germans were ecstatic. Hitler fell onto his knees and 'thanked heaven from an overflowing heart'. Friedrich Beger's brothers soon joined in the frenzied outburst of nationalist aggression and volunteered. Even Stefan Zweig, a cultured Austrian Jew, gloried in the fact that he had been called up to 'cast his infinitesimal self into the glowing mass'. There was an exultant confidence, too, among Germany's High Command. Years before 1914, Feldmarschall Alfred von Schlieffen had hatched a plan for a military campaign that he believed would secure a quick victory for Germany in the event of a European war. It's been called 'the most important official document of the last hundred years'.[7] In its final form, known as the 'Great Memorandum', produced after years of obsessive tinkering by a man without a hobby, von Schlieffen's plan proposed a fast and brutal onslaught against the French. Seven-eighths of the Wehrmacht would attack through Belgium, riding roughshod over that country's neutrality. In just forty-two days, von Schlieffen calculated, the French armies would have surrendered and the Wehrmacht would be free to turn around and attack Russia with equally brutal force. Von Schlieffen died in 1912, but his plan lay in a drawer at Army headquarters like a time bomb.

The Schlieffen Plan was unleashed as soon as the European powers declared war in 1914. It was brutal enough, but it failed. The German Army, in whose ranks marched the Begers, fought its way to within a few miles of Paris but was unexpectedly driven back by the French and the British Expeditionary Force. Von Schlieffen had not anticipated this reversal of fortune, and he was not around to come up with a solution. The Wehrmacht was forced to retreat and then consolidate. Trenches were slashed across the fields of Flanders. A new kind of war had begun that would kill in enormous numbers. It would be protracted and unimaginably bloody. Neither Beger's father nor his two uncles would survive for very long. Friedrich was killed, shot in the heart, on 6 March 1915. Max fell six months later.

Karl was a victim of one of those strange ironies of war and suffered an ignominious end. Strolling past a tavern one evening, he was mistaken for someone else and beaten to death by a vengeful stranger.

Beger's mother Gertrud, like so many other German women, was now without a husband. She had five children and a meagre war widow's pension and Germany itself was fast approaching a crisis. By 1917 there were severe food and fuel shortages which led to bitter hardships. Food prices rocketed, and in the 'Turnip Winter' of 1916–17 there was mass malnutrition. A chronic shortage of coal meant few could keep warm. The Begers were, for a short time, better off than many, but social tensions were rising. Some began to look for scapegoats to blame and there were rumours that 'Jewish speculators' had been profiteering by holding back supplies and inflating prices. Soldiers returning from the front spread rumours that few Jews served on the front line itself and most were officers. An inquiry was launched; when its results showed that these rumours were false it was suppressed. There was a spasm of anti-Semitic feeling, and the genuine fact that many patriotic Jews had been killed on the front did nothing to dampen a *Völkisch* backlash.

It would be scurrilous to imply that Bruno Beger, aged six in 1917, absorbed such ideas so early, but for many Germans a link between Jews and Bolshevism was made during the First World War. In the final part of this book, we will see that the phrase 'Jewish-Bolshevik Commissars' possessed a fearful significance for an adult Bruno Beger. At times during our conversation, Beger came very close to implying that Hitler's war had been a just one because it had been fought against Bolshevism.

After 1917, social chaos and its ugly spawn were quickly followed by military collapse. It had begun in March. General Ludendorff had suffered a nervous breakdown, then mutinies spread through the German Navy and Army. Two million had died; now the rest simply dropped their rifles, picked up their kit bags and walked home. In the Reichstag the politicians finally understood that the war was lost. The Bavarian monarchy was overthrown and the Kaiser forced to abdicate. He fled into exile in the Netherlands where he vented his feelings by felling trees on the aristocratic estates that offered him refuge. The new German Republic sued for peace and signed an armistice on 11 November 1918. Germans of many political persuasions felt betrayed – 'stabbed in the back', according to Feldmarschall Hindenburg. Thomas Mann felt that his people had suffered a mental and physical collapse, 'an unparalleled fall'. The demoralization, he wrote, 'had no limits'.

It was those on the nationalist right in whom feelings of betrayal ran highest and most bitter. Adolf Hitler ranted, 'Did all this happen only so that a gang of wretched criminals could lay hands on the Fatherland?' Germany was convulsed by revolution. In 1919, there were leftist uprisings in Berlin and Bavaria. Troops of mercenaries – the Freikorps Himmler had joined – were used to restore order with the connivance of the government. They killed more than a thousand supporters of the Bavarian Soviet Republic, which the Freikorps leaders called a 'Jewish Republic'. In September 1919 Adolf Hitler joined the German Workers Party, which he soon began to remould as the National Socialist German Workers (Nazi) Party, the NSDAP.

The victorious allies convened in Paris to settle the fate of defeated Germany. They faced a formidable challenge. Europe had been wrecked by war and desperately needed suturing. Four great multinational empires had fallen: the German, the Russian, the Ottoman and the Austro-Hungarian. The destiny of literally hundreds of millions of people had to be resolved. What emerged from the lengthy and acrimonious wrangling in

Paris was the Versailles Treaty. It was bitterly resented by just about every German faction and citizen. There were losses of territory and punitive reparations to be paid. Germany was stripped of its colonies. But what was especially resented was the way in which Germany had been made to accept 'war guilt', and there was fierce and bitter reaction when the victors demanded that the Kaiser should be extradited and tried as a war criminal. The treaty was highly divisive inside Germany. Most conservatives and the far right blamed the new republic for the armistice and its aftermath. The 'Gentlemen of the Swastika' began to seek radical solutions to Germany's problems, and there were many of them, for with military and diplomatic defeat had come economic catastrophe.

Beger's childhood and adolescence were dominated by never-ending financial anxieties which intensified as Germany rode the roller-coaster of defeat. Although the Begers valued academic success, money to afford it would never be easy to find. In their home town of Heidelberg, Frau Beger had, at first, some success with a *Tochterschule* – an upmarket means of educating young girls – on the Hauptstrasse. The school prospered, and she decided to sell the Heidelberg property and build her own, grander school in Neckargemünd. She selected and hired an architect. Then in 1921 the last reparation payment of 132,000 million gold marks was demanded and the German economy went into freefall. The value of the mark plunged. In 1923, Germany was declared in default and the French invaded the Ruhr. Inflation turned into hyperinflation and the value of the mark was slashed again and again. At its lowest, one American dollar was worth 130,000 million marks. This was the year Hitler staged his putsch, and ended up in prison.

The demon of hyperinflation gobbled away at the money Frau Beger had made from the sale of her *Tochterschule*.

Confused and distressed, with no income and her money hourly dropping in value, she turned for help to her sister in Gotha. With her help, Frau Beger managed to extricate herself from the purchase of the new school and buy a much cheaper property in Gotha. All this was accomplished in the nick of time as the mark plunged downwards on the currency exchanges. The Begers moved to Gotha, where his mother survived on a small rental income from the new house.

Times were very hard. Meat was rare, and there was little fuel during the winter. Beger remembers walking to school gnawed by hunger – a memory shared with millions of Germans of that generation. Even so, the family was lucky to have a large garden in which they could grow vegetables. Beger's aunt even taught the children how to hunt for edible plants in the fields on the outskirts of the city. Despite the hardships, the Beger children did well. Bruno won a place at quite a prestigious *Gymnasium* where he excelled in mathematics. To assist his mother, he gave mathematics lessons to his fellow pupils for one mark an hour. As well as numbers, like his dead father, Bruno had a passion for sports.

It is understandable that as he approached adulthood Beger would begin to look for substitutes for his martyred father. By now the young Beger had matured into a striking young man, the perfect Aryan who would always draw the eyes of men and women. He was exceptionally tall, passionate about sports, and his features were highly sculpted, with a powerful aquiline nose. In a nation that measured identity and status in the shape of the skull and skeleton, Beger was a natural aristocrat. When he was still at school, he caught the eye of a sculptor called Hans Lichtenecker who would have a decisive impact on his emerging ideas. At the turn of the century, Lichtenecker had left Germany and built a farm in Namibia. He had fought in von Trotha's savage campaign against the Herero that had proved so valuable for German anthropologists. Lichtenecker's tales of adventure and conquest stirred young Beger's imagination. He began to dream of leaving Germany and becoming, like his hero, a farmer in Namibia – the killing fields of the Second Reich. The dream became even more consuming when, laid up with a sports injury, Beger discovered Hans Grimm's novel *Volk ohne Raum* ('People without Space'). It took him just two feverish days to devour all 1,500 pages of it. As he closed the book, he recalled, he 'wept with joy'.

This episode, with its mysterious passions, brings Bruno Beger's state of mind and his evolving world view into sharp focus. Weimar Germany was an unstable, agitated and fractured landscape inhabited by belligerent interest groups and political movements, all highly vocal and competitively grasping any means at hand to propagate their ideologies. The nationalist right had a powerful supporter in the media and publishing tycoon Alfred Hugenberg, a former director of Krupp. Hans Grimm (1875–1959) was one of his star authors, and *Volk ohne Raum* was a stunning success, selling 315,000 copies – some sources say half a million – between its publication in 1926 and 1935. But it is not by any stretch of the imagination a literary masterpiece. Grimm is dull and repetitive, his prose carved from the hardest mahogany. But then Grimm did not set out to create a piece of fine literature. He wanted to show Germans their true destiny as a people. For Grimm, as for Hitler as he dictated *Mein Kampf* in his prison cell, that destiny involved finding *Lebensraum*. Germans were people without room, and the world would soon have to make room for them.[8]

Grimm makes the point in brutal, simple language: 'The cleanest, most decent, most honest, most efficient and most industrious white nation on earth lives within too narrow frontiers.' The book's hero is Cornelius Freibott, whose experiences Beger closely identified with. In his youth, Grimm makes him the embodiment of true German manhood – a product of the soil but with a deep appreciation of learning. Financial disaster frustrates his desire to become a teacher and, after some convoluted plotting, he ends up in Africa where he joins the Boers in their war against the British – the dastardly villains in the story. Freibott is captured and imprisoned. At the end of the Boer War, he discovers that his former lover has fared even worse and died in a British concentration camp. Freibott then sets off for German South-west Africa, where, in an odd literary touch, he encounters his author in the shape of a trader called Hans Grimm. The Grimm character is able to make sense of Freibott's experience. He is a true German whose destiny awaits him in the new colonies, and he sends him on his way just in time to participate in the bloody suppression of the Herero. Free at last, Freibott buys a farm, but before he can occupy it the colony is overwhelmed by unscrupulous diamond speculators who are, of course, Jews. Diamonds and wealth corrupt the colonists and a dejected Freibott travels on, this time back to Europe and a world war which is ignominiously lost shortly after he arrives. He briefly takes up a career as a political agitator – no guesses as to what he is agitating for – but is murdered by a social democrat. A good editor might have suggested that Grimm turn his novel, with its absurd reversals of fortune, into a comedy. But as propaganda, the odd twists and turns of Cornelius Freibott's life were in 1926 an inspiration for thousands of Germans, both a romantic call to arms overseas and a vision of a new expanded Germany.

Like his hero, Beger experienced his own reversals of fortune. He simply could not raise the six thousand marks he would need to buy a farm. Any other dreams he might have had of an African farm were abruptly extinguished by a decidedly odd chain of events. One of his school friends, and his worst private maths pupil, had developed a consuming passion for the beautiful Frau Lichtenecker, the sculptor's wife. Rather than cultivate his flame of adolescent passion privately, the ardent and apparently simple-minded young man opted to reveal everything to his beloved. It was a disastrous decision. He was rebuffed in no uncertain terms and tried to commit suicide, but he botched the job and ended up mutilated and blinded in one eye. Both Beger and his friend were about to enter the university at Jena, and Frau Beger insisted that her son abandon any further thought of becoming a farmer and look after his damaged friend.

For now, Beger's dreams of staking a German flag in a faraway place had to be put aside. From the winter of 1931, at Jena and then Heidelberg, Beger studied his beloved mathematics and a clutch of natural sciences. He remained devoted to athletics and took a course in sports medicine. He could have had no idea just how valuable his medical skills would prove to be when he travelled to Tibet later that decade.

When I ask him about his time at university, Beger tells me he thought that many of his professors were dull and reactionary; they were poor teachers who sat in cafés day after day talking about 'restoring the Kaiser'. His feelings were typical of many students. They believed that their universities had become moribund, but the transformation they demanded was of a *Völkisch* and frequently anti-Semitic kind. Academic jobs were scarce, advancement sluggish, and many graduates found themselves trapped teaching in schools rather than universities. They vented their frustration, like so many others did, on Jews who were perceived to hold more academic positions than was proper. From 1920 onwards well-organized student bodies demanded quotas for Jews and disrupted lectures by Jewish professors. They restricted the number of Jews joining the *Turnerschaften* (gymnastic clubs) and *Burschenschaften* (fraternities) and stopped them taking part in duels – an essential part of any self-respecting student's time at university. Himmler was proud of his duelling scars, and during our second interview Beger leant forward to show us his own.

In the pretty little town of Jena in Thuringia, the ancient university was especially prone to such sentiments. It had been the academic fiefdom of Ernst Haeckel, who had transformed Darwinian evolution into the science of race. As it now was for Beger, Haeckel viewed 'lovely, small old Jena' as the centre of the world. It embodied all the qualities of German culture; it was a 'fortress of reason'. Haeckel hated cities with their noise and bustle; he associated them with Jews, whom he hated. He loved instead the deep, green valley of the Saale with its picturesque limestone mountains, its villages and brimming orchards. Haeckel's contribution to German scientific culture was to make respectable a racist celebration of the German *Volk* long before Hitler came to power. Hitler himself appropriated Haeckel's thinking in *Mein Kampf* and made him a hero of the Third Reich.

As Beger and his fellow students strolled along the leafy Furstengraben or gathered at the fraternity house, conversation would have turned admiringly to the increasingly successful Nazi Party. Beger, to be sure, did not join the NSDAP until the mid 1930s and says that on the one occasion he saw Hitler before 1933, making a speech from a balcony, he found him rather ridiculous. So did many others. But the stew of *Völkisch* and Judeophobic ideas that seethed and bubbled under the surface of the Weimar Republic had no need of Hitler to keep it piping hot. Germany's academic and scientific community could do that on its own.

Germany's catastrophic defeat and humiliation after 1918 had completely transformed nationalist passions. The state itself seemed defiled by the incompetence of politicians and their abject capitulation, and this conviction prompted the secret crystallization of a new kind of Reich, an inner national soul separate from the normal workings of the state.[9] The Nazis called their cultural magazine *Das Innere Reich*, and its first issue spoke of 'this eternal Inner Germany, the "Holy Heart of Nations" . . .' This 'Inner Reich' was quite distinct from the 'external Fatherland' which had sacrificed so many and then betrayed their memory so shamefully. It was the secret soul of a defeated but resilient *Volk*.

This very odd consequence of war and defeat had an impact on science, too, at least among anthropologists. Whereas before 1914 they had studied and measured native peoples like the Solomon Islanders or the Herero, now they became increasingly preoccupied with their own Indo-German or Aryan race, even with the 'eternal Inner Germany'. Races, according to one anthropologist already known to Beger at school, had souls. Like Madame Blavatsky and the German occult thinkers she had inspired, some German scientists began to investigate the origins of the Aryan race. Crushed by war, Germans could at least celebrate their ancestors and their own uniquely special blood line and inner soul. Furthermore, they could mark out a future *Lebensraum* for Germany by seeking out Aryan cousins in different parts of the world. Once again, Blavatsky and her spawn defined the realm of enquiry. Bismarck's hastily acquired colonies had been in Africa and the Pacific. Now that these had been lost Germans turned instead to central Asia, the land of Blavatsky's Great White Brotherhood. They looked east just as Hitler's geographer Karl Haushofer had demanded. This was a critical turning point in German thinking about the science of race, and one of its most important advocates now became Bruno Beger's teacher at Jena University.

In 1930, a new chair was created at the university, and its first occupant was Professor Hans F. K. 'Rassen' Günther. For the nineteen-year-old Beger, the blunt-headed Günther changed everything. He was much younger than most professors and had, it seemed, bright new ideas. He was perhaps a new, more mature father who could replace Hans Lichtenecker, the mentor of his schooldays. Günther taught an enthralling new science and for Beger it had tremendous glamour. Anthropology relied on the mathematics he loved, but it also conjured up the heady scents of faraway places and the dreams Beger had been forced to abandon. This intriguing science would also, he soon discovered, satisfy the nationalist pride he had inherited from his father. And it would draw him into the dark world of Heinrich Himmler.

Rassen Günther was no scientist, he was a fraud; the chair at Jena University was the gift of Hitler and the 'Gentlemen of the Swastika'. In December 1929, the NSDAP had trebled its vote in the Thuringian state election. What happened next would turn out to be a blueprint for the Nazi seizure of power. Hitler cannily demanded that the NSDAP be given two ministries in the Thuringian government, Interior and Education. This would give him the universities as well as the police, and Hitler said that he would use this power 'ruthlessly and persistently'.[10] He further insisted that one of his old cronies from the failed beer-hall putsch, Wilhelm Frick, take on both ministries. Frick was a notorious thug and his appointment had to be steamrollered through over local protests. As soon as he was appointed, Frick began a purge of schools and universities. He threw out as many Jews and communists as he could find and created a chair of *Rassenfragen und Rassenkunde* ('Racial Questions and Racial Knowledge') for Günther at Jena University.

Günther's rise to power had begun in 1922 when he was invited to take a stroll in the Alps by Julius Lehmann, the publisher and right-wing activist who would play a leading roll in Hitler's 1923 putsch.[11] Lehmann had built his reputation before and during the First World War by producing expensively illustrated medical atlases and texts and he was a vitriolic anti-Semite and *Völkisch* nationalist. In 1917, at the height of anti-Semitic riots in Germany, he had begun to use the pages of one of his widely distributed journals to popularize his ideas about race and 'racial hygiene'. In 1922, inspired by *The Passing of the Great Race* by the American racist Madison Grant, Lehmann was planning a series of books celebrating the superiority of the Nordic or Aryan race. So far, Lehmann had failed to find any reputable academic who was willing to take on the task. Hans Günther was the last name on his list, and his qualifications were not especially impressive.

Günther was a philologist educated in Freiburg, and in 1922 a frustrated school teacher who desperately wanted a university post. He had already published, three years earlier, his eccentric *Ritter, Tod und Teufel*, an 'Account of the Nordic Man' inspired by the famous engraving by Albrecht Dürer 'Knight, Death and the Devil' (1513). Günther had fashioned an unconventional tract that transformed the Knight into a model German. He had all the Nordic qualities: 'talented and beautiful . . . slim, broad shouldered, narrow hipped', but ruthless too, with 'chiselled features . . . shining skin flushed with blood . . . a royal species among men'.[12] The Knight was the superior, pure-blooded leader of the people.[13] One of Günther's most enthusiastic readers was Heinrich Himmler.

Lehmann was certain that he could shape Günther's romantic racism and turn him into a hard-headed advocate of Nordic superiority. He knew that Günther had led a vicious political campaign against the deployment of black French troops in the Rhineland in 1919; he had called them 'the Black Curse on the Rhine'. So as they stopped to take in the view from a high ridge, Lehmann made Günther a tantalizing offer. He wanted him to abandon the romantic nationalism of *Ritter* and turn himself into a committed race scientist. Once he had absorbed the appropriate expertise, Günther would be contracted to churn out a series of lucrative articles and books.

Beger's future professor proved an apt pupil. His first article for Lehmann was 'The Nordic Race and Blood Mixture of our Eastern Neighbours', which was enthusiastically reviewed by the anthropologist Eugen Fischer who was best known for his study of 'bastards' in Namibia. It was followed by his second book, *Racial Lore of the German Volk*, which was an instant popular success. Now Lehmann flooded Germany with racial literature masquerading as science, and Günther became his most prominent and successful author. He produced a torrent of books – eight between 1924 and 1929[14] – and it made him wealthy. He was the darling of the extreme right. Hitler himself attended his first lecture.

Günther turned Beger into an anthropologist. And it is by understanding Günther that we can discover why Himmler sent Beger to Tibet.

Imagine the young Beger in his cramped student digs in Jena. He is a hard-working student when he is not running or jumping, and there are scores of books open on his desk and stacked on shelves and chairs. One is open in front of him. It is Günther's *The Racial Elements of European History*. Physical anthropology, Günther tells his students and readers, concerns itself with the 'calculable details of bodily structure'. From a study of bodily structures, Günther concludes that there are five European races: the Nordic, the Mediterranean, the Dinaric, and so on. But – and this is the fundamental point – 'true breeding human groups' are very rare. Most Europeans, including Germans, are a mixture of blood lines, and the physical anthropologist has the task of calculating the proportion of each race embodied in an individual. This can be determined only by intricately measuring bodies and skulls, recording hair types and eye colour, and then meticulously crunching the numbers. Günther believed that the evidence was worrying; German stock was increasingly mixed. And only the pure in blood could sustain a high civilization.

A great deal of Günther's evidence is subjective. He depends, like most racists, on appearance, and the book contains page after page of mug shots that stand for the different racial types or mixtures of types. Many are anonymous, but others show history's great and good. There is Macchiavelli, 'predominantly Dinaric', alongside Leonardo, who was 'Nordic'; Tennyson was Nordic too, as were Byron and the Duke of Wellington, but Dickens is merely 'predominantly Nordic' since the crinkly texture of his hair betrays the presence of a different strain. Generic American professors (from Yale) and most statesmen are Nordic; marble statues, portraits and antique busts show that Greeks, Romans and Germans too were of the Nordic type. Günther has a rogue's gallery as well. Socialist leader Ferdinand Lasalle is representative of a 'Jew from Germany' and is 'Predominantly Hither Asiatic with Nordic Strain? Texture of hair Negro?' Camille Saint-Saëns is simply a 'Jew from France'.

Günther's conclusion is simple and dangerous. The message of science is that the Nordic or Aryan race embodies all that is great and good. Aryans alone are endowed with a sense of competitive achievement, leadership, highly developed senses of reality, prudence, duty, calm judgement, angelic creativity and 'roguish humour'. What a piece of work is Nordic man! But if the weaker elements betray their inheritance by contaminating its purity, these attributes begin to wither; 'an age of unlimited racial mixture has left the men of the present day physically and mentally rudderless'.

Günther now brings on the villains in the drama of race history. One racial type above all posed the most insidious threat to Nordic culture. The Jews 'give an example of the physical and mental hereditary endowment, for their inherited characteristics are the source of that strangeness which they themselves feel within the racially different European peoples and which these people feel with regard to the Jews . . .'[15] Jews exhibit, according to Günther, particular gestures and traits which, thankfully, make them easy to identify. They are, for example, preoccupied by materialism and have a tendency to obesity and 'lustfully sensual lips'. In his chapter 'Jewish Nation', Günther recommends that a 'worthy and evident solution of the Jewish question lies in that separation of the Jews from the Gentiles . . . which Zionism seeks to bring about'.[16] Thus the scientist became a propagandist.

At the end of the book, Günther tells his readers and students, 'The question is not so much whether we men now living are more or less Nordic; but the question put to us is whether we have the courage enough to make ready for future generations a world cleansing itself racially and eugenically . . . Race theory and investigations on heredity call forth and give strength to a New Nobility: the youth that is, with lofty aims in all ranks which, urged on like Faust, seeks to set its will towards a goal which calls to it beyond the individual life.'[17] Anthropological science, forged in the factories of colonial violence, thus became a rallying call to German youth to purify the race.

From the beginning of the nineteenth century, many had come to believe that the Aryan races had expanded from a central Asian homeland, perhaps in Tibet. Günther turned the idea on its head. According to him, north-west Europe was the original home of the Nordic people, and Günther laboriously followed their trail eastwards to Persia, through the Caucasus and into India. In an echo of the Atlantis myth, Günther's Nords brought with them the art of building and sophisticated social systems. In some regions of the world, they left behind dolmens and stone circles; in India, they created the Hindu *Veda*. But as they spread across Asia, the weaker kind of Aryan began to lust after lesser races and to poison their inheritance. The great Nordic empire collapsed and its people retreated back to their ancestral heartland in the north.

Günther found evidence for this in the *Veda*, which lament the mingling of races. Its proscriptions, he suspected, led to the emergence of the Hindu *varna* system of hierarchical castes that both Günther and Himmler admired. On the other hand, he blamed Buddhism for encouraging mixed marriage. The teachings of the Buddha 'wholly and irretrievably broke down the racial discipline and forethought of this wonderfully gifted people'. This is all strikingly similar to Ernst Schäfer's lament for the tough old Tibet corrupted by Lamaism. According to Günther, the original Aryans had no priests and it was the emergence of a priestly caste that signalled the 'weakening' of their blood. Indian peoples, Günther believed, now contained barely a trace of their original Nordic blood, but he believed that some residual evidence might be found in remote areas of the North-West frontier.[18] This is the key that unlocks Beger's intentions in Tibet.

Beger still has his copy of Günther's *Die Nordische Rasse bei den Indogermanene Aliens*, published in 1933. The maps show dark arrows plunging south then east from the Nordic heartland in northern Europe. They push through ancient Persia and deep into central Asia and the icy peaks of Tibet. In Jena, as he studied these maps, Beger became fascinated by a tantalizing possibility. When he had studied photographs of Tibetan nobles he had become fascinated by their slim, perhaps even Nordic appearance. He later described them as follows: 'tall, with long head, thin face, drawn back cheek bones, springing out straight or slightly bent nose with high nose ridge, straight hair and imperious, self-confident behaviour'. Beger, and his professor, now became intrigued by the possibility that the last Aryans might be discovered on what Kipling had called 'the world's white roof tree' – in Tibet.

But in 1931, Beger had no idea how he might prove his idea. In contrast to his future colleague Ernst Schäfer, who was at that moment striding across the wilds of Kham, Beger was more concerned about how to make ends meet. For him, education was one way to memorialize his slain father, but his mother still needed her sons to pay their way without assistance. And a proper German education took a long time: a typical graduate was at least twenty-seven. After four semesters at Jena, Beger moved back to his home town of Heidelberg for a while, and then followed Günther to Berlin. He found himself a small apartment in Grunewald in a house that had once been the home of a Jewish family. Günther was now head of the Institute for Race Lore, Ethnic Biology and Regional Sociology. As Schäfer had a year earlier, Beger began to see Himmler's SS as a way forward.

The following year, Beger applied to join Himmler's elite. Like Schäfer, but for different reasons, Beger would have been an attractive recruit. He was an anthropologist and a student of Hans Günther whose work was highly valued by the new rulers of Germany. He was a textbook 'Nordic' specimen, as photographs and the film of Schäfer's expedition demonstrate: tall and blond with chiselled aquiline features. 'A typical Slav-face would scarcely be taken into the SS by an SS-Führer,' Himmler wrote. 'The photographs which have to accompany the application form serve the purpose of allowing the faces of the candidates to be seen at headquarters . . . in general we want only good fellows, not louts.'[19] By 1935 his application had been approved, and Beger was an *SS Mann*. In the same year, he joined the Nazi Party, neither an early recruit nor a 'March

Violet' – referring to those Germans who rushed to join the party when Hitler had seized power. More significant was the fact that he now made the acquaintance of Dr August Hirt, a doctor devoted to the Nazi cause. Hirt and Beger would together become involved in one of the darkest episodes of German 'science'.

In the same year that he was accepted into the SS, Beger married and moved from his modest student quarters to a cramped apartment in Marie Curie Strasse near the Zoological Gardens. His first daughter was born there in 1936; two more would rapidly follow. Beger was still a student, and the pressing demands of a young family meant he needed a job, one he could combine with the demands of his dissertation. And he found it inside the SS, in the Race and Settlement Office, the RuSHA. From now on his time would be split between the Anthropology Department on Lentze Allee and the RuSHA on Heidemannstrasse, where he began work on some of the archaeological projects that so fascinated Himmler.

To a remarkable degree, Himmler's ideas had been formed not by politicians but by anthropologists and biologists. Men like Günther had shown, using apparently objective measurements, that certain individuals and only one race was destined for mastery, but that if the blood of the Master Race was mixed with lesser races, it would be weakened and eventually destroyed. Hitler's deputy, Rudolf Hess, called Nazism 'applied racial science'. After 1933, scientists at the prestigious Kaiser Wilhelm Institute found that their ideas were highly valued by Germany's new leaders. Many prestigious scientists became part of the Nazi crusade, even if they despised Hitler in private and were not party members. Among them were well-known biologists and anthropologists like Eugen Fischer, whose work on genetics was highly regarded by Himmler. These scientists fostered, knowingly, the vision of a future where scientific methods of selection would ensure that higher races prospered and lesser ones were weeded out. By pursuing their science, anthropologists nourished the fantasies of others who sought not knowledge but power. Hitler sometimes described himself as a 'physician' whose task was to remove the sickness of modern Germany. In return for scientifically endorsing his metaphor, doctors and anthropologists were offered dazzling opportunities by men who in 1933 seized so much power that they could contemplate what might have been an impossible dream: a purely Nordic future cleansed of impurity. It was a dream of power so radical that it could envision transforming the biological nature of the German people themselves.

So here is Bruno Beger in 1936. He is a fully fledged *SS Mann* and has a new membership card from the NSDAP. He lives and works in Berlin, dashing between the RuSHA and the university, where Günther has given him his dissertation topic. It is his first chance to use in the field the anthropometric techniques he has been taught, and it concerns an historical enigma. The Altmärkische Wische is a small farming region near the Elbe, until 1989 part of the GDR. In the twelfth century, the Altmärkische was plagued by flooding. The local prince, 'Albrecht the Bear', had the inspired idea of drafting in engineers from the Netherlands to build dykes to control the floods. Albrecht's scheme was a great success and the Altmärkische was soon safe, dry and prosperous. The Dutch dyke builders and the families they had brought with them were offered generous legal rights and lucrative tax concessions if they decided to stay on, and many did. Over the centuries, the Dutch community, the Lange Strasse, maintained a semi-aristocratic distance from local German people even after their privileges were eventually taken away from them in the nineteenth century. Beger's task was to take his callipers and gypsum to the Altmärkische and see if he could detect, using anthropological science, whether or not there was any difference between the two groups hundreds of years after Albrecht's clever idea had brought them together. He spent a happy summer cycling around the Altmärkische measuring local farmers, making masks (he must have had considerable charm) and processing the data with a clumsy 'Brunswick calculator'. The question was, who was most German? Could two European 'races' still be detected? And if so, what did that imply?

Beger would never finish his dissertation. One morning in 1937 a postcard was slipped beneath his door in Berlin – it was signed by Ernst Schäfer, the famous explorer.

CHAPTER FIVE

RETURN TO THE FATHERLAND

'How can the peasant in his village, the labourer in his workshop or factory, the employee in his office – how can they all grasp the extent of the total result of their innumerable personal sacrifices and their struggle? . . . All of them . . . will be able to come to the same conclusion: we are truly the witnesses of a transformation more tremendous than any the German nation has ever experienced.'

– Adolf Hitler, September 1937

Shanghai in January 1936 was still a city of brutal contrasts, a deafening tower of Babel, a perpetual motion machine, and, for Ernst Schäfer, crushing after the privations and raptures of the wilderness. Exquisitely attired Europeans, Russians and Americans thronged the *Bund*, the thousand shops of the Nanking Road, the racecourse – the season had begun in November – and the enormous Hongkew Market where you could buy just about whatever you needed or desired. Glittering-eyed traders and dealers were whisked from deal to deal by the city's seventy thousand barefoot rickshaw drivers, although few of them took time to notice any Chinese person unless they could do them a favour or had something to sell. In the narrow side streets, bicycles proliferated and honking American cars competed with overladen carts, wheelbarrows and teams of panting Chinese boys staggering beneath weighty pieces of ivory or lacquer furniture destined for homes on the sedate, tree-lined avenues of one of the European Concessions. At night, any pleasure could be indulged, from dancing to opium to sex (of most kinds and in any combination) – and Brooke Dolan, Schäfer knew, had explored most of them.

While the foreign barbarians made money at Jardine Matheson or Sassoon & Co. and enjoyed leisurely two-hour lunches and nights of doped sensuality, hordes of Chinese refugees, each of whom owned little more than a rice bowl, crowded every day and night across Garden Bridge. They were fleeing unending wars and rapacious armies, and the crippling poverty of the countryside. These bone-thin men, women and children would join hundreds of thousands of others huddled in Shanghai's shanty towns a long way from the *Bund* and the racecourse. The foreign barbarians rarely thought about these glum-faced, starving losers. The wealth of Shanghai's foreigners depended on the weakness of the Chinese, their poverty and their wars with each other and with Japan. A year later, when Schäfer and Dolan were long gone, Japanese bombers would end Shanghai's glory days for ever.

One morning, very early, Schäfer took a stroll along the fog-shrouded *Bund* by the Whangpo. Foghorns sounded across the water, reminding him of conch shells blown mournfully in Tibetan temples – usually a good omen. Schäfer needed to make some hard decisions. He was twenty-five and was already being proclaimed as a new Sven Hedin, thanks to his first book. Now he had completed another dramatic foray into the wilderness and was returning with a rich harvest of zoological spoils.

Like his Swedish hero, he knew that his recent adventures could be mined to yield an exotic drama of exploration and derring-do.

But Schäfer was divided and uncertain. Should he return to Germany? Did he want to? Might the United States offer him more? As the fog cleared on the river, a vista of ceaseless and restless movement unfurled. The viscous brown river was dotted with jostling small craft, junks with spread sails, rusty coasters and steamers, and poised cruisers blithely crossing the sea lanes. Schäfer watched the ships as they sailed or steamed down to the confluence with the Yangtze then upriver into China or out to the Hangzhou Wan and the East China Sea. After the war, Schäfer would claim that he had tried to escape Hitler's Germany, but the evidence implies a more complicated tale.

One of the people who had wanted to meet him in Shanghai was the German consul, General Walther Greibel. Schäfer later told his American interrogators, '[Greibel] was very friendly. I said: "I'm going to America." He said: "That is impossible. You have to go back to Germany. I'll smooth the way for you. I'll write to Germany and recommend you." ' It is true that Schäfer had already been awarded a life membership of the Academy of Natural Sciences in Philadelphia for collecting 'scientific data and specimens of [central Asian] birds and mammals that have never been equalled in size and importance', but back home, he explained to Greibel, it was a different story. His professor, Alfred Kühn, had kicked up a fuss when Schäfer had put his doctoral work to one side to join Dolan and had taken a great deal of persuading before he let Schäfer postpone the completion of his studies. His experiences in Asia were begrudged.

Greibel was so impressed with Schäfer and so alarmed that he might not return to Germany that he immediately sent a letter to the German Research Association (DFG). He told them he had just met a young man who 'could one day become the ornament of our long line of German scientists'.[1] The consul made two suggestions. The first was to award Schäfer an 'honorary doctorate' or to 'bureaucratically facilitate' his doctoral exam. This would prove to be unnecessary: Schäfer was perfectly capable of completing his dissertation without favours. It was Greibel's second proposal that would have the most far-reaching impact. Schäfer had told him that he wanted to lead another, German expedition to Tibet. If the DFG would support this ambitious plan then there was no doubt that Schäfer's loyalty would be guaranteed. The consul's letter came to the attention of Heinrich Himmler who was intrigued by this young SS officer's accomplishments. The Reichsführer would certainly not tolerate Schäfer staying on in America.

Dolan and Schäfer sailed for the United States at the end of the month. In March, Charles Cadwallader at the Academy in Philadelphia wrote to Duncan that 'Brooke Dolan and Ernst Schäfer are now in Philadelphia and all hands are busily engaged in unpacking, cataloguing and caring for the magnificent collections made by the expedition.'[2] Their task must have been immense. They had been on the road for fifteen months, had travelled five thousand miles by caravan and the best part of two thousand by river and had shot and collected every day. Some of the collection was destined for the museum's popular dioramas, which soon boasted a splendid yak 'shot by Ernst Schäfer'. The thousands of other specimens would be meticulously catalogued and 'typed'. Schäfer also spent some time at the Field Museum in Chicago, where he would have seen the panda shot by Roosevelt.

Now a stream of telegrams started to arrive from Berlin. Himmler's assault had begun. The first one congratulated Schäfer on his success and strongly recommended that he return to Germany as soon as possible. Another arrived soon afterwards. This time it was sent from the office of the Reichsführer himself and it informed Schäfer that he had been awarded a flattering honorary promotion to 'SS Untersturmführer *honoris causa*'. Himmler knew his fellow Germans well. Marking academic success with a higher military rank was perfectly harmonized with the national psyche. Militarism, it was said in Germany, 'is the state of mind of the civilian'. The Nazis had simply pushed to its logical conclusion Bismarck's ideal of a *Machtstaat*, or military power state.

After the war, at the de-nazification tribunal, Schäfer took pains to show that his decision to return was not voluntary, yet his reply to Himmler's telegram, written from Dolan's home address in Villanova, Pennsylvania, to the SS headquarters is effusive: 'I am so proud and happy I am not able to express it. I hope I will be able to show my gratitude through my actions. All my expectations were in each and every respect exceeded though the greatest honour for me is to have been promoted . . .'[3]

Even if this is honorific or simply prudent, Germany must have begun to seem more attractive. In the United States, Schäfer would have been a small fish in a big, highly competitive pond. Although he was now widely travelled he was still academically underqualified, and the prospect of starting afresh at an American university would have been daunting. His relationship with Dolan was friendly but the betrayal at Sining would never be forgotten. Schäfer might also have suspected that he would never stop being 'Junge'; the unpredictable but charismatic Dolan would always be in charge. Back home in Germany, if Greibel could be trusted, he would soon have his Ph.D. and could begin preparing his own German expedition. At the very least, Schäfer was a patriot, and he cannot have forgotten Marion Duncan's searing hostility. There was probably a more subtle calculation, too. His books were addressed to a *German* audience. Their deft blend of science and adventure, of natural history and the ecstasy of the hunt, had been knowingly wrought for a readership only just emerging from the humiliation of Versailles and the turmoil of the Weimar years.

If Schäfer had any doubts, his mind was made up by the Academy of Natural Sciences itself. It had no funds to give Schäfer a job, so in June he said goodbye to the Dolans and boarded the SS *Bremen* bound for Hamburg. Hans Schäfer was waiting for him at the quay when the boat docked. As they drove away, his father warned Ernst, 'Be as clever as a snake. It is extremely dangerous.'

Schäfer settled in Berlin and returned energetically to his neglected studies, knuckling down to a doctoral dissertation on Tibetan ornithology. He resumed his popular writing at the same time. *Berge, Buddhas und Bären* ('Mountains, Buddhas and Bears') had been a success in 1933 following the first Dolan expedition; now he started work on a two-volume account of the second: *Dach der Erde* ('Roof of the World') and *Unbekanntes Tibet* ('Unknown Tibet'). And he began to enjoy Germany again. It seemed a good time to be back.

By the 'Olympic' summer of 1936, the Nazis had swept away the last relics of Weimar democracy, and Hitler's brutal New Order seemed to have brought about prosperity and optimism. The Reinhardt Plan had kickstarted the economy with heavy investment in roads, building and industry. Hitler's pet *autobahn* project employed two hundred thousand people and created a dazzling symbol of renewal. New factories sprang up in a golden ring around Berlin, and cafés, restaurants and beer halls boomed. It was said that Hitler was 'the symbol of the indestructible life force of the nation'. However much its prehistoric past might have been revered, the New Germany embraced modernity. Motor cars, sound films and wireless were proclaimed as the gifts of National Socialism. Germans thrilled to Hitler's bold attacks on the hated Versailles settlement. In October 1933 he had withdrawn from the League of Nations. In 1935 an overwhelming majority of Saarlanders voted for integration into the Reich, and on 7 March 1936 German troops marched into the demilitarized zone of the Rhineland. Speer said that Hitler was the leader who 'made a reality of their deeply rooted longings for a powerful, proud, united Germany. Very few were mistrustful at this time . . .'

The Berlin Olympics brought more than a million visitors to the city, including Schäfer's hero Sven Hedin as a guest of honour, and many of them left convinced that the dark stories they had heard about Hitler were untrue. But for those brave enough to look behind Joseph Goebbels' polished screen of propaganda a different kind of world became apparent, one that was dark, chaotic and violent. Hitler ruled through antagonistic rivalry. The dictator spent most of his time, according to Speer, inspecting new buildings, relaxing in cafés, haranguing his colleagues or sleeping. Among his cronies, there was intense infighting between different agencies and power brokers. Nazi leaders were greedy, venal and corrupt. Despite this, repressive measures against Jews and dissidents were brutally effective. In the universities and research institutes, students and academics had welcomed the dismissal of Jewish colleagues and embraced a comprehensive policy of *Gleichschaltung* ('unification') which allowed the Nazi dictatorship to oversee appointments, teaching and research. Doctors and lawyers rushed to serve the dictatorship in overwhelming numbers.

Schäfer was feeling increasingly secure and settled in this environment, so he married. Hertha Volz was, Bruno Beger remembers, '*eine schöne, blonde, groß gewachsene Frau*' – 'a beautiful, blonde, tall woman' – the perfect Aryan match for the stocky young adventurer. She was 'delectable and adorable',

Beger adds, full of laughter. Her family presided over the prestigious Volz'sche Pädagogikum in Heidelberg, which Beger had attended briefly before his family had moved to Gotha, and they had known the Schäfers for many years. After the wedding, the couple found a large apartment at Hohenzollerndam 36 in the smart Wilmersdorf district of Berlin near Nollendorf-platz. Together, the Schäfers enjoyed Berlin's 700th anniversary, which like so much in Nazi Germany was a fiction: there was no certainty at all that Berlin had been founded in 1237. But Berliners revelled in the clubs, dance halls, cinemas and theatres and the elite were fêted by embassy gatherings, dinners and parties thrown by Nazi potentates. For intellectuals who could be of service to the Reich there were other, even more powerful enticements. Soon after his return to Germany, Schäfer was summoned to Prinz-Albrecht-Strasse 8 to meet the Reichsführer himself, Heinrich Himmler.

As he faced Himmler in his poky office, Schäfer revealed his plans for a new expedition to Tibet, this time under a German flag with men of his own blood. Himmler responded enthusiastically and ordered that Schäfer work with the Ahnenerbe, the SS agency dedicated to investigating the ancestral origins of the Aryan race. Schäfer must have shifted uncomfortably in his chair. Although he had spent little time in Germany since 1933, he knew that the Ahnenerbe was a club for crackpots and failures. No-one took its activities seriously and the price of accepting Himmler as a patron could be humiliation. Schäfer appears to have kept his misgivings private. When he drafted a lecture for the British Himalayan Club in 1938, he described his relationship with the Reichsführer in glowing terms: 'Having been a member of the Black Guard since a long time, I was only too glad that the highest SS leader, himself a very keen amateur scientist, was interested in my work of exploration. There was no need of convincing the Reichsführer SS, as he himself had the same ideas; he simply promised to give me all the help necessary . . .'[4] Schäfer addressing an audience of British mountaineers – hardly an occasion at which to exaggerate his loyalty to Heinrich Himmler.

Himmler was indeed interested; a new Schäfer expedition could confer tremendous prestige on the SS, and on the Ahnenerbe itself, which had its own 'expeditions department'. Schäfer himself desperately wanted his own triumph. What must have followed was an elaborate *pas de deux* in which both men sought to extract the maximum advantage and to suffer the least damage. For Himmler, Schäfer's plans had irresistible allure. He was fascinated by Asia and believed, like Hans Günther, that there might be Aryan refugees somewhere in the Himalayas. He was determined to extract from Schäfer's success a propaganda triumph that would seal the reputation of the SS and the Ahnenerbe. Himmler had rivals for political power, but he also resented the cultural status of Alfred Rosenberg, the German Balt who had fled to Germany in 1918 and translated the *Protocols of the Elders of Zion*, the phoney document that implied there was a Jewish conspiracy to seize global power. He called himself a 'Fighter against Jerusalem'; he was called in turn 'a profoundly half-educated man'. He began to churn out voluminous and turgid books such as *Immorality in the Talmud* and *The Myth of the 20th Century*. Like Himmler, he was obsessed with Aryan origins, the fate of Atlantis as well as a clutch of pseudoscientific meta-theories about history. He was also chief editor of the *Völkischer Beobachter*, the Nazi newspaper. By 1936, Reichsleiter Rosenberg had his own rival organization to the Ahnenerbe, known as the Amt Rosenberg, and was a bitter rival of Himmler. A celebrated expedition would give Himmler a powerful advantage.

As Schäfer's plan took shape, Himmler began to pressure him to recruit from Ahnenerbe staff. Schäfer was determined to resist. His reasons had little to do with wanting to occupy any moral high ground. Isrun Engelhardt tells us that 'Schäfer from childhood on hated to yield to authority and resisted being used in any way, be it political or ideological.' And she points out that 'His refusal to oblige the Nazis was not so much grounded in a genuine dislike of Nazi ideology but rather in his own disposition.'[5] Schäfer could never claim, of course, that he had merely followed orders. Over the course of the next year he would wage a guerrilla war with Himmler to protect the identity of *his* Tibet expedition. The Reichsführer was equally determined to mould and influence events. He wanted his own pet theories investigated in the Himalayas. Looking for the Aryan homeland was only one item on his oddball list.

As well as Aryan prehistory, Himmler was also an enthusiast of a bizarre cosmological fantasy called the *Welteislehre* or *GlazialKosmogonie*, the World Ice Theory. The *Welteislehre* had been hatched at the turn of the century by the Austrian engineer, amateur astronomer and inventor Hanns Hörbiger. It was a complete cosmological and historical package. According to Hörbiger, the prime matter of the universe was ice. Cosmic ice threaded its way through the cosmos; the Milky Way and every planetary body, with the exception of the Earth, was sheathed in ice. But this cosmic frost waged perpetual war with gigantic, fiery suns. Every body in the universe was drawn into the perpetual struggle between fire and ice and new planets were formed from the debris of catastrophe and collision. Bigger, more powerful bodies like the Earth ensnared smaller moons in ever-decreasing orbital cycles and the eventual collisions generated floods, earthquakes and volcanic eruptions. According to Hörbiger, *Mondniederbrüche* ('moon breakdown') explained the extinction of the dinosaurs, the biblical flood *and* the destruction of Atlantis. The few survivors fled to form 'asylum' or 'refuge' cultures in Mexico and South America.

When it was published in 1913, Hörbiger's theory was widely dismissed as pseudoscience, but it soon began to attract a cult following in Germany's *Völkisch* community. In this shadowy world, the *Welteislehre* had an alluring eschatological magnetism. The Nordic Master Race had, supposedly, originated in a realm of ice and had been scattered across the globe by catastrophic eruptions, floods and earthquakes. There was a deeper seduction, too: according to Hörbiger, the universe was created from unceasing struggle and destruction, ideas which had a powerful appeal for Himmler.

The *Welteislehre* provided an Aryan alternative to the 'dreadful and mistaken' 'Jewish theories' of scientists like Einstein. Even the usually sceptical Hitler embraced glacial cosmogony. In *Table Talk*, Hitler said he was 'quite well inclined to accept the cosmic theories of Hörbiger' and planned to build an observatory in Linz dedicated to 'the three great cosmological conceptions of history – those of Ptolemy, Copernicus and Hörbiger'.[6] But it was Himmler who most zealously promoted glacial cosmogony, and when he could he silenced opponents of the idea. The German Ministry of Education and Science denounced the idea, and one of Himmler's staff called Polte had actively solicited hostile comments. So when Himmler discovered what he had been up to, Polte was sent 'on leave'. Himmler was a devout believer, and the *Welteislehre* refined his ideas about the origins of the Master Race.

At their first meeting, he had earnestly told Schäfer that the supernatural ancestors of the Aryans had once been sheathed in ice and had been released from their frozen bondage by divine thunderbolts. Many departments of the Ahnenerbe were devoted to 'proving' Hörbiger right – posthumously, since he had died in 1931. It was natural that Himmler would view an expedition to the icy Himalayas as the perfect opportunity for a proper investigation of the *Welteislehre*. His first demand was that Schäfer take an SS officer called Edmund Kiss, an enthusiastic believer in glacial cosmogony.

Schäfer had no idea who Kiss was and began to investigate. What he discovered was dismaying. Kiss had lived in Bolivia in the late 1920s and had become friendly with an Austrian adventurer and rubber maker called Arthur Posnansky. Posnansky had spent more than a decade surveying the ancient city of Tiwanaku in the Altiplano, which was, like Tibet, a plateau surrounded by icy peaks. At Tiwanaku, immense stone blocks lay scattered just as if they had been smashed in some ancient geological catastrophe. The stupendous size of these blocks and their exquisite carving implied that they had been created by some mysterious lost civilization. This possibility intrigued Edmund Kiss, who was well versed in *Völkisch* fantasies. Posnansky was plain wrong, but his peculiar fantasy had been stewed in the poisonous broth of racism and this appealed to Kiss and to his masters in Berlin.

Posnansky violently despised the local Aymara people, who believed – correctly – that their ancestors had built Tiwanaku just two thousand years earlier. Kiss encouraged his friend to rationalize his virulent prejudices and introduced him to German race anthropology. Posnansky began measuring and photographing the Aymara and concluded that they did not have the capacity to conceive and build such an astounding monument. So who had? And when? Although Tiwanaku is less than two thousand years old, Kiss and Posnansky proposed on the basis of some flimsy astronomical calculations that it was a South American Atlantis built by an elite refugee race, abandoned fifteen thousand years ago after calamitous volcanic eruptions and floods. Up on the Altiplano, according to Kiss, everything fitted together. Tiwanaku provided evidence for a lost Master Race and the violent upheavals predicted by

Hörbiger's theory. High in the Andes, Kiss claimed to have discovered a monumental 'Nordic Head' which was more evidence of an Atlantean flight from an inundated world into the Andes. Kiss's head has never been seen by anyone else.

When he returned to Germany, Kiss worked as a town surveyor in Kassel and began to churn out scientific tracts and turgid fiction about Atlantis.[7] For Schäfer they made dire reading. *Frühling in Atlantis* (*Spring in Atlantis*, 1931) is a story about the golden age of Atlantis. In Kiss's fevered imagination, a ruling elite of fair Nordic types called 'Asen' confront a threatening, dark-skinned, Slavic underclass. The Asen leader Baldur Wieborg of Thule, who had been promoting eugenic breeding plans, is eventually murdered. *Die letze Königin von Atlantis* (*The Last Queen of Atlantis*, 1931) is set fourteen thousand years ago and tells the story of the Atlanteans' trek to the Andes, where they practise stringent eugenics and enslave the local people. In his final bestseller, *Die Singschwäne aus Thule* (*The Singing Swans from Thule*, 1939), the Asen embark on a journey back to their Arctic homeland, Thule, under their blue and silver swastika banners. When their ancestors had lived there long ago, Thule had basked in an endless spring, but the Third Moon had made Thule into an icy desert. So the Asen turned south again and founded the ancient Hellenic cultures of the Mediterranean.

Himmler was passionate about Kiss's novels and invited him to contribute 'scientific' works on the *Welteislehre* to Ahnenerbe-sponsored journals. In 1936 Kiss signed the 'Pyrmont Protocol' which bound the Ahnenerbe to support glacial cosmogony, and began to lobby Himmler to allow him to organize expeditions to find evidence.

Schäfer was dismayed by what he had discovered about his future colleague. The suggestion that he collaborate with a fantasist like Kiss, whose work confirmed all his worst fears about the Ahnenerbe, was repellent. But he had to proceed, as his father had advised, with caution. He agreed to meet Kiss, and as soon as he had he realized that there was a way out of his dilemma. He called Himmler and informed him that it would be quite impossible to work with a man who was so much older than he was. His experience in the wilds of Asia had made it clear that the key to success was youth. Nor, he said, did he want his authority questioned by an older man. It was a clever move. Himmler backed down; there would be no Kiss.[8]

Soon afterwards, the balance of power began to tip even further in Schäfer's favour. Shaken by the Kiss experience, Schäfer courageously made a list of twelve conditions that would guarantee his scientific freedom and presented them to the Ahnenerbe head, Wolfram Sievers. Schäfer and Sievers already distrusted each other and Sievers concluded, having read Schäfer's list, that 'The task of the expedition . . . had diverged too far from the targets of the Reichsführer SS . . .' There was another reason for Sievers' capitulation. His official title was 'business manager' of the Ahnenerbe and he was now embarrassed to discover that the coffers of the SS were much depleted (Schäfer was demanding more than sixty thousand Reichsmarks, and presumably not enough of Loibl's illuminated bicycle discs had been sold that quarter). Himmler was furious but there was nothing he could do. So Schäfer's bullishness and the empty Ahnenerbe coffers meant that he could detach his plans from Sievers' grip but still retain the support of Himmler himself.

Schäfer was now faced with a formidable task: he would have to raise the funds himself. But with his father's assistance and his own well-oiled connections he rapidly – 'in no time', he said – accumulated the money he needed. The process snowballed when the Werberat der Deutschen Wirtschaft (Public Relations and Advertising Council of German Business) pledged 80 per cent of the budget. The *Völkischer Beobachter* quickly saw the propaganda potential of Schäfer's expedition and reached into its coffers. The balance was made up by big German companies like IG Farben and the Deutsche Forschungsgemeinschaft (Reich Research Council). Brooke Dolan, perhaps still smarting after Schäfer's threatened bonfire, put in $4,000.[9] Other companies donated otherwise unaffordable scientific equipment, and even a new typewriter, which they hoped Schäfer would be photographed with in the wild.

Schäfer cannily had a letterhead printed. It read DEUTSCHE TIBET EXPEDITION ERNST SCHÄFER in large letters, then 'under the patronage of the Reichsführer-SS Heinrich Himmler and in connection with the Ahnenerbe' (in small letters!). He was careful to remove that second line when he arrived in Gangtok in British India, as his Sikkimese assistant 'German' Akeh Bhutia proved when I met him in 2002. Akeh still possessed the letters that authenticated his involvement with Schäfer; they are simply headed DEUTSCHE TIBET EXPEDITION ERNST SCHÄFER. Some German historians have concluded from this that Schäfer was independent of the SS and was thus able to do 'pure science'. This was not the case. Himmler remained the expedition's patron and Schäfer clearly had no interest in losing his support. Although Sievers had denounced Schäfer's proposal, it is highly likely that Himmler would have approved and released Ahnenerbe funds had they been available. Both men had what they wanted. It would remain an SS expedition, 'in connection with the Ahnenerbe', but Schäfer had made sure that in most respects he would shape its goals. At the very least, the German Tibet Exhibition could enhance the international reputation of Nazi Germany. In many other ways, too, Schäfer's plans remained intertwined with Hitler's New Order.

At a very practical level, Schäfer needed Himmler's support even if he acknowledged this only in small type. The

Reichsführer would provide the expedition with foreign currency, which was extremely difficult to obtain during the Nazi period, and, more importantly, he would grant Schäfer and his colleagues permission to leave Germany.[10] Schäfer would turn to Himmler again, in desperation, at the end of his time in Tibet in August 1939. It is also true that Schäfer's funding, while it did not come from the Ahnenerbe, did come from organizations with very close links to the Nazi state: the Werberat der Deutschen Wirtschaft was part of Goebbels' Propaganda Ministry, and the *Völkischer Beobachter* was the official Nazi Party newspaper. This was not a free society. All this suggests that we need a more subtle account of the ways in which Schäfer's activities were ensnared in the ideologies of the Reich.

To begin with, there was no innate contradiction between a vicious totalitarian regime and science – assuming, in Robert Proctor's phrase, that 'Science is what scientists do.' In Hitler's *Table Talk*, one of the most frequently used words is *Wissenschaft* – science. Although Himmler was fascinated by what can only be characterized as phoney science, and some German scientists like Johannes Stark talked about developing an 'Aryan Physics' to oppose 'Jewish relativity', many different kinds of science were successfully promoted after 1933. Proctor has demonstrated, to take just one example, that the 'Nazi war on cancer' led to outstanding research based on rigorous epidemiological standards.[11] Driving the work on cancer was, of course, the ideal of race health, but bad ideas do not necessarily produce bad science. The chemical and biotechnology industries thrived in the 1930s. No-one develops jet engines, V2 rockets or Zyklon B gas by believing in Atlantis. It is an uncomfortable comment on the amorality of science that the Third Reich was *not* by any means a scientific wasteland. In 1946 the German Physics Society claimed that it had always protected '*die Sache einer sauberen und anständigen wissenschaftlichen Physik*' – pure and decent scientific physics.[12] They were right. Dictators cannot change the laws of nature.

So there really is no contradiction between Dr Ernst Schäfer, zoologist and ornithologist, and Untersturmführer Ernst Schäfer, SS officer and German nationalist. As he developed his plans, Schäfer formulated scientific objectives, chose his small team from the scientific community, and avoided Ahnenerbe cranks. He briefly considered, for example, the archaeologist Dr Erwin Schirmer, who had worked at the Ahnenerbe's Kyffhauser Castle dig looking for '*Indogermanische Volksgruppen*' and the sacred remains of the German ruler who provided the code name for Hitler's invasion of Russia, Barbarossa. Archaeological digs in search of Aryan remains and cult objects obsessed Himmler to such a degree that it provoked even Hitler's scorn. But when Schäfer found out Schirmer's work was considered '*durftig*', that is, inadequate, he simply rejected him.

He chose instead the anthropologist Bruno Beger, the entomologist and photographer Ernst Krause, who would also be the official expedition cameraman, and the geophysicist Karl Wienert. In Schäfer's team only Krause needed to be inducted into the SS, which was a condition of Himmler's patronage; all the others had been SS officers since the early or mid 1930s. Schäfer's right-hand man, organizer and technical expert Edmund Geer was a longstanding member of the Nazi Party and SS. He had served with a Freikorps regiment in the 1920s and Schäfer valued his skills and energy. But despite his faith in Hitler, Geer was often harassed by SS bureaucrats because he could not identify his paternal grandfather. The RuSHA regarded a gap in the family tree as highly suspicious. Could Geer's grandfather have been a Jew? Geer had been born the wrong side of the blanket and was never able to satisfy the SS, who refused to let the matter drop. He was denied a *Sippenbuch*, the precious kin or clan book that every SS member carried at all times, which meant he had a second-class status, even after his return from Tibet.

Wienert's career emphasizes that it was possible to practise conventional science in Nazi Germany, and to have your work rewarded simply for excellence. He was a protégé of the celebrated scientist and explorer Wilhelm Filchner, who had travelled to remote mountain regions to measure and plot the earth's magnetic fields.[13] In the 1930s Germany led the world in geomagnetic research,[14] and Wienert's presence added real lustre to Schäfer's expedition. It is not hard to see why Schäfer would have valued Wienert's involvement very highly. Filchner was as much an inspiration to Schäfer as Sven Hedin was, and his career, which Schäfer followed with intense interest, has much to reveal about a scientific career during the Third Reich.

In 1935, Filchner had embarked on an ambitious 2174-mile expedition across northern Tibet, and in 1937, at a time when Schäfer was making his own plans in Berlin, was reported to be lost somewhere on the southern edge of the Takla Makan Desert. Schäfer and Wienert came very close to changing their own plans and setting off to find their lost hero, but Filchner was rescued instead by the plucky British vice consul in Kashgar, Mr M. C. Gillet, resulting in much German mortification. Once he had recovered from his ordeal, Filchner opened congratulatory telegrams sent to him by Goebbels and the Führer himself. Back in Germany, he was rewarded with the newly created *Nationalpreis für Kunst und Wissenschaft*, which Hitler presented to him at a grand ceremony in the Reichs Chancellery in January 1938. The *Nationalpreis* had been created because Hitler had forbidden any German scientist to accept the Nobel Prize after it was awarded to the German pacifist and 'traitor' Carl von Ossietzky in 1936. Filchner was supposedly in two minds about accepting, but a refusal would have been dangerous, and besides, the award included a cash prize of a hundred thousand marks. Filchner had never been wealthy. He was a genuine and celebrated scientist, and his achievements counted for a great deal in Nazi Germany – and to his student Karl Wienert, who was about to set off for Tibet with Ernst Schäfer.

Science under the Nazis was not just a playground for cranks, then, but that does not mean it enjoyed Olympian independence. Quite the reverse was true: science in Nazi Germany had to serve the state. And there was no disagreement between Himmler and the academics about the importance of the biological sciences and anthropology. No-one in Germany in the 1930s believed that these were in any sense bogus or questioned the precise mathematical study of races.

Schäfer, of course, was a zoologist. His passion was animals. But his apparently innocuous exploration of the animal world had a special value in Hitler's Germany. In *Geheimnis Tibet*, the book he published in 1943, a year after the film, following long wrangles with Himmler, Schäfer explained his scientific objectives. 'On my earlier expeditions, which I had to undertake with Anglo-Saxons,' he wrote with barely repressed contempt, 'I realized a series of mistakes and shortcomings in the one-sided methodology and organization of the expedition.'[15] These mistakes boiled down to excessive specialization: there was no attempt to relate his or Dolan's work as naturalists to the scientific work of other members of the expedition to create a wider panorama of the ecologies they were exploring. Schäfer was determined to yoke together different areas of study: 'The primary objective of my third expedition [*sic*] was to put together a biological picture in the broadest sense creating an overall picture of this mysterious country.' Schäfer is somewhat unfair here to his friend and benefactor Brooke Dolan, who was clearly aiming for some kind of syncretic approach to his first foray into central Asia and had come to Germany to widen the expertise of his team. To be sure, though, the second expedition was much more a *Boy's Own* adventure with the sole purpose of amassing biological specimens, and Schäfer's experience with wild-boy adventurer Dolan still rankled with him. As a German he could do much better – *and* take revenge for that traumatic desertion.

There was much more involved in this than merely on the personal level. In Nazi Germany, the official policy of *Gleichschaltung*, or 'unity', was an imperative.[16] It was the means by which the 'German spirit' could infuse and control every part of the scientific world. If science was to serve the *Volk*, then it had to reject what some called the 'west-European-American path' which had led to a catastrophic fragmentation of science into specialities. Under Hitler, the 'German path' would suture these fragments to spawn a truly Aryan science. Specialization was 'Jewish' thinking and led to a stunting and smothering of the scientific ideal. According to the historian of the Ahnenerbe Michael Kater, syncretic science was a 'romantic-organic ideology', and was most fully realized among the fifty-one departments of the Ahnenerbe. Schäfer reflected this in his plans for his new Tibet expedition, and in his obsessive control of the work done by his colleagues.

The quest for a Nordic empire in central Asia was not, on the surface at least, Schäfer's own obsession. But he had a grand ambition, and it was one he shared with Dolan and other American natural scientists.[17] They were convinced that all species of mammals must have evolved somewhere in between the Americas and Europe – in other words, in central Asia. 'The fact', wrote one influential American scientist at New York's powerful Museum of Natural History, 'that the same kind of animals appear simultaneously in Europe and the Rocky

Mountains region has long been considered strong evidence for the hypothesis that the dispersal centre is halfway between. In this dispersal centre, during the close of the Age of the Reptiles and the beginning of the Age of the Mammals, there evolved the most remote ancestors of all the higher kinds of mammalian life which exist today . . .'[18] The idea of an Asian origin was quickly taken up by anthropologists. Our own species had evolved 'probably in or about the grand plateau of Central Asia', which had become an immense dispersal centre. 'From this region came the successive invasions which overflowed Europe . . . The whole history of India is similar – of successive invasions pouring down from the north. In the Chinese Empire, the invasions came from the West . . .' The Tibetan plateau was a pump, pushing new mammal species, including early men, over the brim of the Himalayas and across the globe. Although Darwin himself had intuited that Africa was the 'cradle of mankind', Asia suited the prejudices of scientists in America and Germany. For many, on both sides of the Atlantic, the possibility that humans had evolved first in the 'Dark Continent' was a repellent nightmare. Both German and American scientists shared a passion for eugenics and race science. Both nations believed they struggled with a race problem.

This idea of a central Asian dispersal centre was embraced by Schäfer. Although it is unlikely that either he or his American colleagues would have admitted to reading Madame Blavatsky and her followers, both *The Secret Doctrine* and the science of human origins sprang from a common source. For both, the key was the Tibetan plateau. Since Schäfer insisted that his new expedition was syncretic and dedicated to *Gleichschaltung*, it followed that he would look for an anthropologist who would endorse the idea of a central Asian origin. There was one outstanding German anthropologist and SS officer with a unique interest in central Asia, and that was Bruno Beger.

Schäfer had another objective that would closely link his scientific ambitions with Germany's war economy. In a letter to the DFG, the German Research Association, Schäfer had argued that Tibet was a region that 'owing to its wealth in original useful plants has been seen as a gene centre and promises a rich yield of new discoveries'. That term 'gene centre' had a precise meaning. It is an ironic fact that German science was powerfully influenced by the experimental work of the Soviet geneticist and plant breeder Nikolai Ivanovic Vavilov (1887–1943). On his travels through the vast expanses of the USSR, Vavilov had become fascinated by regions with an unusually high level of variation among cultivated plants. To him it suggested that they were also 'regions of origin'. These privileged places were natural laboratories which dispersed their botanical gifts to distant parts. Wild ancestral seeds were, he believed, especially fertile and resilient to disease and climate. To prove his theory, Vavilov set off to collect cultivated plant seeds from the Near East, the Caucasus and South America, returning eventually with more than two hundred thousand specimens. In 1927, he presented his findings and theories at the Fifth International Congress of Geneticists in Berlin and inspired an international collecting frenzy that sought regions of origin. Vavilov's work, along with genetics research in the USSR, was purged in 1935 when Stalin swung Soviet science behind the pseudoscientific work of Trofim Lysenko. Vavilov died in a Siberian prison in 1943, but the spirit of his work was most fruitfully cultivated in Nazi Germany.

In *A Rum Affair*, Karl Sabbagh wryly observes: 'Physicists, chemists, biologists, even mathematicians represent in the public mind the potential to do good – or great evil. But you don't expect botanists to win the Nobel Prize and . . . you don't expect them to destroy the world one day.'[19] In Nazi Germany, seeds were a serious matter. As Hitler rearmed with 'blood and iron', many strategists began to think about Germany's ability to feed itself as more resources were diverted into armaments. The news was not good: Germany was already much too dependent on imported foodstuffs. Its agricultural industry, notwithstanding Himmler's reverence for the German farmer, was backward. The Nazi state demanded that German science come up with a solution and, inspired by Vavilov, the search was on for wonder seeds with their miraculous promise of resistance and fecundity. Botany suddenly had a role in the re-armament of the Reich. And there was another, implicit attraction for German scientists and their masters. Seeds, like people, had progenitors; at the root lay a pure ancestral stock. An Aryan Master Seed! Hitler's New Order could create pure seeds as well as pure human stock.

Schäfer himself was very clear that his expedition and his science were politically motivated. In his SS files, which I found in the National Archives in Washington, there is an undated clipping from *Der Schwarze Korps*, the SS in-house magazine. It is a profile of Untersturmführer Ernst Schäfer in which he outlines his views about the role of science in the Third Reich. The interviewer begins rather obsequiously by giving his readers a glimpse of the explorer's world: 'So this is the home of the young German scientist Ernst Schäfer . . . On the floor there are a few preserved animal skins, among them the giant coat of a brown bear. A picture on the wall shows a small herd of wild Tibetan asses. On the desk pile up papers and books . . ' The author then asks Schäfer about science. 'See,' Schäfer replies, 'the same essential ideas motivate me as an SS man and as an explorer and scientist. The ideas of the SS and the ideas of research are identical. Both depend on pioneers, both use selection, both are in their representation and their work based on the values of character and soul that are given to us by our

Germanic heritage . . .' His next point is very revealing indeed: 'I also have to say that my close connection to the National Socialist ideas has evoked loud criticism. What are they accusing me of? They say: You are doing biased science [*Tendenz-wissenschaft*]! . . . Nothing is easier than to destroy such accusations. They say science is international. We don't deny that great achievements of research have to be a gift to the world, but we argue even as passionately that science only grows on a racial basis and that scientists are representatives of a national historical essence [*Substanz*] . . . International science in a liberal sense is out of the question.'

Even when he wasn't being interviewed by SS propagandists, Schäfer was consistent in this identification of science with SS values. He said in another context, for example, that the 'SS-idea and research-idea are one' ('*SS-Gedanke und Forschungsgedanke sind eins*'). He described science as a 'carrier of vigorous German manhood' ('*Trägerin kernigen Deutschen Mannestums*').[20] He then spoke about his expedition: 'We could accomplish more as SS men and do much more for the lack of understanding for the new Germany by being open about who we are, than by travelling under the disguise of an obscure, if neutral scientific academy; after all, we have a clear conscience.'[21] Schäfer might have pushed away the Ahnenerbe cranks like Kiss and relied on his own funding but he was, in 1937, perfectly happy to make himself a spokesman for the SS.

Schäfer had chosen most of his team by 1937, but at that time he was still lacking an anthropologist. His introduction to Bruno Beger came about by chance through a mutual friend, the geologist and hydrologist Rolf Höhne, who had been drawn into the circle of academics and cranks that hovered around Himmler. He was a serious scientist who had, with little enthusiasm, become involved in verifying that a skull unearthed beneath the crypt of Quedlinburg Cathedral was 'Henry the

Fowler', who had supposedly been reincarnated as Heinrich Himmler. Höhne had done his duty and confirmed the identity of the skull, and his work had impressed the Reichsführer. When Höhne heard about Schäfer's plans to lead a new expedition to Tibet, he recommended that he meet his friend Beger who was also very interested in Tibet.

Schäfer urgently sent a postcard to Beger's address in Berlin requesting that he telephone him immediately. But Schäfer had atrocious handwriting, and as Beger pored over his brusque note he misread '*Tibetreise*' ('Tibet journey') as '*Fibelreihe*', a word which in Germany in 1937 had a precise meaning. The National Socialist Association of Teachers was publishing a *Fibelreihe* (series) of educational textbooks about race and racial purity. Beger thought he was being asked to write one of these on race and was mystified as to why the German hero of two celebrated expeditions should undertake to make such a request. Beger ignored the postcard. Three days later, an exasperated Schäfer, his feathers ruffled by Beger's silence, telephoned demanding an answer. Did he want to go to Tibet or not? Beger immediately took the U-bahn to Schäfer's Wilmersdorf apartment.

When he arrived at Hohenzollerndam 36, the door was opened by Germany's most famous explorer. With him in the luxurious apartment, a far cry from Beger's, were Schäfer's right-hand man Geer and his cameraman Krause. For Beger it was a shock. The real Ernst Schäfer was a short, stocky man, not a Teutonic god, but he 'commanded the room' and radiated self-confidence. Beger was almost immediately drawn into the frantic preparations for the expedition, and Schäfer asked him to write a proposal describing what he could achieve. Beger was well prepared. Following Hans Günther, he said that his intention would be 'to study the current racial-anthropological situation through measurements, trait research, photography and moulds [i.e. making face masks] and especially to collect material about the proportion, origins, significance, and development of the Nordic race in this region'.[22] In an uncanny anticipation of later events, he also proposed to search for human fossils and for skeletal remains that could prove a former Nordic presence on the Tibetan plateau. Bruno Beger would turn Schäfer's expedition into a quest for the Master Race.

Beger was by now head of the RuSHA's Race Division (*Abteilungsleiter für Rassenkunde*). In order to be able to accompany Schäfer he joined Himmler's personal staff as a *Referentstelle*, or consultant. On his desk in Marie Curie Strasse, his dissertation lay forgotten.

Then came a macabre and tragic turn of events.

Living in a great cosmopolitan city was not going to stop Schäfer indulging his passion for hunting. Beger, when I interviewed him, seemed to have powerful recall of the events: on 8 November 1937, in the midst of his Tibet plans, Schäfer took his new wife Hertha, the '*geliebten Frau*' of his book *Dach der Erde*, to Schorfheide, a wilderness of forests, lakes and moors a hundred miles north of Berlin. In the history of the Third Reich, Schorfheide has a special significance, for it was the private fiefdom of the Reichsmarschall, Hermann Göring. It was here, among lakes, forests and moorland, that Göring had built Carinhall, an extravagant hunting lodge that commemorated his late first wife, Carin von Fock. On the lake shore opposite his lodge, Göring had constructed a luxurious mausoleum for her. Carin lay inside a massive pewter coffin that her husband imagined would be his last resting place too when the time came. Schäfer must have cultivated Göring as well as Himmler, his bitter rival. Both men, after all, shared a passion for hunting. The Reichsmarschall adored titles, and after the Nazi victory he'd appointed himself the *Reichsjägermeister* (Reich Hunting Master); a year later he'd promoted himself to

Reichsforstmeister (Reich Forest Master). In 1936, Schäfer had shrewdly presented Göring with a pair of Tibetan mastiffs (*Mastiffruden*). It looked like a valuable investment, but on this occasion Hertha would not come back from Schorfheide alive.

Carinhall was surrounded by a game reserve where only Göring, local villagers and privileged guests like Ernst Schäfer were allowed to hunt. Here, the Reich Master of the Hunt and the Forest indulged his passion, decked out in fantastic costumes, with hunting horn and knife and a Scandinavian spear. He once developed a plan to exhibit caged Jews at Schorfheide because 'they were damnably like [the animals] – the elk too has a hooked nose'.[23]

On that cold autumn day, their breath misting the air, the Schäfers took a boat out on the Werbellinsee, one of Schorfheide's two lakes. They would spend the day hunting ducks. It was a far cry from Schäfer's adventures in Asia, but it was better than nothing. Schäfer and Hertha took the boat out into the middle of the lake and waited. In the boat with them was a forest warden. It was a quiet, chilly day with a light breeze that occasionally dimpled the grey surface of the lake. At the stern, Hertha shivered and sipped from her husband's flask of schnapps. There were two shotguns. Schäfer, sitting in the bow, had one; the other rested in the bottom of the boat. Both were loaded.

Just after noon, there was a clatter of wings as a honking flock ascended into the air then turned towards the boat. Schäfer stood up with the urgency he had learnt in childhood and honed on his travels, all his attention focused on the prey as they swung across the sky. Once again he was flooded with a thrilling expectation as he began to squeeze the trigger, imagining the blast, the recoil against his shoulder, the body in motion arrested, falling. He levelled his sights on the leader, relaxing and following, caressing the shape in the air. All his attention was on this moment. There was just Ernst Schäfer and the duck. Then he sensed that the moment had come. But the flock suddenly turned, surprising him. As he swung the barrel, his foot caught the second shotgun, pointing its muzzle towards the rear of the boat. The gun exploded. His young bride caught the full force of the blast and died instantly.

According to Beger, an inquiry was held to determine who was responsible for the tragedy. Schäfer was an heroic figure, at least in SS and party circles, and there was intense interest in the horrifying events at Schorfheide. He was perhaps over-relaxed with guns; he clearly should have known better than to neglect a loaded gun in the close quarters of a boat. After all, he had been a practised hunter since adolescence. But he was visibly racked with guilt and had taken refuge with Hertha's family, so the inquiry exonerated him and blamed the warden instead for negligence. Still, Ernst Schäfer had changed, changed utterly.

Schorfheide is still a wilderness. There are still wolves there, antelopes and many species of duck and bird life. It is a flat green and brown place of silence and calm. Schäfer's feelings that November day are irrecoverable and unimaginable, but on this still lake in the autumn of 1937 a grotesque misfortune seems to have shattered and deformed a 'scientific expedition' and turned it into something quite different. Schäfer emerged a bitter, unpredictable man, haunted by pain and prone to tantrums and rages. The callow youth had become a curmudgeon. From now on he would be feared by his SS comrades, and even more so by his native servants.

As the book was going to press, I received a startling and unexpected piece of information. Isrun Engelhardt had discovered a report by one Wulf Dietrich Graf (=earl) zu Kastell-Rüdenhausen – who had witnessed the death of Hertha Schäfer. It was immediately apparent that Beger had got a crucial part of the story wrong. Schäfer had been invited to hunt ducks *not* at Schorfheide but at a remote estate in the Schweibus district, on the German–Polish border, owned by the Kastell-Rüdenhausens, who had distant connections to Queen Victoria. The report contains chilling new details. The party was, as Beger correctly recalled, duck hunting on a lake. But there were at least five other boats as well as the Schäfers'. Also present was the local Chief of Police. In the 'famous Tibet explorer's' boat were an oarsman and a *Büchsenspanne* (who prepared the guns), Reinhold Graf. But there was no second gun lying in the bottom of the boat. Fifteen minutes after the hunt began, Schäfer was about to fire when he stumbled. His rifle fell against the oarsman's seat, the stock broke and the left barrel fired. Hertha, who was sitting behind her husband, was hit in the head. She died an hour later 'from her severe injuries'. The Chief of Police interviewed all the witnesses immediately, and since what had happened was unequivocally an accident Hertha's corpse was released the same day.

The location of a tragedy might not seem to matter very much. But why should Beger make such a mistake? The reason must be that Schäfer did indeed occasionally hunt at Schorfheide and no doubt regaled his colleagues with stories about his connections to Reichsmarschall Göring. Schorfheide, so close to Berlin, would have been much easier to recall than an obscure estate far to the east. Thus Schweibus became Schorfheide. It was a trick of memory but a revealing one, saying much about Schäfer's connections with the Nazi elite.

PART TWO

PEAKS

CHAPTER SIX

CONFRONTING THE RAJ

'In the final analysis it is, after all, a world empire of the White Race . . .'

– Himmler speaking about the British Empire

'It is always justifiable to be suspicious of inquisitorial travellers.'

– British Minute Paper, 1935

In the courtyard of Dekyilinka, 'garden of happiness', home to the British Mission, a thin, narrow-faced, punctilious Scotsman mounted a scrawny Tibetan pony and nodded to his escort. It was just after dawn. The sky was dark turquoise, brightening in the east. Hugh Richardson led his escort alongside the rugged rocky sides of Mount Chakpori, the 'Iron Mountain', with its brilliantly painted Buddhas and scores of shrines from which poured clouds of aromatic smoke and incense. Already there were throngs of beggars, their hands outstretched, and pilgrims. Then the small party trotted beneath the tall white *chortens* of the Barkokali Gate. High above their heads fluttered dozens of prayer flags. Their dazzling colours – yellow, green, red, white and blue – represented the elements earth, water, fire, cloud and sky. Carried on the same wind that sent the *dharma* prayers spinning from the flags came the solemn roar of temple horns from the Jokhang temple.

Richardson was officially a 'Trade Agent' and head of the British Mission in Lhasa, but trade had little to do with his job. He was in reality a powerful diplomat on the north-east frontier of the British Raj. As he rode on down the poplar-lined avenue that led away from Lhasa, he glanced back, as he always did, at the Potala Palace. Mist was gathering in the Kyi Chu Valley but the early sun was catching the white and red flanks of the palace of the Dalai Lamas. Its soaring roofs glinted turquoise and gold. High on its rocky perch, the Potala was one of the wonders of the world, but behind its thousand sightless, black-bordered windows was an empty throne. Since the death of the 'Great' 13th Dalai Lama in 1933, the power vacuum in Tibet had fomented internal dissent and bitter, sometimes violent struggle. As ever, Tibet was being eyed covetously by greater powers that could also threaten the Raj itself.

As they approached the Dalai Lamas' Summer Palace at Norbulinka, Richardson slowed down and took the salute from a ragged line of Tibetan Army soldiers. Then he rode on quickly; he wanted to be in Gyantse as soon as possible, and his small party sent up a cloud of dust as they sped down the willow-lined highway. He had other obligations before they could take the Chaksam ferry across the Tsang Po and head up towards the Kamba La Pass. They soon passed the Drepung Monastery, which resembled a small city huddled against the side of the valley, and the State Oracle at Nechung with its glittering roof. As they passed the slaughterhouse, already emitting its foul vapours, Richardson reached down for a handkerchief.

Men with yaks ploughed fields; women opened and closed water channels. They passed more pilgrims. By now the Potala had all but disappeared behind the interlaced ridges of the Kyi Chu Valley. At the next corner Richardson slowed and dismounted. A tent had been erected by the road, its roof festooned with prayer flags. Dignitaries from the Tibetan government, the Kashag, were gathered outside, waiting to say goodbye. Richardson motioned his escort to wait and greeted the dignitaries, whose robes billowed in the high wind. He needed to cultivate the goodwill of these men so he spent some time exchanging *kata*, or white scarves, conscientiously making sure that he got right the precise flow of gesture. Such details mattered a great deal. There was small talk and much butter tea, and Richardson was presented with a propitious bowl of rice. Struggling to conceal his impatience, he nibbled a few grains and threw the rest over his shoulder. Richardson could never be quite certain just what the Tibetans thought of him and his British Mission. Sometimes he felt he was just hanging on by his fingernails.

He mounted his pony again and rode on. His most important task lay ahead. At the edge of the city was a new bridge, made of iron and prefabricated in India. Its builder had a house nearby, and it was Richardson's last call. The man he had come to see was one of the richest men in Tibet, a dollar millionaire with bank accounts in Europe. His name was Tsarong Dzasa and he was once an important power broker – and could be again. Tsarong had been a modernist and a reformer but he had moved too quickly for the Dalai Lama and the monasteries. He had lost his power and had turned to making money and building bridges. Tsarong's house was an elegant villa with glass windows – those at Dekyilinka were draughty calico-hung ones – and a large number of potted plants arranged around the front door. Tsarong's most significant gesture towards the twentieth century protruded from the roof: a brand-new radio aerial. Richardson knew that tea and conversation with Tsarong was an essential part of his mission.

Hours later, Richardson was riding along the edge of the Tsang Po River towards the ferry. Tsarong had given him a great deal to think about. A two-year-old boy had been found in a tiny village called Taktse near Kumbum in the north-east of Tibet on the Chinese border. He had responded well to tests. The search party who found him were certain he was the reincarnation of the 13th Dalai Lama, and plans were being made to bring him to Lhasa. A Chinese warlord was causing trouble, too, and as Richardson at last rode up the steep winding road to the pass, he remembered another even more troubling matter. In Gangtok, Sir Basil Gould, the British political officer, had received news that a German expedition was planning to come to India and might attempt to cross into Tibet. It was described as a scientific mission but it was being supported by Heinrich Himmler, Germany's feared Reichsführer. Hugh Richardson's brother was a general and knew very well the threat Hitler represented. Hugh himself had been a fervent supporter of the republican government in Spain and hated Fascism. As Richardson left Lhasa far behind, he resolved that he would do everything in his power to prevent this German expedition from *ever* coming to the Holy City of Lhasa.

From November 1937, Hitler's ambitions had become increasingly aggressive. In *Mein Kampf* he had written, 'Germany will either be a world power or there will be no Germany.' Now he was making good his promise. Apparently fearful about the imminence of his own mortality, Hitler began to accelerate the rolling back of the Versailles Treaty and the expansion of the Reich. The first step would be to realize his Pan German ambitions by forcibly bringing Austria into a Greater Germany; after that he could turn his attention to the other real estate of the future Reich, the Sudetenland, which was part of Czechoslovakia and the Polish city of Danzig, both of which had restless German-speaking populations the Nazis were determined to exploit in pursuit of a Greater German Reich. Hitler launched his first assault on Austria with a strategy of diplomatic aggression and internal mischief aimed at Chancellor Kurt Schuschnigg, who was holding out against being sucked into the Reich. In March 1938 Schuschnigg boldly announced a referendum to decide Austria's fate. Although Göring called this a 'dirty trick' and Hitler panicked, Schuschnigg's gambit would play straight into Hitler's hands.

As these momentous events unfolded, SS Obersturmführer Dr Ernst Schäfer, German explorer and hunter, the conqueror of Kham, recently widowed, watched the mean and grimy suburbs of south London monotonously pass his train window. He had not visited England for four years. Then he had spent his days immured inside the great terracotta treasure house of stuffed beasts and bones, the Natural History Museum in South Kensington. It was while he had sweated over type specimens, 'counting the hairs on a deer', that he had heard about his friend Brooky's troubles in America and had soon afterwards received Dolan's telegram asking him if he would like to return to Tibet. Now he was organizing his own, *German* expedition. Schäfer's destination was the Foreign Office, where he would need to beg the masters of the Raj to help him get across the Tibetan border. In Berlin he had fought the Reichsführer for control of his expedition and he believed he had won the first round. Now he was about to take on the most powerful empire on earth.

The train steamed through sullen Battersea and across the Thames. At Victoria Station it pulled up with a relieved exhalation. Whistles blew, and anxious crowds milled about the echoing concourse. Schäfer picked up his luggage from the rack and walked quickly down the platform and out of the station. Under the stony eyes of Queen Victoria, the former Empress of India, he turned right towards Buckingham Palace and his hotel. The Rubens had a seedy elegance but it gave Schäfer a good enough address from which to launch his assault on the mandarins of the Foreign Office, which was just round the corner. In his room, Schäfer opened his case, arranged his papers and began to plot.

Schäfer's intentions appear to have undergone a perplexing process of metamorphosis and uncertainty. His objective was Tibet, but how was he to cross the border, and once he had, what could he do that would guarantee a glittering success for himself and for Germany? Without any doubt, reaching Lhasa and entering the Holy, Forbidden City at the head of a German expedition would secure immediate glory. Although a number of Europeans had visited the city by the end of the 1930s it still had a magical allure. But Schäfer appears to have prevaricated. Was he genuinely uncertain, or was he instead playing a different, more intriguing game?

In the lecture he had planned to give to the Himalayan Club in London,[1] Schäfer described in clumsily eloquent English an altogether different plan. He recalled the time, in the spring of 1935, when he had been in Ngolok country in north-eastern Tibet with Dolan and Duncan. Schäfer and his companions were at loggerheads, yaks were dropping like flies, and his sherpas were about to mutiny, so he had walked off alone 'to gather together my thoughts for new and hard decisions'. Standing on a nearby peak, Schäfer could see a mass of low cloud 'like a gigantic zeppelin'; behind it, he knew, lay hidden the expedition's 'great aim'. This was Amnyi Machinboro (Amne Machin), the great sacred mountain of the Ngolok people, a 20,610-foot giant that had never been explored or climbed and had acquired a legendary glamour for explorers.

It was Joseph Rock – whose nomadic 'life-de-luxe' Schäfer had encountered on his first Asian expedition in 1931 – who had conjured up the myth of Amne Machin, the 'lost mountain of Tibet'. Rock had discovered the mountain on an expedition through Ngolok country in 1925 and had measured its height using 'an aneroid barometer and inspiration'.[2] He reported that the great pyramid of Amne Machin was 'at least' twenty-eight thousand feet in height. After he published this figure in the *National Geographic* in 1930, the conquest of this mountain, apparently higher than Everest, became a mania.

Like Zarathustra bounding from his cave, Schäfer had experienced an epiphany when he saw Amne Machin for himself. 'I bit my lips,' the Himalayan Club would have heard him reveal, 'I damned myself, and while I sat, as if by Providence, the far distant clouds moved apart, broke and opening, revealed the most imposing and most superb mountain view I have ever seen in all my life . . . No white man had ever set foot on this colossal mountain giant . . .'[3] And nor would Schäfer.[4] One reason for that was political. In November 1936 Germany had signed a defensive anti-Soviet pact with Japan, whose armies would break out of Manchukuo the following year and embark on a genocidal military campaign against the Kuomintang. The Chinese had little reason to be generous to German explorers, and when the German Embassy in Hankow had requested permission for Schäfer to return to eastern Tibet it had been refused. But although the Amne Machin range straddles the fractured and volatile border region between Tibet and China, it could still have been reached from the west.

The real reason for abandoning Amne Machin was sheer competitiveness. The conquest of mountains was an obsession for many in the Reich and, Schäfer realized, too many Germans had made a few too many celebrated climbs in the 1930s. The most spectacular had been the heroic but tragic assaults starting in 1932 on Nanga Parbat, which soars to 26,620 feet at the north-western end of the Himalayas. Germans knew this ice-armoured Mountain of Terror, with its sheer sixteen-thousand-foot South Wall and frequent deadly avalanches, as '*Unser Berg*' – 'our mountain'. Four German climbers had been killed there in 1934 (as well as six sherpas), and the Reich demanded revenge. Yet more Germans threw themselves at the deadly mass of rock. There were two attempts in 1938 and 1939 alone when the Schäfer Expedition was in Tibet. Altogether Nanga Parbat claimed the lives of thirty-one climbers, eleven of them German. Failure was not attractive to the pragmatic Schäfer, and besides, mountaineering was not his glass of schnapps. He was simply not a climber, and striving for the heights of Amne Machin was tilting at windmills, with or without Chinese permission.

Amne Machin would brood under its foggy shroud undisturbed by Ernst Schäfer. Lhasa, by implication, was second choice. That at any rate was the story he planned to tell the British Himalayan Club. But the mystery deepens when the thick 'Political and Secret File' on Schäfer (L/P&S/12/4343), now held in the India Office in the British Library, is closely scrutinized. What is astonishing is that in the first letters and reports concerned with Schäfer up to the autumn of 1938 there is *no reference at all* to travelling to Lhasa. The German Embassy had forwarded to London a map of eastern Tibet and Assam with a letter from Schäfer that asked, 'Would you be good enough to write to Lord Astor that just the uncivilized peoples of Assam are those which attract me . . . the number of travellers who have explored the country of Mishmi and Artor can really be counted by the fingers on one hand . . . Perhaps the Survey of India would be good enough to attach a land-surveyor (pundit) to our expedition as interpreter, because I could imagine that the Indian Government might attach great importance in having this scarcely known land thoroughly cartographed . . .' He added, 'there are, in the secluded mountain valleys, many extremely primitive peoples, who have retained their existence as mere racial fragments . . . In the border territory alone between Szetschuan [*sic*] and Tibet there are no fewer than 18 different tribes . . . These tribes . . . have a strong west-asiatic (or Caucasian) influence.' Here is Bruno Beger's mission in a nutshell. Find the Master Race!

So had Schäfer's plans evolved, or was he being economical with the truth? Or both? And if so, why? Was he inspired by the game that was being played out internationally by the Führer himself, so memorably described by Winston Churchill thus: Hitler, he said, 'had agreed to have his victuals served course by course instead of snatching them from the table'. Schäfer, it seems, began by asking for the hors d'oeuvres and kept the real entrée a secret. Any one of his requested destinations would have allowed him to find a road to Lhasa, either along well-travelled routes from the east or via the Brahmaputra Valley which circles the Assam Himalayas. Long ago Hedin had pulled off the very same trick by saying to the British that he was going one way and then diverting across the forbidden Tibetan border when the coast was clear. If Lhasa *was* always Schäfer's intended but secret objective it raises vexing questions about his motives. A city is an odd destination for a natural scientist. It makes better sense if his mission were political and propagandist rather than 'purely scientific'.

Whatever his real intent, Schäfer's task in London was a formidable one. If Czechoslovakia was a 'far away country' about which little was known, Tibet was much further away and considerably more baffling, indeed an enigma wrapped in a mystery. The British had been perplexed by Tibet for more than a century and viewed it and its borders with a fickle blend of fascination, anxiety, greed and sometimes calculated indifference. British diplomats were confused by Tibet's status and most of all by its relationship with China. Was Tibet an independent nation or a protectorate of China? Did the Tibetans even think of their remote Buddhist realm as a *nation* at all?

What was clearly understood was the critical position Tibet occupied in the complex political map of Asia, perhaps best explained by Indian Foreign Secretary Olaf Caroe's evocation of a 'mandala' of imperial forces.[5] Imagine British India as an inverted triangle. Its base is formed by the Himalayas and the various 'kingdoms of the thunderbolt' – Nepal, Bhutan, Sikkim and northern Assam – with the two corners being formed by Ladakh in the west and Burma in the east. Further to the north is Tibet, and beyond that a crescent of volatile Chinese territory that unfolds like a scroll from Sinkiang through Ch'inghai and Sikang to Szechuan and Yunnan. To the north of this lies another great arc bounded by the USSR and Mongolia in the west and Japan and Japanese-occupied regions of China in the east. From this outer arc, tremendous forces were applied inwards to the other parts of the mandala. Soviet and Japanese pressure pushed down onto China; the Chinese crescent pressed down on Tibet; and Tibet applied its own force to the jewel-like Himalayan kingdoms strung along the border with British India. Tibet was not much of a threat, but it was in a crucial position to resist all that power. In other words, for the British it was a buffer, and according to the diplomat Charles Bell a very superior one. 'Tibet forms a barrier', he wrote to the Foreign Office in 1924, 'superior to anything that the world can show elsewhere.'[6] So the British had a very good idea of what Tibet was *for*, but what it *was* they were not at all certain. Then again that did not matter much as long as Tibet was happy to stand between threatening foreign empires and India.

It is not surprising then that, as Schäfer would discover for himself, British Tibetan policy was a labyrinth of opinions and strategies. The men in the India Office in Whitehall and those others far away in Government House in Delhi frequently adopted different and conflicting positions. The empire was already in decline, racked by crisis under a setting imperial sun, and the views of London and Delhi about the fate of the red splashes on the world map often diverged. When it came to Tibet, some urged that it should be helped to become a strong modern nation with a modern army and modern technology. London preached tactful indifference, fearing that if they treated Tibet as a genuine nation state they would upset the Chinese, even though they agreed that Tibet was a necessary buffer between India and China. It was a mess and only in the British missions at Gangtok and Gyantse did Tibet really matter. Here a unique cadre of 'men on the spot', as the eminent explorer Sir Francis Younghusband called them, lived at the edge of empire spending their leisure hours, as the sun set over the high Himalayan passes, studying Tibetan vocabularies, pondering the mysteries of power struggles in Lhasa and thinking of ways to thwart the Chinese.

Although Schäfer could not have known it at the time, one of the Tibet cadre would become his implacable foe. Hugh Richardson was said to have 'identified himself more closely with Tibetans and Tibetan affairs and . . . gained more insight and respect than any Englishmen [*sic*] since Charles Bell'.[7] Bell was the gold standard among the scholar-diplomats of the British Missions. The 13th Dalai Lama had said of him, 'When a European is with us Tibetans I feel that he is a European and we are Tibetans; but when Lönchen [chief minister] Bell is with us, I feel that we are all Tibetans together.'[8] Bell was still alive, but Richardson seemed to be his reincarnation. But his scholarly interests would not stop him doing everything he could to harass the German expedition and annoy its leader.

In the spring of 1938, London was in a febrile state. Every day the papers carried reports on Hitler's increasingly ominous sabre-rattling over Austria and, at home, furious parliamentary debates about how to deal with the German 'mad man'. Anthony Eden had resigned from Neville Chamberlain's government in February, followed by Duff Cooper in March, both men disgusted with the continuing appeasement of Europe's fascist dictators, but many were still desperate for peace in their time. *The Times* remained openly sympathetic to 'the impossible problem of space allotted to Germany' in 1919 and said it was not a time for 'provocative speaking', but there were also reports on the trial and imprisonment of the anti-Nazi cleric Dr Niemüller and full coverage was given to Leo Amery's speech about a 'situation of terrible danger'. Schäfer visited the Houses of Parliament and heard a 'humane and humorous' speech by Chamberlain. He was just a few feet away when an angry Jew 'boxed the ears' of an MP who had made a speech in favour of appeasing Hitler. Schäfer reported in his diary that the newspapers made the incident much more dramatic than it actually was, but his time in the House of Commons must have provided useful lessons about how much influence the appeasement lobby had. It is no wonder that Ovaltine advertisements took advantage of a tense national mood: 'It's double duty for your nerves these days. Feed your nerves with Ovaltine and note the difference.' Chamberlain must have taken note; after another bruising encounter with Hitler he told 'his people' to 'go home and sleep quietly in your beds' (presumably hastened to their slumbers by a hot steaming cup). Otherwise life went on normally. Schäfer could have heard the Valkyrie at Sadlers Wells or admired John Gielgud's Shylock in the West End.

Lord Zetland, the Secretary of State for India, had breezily informed the German Embassy that the India Office would be 'delighted to see Dr Schäfer at any time convenient to him. Would you therefore ask him to ring up and make an appointment?' After a bitterly cold February, the weather in March was mild and dry, and as Schäfer crossed St James's Park in the direction of the Italianate turrets of the Foreign Office he relished the sight of bar-headed geese that had flown all the way from India. The Foreign Office itself was designed to impress, even overwhelm. From the park, he bounded up the steps alongside its marbled walls and glanced up at a grimy statue of Clive of India. From Whitehall, he turned into the great courtyard and was directed into the India Office itself. High above, statues honoured those Indian princes who had remained loyal during the Mutiny of 1857. In front of him now was a famous statue of a Gurkha soldier, and he was amused to hear civil servants wish it good morning as they passed. Schäfer ascended the deeply carpeted Gurkha Stairs and stole a glance at the opulent Durbar Hall, which ascended three colonnaded storeys. Britain ruled its increasingly fragile empire through pomp as much as through naked military power.

Chastened by the power of the Raj, the young German was directed along a long and lofty corridor to the office of Sir John Walton, the assistant under-secretary of state. Walton was an elderly man who was already scrutinizing the 'Schäfer Case' with an old-boy network of spies who reported back and forth between Whitehall and Delhi. Although any request by a foreign national to travel in Tibet would have come through this department, Schäfer seems to have quickly sensed that he was being treated as if he were a German spy – and he was not at all happy about that, reporting his annoyance to Berlin.

Walton closely examined his young German visitor as he waited for him to get to the end of a long peroration. Then he informed Schäfer that it was not up to the British or Indian governments to give permission for his expedition to travel inside Tibet. That was a decision for the government in Lhasa, the Kashag. He would be happy to forward Schäfer's request to Basil Gould, the political officer in Gangtok, who could forward it to Lhasa. Then it was up to the Tibetans. Walton's reply was cleverly contrived: the British wielded considerable clout in Lhasa and their blessing, or lack of it, made a difference.

Schäfer knew that throughout the 1920s and 1930s another scholar from a fascist country had been able to travel all over Tibet with the sympathetic blessing of the British. Professor Giuseppe Tucci had shrewdly and assiduously courted Basil Gould by scrupulously sending him his itineraries, travel reports and signed copies of his books, which contained fulsome dedications to Mussolini.[9] When another Italian complained to the Government of India that Tucci was quietly making off with valuable Tibetan holy books, it did very little harm to his favoured status. The reason had much to do with Tucci's reputation as a scholar. It might also have reflected the fact that Italian Fascism was scorned as a kind of comic operetta with castor oil.

Germany, on the other hand, was a serious threat in Europe and a German 'scientific expedition' to central Asia would have set off shrill alarm bells. It would have been remembered that in 1916 two German 'experts', Dr Oskar von Niedermayer and Dr Werner Otto von Hentig, were also sent on a mission, at that time to Afghanistan. It became clear that their plan was to persuade the warlord Amir Habibullah to invade British India at the head of 150,000 armed tribesmen. The German 'experts' promised Habibullah military equipment on a fantastic scale as well as an immense budget – the equivalent of ten million pounds.[10] The plan began to founder when the Afghans failed to unite under Habibullah's banner and finally collapsed completely when Germany was defeated in 1918. German infiltration in Afghanistan began again in the 1920s. Schools and hospitals were set up in Kabul, and military training provided. 'Scientific expeditions' were also despatched; according to historian Milan Hauner, 'Scientific expeditions were an important part of German peaceful penetration of Afghanistan . . .' The climax came in 1935 with Inge Kirchiesen's German Research Expedition (*Deutsche Forschungsgemeinschaft*) to the Hindu Kush, where what was supposed to be a 'meteorological station' was built. In the very month Schäfer arrived in London, Lufthansa inaugurated its Berlin–Kabul air service to sustain what was by then the largest foreign community in Afghanistan. Just a year later, Himmler's rival Alfred Rosenberg was even more explicit: Afghanistan was to be used 'for operations against British India or Soviet Russia'. As we will see later, Schäfer himself was drawn into one such plot at the end of 1939.

Such a precedent made Schäfer's scheme to lead a German expedition to Tibet, on the other side of the Himalayas, worthy of caution. He was requesting permission to enter the Assam Himalayas and explore the Lohit Valley, one of the most contested and sensitive border regions in all Asia, so in the India Office Schäfer's plans looked distinctly shady. They could be the first signs of a pincer movement that might threaten the security of British India from the west through the Khyber Pass and from the east down the Lohit Valley in Assam. The entire region was a tinderbox. There were hostile hill tribes who had killed a British political officer in 1911. The Tibetans had sent raiding parties against the rebellious state of Pome or Po and chased its ruler towards the frontier with India. Above all, the British feared Chinese incursions through Assam which would threaten both India and Burma. The problem was that no-one really understood just where the political borders ran in this region of the Himalayas. There was a simmering disagreement over a forty-thousand-square-mile tract of land called the Tawang that Charles Bell *thought* he had acquired from the Tibetans in 1914. The Tawang was forgotten about until the 1930s when someone with keen eyes in the India Office noticed that the Chinese *Shen Pao Atlas* had been changed. It now brazenly showed Tawang as part of Tibet and therefore, at some future time, possibly part of China. The India Office reacted with alarm, and small parties of English botanists suddenly began to take an interest in going to the Tawang. They were spies.[11] One of them, Francis Kingdon Ward, reported that there was a 'menace to [British] India. Sooner or later India must stand face to face with a potential enemy looking over the wall into her garden . . .'[12] Kingdon Ward was arrested in Tawang for illegally crossing the border into Tibet, but had he really crossed a border? The British thought not; the Tibetans were convinced that he had. At the very same time Schäfer was in London, Captain G. S. Lightfoot was leading a small force of British soldiers into the Tawang to assert British claims. All in all, Assam was a mess, and no place to send a German expedition.

Schäfer's curious offer that the 'Indian Government might attach great importance in having this scarcely known land thoroughly cartographed' implies that he had some awareness of the fraught nature of this stretch of the Tibetan border. But to the India Office it must have seemed as if Mata Hari was offering to tidy up their filing cabinets. They knew that from Berlin Himmler was taking a keen interest in Schäfer's progress and that he was being frequently summoned to the German Embassy at Carlton House Terrace. The German press, not for the last time, added to Schäfer's difficulties by loudly crowing that he was a high-ranking SS officer and that the expedition would be, as the British understood the report, organized 'entirely on SS principles'.[13] It did his case no good, and the India Office now had very good reason not to back Schäfer.

Their strategy is spelt out in the 'Political and Secret File'. They would send Schäfer's request to the Kashag in Lhasa but without any attached recommendation. 'We made it clear to the German Embassy and to Schäfer himself, who came over and called at the India Office towards the end of March, that permission to enter Tibet rested entirely with the Tibetan government and it seemed doubtful whether they would give it . . . This was our routine way of dealing with applications from travellers seeking to visit Tibet. We knew that the Tibetans would not grant them unless strongly backed by us and it avoided the risk of foreign governments going direct to the Tibetan government.' The final clause is prescient. This is precisely what a desperate Schäfer *would* do later in the year. Schäfer cannot have known what the Foreign Office was up to behind the scenes, but it is certain that he began to believe that Walton was treating him badly. He felt insulted and upset, so much so that he now complained bitterly to Himmler. For their part, Walton and the other British diplomats who would cross paths or swords with Schäfer simply did not have the measure of his determination. An insulted Schäfer was a primal force, and it was about to come out of its cage.

Schäfer's request filtered down the lines to the Government of India in Delhi, then to the British Residency in Gangtok, where it was received by Sir Basil Gould. From there the request was wired across the Himalayas to the Kashag in Lhasa. News of the 'German Tibet Expedition' soon reached Dekyilinka, the home of the British Mission, and the ears of radio officer Reggie Fox, call sign AC4YN, and Hugh Richardson. The Tibetans would certainly have sought Richardson's advice and he would have been most emphatic that the Germans should not be allowed to cross into Tibet.

When the Kashag did reply, it was with unprecedented speed – a fact that strongly suggests they saw no need to deliberate for very long.

It was by no means the last Richardson would hear of Ernst Schäfer, for he had powerful supporters in England and they would make all the difference to the fate of his expedition. According to the 'Final Report' in the Oriental and India Office's Schäfer file, 'The Expedition was backed by several influential people in this country, including Lord Astor, Mr. Charles Hambro, Mr. Philip Gibb and Professor Cornell Evans . . .' Lord Waldorf Astor and his American-born wife Nancy were at the centre of what came to be known as the 'Cliveden Set', a group of self-appointed foreign policy experts from the upper echelons of British society. Their sympathies were strongly pro-German and they used every opportunity – which usually meant every dinner party – to influence British policy. Nancy Astor was a notorious anti-Semite and Waldorf told anyone who would listen that Germany had a right to a sphere of influence in eastern Europe. The Schäfer family had rather good connections, even in England, and Lord Astor had been vigorously arguing Schäfer's cause through friends in the India Office. In Berlin, Schäfer seems to have met Sir Nevile Henderson, the British ambassador, one of the architects of appeasement, who called Hitler an 'apostle of peace', and Bruno Beger is convinced that Henderson too lobbied on Schäfer's behalf in London. Schäfer's other English backers were even less wholesome.

One evening, Schäfer left his hotel and strolled across St James's Park to Trafalgar Square. He turned into the Strand and walked as far as number 230, known then as 'Link House', where he was effusively greeted by Admiral Sir Barry Domville and ushered into a small lecture hall. For the next hour Schäfer held forth on his adventures and plans 'describing the behaviour and creeds of the natives and illustrating their strange modes of living with photographs'. Domville's son Compton described the event in the July edition of *The Link*, where he informed his many readers that 'Among the hobbies of the scholarly chief of the German police, Reichsführer SS Himmler, is the study of the origin of man and his cultural development. Thus he has sponsored a distinguished expedition . . . led by Dr. Ernst Schäfer, famous German scholar, author and explorer . . .' Domville revealed some surprising facts about Herr Himmler: he had a studious and enquiring mind, for example, 'one of the most enlightened in Germany today', and he found relaxation in 'archaeology, genealogy and kindred fields of research'. On other pages, readers were encouraged to visit German spas where they could enjoy the 'famous smile' of 'Dr. Ley', the brutish and alcoholic Nazi labour leader.

The author of these kind words was one of the most notorious British sponsors of Anglo-German 'friendship'. Domville[14] had been head of British naval intelligence and president of the Royal Naval College at Greenwich. He was an eccentric libertarian who protested about pub closing hours and motoring restrictions; when he visited Germany he discovered unrestrained freedom: 'There are no speed limits in Germany. Even in Berlin you can park your car pretty well where you please.' These relatively innocent convictions were at the top of a slippery slope. Soon he was noting that 'Jewish ways are not our ways, neither are their thoughts our thoughts . . . We have Jacob's Ladders at sea but no Jacobs.' Jews had 'thoroughly impregnated big business and the press'. On his next visit to Germany, Domville was allowed to join Himmler on a shooting trip and found him charming, unassuming and professorial. The Adolf Hitler SS Regiment showed 'splendid physique' and turned out to be 'responsible for eight hundred little Nazis in one year, which were looked after by the authorities if the mothers were true Aryans'. As he usually did, Himmler arranged for international sympathizers like Domville to visit Dachau. He found the camp to be very well organized: 'the administration is excellent'.

Domville first made his charming views public in the *Anglo-German Review*, but he soon came to believe that the *Review* was not merely insufficiently pro-German but was dominated by 'the well-to-do' and 'big business'. He set up a new journal, *The Link*, that would be open to all. It was a shrewd strategy. Branches sprang up all over England from Southend-on-Sea to Birmingham and membership rose throughout 1937 and 1938. Propagandists were despatched from Germany to speak at Link meetings and young men were sent to experience the Hitler Youth in return. The central London branch was fiercely pro-German and anti-Semitic.[15]

They also admired Ernst Schäfer.

Domville was impressed by the energetic German zoologist and was angry that the Foreign Office had, according to Schäfer, treated him poorly. Soon he was arguing Schäfer's case. Domville informed Neville Chamberlain himself that the Ahnenerbe had 'no political connections whatsoever and deals only with History, Folklore, Biology, the Ice Age and Natural History'. *The Link* continued to lobby on Schäfer's behalf with vociferous persistence, and in 1938, at the end of a 'low dishonest decade', the appeasers still had a strong hand to play.

Schäfer had one other crucial encounter before he left London, and it prompted the development of a new strategy to get into Tibet. It was a meeting he never discussed publicly, not even with his colleagues, until many years later. In 1961 he published a second edition of his book *Fest Der Weissen Schleier* ('Festival of the White Scarves'), whose first edition had appeared a decade earlier. In a revised preface, Schäfer had a revelatory new story to disclose.

The fourteenth of March 1938 was Schäfer's twenty-eighth birthday and, away from home, he decided to push the boat out – he does not say with whom, but he had brothers in London at the time. The celebrations were strenuous and he returned to the Rubens late. The following morning he was nursing a hangover and was still in bed at nine when the telephone rang. It was the hotel receptionist to say that someone was waiting for him. Schäfer assumed it was a journalist and asked him to wait. Then he fell asleep again. Fifteen minutes later the telephone woke him once more; his visitor was still waiting. 'Ask him for his name,' Schäfer barked. There was a moment of silence, then, 'Sir Francis Younghusband.' He sat bolt upright. Twenty years later, the memory of that time retained a *Boys' Own* thrill for Schäfer: 'I've never been out of bed and run downstairs faster . . .' There in the lobby sat a bronzed and grizzly man with white hair who turned to fix Schäfer with 'the eyes of a Himalayan eagle'.[16]

Sir Francis Younghusband was one of the great figures in the British imperial adventure, and one of the most paradoxical. On the surface an ardent imperialist with striking blue eyes and a Kitchener handlebar moustache, Younghusband had mixed a soldier's life with intrepid feats of exploration. His most celebrated exploit was a punishing journey from Peking to Hunza across the unmapped Muztagh Pass on the border between India and China. Younghusband had battled to nineteen thousand feet through snow and ice using knotted turbans and reins for rope.[17]

In 1903, Lord Curzon, the Indian Viceroy, had become concerned about reports of Russians infiltrating Lhasa and bending the ear of the 13th Dalai Lama. Curzon's letters demanding an explanation were returned from Lhasa unopened. Increasingly frustrated, Curzon despatched Colonel Younghusband to sort out the obstinate Tibetans. His mission turned into a bloody invasion. Thousands of Tibetans were killed and the Dalai Lama fled to Mongolia. In Lhasa, Younghusband forced a treaty on the Tibetan government but it was quickly repudiated by the British government. He returned to England a popular hero but a political outcast. His most important achievement was perhaps taking London journalists to the Forbidden City; their reports became the first detailed accounts of a hidden and secretive world. Schäfer read all of them and took copies with him to Tibet. After this ignominious episode, Younghusband took refuge in religious mysticism. In Lhasa he had experienced some kind of epiphany as he watched the sun go down on the Potala Palace, bathing it in a 'rosy glowing radiancy'.[18] At the time he came to meet Schäfer his reputation was quite diminished and he was known, if at all, as an obscure mystic and the author of *Life in the Stars: An Exposition of the View that on Some Planets of Some Stars exist Beings higher than Ourselves, and on one a World Leader, the Supreme Embodiment of the Eternal Spirit, which Animates the Whole*.

'So this was the man who had lifted the curtain of silence from the Forbidden City . . .' Schäfer reflected. He must have opened his heart to the strange old man and denounced the India Office and its machinations, for Younghusband gave Schäfer some advice, his wrinkled hands grasping his silver-topped walking stick and rapping it on the floor to emphasize his every sentence. 'Sneak over the border, that's what I should do – sneak over the border. Then find a way round the regulations.' The old man slowly got to his feet and went into the adjoining room where there were writing desks for guests. He returned some minutes later with a sheaf of letters. They were references for the governors of Assam and Bengal, the British-Indian foreign secretary and for Lord Linlithgow, the Viceroy.

'Why was he helping me, a young German?' Schäfer asked. 'Our civilization went the wrong way,' was Younghusband's bitter answer, according to Schäfer; 'In our country the pioneering spirit has died, our young people only want to dance, to enjoy themselves. But there is no status quo, everything goes on, everything changes . . . I believe you understand me.' Schäfer was elated by the unexpected meeting, and intrigued by Younghusband's advice.

Younghusband's ideas and activities at the end of his life (he died in 1942) were so peculiar that it is not difficult to imagine him endorsing the youthful vigour of Germany and deprecating a malaise afflicting young Englishmen. It had nothing to do with politics. Years before he had done the same favour for Schäfer's mentor Sven Hedin.[19] The two men had first met in Kashgar in 1890 and then a decade later in Kashmir when Hedin was preparing to set off on a journey into southern Tibet and, he hoped, Lhasa. At the last minute the British government tried to stop the expedition entering Tibet, but Younghusband secretly delayed the crucial telegram and Hedin blithely headed off to cross the Tibetan border. 'Sven Hedin put his arms around my neck as he left and if I had given him the slightest encouragement wd. have embraced me!' Younghusband wrote primly to his wife. With Younghusband's connivance, Hedin had run rings around the British.

Schäfer knew that Hedin distinguished between his 'ordinary morals' and his 'geographical morals'. In the case of the latter, he admitted that 'my moral is very, very bad'. As Schäfer set off for Germany, he was haunted by Younghusband's advice: 'I couldn't get this "sneak over the border" out of my head.' Schäfer, too, would use 'geographical morals' to reach the Holy City. And in March 1938 Adolf Hitler was applying the same 'morals' in Austria.

While Schäfer was in London, Chancellor Schuschnigg had

received a telegram from Lord Halifax stating that 'His Majesty's Government are unable to guarantee protection.' Shamelessly abandoned, Schuschnigg resigned. Austrian Nazi mobs rampaged through Vienna. Seizing on the disorder, Hitler and Göring gave the Wehrmacht the order to march. At the head of a fleet of grey Mercedes, Hitler drove across the Austrian border at Braunau am In, the small village where he had been born. He was greeted with astonishing enthusiasm. He drove on to Linz, where his reception by screaming crowds and pealing bells made him weep. Two days later Hitler was in Vienna and the *Anschluss*, the welding together of Germany and Austria, was complete. American journalist William Shirer was there: 'The Nazis are in . . . Hitler has broken a dozen solemn promises, pledges, treaties. And Austria is finished. Beautiful, tragic, civilized Austria. Gone. Done to death in the brief moment of an afternoon. This afternoon.'

Soon afterwards, on the orders of Adolf Eichmann, the enemies of the Reich were rounded up. Jews, communists and socialists were arrested. Jewish shops were attacked and plundered. Jews were forced to scrub pavements, watched and assaulted by baying crowds. When Hitler returned from Vienna, he was soon greedily scrutinizing maps of eastern Europe. 'First now comes Czechia,' he said to Goebbels. He brooded for hours, reliving the triumphs of the *Anschluss* and relishing the admiration of the German people. Now he wanted more, and it seemed as if the democracies were too frightened of war to act against him. The dream he shared with Himmler of a great Germany occupying the old lands of the ancient Teutons and more, seizing for the *Volk* the *Lebensraum* it demanded – all this was now possible.

As Hitler deliberated over his maps, Ernst Schäfer returned to Berlin to make final preparations to leave for India. He had returned from London empty-handed and angry, but neither he nor Himmler was prepared to give up. In Berlin, Edmund Geer had been supervising preparations in a warehouse on Potsdamerplatz loaned by Schäfer's father. There was much to do and to acquire: Karl Wienert's needs included theodolites, chronometers, stopwatches, earth inductors, shortwave radios and a robust German invention called the *Feldwaage*. All these had to be donated by, purchased, borrowed or begged from companies all over Germany. Bruno Beger too had more than a hundred cases. Inside was an armoury of callipers, eye-colour charts, bushy sheaves of hair types, packets of gypsum to make masks, fingerprinting apparatus and scores of custom-designed data-recording notebooks. Ernst Krause was taking hundreds of rolls of movie film and 16mm and plate cameras as well as his butterfly nets and specimen jars. There were crates containing tents and tables, bottles of schnapps and Pils, thousands of cigarettes. The cases were all custom-designed and insulated with rubber to survive the extremes of heat and cold, the drenching monsoon rains and the sopping humidity while on the rolling back of a mule or temperamental yak.

Everyone knew that Schäfer had been humiliated in London. There was no answer from the Kashag in Lhasa and Walton had made it clear that good news could not be expected. But Schäfer had seen the flabby, appeasing side of the British and sensed they would not resist too much if he pressed his case hard enough on the spot. Both Schäfer and Himmler knew that they could afford to be provocative – for now. The poison of appeasement meant that no-one in London or Delhi could risk offending Germany. There was to be no turning back. At no point did Schäfer reveal to his colleagues that he had another plan. Younghusband's potent advice that he should 'sneak over the border' was a card he would play when the perfect moment came.

CHAPTER SEVEN

TRAPPED

'He must go–go–go away from here!
On the other side of the world he's overdue.
Send the road is clear before you when the old springfret
comes o'er you,
And the Red Gods call for you!'

– Rudyard Kipling, 'The Feet of Young Men', 1897

On 18 April 1938, Bruno Beger, Karl Wienert and Ernst Krause boarded an express bound for the northern Italian port of Genoa.[1] A German *Schnelldampfer* (fast steamship) called the *Gneisenau* had been loaded with the expedition equipment in Hamburg and was already on its way to the Mediterranean. On this first leg of their journey they were chaperoned by Käthe Blaumen, a pretty young woman from Hans Schäfer's Phoenix company who would travel with them as far as Genoa. Beger chose not to introduce her to his wife, who had come with her husband to say goodbye. Everyone was in high spirits. Wienert had brought a hubble-bubble pipe which they smoked throughout the journey, much to the disgust of other passengers.

Schäfer and Geer caught a later train. From the very start, Schäfer chose isolation to assert authority. Packed in the hold of the *Gneisenau* was his own superior one-man leader's tent. He had an instinctive belief in the *Führer Prinzip* and he would never let his comrades forget that his was the superior rank.

In Berlin, Beger had had one last encounter with the sinister world of their patron, the Reichsführer Heinrich Himmler. He was working late at the Ahnenerbe offices in Dahlem and in the early hours of the morning went in search of a suitable place for a nap. He found an unlocked and empty office equipped with a large and inviting sofa. The building was quiet; Beger stretched out and rapidly fell asleep. He awoke suddenly to find an old man sitting at the end of the sofa regarding him intently. It was Karl Maria Wiligut, or 'Weisthor', Himmler's Rasputin. Wiligut was by now disgraced and probably mentally ill; his obsession with runic law and his millennia-old ancestral race memories were indulged only by Himmler. Beger apologized and began to leave the office, but Weisthor knew who his intruder was and had some requests. Beger must find out as much as he could about marriage customs in Tibet. Women were said to take a number of husbands. Would this practice, if it was adopted by the SS, permit the biological manufacture of yet more pure-blooded Aryan SS men? Weisthor had also heard an intriguing legend: Tibetan women were thought to carry magical stones lodged inside their vaginas. Would the expedition please find out if this was true? Then this peculiar old man said goodnight and shuffled painfully away through the dark Ahnenerbe offices.

In Genoa, the Germans took a taxi from Brignole Station to the grubby, swarming port. Only Krause, at thirty-eight the oldest member of the expedition, and Schäfer had spent any time outside Germany, so for the other three this was a breathtaking first experience of being abroad. It was a brilliant spring morning and the Mediterranean glittered invitingly. Genoa, the birthplace of Columbus, is encircled by hills and squeezed tight between them and the sea. On the Via Garibaldi are the high palaces of the city's grand old families; behind the port is the twisting warren of the Old City. For Henry James this had been the 'crookedest and most incoherent of cities'. There were a few posters of Mussolini but little else that celebrated Europe's oldest fascist state. Here, money, food and trade had always been more important than politics. On 21 April, the five young German men boarded the *Gneisenau*. Customs arrangements had been cleared by Himmler's staff. On the quayside, Käthe Blaumen waved goodbye and turned back towards the station and the train to Berlin.

The following day the *Gneisenau* steamed into the Mediterranean taking the Ernst Schäfer German Tibet Expedition east towards Suez, the Red Sea and the Indian Ocean. Schäfer was determined that the expedition should make the right impression and he had splashed out on first-class tickets. Their companions were diplomats and German businessmen and their wives en route to India and China. In this exalted company even rugged explorers had to change three times daily and could only play deck games if they were appropriately attired. Beger and Wienert boxed in the *Gneisenau*'s gym. Beger had the longer arms, and his damaging assault on his comrade provoked the first of Schäfer's tantrums when Wienert sat down to dinner with a bloody nose and swollen mouth. As the *Gneisenau* ploughed through the waves getting further and further away from Germany conversation at dinner became much freer. Beger discovered that not all Germans supported Hitler and that many of his fellow passengers feared for the future.

That month, as the Schäfer expedition set off for India,

Hitler had turned his attention to Czechoslovakia. It was a mongrel nation that had been cobbled together from leftover bits and pieces of the Habsburg Empire. Its people were a polyglot and restless mixture of Czechs, Hungarians, Poles, Ruthenians and, in the Sudetenland, Germans. They were naturally of great interest to Hitler. He hated Czechs – a typical prejudice in the Habsburg Empire – and the very idea of '*die Tschechei*' as a bastard creation of Versailles. Its very existence was 'intolerable for Germany'.

Hitler began the game of conquest by championing the rights of the allegedly downtrodden and oppressed Germans in the Sudetenland. He encouraged Konrad Heinlein, leader of the Sudeten German Party, to demand autonomy from the government of Eduard Beneš. As well as stoking up the passions of the Sudeten Germans he also encouraged the Slovakian leaders to pull away from Beneš's central government. To the appeasers, Hitler genuinely had at heart only the interests of the Sudeten Germans, trapped as they were behind a much-resented border. Even the London *Times* agreed that the Sudetenland was properly part of Germany. But Hitler's strategy was of course ambitious and destructive. He told his generals, 'I am utterly determined that Czechoslovakia should disappear from the map.'

The Wehrmacht had already produced a plan for the invasion of Czechoslovakia (in 1937) called 'Case Green'. The Czechoslovakians were in theory protected by treaties with France and the USSR, but in reality the country was, in historian Ian Kershaw's words, 'exposed and friendless'. Hitler calculated that France and England wanted to avoid war, and he was for now proved right. In May 1938 there were reports of German troop movements near the Czech border and Beneš ordered a mobilization. 'Everyone awaits what is coming,' Goebbels wrote in his diary. From the *Gneisenau*, Schäfer followed events closely. If war broke out before he arrived in India his expedition would be over. He depended for now on that 'humane and humorous' English gentleman Neville Chamberlain.

While the German Tibet Expedition steamed across the Mediterranean towards the Suez Canal, Schäfer's supporters in England had continued to lobby the India Office and Lord Linlithgow, the Viceroy himself. Himmler had heard Schäfer's side of the story and now weighed in with aggrieved outrage and crude threats. He sent a letter to Domville, who passed it on to the Prime Minister:

> You know yourself that up to now my attitude towards every Englishman who has come to Germany has been entirely friendly. For that reason I am the more astonished that the English should treat one of my men in a brusque, wounding and unfriendly way. I cannot imagine the authorities are so stupid as to see in the scientist Dr Schäfer, officially dispatched by me, a spy. For the English Secret Service cannot believe me to be so stupid as to dispatch such a man officially and under my name if I really was engaging in espionage. You can imagine that this kind of treatment has upset me personally very much and has given rise to the thought that apart from personal friendship, such as ours, there is no point in treating British subjects in Germany in a comradely way, since on the other side such treatment has not the slightest echo.

Number 10 forwarded Himmler's rant to the India Office. It put them in an awkward position. They had considered Schäfer's request to travel through the Assam Himalayas and turned it down on the grounds that 'tribal unrest' made it too dangerous. This was window dressing; the reason was that disputed and fractious border. There was still silence from the

Kashag, but Walton was certain that it would not be positive. Now the Foreign Office realized it had been outmanoeuvred. Schäfer was at that moment steaming towards India and Himmler's letter threatened an embarrassing international incident if he was turned away. Chamberlain had given Lewis's department stores a 'high powered rocket' for boycotting German goods after the *Anschluss*; now the India Office feared admonishment for thwarting the 'scientific ambitions' of one of Himmler's protégés.

So they telegrammed Gould indicating that there was a need to find some compromise. It was 'politically desirable to do anything possible to remove any impression that we have put obstacles in Schäfer's way'. Gould's solution was adroit. Schäfer could be given permission to travel north to Sikkim, but no further. There, the Germans would find plenty to occupy their time – birdwatching or whatever else took their fancy. They could be kept under close surveillance by Gould himself from Gangtok. The strategy was perfectly in keeping with the spirit of appeasement. But in the same way that Chamberlain had believed that Hitler would be satisfied with the Rhineland and then Austria, so too Gould imagined that Schäfer would be happy with Sikkim and a peep into Tibet. Gould would be just as mistaken about Schäfer as Chamberlain was about Hitler.

The news from London was telegrammed to Schäfer on board the *Gneisenau*. It closed the door on Assam and the Lohit Valley route to Tibet, but opened another front. Sikkim was a tiny and isolated mountain kingdom richly endowed with unique flora and fauna. Its peoples were diverse and included a Tibetan elite, the Bhutia. But most important of all, Sikkim was a gateway to Tibet. The road to Lhasa began in Kalimpong, followed the Tista Valley to Gangtok then climbed fourteen thousand feet to the Natu La Pass on the threshold of the

Forbidden Land. In 1904, Younghusband had taken this road all the way to Lhasa. Schäfer also knew that the year before the British had crossed *another* pass and marched to a Tibetan stronghold called Khampa Dzong. When Younghusband's negotiations had reached an impasse he had retreated back to Sikkim. So Sikkim, the gift of Gould's appeasement, could be the key to Tibet and to Lhasa.

But then another telegram arrived, this time from the German consul general in Calcutta, von Plessen. For Schäfer, it felt like a stab in the back. The consul advised Schäfer to turn back immediately. The British believed they were spies, and from the consul's point of view they had become an embarrassment. In the files of Indian Political Intelligence, I discovered that von Plessen was suspected by the British to be an anti-Nazi who had 'incurred the displeasure of Party leaders',[2] so it is unlikely that he would have welcomed men he probably perceived as emissaries of Himmler. The opening of this second hostile front, inside the German Foreign Office, was a bitter blow and Schäfer once more protested angrily to Himmler. Beger remembers that Schäfer became 'like a man possessed'. While his comrades practised their English, played games or relaxed on deck in dashing white flannels chatting to 'important people', Schäfer brooded alone. In the evenings, as the *Gneisenau* steamed through the Suez Canal, Schäfer watched the steel bow slicing through the cobalt-coloured, white-capped waves and plotted his next move. On all sides, the desert stretched away and the wind brought with it the first breath of the Orient.

The *Gneisenau* docked at Colombo, from where Schäfer and his colleagues caught a freighter north to Madras and then another on to Calcutta. Now Schäfer faced further setbacks. On 4 May the Kashag had given their answer. No-one was surprised that they refused to give Schäfer permission to enter

Tibet. The speed of the response strongly implied the interference of Gould and Richardson, and Schäfer also discovered that stories were appearing in newspapers, including the *Times of India*, with headlines like A GESTAPO AGENT IN INDIA. It was a blow which put in jeopardy his delicate arrangement to travel on to Sikkim. Calcutta was the commercial hub of the British Raj and wherever the party went they received a chilly reception. Schäfer contacted the German consul, whom he berated for his lack of support, and his Indian representative Hans Gösling who was a trade agent for Agfa in Calcutta. He had met Schäfer during the second Brooke Dolan expedition. The consul, now under pressure from Berlin, lobbied the Viceroy's office for a meeting to confirm that the German Tibet Expedition could travel on to Sikkim. In the meantime, Gösling, Schäfer and Geer waged war with customs officers and bureaucrats to get their hundreds of cases unloaded ready for the journey north. They had to leave before the monsoons came in July and every delay was agonizing.

Fosco Maraini's 'metropolis of tooth and claw, tyranny and blackmail, suffering, evil and asceticism' itself seemed to conspire against them. In the summer, Calcutta and its polyglot citizens are scorched by the fierce, unrelenting heat that flows down to the Bay of Bengal from the flat, steaming rice lands of the Plain of Bengal. Inside the cauldron the Raj flaunted its imperial power and glory, taunting the Germans who waited impatiently for news. Krause took his camera on the tramcar that rattled along Old Court House Street. Through his viewfinder passed Boots the Chemist, Lloyds Bank, the stately Government House and the great blocks of government offices where the affairs of empire were decided. On the emerald-green *maidan*, statues of past viceroys swept past sharing space with scarlet-blossomed *mohur* trees. Men, both Indian and English, played cricket in spotless white flannels. Along the swift-flowing Hoogli, merchants bustling along the wharves and bargaining in warehouses proclaimed the wealth of empire at the tops of their voices. The Germans observed too the raw contrast between palace and hovel, grandeur and squalor; in the poorer parts of the city they held their noses as they walked through the tangled labyrinth of unpaved backstreets with their fearsome howls of despair. At night, after the mauve and silver hues of sunset had subsided and the twinkling lights on the Strand were reflected in the darkly flowing Hoogli, they sipped whisky with Dr Oswald Urchs, the Nazi Party leader in India, and Subhas Chandra Bose, the radical Congress Party member. Bose was seeking German or Japanese backing in his fight for Indian independence. Beger would meet Bose again in 1941 when he fled to Berlin to try to persuade Hitler to support his cause.

Schäfer, usually alone, took refuge outside the city. 'Sometimes,' he wrote, 'when the haste and hurry become too much, when the problems become too unfamiliar, too incomprehensible, too involved, when it is difficult to come to conclusions because of constantly changing opinions, I grab my shot gun and flee . . . into nature . . .' Despite his wife's violent death, the gun was still a consolation. Beger's diary makes it very evident that Schäfer was very often difficult, abrasive and solitary. Until he formed a most unusual relationship after they arrived in the Sikkimese capital Gangtok, he proved to be a dark and bitter companion prone to frequent rages and tantrums. He rampaged through Calcutta like an angry bear. Schäfer was, as everyone knew, still racked by guilt, but his energy was unrelenting, and for this he never lost Beger's respect. He seemed to channel all the sorrow and anguish into a grim armour of determination. First Sikkim, then Tibet.

The Viceroy finally relented in June and Schäfer was summoned to the Viceregal Lodge in Simla, the summer capital of British India. But what he had long dreaded was about to come to pass. From his hotel window he could see colossal flotillas of clouds building high over the Bay of Bengal. Now the dense green foliage sprouting from every nook and cranny in Calcutta was quivering in a light breeze. The monsoon was coming. Schäfer had little time to lose. He found a dark suit, then took a taxi to the Howrah Station; he caught a train to Kalka, then changed on to the Simla line. For the first time he could see, hundreds of miles to the north, the endless ramparts of murky cloud that signalled the presence of the Himalayas.

Schäfer had plenty of time to mull over his tactics as the train, swaying on its narrow-gauge track, chuffed for six bone-rattling hours up into the Himalayan foothills through 103 tunnels, over 800 bridges and round 900 bends to Simla Station. From his window, as the steam cleared, Schäfer could see Mount Jakko dotted with tiny villas, the prickly spires of Christ Church and the Viceregal Lodge itself. A flag signalled that the Viceroy and Vicereine were in residence. For some, Simla was an Indian Mount Olympus; for others less enamoured by this little England perched on a Himalayan hill top, it was the Abode of the Little Tin Gods. Up here the nerves of the Raj were calmed and soothed by honeysuckle- and rose-scented memories of home, or by the sight of pines in the mist and the call of cuckoos and thrushes. The gossip was of flirtations and theatricals, and in the words of one exasperated English man, there were 'balls here, balls there, balls to the Society, balls by the Society'. For a young German burdened with a sense of imperial disappointment, this exclusive fairy-land of empire must have prompted ambivalent feelings. It was a world to be envied through gritted teeth.

Leaving the station, Schäfer hailed one of the jostling rick-shaws and was rushed down the Mall, past the Swiss chalet-style Post Office and the Tudor-style Gate of Christ

Church, then up the winding approach to the Scottish Hydro-style Lodge that stood with stolid arrogance on Observatory Hill. As he jumped down onto the gravel drive and crunched his way towards the lodge, Schäfer knew that the rose pergolas and terraced lawns, the click of croquet mallets and the distant strains of music-hall songs from a gramophone were window dressing; in the summer, the Viceregal Lodge became the engine of imperial power. Waiting for Schäfer in the soaring teak- and walnut-encrusted entrance was the Viceroy's secretary, J. G. Laithwaite, who took his guest through the ballroom and on to the veranda. Here the 'Grand Ornamental' himself, his six feet five inches of ungainly body folded into a basket chair turned towards the viceregal lawns, awaited the pleasure of Obersturmführer Schäfer's company.

Victor Alexander John Hope, Lord Linlithgow, the man Schäfer now faced across a silver tea service of exquisite luxury, was a chilly, cautious and self-assured man who was not universally liked. Some viewed him as uncouth. The Indian statesman Jawaharlal Nehru said he was as solid as a rock with 'a rock's lack of awareness'. Few were allowed to know that his awkward physical manner was the result of polio; he had to support his chin with his left hand while drinking tea and could only turn his head and shoulders at the same time. He dropped the final 'g' from participles and loved the rough comedy of Bud Flanagan and 'Monsewer' Eddie Gray. As his wife hated Simla's thin air and spent most of her time resting in her room, the Viceroy had plenty of time to reflect on the truth that in the administration of India 'every pigeon-hole contains a potential revolution; every office-box cradles the embryo of a war or death'.

In that summer of 1938, Linlithgow was much preoccupied with escalating violence between Hindu and Muslim, a campaign of terror and assassination that had broken out in

Bengal, and with what Mr Gandhi or Mr Bose might do next. The German Tibet Expedition was a minor annoyance. Schäfer, who was such a difficult companion, was now persuasive and charming, and Linlithgow had a passion for butterflies and nets and collecting jars that Schäfer was able to admire. The message from the Foreign Office was to appease Herr Himmler, whose feathers had been ruffled by Schäfer's experiences in Whitehall. The expedition seemed harmless enough. Why not let them do a little bird spotting and butterfly collecting in Sikkim? He gave them six months, then said goodbye to Schäfer and returned to real problems. Were the Japanese planning to invade Burma? Were the gun batteries in Singapore pointing the wrong way? Of course, it is very likely that the British strategy was simply designed to aggravate Schäfer by making him wait then dragging him all the way to Simla. Every step of the way, British pomp and power, however insecure, would have been thrust in the young German's face.

Schäfer returned to Calcutta and the monsoon arrived soon afterwards. Now snakes slithered under houses, mosquitoes rose in whining clouds from rivers and creeks, regiments of stink beetles crawled from beneath dank vegetation, jute flies swarmed and shoes left out to be polished rotted overnight on hotel verandas. Calcutta had exhausted everyone, and no-one was sorry when Schäfer ordered them to be ready to leave for the north and, in Beger's words, 'the stronger and rougher sons of the high plains of Inner Asia'. At the station, they loaded their tons of equipment and supplies onto a night train that after the usual delays began its journey north towards the railhead at Siliguri. As dawn approached, shadowy forms on the interminable Plain of Bengal were slowly disclosed and Krause unpacked his camera. They passed groves of misty olive-green bamboos and banana plants whose wide leaves had been slashed and ripped by the rains. It is said that the detritus brought down by the rivers that rise on the Tibetan plateau is so churned by the tumbling waters that not one stone on the flat, hot plain is bigger than a baby's hand. As the sun burnt off the mist, they could see thatched mud huts and water buffaloes; for mile after mile flat rice fields mirrored the bleached sky, all neatly separated by low mud walls. Rain clouds scudded overhead. On the horizon they could see a rippling slash of white snow: the Himalayas.

At Siliguri they found a ramshackle village dotted with mango trees. At the station, though, they could eat eggs and bacon. From the railhead the expedition took the Darjeeling Himalayan Railway, known to everyone as the 'toy train', to Ghoom Station. Like a clockwork railway from a Victorian childhood, this Lilliputian train huffed and puffed up 7,407 feet on two-foot-gauge rails – the logical engineering solution to severe gradients and endless switchbacks. Like a well-behaved school party, Schäfer and his comrades took their places in curtained trolleys. Their supplies had been loaded onto covered wagons at the rear that would return to Siliguri later, packed with tea. Only Schäfer was not awed by the tropical forest, thick with orchids, through which they now steamed. Tree ferns and wild bananas made an arch over the line. Bamboo stood in dense hundred-foot-tall tufts.

A little over halfway, as the train chuffed resolutely forward, climbing steadily higher at a startling twelve miles an hour, there was a commotion from the engineers. The train squealed to a halt and everyone leant out to see what was wrong. A mud-slide had blocked the tracks. This, as Schäfer knew very well, was the cost of travelling during the monsoon. Now the expedition would be bedevilled by collapsed mountain roads and frequent, terrifying mudslides. As the train engineers excavated the track, Schäfer stepped across the tracks, leaving the others on the train. He pushed his way into the dense, wet jungle known in the

The expedition with the Maharaja or Chogyal of Sikkim.
From left to right: Beger, Schäfer, the Chogyal, Geer, Krause, Wienert.

ABOVE LEFT
Kaiser Bahadur Thapa, Schäfer's favourite – who might have ended up in Berlin.

ABOVE RIGHT
Geer and Krause in Gangtok: note SS insignia on pith helmet.

LEFT
The expedition in the field. Left to right: Wienert, Beger with native 'subjects', Geer.

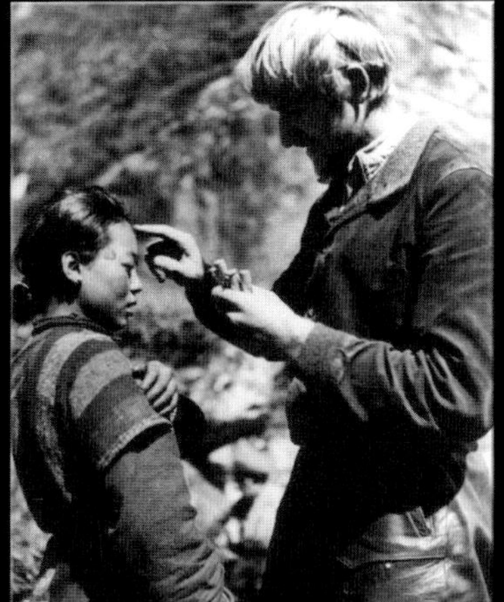

ABOVE

Bruno Beger at work measuring the peoples of Sikkim.

BELOW

The snowbound German camp in northern Sikkim.

ABOVE LEFT

The Tering Raja and his wife. He lobbied the Tibetan government on Schäfer's behalf; she was concerned about the British response.

ABOVE RIGHT

The 'Minister' of Tering, who encountered the desperate Schäfer in Sikkim.

BELOW

Schäfer in extremis 'sneaking over the border' into Tibet to see the Tering Raja.

ABOVE
Schäfer and his party hunting for shapi.

ABOVE
One of Schäfer's guides sneezing into the snow to maintain silence during the hunt.

RIGHT
Schäfer's great prize: a dead shapi, an animal unknown to science, with Sikkimese hunter.

LEFT
The German Tibet Expedition winding its way up to the Natu La.

BELOW
The expedition encamped at night. Left to right: Krause, Schäfer, Beger, Geer, Wienert. Sikkimese members of the expedition in row behind.

Kaiser Thapa on the Tibetan plateau. Later Schäfer cruelly misused Kaiser's horse.

TOP RIGHT
Karl Wienert was forced to take his geomagnetic readings undercover. The tent behind him in this photograph conceals his equipment, which he had been forbidden to bring across the Tibetan border.

MIDDLE RIGHT
Akeh Bhutia in hunting garb in 1938. He and Bruno Beger are the last surviving members of the expedition.

BOTTOM RIGHT
The Dzongpon's wife, whom Beger was told enjoyed 'medical examinations'. Beger celebrated her body in his diary.

Ernst Krause filming. He, or rather Schäfer, was determined to return to Germany with outstanding motion-picture film and often took risks to obtain the most dramatic pictures.

Himalayan foothills as the Terai. The ground was swampy underfoot and the air was scented with the hot-house aroma of orchids. Schäfer walked a few yards and stopped, listening. He hoped to glimpse some sign of the forest's legendary beasts, but among its innumerable pale tree trunks there was little movement. Far away, a parrot screamed unseen. A waterfall roared. The whirring of millions of insects rose and fell as if the forest were breathing. His reverie was interrupted by a piercing blast from the train whistle. When he returned, he reported that the jungle was 'like a cemetery'.

At the end of the line, Darjeeling was another British hill station huddling in the foothills of Kangchendzonga, Sikkim's holy mountain. Its peaks were veiled in cloud but tier after tier of ever-heightening ridges could be seen marching away towards the north. At the beginning of the eighteenth century Darjeeling, originally Dorjé Ling, was part of Sikkim and was frequently attacked by the Gurkhas of Nepal. The British East India Company was interested both in pushing back the Gurkhas and securing the trade routes into Tibet, so in 1835 they compelled the Sikkim ruler, H.H. Sri Sri Sri Sri Sri Maharaja Tsugphud Namygal, to cede Dorjé Ling to the company. It was the first of many assaults on the tiny kingdom, and like the others had never been forgotten.

Younghusband had written of Darjeeling, 'This is a funny quiet sleepy little place . . .' but it was where he first saw Kangchendzonga 'clear and clean against the intense blue sky . . . the culminating peak of lesser heights converging upward to it and all ethereal as spirit . . . We are uplifted.'[3] Schäfer's experience was rather different, for it was here in Darjeeling that he met face to face for the first time with Hugh Richardson. It was to be a humiliating experience.

Richardson was already an angry man. He had received this personal telegram from the Viceroy: 'I have to ask you *to do what you are asked* because the Foreign Office have been approached by Himmler and it is his special wish that the mission should go ahead.' For the British Mission officer in Lhasa to receive a telegram directly from the Viceroy, rather than from Sir Basil Gould, his superior in Gangtok, was unprecedented. Evidently, Richardson remained resolutely opposed to any co-operation with Schäfer, and he had resolved to make their stay as unpleasant as possible. To be sure, Gould said Richardson was 'critical by nature',[4] but behind the civil servant's tight-lipped façade Richardson was opposed to what he viewed as appeasement on the spot. So as soon as he knew Schäfer had arrived in Sikkim, Richardson summoned the Germans to his private office in the Hotel Mount Everest. There, the tall, slender, dark-haired Scot harangued them for thirty minutes without pause, to the accompaniment of rain drumming on the veranda, about what they could and more particularly could definitely not do in Sikkim.

The meeting revealed to Schäfer what he was up against. This was the man he needed to beat if he wanted to get to Lhasa. But it was Bruno Beger whom Richardson singled out that afternoon in the hotel. He had taken the trouble to find out what each member of Schäfer's expedition was planning to do and he was disturbed that Beger was going to wander hither and thither forcing local people to submit to his callipers. Richardson knew this might cause grave offence and he demanded that Beger take especial care. In fact, he would prefer that no measurements be made at all.

Beger already knew that collecting anthropometric data from real people was often tricky. In the Altmärkische, even German farmers had been suspicious when he brought out his callipers, eye-colour charts and all the other paraphernalia of a travelling anthropologist. He had been forced to perfect techniques of gentle coercion and, when he could afford it, bribery. Now he faced a new obstacle: hostility from a powerful British civil servant whom he sensed could make his work very difficult. But as Beger mulled over Richardson's tirade, he began to see the glimmerings of a solution. In Calcutta and during the journey to Sikkim he had frequently observed people afflicted with ugly rashes and infections, the painful symptoms of chronic malaria, as well as everyday sprains and fractures. He had spent a year studying 'sports medicine' in Heidelberg and knew he could treat these simple diseases very effectively. He was glad that he had persuaded Schäfer to bring along the best medicines Germany could offer. He wrote, 'I had to win the trust of these people. And our medicine chest gave me the tools for this.' He decided he 'would have to become a respected "medicine man" for the people here. My natural and sincere helpfulness would have to pave the way for fruitful research.' It was a callous calculation, but it would reap tremendous benefits for Beger in the months to come.

Schäfer did not stay long in Darjeeling. Equipment and stores were loaded onto oxen while the expedition travelled by car towards the Sikkimese capital, Gangtok. They had hired Nepali drivers who insouciantly negotiated a vertiginous ladder of hairpin bends that took them slowly up the Tista Valley, through the jumbled spurs of the Himalayan foothills. The monsoon rains were unrelenting and the cars frequently had to be extracted from viscous mud.

Sikkim can be imagined as a thin wedge sharply tilted from a few hundred feet above sea level in the south to more than twenty-three thousand feet on the Tibetan border. Cut deep into the wedge is the Tista Valley. Its sheer rocky flanks are sheathed with tightly packed ferns, bamboo, oak and giant magnolia that shut the narrow strips of road inside a dizzying green corridor. Schäfer described Sikkim in *Geheimnis Tibet*: 'It brings together in a vertical graduation all the *Lebensraum*: the tropical jungle zone, the sub-tropical with its uncounted orchid species, the temperate zones with pale birch forests and dark firs which recalled our homeland, the great rhododendron forests at the tree line, the alpine meadows, the desolate realm of stones – and finally the eternal snow.' The lower reaches of the river were once much-feared cerebral malaria country. 'Haunting suspicion of fever', Younghusband had noted in his diary in 1903. Schäfer knew that when Younghusband had brought his troops through here in 1903, hundreds of his pack animals had died as they struggled up the valley, slain by a deadly zoo of microbes including anthrax, rinderpest and foot and mouth disease. Still others were poisoned after eating a wild plant called aconite (also known as monkshood or wolfsbane). In Gould's time, there was an outbreak of black plague (kala-azar) in the Tista Valley, a deadly and debilitating disease with symptoms like malaria. Like Schäfer, Younghusband's troops had been forced to travel in the rainy season, and as well as sickness they too were plagued by mudslides and avalanches that swept away animals and men and often blocked roads for days on end. But for Schäfer, this time, the journey to Gangtok passed without serious incident.

Krause was elated by the dazzling profusion of large and brilliantly coloured butterflies that hovered scarlet, green and blue over every patch of moisture in the road. For Beger, too, Sikkim promised to be a rich anthropological laboratory. Although this tiny kingdom is a mere eighty miles from north to south and forty miles wide, its population is extremely diverse. It was originally settled by Lepchas (who call themselves Rongpa) and by Bhutia who came across the mountain passes from Tibet. Tens of thousands flooded in from Nepal in the nineteenth century and, according to one patronizing British traveller in 1937, 'nowadays . . . the pure Lepcha is rarely seen. He is a guileless gnome-like person with a great knowledge of the trees and plants of the forest.'[5] By the time the German Tibet Expedition arrived the majority of Sikkim's people were Nepali, but the Bhutia remained Sikkim's rulers and had many close relatives among the aristocracy of Lhasa. It was a convention that one son from a Bhutia family should enter the priesthood, and the Buddhist monasteries dominated education and culture. Sikkim was, as a result, unmistakably 'Tibetan'. For Schäfer, the monasteries and lamas, the prayer wheels and prayer flags and *chortens*, the endless ringing of monastery bells, the sound of conch shells and the chanting of *Om Mani Padme Hum* stunned him with nostalgia and sadness.

As the expedition drove across the new suspension bridge into Gangtok ('High Hill') they could see a large village straddling a densely forested ridge whose sides fell steeply to the river. At one end of the ridge was the royal palace and the private temple of the Chogyal, whom the British always referred to as the Maharaja. The British Residency faced the palace on higher ground, discreetly hidden behind pink tree dahlias and green ferns but approached along a grand concrete road with electric lighting. According to Gould, the residency was 'the most attractive medium sized house in the whole of India'.[6] Like the Viceregal Lodge in Simla, it was also a mask for imperial power.

This was the home of Sikkim's political officer, and as he was driven into the city Schäfer regarded it with wary ambivalence. He would discover that at least some of his feelings were shared by the Sikkimese, who had difficulties accepting the treatment meted out to their country by the British. Centuries ago, Sikkim was an independent Buddhist kingdom ruled by a Bhutia king, the Chogyal. In the nineteenth century the British, eager to extend their trading empire, began to fret at Sikkim's borders. In 1861 they annexed the region around Darjeeling in the south and began to bring in Nepali workers, who were alleged to be 'stronger' than the native Sikkimese. The result was unrest and conflict, so in 1888 the British sent troops to mediate between the warring factions and succeeded in seizing more territory and more power. The British political officer John Claude White then turned Sikkim into a private fiefdom. He and his soldiers raided the palace of the Chogyal, Thutob Namygal, who was a diffident, reclusive man 'much disfigured by a bad hair lip'.[7] White stripped him of any power and sent him and his consort, the charismatic Yeshe Dolma, into exile. More Nepalis arrived and White insisted on replacing Sikkim's national symbol of the prayer wheel with the Gurkha *kukri*. He also tried to rein in the Chogyal's two sons and make them puppets. One of them was so terrified by the dictatorial British political officer that he fled to his estates in Tibet and never came back. This man, the Tering Raja, would turn out to be Schäfer's salvation.

White would never be forgiven, even after 1918, when the British allowed Tashi Namygal, the new chogyal, to govern Sikkim as a British protectorate. The new ruler was, at least on the surface, on very good terms with the British, but Schäfer soon made friends with him, calling him 'a nice little man in his middle years' who was very conscious of the 'iron power' of the British. Sir Tashi Namygal was a modest, spiritual man who spent much of the day painting or praying. Fosco Maraini gave this memorable description of him: a 'perfect representative of the small, secretive type of humanity that peoples the valleys at the feet of the giants of the Himalayas'.[8] He loved fine things, rare stones, lacquer and jade, which he caressed with 'the thin fingers of a refined ascetic'; he passed quietly from room to room of his palace 'as if by levitation'.

Sir Tashi invited Schäfer and Krause to film the Pang Lhabsol Festival, the War Dance of the Gods. It was the first of scores of such festivals Krause would photograph at tedious length over the next year. The dance was dedicated to the holy mountain of Sikkim, Kangchendzonga. Its name means 'Five Storehouses of the Great Snows', and each of its five peaks is thought to conceal sacred minerals, grains, salt and rare holy scriptures. Later, Schäfer enthusiastically told his readers that Kangchendzonga was a martial god; the dancers were helmeted and waved swords. As the Germans watched, the cymbals, flutes, ringing bells and booming drums of the orchestra mingled with the shrieking bagpipes of Nepali soldiers. The War Dance of the Gods was a bizarre display of warlike pomp and Buddhist calm. All in all, it was 'ecstatic, wild, and terrible'. As the dancers whirled in front of them, one of the Bhutian aristocrats confided to Schäfer, 'We only marry among ourselves and detest commingling with other races. When we cannot find suitable girls in Sikkim, we travel to Tibet and get ourselves women from families of equal status . . . The Lepchas were not born to be leaders. Though they are good subjects, modest, hard-working and adaptable, they aren't fighters: they avoid any danger and that is why they are where they are, in the middle of the jungle, where they are in nobody's way.' To the German expeditionists, these must have seemed admirable sentiments. The text of *Geheimnis Tibet* shows very clearly that Schäfer and Beger shared the same ideas about race: when Schäfer discussed the Nepalis he described them as 'part Indo-Aryan, part Mongoloid', 'intellectually very superior' and 'biologically robust'. The closer to the Aryan source, the better the blood.

Schäfer soon met Sir Basil Gould, the political officer. On the surface he seemed a soft touch compared with Hugh Richardson, but the truth was that he was a very experienced and wily operator who quickly had the measure of Schäfer and, most importantly, knew how to get him to talk. This was essential: no-one really understood just what the SS party wanted or intended to do. Gould, as the documents in the India Office collection show, could make the young German sing like a canary.

Once they had made camp at a nearby lodge called Dilkushka, Geer and Schäfer began hiring porters, many of them sherpas.[9] Gould cleverly let him use the grounds of the British Residency where he could keep an eye on his activities. There were the usual problems. A cook was insolent to Schäfer and returned drunk from the market where he had been sent for supplies. Schäfer sacked him on the spot, but the man said, cannily, that he was going to inform Sir Basil. It is a measure of Schäfer's anxiety that this made him retain the chef, who immediately returned to the village and resumed drinking. When he came back this time he was sacked, and Schäfer laughed at him when he returned the following day, sober, pleading to be taken on again. On another occasion, Schäfer discovered a man riffling through his books and papers, which meant that Gould was going to do all he could to spy on the Germans. A young man called Akeh Bhutia also turned up one day claiming to be an expert hunter. Schäfer tested his marksmanship and then made him head porter. Today, Akeh Bhutia lives just down the hill from the old residency and is known to everyone as 'German Akeh'. He would be Schäfer's infuriating, libidinous shadow for the next year.

Then a young, rather slight Nepali Gurkha wearing a blue suit appeared at the German camp and asked for an interview. His name was Kaiser Bahadur Thapa and he immediately attracted Schäfer's attention. Soon he would be the 'Kaiserling, shy boy and favourite of us all . . .' He had been to Gangtok High School and was clearly very bright. When he met the Germans, Kaiser was holding down a humdrum job in the Sikkim civil service, twiddling his thumbs in an airless cubby hole, and he longed for adventure. And he knew his worth: he asked Schäfer for a higher salary than anyone else. So impressed was Schäfer that he took him on as a translator without much fuss. Much later it would become evident, at least to the British, that Kaiser's Tibetan was poor, but the young man's value to the expedition and to Schäfer himself would far outweigh his failings as a linguist. Schäfer called this 'delicate, handsome, shy, wiry and intelligent' youth 'my selfless, courageous, yes, almost indispensable comrade'. Beger remembers, with some rancour, that Kaiser always knew more about Schäfer's plans in advance then he or Geer ever did. Kaiser alone would be immune from Schäfer's frequent rages, and he would receive most of his attention.

Kaiser had been born in 1918, and the Germans were naturally curious about his name. Why on earth was he called Kaiser? It turned out that his father had enlisted in a Gurkha regiment and been sent to France to fight the Germans. He might, then, have been expected to christen his son 'Haig' or 'Kitchener', but according to Beger's account Thapa senior revered the Kaiser as a fellow warrior. At any rate, the matter was decided when it was observed that the constellation Indians call Kag (or Kuk) had risen brightly in the evening sky as the boy emerged howling into the world. According to custom, he had to have a name that began with the letter K. In 2002, I discovered that Kaiser's son Taj had a different story altogether. Kaiser got his name on the principle that 'your enemy's enemy is my friend'. Kaiser was called Kaiser because his father had come to dislike the British.

Kaiser's father had died in 1924 and ever since then he had been responsible for looking after his mother and three sisters. He sent all his earnings home. By 1938, Nepalis like the Thapas had secured their position as Sikkim's secular elite, but when Beger visited the Thapa family home he was repelled by what he saw. There were 'tasteless pictures' on the walls, badly made family photographs jumbled up with 'disgusting' prints of gods, saints, even fashion models and Western advertisements. Everything was 'dirty and dusty' – a canonical refrain among most Europeans in Asia – and representative, Beger believed, of an elite that was desperately imitating its rulers, 'badly digesting' their culture and ignoring the values of its own. The Thapas represented a kind of *Mischlinge* or mixed-up culture that Germans despised.

Many of the men they hired would stay with them for the next year. Schäfer also took on Mandoy, a Hindu and a Dalit, or 'Untouchable', as his taxidermist. Mandoy was a hard-working man who slowly lost his feelings of inferiority, Schäfer says, in the company of Europeans who valued his meticulous work and happily shared their camp fire with him. At night Mandoy worked with Krause, both men bug-hunting with a light trap and ensnaring hundreds of moths, spiders, mantises, beetles and butterflies. A scene in *Geheimnis Tibet* shows Mandoy working with Schäfer in a charnelhouse of animal body parts and discarded horns and skins that was the expedition's open-air natural history laboratory. And there was Lezor the cook, who served the same food day after day until Schäfer threw a plate at him (Akeh, now the caravan leader, doubled as cook) and 'fearless and reliable' but frequently intoxicated Pänsy, Schäfer's servant.

Schäfer began hunting immediately, at first without official permission from the Chogyal. He bagged a vulture and an eagle and brought them back to Dilkushka. The lodge was already cluttered with the expedition's equipment, and one morning Schäfer was surprised by a visit from the Chogyal's secretary. Everything was hidden, the dead birds dragged on to the veranda. Later, Schäfer was on good enough terms with the Chogyal to ask his permission to hunt officially. This time he got what he wanted. When I met the naturalist Mr K. C. Pradhan in Gangtok, he showed me his father's diary: he'd recorded meeting Dr Schäfer and granting him permission to hunt following approval from the Chogyal. Schäfer took advantage of his permission as soon as possible and would face the Chogyal's wrath for excessive zeal on his return the following year.

It was in Gangtok that Beger began his anthropological work. He wanted to experiment making a head cast or mask – a difficult and time-consuming process which demanded of the subject considerable patience and endurance. Beger had made an arrangement to work with Akeh, but Schäfer sent him hunting instead so Beger was forced to use Passang, another sherpa, who, he realized, was unwell following a bad head injury the previous week. Despite this, Beger and Geer pressed ahead, with Kaiser helping them translate. It was a reckless decision, one that would bring the expedition to the brink of disaster.

The rushes of *Geheimnis Tibet*, held by the Library of Congress in Washington DC, show the making of an anthropological mask in detail. The raw gypsum has to be mixed with water and disinfectant and then globs are plastered over the unfortunate subject's face. Two straws are usually inserted into the nostrils, although they do little to relieve the feelings of intense claustrophobia. When the mask is finished, the subject has to sit completely still, resembling nothing so much as a mummy from a horror film. Every now and then, in Krause's film, he turns without expression to the camera. When the mask is at last removed it forms, of course, a negative, a reversed image of the subject's face, so the final stage is to mix a synthetic rubber solution which is poured into the mask. When it has set it is peeled away, revealing a precise simulacrum of the subject's face – a portrait in latex.

On that day in Gangtok, nothing went to plan. Beger

prepared the plaster and smeared it meticulously over Passang's face, but he failed to insert straws and merely wiped the clay away from the nostrils. Passang soon began to experience difficulties with his breathing. As Beger covered his eyes he saw he was very frightened, but he decided to continue. With most of Passang's face completely covered, they all settled down to wait. Beger held a stopwatch and smoked a cigarette. Then he realized with horror that Passang's head had begun to jerk grotesquely and the fragile globular mask had begun to break apart. Passang was, he could see with horror, having an epileptic seizure. Gurgling and foaming through the clay, he fell to the ground, his body arcing upwards then slumping violently down. He was sucking the wet clay into his mouth and nostrils and turning blue. Beger began to scrape the mask away from his face, plunging his fingers into Passang's throat. It was a scene of repulsive horror, but Passang was saved. He explained to his companions, Beger reported, that 'he was taken over by thoughts of torture . . . Everything started to rotate around him when the clay flowed into his nostrils . . . The mountain god Kangchendzonga had appeared before him, seized him and shaken him violently.' Beger's inexplicable (to him) activities, which he had tolerated full of fear and suspicion, had transported him into a world of demons.

Passang and the other porters found a picture of a grotesque demon god and showed it to Schäfer. It was a warning to unbelievers. Schäfer was outraged and turned on Beger. By this time, Geer and Kaiser had set off to find the local doctor and Schäfer was fearful of the repercussions. If the British – if *Hugh Richardson* – discovered what had happened the Germans could be expelled. There had been a confused discussion about whether getting a local doctor was in fact a good idea, but Kaiser and Geer failed to find him anyway. Schäfer gave Passang one of his best white shirts, which seemed to pacify him, and told his men that they would be sacked without pay if anything was said to outsiders. And no more face masks would be made in Gangtok.

Towards the end of June, after two weeks, they prepared to leave. On the morning of departure, the sound of gongs and booming wind instruments rose from the monasteries. The garishly decorated mules, tethered with yak hair, were readied for departure. Kaiser now showed his worth by expertly organizing the porters and their animals. There was a confused clamour. The scarred backs of the animals were draped with felt and crude wooden saddles were securely strapped on top; the expedition's boxes were then roped on in pairs. Kaiser and Geer darted between the docile mules, with their tinkling bells, making sure that their precious cargo was secure. Schäfer, by now the grizzled explorer again, drove them all hard. Everyone had seen at least one of his explosive rages and dreaded another.

The caravan set off, zig-zagging out of the village, past the Sikkim State Gaol, whose inmates gazed dolefully from barred windows and up into the hills that curved around the village. Occasionally a load would become entangled or a mule would take a wrong direction, but the German Tibet Expedition was, at last, en route. On the other side of the ridge, Schäfer turned directly north up the Tista Valley and away from the road that led to Lake Changhu and the Natu La Pass. This was the road to the Forbidden City. That morning it began to rain early and it was very hot. Birds shrieked and distant monastery bells chimed. They passed Lepcha huts made of woven bamboo and clearings where hump-backed cattle fed on the lush wet grass. Villagers watched the expedition impassively. As they climbed higher, the valley bottom disappeared in a chasm of sullen cloud. It was 21 June 1938.

Schäfer headed first for Chungtang, where the Tista Valley splits. One branch heads for Lachung, the other towards

Lachen and Thanggu, where Schäfer planned to make his base camp below Kangchendzonga. Although he had left the Lhasa road behind, he knew that Younghusband had first taken the road north through Lachen, crossed the Himalayas into Tibet and marched to Khampa Dzong. This surely is what he must have been referring to when he urged Schäfer to 'sneak over the border'. Unlike the Natu La, this pass was usually unobserved.

During the monsoon the Tista Valley is foggy and damp, its sides scarred by landslides. Entire mountainsides seem to fall away. Just after dawn, the towering serrated and snowy peaks of the Himalayas and Kangchendzonga are sometimes unveiled with startling clarity, resembling another rocky world beyond the horizon. The monsoon made travelling hard. The party was frequently halted by landslides – on one occasion Wienert faced a river of mud over two hundred feet across – and forced to wait while a new route was hacked out. Everyone was sodden. They were soon being feasted upon by that insidious tropical pest the leech. On a single day Schäfer counted fifty-three blood-bloated creatures latched onto his right foot, and forty-five sucking away on the other. Still more leeches were blindly and greedily making their way from trouser to sock and then over the rim of his boots, where they lodged until the evening. Krause discovered that any attempt at botanical collecting meant fending off a horde of leeches, all furiously aiming for the soft flesh between his fingers. And so the blood of the Master Race entered the leeches of Sikkim . . .

They reached Dikchu, the Devil's Water, where the Tista makes a dash through a narrow gorge. The old rope bridge was down and Krause filmed roll after roll as a brand-new bridge was yoked together from cane rope and tree trunks and flung across the bloated torrent. The caravan of mules and men then delicately crossed the wobbly structure. It was an exquisitely uncomfortable journey. The path was streaming wet and hemmed in on one side by a terrifyingly sheer drop to the seething river below and on the other by a vertical wall of rock laced with cascading waterfalls, fringed with maidenhair, which sprayed the already rain-sodden road. The thick and feverish monsoon air was impregnated with moisture and seemed to seep under the skin. After hours of climbing Schäfer was high enough to see the eastern slopes of Kangchendzonga ahead – a dark rocky mass in the late afternoon. At twilight, they made camp and sat around the fire ritually squeezing the blood from their socks. The puncture marks would itch maddeningly for days.

Although Schäfer was often a gloomy and bitter companion, life in camp settled down to a routine. It was a new experience for most of the Germans. One of their cases usually served as a dining table, writing table, smoking table, cartridge shelf and candle holder. Scattered around, but easily to hand, were scientific instruments, cameras, rifles, insect jars, books, eating utensils, cartridges, cases, tea kettles and pans. At night, Schäfer insisted that diaries were read out; in his book, he says this was to remind themselves that they were 'correct people'. At other times, they merely cursed the weather or stared out into the fog.

The rains usually began at five o'clock and lasted throughout the night. Schäfer lay awake tortured by 'painful uncertainty', listening to the big drops glutinously beating on the canvas. It was a peculiarly dispiriting sound. Mornings were always misty and damp, but as they travelled deeper into Sikkim, following the Tista up towards its glacial source, they were astonished by the fecundity of the landscape as it modulated from tropical forest into the magical alpine realm of the Yumthang Valley. There they walked through fields of gentians, blue poppies and wild strawberries. Occasionally the snow fortress of Kangchendzonga deigned to reveal itself, a dazzling apparition of red granite cliffs laden with ice and white spires climbing into startling cobalt-blue skies. When they looked over their shoulders, they could still see the distant Plain of Bengal shimmering in blue, pinky mauves laced with glittering silver bands: India's rivers in flood.

Schäfer's diaries are full of complaints about everyone except Kaiser. Although Akeh was an excellent shot and highly valued as a hunting partner by Schäfer, he was lazy and unreliable. Schäfer grumbled about 'the bad behaviour of our people when I am not there. Akeh is always the troublemaker of that lot: they don't even carry their own sleeping bags.' Then one day Akeh showed Schäfer a letter. 'Dear Son,' it read, 'Your wife died yesterday: come quickly then you will be here for the cremation . . .' Akeh's wife had, it seemed, been poisoned, possibly by her first husband. He cried bitterly and told Schäfer he had had a dream about 'a beautiful tree falling in front of his eyes'. An hour later he had gone. It seems he was not inconsolable for long. Later, his father reported that his 'wife' was in Gangtok doing housework. Akeh had lost little time finding himself a new companion.

Beger was now doing everything he could to impress the Sikkimese with his skills as a 'medicine man'. His motives were not entirely humanitarian. As his reputation spread, he was able to make anthropometric measurements and masks with much less difficulty. He simply used his patients. Beger had begun by treating the caravan's porters, but soon others heard about his powers and there was usually a queue of patients waiting as they passed through small hamlets and villages. He had a wide-ranging collection of drugs and medicines and he impressed on everyone the power of German science. Many of his patients were the higher Bhutia class who were less inclined to rely on traditional medicine than the Lepchas. Beger offered treatments for malaria, diarrhoea, eye infections, sores and skin problems, rheumatism and broken limbs. His work, however, sometimes brought him into conflict with monks. On one occasion he was asked to treat a young woman who was suffering from an abscess behind her knee. He prescribed an antiseptic ointment. When he returned a day or so later he was turned away by the young woman's father who angrily told the stupid European that her leg was possessed by a demon. A monk had taken charge of her treatment. He had forbidden her to sleep and there was pandemonium as everyone banged drums and blew trumpets to scare away the demon. After his experience in east Tibet, where gonorrhoea and syphilis were endemic, Schäfer had made sure that Beger carried treatments for venereal disease, and he would discover that even monks would be in need of this particular service.

The Germans took a keen interest in the sexual mores of native people. In his anthropological notes, Beger recorded some of his discoveries:

> The Sikkim-Bhutia say that their women start masturbating when their husbands are absent for a longer period of time by rubbing their heels against their vaginas. But this only applies if the women are faithful. Masturbation by women is unknown to the Lepchas, the Lachen-people and the Tibetans. Masturbation of men and boys also seems to be pretty much unknown. While riding from Chungtang to Lachung, Untersturmführer Krause observed a ca. 15 years old girl, who had lain down on a carved beam, moving rhythmically. There is a saying in Sikkim: 'When a girl has feelings in her vagina, she sticks her heel in; this way she gets dirt in it and then it itches even more . . .'

Karl Wienert, too, was hard at work in his attempt to quantify the mysterious power of the Earth, which proved to be as tricky as measuring its people. Wienert's teacher Wilhelm Filchner had completed a number of gruelling geomagnetic and topographical surveys across the high interior of Asia, the first in 1903 and the most recent between 1935 and 1937. He had returned with spectacular new data, the pride of German science. Filchner had established a chain of magnetic stations across the northern borders of Tibet in the Kunlun Range; Wienert's task was to do the same in the Himalayas, to the south.

In the nineteenth century, unmapped regions of the world were simply shown as white spaces. The explorer's mission was to fill in those provocative lacunae, 'to trace lines upon the unknown corners of the earth'.[10] For geophysicists, Sikkim and southern Tibet were magnetic white spaces. The problems were, of course, intertwined. For the last seven hundred years, explorers and navigators have been able to exploit one astonishing property of the Earth. Inside its core is a mass of liquid iron which slowly rotates below the crust. Its slow movement works like a dynamo, turning the Earth into an immense magnet with a magnetic field and a north and south pole. The invention of the compass some seven centuries ago made it possible for navigators and explorers to fix their direction of travel in relation to the north magnetic pole – the direction in which the tiny needles of their compasses always pointed. These magnetic poles lie close to the geographic North and South Poles, but hold a compass in the palm of your hand in Berlin and its needle will point four degrees away from north to the west; in San Francisco, twenty degrees to the east. This is the declination. If your compass was constructed so that its needle could hang freely in space it would not only be in error horizontally but vertically too – this is called the inclination. Scientists like Filchner and Wienert measured these discrepancies to create a three-dimensional image of magnetic variation. It was also realized that magnetic readings varied over time, so Wienert had to record both exactly where he was and the precise time when he made the measurements. In the field, quite complicated and cumbersome apparatus is needed to record as precisely as possible declination and inclination as well as the exact location and time of each reading.

Almost everything scientists like Filchner and Wienert were measuring was connected with that liquid iron dynamo slowly rotating deep down in the Earth's core. So, standing in the Himalayas, not far from the highest place on the planet, Wienert was actually measuring something that was being generated near the planet's centre. But when Wienert was taking his measurements in 1938 scientists knew virtually nothing about the core; Wienert probably did not understand where or how the magnetic field was generated in the first place. In effect, then, he was making measurements in the dark, blindfolded, hoping that a few extra statistics would somehow throw light on this great mystery of the Earth.

But his measurements would be of more immediate practical use for future travellers or mapmakers in Tibet, who might need to rely on a compass. As an explorer moved across a landscape, filling in the blanks on his maps, he had to be aware that his compass needle was fickle, and the geomagnetic data gathered by men like Filchner and Wienert allowed him to make appropriate adjustments. German scientists were very good at geomagnetic measurement; the unit of magnetic force, the *Gauss*, was named after one of the most outstanding of all scientists, Carl Friedrich Gauss. And, of course, there is nothing intrinsically sinister or 'Nazi' about measuring earth magnetism. It is conceivable that Himmler believed Wienert's work could make some contribution to the *Welteislehre* (the World Ice Theory) – after all, Wienert was in the very region where the Aryan ancestral race, wrapped in icy shrouds, was alleged to have descended to Earth – but Beger remembers that Himmler's 'theories' about human origins were often discussed around the camp fire and were much valued as comedy, so presumably if Wienert had any interest in glacial cosmogony it involved a tongue and a cheek as well as a theodolite.

But it would be a mistake to conclude that as Untersturmführer Wienert tramped up mountains in Sikkim his activities had nothing to do with Germany's New Order. From the turn of the century, German geographers had played a vital political role in defining ideas about *Lebensraum* and the *Drang nach Osten* – the push to the east. Along with anthropologists like Günther and Ludwig Ferdinand Clauss, geographers had insinuated into intellectual life ideas about the intimate connection between the land and the *Volk*, between blood and geographical space. After 1933, these ideas were endorsed by Hitler and Himmler, their racial bounty drawn out like poison from a snake. The German *Herrenvolk* demanded space to live, in the East or in Africa, which it deserved as a sacred right; geographers were called on to define not merely Germany as a state within political borders but also as a *Volksboden* and a *Kulturboden*, an ethnic and cultural territory, which stretched minds to thoughts of colonization and conquest. Geographers surveyed places and regions, anthropologists measured and calibrated living people, but both could come to the same conclusions about races and landscapes: that they belonged together, fed each other. A pure-blooded *Volk* was naturally wedded to a landscape; mixed races were estranged. Jews and gypsies were victimized by these ideas because they were viewed as races without a homeland. In fact, most geographers welcomed the new regime in 1933; very few were driven into exile. One claimed that 'German geography today is proud to make its results and its work . . . available to the leadership of the state.'[11] After 1939, German geographers worked hand in hand with

German conquerors, mapping new conquests as 'Germandom' expanded in the wake of the tanks and Stukas of the Reich.[12]

Every morning, Wienert closely supervised his porters as they packed and strapped to the back of mules his two Kleine Hildebrandt theodolites, two chronometers, a shortwave radio for time signals, a hypsometer and four aneroids to measure atmospheric pressure, two boiling-point thermometers, and a magnetometer specially designed for the travelling geophysicist by Gustav Schulze of Potsdam. Inside their gleaming brass carapaces were delicate mechanisms that were intolerant of a lurching ride up stony, treacherous paths, but during these monsoon months rust was Wienert's greatest enemy. For most of the day the heat and the humidity were punishing, then the rains came, drenching his cases.

As they struggled higher into the outlying ranges of the Himalayas, Wienert was frustrated by cloudy skies, frequent storms and bitterly cold weather. It took him a month to feel comfortable at high altitude. He later wrote that 'perfect work was nearly impossible'. It was fortunate that Wienert was blessed with a dry Prussian sense of humour. The work itself was useless if it was not meticulous. Alcohol was a frequent solace. Beger's diaries record an episode when both he and Wienert had imbibed a great many Tibetan beers. Long after midnight they uncertainly made their way back to Wienert's 'measuring tent' and proceeded, much the worse for wear, to make geomagnetic 'swing measurements'. 'One, two, Achtung stop! I had to say this 168 times in the course of one measurement. It may have been the 73rd time that I forgot the "Stop!" The alcohol and the exhaustion! Then we pulled ourselves together once more, the measurements were repeated and the whole thing completed properly . . .'

At the end of June, Schäfer led his men north to Lachen, where they made camp in the garden of an inn. It was an idyllic few days in a village that reminded them of the Tyrol. Doctor-sahib Beger dispensed his medicine and was able to take scores of measurements, and to make face masks without incident. He had one problem, though: the local farmers 'were very dirty and smelt so badly that at first I had great difficulty overcoming my disgust'. In camp, damaged equipment was repaired, and Schäfer spent days furiously typing the first chapters of what would become *Geheimnis Tibet*. What made Lachen unusual was the presence of a Finnish Missionary Station, although during this visit the German Tibet Expedition disdained to have much contact with the missionaries since they all professed to despise evangelical Christians. In early July, members of a British Mount Everest Expedition, one of many in the 1930s, passed through the area and Schäfer invited them to join them for a meal. One of the Everest team, Peter Lloyd, spoke good German and there was heated debate about Hitler. It turned into an uncomfortable evening, and was another reminder of how vulnerable were their reputations as 'pure scientists'.

After Lachen they worked their way higher towards Thanggu, where they would make their first high-altitude – or alpine, as Schäfer called it – base camp. Now they took on yaks as well as mules, because yaks are adapted to altitude. They were just fifteen miles from the Tibetan border. The journey through forests of rhododendron and walnut towards the tree line had been tough. Everyone was suffering from the altitude, and daily rains continued to make their lives miserable. The mule tracks were slippery and treacherous; paths were frequently blocked or had been swept away. They had to cross replete, foaming rivers on terrifying bridges made from plaited branches and creepers. Krause was injured in a rock fall. The porters were exhausted, and making sure the caravan kept moving onwards and upwards was a daily fight. Local Bhutia villagers in the north were angry that all the animals had been hired in Gangtok and were threatening to withhold food. Despite this, their first alpine field camp was built close to a small monastery in the shadow of Kangchendzonga on the great curving tongue of the Zemu Glacier.

To everyone's relief, Schäfer had his own tent, but there was little escape from his dark moods and fits of bad temper. In the evenings, his colleagues read out their diaries, usually to much hilarity, while Schäfer brooded in his tent and read *Faust*. Only Kaiser knew what he was planning next. The porters had names for everyone: Schäfer was Bara-sahib, or Great Master; Geer was Store-sahib (because he was in charge of provisions); Beger was Doctor-sahib; Krause was Picture-sahib. Karl Wienert was called Tar-sahib apparently because he operated the radio, although the derivation is not clear.

Beger recorded that on their first night in the alpine camp it rained continuously, but he awoke to virgin snow which covered the plateau to the horizon. The temperature had plummeted; it was time to get out the warm underwear and heavy leather coats. Schäfer and his comrades were now in the realm of the mythical Yeti, or Migyud the apeman god of Buddhist mythology, or, as Schäfer knew, in reality the Tibetan bear. Not far from their camp was a lake whose water modulated through every shade of green as the sun arced across the sky. Green Lake was, according to local legend, the lair of the Migyud, and the camp's proximity to the legendary creature's alleged home led to much whispered speculation and anxiety. For the rest of his life Schäfer would poke fun at believers in the apemen of the Himalayas. In 1938 he became exasperated as day and night his men fearfully discussed Migyuds, and he took to playing tricks on them by faking its footprints in the snow.

Thanggu had a bad reputation even among hardened travellers. Some blamed the water, but it was simply the altitude. At twelve thousand feet everyone was severely altitude sick for weeks. It is one of the most disagreeable conditions. The sufferer endures perpetual nausea and dizziness; bending down to tie a boot lace feels like a tumbling, vertiginous fall. The heart pounds violently as if it is struggling to escape. Walking brings on pains in the chest and throbbing headaches, even sudden fits of weeping. A few of the porters were so ill that they visited a *tulku* – an incarnate lama – in the little monastery. They had scant interest in Beger's medicine chest this time.

Now that he had his base camp, Schäfer was, as ever, determined to reap a mammalian harvest for the museums of the Reich. He had already shot gorals near Chungtang by stripping off, he said, the veneer of a 'civilized man' and becoming an animal, thinking and feeling with the beast he would kill. At Thanggu he wanted to film and then shoot the mysterious bharal, or 'blue sheep'.[13] The bharal is neither blue – although some describe it as being slate-blue – nor a sheep, and its biological identity still vexes naturalists. It is a rather noble and sure-footed animal with large horns and is usually hunted by the snow leopard. Every morning Schäfer, Kaiser, Krause and his servant Mingma set out with rifles and camera in search of the elusive animal. It was often foggy, and climbing the wet rocky slopes was difficult. Krause was soon exhausted, panting heavily, and Schäfer feared he was on the point of collapsing. He was becoming impatient with the differing abilities of his small team, although he described the consequences with some humour: 'Krause wants me to climb slower. I want him to climb faster. One of us sees the landscape and is on the lookout for sheep. The other observes every flower and when he sees a rare bee, then he forgets all the blue sheep in the world.' The frustrating chase went on for weeks. As Schäfer hunted, Beger measured the occasional passing Tibetan or assisted the hard-pressed Wienert. Finally, after several frustrating days, Krause succeeded in filming the legendary bharals: 'At last Krause is laughing and Geer is laughing and Pänsy and we are all laughing. It's like a salvation when you are eventually victorious after three weeks of struggle with the mountains.'

As the weeks passed, Schäfer shot many bharals and extended his hunting grounds into the valley of the Zemu Glacier on the north side of Kangchendzonga. He had at first been unwilling to do this because it had been explored so many times by climbers, including the 'Great Beast of the Apocalypse' Aleister Crowley in 1905 and the German Paul Bauer in 1929. Bauer had climbed and tunnelled through the Zemu Glacier before being beaten back by blizzards at 24,150 feet. One morning, Schäfer stumbled on Bauer's old camp and its depot of untouched tinned food.

Schäfer hunted with a relentless passion, Akeh and his porters dragging his bloody trophies back to the camp. He bagged argali (wolves) and beautiful wild kiangs. As Younghusband marched towards Tibet in 1903 his men had also seen these lovely animals and 'At first we mistook them for detachments of Tibetan cavalry, the wild horsemen of the Chungtang, as they came galloping in a whirlwind of dust, then executed a perfect wheel around . . .' A lone kiang attempted to escape Schäfer's fire by galloping into the expedition camp, only to be attacked by mules. Schäfer ended its agony quickly, feeling 'like a murderer'. When I visited Lachen in 2002 I met Kelsang Gyatso, a retired school teacher who remembered the Schäfer party. He told me he had heard that the Germans drank blood. I was told the same in Gangtok – and Bruno Beger confirmed the story. It seems that Schäfer did indeed cut the throats of some of the animals he killed and drank their blood. It conferred strength and potency.

Beger told me another odd story. One morning, Schäfer

stalked out of his tent carrying his gun. As the others watched, he stomped through the snow towards the horizon. It was the anniversary of Hertha's death. Beger watched with foreboding. On the ridge, Schäfer froze and swung his rifle stock up to his shoulder. Beger saw an unusually bright flash, and Schäfer reeled backwards, his hat flying through the air, the rifle falling into the powdery snow. Now the other Germans ran up to the ridge. They found Schäfer picking himself up and turning over the broken rifle. There were powder burns on his cheeks. He had forgotten to remove the cleaning brush and the breach had exploded, sending a fragment of steel ripping through his hat. Beger still possesses that shattered piece of steel – a macabre memento of Ernst Schäfer's memorial to Hertha.[14]

From Thanggu, Schäfer pressed on further north to Gayokang, which was high above the tree line. This meant that their already overburdened mules and yaks now had to carry firewood in addition to their normal loads. Schäfer had been delighted to see yaks again, but as pack animals they are less reliable than mules. Their Latin name, *Bos grunniens*, means 'grumbling ox', and it is deserved. When their packs are being loaded they can be temperamental. After that, they make slow, disconsolate progress.

High on the flanks of Kangchendzonga, it was hard to find level ground to pitch their tents. Schäfer's much smaller *Führer* tent ended up on a slope, much to his irritation. During the long freezing night, he rolled out into the snow. It was an offence to his vanity and his comfort, and in the morning he was furious. Even Wienert, who was most loyal to Schäfer, was repelled by his rage. That same day he had a bitter argument with Schäfer that damaged their friendship for ever. The argument, Beger believes, was over Schäfer's treatment of Kaiser's horse. He had quite simply ridden it to death. 'He had a relationship to horses I didn't like,' Beger recalls. Schäfer's equestrian sadism tested even Kaiser's loyalty. When he acquired a new horse, he made sure it was ridden only by himself and Beger.

Although the expedition was tantalizingly close to the border with Tibet, there was still no sign that they would ever be granted permission to cross, let alone to travel as far as Lhasa. So far, Schäfer's expedition had accomplished nothing to compete with Brooke Dolan's. When Schäfer had travelled to Tachienlu and beyond, there had, to be sure, been problems with local warlords but the border between China and Tibet was in flux and Chiang Kai-shek's Kuomintang had little if any authority on the far reaches of his fragile empire. So in practice the border with Tibet was quite permeable. Here in Sikkim, the British presence combined with Tibetan protectiveness now made for a potentially intractable barrier. Schäfer kept up the pressure, though, applying to Gould for a 'trade route pass' that would allow him to travel as far as Gyantse, and then making another bid for Lhasa. There were many plans still in play – even Assam came up again – but no sign that any of them would be realized. It was only July, and Schäfer was already facing the chilling prospect of having to return to Germany and the office of the Reichsführer empty-handed. Then the Finnish missionaries they had regarded with such contempt in Lachen inadvertently offered a way out.

Fearing he would never see Lhasa, Schäfer had begun to make profligate use of his resources hunting in the high glacial valleys of Kangchendzonga. After one long-drawn-out pursuit of takin (large Tibetan horned ruminants) he ran out of provisions, so a sherpa was sent back south in search of more supplies. When he arrived in Lachen, he told the much-despised Finnish missionaries about Schäfer's plight. The missionaries sent their own servant with food, and blessings, to Schäfer's beleaguered camp. Their saviour turned out to be a young Christian Tibetan called Timothy,[15] and Schäfer took an immediate liking to him. He invited Timothy to join him and his comrades around the camp fire and they began to discuss local hunting. Timo, as Schäfer took to calling his new friend, told one story that was very interesting indeed. Timo had heard many tales about a secretive goat-like creature that had been occasionally spotted near Chungtang. The Lepcha believed that it lived in a hidden place of precipitous and rocky cliffs, and they called it the shapi.[16] For them, Timo said, this 'black mountain ghost' was a sacred animal, a god that no-one must harm or even speak about; it had been created long ago as a wedding present for the god of Kangchendzonga to present to his daughter. (Oddly, 'shapi' is also a term of abuse. Being told that you have 'a face like a shapi' is not a compliment.)

Schäfer's reaction to Timothy's tale, which he made him repeat a number of times that evening, was to say the least enthusiastic: 'Now I am frantic and ecstatic. I am ablaze – as if a fire was burning inside me. *Shapi – Shapi – Shapi.* I bellow like a bull, run up and down obsessively, call all the Sahibs [his colleagues] into my tent . . .' Timothy is made to repeat his story yet again, and Schäfer made it very clear how the shapi could contribute to the greater glory of the expedition. 'I jump to my feet. I believe this fellow – all this can't be fiction. Gentlemen, this will – it has to be – the greatest scientific discovery of the expedition. Devil, Devil [*sic*] this is going to be a success for Germany.' Then came his most revealing words: 'But what will the *English Gentlemen* say? They who believe they are so clever [in German, the phrase is '*die Weisheit mit Löffeln gefressen haben*', which means they who 'have spooned up wisdom'] and think they know the Himalayas and Tibet better than anyone else.' In a calmer frame of mind, he added, 'It is as I have suspected for a long time. There is a new great animal in the mountains. All biological findings point in that direction.'

Having resolved that a dead shapi, if one could be successfully bagged, would be good for Germany, Schäfer even began dreaming about this unfortunate, ugly animal that was no doubt skulking in its rocky hideaway in blissful ignorance of the German's plans. 'A shapi ram, black as Satan, is standing on the peak of a rock. I'm lying in front of him and shoot . . . shoot . . . shoot but all the bullets rise too slowly and I see them fall into the snow. The shapi merely quivers and disappears in a cloud.' It is not necessary to be pruriently Freudian to suspect that Schäfer felt his manhood was at stake. Timothy further tantalized Schäfer by showing him an ancient hide from a shapi that had been killed long ago. Its odour suggested that it was related to the tahr, another goatlike native of the region.

Now the shapi hunt began in earnest. Schäfer decided to split the expedition; only he and Geer would hunt the shapi, because the route was extremely dangerous. Because Krause had shown himself to be a less than adventurous climber, there would be no filming. This implies that Schäfer wanted complete control of how the shapi story would unfold and how it would later be represented. The hunting of the shapi would be his tale and he would be its hero. Geer was his most devoted and loyal colleague – a simple man, schooled in military obedience, who was patient and calm where Schäfer was tense and excitable. Geer had impressed the Sikkimese when faced with one landslide: he had held up his bamboo walking stick and appeared to stop a boulder in its tracks. After this incident he was called the 'German Lama' and the magical bamboo stick would be brought out whenever there was trouble.

Geer and Schäfer returned to Chungtang, where they hired – and this is significant – fresh porters. This was going to be Schäfer's show, but he was taking a risk. The fourteen new men were all Lepchas, who might decide that their wages were not worth the destruction of a sacred animal. The party headed out of Chungtang towards a little-known region between the Talung and Lachen Valleys and everyone hoped that the shapi would be at home.

The land of the shapi turned out to be much more difficult and dangerous to reach than Schäfer had imagined. From the valley bottom the men had to climb sheer rock faces sheathed in dense bamboo jungle. For some reason, they had left all their rope in Chungtang and were therefore in constant peril, climbing 'like flies on a wall' and camping on narrow rock ledges. The bamboo gave way to rhododendrons, which grew here as great trees with scaly red bark and emerald-green foliage. They struggled through dense forests of thorny trees, gloomy swamps and, as they got even higher, great fields of barren, fog-shrouded stones. On the other side, they descended into clumps of trees hundreds of feet high with swooping, clinging tendrils. It was either hot and humid – or bitterly cold. Underfoot was a perilous carpet of decaying vegetation which often gave way. Timo and his Lepcha companions, however, knew how to track. They understood that silence was essential. To maintain it, they would even kneel down and cough into the snow, to muffle the sound.

When they at last reached the plateau, Schäfer almost immediately spotted tracks and hair which he was convinced had been left by a shapi. He was exhausted but very excited. Soon afterwards he caught sight of his first shapis – they look like horned black goats – and started shooting. Six times he missed, and he began to wonder if the unsightly, sacred animal was somehow invulnerable. After that the weather closed in, shrouding the plateau in fog and snow. The intrepid hunters retreated to a cave still known to local villagers as the 'German Cave'. A powerful storm buffeted the mountain, sending flurries of snow and showers of ice particles into their shelter. Schäfer passed the time by declaiming verses from *Faust*:

> *How strangely through the hollows glimmering*
> *Like a false dawn the dull light glows!*
> *Into crevasses glinting, shimmering,*
> *Into each deep abyss it goes.*
> *Clouds drift, a vapour rises, yet*
> *Through veils of mist that radiance gleams . . .*[17]

Geer was soon asleep.

For five days the snows came down, then they resumed the hunt. Conditions worsened, although Schäfer wrote that he faced them with 'devilish lust'. In a 'Satan abyss' of cliffs, rock falls, precipices and knife-edged peaks, the little party struggled on. The Lepchas 'crawled like squirrels after us'. 'Arrogant' boulders crashed down the mountainsides, narrowly missing the hunters. They made camp above a roaring waterfall, where Geer endured more readings from *Faust*.

A week passed before they so much as glimpsed another shapi, and then only fleetingly and at a distance. Schäfer missed again. It became obvious that the Lepchas – 'wild, animal like people', according to *Geheimnis Tibet* – were not helping. When Schäfer demanded to know the identity of some dung he had discovered, he had to force one of them to confess that it was indeed shapi spoor. They had to be getting close. Climbing was now very hard, especially with no ropes and unsuitable boots. Schäfer forged ahead while Geer ruthlessly drove on the rest of the party behind. On the rockiest slopes they made improvised ropes with bamboo shoots. At night, Schäfer became haunted by the 'enchanted forest' and imagined himself surrounded by cunning goblins and malicious gnomes – memories from his childhood introduction to the magic of the hunt by Herr Direktor. But soon, Schäfer found his own shapi hair; he was 'radiantly happy' and sat for some time gloating over his prize and chewing boiled rice from a thermos. When he finally saw the legendary goat, it was an epiphany, a 'picture for the gods'. The shapi had curved, sweeping horns, long manes and jet-black, muscular bodies. They quickly fled, bouncing across the rocky terrain like rubber balls. More adventures followed, the men sustained only by apples and onion soup, but a few days later he had a shapi in his sights and Schäfer pulled his trigger. 'The first, royal [*sic*] Shapi falls freely hundreds of metres, with a bullet in his right eye – and lands with a great thud . . .' Soon he had bagged two more males and three females.

Schäfer and Geer returned in triumph to the camp. German scientific pride had been satisfied, and the shapi would eventually be named *Hermitragus jemlahicus schäferi* when its stuffed carcass was delivered to the Berlin Natural History Museum a year later. Schäfer's claim, made in desperate times, has since been disputed; the shapi may not be much different from the tahr, another goatlike mammal. (Just fourteen shapi survive today in the same valley where Schäfer discovered them in 1938.)

Every evening as the sun set, Schäfer and his colleagues could gaze north across the humpbacked ridges of Sikkim, sculpted into fantastic shapes by the long shadows, to the five soaring peaks of Kangchendzonga. Other giants lay beyond: Everest, Kangcherjhau, Pauhunri and Chomolhari. Then, turning to the north-east, Schäfer trained his binoculars on a lower line of jagged, snow-covered spires and focused on a thin grey wedge that sliced into the snow and rock. It was the Natu La Pass, piercing the Himalayan wall at over fourteen thousand feet. On the other side lay the Chumbi Valley, and then Tibet. Beyond were 380 miles of rocky passes, salt lakes and bleak treeless plains before the stony trail swooped down to the slow, yellow waters of the Tsang Po and the road to Lhasa.

As the last light faded to aquamarine over white snow, Schäfer put down his binoculars. In that summer of 1938, he might as well have been contemplating a trip to the moon. It was time to launch the Younghusband Plan.

CHAPTER EIGHT

BREAKOUT

'I did not hesitate for a moment . . . I would not retrace a single step of my trail. I was swept away by the irresistible desiderium incogniti *which breaks down all obstacles and refuses to recognize the impossible.'*

– Sven Hedin

According to legend, Kangchendzonga, the great God Mountain of Sikkim, makes many promises. In the limpid depths of his glacial lakes reside the gods of fertility, and women once made pilgrimages there to secure their blessing. Legends told of a golden palace locked away behind sheer walls of ice; hidden inside were all the treasures the mountain god had accumulated and hoarded.

On a July afternoon in 1938, Ernst Schäfer, enthroned in his new camp, resplendently bearded and with his diary open in front of him, observed the arrival of his third spring in a single year. The first had brought daffodils to St James's Park as he'd argued with Foreign Office officials in London; a few weeks later, spring had come to Berlin as he'd made preparations to leave for India; now, at last, it made a 'wild, exultant cry' in the Himalayas. The monsoon was finally sputtering out in brief flurries of snow and evening rains.

Schäfer tilted his head up towards the jagged peaks of Kangchendzonga, now turning from pink to dazzling white, then began writing in his execrable hand: 'We are at Tibet's frontier. It is the realm of our most powerful yearning. Up there, not far away at all, is the border pass.' This, Schäfer knew, was where Younghusband had first crossed into Tibet on 4 July 1903: the Kangra La Pass to Khampa Dzong where Lord Curzon had instructed him to meet and negotiate with the Tibetans. Schäfer went on: 'There are neither guards nor sentinels, neither barrier nor gates – at that lonely altitude, there is only an obo [a heap of stones, or animal bones] wrapped in prayer flags . . . I have promised the Viceroy . . . not to cross the Tibetan border . . . without "Official Leave". And as a German I am not willing to break a promise. But what does "Official Leave" mean?'

Schäfer's diaries show how he struggled to make the best of long months in Sikkim. He described it as a unique biological laboratory hemmed in by Nepal, Bhutan, India and Tibet. Its valleys and ravines were like greenhouses that had preserved unique and little-known species of animals and plants, which would be studied thoroughly 'in the German manner' over several months. He appears to have forgotten that the English botanist and explorer (as well as amateur geologist, geographer, meteorologist and cartographer) Sir Joseph Dalton Hooker had used almost precisely the same words in 1848. Hooker had thoroughly explored Sikkim with a team of fifty-six plant and bird collectors and porters. Sikkim was by no means a 'white space', and Schäfer must have known this in his heart. He closed his diary, grabbed a rifle and stalked off into the snow to hunt.

Later that afternoon, it began to rain. Bruno Beger was alone in camp working on his anthropological notebooks. Looking up through the open flap of his tent, he noticed a splendidly attired man riding past the camp in the direction of the Kangra La. He suspected, rightly, that he was an official of some kind and invited him to take shelter and share some tea. The official was very pleased to get out of the rain, and he and Beger got along famously. It soon emerged that he was a minister for the man the Germans would always call the 'King of Tharing'. The minister even allowed Beger to measure him and gave him *tsampa* bowls and dried meat as presents.

When Schäfer returned to camp, Geer told him what was happening. Although Beger must have already come to the same conclusion, Schäfer immediately understood that fate had delivered him a way of acquiring 'Official Leave' and trumping the 'English Gentlemen'. He asked Beger to keep the minister happy while he, as expedition leader, prepared an even grander display. There was an urgent, whispered conference, then Krause, Wienert, Geer and their servants rushed off to prepare a theatre of seduction in Schäfer's tent. They brought their cameras, theodolites, lenses and altimeters and piled them high in a gleaming pyramid while Schäfer searched desperately for matching socks and a proper suit. They brought out sacks of provisions, boxes of biscuits and other delicacies, and made tea. Finally, Schäfer, who was shorter than Beger, inflated a rubber cushion, placed it on his camp stool, sat on it in elevated splendour – looking like, in Schäfer's words, a 'wholly great man' – and sent Kaiser to bring the minister into his presence ('the curtain rises, the performance can begin').

Their visitor must have had sharp eyes. However impressed he was with Schäfer's display, the conversation turned immediately to vegetables. His employer, the Tering Raja, had a passion for them, but it was difficult to obtain any at his palace in

Doptra, just over the border on the shores of Lake Gayamtsona (Tsomo Dramling). The Germans had, he could see, plenty of vegetables; could he return with some for the king? His request was granted with enthusiasm; their best green vegetables, eighty kilograms of potatoes and some choice German delicacies were quickly packed. Schäfer now broached the subject of the border. He told the minister about his travels in the East and, as he always did when he met any influential Tibetan, his meeting in 1935 with the Panchen Lama. He then ordered more presents to be piled in front of the minister: they included chocolate, biscuits, medicine, sugar, rice, leather gloves, woollen gloves, woollen socks, towels and soap, wellington boots, leggings, a rubber mattress and a rubber pillow, and an enticing tube of Nivea cream. It was a magnificent spread. The minister asked Schäfer to compose a letter addressed to the king making his case; he promised he would take it to Doptra the following day. Schäfer ordered Kaiser to accompany the minister and promised him a pay rise if he came back with permission to see the 'King of Tharing'. Kaiser and the minister left, with the vegetables and the letter, the following day. Schäfer celebrated with a thick but mouldy cigar, and waited.

He spent most of the time shooting and collecting in the mountains while Beger measured and made masks. He and Wienert occasionally set out on geomagnetic missions. A spell of beautiful weather gave Krause an opportunity to photograph some of these activities, which are shown briefly at the beginning of *Geheimnis Tibet*. What Krause filmed can be seen at length in the rushes, confiscated in 1945 and now held in the Library of Congress in Washington DC. The subject for the head cast was Pänsy, Schäfer's servant. He was extremely nervous: the Gangtok disaster had not been forgotten. Beger's victims always feared suffocation, and if they survived the ordeal to them the mask itself resembled the 'demon masks' of

Tibetan festivals. So as he smeared the gypsum over Pänsy's face, Beger could hear him breathing loudly and fearfully. With his face entirely covered, they waited for the mask to set, but Pänsy's head rolled backwards alarmingly. Krause had to stop filming to support him. But this time all went well. The mask set perfectly and was easily removed. Beger then poured in the latex and, like a conjuror, drew out the finished face mask. It was a great success. Everybody loved recognizing Pänsy.

Beger had more difficulty with a striking young woman he began measuring that same day. In the rushes, we can see that at first she giggles and pushes Beger away quite playfully, but as he insistently and probably painfully takes his callipers to her arms and then starts to measure her hips, she indignantly lashes out and strikes him across the face. These moments were edited out of Schäfer's film, but the real-time event is still preserved in the rolls held by the Library of Congress. They demonstrate that violence underpinned the practice of physical anthropology. Measuring bodies and making masks was not much different from possessing them or turning them into lifeless cadavers.

There is another ingredient in these scenes, of course, and that is sex. Anthropologists had always been fascinated by the sexuality of their native subjects, and by their own responses to it. In the nineteenth century, photography and the need to make scientific measurements gave European anthropologists access to naked bodies in the field – an experience that was repressed in their Victorian homes. Anthropological expeditions were voyages that took scientists out of the drawing room and lecture hall and into the realms of desire. Beger was certainly not immune to native charms. One evening he 'sat next to a pretty female sherpa around one of the fires, very close as there was little space. She looked at me in a way which made me feel very odd and indicated that her bare knee was cold and stiff. I could only comfort her by caressing it – then she took my hand and played with it. Oh well, we sahibs are only human after all – forced to exercise iron restraint.' Beger discovered later that the woman had a polyandrous marriage; her two husbands were also members of the expedition.

Late one afternoon, Kaiser returned. Schäfer was in the hills shooting and filming with Krause, so Mingma, Krause's assistant, ran to fetch them back to camp. Schäfer sent everyone ahead. 'Superstitiously, as we half-wild children of nature are, I let my comrade climb down to the camp alone – and I convince myself it is good will power training to repress my curiosity.' Kaiser did have good news. He had returned with a letter from the 'king' wrapped in a white *kata* scarf; it invited them all to spend three days at his summer residence. Schäfer wrote, 'the joy was inconceivable'. He decided that there was 'no time' to inform the British, or his own consul in Calcutta.

Schäfer knew that there was still no invitation to visit Lhasa. The Tering Raja might only be the first step on that much tougher road, and he was running the severe risk of antagonizing the British when they eventually found out, as he knew they must, about his incursion. So Schäfer made some hard calculations. He would take only Kaiser and Krause with him to Doptra, not the entire expedition. Beger and Wienert would continue their scientific work in northern Sikkim; Geer would begin re-provisioning the expedition. Schäfer could claim, if need be, that he had merely responded to a personal invitation – one 'king' to another – and the activities of his comrades would serve as a diversion. By taking Krause he ensured that he would return to Germany with at least some film of Tibet and its culture in the event that they did not make it to Lhasa.

On 30 July, Schäfer, Krause, Kaiser and a little caravan of porters and servants set off towards the border. For some time they followed the icy flanks of Kangchendzonga, and then began climbing up towards the Kangra La Pass. The valley was pastel-coloured, barren and desolate except for low scrub and dwarf rhododendrons. Then at seventeen thousand feet they crossed the border into Tibet. In front of them lay an immense plain completely devoid of trees. At this moment Schäfer was, according to the British files, 'committing an offence under Regulation 5 of 1893', but for Schäfer and Krause it was a transcendent moment. They began to ride down the other side of the pass into the Forbidden Land in the footsteps of Sir Francis Younghusband.

There must have been some envy among Schäfer's colleagues. Wienert and Beger took another route to the edge of Tibet the same day, shadowing Schäfer's trail. Following a stone pillar on the horizon as a sight line – it turned out to be a colossal boulder when they reached it – they struggled up to sixteen thousand feet. In front of them stretched the Tibetan highlands, range upon range of rust-red mountains with snowy peaks and beyond them yet more ranges dissolving into the extreme distance. 'How much we longed for this!' Beger wrote in his diary. The air was very clear. They could make out Schäfer's little expedition and even Khampa Dzong itself with its towering fortress (the *dzong*) – a halfway point on the road to Doptra. Beger and Wienert knew that everything depended on the tiny figures they could just about see miles below them.

Schäfer later recalled riding down from the Kangra La into a 'lunar landscape' – the immense Tibetan plateau that stretched ahead of them like an ocean, 'monotonous, deep, fantastic and wild'. By mid morning the sun was bright and hot in a violet-blue sky. For the first day they rode in silence until the long shadows cast by the dark ochre mountains lengthened, metamorphosed into a deep red then faded to black. They made their first camp and sat round the fire eating *tsampa*, thrilled by their illicit journey. In the morning, Schäfer insisted that

Krause film as much as possible when they reached the first Tibetan settlements, so progress was slow. They spotted Everest ninety miles to the west. After crossing a cold, desolate plain, they turned towards the county capital Khampa Dzong. Long before they arrived, the towers of the *dzong* itself were clearly visible on a lofty crag above the village, as impressive as any Teutonic fortress. The three men rode into town that evening. Schäfer watched the sun falling towards the horizon in a 'yellow-green unreal glow', 'not the mild sunset of the Nordic sky at home and not the flaming scarlet of the south. It's the icy sky of the Himalayas.'

There was disconcerting news in Khampa Dzong. The local *dzongpon*[1], or governor, of the region was not at all happy about the presence of the foreigners, so Kaiser found them lodgings and asked to meet him immediately. Ominously, the local military commander and some of his men also appeared. The meeting was tense and, as Hugh Richardson had suspected, Kaiser did *not* speak fluent Tibetan. Conversation was excruciating, and Krause, still greedy for pictures, offended his hosts by focusing a bright flashlight on them as they ate. They blinked and snorted in disgust. Schäfer said that the governor sat 'like a stuffed dummy staring poker faced into space with an angry look and not saying another word'. Then Krause knocked over a valuable Chinese vase and the meeting broke up with little result.

The following morning Schäfer was summoned to see the governor again. This time, the commander of the local fortress and a noble from Shigatse were also present. As usual when Schäfer faced catastrophe, he fought back hard, and this time he made sure he had a decent interpreter; he also wore his best pith helmet with SS thunderbolts on each side. He spoke for an hour and a half, stopping only when the interpreter needed to catch up, about his experiences in Tibet and how much he esteemed the Buddhist traditions. Again, he exploited that meeting with Chokyi Nyima, the Panchen Lama, and said that one of his own books contained a splendid photograph of the Panchen Lama which had made him revered all over Germany. In Khampa Dzong, this was a very shrewd move. Although the Panchen Lama had died in 1937 and had been a thorn in the side of the Tibetan government, they were close to Tashilunpo, the great monastic city and the ancient seat of the Panchen Lamas. Chokyi Nyima would have been especially revered so close to his monastery. Schäfer's speech was a brilliant success. His knowledge of Buddhist doctrine and experience of the wilder regions of Tibet were warmly praised, and the governor agreed that the party could travel on to the palace at Doptra. It is revealing that he also said that he would need to refer his decision 'up' to the Kashag, and requested that Schäfer not disclose to anyone that he, Schäfer, was obliged to him. Bucks were clearly being passed.

They left the next day, but no-one had told Schäfer that his animals would not be fed overnight because they were 'foreign'. Schäfer's mount collapsed five hours after leaving Khampa Dzong. They all dismounted and started to walk, Kaiser leading the horses at the rear. Then it began to rain, slowing progress further. They were still struggling across the treeless plain when night fell and a thunderstorm began to flicker and rumble in the sky. 'Truly,' Schäfer said later, 'you can understand why Tibetans describe their country as the stronghold of the gods.' There was no sign of Doptra so they decided to make an emergency camp for the night. Kaiser had not yet caught up with the two Germans so Schäfer and Krause spent an anxious night under canvas. The following morning was foggy and the storm still rumbled ominously from the invisible mountains. Kaiser turned up shortly afterwards with the two horses, behaving with impeccable sangfroid as befitted a proud member of the Nepali warrior caste. Schäfer said that 'with his face of a child, he has turned into a brave man'. As the fog cleared they could see that their camp was close to Lake Gayamtsona, and this meant they were close to Doptra after all.

They made *tsampa* with lake water, but something made Schäfer sick and dizzy. He had diarrhoea and was doubled up with abdominal pain but he pressed on, and with Kaiser and Krause behind him began to urge his horse forward across a desolate fen (Schäfer calls it a '*Schwemmoor*', or big water fen). There were no tracks and they all splashed blindly through this waterlogged plain for hours until they reached a wide, shallow river. It did not look difficult to cross, so Schäfer and Kaiser trotted confidently into the flow. But hidden on the river bed was thick, viscous mud and their horses were instantly trapped. Schäfer dismounted and began to pull the horse clear by its tail. By now, though, he was very sick indeed. He frankly describes what happened next: 'I have never felt such pain before and my bowels are exploding . . . I am too weak to move a single limb and sink down, on my saddle, into the middle of the river. I sweat profusely; I lose control [of his bowels]. Lethargically, fatalistically. I don't care any more. It's only when I regain consciousness that I am disgusted with the state I am in . . .' And then he writes, 'Kaiser helps me with affecting love ['*Kaiser hilft mir in rührender Liebe*'] to clean myself and then we return to the river bank and sit down together.' Schäfer had never been as close to any of his companions as he was at that moment to Kaiser.

Schäfer and Kaiser rode downriver and were able to successfully cross the river, but the *Schwemmoor* still stretched away ahead and on either side of them, a stinking, sucking quagmire of silt and mud. It was a torment to cross and the animals were frequently stuck, but after hours of slow and tortured progress Schäfer reached a small elevated 'island' where he let the exhausted horses graze. Behind them they could just see Krause and the rest of their small caravan battling through the fen on the other side of the river; Kaiser, the 'faithful, shaking Nepalese, who [was] almost melting in tears', made his way back to show Krause the way across. By now everyone looked 'disgusting', Schäfer wrote; 'we were covered in mud and encrusted in thick clay'. Then the minister to whom they had presented their vegetables appeared, walking barefoot across the fen. They were just a few miles from Doptra. He would now escort them to the palace of the 'King of Tharing'.

Schäfer and Beger had both realized who the Tering Raja was and hoped that he might be persuaded to help them.[2] It shows they had done their homework about the dark side of Sikkimese history and the dastardly role of the British. When the first British Mission officer John Claude White had been persecuting the hapless Chogyal Thutob Namygal fifty years before, he had come up with a plan to replace the Chogyal with one of his two sons, Kumar Sidkeong Namygal or his half-brother Tsodok Namygal. But White had a problem: both sons were terrified of him and had fled from Sikkim. Tsodok had estates at Tering near Gyantse and a summer residence at Doptra. Because he refused to co-operate with White, he was banished from Sikkim and remained in Tibet. This was the Tering Raja, the 'King of Tharing'. Sidkeong, the other son and an incarnate lama or *tulku*, succeeded in his place, but died in mysterious circumstances in 1915. Schäfer had every reason to hope that the embittered Tering Raja would help him thwart the British. What he as yet did not know was that the Raja's son Jigme Tering was one of the most important young men in Tibet and an important ally of the British.

Doptra turned out to be a small village with a ruined *dzong*; the Tering Raja lived nearby on a modest estate with a well-tended garden behind a mud wall. He had been watching the group's struggles through a pair of binoculars, and came to meet his guests, accompanied by his 'queen' and 'princess', as soon as the German visitors arrived. He was a dark-skinned man who wore a conical hat and silk robes decorated with flowers. The Tering Raja had prepared tents, English style, where Schäfer and his companions could wash with hot water and Japanese soap. White towels had been thoughtfully laid out on their bunks. The next two days, Schäfer said, were 'like a dream'. As if to reciprocate for the vegetables, which the Tering Raja had so much desired, they were fed delicacies from all over Tibet as well as Bhutan and Nepal. The Raja knew Schäfer had been ill so he personally wrapped him in a woollen blanket. Krause filmed Schäfer in his pith helmet with the SS insignia presenting *kata* (white scarves) to the Raja. Schäfer would place these images at the very beginning of his film *Geheimnis Tibet*, for the meeting changed everything.

In the evening they drank Tibetan beer and Schäfer and Krause sang raucous German songs; Kaiser sang a delicate Nepali love song. Schäfer took every opportunity to convince the Tering Raja that he was a devoted student of Buddhism: he knew that they could not simply continue to live like Nordic lotus eaters at the court of the Raja. The Tering Raja had to be persuaded, and quickly, to write a letter of recommendation to the Kashag. But the problem seemed not to lie with the Raja himself. Schäfer was forced to play a confounding cat-and-mouse game with the 'Queen of Tharing', who appeared determined to frustrate his plans. The fact was that she was trying to protect her husband's interests: the family had extensive British as well as Lhasan contacts and they could pay a heavy price for this fraternization. The solution to the impasse seems to have been more presents, this time a ten-piece binoculars set, a medical kit and – the *pièce de résistance* – a large metal mirror for the queen herself. Schäfer finally convinced her of his good intentions, and the letter was at last written and sent to Lhasa.

That done, Schäfer took his men over the mountains and back to camp – and waited. He sent presents to the Kashag and the Regent and continued to badger Basil Gould, who reported Schäfer's activities back to London. Gould and the British were, naturally, infuriated when they discovered that Schäfer had crossed into Tibet; they might have been even more annoyed if they'd known the idea had come from Sir Francis Younghusband, who was once one of their own. And there were repercussions. Beger reports in his diary that his assistants were insulted by one of the Tering Raja's inspectors, which strongly implies that either the British or someone in Lhasa had, as the 'queen' must have feared, vented their spleen on the hapless 'King of Tharing'. The secret files in the India Office do show that Gould had indeed communicated with the Raja. In a letter to the Government of India, he wrote, 'Actually Raja Tering much resented the visit, and feared that the Lhasa government might find some unpleasant method of indicating its disapproval.' Since there are no Tibetan records of what kind of debate took place after the Tering Raja wrote to Lhasa on Schäfer's behalf, it is possible only to hazard a guess that the British – meaning probably Hugh Richardson – were busy stoking up hostility to Schäfer and someone in the Kashag 'punished' the Tering Raja in some way. But the Tibetan government rarely achieved unity on any issue, and such conflict could turn out to be in Schäfer's favour. Not everyone in Lhasa favoured the British, as Hugh Richardson knew very well. That is one possibility. The other, of course, is that the Tering Raja was simply fobbing off Gould with a sob story. At any rate, it was up to the Kashag to reply, and Schäfer waited anxiously for news.

In their remote mountain hideout the Germans were tuning in to Wienert's radio with increasing frequency. Far away in

Europe, events seemed to be rapidly approaching a climax. In September 1938, Hitler urged his generals to prepare for 'Case Green', the military destruction of Czechoslovakia. Appeasement continued to dominate British tactics. Chamberlain sent Lord Runciman to pressure President Beneš to settle the grievances of the Sudeten Germans, but that was not what Hitler wanted. Suddenly there was no excuse for the all-out war he desired so he demanded that Konrad Heinlein, the leader of the Sudeten Germans, stage some provocations. This Heinlein duly did, and his Sudeten German Party engineered violent clashes between Czechs and Germans. When Beneš appealed for calm, Heinlein ordered riots and Germans began attacking Jewish shops. On 15 September Chamberlain, desperate for peace, flew to Germany to meet Hitler once more. After a bruising encounter at the Berghof he appeared to secure Hitler's promise not to take immediate military action *if* the Sudetenland was ceded to Germany. Without saying a word to the unfortunate Beneš, Chamberlain worked out a deal with the French to let Hitler have what he wanted; Beneš was presented with an ultimatum if he did not agree. Bitter, angry, hurt and powerless, poor Beneš agreed. But now Chamberlain discovered what appeasement really meant. Whatever he gave Hitler was never enough; he simply added more demands. Now that the Sudeten Germans had what they wanted, other nations wanted a piece of Czechoslovakia, and that suited Hitler very well. He insisted that no final agreement was possible until the demands of Hungary and Poland for territorial concessions in Czechoslovakia were also met. At the same time, he told an appalled Chamberlain that he would send troops into the Sudetenland if the Czechs had not removed themselves by 1 October. In Prague, Beneš mobilized the Czech Army; Hitler responded by moving up the date of his threatened invasion to 28 September. War seemed to be very close. All over Europe, anxiety and foreboding rose to fever pitch.

Believing that he must 'try, try and try again', Chamberlain shuttled between London and Germany and appealed to Benito Mussolini. The Italian dictator was also fearful of a war and urged Hitler to stop his invasion. Hitler called Chamberlain back to Germany for a conference in Munich. The events that followed are, of course, infamous. The French, British, Germans and Italians, with no Czech representative present, met at the Brown House in Munich, where they dismembered 'a faraway country' about whose 'people [they knew] nothing'. Chamberlain was fêted in London and Germany as the hero of the hour, but the real victors were Hitler and Mussolini.

William Shirer was in no doubt that the dictators believed they had won. While the foolish Chamberlain looked 'pleased with himself', the French premier Edouard Daladier was 'a completely beaten and broken man'; Hitler, in contrast, 'brushed past me like the conqueror he was', and Mussolini was as 'cocky as a rooster'. On the train back to Berlin, Shirer described the gleeful German press 'gloating over it, buying out all the champagne in the diner, gloating, boasting, bragging . . . When a German feels big he feels *big*.' In London, Chamberlain basked in fatuous glory; in Parliament, Duff Cooper and Churchill were the lone voices recognizing that Hitler, who had gambled on the democracies' fear of war, had won another round. Instead of averting war, Munich brought a European catastrophe closer.

In Sikkim, the German Tibet Expedition shared in the elation that there was 'peace in our time'. But Schäfer was no nearer to Lhasa, and he must have absorbed a few lessons from the Munich crisis. As he waited at camp, Schäfer continued to cajole and pressure Gould, resorting to an old trick. 'A few days after [Schäfer] left me,' Gould reported following one meeting, 'he wrote enclosing a somewhat blustering letter from Reichsführer Himmler which was apparently intended as a hint that should permission from Lhasa not be forthcoming, consequences might be awkward . . . I learn that Herr Schäfer thought fit to report the German consul general at Calcutta for inefficiency, because he did not push through quickly enough all that Herr Schäfer desired: and from what I have seen of Herr Schäfer – and it is a good deal – I have no doubt that I was intended to regard Herr Himmler's reference to procrastination as a warning.' Himmler's awkwardly translated letter is attached: 'My Dear Schäfer, I am glad that the expedition is so well off and that it is a disciplined body bound together by comradeship. When I heard . . . there was procrastination with the English authorities, I immediately cared for an explanation in England, which, as I saw from the answers was of use and has cleared the air . . . I very often think of you. Heil Hitler.' Gould was clever enough to see what was at stake: 'Actually Schäfer is perhaps nervous that if he fails to get all he asks for, his credit in Germany may wane.'

With no reply from the Tering Raja, a tense and increasingly bad-tempered Schäfer pushed his team to get more results. Krause filmed what he could, collected Sikkimese orchids and hunted for butterflies and moths; Wienert fought wind and snow to get his magnetic readings; Beger measured and fingerprinted local people and passing wool merchants. He had taken to playing gramophone records to attract potential subjects. What was even more useful, though, was his success as a highly effective 'medicine man'. And his medical work led to some interesting discoveries about the lives of Buddhist monks.

After a visit to the Pemayangtse Monastery, Beger was approached by three rather contrite monks. After some dissembling they opened their robes to reveal their genitals. Beger realized they were all suffering from untreated gonorrhoea; the symptoms were unmistakable. 'Even celibate monks', Beger noted in his diary, 'could not control their natural desires.' It was 'like a plague', he said. Most of his patients called a venereal infection the 'Chinese Disease'; monks claimed they acquired it by 'sitting in long grass'. Traditional medicine had no remedy for venereal infections, although marijuana was sometimes used. Beger, of course, had no antibiotics and had to treat the monks with arsenic compounds like Salvarsan. These could be brutal in their effects and had to be taken over a long period of time. So pleased were they after their first treatment, the monks asked to have their photographs taken.

In November, a lunar eclipse was predicted by the astrologers. The Germans watched as hundreds of villagers gathered to bang drums and shout at the tops of their voices. According to one villager, Beger wrote in his diary, an eclipse happened when the moon was attacked by a demon; if the demon was not scared away the moon might vanish for ever. Beger, who frequently felt exasperated by such superstitions, tried to explain to one of the villagers what was really happening, but he was politely ignored. He was, however, able to convince the villagers that they were six hours early, and they all went away. At midnight they returned and the cacophonous ceremony began all over again. Beger described what happened:

> Ghostly shadows settled on the immense mountains, and the peaks disappeared in darkness. Yes, this was about the light – the light and the life – especially here in the depths of the valley. It was vital to stay awake, to fight the demonic animal that threatened the natural order. It sank its teeth into the moon and almost swallowed it. How tortuously slowly! At last a thin silver trickle poured from its hungry lips. All hell broke loose.

> Everyone made as much noise as possible to rescue the moon from the demon and protect her light. At the end of the eclipse when the sickle of light grew and began to return, there was a single scream that died away slowly . . .

After the eclipse, the winter snows arrived, and the expedition was often marooned for days on end. The stress was punishing for the already fragile Schäfer. There was no news from Lhasa and he felt trapped like an animal. There were tantrums and sulks. If he could have slammed his tent flap he would have done so frequently. In their tents, the others discussed his erratic and difficult moods late into the night, but, Beger added, 'This was nothing new. It had been our constant companion from the start. It was the crowded conditions and sitting around idly that made it almost impossible to bear and threatened to destroy our community . . .'

Then, in December, as Schäfer was returning to camp, he heard Geer uttering a 'wild victory cry'. In his hand he held a letter with five seals from Lhasa.

> To the German Herr Dr. Schäfer (Doctor Saheb Sha-phar) Master of 100 Sciences.
>
> Thank you from the heart for your letter from the 12th day of the 9th English month together with two boxes, which contained a gramophone, records and two binoculars each.
>
> Concerning your request to visit Lhasa and to view the holy monasteries together with the other Germans in your company Hr. Wienert, Hr. Geer, Hr. Krause and Hr. Beger (together not more than five people), we inform you that in general entrance into Tibet is forever prohibited to foreigners. Although we know that if we allow you to enter, others might come the next time, it nevertheless appears from your letter

that you intend only friendship and to see the holy land and its religious institutions.

Knowing this, we grant you permission to enter Lhasa and stay there for 14 days, but only under the condition, that you promise not to do any harm to the Tibetan people and that you consent not to kill any birds and mammals, which would deeply hurt the religious feelings of the Tibetan people, both clergy and lay.

Please take this to your heart.

Sent by Kashag,
the Tibetan council of ministers,
on the auspicious 3rd day of the 10th month
of the Fire-Tiger-Year.

The elation, Schäfer said, was indescribable. The Kashag had now issued the invitation the British had always demanded and assumed would never come. This was the longed-for 'Official Leave', but Schäfer still needed Gould's permission to cross the border officially and to take the 'trade road' through Gyantse to Lhasa. This was the fiefdom of the political officer in Gangtok. Getting Gould to agree would now take up much of Schäfer's time in the course of the next frustrating month. He lost little time in writing to the Viceroy's office crowing that Richardson had been given a sealed letter from the Kashag which told him that the expedition could visit Lhasa for fourteen days 'on condition that it is a pleasure trip only and with the usual prohibition of shooting in Tibet'.[3] Schäfer added, 'This is one of the most happy days in all my life and I herewith like to express my deepest and most cordial thanks for all your kind help . . .'; he would now be able 'to celebrate Christmas in the land of the lamas'. He went on to show off his accomplishments in Sikkim, emphasizing, as usual, that they were purely scientific: Karl Wienert had taken measurements at two hundred terrestrial magnetic stations and Schäfer himself had had 'one very nice result . . . as I was able to find a new species of big game, known only to five or six lepchas before . . . It is the Shapi related to the "Thar" [tahr] but nearly black, much bigger and with strongly bent horns unlike those of the common Thar . . .'

There was still a problem. In the India Office files, Gould's revealing response to Schäfer's letter is attached: 'The gist of this is that Dr Schäfer has only been permitted to visit Lhasa as a tourist. [We have] insisted that they should leave their scientific instruments behind with [us], lest the Tibetan authorities . . . make trouble for them.' Regarding 'the matter of meteorological observations', Gould added that 'the Tibetans would be likely to be resentful if they found that any sort of survey had been done without their permission'. So, no shooting and no geophysical measurements.

Examined more closely, the Kashag's letter represented something of a Pyrrhic victory. If Schäfer followed the letter of the law, he would *not* be leading a 'scientific expedition' to Lhasa, and their stay there would be limited to a mere two weeks. This meant that Beger would have very little time in which to complete any serious examination of the Tibetan aristocracy – and that was the most important task of the German Tibet Expedition. Schäfer could not shoot anything and Wienert would be twiddling his thumbs. Gould and the Government of India were very anxious that Schäfer should comply with these conditions. Richardson, who must have found the Kashag's letter especially galling, consoled himself by observing that 'it is a pleasure trip only with the usual ban on shooting etcetera . . . He may be advised to leave firearms and Scientific instruments in Sikkim . . .' And the Viceroy's secretary, writing from Delhi, rammed home the message in another letter to Schäfer that the Tibetans 'would be likely to be resentful if they found that any such scientific work had been done without their express permission'. The British, especially Richardson, derived satisfaction from the fact that while Schäfer had gambled by making a move behind their backs and won he would now be travelling to Lhasa with his hands tied and be back in Germany in a matter of weeks, soon after the New Year.

It will be no surprise to learn that Schäfer had no intention whatsoever of abandoning his scientific aims or of staying in Lhasa a mere fortnight. Once again, he was applying the lesson of the past that if he was to have his 'victuals' then they could come 'course by course'; there was no need to 'snatch them from the table'. These were the lessons of appeasement, and only Hugh Richardson, it seems, understood the game that was being played. From the British Mission in Lhasa, he too had been watching the slide to barbarism in Europe with increasing dismay.

On the evening of 27 October 1938, a Jew of Polish origin who had settled in Hanover, Sindel Grynszpan, had been rounded up with his family and transported, with twelve thousand other Jews, to Zbaszyn on the rail line between Berlin and Warsaw where they were dumped in stables and pig sties and whipped until they bled by SS officers. Herschel, the Grynszpans' youngest son, was studying in Paris and escaped deportation. His father managed, somehow, to contact him from Poland and told him what had happened. Herschel purchased a revolver, walked to the German Embassy and shot Ernst vom Rath, the Third Secretary, twice in the stomach. Vom Rath died a few days later. Goebbels immediately claimed that the killing in Paris was proof of a world conspiracy organized by Jews against the Reich. Himmler made a speech to his SS Gruppenführers insisting that 'In Germany the Jews cannot hold out . . . We will drive them out more and more with unexampled ruthlessness.' On 9 November, attacks on Jews began taking place all over Germany. It was a spasm of racial hatred organized from the heart of the Nazi dictatorship and described in secret memos as 'lightning, urgent, immediate action . . . on account of the assassination of the Leg. Sec. v. Rath in Paris'.[4]

Reichskristallnacht had begun. Jews were murdered in the street and even taken from prison cells and battered to death. Synagogues were burnt, precious books and Torah scrolls were destroyed. Thousands were arrested and transported, until the camps were bursting at their barbed-wire seams. By the time the Reichskristallnacht was over, thousands of Jews had been killed and nearly three hundred synagogues destroyed. There was, naturally, international outrage, but nothing was done to stop the march of the Racial State. Schäfer's patron Himmler moved closer to the centre of power. It was no longer possible, for men like Richardson at least, to ignore the despotic cruelty of Hitler's dictatorship.

In Sikkim the following month, there was a flurry of exalted preparation. Geer and Krause travelled all the way back to Calcutta for supplies and returned to Gangtok to hire more men. Schäfer ironed out the last arrangements with Gould. To thank him for his efforts, Beger presented Gould with the face mask of a young Tibetan woman they had both admired.

Although a winter journey to Lhasa across the Himalayan passes could be perilous, the worsening international crisis now compelled Schäfer to act with the utmost urgency. The deck of appeasement cards was depleted; he knew that at any moment he and his British friends could become hostile combatants. Beger noted, 'The political situation in Europe was giving us cause for concern. We discussed this late into the night – thinking about what we could do in case war broke out. Fleeing into Tibet could give us a chance to avoid British imprisonment.' By mid December Geer had completed most of their preparations, and on the 20th the German Tibet Expedition set out from Gangtok for the second time, on this occasion heading east towards the Natu La Pass. It was the road to Lhasa at last.

They had more than fifty pack animals this time and a new interpreter called Rabden Kazi. They all suspected he was spying for Gould. Kaiser's role by now was more colleague than translator. At the last moment, there was trouble with the young woman whose mask Beger had presented to Gould, and it involved Akeh. Because he had been recently widowed, custom required that he abstain from sexual contact for a year, but it was he who had insisted on bringing the young woman on the expedition and he'd been 'unable to contain himself'. Rabden informed Schäfer that local gossip said that the Germans were travelling with a prostitute, and when a search was made Akeh and the young woman were discovered vigorously *in flagrante*. Schäfer was terrified that Gould would find out and accuse him of immorality, so he ordered the woman back to Gangtok and administered a beating to the unfortunate Akeh.

As they followed the telegraph line towards the Natu La Pass, they seemed 'to float between heaven and earth'. Looking back, they could see the Chogyal's palace and the British Residency apparently floating in the clouds. Everything else was invisible. They passed small Buddhist monasteries, each with its *mane*, or painted prayer wall, at the edge of the road which the devout passed on the left. At the river's edge were the homes of the local landlords painted in red, white and blue stripes, with prayer flags at each corner. Dogs were chained outside every house and barked viciously as the expedition passed. As they climbed higher out of the valley, the air thinned and the temperature dropped steadily. They made rapid progress, only occasionally slowed down by Tibetan wool merchants and their caravans coming the other way from Gyantse on narrow mountain paths.

Akeh was trying to prove his worth again and attacked one of the mule drivers with a stick. The man drew a sword. Schäfer lost his temper and stepped between the two men, pushing them apart, and the expedition moved on.

Two days later they stopped in a cup-shaped valley by the still, grey waters of Lake Changu. They had reached 12,500 feet and it was bitterly cold with flurries of snow. Here the tree line ended. On one side of the lake birch and rhododendron scrub ran down to the edge of the water; on the other there was treeless and rocky hillside. Beyond the lake the road ran on into a damp, dispiriting fog. Two thousand feet above them was the pass.

Akeh told them a story about a 'progressive' Sikkimese official who had tried to build a trout farm there. When the fish were released into the lake, the water boiled and bubbled in protest. He had not known, of course, that Changu was 'the resting place of poor souls' whose slumber the foreign trout had disturbed. Twelve high lamas were brought to exorcise the unquiet ghosts of Changu. They prayed ceaselessly, and after seven days and seven nights the boiling lake calmed. But the trout were never seen again. The disillusioned official returned to Gangtok. Schäfer enjoyed hearing these stories, but he dismissed them as idle superstition.

It was the winter solstice, and that night he and his comrades celebrated their own brand of paganism. Since 1933, the Nazis had aggressively promoted the celebration of pagan festivals to wean Germany off its 'Jewish' Christian habits. That December night in 1938, high in the Himalayas on the edge of Tibet, as the sun dropped into the incandescent waters of the lake, Schäfer and his comrades built a towering pile of logs and dry scrub. Then they stood in a ring and sang 'Flamme Empor' ('Flame Uprise'), an old military song which had become a talismanic anthem for the Third Reich.

Flamme empor!
Steige mit loderndem Scheine
Von den Gebirgen am Rheine!
Glühend empor!

Siehe wir stehn
Treu im geweiheten Kreise,
Dich zu des Vaterlands Preise
Flamme, zu sehn!

Heilige Glut,
Rufe die Jugend zusammen
Daß bei den lodernden Flammen
Wachse der Mut!
Auf allen Höhn
Leuchte, du flammendes Zeichen
Daß alle Feinde erbleichen
Wenn sie dich sehn!

Leuchtender Schein!
Siehe, wir singenden Paare
Schwören am Flammenaltare
Deutsche zu sein!

Höre das Wort!
Vater, auf Leben und Sterben
Hilf uns die Freiheit erwerben!
Sei unser Hort!

Flame uprise!
Rise in blazing light
From the mountains along the Rhine!
Rise shining!

See, we are standing
Faithful in a blessed circle,
To see you, flame,
And so praise the Fatherland!

Holy Fire,
Call the young together
So that next to your blazing flames
Courage grows! . . .

Etc., etc.

As their voices faded across the lake, the light vanished altogether. Then Schäfer climbed a rocky outcrop, holding aloft a burning branch, which he hurled into the bonfire. The wood and scrub caught quickly. Flames roared into the dark sky and were reflected on the dark surface of the lake, turning it blood red. Schäfer spoke 'from the heart'. They must all work together, he shouted, to make the German Tibet Expedition a success and the *Vaterland* proud of their achievements. *Einer für alle und alle für einen! Lhasa Lo!*

Wienert tuned in his radio, not to check the time as he usually did, but to hear the words of Heinrich Himmler broadcasting from the Sudetenland. With grizzled faces illuminated by the leaping flames of the bonfire, the men listened solemnly to the 'calm voice' of the Reichsführer. Then Schäfer took a burning log from the fire and, holding it aloft, led his comrades in a procession down to the lake. Standing on the edge, he hurled the flaming torch across its dark surface.[5]

The next morning the German Tibet Expedition began the climb towards the Natu La Pass. Schäfer had strapped SS pendants to the back of a donkey, and they fluttered wildly in the high, freezing winds.

CHAPTER NINE

ON THE ROOF OF THE WORLD

*First Soldier: I thought Tibet was a f***ing table-land?*
*Second Soldier: So it f***ing is, you silly c**t. This is one of the f***ing legs.*

– soldiers' conversation reported during Younghusband mission, 1903–4

On 22 December 1938, five heavily bearded men, by now barely distinguishable one from the other, panted hard in the thin, cold air as they pulled their small Tibetan ponies up the zigzagging trail towards the Natu La Pass that lay somewhere in the swirling clouds above them. Strung out behind them were their servants and porters and a caravan of yaks and ponies, piled high with boxes. It was wet and misty with light snowfall. The trail was steep, like the side of a house, and strewn with icy boulders. Even their surefooted animal slipped. There was another tense encounter with a wool caravan coming down from the summit and heading for the great wool market at Kalimpong. This time, Schäfer's men pushed two of the wool caravan's mules off the path and into a ravine. The two parties faced each other 'like rabid dogs', but it was a victory for the

Germans. At the summit, a harsh saddle of stone, the mist had cleared. There were hundreds of trembling prayer flags and a big cairn of stones. As Schäfer's men filed past they added their own stones and cried out, 'So-ya-la-so!' Ahead of them lay the Chumbi Valley and the road to Gyantse.

Today, the Natu La Pass is the world's highest international border. It is a tense junction between China and India, an ugly jumble of barbed wire, trenches and a military post. For the soldiers who have to guard India's frontier, there is a telephone box offering special rates. A sign warns in Chinese, Hindi and English:

Halt! Don't move! Throw down your weapons
Don't cross the wire fence
I'll shoot if you do not follow instructions.

In 1962, China took advantage of the Cuban missile crisis and sent the Red Army down the Chumbi to humiliate the Indians. No European has travelled here for more than forty years; the Chumbi is a lost world. The valley can be imagined as a thin tongue of land sandwiched between Sikkim and Bhutan, and for many centuries it had been the traditional route from India to Lhasa. Only at its northern end does the road lead upwards to the Tibetan plateau itself.

Schäfer and his comrades stood in silence, gazing down into Tibet awestruck and hungry for conquest. Ahead of them they could see a great cathedral of snow. It was the soaring spire of Mount Chomolhari, the Mountain of the Goddess, Bhutan's westernmost peak on the edge of Tibet. Chomolhari would now preside over their journey, replacing the mountain gods of Kangchendzonga. They could see lakes, too, covered with ice, and hear the deep roar of the river in the valley far below. Men, mules and yaks now set off down the other side, descending along a frozen, muddy and slippery track through bare rhododendron bushes and uncanny six-foot spikes of wild rhubarb.

Younghusband had crossed the Himalayas on 13 December 1903 through the Dzelap La Pass, which slices through the Himalayas to the west of the Natu La. Led by a sepoy with a Union Jack, his 'escort' of two thousand troops had an arduous climb, with full kit, over broken rock and shale up to the summit. They were followed by ten thousand coolies, seven thousand mules, four thousand yaks and five newspaper correspondents. Twenty-nine containers were crammed with Younghusband's 'kit', which comprised, as Patrick French discovered,[1] sixty-seven shirts, nineteen coats (including a Chesterfield and a Chinese fur coat), an imperial cocked hat and other varieties of headgear as well as tents, field baths, rifles and swords. From the summit, the journalist Edmund Candler saw that 'Behind us and on both sides was a thin mist, but in front my eyes explored a deep valley bathed in sunshine. Here then was Tibet, the hidden, the mysterious.'[2] Then Younghusband's men slithered down the other side, as slippery as ice, into the Chumbi.

Schäfer needed to be much more secretive than Younghusband had been in 1903. Inside the boxes strapped to the backs of his mules and yaks Schäfer had concealed his rifles as well as Wienert's geomagnetic equipment. Schäfer was never going to accept his enforced status as a mere 'tourist'. On their first night (officially) in Tibet the expedition camped at the Champithang rest house, one of a chain constructed by John Claude White all the way to Lhasa. It must have been an odd experience for these servants of the Reich. On the walls were pictures of pretty cottages in Surrey and Berkshire; the roughly made tables were littered with old copies of *Punch*; everything seemed, however casual, to be designed to evoke an England that was lost even to the English. Champithang's guestbook,

Schäfer found, was inscribed with the initials or signatures of British officers and travellers who had crossed the pass into the Chumbi Valley, including the men who had gone with the Younghusband mission.

Historians have often been perplexed by the intricate combination of motives that drove Younghusband over the border. The instigator of the mission, as the invasion was euphemistically called, was the Indian Viceroy Lord Curzon, who resented the 'Cinderella like' status of India's North-East Frontier and was increasingly exasperated by Tibetan relations with his government. There had been repeated trespasses into Sikkim, border stones had been overturned, treaties had been obstructed and the Dalai Lama had returned Curzon's letters unopened. But the Dalai Lama seemed to be on very good terms with the Russians, and it was Tsar Nicholas II's imperial ambitions in Asia that troubled Curzon most deeply. He was especially exercised by the mysterious activities of a Buddhist monk called Agvan Dorzhiev[3] who, it was reported, flitted between Lhasa and the Russian imperial court, where he was reported to be friendly with the Tsar's 'Tibetan Adviser'. All this must have been well known to Schäfer because his hero Wilhelm Filchner had produced a racy account of the Younghusband mission in *Storm Over Asia*.[4] He had claimed that another shadowy Russian called Zerempil had been supplying the Dalai Lama with machine guns. In 1903, the Tibetans arrested and tortured two Sikkimese scouts and then committed an obscure act of aggression against some Nepali yaks. These 'provocations' on top of yet more rumours and counter-rumours about Russian agents gave Curzon ammunition to force the hand of the Balfour government in London. Colonel Younghusband was given permission to advance into Tibet as far as Gyantse. It would be the last imperial adventure, 'forward policy' at its most belligerent.

As Christmas approached, Schäfer and his caravan followed Younghusband's trail down towards the labyrinth of deep forest-clad valleys that lay ahead. In spring, their route would have taken them through a natural rock garden of primulas, orchids and azalea, but now it was bleak and cold, although milder than the winter the British had endured in 1903–4. They passed the overgrown *mane* wall of the Kargyu Monastery that overlooked the valley from a rocky spur dotted with numerous *chortens*. As the expedition descended deeper into the valley, the Germans commented on its alpine qualities; even the villages had a Tyrolean look about them with their wide eaves meeting over narrow streets. There were more dogs: mastiffs chained to doors, obviously well fed, which ran barking at their visitors, and other beasts that were merely skin and bones and often unable to do more than limp towards the caravan and growl as it passed.

After riding through Pipitang, where the telegraph line runs down from the Dzelap La Pass to join the road from Natu La, they rode alongside the Amo-chu itself which flowed icy green between empty wheat and barley fields. The Tibetan name for the Chumbi is 'Tromo', which means 'wheat district'. The local people are known as Tromopos and made a good living from the wool caravans that passed through on their way from Gyantse to Kalimpong in Sikkim. Schäfer thought they resembled 'alpine peoples' in Europe and he speculated with Beger about their origins. 'Don't they have the same lively blood? Mere convergences, some would say, while others refer to the migrations of prehistory ...' There were prayer flags everywhere and almost everyone they passed twirled a prayer wheel. One imposing building on the river's edge housed three tremendous water-driven wheels which revolved on axles and were crammed with prayers written on tightly folded pieces of paper. *Om Mani Padme Hum* . . .

The Chumbi Valley was a memorial to many different histories. In 1910, China's 'foreign' Manchu Ch'ing dynasty, in a decaying spasm of aggression, had sent two thousand troops under General Chao Er-fang across the border into Tibet. When they arrived in Lhasa they fired on the crowds who had turned out to greet them. On 12 February the 13th Dalai Lama fled towards India pursued by two hundred Chinese cavalrymen, and rode to Phari and then Yatung in the Chumbi Valley, where he was given protection in the Trade Agency and fed chicken soup, roast mutton and baked custard pudding. But the Chinese were hot on his heels and he was forced to move on, over the Dzelap La Pass and into Sikkim. He was closely followed by twenty-four-year-old Chensal Namgang, disguised as a mail runner, who would become better known as Tsarong Shapé, one of the most important secular officials in Lhasa. Some would call him the 'uncrowned king of Tibet'. During the next three years, the exiled Dalai Lama would form close friendships with some of the great figures of the 'Tibet cadre', in particular Charles Bell and David MacDonald. At least until the Dalai Lama's passing on in 1933, the British name 'stood high in Tibet'.[5]

On Christmas Eve the Schäfer Expedition reached Yatung, where there was a small barracks, a post office and the low, red-roofed bungalow of the British trade agent. Beger writes that an American – Beger simply calls him 'Grant' – caught up with them here. He had strong republican views, according to Beger, and said 'he didn't hold "heroes" in high regard [meaning the European dictators] – there was nothing good behind such people, their work was not lasting and their words empty. He tactfully only named Mussolini as an example.' They all stayed at the Dak bungalow. There were signs of British interests everywhere; the trade agent had 'a most delightful house', according to the official diary of Gould's mission to Lhasa in

1936. In 1903 in Yatung, Younghusband had encountered a wall built across his path commanded by a Tibetan general. The general ordered the British to return over the pass to India. Realizing that a door in the wall had been left open, the British mission simply marched on through, ignoring the general, who made a futile lunge at Younghusband's bridle.

There were bears and bharal in the area but Schäfer knew that he could not risk hunting, not yet at any rate. For Germans, Christmas Eve, *Heilig Abend*, is the time for feasting and present giving. Schäfer found a tree that would make do as a *Tannenbaum* and that evening the expedition feasted on tinned asparagus and sausage washed down with strong Tibetan beer. They played gramophone records, sang *Weihnachtslieder* and became increasingly sentimental and homesick. Their new translator, Rabden, declared that he would follow them anywhere whatever their political goals – a remark Schäfer regarded with considerable scepticism. He remained convinced that the young Sikkimese *kazi*, or noble, was reporting back to the British and was perhaps resentful that Rabden had taken on the role he had intended for Kaiser until his inadequacies had been exposed in Khampa Dzong. The class distinction between Rabden and Kaiser is intriguing: Kaiser was Nepali; his competitor was a high-born native Sikkimese. In the following months, Schäfer would develop an irrational fear that the *kazis* of Sikkim were conspiring against him, an anxiety that must have been connected with the wily Rabden.

After the celebrations, most of the expedition turned in to sleep off the excesses of the night, but Beger and Wienert had work to do – in secret. They silently left the Dak bungalow and retrieved Wienert's geomagnetic equipment. Now that the expedition had crossed the Tibetan border, it was imperative that Wienert take special care. Officially they were tourists, not working scientists. Very few of their companions could be completely trusted but the Christmas celebrations provided good cover. With only the moon to guide them, they stumbled along a path they knew led into a side valley, their boots crunching through ice and snow. They crossed a stream and ended up on a narrow ridge with a good view of the night sky and a brilliant vista of stars.

As they knew well from experience, taking astronomical sightings and using the complex magnetometer were not easy tasks after numerous glasses of Tibetan beer. It was bitterly cold too, and their fingers were stiff and clumsy. They tipsily set up Wienert's equipment and somehow, in spite of the Tibetan beer, the cold and the dark, took readings; Yatung is there in Wienert's data at 9,780 feet, latitude 27°29′, longitude 88°54′. He was always meticulous, however challenging the circumstances. As they travelled closer to Lhasa his work would become much more difficult, and a great deal was at stake. 'If these activities had been discovered by the Tibetan authorities,' he wrote, 'this would have meant the end of the expedition. The Tibetan as an individual is rather harmless and extremely helpful, but in congregations, especially when involved in religious service, he becomes easily excited and dangerous.'[6] Despite this, between Yatung and Lhasa he found ways to set up fourteen geomagnetic stations, most often working in the very early hours of the morning. During the day Wienert often let the rest of the caravan pass by, and as soon as he was out of sight would seize another opportunity to set up his tripod and magnetometer. Whenever he *was* discovered, one of the sherpas would strike poses as if Wienert were taking photographs.

On Christmas morning everyone felt ill and bad-tempered so Schäfer, with aggressive bonhomie, forced them all to play games. His dark mood appeared to have lifted, at least for now. He handed out gifts of new wellington boots to the porters and a few extra rupees. From Yatung, Schäfer followed the Chumbi towards Phari with, he wrote, 'a new caravan'. This needs some explanation. Geer and Schäfer had recruited permanent staff in Sikkim – Kaiser, of course, and Akeh Bhutia, as well as Mingma, Lezor, Pänsy and the enigmatic Rabden – but other porters came and went as the party progressed from one big town to the next. And at each stage, yaks and mules were replaced. What lay behind this confusing state of affairs was the Tibetan transportation corvée system.[7] All the great routes that criss-crossed the Tibetan plateau were divided into *satsigs* – relay stations at intervals of a half-day's walk. At each *satsig*, villagers were obligated by the government to provide animals and shelter on presentation of a *lamyik*, or travel permit. Marion Duncan referred to this as '*Oolah*',[8] and he was a wily manipulator of the system. But it placed a tremendous burden on Tibetan peasants who had at all times to keep large numbers of animals available for travellers. Tibetans would always try to extract money from foreigners, and in practice 'Oolah' usually led to protracted and heated negotiation. Geer and Schäfer also faced wrangling about the most propitious travel times with any peripatetic lamas who had attached themselves to the caravan, with the result that every departure felt like a hard-won miracle.

On 26 December the new caravan pushed on down the Amo-chu and began climbing again. Now their mules and yaks had to carry firewood because they would soon be above the tree line. Snow-clad peaks began to appear above the fir-lined hills of the valley. Travelling at the same time of year, one of Younghusband's journalists, Edmund Candler, described an orgiastic profusion of gentians, anemones, eight varieties of primula, wood sorrel, wild strawberries and, of course, yet more rhododendrons 'glowing like coals in the firs'. For some hours they rode alongside the Amo-chu, now a raging Himalayan torrent, then ascended through a gorge layered with scrub and jungle. Above on either side were bare rocky peaks.

As Schäfer rode on, all at once it seemed the valley became dead level for many miles. He had reached the Lingma Thang. This miniature tableland had been created when a landslide had blocked the Amo-chu; a lake had formed, then silted and dried. On either side were bare craggy uplands dotted with monasteries and their hermitages, including the imposing Gompa of Donka, or the Kargyu Monastery. Big white *chortens* dotted the valley ridges. These walled towers – the word *chorten* means 'receptacle for offering' – usually contained the remains of saints. They were also symbolic structures representing the Earth and the elements: *chortens* are usually crowned by a crescent moon and a sun that represent fire and air.[9] From the roof of the monastery, curious 'Yellow Hat' monks watched the procession of foreigners below and wondered how they had dared enter Tibet. They blew their great horns as if to warn them away.

The Chumbi became increasingly wild and rugged as they travelled on, always climbing, through claustrophobic gorges hemmed in by steep, grey slopes of scree. They passed pilgrims and monks and more caravans. Eventually the gorges ended and they emerged high on the Tibetan plateau. They had crossed another frontier. The Chumbi Valley was only marginally Tibet, and its people were not Tibetan. Here, guarded by the sentinel peak of Chomolhari, was the true edge of the 'roof of the world'. Schäfer and his comrades were standing near one of the most remarkable frontiers on the surface of the Earth.

Twenty-five million years ago, after a six-thousand-mile journey across the Pacific, the geological plate that carried the Indian subcontinent smashed into Eurasia. Between the two brutish masses lay the Sea of Tethys. The massive collision threw the sea floor upwards many thousands of feet. It became a plateau the size of western Europe – Tibet. For a few million years the great plateau was hot and wet, but the battle of the continents intensified and Tibet was lifted to higher and much more arid altitudes. At the same time, the colossal forces released by the collision threw up tremendous chains of mountains that rippled out from the impact zone. Tibet became a natural fortress buttressed to the south by the Himalayas, the youngest and highest mountains on earth that continue to rise five millimetres every year even as they are fiercely eroded by water, wind and snow. The Karakoram and the Kunlun arc from west to north where they join the Altyn and Quilian Ranges that sweep to the east. Much of Tibet is above twelve thousand feet and altitude above all has moulded the land and its peoples. Only in the north-east is Tibet easier to penetrate. Here, in the Amdo and Kham regions, lower-lying plains merge into the Asian steppe and Chinese highlands – a fact of geography which would have a deadly historical penalty.

The Tibetan plateau tilts downwards from north-west to south-east like an immense rocky and dripping plate. All the great rivers of Asia originate on the plateau. In the east, the Yellow and the Yangtze, the Mekong and the Salween drop many thousands of feet from the rim of the plateau, gouging out tremendous ravines then flowing more than three thousand miles across China and south-east Asia. Between the Himalayas and the Nyanchengtangla Range north of Lhasa, which Hedin called the Transhimalaya, is the Tsang Po River, which when it reaches Assam dives to the south and tears through one of the deepest and most perilous gorges in the world to become the Brahmaputra. The headwaters of the Tsang Po are close to the sacred mountain the Tibetans call Kang Rimpoche, the Indians Mount Kailas. One of the most sacred places in the world to Hindus and Buddhists and Jains, this is where the Indus, the Ganges and the Sutlej Rivers have their icy beginnings.

This was the new world Schäfer and his party now faced. Ahead for mile upon mile, grasslands stretched away across rounded stony hills towards an undulating horizon. There was not a single tree. Enormous herds of yak grazed in dark clumps and there were many columns of blue, greasy smoke rising from the dung fires of their herdsmen squatting outside their black yak-hair tents. Himalayan vultures and kites hovered high overhead. They could give their wild little ponies their head here. It was getting dark as the rolling hills gave way to a flat plain but they could still see the road leading dead straight across the dun-coloured earth to the great *dzong* at Phari. As the German Tibet Expedition rode into town they were greeted by Tibetans with protruding tongues. It was a traditional greeting, intended to show that they did not have the black tongues associated with the old Bön religion of Tibet.

Phari commanded the head of the Chumbi Valley but it was a scrappy place of flat-roofed dwellings surrounded by seemingly limitless space and dominated by Mount Chomolhari. It was the meeting place of the road from Sikkim and the 'Tremo La' from Bhutan, and at fifteen thousand feet was the highest human settlement in the world.[10] But its reputation among European travellers had little to do with its strategic setting or record-breaking elevation. Little, flat-roofed Phari was simply the Capital of Grime. 'Dirt, dirt, grease, smoke' were the words that dominated one early visitor's account. Perceval Landon, one of the correspondents who arrived with Younghusband, savoured every last drop and dollop of excrement, 'heaped up . . . to the first floor windows. In the middle of the street runs a stinking channel, which thaws daily. In it, horns and bones and skulls of every beast eaten or not eaten by the Tibetans lie till the dogs and ravens have picked them clean. The stench is fearful. A curdled and foul torrent flows, in the daytime, through the market place. The men and women have never washed themselves . . . and the disgust of all this is heightened by the everlasting snows of Chomolhari – a huge wedge of argent a mile high.'

The filth of Tibet and its people was a steady refrain in travellers' accounts, and Phari seemed to collect, to the colonial mind, every excrescence ever deposited on the roof of the world. It is hard to know whether Phari was encrusted with excrement or simply myth. Schäfer had discovered for himself that it was a scurrilous fairy tale that Tibetans never washed, but although he admitted 'I myself love the odour of yak dung more than anything', Phari surpassed expectations. As the expedition rode in, the yaks and mules kicked up a deep layer of dried excrement both animal and human which rose in choking, stinking clouds. Schäfer and his comrades pulled out handkerchiefs and held them tightly over their noses. People, it appeared, defecated everywhere and their efforts actually raised the street level. The houses were built with mud cement, which was slowly blown away in the cold, dry air.

Schäfer asked Rabden to find out if he could pay his respects to the *dzongpon*, but his enigmatic interpreter came back with a negative reply. In malodorous Phari, the European visitors, who seemed to have miraculously brought a mild winter in their wake, had a much too elevated status. Or were the Tibetans playing hard to get? British visitors were often met by officials bearing the traditional white silk scarves of greeting. In 1936, Gould had met all the local 'celebrities' in Phari and been presented with these *kata*.

For Younghusband, Phari had been the scene of an unintended change of tactics. His army had been unopposed all the way down the Chumbi Valley, but no Tibetan had come forward to negotiate. Because officially Younghusband was being escorted, his troops had to have an official commander. That man was Brigadier General James MacDonald, and he fought Younghusband's ambiguous authority every foot of the way. In Phari, tensions between the British commanders boiled over. Younghusband had assured the Tibetans that he would leave the Phari *dzong* untouched, but MacDonald countermanded his order and galloped into the town, where the small Tibetan garrison politely surrendered. The action made military sense, but Younghusband was furious, for he could no longer claim he was leading a peaceful mission.

Now that they had left the Chumbi Valley behind and arrived on the Tibetan plateau, Schäfer could no longer restrain his passions. Just as his comrades would continue their work, using equipment theoretically banned by their agreement with the Tibetans, he would find a way to hunt and collect. Although he is secretive about this transgression in his books, Beger tells us that his first idea – probably inspired by the slingshots carried by Tibetan herdsmen – was to make catapults from the rubber lining in their cases. The catapults were surprisingly powerful and allowed Schäfer to furtively shoot down small birds and the mouse-hares, voles and other rodents that scuttled about wherever they travelled. Schäfer, it will be recalled, had another task to perform for the Reichsführer on the fertile Tibetan plateau: he needed to collect barley and wheat seeds – progenitors, he hoped, of hardy new breeds that would feed the Reich when war came. Now that they had entered one of the most fertile regions of the plateau, Schäfer would frequently send Kaiser out on seed-hunting forays. By the end of the expedition they had acquired more than fifty new varieties for the Reich.

Beger, in search of human quarry, set off to explore Phari and take photographs. At the end of a road choked with mud and littered with dead and decaying dogs and mules, he found himself facing the grey-walled Phari *dzong* itself. It was a colossal, rambling structure constructed from big stone blocks and rising six storeys. He walked through the massive main gate into a courtyard which had become a storehouse for what seemed to be instruments of punishment. Stocks, wooden collars, iron fetters, thong whips and the like were all stacked higgledy-piggledy around the walls. Looking up, Beger could see imposing machiolated galleries and projecting bastions. These castles fascinated the Germans. For Schäfer, they stood as symbols of Tibet's imperial past, a time when its peoples were warriors.

After tying a handkerchief over his face, Beger squeezed through a tiny cavity into a claustrophobic warren of stairs and passageways. He climbed up to Escher-like landings and peered into dark, empty rooms with narrow slit windows. The enormous structure seemed to be deserted, but in every nook and cranny were the putrid secretions of centuries of occupation. Bugs and beetles engaged in noisy and ceaseless activity, darting from one pile of dirt to the next. Wind from the plateau blew through the narrow windows and broken walls. Dust stuck to Beger's clothes and blew into his eyes. In 1903, the British had discovered rooms full of shields and breastplates, old matchlocks, slings, and bows and arrows. For a week they had set eighty coolies to work clearing the rubbish from the fort. The wind simply blew it all back. When he re-emerged, smeared with noxious grime, Beger was pursued by a decrepit man who appeared to be deranged. He was persistent, so Beger raised a stick. A small crowd gathered and one man lifted the beggar's shirt to show Beger a livid mass of bruises. 'How often had this man been beaten?' Beger reflected, then commented, with astonishing irony, 'So this is how mentally ill people are treated here.' In Germany, the first killing of a handicapped child had taken place that year, and the T4 euthanasia programme was initiated in 1939. Forced sterilization of the 'unfit' had been taking place since 1933.

While Wienert – 'our indefatigable geophysicist', as Schäfer later called him – continued to work mainly at night, usually dressed from head to toe in leather so as to endure the cold winds, Beger resumed his anthropometric work, taking advantage of the rich diversity of people passing back and forth through the little village's fetid streets. There were Bhutanese traders who bustled around in kilt-like robes carrying straight swords sheathed in silver; Mongolian Buddhist pilgrims and Tibetans from Amdo too, with their rolling gait and reddish dark skin; Indians, Nepalis and Bhutia all came through Phari trading cotton, precious stones, needles or soap for Tibet's wool, musk, yak-tail fly whisks and gold dust. Close to the *dzong* was a bazaar selling mirrors, jewellery, bricks of tea, spices and tea cups, where everyone came. It was an anthropologist's dream, but the persistent wind and foul dust made working conditions extremely difficult and Beger was disappointed that so many people ran away whenever he tried to photograph them. The Phari women were especially hard to capture. They smeared blood onto their cheeks as protection from the sun and Schäfer described them as 'disgusting', 'witches' and 'the scum of the earth'. Krause had a more generous eye. His rushes are full of smiling women with hooped head-dresses and elaborate costumes.

The expedition had set up camp far enough away to avoid the stench of Phari. New Year was coming and their talk often turned to Germany and their eventual return. By now, they were aware that a European war was likely, and Geer argued that they should plan to return overland rather than through British India, where they could be interned. Schäfer would become increasingly unhinged by these fears and vented his spleen about the British in a newspaper article he was drafting for the *Frankfurter Zeitung*. Beger and Wienert were taking it in turns to type it up for him on the expedition typewriter. It would cause him no end of difficulty when it was translated for the Foreign Office the following spring.

And he had developed another fixation. He now wanted to take Kaiser, who shadowed Schäfer's every move, back with him to Germany when the expedition was over. In Berlin, they would share an apartment and Kaiser would get a German medical education. After that he would be free to return to Sikkim. The nature of Schäfer's passion for Kaiser is not easy to make sense of, and the most detailed accounts of his state of mind come not in his own writings or those of other expedition members but from the British records. These are hardly objective, written as they were by men who had experienced the very special education provided by England's public schools. Their account has to be read with some care, as we shall see shortly.

The expedition was still hundreds of miles from Lhasa. Between Phari and the Holy City stretched the forbidding plateau and a double barricade of mountain ranges before they could descend to the Tsang Po and the final leg to Lhasa. After a few days at Phari they set off again, this time towards Gyantse. The night had been stormy and the winds blowing across the flat plain were still fierce. The temperature was –5°C. As Schäfer's caravan joined the long wind-blown line of traders, yaks, donkeys, oxen and pilgrims on the road to the Tang La Pass, they are unlikely to have looked back over their shoulders with regret, all too pleased to see the last of the hovels of Phari. To the west, rising abruptly from the grassy plain, glowered the dark cone of Chomolhari. Clouds raced across its tremendous snow-clad flanks, dramatizing the mountain's height and power and reminding the Germans of the Matterhorn. On the other side of the plain was the snow-clad mass of Pauhunri whose peaks seemed to have been smoothed by some primeval force so that it resembled Chomolhari's humble companion. Other mountains loomed ahead. The Germans were awed by the colours. Rock was red, yellow and ochre, sometimes laced with bands of green and white quartz. There was a softer green where the glaciers dipped down towards the plateau and grass grew in the melt water. Higher up there was the gleaming snow against the intense blue of a sky that was closer to the sun than anywhere else on Earth. Always, as Fosco Maraini also recalled, there was wind, sometimes stroking, sometimes punishing; the sound of the yaks and mules; the porters talking and laughing. The climb up to the Tang La, which means 'level pass', was not especially arduous and only the usual prayer flags and cairns of stones made it apparent that they had crossed over. On the other side, the road gently sloped down to a barren and stony expanse which stretched for many miles in all directions – this was the Plain of the Three Brothers. From the Tang La a road split off in the direction of Khampa Dzong, and the main route led through a scattering of tiny hamlets towards Gyantse.

It remained cold and stormy for days. On New Year's Eve, the caravan rode past Dochen Lake – also known as the Rham Tso – which was covered with shards of ice. The Tibetan plateau is pockmarked with many lakes, all relics of the ancient Sea of Tethys. The expedition sheltered at another Dak bungalow nearby and celebrated the turning of the year with anxious talk and a great deal of alcohol. Wienert slipped out into the storm to collect more data. Clad in his leather coat, he worked for hours in his swaying tent battered by wind and dust. In the morning, he took astronomical sightings. Schäfer was satisfied that thanks to Wienert's scrupulous secrecy 'no Tibetan knows that we have sinned against their gods'. A violent storm engulfed them on New Year's Day and it was impossible to travel further. On the 3rd the mail was brought by runner and they had news of home – and it was very worrying indeed.

After the Munich Conference, very few of the Western democracies had believed that Hitler's demands were at an end. War was unavoidable, and Britain and France were now committed to breakneck rearmament. In Germany, however, there was debate and indecision about the next move, and Hitler regretted that he had not smashed the Czechs as he'd originally intended in the autumn. For now, he contented himself with fomenting division in Ruthenia, the mountainous Czech border with the Ukraine, and made plans to take back an obscure German territory (with a Lithuanian minority), the Memelland. The destruction of Czechoslovakia was inevitable sooner rather than later and Hitler was also looking greedily at Danzig, the German port on the Polish coast. Most of the Nazi elite were consumed by imperial ambition. Himmler, who had been building his military wing, the Waffen-SS, longed to seize the territories of the East.

Furious rearmament, however, had generated an economic crisis in Germany. High wages and a shortfall in consumer goods meant that the banks sent Hitler an ultimatum warning that the spectre of inflation was threatening to overwhelm Germany. Hitler fired the president of the Reichsbank, but the crisis merely got worse. Hitler hated Versailles and despised the Czechs, but the phenomenal industrial wealth and natural resources of Bohemia and Moravia as well as Czechoslovakian gold and currency resources made conquest even more desirable. It was just a question of time. In the winter of 1938 to 1939, pressure was increased on the Poles and her foreign minister was summoned to the Berghof for the usual bullying negotiations. In January, Hitler made a series of speeches to the Wehrmacht promising them untold power as conquerors. Their loyalty was essential and difficult to guarantee, but the meetings went very well. Afterwards, celebrating officers vomited happily in the corners of the new Chancellery.

In Spain, Franco's forces finally smashed the Republicans thanks to aid and arms from Hitler and Mussolini. And in Rome Pope Pius XI died, and was replaced by Cardinal Eugenio

Pacelli. The new Pope was an admirer of all things German and was resolutely opposed to any confrontation with the Nazis. Intent on conquest, Hitler issued a warning to the Jews: if their machinations led to a war, the result would be their own annihilation. At least on paper, the gloves were off. Nietzsche had said in 1887 that in a nation founded on order and obedience, held in check by custom and obedience, used to spying on one another and believing too strongly that it was a noble race, 'we cannot fail to see the blond beast of prey . . . avidly prowling round for spoil and victory . . .' He had warned, 'The beast must come out again, must return to the wild.' By the beginning of 1939, the beast was loose.

In the wilds of Tibet, apparently far removed from the crisis in Europe, Schäfer digested the news from Germany and must have realized that time was running out. On 3 January the expedition had begun to cross the immense plain below the Tang La Pass. The journey inspired some of Beger's most lyrical diary entries: 'We had to look back again and again at the [lake] which looked as beautiful as a painting in the early morning light. Overall, this stretch seemed the most beautiful of the Highlands: the deep blue surface of the lake was framed by gentle, light brown hills, that seemed to be covered with velvet . . . Above them was the lighter, pure blue of the sky with a few white clouds. Far away in the haze were the gigantic snow-covered peaks we had passed days ago. We would remember this stunningly beautiful landscape and long to return here after we had returned home.' They passed a red-walled monastery where Indian Viceroy Warren Hasting's emissary George Bogle[11] had stayed nearly two hundred years earlier on his way to meet the Panchen Lama at Tashilunpo. On the edge of a tiny village called Chu-gya (which means 'frozen stream') the caravan halted in solemn respect. A grand rimpoche[12] from Lhasa cantered past, clad in a golden helmet and protected by a splendidly attired entourage running in his wake. It was their first glimpse of a frozen medieval world.

The German Tibet Expedition was now approaching the villages of Tuna and Guru. They were little wind-blown hamlets with hot springs, but in Tibetan memory their names conjured the same dread as Nanking or Guernica. It was here in 1904 that Younghusband's mission brought violent death to the Tibetan plateau. Schäfer knew this very well, and noted in *Geheimnis Tibet* that 'The Tibetans remember this time with fear and bitterness.' The chain of lethal events was as follows. The Tibetan government, which will be described in more detail in the next chapter, was bitterly divided about how it should respond to Younghusband's mission. The most progressive ministers understood that the Tibetan Army was not equipped to resist the British on the battlefield. Diplomacy and compromise were, in their opinion, the only workable responses to a very serious threat, but these men lost out to conservative factions who believed they could rid themselves of Younghusband just as they had other intruders in the past, by force. So in the winter of 1903–4, the Kashag ordered the mobilization of more than two thousand Tibetan militia and despatched them to Guru. They constructed a wall at a place called Chumi Shengo, complete with sturdy block houses called *sangars*, across Lhasa road all the way from the range of hills above the road and running in the direction of the Hram Tso Lake. But they made a fatal error. At one end the wall was securely buttressed by rising ground, but closer to the lake there was easy access across the Tibetan flank.

To be fair to Younghusband, it is clear that he wanted to negotiate rather than wage war, even though he spoke of 'smash[ing] those selfish filthy lecherous lamas'.[13] His troops had halted and made camp near Tuna where, in this treeless wasteland, firewood was a luxury and they were forced to endure, as Schäfer had, ferocious storms at night and bitterly cold winds during the day. High on the Tibetan plateau, a stalemated mission now froze solid. Supplies came over the pass and up the Chumbi Valley with maddening slowness. The Tibetans had sealed the valley, but in March 1904 the mission began to move further up it. Very soon Tibetan blood was being shed on the grasslands of Tuna. As the two very unequal armies confronted each other a stone was thrown – or so one version has it; other accounts say the British simply opened fire. What is certain is that their superior firepower killed more than six hundred Tibetans and wounded two hundred more. A Lieutenant Hadow 'got so sick of the slaughter that I ceased to fire'. The British fired 1,400 machine-gun rounds and 14,351 rifle rounds.[14] Candler, one of the journalists, observed that the defeated Tibetans 'walked with bowed heads as if they had been disillusioned with their gods'.

Younghusband, it is said, was appalled, but he blamed the massacre on the incitements of a fanatical lama and the silliness of the Tibetans. The Dalai Lama, in short, 'deserved to be kicked'. The London press was outraged by the incident, but the mission continued to advance towards Gyantse. Schäfer followed in their path in the winter of 1939. When the expedition camped near Guru, where it was still possible to see traces of the Tibetan wall, it is not difficult to imagine Schäfer telling his comrades about the bloody events that had taken place here just a few decades before. The Tibetans who were travelling with them and others whom they met en route would have had their own stories to tell, full of 'fear and bitterness'. Younghusband had haunted Schäfer's journey from the start. His advice to 'sneak over the border' had resulted in a stunning success – but his reputation served Schäfer in another, completely different way. In Tibet, the British had blood on their hands; Germans did not.

After they had passed through Guru, Schäfer travelled on across the monotonous grassy plain, the caravan hugging the edge of wide, silvery lakes. These were Bham Tso and Kala Tso whose icy waters were shrouded by a multitude of wildfowl. Bogle had hunted here two centuries earlier, but the birds had no sense of humans as predators. Schäfer could not resist the opportunity, although whether he used a catapult or rifle is not known. Krause filmed more kiangs, Schäfer chasing the herd towards his camera. Then the expedition turned off the plain and entered the valley of the Nyang Chu, which flows down to Gyantse.

Now they rode past ruined houses and crumbling forts as well as untended irrigation ditches; fewer people came to the roadside to greet them. Different theories were offered to explain this eerie desertion: there had been plague in the area, or raids by Bhutanese bandits. After thirty miles, the sides of the valley abruptly narrowed. They had reached the Red Idol Gorge. In 1904, another Tibetan force had hastily thrown up a wall here and hundreds more were killed as the British forced their way through. The walls of the gorge soared above the caravan as men, mules and yaks plunged down the tortuous path alongside the river. The sheer walls of the ravine were honeycombed by recessed carvings of the Buddha daubed in red paint and bristling with countless prayer flags. At the foot of the gorge there was a towering Buddha carved from solid rock. From here the road led through lush fields of barley and mustard towards Gyantse. As the road dropped down to the river, they could see the Gyantse *dzong* rising above the city like a big broken giant's tooth.

Beger noted many swastika designs on the sides of houses, and even what he called 'Rune-like' figures, which implies that he had listened to Weisthor or the other SS mystics more than he cared to recall later. Schäfer travelled with swastika flags and SS banners whenever he was not observed by the British, as his film shows very clearly. In Tibet, the swastika is called a *yungdrung* and is represented with its arms both clockwise and counter-clockwise.[15] In its oldest form it is an image of the wind turning aside the rays of the sun; later, it came to represent good fortune. The Chinese call it *lei-wun* ('thunder rolling'), and Indians call it the *swasti*. You see them everywhere today. Charles Allen, whose account I am using here, calls the swastika the 'crux grammatica' in Asian religion. Swastikas adorn temples, houses and even lorries – when I visited the Ganden Monastery in 2002, a monk was happily polishing his swastikas on a brightly painted lorry. The main construction company in Sikkim is called Swastik. In Tibetan temples they are often made from Chinese money and pasted on walls. For the German occult mystics the swastika stood for Eastern wisdom. The Nazis had turned it into a sign of brutal aggression, but Schäfer shamelessly used his swastikas and thunderbolts to imply a cultural link with the Tibetans.

On 5 January the German Tibet Expedition crossed the massive stone bridge into Gyantse and rode past the Changlo, the British Trade Agency, the scene of fierce fighting in 1904. Gyantse is Tibet's third largest town and boasts one of the most remarkable monuments of Buddhist culture: the great *mandela* of the Kumbum. It means 'the hundred thousand images', and Fosco Maraini called it the Assisi of Tibetan Buddhism. The Kumbum is the biggest *chorten* in Tibet and rises to a tower with two painted eyes. Below are four platforms. Inside are seventy-three chapels whose walls are painted with an exhaustive representation of the entire Buddhist universe. The foundations measure precisely 108 cubits. The number is of special significance in Tibet: there should always be 108 votive candles, there are 108 signs of Buddhahood and the *Kangyur*, one of the Buddhist scriptures, comprises 108 volumes, as the expedition would discover.

Gyantse is set in an amphitheatre of hills crowned by the *dzong* and a chain of red fortresses called the Dragon's Back. It was also a commercial hub, and the mercenary and spiritual were tightly woven. The wool market was held in the monastic compound and the stalls were rented out by monks, who could make big profits. Roads from Lhasa, Shigatse and Sikkim all met here, and the seat of the Panchen Lama was not far away. The British had a garrison here too, manned by fifty Indian troops, and it did not take long for them to pick a fight with Schäfer.

His first antagonists were Major Mackenzie and Captain Clifford. The latter was a notorious drinker and an aggressive drunk. The Germans were invited for lunch at the agency's fort. When they arrived, Mackenzie took his guests upstairs to the mess, pointing out the two big guns left over from Younghusband's mission. For Schäfer it was a not very subtle reminder of the military power the British could deploy if they so wished. In the mess the British officers and the SS men stood shivering around the wood stove and made awkward conversation. Clifford began to consume prodigious quantities of stout with gin chasers. At a lung-scorching 13,500 feet, Gyantse was a hardship posting in winter with sub-zero temperatures at night and dust storms in the day. Schäfer now learnt that Hugh Richardson was due to ride down from Lhasa in two days and had ordered that the expedition wait for him before they travelled any further. It was not welcome news.

As lunch was served, Clifford launched into a slurred rant against Nazi Germany which reached a climax when he knocked over a glass of stout. He began with Munich, and bellowed at his guests, 'Nobody trusts Germans!' which infuriated them all. Schäfer, Beger wrote, ignored Clifford and talked across him to Mackenzie, trying to 'give a better image of Germans'. Increasingly red-faced, Clifford raged that *Mein*

Kampf had been deliberately translated with mistakes and omissions so that Hitler's real aims were never understood. But Germany would lose a war, and in spite of Goebbel's anti-Semitic propaganda only half the German people supported Hitler. He concluded with a triumphant 'I have beaten you!' and slumped over his plate.

The meeting with Richardson a few days later was stone-cold sober but very tense. He ticked them off for insulting a postal runner then demanded to see their papers. These he minutely examined before handing them back, claiming that they contained mistakes. Richardson also ordered Schäfer to stop displaying his swastika flag. Rabden must have informed him about this, and presumably Richardson had met Gould's 'plant' before meeting Schäfer. There is no evidence to suggest that Schäfer ever complied with Richardson's wish when out of his sight, especially when his swastikas had become such useful calling cards with Tibetan dignitaries. Richardson reasserted the prohibition on shooting and measuring, too. It is certain that Schäfer would have made sure that Rabden was not present when his men did their science: and concealment was always tricky.

Schäfer might have been amused if he had known about the favourite activity of one of Gyantse's former trade officers. Mr F. M. Bailey revealed much about life at the Trade Agency for *Blackwoods Magazine*[16] and began by describing his breakfast ruminations: 'What is to be done today? . . . the obvious answer to the question has just presented itself – *Let us kill something.*' The Dalai Lama had banned hunting in 1901 but Bailey was able to pursue his passion without restraint. He even built a zoo to accommodate the orphaned offspring of the animals he bagged and, just as Dolan and Schäfer had done, supplied museums in England with skins and specimens. As late as 1940, an escort officer reported hooking a dead baby from a Tibetan river while fishing. For the British to enforce a ban on hunting by German travellers looks like hypocrisy. Their strategy was to harass Schäfer and to prevent Wienert gathering useful geographical information. When they finally reached Lhasa itself the Germans and British would wage cold war until August 1939 when Schäfer had few choices left.

There were much more congenial encounters with Tibetan officials. They had tea with the 'Eastern' and 'Western' *dzongpons* and invited one of them to lunch. This was probably Tendong, who spoke English, having been educated at Frank Ludlow's short-lived English School in Gyantse which, among other small achievements, had introduced the Tibetans to football.[17] According to Beger's diaries, Schäfer 'led the conversation with glowing reports about Germany and news about new technology which met with amazement . . .'

Beger had been informed by the smirking Captain O'Malley, the British medical officer, that the *dzongpon*'s wife 'liked to be examined'. There is a photograph taken by Krause of the *dzongpon*'s wife which shows a very pretty young woman with a radiant smile. Unused, perhaps, to British humour, Beger saw an opportunity to advertise the skills that had given him such a high status in Sikkim, so while Schäfer was promoting the Reich, Beger would represent the Master Race in another way. He described the episode frankly in his diaries. His first task was to treat the *dzongpon*'s digestive problems so, as he usually did, he prescribed a harmless placebo and suggested dietary changes. Beger then asked after the *dzongpon*'s wife's health. The *dzongpon* replied somewhat briskly that his wife was perfectly fine, but she stepped fearlessly up to Beger and requested, as O'Malley had anticipated, an 'examination'. Here is what happened: 'With Rabden to translate, I took her to a side room where I had all my gleaming instruments laid out on a little table. Without wasting any time or showing any embarrassment, she exposed her upper body and lay down on the bed. I listened, tapped and checked her all over while she looked at me all the time in a relaxed and beguiling manner. Or so it seemed to me. She had a tender and petite body with small, firm breasts and charming nipples.' Beger concluded his entry with some regret: 'Yet I asked her to get dressed again and gave her some medication for future use with exact instructions.'[18] Few anthropologists have made their relationship to the unclothed native body more explicit than this.

On 11 January the German Tibet Expedition left Gyantse and travelled on towards Gobshi. The expedition was just over halfway to Lhasa. The toughest pass lay ahead of them, and then the long descent to the Tsang Po. They stopped after about six miles to renew their friendship with the Tering Raja – Schäfer's 'King of Tharing' – on his country estate just outside Gyantse. Just as he'd been at Doptra, the Raja and his family were generous hosts. In a grand room full of rather stuffy European furniture and Chinese hangings they plied the Germans with an endless succession of dishes. The Terings had a fondness for crème de menthe.[19] But the Raja was nervous and uncomfortable. As *chang* (barley beer) was poured from a silver jug, he confessed that he had informed on Schäfer to Gould about his 'sneaking over the border'. This confirmed what Schäfer had suspected ever since Beger's assistants had been 'insulted' by the Raja's men in Sikkim; the Raja had almost certainly been embarrassed in some fashion either by the British or by the Kashag. Still, Schäfer knew that he owed a great deal to the Raja's intervention, however unwise it had been. They parted on very friendly terms.

The caravan travelled on down a stony valley and stopped for the night at Gobshi. Although the village lay at the junction of a number of valleys, it was ruined and deserted. A dilapidated fort stood on a rocky outcrop nearby. They had an uncomfortable night and sang rousing German songs to cheer themselves up. Later, a young woman drifted into the camp. The *dzongpon*'s wife must have stirred tired German libidos, for as she squatted demurely in the firelight the young men were captivated. The following morning she was asked to travel on with the caravan as a 'maid'. After leaving the desolate village, the caravan rode through the Nyang Chu Gorge and reached Ralung by the evening. Above the river valleys here, the landscape was dry and parched. From Ralung they could see the shimmering glaciers of the Karo La, the next pass. It was more than thirty miles away so Schäfer decided to push on as fast as possible across the snow and ice. He rode the caravan hard. By nightfall they had arrived in Nangartse, on the threshold of the pass, making this the longest day's march. Schäfer was exhausted and feverish and immediately went to bed with three pans of hot sheep dung. He was in no mood for company.

He had barely closed his eyes when Kaiser shook him awake: the *dzongpon* himself had arrived with two other officials and was waiting to see him. Cursing, a grumpy Schäfer pulled on his pith helmet with its SS insignia and stumbled across the icy ground to the *dzongpon*'s house. A number of Tibetans were gathered in the courtyard. The *dzongpon* presented gifts of dried meat and eggs and invited the Germans into his residence, where he showed them an impressive canopy. It served as a place of honour for visiting dignitaries, or even a Dalai Lama should he come this way. Beer and *tsampa* were served, but the *dzongpon* had more than hospitality on his mind. The conversation turned to the dilemma of the new Dalai Lama, a mere child who had been discovered at the Kumbum Monastery in Amdo on the Chinese border more than a year earlier, in 1937. The Muslim governor of Sining, General Ma Pu-fang, who had made life so difficult for the second Dolan expedition, was holding the boy and the search party hostage.

In the meantime, all Tibet was waiting for the new Dalai Lama to be proclaimed. And now the *dzongpon* came to the point: the ban on hunting would be enforced with special stringency, and neither could there be any 'scientific' work. Somehow, intelligence about the expedition had raced ahead of them. Even if Rabden Kazi was not spying on them, Schäfer himself reported that when they had passed through the village of Ralung the local people were especially hostile to 'scientific work' and feared it would bring plague and famine. Despite taking every care, both his and Wienert's forbidden investigations were no longer a secret. Schäfer promised to honour the *dzongpon*'s request, but all he told Wienert and Beger was to take more care.

The following morning Schäfer was invited to a banquet by the *dzongpon*, but he sent Beger alone as a diversion and 'explored' the area with Kaiser. Beger rather cryptically notes that at the banquet he requested the *dzongpon* 'not to visit them' that afternoon. Although Beger was able to take a number of photographs in Nangartse that day, Wienert records a series of data entries for Gyantse, Gobshi and Ralung but then 'jumps' Nangartse and picks up again at Pede Dzong, on the other side of the Karo La. Schäfer had clearly decided not to risk discovery by the inquisitive *dzongpon*.

'Oolah' at Nangartse was very poor and the expedition was forced to continue on the sore-encrusted backs of low-quality animals. These sorry mules were the *dzongpon*'s last gift. According to the British files, 'The Germans made themselves unpopular at Dochen, Tuna and Phari by demanding supplied [*sic*] for which they paid at less than current rates, and by allowing their Sherpa servants, recruited in Darjeeling, to abuse and beat the people. There are also complaints in regard to anthropometrical measurements.' Making sense of these different accounts is not easy. The most plausible explanation is that Richardson had poisoned the well of goodwill on his way back to Lhasa, but reports of the Germans paying low wages and letting their men treat the Tibetans high-handedly are very consistent. Richardson *was* fighting a rearguard action and Schäfer was an aggressive expedition *führer*. Both sides were on a collision course.

On the threshold of the Karo La, Schäfer decided to reward his comrades with the last ounces of coffee. Lezor the cook boiled up the water and handed round steaming cups. Schäfer went first, raising this sacred last cup to his lips, but as soon as he took the first sip he violently spat it out on the ground. Now it was the others' turn, but they too gagged on then spat out the foul-tasting brown liquid. Schäfer angrily turned on Lezor, and the cook quickly fingered the real culprit – none other than Rabden Kazi, who had, he confessed, washed his face in the coffee pot. 'Oh this son of Satan!' Schäfer cursed. 'Rabden, you idiot, what have you done to us? Washed your dirty face and ruined our whole day . . .' He must have enjoyed humiliating the man he so mistrusted. It was a delicious moment for Kaiser too, who resented Rabden's enforced closeness with Schäfer.

There was busy traffic on the road as they climbed coffeeless up towards the icy summit of the Karo La. Fractious yaks were strung out along the path, swaying fluffy mountains of wool tied to their backs. The temperature was –10°C and it was stormy as Schäfer rode up ahead with Kaiser. He tried to photograph some blue sheep but was unable to hold the camera steady in the freezing wind. On either side were towering mountains sheathed with snow and with formidable glaciers tonguing down towards the valley floor, creaking in the bright sunlight. When they reached the great collection of cairns and prayer flags at the summit of the pass, their men shouted, '*Lha Gyo-la!*' ('God be praised'). In 2002, there were masses of Tibetan beggars here who wanted money to be photographed.

Schäfer led the expedition down towards the Yamdrok Tso ('the lake of the upper pastures') which glistened, like an immense blue scorpion, in the twilight. Lhasa was not far away.

For the Tibetans who travelled with the Germans, Karo La was a haunted place. Here in 1904 the Tibetan Army had made its last stand, and travellers were still stumbling on their bones in rocky clefts above the road in the 1930s. In April 1904 Younghusband had sent Colonel Brander and a small force up into the Karo La, where he had discovered yet another wall across the road manned by three thousand Tibetan soldiers who immediately opened fire. Brander ordered the Maxim machine-guns to reply and an infernal racket echoed through the pass. Battle had never been joined at this altitude in military history, and this close to Lhasa the Tibetans fought with desperate courage. Back in Gyantse, the Tibetans had stormed the *dzong* and had only been ejected after a bloody fight. The British raced up the now reoccupied Karo La Pass and swept aside the last defenders. The road to Lhasa was now open before them, and on 30 July the 13th Dalai Lama fled to Mongolia accompanied by the mysterious Russian agent Agvan Dorzhiev. What Younghusband could not know is that Curzon's political star was now waning, and with it his own.

In the winter of 1939 the weather continued to be cold and stormy as Schäfer and his men skirted the edge of the Yamdrok Tso in the direction of Pede. Tibetans called this the 'Turquoise Lake', and its colour, Younghusband noted, was never stable, modulating through every shade of violet to 'the blue of heaven' and then a deep greeny-blue. Snow-draped peaks of the central Tibetan ranges were reflected on its surface, which was flecked with long, blue rafts of ice. Fish teemed in flickering, darting shoals. Nearby was the nunnery of one of the most remarkable of all Tibetan incarnations, Dorje Phagmo or 'Thunderbolt Sow'.

At Pede, where a ruined *dzong* stood on a tongue of land projecting into the lake, the expedition was warmly greeted by the *dzongpon* and presented with friendship scarves. As they got closer to Lhasa, Schäfer grew increasingly optimistic that they would be received with appropriate pomp. A fear of injured pride dominated all his relationships, whether with Tibetans, the English or his fellow Germans. The next morning they were all fed eggs; they estimated that during the previous six months they had consumed at least ten thousand. From the Yamdrok Tso, they climbed again, crossed the Kamba La and saw for the first time the valley of the Tsang Po – the Tibetan name for the Brahmaputra, which had flowed from Tibet's holy Mount Kailas, eventually draining into the Bay of Bengal. The Tsang Po and its tributaries nurtured the first Tibetan kingdoms, which emerged in the Yarlung Valley to the east of Lhasa. It is the Nile of Tibet, a resemblance that is reinforced by the tremendous sand dunes that rise along its flanks. Schäfer halted the caravan above the Tsang Po and the Germans squatted on the ridge looking down at the great brown river below 'in silent devotion and overwhelmed by inner joy' until it was dark. Even a phlegmatic British observer standing on the same spot had felt that he had 'come through the desert to Arcady'. Lhasa was now just three days away.

The German Tibet Expedition crossed the river at Chaksam, where there were two long, flat ferries operated by monks, and yak-hide-covered coracles that were paddled with what looked like ping-pong bats attached to poles. In 1904 the British had taken more than three days to cross and an officer had drowned. Schäfer and Krause were off 'filming birds', so Beger handled the crossing alone and impressed the ferrymen by rowing some of the way himself across the wide, yellow waters. A storm rumbled from the mountains before the caravan had crossed, but for now the thunder gods were content just to growl.

From Chaksam, the road led to Chu-Shur, where rocky spurs cut into the flow of the river, turning it into a foaming torrent. Here the Tsang Po is joined by the Kyi Chu, and the road to Lhasa. Where the rivers met, Schäfer was greeted as usual by the *dzongpon* and other local officials. They introduced Schäfer to a monk who had travelled down from Lhasa to make arrangements for the Germans' arrival. He told Schäfer that a party of secular and religious officials would meet them outside the city in two days' time. Schäfer was, once more, encouraged that both the Kashag and the religious authority, the Yigtsang Office, acknowledged the high status of these potentates from the Reich. There was no reason for him to foresee any calamity.

They eagerly turned into the valley of the Kyi Chu, which means 'Middle River' or 'River of Happiness'. For the first day they travelled between irrigated oases and sandy desert. Interlocking spurs masked the way ahead, increasing their excitement. At the head of the valleys that drained into the Kyi Chu were small villages and monasteries. They passed one young woman drying herself naked in the sun. The city itself and the Potala Palace were screened from view by interlocking ridges, but the road was busy and crowded. There were trade caravans, of course, but now there were as many monks travelling alone or in groups, sometimes mounted but most often on foot. There were prostrating pilgrims, too – a sight so astonishing that Krause stopped to film one man for hours.

Prostration is fundamental to Buddhist religious practice. The pilgrim stretches out with his forehead touching the rocky ground and his arms outstretched. He usually carries wooden boards to protect his hands and binds his knees with rough cloth. A mark is made where the pilgrim's extended hands touch the ground. Then he stands up, places his hands together in the praying position and advances a few steps, positioning himself like an actor on the mark he has just made. Now he prostrates again, touches his forehead again, marks the position of his hands again, stands and prays again – and so on. For some pilgrimages from Mount Kailas or eastern Tibet all the way to Lhasa, the devout would measure their length on the ground over many hundreds of miles. Some even performed prostration sideways and advanced a mere body width each time. The man Krause photographed told Schäfer that he was from Amdo on the Chinese border in east Tibet. He claimed he had been walking and prostrating for eight years, 'through frost and storms'. Now he was close to the end, to Lhasa. Schäfer could not resist, when he wrote about the meeting later, a homily. He himself was a pilgrim approaching the end of his journey after eight years of restless wandering. His, though, was a 'pilgrimage of the highest science', not of 'fanatical faith'.

Their last stop was at Nethang. Here, Atisha, one of the great sages of Tibetan Buddhism, was buried in a grand tomb. The night was cold with a clear view of the stars; they listened to the drums and horns from nearby monasteries and the eerie cry of cranes. At dawn, everyone was ready, dusting down their saddles, and pressing ragged clothes and trimming beards. Schäfer would always remember this moment. The morning was unusually bright with a clear blue sky; he sniffed the mingled scent of burning juniper wood, leather and yak dung. Horses snorted and stamped, there was hurried praying from the servants' quarters and, barely perceptible, the cry of an owl. Then they set off, the Germans riding ahead with Rabden and Kaiser just behind. In the rear came their servants, the caravan leaders and finally the muleteers and baggage. It was 19 January 1939.

The plan was to meet their reception committee when the 'holy sun throws the shortest shadow'. At a distance of ten miles, as they ascended a ridge they caught sight of the golden roof of the Potala Palace for the first time soaring above its rocky hill-top foundation. It was a highly charged moment, and Schäfer halted and knelt for as long as he dared to savour the spectacle of the Vatican of Tibetan Buddhism. Today, no such vista is possible. The road into Lhasa is a wide Chinese highway punctuated by advertisements for mobile telephones. At the end of the avenue the Potala is hidden behind a massive billboard.

The German Tibet Expedition passed the great Drepung Monastery, which resembled a fortified city huddling in the hills, and the State Oracle at Nechung. More profane was the nearby abattoir, which was busy even at that hour, its *ragyapa* (untouchable) slaughterers heaving carcasses of meat onto hooks and slashing them with long and bloody knives. By now the road was running on top of a causeway between low walls clad in clematis. In the marshy land stretching down to the river on their right, Schäfer could see thousands of the black-neck cranes that spent every winter near the Holy City, as well as redshanks and teal. He reminded himself that this close to Lhasa every one of them was especially sacred. To the right of the Potala was Chakpori, the Iron Hill crowned by the yellow-walled Medical College. They passed the *lingkas*, or parks, which were lined with white poplars and willows. On the edge of the city was the Summer Palace of the Dalai Lamas, the Norbulinka. Everyone was in high spirits, 'eyes wide open to take it all in'.

Then they heard a clatter of hooves approaching rapidly from behind. Schäfer twisted in his saddle and saw two very familiar figures riding at a lick in the same direction and obviously determined to overtake the German caravan. It was Hugh Richardson and Captain Clifford. Schäfer made to raise his hand in greeting but the two men rode past, kicking up a cloud of dust. Richardson barely acknowledged the Germans, muttering only a curt hello. It was a gesture none of them ever forgot; it still rankles with Beger more than sixty years later. There was worse to come.

A few miles from the city, Rabden was sent ahead to scout out the reception committee. He returned with unsettling news: a single official was waiting for them, and a lowly one at that, Rabden was certain. He had requested that the five Germans meet him one by one, not as an official party. They were being welcomed, that was obligatory, but the German Tibet Expedition was most definitely not being acknowledged. It was a stinging insult. 'Unacceptable!' Schäfer stormed, but he was helpless to change anything. He rode on stoically and accepted, smiling and bowing, the solitary official's welcome to Lhasa. He had more crushing news. The Regent, the most powerful man in Tibet if there was no Dalai Lama, could not meet them today or at any time in the near future because he was, so he claimed, enjoying a spiritual retreat. The official then took Schäfer to meet officials from China and Nepal who ceremonially presented the Germans with white scarves in the Tibetan manner. It was a less than subtle rebuke to the British. The Chinese, some in uniform, then accompanied the Germans through the Western or Barkokali Gate, which cut through the middle of three white *chortens* built between the Marpori and Chakpori Hills. Now the German Tibet Expedition at last entered the Forbidden City. There were no fanfares; only small bells strung across the Barkokali Gate chimed in the breeze. A greeting party of beggars swiftly surrounded Schäfer's caravan, stretching thin and twisted arms towards the mysterious European visitors.

When Gould had arrived in Lhasa with a large party in 1936, they had been greeted first by Möndro, an important monk official and one of the Tibetans the British had sent to Rugby School, then by numerous other high-ranking members of the Kashag, all of whom presented white scarves on behalf of the Lönchen, who was something like a prime minister, and the Regent. They were then served tea and biscuits in the Garden of Mystics.[20] After tea, they were taken to inspect a guard of honour and were greeted by 'half the population of Lhasa'. This was an important diplomatic visit, to be sure, but Schäfer as a representative of the Reich was expecting a grander reception.

Inside the city, the white- and wine-coloured walls of the Potala Palace soared above them. A few citizens had come out to see the new arrivals and clapped loudly, which revived Schäfer's spirits. But, as Kaiser pointed out, they were merely trying to rid the city of evil spirits. In 1904, the 'rosy radiance' of the Potala Palace had inspired Younghusband to flights of mystical ecstasy, but on that January day in 1939 its impact on Schäfer and his comrades was muted by this sorry reception. To their right was the old village of Shöl, and ahead, across meadows and fields, they could see Lhasa Old Town clustered around the golden roofs of the Jokhang Temple. There was more humiliation to come.

Schäfer had been led to assume that the expedition would be offered accommodation in one of Lhasa's grand aristocratic mansions, but instead they were led to the Tredilinka, a drab and poky official residence near the river whose rank air was unpleasant testimony to the hygienic standards of its most recent occupants. This final blow made them depressed and angry, Beger admitted.

They now understood very clearly what Richardson had meant to convey when he rode past them, with such roughshod manners, into Lhasa. This was his city, and he wielded power the German intruders could not afford to ignore. Schäfer was determined to prove Richardson wrong, but he had only fourteen days in which to reverse his fortunes.

CHAPTER TEN

WEIRD BARBARITY

'The veil has been torn aside and the naked city [of Lhasa] has been revealed in all its weird barbarity.'

– Colonel Sir Thomas H. Holdich, 1906

'In particular we must guard ourselves against the barbaric red communists, who carry terror and destruction with them wherever they go . . .'

– Testament of the 13th Dalai Lama

Ernst Schäfer had entered a strange and perplexing world. Tibetans frequently complain that Westerners have turned Tibet into a spiritual Disneyland. Donald Lopez, an American scholar of Buddhism, has called Tibetans 'Prisoners of Shangri-la'. His reference is, of course, to the famous book by James Hilton published in 1933, soon turned into a Hollywood smash hit. Hilton represented Tibet as a kind of theosophical retreat which provided just about every spiritual solace except colonic irrigation. But his fiction simply gave a name to a long tradition. Scholars, travellers, diplomats as well as a lunatic fringe have for centuries pictured Tibet as a spiritual fastness, isolated, unchanging and pure. It was never anything of the sort, and it certainly wasn't in 1939. The story of that restless, bitter decade in Lhasa begins at the end of 1933.

On 12 December that year, Thubten Gyatso, the 'Great' 13th Dalai Lama, was reported to be feeling unwell.[1] His monks were informed that he could no longer appear for public audiences and instead he would be represented by a ceremonial robe placed on his throne. This was known as a 'throne audience', or 'inviting the clothes'. Many monks found his absence very distressing and became fearful about the condition of Tibet's spiritual ruler. They were right to be concerned. Inside the Dalai Lama's Norbulinka Palace there was intense and highly secretive fear. Tibet's theocratic ruler had been ill for twelve days, complaining of a poor appetite, shortness of breath and difficulty walking more than a few steps. When it became widely rumoured that the Dalai Lama had still not recovered some days later, monks in the monasteries that encircle Lhasa began continuously to chant 'The Prayer of Long Life' night and day, stopping only to relieve themselves. On the 16th, the Dalai Lama's favourite, Kumbela (Dechen Chödrön), entered the Dalai Lama's quarters and discovered his master panting for breath. He immediately summoned the State Oracle from Nechung.

Other important lamas now came running to the palace to urge the Dalai Lama to 'remain in his body' – that is to say, not to pass on to another incarnation. The Nechung Oracle also made a more practical recommendation: the Dalai Lama must take a medicine called 'the seventeen heroes for subduing colds'. For reasons that will never be known, the Dalai Lama refused. The Oracle insisted and poured a dose of 'seventeen heroes' down the Dalai Lama's throat himself. The condition of the patient immediately worsened and he lapsed into unconsciousness. The Great 13th, the spiritual ruler of Tibet, never spoke again and died on 17 December at 6.30 p.m. On the roof of the Potala Palace butter lamps were lit to signify that a death had taken place and the *dama* drums began tolling.

To say that the 13th Dalai Lama had experienced an eventful and turbulent life would be a gross understatement. He had been born in 1876 and acknowledged as Dalai Lama three years later. Until he reached his majority, a man called Demo Rimpoche was the de facto ruler of Tibet. Many of the Dalai Lama's predecessors had died young in mysterious circumstances and Tibet had been ruled by a succession of such regents for two centuries. Most of them were subservient to the Chinese, so it was very likely that these new incarnate rulers had been murdered by the Chinese faction in Lhasa. Almost as soon as Thubten Gyatso had become Dalai Lama, Demo Rimpoche attempted to kill him with a Buddhist black magic mantra sewn into a boot, but the plot was foiled by Sogya, a lama from Kamba, and the Nechung Oracle. Demo was arrested and drowned in a copper water vat. The foiled plot tempered the character of the new Dalai Lama and he grew into an effective and highly intelligent ruler after he reached his majority and took real power in 1895. It fell to him to steer Tibet into a new century, and it was the 'Great 13th' who had moulded the Tibet Schäfer entered in 1939.

It is often said that Tibet was a frozen feudal society and that to travel to Lhasa was to take a journey back into time. It was an image encouraged by the endless ceremonies and rituals of the Tibetan year, which were avidly photographed and described by Western visitors. Across the movie screens of Berlin or London passed an endless procession of monks and dignitaries in exotic costumes; behind them came helmeted men in chain mail and armour mounted on handsomely dressed horses. Tents were thrown up in front of the Potala Palace and warriors sought glory by winning prizes for feats of archery. But it would be a mistake to judge British political life by the most arcane parliamentary rituals, or to view morris dancers as typical English citizens. I pointed out at the beginning of this book that Schäfer exploited the old warrior Tibet in the documentary he released in 1942. To view *Geheimnis Tibet* today is to see, in the ceremonies and festivals Krause filmed in Tibet, a simulacrum of the folksy medieval parades organized by the Nazis in towns and villages all over Germany. To German audiences in 1943, Tibet must have looked oddly familiar.

What lay behind the surface, in both cases, was quite different. Tibet certainly resembled a feudal society. Its wealth came from agriculture and pre-modern industrial activities like wool manufacture. The countryside was dominated by manorial estates owned by the aristocrats (who so fascinated Bruno Beger), monasteries and lamas. These estates were hereditary and were dependent on labour performed by 'bound' serfs. They received only seed and plough animals from their lord and were usually obliged to perform other tasks like that onerous transportation corvée. Serfs were also taxed, and their children could be drafted as monks, servants or soldiers. Some were wealthy, but they had very few rights and no political power.

But there was a fundamental difference between a seemingly 'medieval Tibet' and Europe in the Middle Ages. While the Catholic Church was immensely powerful, the Pope was not a head of state. The Vatican had power, but it was not the residence of a king. Dalai Lamas were both pope and potentate and were powerful theocratic rulers. Tibetans used a phrase, *chösi nyitrel* – it meant religion and political affairs joined together. Like Siamese twins, state and Church occupied the same body, that of the Dalai Lama. He was both head of state and an incarnate god. The Potala Palace was, as Schäfer said, the 'Vatican' of Asia, but it was also where the Dalai Lama convened the National Assembly and imprisoned his enemies. It was also his private home and treasure house. And it was a mausoleum that housed the remains of previous Dalai Lamas in immense and lavish tombs.

The men who lay embalmed inside the vast silver- and jewel-encrusted tombs were not blood ancestors. In Tibetan Buddhist belief, the Dalai Lama was the earthly embodiment of the Bodhisattva Avalokiteśvara who ruled through divine not genetic inheritance. When a Dalai Lama passed on, the deity 'emanated' into a foetus, invariably male, a stranger who would be born as the next Dalai Lama. Incarnation was the engine of the state, ensuring that power could be dispensed only through the Church and that no earthly ruler could ever pass it on to his descendants.

Schäfer believed that the power of the old warrior Tibet had been sapped by Buddhism, but Buddhism when it first arrived in Tibet had become the religion of empire-building rulers. It was the machinations of monastic power brokers more than five hundred years after the decline of the Tibetan empire that made Tibet unique, and uniquely weak.

At the end of the twelfth century, a Mongolian aristocrat called Temujin was proclaimed Chinghis Khan – 'Universal Ruler'. He had savagely yoked together the warring Mongolian tribes and recruited a swift and ruthless army which he sent to conquer Asia with savage success. Tibet was more fortunate for, distracted by other campaigns, Chinghis Khan refrained from crossing its borders and then died. But it was only a temporary reprieve. In 1239, the new Mongolian khan returned to complete unfinished business and sent his armies to mass on the Tibetan border. By now, the most powerful men in Tibet were the abbots of monasteries; they have been called 'prince-bishops in the land of the snows'.[2] Bitter power struggles between warring Buddhist sects had been won by Lama Kunga

Gyaltsen of the Sakye Monastery, and it was he who faced the Mongolian threat. With considerable political cunning, he negotiated a deal that kept the khan's armies out of Tibet but made him, as Fosco Maraini puts it, 'the viceroy of a Mongolian protectorate'. In 1260, the Mongolians conquered China and the new Manchu emperors inherited the special relationship with the Sakya-pa abbots. China now became a 'patron', and Tibet a 'client'. Tibetans called this *cho-yon.* It meant that a powerful secular power guaranteed the safety of a spiritual ruler. It was a unique and to Europeans incomprehensible bond that would, many centuries later, destroy Tibet.

Religion and power were now inextricably bonded, and enormous fortress-like monasteries dominated the power struggles in Tibet. This was Tibet's Dark Age, a time of confusion and often bitter fighting as a bewildering succession of Buddhist sects squabbled, each one vying for the attention of Tibet's Mongolian or Chinese Manchu 'patrons'. Far from corrupting Tibet's ancient warrior spirit, the monasteries embodied it, and with a vengeance. From their fortress-like seats, the abbots and their fighting monks did battle with one another, with petty aristocrats or with decayed relics of the royal line. Just as inside the great monasteries of medieval Europe abbots of whatever sect had become venal and despotic, many of their monks were corrupt too.

In the smaller monasteries and in the more remote parts of Tibet, voices began to call for reform. The Martin Luther of Tibetan Buddhism was a man called Lobsang Drakpa. He was born in 1357 in a place called Tsonkha, meaning, somewhat prosaically, the 'land of the onions', and he would always be called Tsonkhapa, 'the man from the land of the onions'. Lobsang Drakpa did not nail a proclamation to a temple door or preach loud and fiery sermons; instead, he quietly founded a new sect with a handful of disciples. They called their new sect the Gelukpa, and because they adopted yellow headwear became known as the 'Yellow Hats'. Lobsang Drakpa taught discipline, austerity, abstinence and celibacy – all abandoned by Red Hat sects like the Sakya-pas. His disciples laid the foundations of future power by building between 1409 and 1419 what would become the biggest and most influential monasteries in Tibet. These were known as the 'big three', and all were clustered around Lhasa: Drepung, Sera and Ganden.

It was not until the sixteenth century that a unique combination of circumstances led to the ascendancy of Tsonkhapa's obscure little sect, and it was a Mongolian prince who again opened the road to power. After the death of Kublai Khan, he of the 'stately pleasure dome', the Mongolian empire had decayed and the old ties with Tibet fallen into disuse. Then a prince called Altan Khan launched a new military campaign to restore the empire of Chinghis Khan. He crushed his Mongolian rivals and once more rivalled the power of China. In a battle with the Ordos Mongols, Altan Khan had acquired two Tibetan monks as booty and both he and his nephew were converted to the Buddhist faith by these two very persuasive monks. To reinforce his power, and to add lustre to his new religion, Altan Khan, like his ancestors, sought out a Tibetan master who would accept him as a patron. His nephew recommended the charismatic abbot of the Drepung Monastery, which was the power centre of the Gelukpa sect, and an emissary was sent galloping across the steppe to Lhasa to invite him to meet the Mongolian ruler.

The master's name was Sönam Gyatso. Like the Sakya-pa abbots centuries earlier, he immediately appreciated the opportunity being presented by the Mongol ruler's messenger. Gyatso and Altan Khan met on the Mongolian border in 1578. Gyatso had little hesitation in accepting a deal and Altan Khan heaped him with gifts and privileges. Above all, he named him *Dalai Lama*, meaning 'Great Ocean' in Mongolian, and the two men also agreed on a principle of succession that would become essential in Tibetan religious and political life.

Sönam Gyatso was not, in Buddhist doctrine, any ordinary mortal, he was the latest bodily incarnation of religious leaders who had died long before.[3] The first of them was Gedun Drub, a disciple of Tsonkhapa and the founder of the Tashilunpo Monastery near Shigatse, whose incarnate successor had been recognized after his death in Gedun Gyatso and, when he died, in Sönam Gyatso himself who was, backdated, the 3rd Dalai Lama.

In Madhyamaka Buddhism selfless individuals called Bodhisattvas can interrupt their own journey to enlightenment by returning to ordinary life – becoming incarnate – and assisting others. In 1283, when the leader of the Kagyu-pa sect died, his disciples decreed, on the evidence of omens and tests, that a particular male infant was his reincarnation. Soon other monasteries followed the Kagyu-pa's lead and incarnate lamas were being discovered all over Tibet. As a doctrine, reincarnation proved to be of great value. It allowed the monasteries to dispense with any biological or dynastic obligations and manage the succession for themselves.

Altan Khan and the incarnate Sönam Gyatso understood the bigger picture very well. The Dalai Lamas, incarnate Bodhisattvas, would become the spiritual rulers of Tibet, in effect god-kings, and their power both spiritual and temporal would be passed on to successive incarnations. In return for supporting Sönam Gyatso, Altan Khan was himself rewarded by being recognized as the incarnation of his illustrious precursor Kublai Khan. A decade or so later, his grandson was recognized as the incarnation of Sönam Gyatso himself, and so a Mongolian prince became the 4th Dalai Lama.

The power of the Dalai Lamas was thus completely

dependent on *cho-yon*, and it would prove to be a dangerous doctrine upon which to build a state. It became especially perilous when the Chinese Manchu Ch'ing emperors replaced the Mongolians as patrons of the Dalai Lamas in the eighteenth century. The history is complex and cannot be rehearsed in detail here, but three events reveal the emerging power of the Chinese empire in the affairs of Tibet. In 1698, the Manchu and the Russians signed the Treaty of Nerchinsk, which allowed the two powers to carve up central Asia between them. Mongolian power was crushed and Tibetan autonomy severely reduced. Between 1715 and 1717, the Manchu emperor commissioned a Jesuit priest to map all of their domains. The Jesuits trained two lamas in geometry and arithmetic and sent them into Tibet. The resulting Ch'ing maps of China clearly show that the Manchu believed Tibet to be part of China. Then in 1720, the forces of the Ch'ing emperor marched into Lhasa ostensibly to protect the 7th Dalai Lama from a rebellion. Instead, it signalled the beginning of Ch'ing control of Tibet. They established a new organ of government called the Kashag and appointed a supervisor who would remain in Tibet after the Chinese troops withdrew. This was the *amban* – or, as Younghusband's men called him, the 'Hambone'. The Chinese remained in control of Tibet until the beginning of the twentieth century. They also tried to Sinicize Tibet by banning, for example, sky burials. They insisted that new incarnations of both the Dalai and Panchen Lamas would be chosen by lot under the supervision of the *amban* using a golden urn. These reforms were implemented only unevenly and Chinese control waxed and waned. The *ambans* became venal exploiters rather than dictators and Chinese sovereignty became increasingly vague and, for Europeans, hard to understand. Inside Tibet, the Chinese reforms counted for very little. Tibetan society remained frozen in time.

In Lhasa, the main secular office, which has been frequently referred to, was the Kashag, made up of four officials called *shapés*, only one of whom was a monk. The Kashag was the secular hub of power and its seal was demanded on any formal government policy. The office became considerably more powerful during a regency, in the absence of a Dalai Lama, and it was, of course, to the Kashag that Schäfer directed all his demands to be allowed to travel in Tibet. Although one of the *shapés* was a monk, there was a separate office concerned with religious affairs, the Yigtsang, headed by the Chigyab Khembo and staffed by four monks called Trunyichemmo. The Yigtsang Office controlled appointments and promotions of monk officials but also took part in the National Assembly with *shapés* from the Kashag. Despite a degree of separation of powers, it was simply not possible for the Tibetan state to make secular decisions or enact policies that were not connected to religion in some way.

This was reinforced by the stunning power of Tibet's monasteries. Lhasa itself was ringed by the 'big three' – Drepung, Sera and Ganden – and they were known as the 'Densa Sum', the 'Three Seats' that presided over the entire monastic system. Any traveller in Tibet would see literally thousands of monasteries, both big and small. Even so, the astonishing nature of Tibet's mass monk society can only be properly appreciated with some statistics. A survey carried out in 1733, when the population of Tibet as a whole was 2.5 million, showed that there were 319,270 monks. This was 13 per cent of the total population and an astonishing 26 per cent of male Tibetans. In 1951, Drepung, the largest monastery, was home to 10,000 monks, Sera held 7,000 and Ganden 5,000. By becoming a monk, a young man did not join an elite but participated in a mass movement. Many were devoutly religious, but boys as young as seven were placed in monasteries by families desperate to reduce family size, and they did not tolerate resistance. Escapees from monasteries were usually returned by their fathers. Once inside the monastery the boys faced a lifelong commitment to religious observance and celibacy. A monk could only be expelled if he committed murder or had heterosexual sex. Homosexuality was tolerated, or simply accepted as inevitable, as long as no orifice was penetrated. Bruno Beger's investigations showed that the preferred mode of intercourse involved the dominant monk inserting his penis between the arm and torso of the other. In theory, at least, all monks were celibate.

A monastery's wealth was not simply dished out to its thousands of monks. They had to earn their daily *tsampa* or a share of donations by taking part in the daily cycle of prayer sessions and religious ceremonies. The more prayers a monk uttered and the more ceremonies he took part in the better his income. Because there were so many thousands of monks, the monasteries fought hard to extend their estates and increase their endowments and they resisted any attempt to reduce their revenue. Even the doctrine of incarnation had a business side to it. An incarnate lama like the Dalai Lama possessed a *labrang*, which was the accumulated wealth of his line of incarnations. When a lama passed on and his new incarnation was discovered, the new incarnation would inherit the *labrang*, and so on for incarnation after incarnation. Some were very wealthy indeed.

The monasteries also possessed the means to defend themselves and resented the existence of a separate Tibetan Army. Schäfer would discover the brute force of the monasteries not long after he arrived in Lhasa. At least 15 per cent of the monks were *dobdos*, or 'fighting monks'. *Dobdos* were trained in combat, dressed to kill and usually acted as bodyguards. They far outnumbered the ill-equipped Tibetan Army, which could muster a mere fifteen hundred ragged soldiers. It was the *dobdos* who fought hardest against Younghusband, and when a member of Gould's 1936 mission, Brigadier Neame, reported that 'Tibetans as a nation are absolutely non-military', he cannot have had a force of *dobdo* monks in mind.

The Great 13th Dalai Lama did not set out to completely remould this glacial world. What he did struggle to change to his advantage were Tibet's relations with foreign powers. It is tempting to think that this remarkable man, one of the great figures in twentieth-century history, was responding to the nationalist aspirations that had swept Europe and, later, China, but the old idea of *cho-yon* meant that his hands were tied by history, and by the Chinese. And he would be defeated, perhaps poisoned, by the great monasteries, who were perfectly happy with Chinese power and saw any sign of modernity as a threat. There is a savage irony in the fact that it was the Chinese, welcomed by many of the monasteries, who brutally thrust Lhasa and Tibet into the twentieth century after 1950.

China was not the Dalai Lama's only concern. The British empire had begun pushing at Tibet's southern borders and its diplomats had hatched up a plan to end Tibet's frustrating isolation by sending a mission to Lhasa. The Kashag responded quickly and aggressively: they sent an armed force across the Sikkimese border to thwart the mission and to assert their rights in Sikkim, which had been annexed by the British. In March 1888, the Tibetans were expelled, but the border remained tense. At this point, the Chinese intervened, sending their representative in Lhasa, the *amban*, to sort out the conflict. After much debate, the Chinese and the British signed a convention that recognized Sikkim as a British protectorate and established a trade mart at Yatung inside Tibet.

At no time were the Tibetans themselves consulted, and from the turn of the century the 13th Dalai Lama began to fight back. His most important tactic was to initiate discussions with the Russians, the one great power that seemed to offer support both against China and the British. Historians have sometimes viewed the Russian connection as an opportunist figment of Lord Curzon's imagination, but as Alistair Lamb has convincingly shown, contact between the Dalai Lama and Russian imperialist hawks was very real indeed. So Curzon sent Sir Francis Younghusband to sort out the Tibetans. As we have seen, the 'mission' was disastrous. The Dalai Lama fled to Mongolia and Younghusband's deal with the Kashag was repudiated by the British government. The invasion provoked the Chinese, who now feared that Tibet would become a British protectorate. They reacted first in the east by crushing the Tibetan presence in Kham and then advanced on Lhasa.

In 1904, the Dalai Lama fled south from Mongolia through the Chumbi Valley. As a consequence, the Chinese deposed him, declaring he was 'guilty of treachery and has placed himself beyond the pale of our Imperial favour'.[4] He had, in other words, broken the rules of *cho-yon*. Now the Dalai Lama turned to the British for help, but with mixed success. He was given refuge in Sikkim and formed an important friendship with Sir Charles Bell, a scholar-diplomat who urged Delhi and the Foreign Office in London to back the Dalai Lama. But British policy was confused and divided. They were never quite sure how and why the Chinese believed they had power in Tibet, and although they feared the Chinese they were also concerned not to offend them. The British refused to assist him directly. The Dalai Lama turned again in despair to the Russians, but this time the British had sufficient clout in Moscow to stymie his desperate last move.

Then events turned, at last, in the Dalai Lama's favour. In 1911, the Chinese people rose against the despised and feeble Manchu Ch'ing dynasty. The following year the child emperor Pu Yi Hsüan-t'ung abdicated and declared a republic. From

exile in India, the Dalai Lama sent Tsarong Shapé, the hero of his flight into exile, to stir up revolt in Lhasa. China's three thousand troops and officials were expelled in disarray, and in January 1913 the Dalai Lama returned in triumph to Lhasa. For the first time since the eighteenth century, Tibet was free of Chinese troops and officials.

For the British, a unique opportunity had now presented itself. The collapse of Chinese power meant they could deal directly with the Dalai Lama and Tibet as a 'favoured nation'. Tibet's borders could be opened for trade but closed against any foreign power that might imperil the Raj. For his part, the Dalai Lama had forgotten neither his friendship with Charles Bell nor his abandonment by the British government. This ambivalence would mould and sometimes sour relations between the British and the Tibetans for the next two decades, and in the view of some historians made inevitable the catastrophe of 1951.

Ensconced back in the Potala Palace, the Dalai Lama began to look for ways in which to modernize Tibet and to protect its new independence. Tsarong Shapé, the man Schäfer would call Tibet's 'uncrowned king', sensed the new mood and lobbied for increased spending on the Tibetan Army and police. He appealed to Charles Bell, who wrote to Delhi, 'we should allow them to procure a few machine guns and mountain guns . . . We cannot profess real friendship with Tibet if, in spite of her frequent requests, we continue to prevent her from buying guns . . .'[5] It was to no avail. The British would not sell arms to the Tibetans nor allow Tsarong to import any through India. Tsarong also encountered bitter opposition to his plans inside Tibet, and from a very powerful faction. The 'big three' monasteries saw Tsarong's ambitions as a threat to the very foundation of Tibetan society and were resolutely opposed to any increase in military spending. For the monastic segment, the state existed only to further and protect the interest of the

Gelukpa sect and was certainly not permitted to develop in its own right. 'Tibet' existed only as a conglomeration of monasteries, not as a nation state. That was one reason for opposing Tsarong. Another was the threat to monastic wealth. If the army was strengthened and modernized, as Tsarong wanted, its costs would inevitably rise. This would push up taxes and threaten the prosperity of the monastic estates, and that was intolerable.

Tsarong provoked the monasteries in other ways. He and his fellow officers took to wearing British uniforms and showing their legs 'like monkeys'. They played tennis and polo, shook hands and drank sweet tea. Tsarong developed a passion for motor cars and invented a Tibetan typewriter. All in all, he was seen as a dangerous emissary of the heathen British. Even more disturbing was evidence that the Dalai Lama himself had begun to share Tsarong's enthusiasm for the army. A way had to be found to smash Tsarong's power.

In May 1924 a policeman was killed by a group of soldiers in Lhasa. Tsarong himself severely punished the offenders on the spot: one had his leg amputated, the other lost an ear. Protests were made to the Dalai Lama about this high-handed and brutal punishment and Tsarong was rebuked. In an atmosphere thick with rumour, a group of army officers now signed a petition supporting Tsarong. The move played straight into the hands of his enemies. A petition meant revolt, and the Dalai Lama began to suspect his favourite. A few months later, another incident involving the police stirred up the murky waters of conspiracy. A key player was Möndro, one of the Rugby boys who would become very close to Schäfer in 1939 and was in 1926 in charge of the police force. The story began with a fight between policemen and monks on a road near Lhasa. Things escalated when the monks were arrested, and became explosive when a magistrate assaulted the policemen.

PREVIOUS PAGE *The Regent of Tibet, Reting Rimpoche, who became Schäfer's ally in Lhasa.*

ABOVE FROM LEFT
Möndro, one of the Tibetan boys sent to Rugby School in England, who became very attached to the German party.

Tsarong Dzasa, the 'uncrowned king of Tibet', who helped Schäfer stay in Lhasa for months rather than weeks.

The 'Great 13th' Dalai Lama, Thubten Gyatso, who died in 1933 and whose reincarnation was trapped in China when Schäfer was in Tibet.

The 14th Dalai Lama, Tenzin Gyatso, who was brought to Lhasa after Schäfer had returned to Germany.

BELOW
The German Tibet Expedition outside Lhasa in early 1939. From left to right: standing, Rabden Khazi, who was spying on the Germans for the British, Kaiser Thapa, Schäfer; seated, Krause, Geer, Wienert, Beger.

OPPOSITE
Bruno Beger providing medical assistance in Tibet, much to the annoyance of Hugh Richardson.

ABOVE
The Potala Palace in Lhasa, 1939.

BELOW
The village of Phari, which was said by some travellers to be the dirtiest place in the world.

ABOVE
A Tibetan aristocrat: for Beger an Aryan cousin.

BELOW
Border stones on the edge of Tibet.

ABOVE
Time for negotiation: Sir Basil Gould with the German Tibet Expedition. From left to right: Geer, Beger, Gould, Schäfer, Wienert, Krause.

BELOW
The expedition entertaining some important Tibetans in Lhasa: Tsarong Dzasa is at the head of the table with Schäfer; one of the Shapés (government ministers) sits far left, alongside Beger and Geer; on the right are Wienert and Möndro.

RIGHT
The Regent blessing Beger. Reting demanded that the tall German anthropologist stay on in Tibet as a bodyguard.

BELOW RIGHT
A dog for Hitler? The Regent wanted to send such a beast to the German dictator, but Schäfer was offended by the quality of the miserable animal.

BELOW
A sky burial in progress with ragyapas dismembering a corpse and pounding and mixing body matter with tsampa. Schäfer paid Akeh to obtain skulls from the ragyapa.

The Yumbu Lagang, reputedly the most ancient building in Tibet. The Germans were given permission to enter this highly symbolic tower – a privilege denied to Richardson.

Tsarong began to look even more dangerous. Möndro was banished to the Ladakh border and Tsarong was sacked as commander-in-chief of the army. In 1930, he lost his position as a *shapé*.

Tsarong Shapé never regained the power he once held. As plain Tsarong Dzasa he devoted his time to making money and building up the Trapchi Lotrü Laygung (Trapchi Electrical Machine Office), a haven of modernity three miles from Lhasa. The Lotrü Laygung meshed together the Tibetan mint with the national armoury and was powered by a hydro-electric plant. In 1939, Tsarong remained an impressive and charismatic figure in Lhasa. The Dalai Lama did acquire two Baby Austins (Dalai Lama 1 and Dalai Lama 2) to nip around Lhasa in, but by the time of his mysterious death the poisonous conflict between the modernizers and the powerful monasteries remained highly toxic.

After the Dalai Lama's death in 1933, Tibet entered a turbulent interregnum while his 'consciousness' sought a new incarnation. One would not be born until July 1935, and in the meantime Lhasa was consumed by violent spasms of struggle and brutal violence. In the background, the Chinese remembered their claim on Tibet. On the day of his abdication, the child emperor Pu Yi had declared that the new government would eventually forge 'one Great Republic of China by the union as heretofore of the five peoples, namely Manchus, Chinese, Mongols, Mohammedans and Tibetans, *together with their territory* [my italics]'. Now, with the Dalai Lama *in absentia*, the Chinese began to think once more about 'the Fifth People'. As Schäfer himself had witnessed, a new force had emerged alongside the Kuomintang: the communists, who had been marching through Kham and Yunnan when Schäfer was heading for Shanghai and his confrontation with Dolan. Although between them Mao Tse-tung and Chiang Kai-shek were tearing China apart, both forces sent tremors of alarm through Lhasa and down the Chumbi Valley to the British Residency in Gangtok.

Bell had instituted his unusual educational experiment of sending four Tibetan boys to Rugby in 1913. One of them we have already met: Khenrab Künsang Möndrong, better known as Möndro.[6] Their chaperon was the exceptional lay official Tsipön Lungshar (Dorje Tsegyal) who was a doctor and mirror diviner as well as a skilled and worldly politician. Lungshar was an arrogant, clever man who like Tsarong hoped to become a modernizer. When he returned to Tibet he immediately sought power and worked his way into the Dalai Lama's inner circle. He was appointed to the important post of *tsipön* and unleashed an attack on both the monastic and aristocratic estates, confiscating some and racking up taxes on others. He poured this new revenue into the army, recruiting more than two thousand extra troops and dressing them in Tibetan not British uniforms. Soon Lungshar was one of the most unpopular men in Lhasa, hated by the abbots.

His main rival was the Dalai Lama's personal attendant, Kumbela. He was a formidable opponent. His family were serfs and he was born Dechen Chödrön, a name usually given to girls, but the Dalai Lama recruited scribes from such lowly families and the bright young lad was ordered to Lhasa when he was twelve. He was a precocious pupil and matured into a 'tall rather good looking man'. He became extremely close to the Dalai Lama, who gave him his monk's name, Thubten Kumbela. He was soon 'next to the Dalai Lama the most powerful person in Tibet . . . extremely clever and intelligent'.[7] After the Tsarong affair, a sign of Kumbela's success was the fact that the Dalai Lama encouraged him to create a crack new regiment. It was called the Trongdra Regiment because its soldiers were recruited as a tax from *trongdra*, or 'better families', and were forced to cut their hair. Kumbela spent lavishly on his new toy, purchasing their uniforms in Calcutta, designing gold insignia and frequently showing them off to the Dalai Lama. One of the Trongdra's commanders was Jigme Tering, son of the Tering Raja.

After the death of the Dalai Lama, Lungshar and Kumbela clashed immediately. Lungshar's strategy was simple, brutal and effective: he accused Kumbela of poisoning the Dalai Lama. There was no real evidence, let alone proof, but Kumbela was arrested and locked inside the Potala's notorious Sharcenchog Prison. Finally, he was dragged through the streets of Lhasa and banished. A street song commemorated his downfall: 'The powerful person, conqueror of all places / in the British car / That favourite who is a son of the gods / please tell me where he has gone?'

For now, Lungshar was triumphant, but his fate was to be even more brutal and violent. The chain of events began when the National Assembly finally selected a regent. Because they couldn't agree between a number of candidates, they resorted to a *senriy*, or divine lottery, which took place on 24 January 1934. The lottery selected a slight young man of twenty-four. Despite his age and inexperience, he was the abbot of the Reting Monastery and an incarnate rimpoche. His name was Jampey Yeshe, and he had once been singled out by the Dalai Lama during a visit to the monastery. He, too, would have an intriguing part to play in the story of the Schäfer Expedition and its aftermath.

There is a photograph showing the diminutive Regent next to two looming *dobdo* bodyguards. A British visitor described him as 'an anaemic looking young man . . . Large head, protruding ears, no chin, weak mouth'.[8] Lungshar realized that the Kashag was now in a uniquely powerful position. It could easily dominate the callow young Regent. He decided to seize control of the Kashag, but the tables were turned in scenes of high drama.

In May 1934, the Kashag summoned Lungshar. He marched into the Assembly Hall 'swaggering characteristically' with an armed retinue. It was an extraordinary provocation, so the ministers ordered his arrest and accused him of trying to install a Bolshevik dictatorship. The accusation may sound far-fetched, but the 13th Dalai Lama had warned that 'this present era is rampant with the five forms of degeneration, in particular the red ideology . . .' As he was led away, Lungshar made a lunge for a pistol held by one of his servants. In the ensuing struggle a giant monk broke Lungshar's arm. His official dress was torn off and his gold charm box, which was bound into his topknot of hair, taken away. As his honorific boots were being taken off, a piece of paper fluttered to the floor. Lungshar, despite his injuries, lunged after it and tried to put it in his mouth, but the burly monk tore it from his fingers: on it was written 'Trimön Shapé', the name of the leading *shapé*. A magical way of doing harm to someone was to trample his name underfoot.

In a shockingly brief time, an investigating committee sentenced Lungshar to be punished in a uniquely horrible manner. First of all he would be blinded, for it was feared that execution would result in visitations from Lungshar's vengeful spirit. Mutilation was traditionally carried out by Tibet's untouchables, the *ragyapa*.[9] On 20 May, they entered Lungshar's cell, ordered him to kneel and placed a yak's knucklebone against each of his temples. These were then tightened around his head, using leather thongs, until one of Lungshar's eyeballs burst out of its socket; the other was then hacked out with a knife. The sockets were cauterized with boiling oil. Although Lungshar was drugged, the pain was, he admitted, severe. In the streets of Lhasa it was sung that 'he has given his eyes as alms'.

Lungshar died a year later. His savage punishment brought any serious reform to an end in Tibet. But now Tibet was forced to deal with a new threat from the Chinese. In 1931 there had been bloody fighting in eastern Tibet between Tibetan forces and a Chinese Army under General Liu Wen-hui and the Muslim warlord Ma Pu-fang. Schäfer had seen some of the fighting for himself during the first Dolan expedition. The Tibetans were badly defeated. The British were persuaded to make mild protests, but what got the Tibetans out of trouble was the Japanese invasion of Manchuria in the same year. In 1933, the Chinese saw another opportunity. After the death of the Dalai Lama, they demanded that they be allowed to send a mission of condolence to Lhasa. The request was greeted with alarm in the Kashag, which suspected the motives of any Chinese incursion across Tibetan borders, but this outraged the monasteries. In their view the Chinese had every right to come to Lhasa; they were pilgrims and worthy of proper courtesy, not suspicion. And the monasteries' view prevailed.

On 28 August 1934, eighty Chinese officials and soldiers under General Huang Mu-sung rode into Lhasa. They brought gifts of tea and silk, and for the first few days the general behaved with ostentatious piety. He had also brought with him something that would prove considerably useful for Schäfer five years later – a wireless set that could be used to communicate with Nanking, at that time the Kuomintang capital.

Chiang Kai-shek had set down the Chinese negotiating position. 'Tibet must accept inclusion into China' was the first point, and Tibetan issues would therefore be Chinese issues not requiring 'interference' from the British. Huang repeatedly asked the National Assembly to decide what relationship Tibet wanted with China. The enticement was an end to the border dispute in eastern Tibet, which was draining Tibet's coffers, and a solution to the dilemma of the Panchen Lama, who was exiled in China – where Schäfer had had an audience with him in 1934 – and wished to return to Tibet with a large Chinese escort. In Lhasa, this was viewed with considerable alarm. The National Assembly refused Huang's demands, but in an ambiguous way that reflected the divisions and discord within the Tibetan government. Huang did not go away empty-handed. Since he could claim that his mission had led to 'dialogue', he persuaded the Tibetans to allow some of his colleagues to remain in Lhasa with their wireless. One of them would greet the humiliated Ernst Schäfer outside Lhasa five years later. His name was Chang Wei-pei, and he was said to be something of an oddball and an opium addict. The men left behind by General Huang would make very good use of their wireless. News and propaganda were broadcast from Nanking and Tibetan nobles, merchants and monks all queued up to talk to trade agents and friends in China. In the most subtle way, Tibet had been drawn closer to the modern world and to the new China. Far-sighted Tibetans like Tsarong realized that this was a troubling development, so they turned to the British again.

In Delhi, and to a lesser extent in London, all this was very bad news indeed. Once again the British would need to debate what kind of Tibet they wanted and how much support they could offer it. A response was demanded but the political officer in Sikkim was pessimistic that one would be forthcoming: 'we should I think do what little we can. Our intentions are honest enough. We merely want her to be completely independent in substance even if she is merely "autonomous" in name.' More practically, the political officer urged that the Tibetans be granted a 'disguised subsidy' – which Schäfer would later call the 'British bribe' – and that a well-funded British Mission be established in Lhasa.

So in August 1936 the British sent the new political officer,

Sir Basil Gould, on a mission to Lhasa. He was accompanied by Hugh Richardson and F. Spencer Chapman, his private secretary, and a military contingent led by Brigadier Philip Neame. With him were Lieutenants E. Y. Nepean and S. G. Dagg of the Royal Corps of Signals. It was their job to set up a British wireless station in Lhasa to counter the Chinese radio left by Huang. Gould's caravan was impressive. As well as the six Englishmen, they were accompanied by Nordhu Dondup, a Tibetan admired and trusted by the British, as well as numerous servants, pony men and 145 pack animals. The radio equipment alone took up twenty-five ponyloads. Gould's plan was to establish a mission at Dekyilinka in Lhasa, then to tackle the exiled Panchen Lama in Jyekundo. The Chinese were not informed. What Gould discovered was disturbing. The Tibetan government was unstable and the Regent, Reting, an enigma. Trimön Shapé had seized power after the fall of Kumbela and Lungshar and was prone to periodic bouts of insanity, and Tsarong, who everyone had hoped would turn out to be the 'strong man of Tibet', was sidelined at the Trapchi mint and arsenal. Apart from Jigme Tering and one of the old Rugbeians, Rinzin Dorje Ringang, there were few Tibetans with power and influence who were wholeheartedly British sympathizers.

It was only by exploiting the Tibetan New Year in February 1937 that Gould was able to stay on in Lhasa at all, declaring that it would be rude to leave. His final task was to try to persuade the Kashag to allow Hugh Richardson to stay on at Dekyilinka. With his health failing, Gould did what he could, but he never got an official agreement. Instead, he simply informed the Tibetans that he was leaving Lhasa to return to Gyantse and that Richardson would remain behind to deal with any other matters arising in his absence. It was a sleight of hand, but the British now had their mission, however fragile, and the Union Jack would flutter over Dekyilinka until

1947. As well as Richardson, Nepean's wireless also remained in Lhasa. It would be operated by Reginald Fox, a civilian who had replaced the Signals Corps, and Gould promised that 'listening sets' would be given to the Regent and other important Tibetans. The battle of the radios had begun.

In the meantime, the wandering 'aspect' of the 13th Dalai Lama had become incarnate once more. Somewhere in Tibet lived and breathed a male child who was the new Dalai Lama. Where and who he was no-one knew, and the answer would come only in signs and omens. In August 1935, the Regent Reting set off on a long pilgrimage to the Chökhorgyal Monastery in southern Tibet, which had been founded by the 2nd Dalai Lama, Gedun Gyatso. Close to the monastery was the sacred Lhamolatso Lake. According to legend, prophetic pictures could sometimes be seen in its shimmering blue waters, and the Regent and his party hoped that Lhamolatso might offer enlightenment about the identity and whereabouts of the new Dalai Lama.

The Regent's party pitched their tents on a hill above the lake. Monks chanted prayers and played solemn music. Reting and Trimön Shapé rode down to the lake on yaks, but when they returned they said there was nothing to be seen. The monks prayed with yet more enthusiasm, blew their great horns and conch shells, banged gongs and spun their prayer wheels, but Lhamolatso remained impassive, a blank screen. The Regent now went to the water's edge alone. He was gone for several hours. Years later he would tell Schäfer that 'the waters began to live'. Signs and wonders appeared. At sunset, when he returned to his tent, he was silent and preoccupied but revealed nothing to his companions. After the visit to the lake, he travelled on to his birthplace in Rame. Tsepon Shakabpa recalled that he was astonished when he met the Regent's 'economically deprived and physically unattractive relatives'.[10] Incarnations had no respect for status or looks.

In Rame, the Regent and Trimön had a number of long, secretive meetings before riding on to the Taklo Monastery, where Shakabpa was given some disturbing news. Both the Regent and Trimön had decided to resign. What happened next was the first obvious sign that Reting, this odd and diffident young man, was intoxicated by power. The pact with Trimön was a crude trick; Reting had no intention of giving up power but was only too pleased to accept Trimön's letter of resignation. A powerful rival was quickly dispensed with. Trimön lost more than power, though. He became manic and began wandering the streets and markets of Lhasa playing and singing music and wearing the white robe of an ascetic lama.

Just under a year later, in the summer of 1936, the Regent convened the National Assembly inside the Potala Palace. For the first time he revealed what he had seen in Lhamolatso: a monastery with a three-storeyed turquoise roof and a gilded top like a pagoda, a trail leading east from the monastery to a bare hill, shaped like a *chorten*, a poor one-storey house with 'strangely shaped guttering', and the letters *A*, *Ka* and *Ma*.[11] (It is amusing to note that some Tibetans have thought the letters stood for 'Amerika'.) Reting told the Assembly that he was certain that the *A* stood for Amdo. This was a shock. Although ethnically Tibetan, Amdo was part of China's Tsinghai province. If the Dalai Lama were discovered there it would surely give the 'claws of the dragon' an even more powerful hold over Tibet. But Reting had other supporting evidence. The oracles had revealed many omens and signs implying that the new incarnation would be found in the east. As the Dalai Lama's body was being embalmed, it was wrapped in gauze and placed on his throne facing south. The following day, the Dalai Lama's head had twisted, to face east. It was also noted that an enormous star-shaped fungus had formed on a wooden pillar on the east side of the throne room. The National

Assembly found this persuasive and so search parties would be sent east. In Tibet there was intense interest in the news. Every mother in Tibet was hoping that her little boy might be the new Dalai Lama.

Reting's choice of Amdo, assuming that people are not reincarnated and that lakes are not celestial televisions, has never been explained. It could suggest he was hedging his bets with China or, on the contrary, staking a claim to eastern Tibet and the disputed border. The evidence is inconclusive, but we do know that in 1945 Reting was making overtures to Chiang Kai-shek at a time when he was fighting to regain power, and that he sent two aides to Nanking. Two years later, a coded message was intercepted by the Kashag. It showed that Reting had asked for Chinese military aid to topple the regime in Lhasa. The discovery of these documents led to Reting's arrest and imprisonment. He was fatally poisoned in May 1947 in circumstances all too reminiscent of the death of the 13th Dalai Lama.

Back in the autumn of 1936 three search parties were despatched in easterly directions. The Amdo party was led by Ketsang Rimpoche. As well as various signs and omens, the searchers also needed to be on the lookout for an odd collection of physical peculiarities in any candidate: for example, marks as of a tiger skin on his legs, long curving eyebrows, large ears, two pieces of flesh near the shoulder blades, an imprint of a conch shell on his hands . . . When Ketsang Rimpoche arrived in Jyekundo in eastern Tibet he was invited to visit the Panchen Lama – and here the plot thickens. The Panchen Lama had, as already noted, spent many years exiled in China and Mongolia and was now demanding that he be permitted to return to his seat at Tashilunpo with a Chinese escort. This had been refused by the Kashag and the matter remained unresolved. But he still wielded spiritual power and he reported to Ketsang Rimpoche's party that while he had been staying at the Kumbum Monastery he had taken an interest in unusual male births. Three boys seemed especially interesting. And surely the *Ka* the Regent had seen in the waters of Lhamolatso might refer to Kumbum?

Ketsang Rimpoche rode on to Kumbum and arrived there in May 1937. As soon as the party saw the Kumbum Monastery, whose roof was tiled in gold and turquoise, they sensed that it was the building the Regent had seen at Lhamolatso. It did not occur to them that the Regent might have been familiar with the appearance of such an important and famous Tibetan monastery. In Amdo, the search party was careful to present gifts to the local warlord General Ma Pu-fang, who would soon cause the Tibetans no end of trouble, and for the next month Ketsang Rimpoche searched the region around Kumbum. One boy in particular, born on 6 July 1935 in the village of Taktse, seemed very promising even though his family spoke Chinese as a first language. His name was Lhamo Thondup.

The 'Taktse Boy', as he was called, had also been on the Panchen Lama's list and most of his brothers had already been accepted as incarnations by the Kumbum Monastery. His home had strangely shaped guttering and seemed to match the Regent's vision. But were blue roofs so rare in Amdo? With mounting excitement, the search party exchanged clothes with their servants to disguise their intent and the boy was tested in the traditional way.

The tests were well rehearsed. Matched objects (pairs of walking sticks, rosaries and what not) were set out on a long table. One of them had belonged to the Dalai Lama, the other was a 'control'. The description of what followed is a fascinating example of how unconscious suggestion can guide behaviour. The search party would naturally wish that the boy they now favoured was the incarnate Dalai Lama, so when they showed him two rosaries or two walking sticks, a variety of behaviours on their part could guide the boy's choice with neither he nor the search party realizing what was happening. Especially suggestive is the fact that when the boy reached for the wrong walking stick he quickly put it down and picked up the right one. He must surely have sensed 'negative feedback' from the search party. The final test involved two small drums. One was exquisitely decorated, the other was plain. The boy correctly chose the duller object and ignored its more beautiful counterpart. This was, for Ketsang Rimpoche, the clinching moment in the test, but it could simply have been an indication of the boy's precocious shrewdness.

Ketsang cabled Lhasa with the momentous news. The Regent and his advisers were equally enthusiastic about the Taktse Boy. They wanted him brought to Lhasa, alone, immediately, for further examination. No other candidate was to be considered. Tibet was on the threshold of historic change, but now Ketsang discovered that he was in serious trouble. Ma Pu-fang refused to let them leave Amdo and the Kumbum Monastery knowing, of course, the immense benefits that could be reaped from the discovery of the incarnation on his doorstep. He demanded that the search party confirm they had discovered the Dalai Lama before they departed. Some of the monks became very angry and threatened to assault Ketsang and his party.

When Ernst Schäfer and the German Tibet Expedition rode up to Lhasa's west gate in January 1939, the three-year-old Dalai Lama was still trapped at the Kumbum Monastery in Amdo.

Although Schäfer had been humiliated at the gates of Lhasa, he would soon find out for himself that Richardson and his masters in Sikkim and Delhi were neither secure not universally admired. In the eyes of many Tibetans, the greatest sin of the British was their tepid and uneven support for a genuinely independent Tibet. In the great monasteries they were regarded as heathen modernizers. Tibetan society was itself unstable and fractured by many self-interested factions and individuals. The Regent himself was increasingly despotic. It was a unique moment in Tibetan history, and Schäfer was determined to make the Third Reich a player in the game.

CHAPTER ELEVEN

THE WHITE SCARVES

After eating the mountain, hunger is not satiated.
After drinking the ocean, thirst is not quenched.

– Tibetan proverb

'The strangers who came from far away across the sea do not treat you like children: they love our teachings, but they are also carrying something else – be patient with them, because they enjoy the Great Prayer.'

– the Nechung Oracle, referring to the Schäfer expedition, quoted in *Festival of the White Scarves*

One spring morning in 1939 Hugh Richardson and his confidential adviser Sonham Kazi sat down to an English breakfast on the veranda of the British Mission in Lhasa. In the gardens of Dekyilinka, salmon-coloured hollyhocks were blooming and vegetables were ripening – testimony to the care the gardeners had lavished on them during the harsh winter months. As he decapitated a boiled egg, Richardson mulled over the secret report he would shortly have to send to Gould in Gangtok.

He would relish informing him that he had 'lunched with the Schäfer party. They have a collection of Tibetan mastiffs, cats and monkeys . . . They do not have a very large or comfortable house nor have they a good cook. In fact they find it easier to live mainly on raw minced yak steak . . .'[1] There is an irony here that only the British would have understood. On 22 January, Gould had complained to the Indian government in Delhi about their own residence. Dekyilinka compared unfavourably with the Chinese and Nepali missions; it was not conducive to 'health and efficiency' and was 'incompatible with dignity'.[2] Richardson also reported to Gould that 'by their dress, beards and behaviour the Germans so stressed the difference between themselves and us that they created an unfavourable impression in Lhasa . . .' He was being parsimonious with the truth. Schäfer's 'official leave' had specified that he could stay for fourteen days in Lhasa 'as a tourist'; as Richardson mulled over his report, the German Tibet Expedition had only just left Lhasa. They had spent three months in the Forbidden City and were now on their way to inspect a Tibetan monument the British had never been allowed to visit. The truth was that Schäfer had done rather well in Tibet, and Richardson needed to save face. His report on the German Tibet Expedition would be a pack of lies.

Richardson smeared butter over a triangle of toast and scooped a spoonful of marmalade from a dish. He had other concerns, too, which he spelt out to Gould: 'Although the mission's outward relations with all the members of the present Kashag are cordial, we cannot claim to have any enthusiastic supporter . . .' The Regent was a 'man of scarcely adequate calibre . . . apparently content to get what he can both from the Chinese and ourselves . . .' Richardson noted that the war in

China had relieved the pressure on Tibet for now, but the conflict brought fresh peril. What would happen if the Japanese defeated the Chinese? What would happen to Tibet then?

He filled a mug with tea and sat back. Richardson might have been even more concerned if he could have known that in May 1939 an intelligence officer from the Imperial Japanese Army called Jinzo Nomoto would cross into Tibet disguised as a Mongolian and remain for eighteen months gathering information. There is no evidence Nomoto had any contact with Schäfer's party, but Richardson is not likely to have forgotten that since 1936 the two most aggressive foreign powers in the world had been joined in a world-embracing pact. Waving to his radio operator Reginald Fox, who was strolling with his Tibetan wife and young children among the hollyhocks, Richardson rose from the table and walked into his study to begin crafting his report. At the beginning of the year, it had all been very different. When the Germans had arrived Richardson had been able to demonstrate his power. But somehow it had slipped from his hands.

After his humiliation outside Lhasa, Schäfer had spent some time nursing his bruised ego. Despite his tense relationship with his fellow Germans, he now claimed to espouse Tibetan values: he would 'show calmness and sedateness, be tolerant with irony, laugh, smile, help, flatter'; he would not 'judge, play the self righteous westerner and not give in to the temptations of energy . . .' The Germans spent their time making Tredilinka habitable, playing football and exploring the streets and monuments of Lhasa. There were consolations and congratulations from Himmler. They were, after all, the first purely German expedition to enter Lhasa. Schäfer had trumped Hedin and Filchner, but he could not forget that his 'official leave' meant he was a mere tourist forbidden to do any science. He faced an implacable foe in the shape of Hugh

Richardson who seemed to have considerable influence with the Tibetans.

They did what they could. Krause re-staged their arrival for his cameras and made them look like conquering German heroes. If Schäfer was to be a tourist then he would be one in the German manner. They would make a thorough exploration of the city. The Germans set out on daily forays, with Krause filming as much as he could. The film and photographs that the expedition took in Lhasa would be some of the last that showed the city before the Chinese invasion. Lhasa was like a small solar system spinning around a double star formed by the Potala and the Jokhang. On the other side of the Barkokali Gate, directly in front of the Potala, was Shöl, a small hamlet whose unsanitary habits had, like the village of Phari, always inspired Europeans to heights of wordy disgust. Here, for example, is Manning, who arrived with Younghusband in 1904: 'There is nothing striking, nothing pleasing about Lhasa's appearance. The habitations are begrimed with smut and dirt. The avenues are full of dogs, some growling and gnawing bits of hide that lie about in profusion and emit a charnel house smell; others limping and looking livid . . . others starved and dying and pecked at by ravens . . .' Candler 'found a city squalid and filthy beyond description, undrained and unpaved. The streets after rain are nothing but pools of stagnant water frequented by pigs and dogs searching for refuse . . .' All agreed that the Potala Palace drew the eye like a magnet, and 'in the morning, the sun [strikes] the golden roof like a beacon for the faithful'.

As the Germans toured the city at the beginning of 1939, watched by innumerable pairs of curious eyes, it was the dirt and the beggars and the dogs, dead or alive or dying, that they noticed first. From Shöl, the Germans crossed the Yuto Sampa or 'Turquoise Bridge' with its crowds of beggars, and after that a wasteland heaped with piles of refuse. Schäfer saw small pigs rooting in mounds of excrement or gnawing on discarded bones and rotten horses' heads. Nearby they found the Post and Telegraph Office which had been built inside the ruined Tengye-ling Monastery, destroyed after its abbot had sided with the Chinese in 1912. From there they skirted the only, and unused, public latrine in Lhasa and the old palace of the Chinese *amban* with its two granite lions. All this has been levelled since 1959 and replaced by a sterile plaza, ringed by picture-processing emporiums and decorated with a full-scale MiG fighter. Shopping streets radiate outwards full of those gold-encrusted novelty stores so beloved in the new China. After the military invasion and the genocide of the Cultural Revolution, China assaulted Tibet again, this time with its own unique brand of capitalist acquisitiveness.

Soon they were inside the city of Lhasa itself, and Beger especially was enthralled by the multitude of Asian 'races' funnelled into the narrow streets that radiated from the great 'Cathedral' of Jokhang, the holiest pilgrimage site in the city. These must have been especially frustrating weeks for Beger. He needed to return to Ahnenerbe headquarters in Berlin to prove a connection between Tibetans and his own race, but his data so far was spotty and inconclusive. Here in the streets of Lhasa surely were clues to the origins of the Aryan race. Lhasa promised to be the human laboratory his peers and professors could only dream about.

One visitor to the city listed Tartars, Chinese, Muscovites, Armenians, Kashmiris, Hindustanis and Nepalis. As Beger stood wide-eyed he could see nomads from Kham, Ngolok and the Chungtang as well as Chinese officials, hundreds of scurrying monks in dark red robes, and merchants and traders from all the kingdoms of the Himalayas who had their own separate quarters in the Old City. Aristocrats, his special interest, strutted past in gold-embroidered robes, their long hair tied in a double topknot. In their wake came their wives in big head-dresses, tottering carefully in their silk dresses layered with silver jewellery. Lhasa women wore their wealth. The Jokhang was encircled by a pilgrimage route called the Barkor. There were pilgrims everywhere, prostrating themselves in front of the holy shrines and walking solemnly around the temple.

Here were the three-storey whitewashed mansions of the aristocrats with their black-bordered windows. There was also a multitude of stores. The most prestigious were owned by Nepali merchants, who wore tight white trousers and brimless hats and sat by their doors smoking shishahs while their wives sold everything imaginable: vegetables, spices, bricks of tea, charm-boxes, cups and jugs full of holy water, soap, shoes and boots, electrical torches, mirrors, medicinal herbs, yak tails, salt, borax, toys, silks and furs, horses, rare animal skins, aluminium pots, and even German beer from Bremen. The 'Forbidden City' was certainly not closed to free trade. There were beggars, pilgrims and convicts in leg shackles, their necks locked inside wooden boards called *cangues* upon which their misdeeds had been inscribed. To the south of the Jokhang was a large square. Here stood the Treasury and other government buildings, including the Kashag.

In Lhasa's crowded streets, women outnumbered men. Many were prostitutes. Driving this conspicuous imbalance were the great monasteries that sucked in so many thousands of young men and demanded that they become and remain celibate. The other reason was the practice of polyandry, which so fascinated Himmler. In the Tibetan countryside, men of all classes shared wives. A single woman could be married to two or more brothers so that few children knew who their biological father was. Polyandry probably emerged among pastoral nomads who were usually too poor to support a family alone and were frequently travelling. The benefit was that if all the sons took a single wife the men's inheritance would be preserved and no one son would have to bear the entire burden of the marriage. As a result, many women failed to find a husband and drifted into the villages and towns, where they often turned to prostitution. Their clients came from the trading caravans that always filled the roads crossing the Tibetan plateau – and, it has to be said, from the monasteries.

One evening when they returned to Tredilinka, Beger reported 'strange, inexplicable' sounds coming from the ground floor where their men were quartered. When Schäfer stormed in he found that Akeh had 'ordered girls' and had spent the evening drinking *chang* and singing songs; then they had all gone to bed with the 'lovely children' in pairs. In the straw-filled room Schäfer was presented with a fine display of Tibetan rear ends rhythmically rising and falling. His response could be heard streets away. He barrelled into the panting throng, pulled his men from their paramours and roughly dragged the terrified, naked women up the stairs and threw them into the street. The outside temperature was –13°C. Schäfer's diary records that 'all hell broke loose, and two days later Akeh had a wonderful golden tooth'. The reason was that Schäfer had knocked one out in the brawl and he later contritely offered to replace it. Akeh is happy to show the prize to visitors today.

For most of the time the expedition stayed in Lhasa, Tredilinka was frequently besieged by prostitutes hoping to seduce the gruff, bearded foreigners. In his books, Schäfer pictured the Tibetan as 'happy like an animal' with no 'effeminate men' or 'hysterical Suffragettes', but he was puzzled by the way free libidos did not lead to free minds. Everyone he met seemed to accept an 'egotistical lamahood' that denied education and demanded slavish obedience. Schäfer's comments reflect the SS's distrust of religions without an Aryan pedigree. For him, as we have seen, Tibet was a twisted mirror in which he saw reflected the paradoxical progressivism of Nazi Germany. Tibet was weak; Germany was strong. Tibetans were corrupted by religion; under Hitler, Germans had rejected the Church and revived older, more potent gods. The SS was, at the same time, an occult order dominated by ritual and mysticism. Himmler himself was both policeman and magus. Nazi Germany was ruled by men who had come to believe that they were gods with power over life and death – more than any Dalai Lama ever claimed.

It is not at all surprising that we find Schäfer becoming just as fascinated as Madame Blavatsky by the occult goings-on in Lhasa. He took to visiting the gloomy and claustrophobic Jokhang Temple and interviewing its priests. Every morning, he would slip inside the narrow, greasy entrance and watch the pilgrims prostrating themselves on worn stones or spinning the long racks of prayer wheels in the Nagkor, the inner of Lhasa's three circulatory routes. Vats of butter kept the thousands of candles burning. The floor was slippery with congealed grease and the air thick with the perfume of butter mixed with burning incense. The monks showed him to the shrine of Palden Lhamo, a goddess the Tibetans believed had been reincarnated as Queen Victoria. Behind a door made from iron chains, in a chapel illuminated only by oily butter lamps, Schäfer was shown her effigy, which was usually shrouded. Palden Lhamo was depicted as a monster wearing the skins of her human victims and eating a brain from a skull she clasped in her twisted fingers. Surrounding her were images of disease and death and an odd collection of antique firearms. In a neighbouring shrine she was shown in a better frame of mind, surrounded by gold and gems. Both shrines were teeming with tiny mice that were thought to be incarnations. Their skins were believed to be arrow- and bulletproof. Schäfer caught one and closely examined it until a guard ordered him to set it free. He was, though, able to buy a 'shabby pelt' at an inflated price. The shrines, with their multitudes of different manifestations of the Buddha, were, he concluded, a 'horrible realm'.

Some of the monks were happy to talk about the tantric mysteries. Some of the more adept, they claimed, could control their 'inner heat' and spend days sitting in icy streams; others lived for years in caves without light. Sexual ecstasy was cultivated to achieve the highest enlightenment, and the masters of secret teaching 'addicted themselves to sex', Schäfer said, making sure their students offered them their wives, lovers or daughters. Ejaculated sperm was the physical form of enlightened thought. One practitioner asked him if he had seen the Himalayan snow frog, which had rejuvenating powers. Tibetan priests sometimes told Europeans what they wanted to hear, but there is a Buddhist tradition of black magic, such as that used against the young 13th Dalai Lama, and Schäfer was given a rather lurid version in the smoky shrines of the Jokhang.

Lhasa was ringed by processional paths that began in the cloisters of the Jokhang Temple then extended outwards like ripples of devotion. Inside the 'cathedral' the devout perambulated clockwise round the cloisters, turning great banks of prayer wheels that stood in long wooden racks. Beyond the temple itself was the Barkor, marked out by immense wooden poles decorated with yaks' tails where pilgrims threaded their way through clotted crowds of traders and merchants. Smoking was forbidden here, as Schäfer discovered when he re-emerged one day from the Jokhang and lit up. People began throwing stones, forcing him to take refuge inside the mansion of a Lhasan aristocrat who told Schäfer that he would 'forfeit his life' if he disturbed the gods in such an unpleasant manner again.

Circling the city and the Potala Palace itself was the Lingkor, the sacred way. Buddhists had to circle the city once a day, and for Schäfer and his comrades such perambulations provided both insights into Tibetan life and opportunities to meet any useful officials. From Tredilinka, the path ran alongside the meandering and marshy banks of the Kyi Chu River. On the western side of Lhasa, near the road that led to the Dalai Lama's Summer Palace at Norbulinka, the Lingkor turned north towards the Potala and the Germans passed directly in front of a mud-brick archway that led into Dekyilinka, the British Mission. The Union Jack fluttered gaily from its roof. On holy days, the Lingkor was busy with pilgrims and the devout, mixing with gangs of workmen and an army of beggars. Everyone walked clockwise, spinning their prayer wheel in the same direction. Anyone walking the other way would be marked out as a practitioner of Bön, the old religion of the Tibetan kings.

Not everyone *walked* the Lingkor. Some of the prostrating pilgrims were probably being paid for their services by a high official or aristocrat who hoped to annul his own transgressions. One lama Schäfer described claimed he had been circling Lhasa for fifteen years without stopping. The sacred road was five or six miles in length, which would mean at least three thousand obeisances, and the lama had developed a lump the size of an egg on his forehead. Pilgrims still circle Lhasa on the Lingkor, although only short sections of the sacred way are anything like the one Schäfer knew. But there is something powerful and moving about the sight of devout Tibetans, usually nomads from the east, crossing a busy intersection with their prayer wheels and packets of powdered yak butter. This modern road with its Chinese traffic lights and billboards may no longer resemble the Lingkor of old, but it is no less impressive for that.

For pilgrims in 1939, cairns marked positions from which the Potala Palace could be seen and venerated. Built by the 5th Dalai Lama in the seventeenth century, this wonder of the world resembled, according to Giuseppe Tucci, 'a diamond secured to its setting'. The soaring red and whitewashed walls of the palace appeared to grow from the rock itself. They leapt upwards 440 feet and were crowned with golden roof pavilions. Up there, guarded by monks who chanted in time to solemn drum taps, were the tombs of the God-Kings of Tibet. The greatest is that of the 'Great 13th' Thubten Gyatso, which was constructed from more than a ton of gold and rises from foundations many floors below. The sheer walls of the Potala Palace were punctuated by ziggurat-like stairways and hundreds of tiny shuttered windows. Nearly all the Tibetan ceremonies took place inside the Potala's bastions and every official in Lhasa would have to meet in the Assembly Hall and drink yak butter tea at least once a day. In January 1939, the Potala was without a Dalai Lama. Its insecure ruler was for now Reting Rimpoche, the Regent.

A wool caravan was setting off for India when the Germans reached the junction between the Lingkor and the Kaling Chu aqueduct. Here the sacred road narrowed as it skirted a rocky outcrop whose crumbly stone was believed to be a cure for rheumatism; few could resist self-medicating as they passed. Sacred cocks from a Chinese temple strutted about, and beyond the Kaling Chu was the whitewashed wall of the Snake Temple, dedicated to placating the water demon of the lake Lhasa had been built upon.

The Lingkor now ran across marshes and barley fields in the direction of the Regent's summer palace, passing the Elephant House or Langkhang where the 13th Dalai Lama had kept four elephants presented to him by the Chinese government. Their bones were found when the building was demolished in 1997. Nearby was the Naga Lake, where Schäfer found a 'secret place' to which he often returned in the following weeks in order to use this marshy refuge as a 'private hunting ground'. It was, he said, an idyllic place of streams and twisted old willow trees replete with gulls, geese and Brahman duck.

As the Germans followed the Lingkor as it swept back towards Lhasa, they had an altogether different encounter, for here were the mud-brick and greasy yak-hair hovels of the *ragyapa*, Lhasa's untouchables. Schäfer called them *der Abschaum*, which means literally 'offscouring', 'dregs', 'scum' or 'skimmings'. They could be seen every morning setting out with the dead of Lhasa stretched on their backs. At some distance from the city they would perform the sky burial ritual as witnessed by Schäfer and Dolan in 1935. On one occasion, Beger watched them working on the body of a young woman. As the corpse was expertly torn apart, a foetus was pulled from the uterus and smashed to pieces alongside its mother. The *ragyapa* had other tasks too. They could be sent in pursuit of thieves, and often demanded payment from visitors to Lhasa on arrival and departure. Some were quite wealthy. The better off wore earrings beneath saucer-shaped hats and lived in houses decorated with yak horns. (When I met 'German' Akeh in 2002, he told me that Schäfer had given him a hundred rupees – quite a sum – with which to acquire human skulls from the *ragyapa*. When I asked was this definitely Schäfer, not the anthropologist Beger, he was emphatic that it was Schäfer.)

There were other marginal people. Near the Ladakhi Mosque were the slaughterers and butchers who worked in the Lhasa abattoir. A mile or so further on there was a village of leather-workers. They allowed Buddhists to eat meat or wear leather clothes without taking life themselves. Around their rough hovels, the ground was littered with bones, horns and skulls.

Sightseeing and clockwise perambulations could not occupy Schäfer for long. Gradually, the expedition began to find friends among Tibetans, much to Richardson's chagrin. Kaiser had been very active on Schäfer's behalf. He had visited Jigme Tering and told him that the Germans were not happy with their residence. Jigme had then approached the Lönchen, whom Schäfer called the 'Prime Minister', and he had come back with an offer of alternative accommodation. This Schäfer politely refused. They had turned Tredilinka into an efficient headquarters and a comfortable German home from home. Humility, anyway, was a very clever tactic. Soon afterwards, a high-ranking monk official called by and presented the Germans with white scarves. The monk, who was fascinated by Schäfer's swastika flags, was accompanied by a small entourage bearing very generous gifts, all of them proudly listed by Schäfer: flour, corn, beans, rice, big lumps of butter sewn into yak skin, bricks of tea, hundreds of eggs, dried sheep and pig, half a yak, carpets, Tibetan artefacts and holy texts. Ordinary people who had seen the Germans walking about in Lhasa also came bearing gifts until there was no more room left inside Tredilinka.

Not long after the monk's visit, a mail runner called with another, much more momentous invitation. Reting Rimpoche had ended his retreat and wished to meet the German expedition. Schäfer ruthlessly drilled his comrades in Tibetan etiquette, with Rabden and Kaiser judging the results. Especially difficult was the subtle ritual of the white scarves, or *katas*. There was a complicated protocol and mistakes could easily be made. A high-ranking official expects a *kata* from someone of lower rank but will not give one in return. People of equal rank simply exchanged *katas*, but some care had to be taken. One held the kata towards one's guest and deftly took his underneath. The etiquette was subtle and hard to get right.

It was also essential to bring gifts. Schäfer and Geer made a careful selection of optical instruments, German china, amber (which Tsarong Dzasa had used to decorate his house), medicines with new Tibetan labels, various delicacies and a radio that would end up being placed on an altar. They also did what they could to look as sartorial as possible. High officials in Lhasa were used to seeing their British guests in full diplomatic uniform with a cocked hat and decorations or, at the very least, a morning-coat and topee. These outward forms and symbols were the bedrock of prestige for the British, although behind their smiles the Tibetans were rarely impressed.[3]

At dawn the next day, the five Germans marched from Tredilinka to the Potala Palace and climbed the great flight of stairs that led upwards to the entrance. A flustered troop of monks and officials were waiting for them, and took them across the Deyang Shah courtyard and into the Red Palace, the heart of the Potala. Schäfer knew that he faced a severe test. He was certain that Rabden would have reported their success back to Richardson, and he could not afford to falter now. Their escort led them along narrow twisting passageways that burrowed inside the palace. They passed richly coloured murals and incense-filled chapels with opulent golden statues of the Five Supreme Buddhas or the kings of Tibet. Many were encrusted with jewels and draped with silk *kata*. There were peacock feathers and flickering yak-butter lamps. Monks prostrated themselves, muttering their secret incantations. They found the Lönchen waiting for them outside the Regent's quarters. He ushered them inside and the Germans prepared their *katas* with sweaty fingers.

Enthroned before them on a cushioned seat, flanked by *thankas* (religious wall hangings) and a collection of antique Belgian pistols, was a frail, thin young man with very prominent ears which Schäfer called 'mystical antennae'. He was dressed in a yellow suede jacket. *Kata* were successfully exchanged, the Regent blessing each one with both hands. His throne was guarded by two enormous monks with padded shoulders who stared fixedly at Schäfer's party throughout the audience. Reting's hair was very closely cropped, and when he frowned curious hornlike creases of skin appeared on his forehead. Schäfer was struck by his large, dark eyes. Reting was joined by a 'delicately beautiful young man', probably his 'favourite' and monk-lover, Phünkang Jetrungla; Beger noted that 'it seemed to me he was serving inverted desires'.[4] The conversation was halting at first, but the Regent slowly relaxed and began to express an interest in Schäfer's claim that 'Europeans could fly, make clothes out of wood and gems from air'. The Regent told them the entire story of the discovery of the new Dalai Lama, who was still in Kumbum. He took them to see the mysterious fungus-like growth in the Dalai Lama's throne room, the 'divine finger' that had pointed towards the east and was now enshrined behind glass.

For his part, Reting was very taken with the Master Race. He was particularly fascinated by the tall, blond Beger. At the end of the audience, he requested that Beger be left behind in Lhasa as his bodyguard; in return, a monk could be sent to Berlin to convert the Germans to Buddhism. Polite refusal was simply ignored and Beger frequently had to fend off the insistent young ruler whenever they met. German beards provided another potent thrill for Reting. At one point he leant forward and began to stroke Schäfer's and to pluck hairs from the back of his hand with 'tender fingers'. The Regent had also asked Hugh Richardson to procure bearded Sikh bodyguards from India, and he made many enquiries about medicines that could encourage the growth of facial hair in Tibet. Schäfer liked the Regent but was surprised and disappointed by his knowledge of Buddhism. Religion did not seem to interest the young ruler of Tibet.

Schäfer's account rings true. After Trimön's resignation, Reting had made himself the most powerful man in Lhasa. This inhibited, reserved man eliminated all other rivals for power one by one and revelled in his role as the discoverer of the Dalai Lama. His lifestyle became increasingly hedonistic.[5] He had an appetite for both men and women and spent his time frittering away his *labrang*, flying kites and shooting. A British official reported that Reting was 'hopelessly venal'. He worked his way through the prettiest monks and shamelessly seduced the wives of senior officials. The problem was that everyone in Lhasa knew what he was up to, and sex would contribute to Reting's undoing.

Another curious event took place that day. As the Regent relaxed, Schäfer set up his camera and began to take photographs, which Reting seemed to enjoy, but he strongly resisted being filmed by Krause. While the Regent was distracted by his favourite, Krause switched on the camera as surreptitiously as he could. By the end of the day he had succeeded in shooting the Regent in colour and black and white, with wide-angle and telephoto lenses, and had even caught him stroking Schäfer's beard, to which Reting had become very attached.

As soon as he could, Krause sent his rushes back to Berlin. Months later they received a decidedly rum technical report. Among the flaws noted were 'Regent blurred' . . . 'Regent not recognizable, but companions on left and right pin sharp' . . . 'Regent stroking beard good and sharp'. Krause must have been having problems with his lenses, possibly as a result of the elements being jarred, or he had simply found the low lighting conditions too challenging, but it led to some absurd correspondence with Himmler's scientists. Dr Eberhard Cold sent Schäfer his analysis: 'The Regent is not transparent but blurred. That means that the photosensitive layer has not been exposed to the normal imprint of the Regent but to something else not visible to the human eye – or your eye.' Cold called this the 'phenomenon of the halo' or the 'aura'. In Buddhist art, saints are often shown with a corona of light or 'body halo' signifying the radiance of the soul. The emanation caught by Krause's camera was, Cold suggested, a healing force. It is surprising that Schäfer should engage in this kind of nonsense. Was he pulling the Ahnenerbe's legs?

The meeting with the Regent, whether he was blurred or sharp, was a great success. It elevated Schäfer's status in Lhasa and began to confound all Richardson's efforts to blacken his name. Over the next week, the expedition had meetings with most of the important people in the Kashag, including the Lönchen and all the *shapés*. They began to see Jigme Tering frequently, as well as two of the Old Rugbeians, Rinzin Dorje Ringang and Khenrab Künsang Möndrong, both of whom spoke perfect English. Schäfer discovered that Jigme shared his passion for hunting, despite his Buddhist faith. Another important contact was the Nepali representative Major Bista, who became very friendly with the Germans. It is an interesting fact that in 1940 Adolf Hitler presented King Tribhuvan of Nepal with a 1939 Mercedes – was this gift suggested by Schäfer? Very little science was done in Lhasa. Wienert records only four data sets for Lhasa, taken between the end of January and the beginning of March. Beger was too busy with his patients, and Schäfer became an explorer who lunched. As war in Europe became more certain, he evolved from a zoologist into a politician. He admits as much in his book: 'I was successful', he wrote, 'in destroying all the intrigues that had been spun around like a spider's web.' For Schäfer, the war had already begun.

Their most influential friend would turn out to be Tsarong Dzasa, who had once been the commander-in-chief of the Tibetan Army and a *shapé* until his fall from grace in 1930. Schäfer visited Tsarong at his very modern house on the outskirts of Lhasa, a big concrete structure with a modern library, glass window panes and even a working bathroom. A radio aerial protruded from the roof. In 1946, Heinrich Harrer and Peter Aufschnaiter, who stayed with Tsarong after their escape from Dehra Dun, found that Tsarong's radio 'gave one all the stations in the world' with no atmospheric disturbance. All these Tibetans were close to the British and were ceaselessly cultivated by Hugh Richardson, but every one of them had been caught up in the struggle to make Tibet a modern nation, and some were disappointed and frustrated. They admired and liked Richardson and Gould but knew that these 'men on the spot' had been unwilling or unable to persuade the Government of India and Foreign Office to support their cause. As Richardson admitted, he could not claim that he had a single 'enthusiastic supporter' in the Kashag. Schäfer became an expert on these tensions and did his best to exploit them.

The Germans saw themselves as representatives of a new and modern Germany. They extolled the virtues of German technology at every opportunity, and Schäfer also began to look for ways of getting the Regent to think of Germany as a more powerful patron than the British. At a later meeting in the Regent's palace, Kaiser was attacked by a guard dog which shredded his trousers. Instead of complaining, Schäfer praised the nasty little beast's diligence and 'Reting had the dog brought to us as a present for Adolf Hitler. Yet it was so aggressive that our men were terrified of him and shoved his food at him at the end of a long stick even when he was securely tied up.'[6] On another occasion a delighted *shapé* noticed Schäfer's 'good fortune flag', the swastika. Schäfer was clever enough not to make anti-British remarks to officials, although he could not help venting his feelings in the company of his own men, and his remarks were sometimes reported to Richardson.

On 26 January Beger recorded that the first mail from

Germany had arrived in Lhasa, via Gyantse; he learnt that his brother had marched into the Sudetenland with the Wehrmacht to be 'greeted jubilantly by the population'. Mail became a bitter source of dispute between Schäfer and Richardson. Because the British controlled both the post and the telegraph, any letter the Germans sent home was read at Dekyilinka. We know, for instance, that Richardson informed Gould about the warm greeting Schäfer had received from Himmler. Schäfer therefore began cultivating the Chinese, and was so successful that they began to let him use their wireless transmitter. Frustratingly, little is known about what messages were sent to Berlin. As Schäfer's status in Lhasa became more secure, he and Kaiser devised another way round the British. They bribed a telegraph lineman to pass their mail to a coolie who would take it out of Lhasa. The arrangement worked well until the bribe ran out in March and the system collapsed. Schäfer suspected Richardson of sabotaging his arrangement and threw a spectacular tantrum. Kaiser quietly slipped the lineman more money.

While Schäfer socialized, Beger did even more to add lustre to their status. Within days of his arrival, his reputation as a medicine man had spread among the Lhasan aristocracy. He turned Tredilinka into a dispensary and consulting room and was soon very busy indeed. He was, he said, 'overrun' by patients. 'Already very early in the mornings and very late in the evenings sick persons and petitioners came for medicines. There were days when they were already in front of the gate before dawn.' In letters to his wife he complained that he had no spare time for either his scientific work or for his diary and seemed perplexed by his success. There were many local practitioners and a doctor attached to the British Mission who supplied free medical care to encourage Tibetan goodwill, but Beger had a surprising advantage: the mission doctor was

Sikkimese, and to the people of Lhasa he simply did not possess the allure of the German medicine man even though the treatment offered at Dekyilinka and Tredilinka was almost certainly identical. The people of Lhasa deserted the mission doctor in droves, which infuriated Richardson and led him to try to prevent Beger getting fresh medical supplies. After this, Gould applied to Delhi for a permanent European medical officer to be stationed in Lhasa.

Beger worked for free, too, and was inundated with gifts of a quite remarkable diversity. The poorer among his patients offered eggs and tea, but the nobility brought artefacts of great cultural value. One of the most impressive was an entire suit of armour presented to him by the Phala family. He treated a variety of minor complaints, sometimes using placebos, but spent most of his time examining the ulcerated and suppurating genitalia of Tibetans of every rank and age – monks and laymen, aristocrats and peasants. Venereal diseases were even more prevalent in Lhasa than in the countryside. It was not always pleasant: 'Unfortunately,' Beger wrote, 'the time here in Lhasa put me off from becoming a registered doctor.' The Tibetans regarded Beger as a magician and presented him with a horse so that he could get to the sick outside the city. Mistakes were usually forgiven. On one occasion he was treating a woman with venereal disease and spent some time struggling to insert a catheter into her urethra; he discovered that he was inadvertently stimulating her clitoris, much to his patient's surprise (and, presumably, pleasure). Even when one of his patients died he was forgiven, indeed praised for prolonging her life. Beger was even asked if he had a medicine for eternal life.[7]

In spite of these successes, Schäfer had not resolved his most pressing problem. There was no indication, despite the daily round of lunches and dinners, that his permission to stay in Lhasa would be extended. The Tibetan New Year was approaching and he was regularly informed that the expedition would have to leave Lhasa before the ceremonies began. With just days left, Schäfer launched a new assault on the Lhasa officials. Both he and Beger had become close to Khenrab Künsang Möndrong, the monk official in charge of the police whom they called Möndro. During their first encounter, this Rugby-educated Tibetan had pretended not to speak English and had eavesdropped on their conversation with other Tibetans, and at first was probably reporting back to Richardson. But as he became closer to Schäfer he began to share rather critical views about Tibet and the lamas. Möndro was a lost soul. The 'Rugby Boys' had achieved little after they returned to Tibet and the Dalai Lama regarded Bell's experiment as a failure. Like their chaperone Lungshar, who had been punished so brutally for trying to change Tibet, the boys turned into disappointed, even bitter men. Möndro had headed the police in the mid 1920s but had been exiled to the Ladakh border following the fall of Tsarong.[8] (He was forgiven in the mid 1930s and staged a comeback.)

Schäfer sensed the bitterness in Möndro, perhaps identified with it, and the Tibetan began to open his heart. He told Schäfer about his plans to mine gold in Tibet and how he had been thwarted by priests who believed he would disturb the demons of the earth. Möndro was nostalgic about his time in England (and in Cornwall, where he had been sent to study mining) and bored. In the early 1930s he'd purchased a motorcycle in India and brought it to Lhasa. He'd taken to hurtling around the city like some proto beatnik driving away the demon of ennui, his robes fluttering behind him. Sometimes he'd taken the Dalai Lama for rides around the Lingkor. But these motorized pilgrimages had come to a bad end when in a moment of exquisite symbolism Möndro's motorcycle had scared the horse of a minister who was unceremoniously thrown to the ground.

Möndro liked Schäfer, but he was obsessed with Bruno Beger. He took to visiting the Germans every day to chat, smoke German cigarettes, sip whisky and try to seduce the tall, blond German. The outcome was a most unusual bedroom farce. Realizing how much he stood to gain from this friendship, Schäfer ordered a telescope from Calcutta and presented it to Möndro as a gift. Möndro reciprocated with rare artefacts from his own collection which Beger, in particular, highly valued. Möndro and the Germans celebrated with a great deal of whisky and Tibetan beer. At the end of the evening, the tipsy Möndro, his passions thoroughly inflamed, asked Beger to come home with him. Beger, probably mulling over what else the English had taught the young Tibetan at Rugby, agreed only after much prevarication and on condition that Geer accompany him. They took their ponies to Möndro's residence, where more rice wine and *chang* was consumed. Möndro showed Beger a 'comfortable room to which he no doubt intended to retire with me later'; Geer was provided with one of Tsarong's maids. The other servants discreetly melted away. It was vital not to offend Möndro, so Beger pretended to pass out. Geer apologized for his friend and dragged him out of the door, but Möndro would have none of this and threw himself on Beger. Geer was stronger, however, and succeeded in dragging his comrade out through the front door, shouting an emphatic 'Goodbye!' Beger recovered quickly and they mounted their horses and galloped away. They saw Möndro as usual the next day and there was some awkwardness, but the German's high spirits won Möndro over.

Möndro now offered to help Schäfer extend the period of time he was allowed to stay in Lhasa. There was only one person with the clout to change the Kashag's mind, and that was Tsarong Dzasa. They would invite him and other important officials to Tredilinka and seduce them with a feast. Schäfer made sure it was a sumptuous affair – after all, Tsarong's own chef had been acquired from a top hotel in Calcutta and was famous for his roasts and confectionery. As well as Tsarong, Jigme Tering, Möndro, his fellow Rugbeians Rinzin Dorje Ringang and Wangdu Norbu Kyibu, and Chang Wei-pei, the opium-addicted Chinese radio operator, all turned up. By now Schäfer had become a master of this kind of theatre. When his guests arrived at Tredilinka he showed off their zoo with its mastiffs, cats, monkeys and the Regent's vicious dog, and Wienert tuned in the radio he had constructed in an old Maggi box. Two SS flags were hung over the dining table. After a long meal in the Tibetan style, they settled down to drink whisky and *chang* and listened to gramophone records. The Germans began singing Wandervogel songs, which were a great success. When Heinrich Harrer arrived in Lhasa seven years later, he was surprised to hear these songs being sung by people in Lhasa and in Tsarong's house, where he stayed.

Tsarong had many stories to tell about his long and eventful life, and the Old Rugbeians reminisced about their time in England, which had not always been happy. After the gramophone records and the songs, the *chang* and whisky, Schäfer came to the point. How could his expedition stay longer in Lhasa? According to Beger's diary, Tsarong and the others unanimously promised to help. When the others had left, Möndro stayed on, crumbling cigarettes between his fingers. Schäfer taught his Tibetan friend how to sing 'Forty Green Bottles', then he and the others helped Möndro home, walking arm in arm with him through the dark streets of Lhasa.

The next day their good friend returned with mixed news: their stay had been extended by eight days but they would have to leave Lhasa after the second day of the New Year because their safety could not be guaranteed when thousands of monks poured into the city. It was Beger who held the key to an even more generous concession. Möndro explained that they had failed to include one important *shapé* on their invitation list, and it was this man who had blocked their request for a longer stay. Schäfer decided to visit the *shapé* at once. He discovered that the man's wife was sick with influenza and running a very high temperature so he sent for Beger and his medicine bag. They soon had the *shapé*'s wife feeling more comfortable. 'I knew how to use an aspirin,' Beger said when he told me about the incident. Just days later their permit was extended again, this time until 8 March. Richardson's reaction can only be imagined. The war of words increased. Schäfer did his utmost to annoy Richardson with provocative nationalist slogans and Richardson began playing radio news about Nazi aggression very loudly from the veranda at Dekyilinka. Tibetan officials began to fear inviting the two parties to the same events.

Now, of course, they would have the opportunity to experience and photograph one of the most remarkable events in the Tibetan calendar: the New Year and the Great Prayer or Mönlam, when thousands of monks flooded out of their monasteries and took command of Lhasa. Up to 1936, the only Europeans to have witnessed these remarkable ceremonies were Charles Bell and his doctor. Spencer Chapman and the Gould party were guests of honour in 1937, and they took hundreds of photographs and a great deal of film, although only Richardson stayed on for Mönlam. Schäfer's own accounts are extremely detailed; the New Year was, for the German Tibet Expedition, the high point of their time in Tibet. But it would end in a most unexpected and violent way.

The New Year began with the arrival of tens of thousands of pilgrims from all over Tibet. Buildings were whitewashed and thousands of prayer flags sprouted from every roof top. In every home, people chased away the evil spirits of the old year.

There was incense burning on every street corner and the air became thick with smoke. The Germans were invited by the Regent to attend the Devil Dance inside the Potala Palace on the last day of the Tibetan twelfth month. It was a potent sign of their new status. The dance would take place in the eastern courtyard, which had been hung with immense red, green and gold curtains decorated with dragons, and here, with Möndro's assistance, Krause set up his cameras. The Lhasa elite paraded around in glistening brocade and brightly patterned robes, mingling with crowds of warriors who resembled medieval knights in rusty helmets and armour with clinking chain mail and held aloft fluttering pennants. In their wake came brown-clad bowmen with conical hats. It was said that these warriors commemorated the defeat of a Muslim army overwhelmed by blizzards as it marched towards Lhasa. The armour they wore, it was said, had been taken from the frozen corpses of the invaders and carried in triumph to Lhasa. Tsarong entered resplendently, and he waved to his new German friends as he was led to his place of honour.

As Krause's rushes show, policemen with leather thongs waded in and out of the crowds, lashing out when anyone misbehaved. Trumpets and horns blasted from all directions. Butter tea and *tsampa* were handed out and were very welcome because a cold wind was now blowing through the palace gates. Hugh Richardson, looking more gaunt than ever, gave the Germans a tight-lipped smile. Schäfer could see that the *shapés* and other lay officials had assembled on one balcony, and as he glanced back the Regent himself rode past, his bodyguards wearing dark glasses. He smiled sweetly at Schäfer, who rather self-consciously stroked his beard. Reting disappeared inside the White Palace which bounded one edge of the courtyard and reappeared with the Lönchen at the Dalai Lama's window on the sixth storey. It was a signal for the horns and drums to begin the music for the Devil Dance.

What followed was a spectacular pantomime that blended Buddhism with the old Bön religion and even Hinduism to drive out the old year and bless the new. Down the palace steps came a corpulent figure clad in vermilion and gold wearing a big, grinning mask: this was Hushang, or the Laughing Buddha, who would sit on the sidelines nodding his great round head for the rest of the day. After him came the demon dancers, their arms outstretched in long-sleeved robes, wearing papier-mâché masks of fanged demons, bulls and stags. As they danced, hopping and turning, an effigy of a corpse was dragged into the centre of the courtyard. Now, with the crowd whistling and stamping, the 'skeleton dancers' ran into the courtyard, showing off their skull-like heads and bony fingers and dancing with abandon around the 'corpse'. As the dance reached a climax of frantic movement, yet another figure appeared. This was the Ancient Man. He wore the deeply lined mask of age, with downturned mouth, shaven head and long grey beard. He tottered round the courtyard, sinking every now and then to the ground but then rising again and struggling on. The crowd rushed him at one moment and were driven back by the rubber-thong-wielding attendants. Finally, the Ancient Man engaged in a life-and-death struggle with a tiger-skin rug and expired. Tsarong told Schäfer that the Ancient Man had been added to the ceremonies by the 13th Dalai Lama after a dream.

After the Ancient Man had gone, an extraordinary figure stalked down the palace steps. This was the Black Hat Magician, who commemorated the ancient struggle against the Bön religion when a Buddhist lama dressed in black slew Langdarma, the heretic king of Tibet. The lama escaped by reversing his coat, which was white inside, and slipping away. The Black Hat Magician wore an enormous woven hat and robes that billowed in the bitter wind that had begun to sweep in from the mountains. In his hands he clasped a dagger and a skull. He was followed by a troop of monks blowing high-pitched silver trumpets, and then twenty more Black Hat dancers. They performed for many hours and some of the crowd disappeared before the dance was completed. Then a tiny acrobatic figure dressed in silver and wearing a stag's head leapt centre stage and squatted over the figure of the corpse. In the meantime, a bubbling cauldron of hot mustard oil had been prepared, and the first Black Hat approached it slowly, holding out the skull. He poured something – Schäfer said it was wine – into the hot liquid and there was a tremendous flash and explosion. It was a signal that the ceremony was over. The devils of the Old Year were dead and the New Year could begin at last.

By now it was dark and stormy. A thunderstorm flickered in the mountains. Inside the palace an enormous procession formed, led by the Regent. It slowly made its way out of the courtyard and down the great flight of stairs to the city. The warriors fired their old muskets into the air. The Germans returned to Tredilinka and listened to the drums pounding on the Potala roof.

The next day was New Year, and Schäfer was awakened by his men. Each of them laid a *kata* across his sleeping bag. During the days that followed, many different ceremonies and rituals took place in Lhasa and in the Potala. Schäfer and his comrades were given honoured positions, and often found themselves facing Hugh Richardson, who glowered at them over tables groaning with food. On one of these occasions Schäfer presented another *kata* to the Regent and noticed that 'his eyes gleamed with pride. He affectionately squeezed both my hands and blessed me with a fond smile.' Reting's tea, they noticed, was tasted first by a monk. All these events were strictly policed by lamas armed with truncheons who punished the slightest transgression. One stood over Beger 'with evil eyes' after he had innocently adjusted the position of a cramped leg.

This first part of the New Year ended with a mass feeding of the city's beggars. An immense pyramid of food – cakes, sweets, dried fruit, bread, tea, butter, flour, *tsampa* – was constructed inside the Dalai Lama's throne room and two dried yaks placed on either side; then the doors were pushed open and a crowd of the poorest, dirtiest and hungriest citizens in Lhasa poured through and set about consuming every morsel. The first to reach the trove of delights dived in and threw whatever they could lay their hands on over their shoulders to relatives. They kicked and bit one another. The police, inevitably, waded in wielding their leather thongs. For those watching it appeared to be pure entertainment. In fewer than fifteen minutes the food pyramid has been devoured and the beggars sent on their way, bruised but satiated.

Now came the Mönlam Chenmo. It means 'Great Prayer', but this is a ridiculous misnomer for the violent and terrifying events that followed the New Year. The Mönlam combined the frenzied zeal of an auto-da-fé with the ethics of a riot, for this was a time when the hordes of monks from the 'big three' monasteries strode down from their mountain strongholds in their tens of thousands and seized control of Lhasa. Mönlam was a Bacchanalia of monkish terror. Robbery and even torture were common. The richer aristocrats locked away their valuables and usually left the city to the rapacious monks. The fighting *dobdos* came to enforce the will of the monasteries, but ordinary monks fought one another as well to make sure their own monastery had the upper hand.

When Charles Bell visited Lhasa in 1920–1, the Drepung Monastery took advantage of the Mönlam to attack both the British and Tsarong, who was then a *shapé* and commander-in-chief of the Tibetan Army. Bell was hated by the monasteries because of his annexation of the Tawang Tract and its monastery and his support for increased spending on the Tibetan Army; both strategies threatened to reduce the power and income of the monks. Placards were pasted on the walls of Lhasa calling for Bell and Tsarong to be assassinated. At the height of the crisis, Bell fled the city and the Dalai Lama was forced to send what troops he could to blockade the Drepung Monastery and its unruly monks.[9] After this experience, the Dalai Lama struggled to turn Mönlam back into a religious festival rather than a time when 'the lunatics took over the asylum', but after his death, as Schäfer put it, the lamas 'turned into little tyrants again'. Mönlam was a perilous time for foreigners, and even for the lay officials of the Kashag. Tsarong made sure that the Germans had bodyguards.

On the third day of the New Year, the five Germans watched from a rooftop as the monks came to Lhasa. Across the Kyi Chu Valley they could see columns, at least a mile long, of monks converging on the city 'like hungry swarms of locusts . . . predators who have the chance to play for a short while'. They came from all directions and for hour after hour poured through the Barkokali Gate. At their head came the preceptors, who carried silver maces that symbolized their temporary but absolute power in the city. They were flanked by six-foot-tall *dobdo* monks wearing padded robes and platform shoes and wielding formidable sticks and whips. Many had blackened their faces with soot.

Schäfer knew it was a once-in-a-lifetime opportunity and insisted that Krause get as close as possible with his camera. Ringed by his bodyguards, they found a position in the Barkor near the entrance to the Jokhang, but some of the monks realized what was happening and started to lob stones at the foreigners and their cameras. Krause retreated quickly. For the rest of that first day he filmed from rooftops. Schäfer was disappointed, and was determined to find a way to get better pictures.

Inside the Jokhang there was a great orange crush of monks. Some were suffocating and had to be passed to safety over the heads of the others. Schäfer claimed that when they were not praying and chanting inside the holy sites, the monks indulged in every excess: drinking, smoking, gambling and arranging orgies with Lhasa's prostitutes. All over the city fires were lit on street corners to cook *tsampa*, and the streets became slippery with excrement.

The most important event during the Mönlam was the yearly prophecy of the State Oracle that took place at the Nechung Monastery outside the city. There were three oracles in Tibet and they were all taken very seriously. The entire National Assembly of lay and monk officials rode out to hear what the medium, or *kuten*, had to say. It was a bright, cold morning. Krause and his bodyguards managed to clear the crowds from a section of the Barkor to film this remarkable sight – 'Like a vision from ancient times . . . glittering and glistening.' At the head of the procession was the Regent, carried in his palanquin and accompanied by more than twenty attendants in bright red hats and by his latest pretty monk. As Reting was carried past, he gave Schäfer and Beger a 'secret smile'. On the road outside the western gate monks were still streaming into Lhasa from the opposite direction, and some insolently refused to move aside for hated lay officials like Tsarong, who was forced to ride around them.

Nechung was on the road to the Drepung Monastery and stood surrounded by big willow trees. The ceremony took place inside a courtyard hung with dark drapes which stirred fitfully in the wind. It began when the Regent and the *shapés* took their places. Horns blared, drums banged and cymbals clashed monotonously. There was another Devil Dance, designed to lure the spirit of prophecy to the temple. Schäfer had already met the Oracle, Ta Lama Rimpoche, and noticed him slipping into an inner chamber dressed in gold and wearing an immense jewelled and feathered head-dress. There he prepared for his trance. He had already fasted for many days.

Outside in the courtyard, the music and dancing stopped. Gongs and drums continued to sound from inside the monastery, building in a crescendo. A commotion erupted on the steps and the Regent and government officials dashed forward. The Oracle had appeared, already red-faced, his whole body shaking, his arms outstretched and supported by monks. The spirit of prophecy had taken possession of Ta Lama Rimpoche. The plumes of his head-dress quivered as the trance became deeper and more violent. Sometimes he lashed out, making it hard for his attendants to hold him upright. After a while he became calmer and more meditative and began to dance. Now the questions could be put to him by the Regent. This is how Schäfer reported the Oracle's prophecy: 'Watch the mountains which are on the border: flying people will approach the land of snow through the sky. They come with beautiful gifts, and their speech will be as sweet as the cooing of pigeons – but they bring false dogma, which does not come from heaven. Peace will pass by in the land of snow, if the new Dalai Lama does not come to the Holy City this year. Then happiness will return. Protect the teaching, make sacrifices, be friendly to strangers, but reject their gifts, because they won't help the living. A dragon rules their world . . .'[10] The Oracle also had a prophecy for Schäfer: 'The strangers who came from far away across the sea do not treat you like children: they love our teachings, but they are also carrying something else – be patient with them, because they enjoy the Great Prayer.' What else the Germans were 'carrying' with them is, of course, the great puzzle of the German Tibet Expedition.

In the days that followed there were more ceremonies and parades around the Barkor. In the butter-lamp-lit streets of Lhasa there was an eerie, threatening atmosphere. Fireworks were let off, crowds of monks surged through the streets, guns were fired. Later, big tents were pitched on the Kyi Chu plain in front of Lhasa. There were archery contests, which Krause filmed at tedious length, and more of those parades of armoured warriors that Schäfer admired. Mock heroics sometimes turned into real violence. One man was shot point-blank in the face; a Devil Dancer lost a finger. On the fifteenth day came the butter feast when sculptures called *torma* made out of butter were paraded all over the city. There was even a butter puppet theatre.

Both Krause and Schäfer continued to film as much as they could. They knew the value of the remarkable pictures they were getting and anticipated the glory they would bring when they returned to Germany. But they were often stoned and cursed. They were very dependent on their bodyguards, and on the police, who were frequently forced to intervene. Still, Schäfer became increasingly reckless. After the butter festival he was determined to film the arrival of the Nechung Oracle at the Meru Nyingha Monastery, which was his town residence.

Krause and the rest of the expedition, along with their bodyguards, first took up positions on a roof overlooking the entrance to the monastery. The Oracle visited the Jokhang then processed towards Meru Nyingha following a large *torma*. There was intense and rising excitement among the crowds of monks lining the way. Drums pounded and cymbals crashed. As the Oracle approached, the Germans were spotted filming on the roof and the first stones were lobbed in their direction. In the street, the Oracle had entered another trance and was lashing out at his companions. He started dancing, but then ran towards the monastery shooting arrows at invisible enemies before collapsing and being carried into the entrance. Schäfer, with Akeh, Krause and his camera in tow, impulsively rushed down the steep ladder in the house they were using and tried to follow the Oracle. As he emerged on to the seething Barkor he must have known very quickly that he had made a terrible mistake. Now the crowd of black-faced monks turned on the Germans and their terrified bodyguards like 'a snarling beast, full of hatred and fury'. Schäfer stopped moving and they all gathered in a tight circle. No-one spoke. The monks began to whistle – a high, soul-searing sound from another world. Then it stopped as suddenly as it had begun and the stones began to rain down.

In his books, Schäfer gives a rather clichéd and unconvincing version of events. They were 'five against thousands'. By 'fixing the monks' eyes' he managed to stop some of them throwing their 'vicious little pebbles'. He claims he grappled with one or two and made the rest retreat. The account in his diary, however, has a raw authenticity: 'We are "great men" and must not show any weakness. But I think: the bird hunting [with a catapult] has trained me to be a good stone thrower. I killed more than one bird with a single stone's throw. In front of me lies a big stone with which I could at least smash these devils' skulls . . . Akeh sees this. He has helped me hunting birds in the holy land and understands me. He is not a coward. He bends down to pick up the stone. He draws back [his arm] and aims . . . Off goes the stone; the man folds like a penknife . . .' With their bodyguards' assistance, Schäfer, Krause and Akeh clambered over a wall and ran pell-mell through the back gardens of the Barkor until they could cut back round to Tredilinka and safety. They were all bruised and cut, and fortunate to be alive. Krause had lost a camera and one of his lenses was badly damaged.

When the faithful Möndro visited them that evening he

found Schäfer in his sleeping bag covered with bandages, his face bruised and bloody. The Tibetan was mortified and apologized many times, consoling Schäfer by telling him that even the 13th Dalai Lama had once been assaulted by monks at the Drepung Monastery. But Schäfer's injuries were not quite what they seemed. According to Akeh, he had daubed his face with red dye and made sure that the *shapés* saw the result. In his reports, Richardson claimed that the Germans had experienced a humiliating catastrophe, but Schäfer won yet more ground. He soon received an official written apology from the Kashag addressed to 'The Master of 100 Sciences', and not long afterwards Krause began filming again.

Some Ngolok people from Kham had set up camp near Lhasa for the New Year, so Schäfer paid them a visit. Krause filmed them eating *tsampa* together. But then Schäfer got into a scrap with an elderly Ngolok man and, according to Beger, 'shouted at the men so violently that he trembled then apologized . . .' For Beger, still busy with his medical work, it was a frustrating time. He had been able to do little if any scientific work in Lhasa, and Mönlam would have made any measuring provocative and foolhardy. He had to be content with taking photographs. It was tormenting to observe among the visitors to Lhasa 'many beautiful and tall people with even features' – traces of the Master Race which threatened to elude him for ever.

By now the expedition had spent more than two months in Lhasa and they had become honoured guests and friends of the city's elite. Krause's film of the New Year and Great Prayer had provided them with extremely valuable material to take back to Germany and present to the Reichsführer. In addition, Beger had acquired an impressive collection of ethnographic artefacts, including a copy of the 108-volume *Kangyur*, one of the holiest of all Tibetan religious texts. Lhasa had given up many of its secrets and it was time to move on, but to where? As the political situation in Europe deteriorated they began to receive messages urging them to come home. Schäfer still hoped to get to Nepal or even Kashmir – a prospect that caused shockwaves of alarm in the Foreign Office. As a result of the stoning, the Kashag had offered the expedition another two months in Tibet. After much discussion it was decided to remain within Tibetan borders and travel east to Tsetang and the Yarlung Valley and then return west along the Tsang Po to the great city of Shigatse. After that they would hopefully head south back to Gyantse and the Indian border – if the British would allow it.

Before he left the Holy City, Schäfer had one last request to make of the Regent, and Reting, too, had something on his mind. By now the Germans were on very good terms with Reting. It was conventional to make a request to see him three days in advance, and then, as Richardson found, the audience lasted a mere ten minutes at most. But Schäfer's diaries show that he was able to meet the Regent at almost any time and to spend two or three hours in his company. Shortly after the battle in the streets, Schäfer had another audience with the Regent during which two abbots were forced to apologize on behalf of their monks. No mention is made of this in Richardson's report. At either this meeting or at another not long afterwards, the Regent made a breathtaking request: he asked whether Schäfer could supply him with guns – German guns. It can hardly have come as a surprise; Schäfer's long conversations with Tsarong would have provided invaluable history lessons. Tsarong's struggle to modernize and properly equip the Tibetan Army had met with hostility from both the monasteries and the British. The future of the Tibetan Army had also been at the centre of the bitter politics inside Tibet that had so preoccupied the 13th Dalai Lama and had then erupted in violence after his death. Beger also records being summoned to see Lady Lhalu, the widow of Tsipön Lungshar, another modernizer who had been so brutally punished five years earlier; she would have left him in no doubt about the nature of Tibetan politics. In eastern Tibet and on the border with China Tibetan forces had fought hard but could never sustain an assault on the better-armed Chinese, whose officers had been trained, ironically, by German staff officers. So the Regent might have wanted the guns to defend Tibet or to advance his own power struggle.

Beger's diary records unequivocally that Schäfer refused the Regent's request, but this is not surprising. Both the Chinese and the British would have reacted very strongly to any rumour that the Germans were bringing guns into Lhasa, and although Schäfer enjoyed torturing Richardson, he could not afford to fall out with Gould as well. Even so, the plot now began to thicken.

The German Scholar Dr Isrun Engelhardt has shown that Schäfer had begun to discuss officially inviting the Regent to Germany.[11] The idea was to send a plane from Berlin, pick the Tibetan ruler up in Calcutta and then fly him to Germany where he would, presumably, meet Hitler and other members of the Nazi elite. Other Tibetan aristocrats had also expressed an interest in visiting Germany – but the Kashag bluntly vetoed the idea of anyone going to Germany and that was that. Schäfer did not give up and now suggested that the Regent write a letter to Hitler.

Engelhardt has translated what resulted as follows:

> To his Majesty Führer Adolph, Hitler, Berlin, *Germany*.
> From: The Regent of Tibet.
> On the 18th day of the first month of Sand-Hare Year.
>
> Your Majesty,
> I trust your Highness is in best of health and in every progress

with your goodly affairs. Here I am well and doing my best in our religious and Government affairs. I have the pleasure to let Your Majesty know that Dr. Schaefer and his party, who are the first Germans to visit Tibet have been permitted without any objection, and every necessary assistance is rendered on their arrival. Further, I am in desirous to do anything that will help to improve the friendly tie of relationship between the two Nations and I trust your Majesty will also consider it essential as before.

Please take care of Your good self, and let me know if Your Majesty desire anything.

I am sending under separate parcel a Tibetan silver lid and saucer with a red designed tea cup, and a native dog as a small remembrance.

Sincerely Yours,
Reting Ho-Thok-Thu.[12]

This letter has been used to suggest a Tibetan interest in Nazism.[13] Engelhardt, however, notes that Tibetan correspondence usually follows strict rules – and in the Regent's letter a number of them are carelessly broken: 'the letter seems to have been hastily written . . .' is her conclusion. It is 'not a letter to an equal but from someone slightly superior to an inferior.' The implication, according to Engelhardt, is that the Regent was *disinterested* – and not at all fascinated by the Nazi leader. But in the early 1940s, a German scholar, who was seeking employment with Schäfer's 'Sven Hedin Institute' (unsuccessfully as it turned out) translated the letter to make it appear more obsequious than it was, thus implying that the Regent was eager to forge some connection with the German Dictator. Even today, writers like Victor and Victoria Trimondi continue to use the mistranslated version of the letter as evidence that the Regent as well as other Tibetan leaders and even the 14th Dalai Lama were sympathetic to Nazi thinking. The truth is that in 1939, the Regent may have had only the vaguest idea just who 'Herr Hitler' was – and this is very clearly implied by the tone of the letter that Schäfer solicited.[14]

In brief, research by modern scholars (like Dr Engelhardt) has demonstrated that Tibetans like the Regent had very little curiosity about the ideologies espoused by Ernst Schäfer and his German masters; they certainly wanted something from Schäfer but not a dose of Nazi thinking. It is much more likely that they wanted to show their English friends that the British Empire was not the only non-Asian power they could exploit. So much for the Regent himself: but what was Schäfer up to?

The letter incident provides further evidence that Schäfer had *political* interests in Tibet – not simply 'scientific' ones. To be sure, returning to Germany with a letter from the ruler of Tibet addressed to the German Chancellor would have added lustre to Schäfer's reputation in the Third Reich. But even more than that, other evidence suggests this odd letter was an opening salvo in Schäfer's own undeclared war against the British. By the time the Regent was writing his notorious letter, every foreigner in Lhasa was sharply aware that a European war was increasingly likely, if not inevitable.

At the very moment Schäfer was preparing to leave Lhasa, Hitler was making his last move in the destruction of Czechoslovakia, that 'miserable little nation'. On 14 March, Hitler summoned the Czech President Dr Emil Hácha to Berlin. Slovak unrest and military action by the Czechs had given Hitler his longed for excuse to move against the hated 'Tsechia' and the Wehrmacht was already poised on the border ready to carry out 'Case Green'. The ailing Hácha was too terrified to get on board an aircraft, so he took a train to Berlin, accompanied by a small entourage that included his daughter. When he eventually arrived at Speer's Chancellery building, he was kept waiting for hour after humiliating hour while Hitler enjoyed a film with his inner circle.

Finally at one in the morning, Hitler had Hácha, sick and exhausted, dragged into his enormous study where he treated the increasingly distraught Czech leader to an hysterical tirade, the upshot of which was that German troops were about to cross the border into Czechoslovakia. Hitler demanded Hácha order the Czech Army to lay down their arms. When the panic-stricken Hácha was told that the Luftwaffe was already in the skies over Prague – they were in fact grounded by severe weather – the Czech leader fainted. Hitler's doctor gave Hácha an adrenaline shot – and when he had regained consciousness he telephoned Prague and did Hitler's bidding. Both the man and the nation were brutally snuffed out. 'This is the happiest day of my life,' Hitler told his secretaries, 'I have achieved the union of Czechia with the Reich . . .'

By 9 a.m. on 15 March the first German units rolled into Prague. There was no resistance. That evening, Hitler was driven to the Czech capital where he entered the Hradcany Palace, the ancient seat of the Kings of Bohemia. Here he finalized the absorption of the 'Bohemian and Moravian lands' into the Reich. The Slovakians soon suffered the same fate: Ruthenia was handed to Hungary. In Berlin, there was the usual hero's welcome when Hitler returned to the Chancellery. Göring swiftly lapped up the riches of the new 'German' provinces relishing especially the Skoda munitions factories which the Nazi imperialists had long dreamed of possessing.

Far away in Lhasa, the consequences were at first comic. Schäfer and his men clustered round their battered radio and struggled to hear what was happening in Europe. But the transmission broke up continuously and everyone was confused and probably very anxious. Something momentous had happened –

but what? For Schäfer, there was only one course of action. He dashed out and headed towards the British Mission: his arch enemy, Hugh Richardson, would surely know the truth.

Richardson was quite surprised to see his visitor who arrived 'soon after breakfast . . . breathless with excitement'[15]. Richardson ('coldly', he remembered) clarified what had happened and Schäfer said, 'Good, good: your government will make that all right, won't they?' Schäfer was manifestly trying to discover both whether Britain would let Hitler get away with the invasion (as they did) – and whether his expedition was in peril. Richardson later wrote that he gave him short shrift: 'I hope they will not [make that all right] and I do not wish to see you again.' Geer had accompanied Schäfer and talked to Reg Fox, the radio officer. According to Richardson, Fox was 'less diplomatic than me': 'You bloody Nazis, you had better take care; we have troops at Gyantse'. A flavour perhaps of 'Dad's Army' here – but feelings were running very high.

Richardson's papers, which give such a vivid sense of that day in the spring of 1939, became available in the summer of 2003 – after this book had been published. They reveal a rather different Ernst Schäfer and they have led me to conclude that I had given this puzzling man more benefit of doubt than he deserved. Although Richardson was hostile to the German Expedition from the beginning, there is an authenticity to his recollections and little reason to doubt the detail of what he relates. I had imagined Schäfer as, above all, an opportunist: someone who could stand aside from Nazi ideology and yet make use of the opportunities his SS membership and friendship with Himmler could bring him.

But Richardson met a man who was openly fascinated with 'Aryans' and was as he put it 'Anti-Jew'. For example, he recalls 'a long talk [with] Schäfer who was emphasizing the Aryan line with an extraordinary theory that *the Germans and the British and some other favoured nations were descended from some sort of cosmic ice, and arguing that we should stand together against lesser breeds.* I was not impressed . . . [my italics]'. It is very unlikely that Richardson would have had knowledge of the 'World Ice Theory' (described in Chapter Five) *and* that he would have put these words into Schäfer's mouth. I can only conclude that these *were* Schäfer's views in 1939. His later contempt for Himmler and his cranky theories, expressed to Schäfer's American interrogators, should, therefore, be read with even greater caution than I had realized. While it is very clear that Bruno Beger had been completely immersed in Nazi racial theory, Schäfer's interest in these ideas seemed to me, at first sight, to be half-hearted, opportunist. But the Richardson papers provide potent evidence that Schäfer really was that 'high priest of Nazism' – and not a fellow traveller.

As Schäfer fled from Lhasa in a panic, appeasement – the cowardly policies that had proved so useful for his plans – had been mortally wounded, if not quite killed off. Even Chamberlain began to see that Hitler's invasion of Czechoslovakia was the first big step towards European domination. On 22 March Hitler mopped up the Memelland, without resistance, and quickly turned his full attention to Danzig and the eventual liquidation of Poland. He demanded that his generals finalize plans for 'Case White' in order that what Göring called a great 'chorus of revenge' would descend on Poland. Britain and France intensified their rearmament programmes, and on 31 March Chamberlain signed a mutual assistance pact with the Poles. This time the German dictator would not prevail so easily if he decided to send his forces across another frontier. Unnerved by this development, Hitler defiantly told his staff, 'I'll brew them a devil's potion'. The war against lesser breeds was about to begin.

In Tibet, Ernst Schäfer and his colleagues faced a new crisis:

time was running out fast and there was still much they had to accomplish. The ancestors of the Master Race were proving distinctly shy.

CHAPTER TWELVE

ESCAPE FROM THE RAJ

'I hope that Schaeffer [sic] *will not be a nuisance . . . I cannot believe that the Nazi government would stand any nonsense in such circumstances, and, while I have no disposition whatever to adopt a rabidly anti-German attitude, I suspect that we are reaching a stage at which, unless international relations improve, good nature on our part may be taken for weakness by Germans and pro-German sympathizers; and may be entirely misunderstood by the Indian public.'*

– Lord Linlithgow, Viceroy of India

On 20 March 1939, five young German scientists set off in a north-easterly direction along the edge of the Kyi Chu River in Tibet at the head of a long caravan of servants, muleteers, yaks and ponies. Had they looked over their shoulders they would have seen, for the last time, the golden roof of the Potala Palace catching the early-morning sun, then rapidly disappearing behind the cloud of dust kicked up by a hundred hooves. The five young men had not seen the Fatherland since the spring of 1938.

As this curious expedition wended its way below the craggy tan hills of the Kyi Chu Valley, it was obvious to passers-by that the animals were all heavily burdened. Large cases, custom-designed in Berlin, were fastened across the back of every yak and mule. What they contained was a mystery, because this was not just another wool caravan meandering on its way towards Kham or Amdo. The heavy, tightly locked boxes were swollen instead with prized animal skins, including one creature unknown to science, hundreds of reels of film, heavy-duty tripods, magnetometers and theodolites, several radio receivers, and all 108 volumes of the Tibetan Buddhist 'Bible', the *Kangyur*.

For thirty miles the road ran dead flat along the edge of the wide valley with its lazily meandering waters, but when the caravan reached the crumbling walls of an old fort, the Dagtse Dzong, Schäfer signalled that they must now turn away from the Kyi Chu and head into the mountains towards the Gokar La Pass. As they began climbing away from the valley, dark, snow-covered peaks appeared ahead of them and the temperature fell. As the track steepened, mules and yaks stumbled on the icy path that climbed into the clouds. When they finally reached the summit of the Gokar La, the Germans added stones to the cairns that marked the crossing. Prayer flags fluttered wildly, spilling their magic formulas and blessings into the cold wind, and the men all shouted '*So-ya-la-so!*'

Heavily bearded, enfolded in long, dark leather coats, the Germans resembled the high priests of a religious order. Ernst Schäfer had been denounced as a 'priest of Nazism' by the British, but as he crossed the pass on that spring day he had reason to be pleased with his accomplishments as an emissary of Germany's New Order. Given permission to spend two weeks in Tibet, he had extended his stay in the once Forbidden City of Lhasa to over two months. He had thwarted the efforts of the

British to tarnish his reputation among the Tibetan nobility and now counted some of Tibet's most powerful men as close friends and informants. One of them, Khenrab Künsang Möndrong, or just plain Möndro, was now part of the expedition, a British public schoolboy turned honorary German.

In Lhasa, Bruno Beger had become an overworked amateur doctor, but he had little interest in the health and well-being of the Tibetans or anyone else for that matter. Beger was in search of the Master Race, and he sought it by measuring the heads and bodies of men and women who belonged to the Tibetan nobility. Their unusual appearance could only be explained, he believed, if they were kin to the Aryan race. In Lhasa, Beger had been too busy to continue his scientific work; now, as the expedition rode down through the clouds, he knew he had much to accomplish and many bodies to measure.

As the German Tibet Expedition descended through flurries of snow down the stony track on the other side of the pass, the Nazi leader Adolf Hitler was returning to the Reich Chancellery in Berlin, where he was greeted by roaring crowds and a tearful Hermann Göring. The Unter den Linden was a spectacular tunnel of light and fireworks burst in radiant splashes of colour over the Tiergarten. 'I will go down', Hitler said, 'as the greatest German in history.' War was now inevitable. The policy of appeasement that had been designed to contain Hitler's ambitions was discredited. The governments and people of Great Britain and France knew that Hitler had to be confronted. For Ernst Schäfer and his SS scientists, time was running out. They knew that within a very short time they would be transformed from mere irritants into enemy aliens and would face internment or worse. Schäfer's remarkable success had been the gift of appeasement. Now his luck was about to end.

The German expedition spent two days crossing the mountains and then descended towards Samye, Tibet's oldest monastery, which had been founded by King Trisong Detsen in the eighth century. They travelled on towards the Tsang Po River, which they had first crossed upstream near Lhasa in December 1938. A ferry took the Germans and their animals and porters across the river and landed them close to the regional capital of Tsetang. Schäfer now turned south and led his expedition into the Yarlung Valley, the ancient heart of Tibet. The landscape was infused with mythic history. As they left Tsetang, they could see to the east the mountain of Gangpo Ri. Here, it was said, Avalokiteśvara or Chenresig, the Bodhisattva of Compassion – who would be endlessly reincarnated as successive Dalai Lamas – had descended from the heavens as a rock monkey and retreated to a cave. Chenresig was tempted into the world by an ogress whose attractions were so powerful that between them they produced six children. These malformed creatures were the first Tibetans. Half men, half apes, they became fully human only when Chenresig brought them 'six kinds of grain' and instructed them to become farmers. Close to the foot of Gangpo Ri is Sothang, the legendary 'First Field' where the seeds were planted and harvested. It is now the more mundane 'Commune Number Nine'. Schäfer had a special interest in those grains: he hoped they would feed the Fatherland.

Due south was the Yarlung Valley, flat, fertile and green, stretched like a bow string between dry brown mountains. As Schäfer led his caravan south, Tibetan serfs planted and hoed the lush and fertile fields, their yak-drawn ploughs slicing into the rich earth. A few miles south of Tsetang, the Yarlung bifurcated. To the east, the Chongye Valley led to the funerary mounds of the first Tibetan kings; to the west was one of the most remarkable of all Tibetan monuments, and it fascinated

Schäfer and his colleagues. This was the Yumbu Lagang, a hill-top fortress and reputedly the most ancient building in Tibet. According to legend, Buddhist texts had rained down on its roof in the second century after Christ. No-one could read them, but they were kept as a *nyenpo sangwa*, or 'awesome secret'. For two days Schäfer camped at the foot of the rocky spur, the Yumbu Lagang towering above them. They spent days measuring and photographing. For Schäfer, the Yumbu Lagang was another point scored against the British. The Tibetans had never permitted them to visit this jewel of a building. It had an almost talismanic power for the Germans. As clouds dashed pell-mell across the hills and mountains, the Yumbu Lagang glowered and shimmered on its granite crag. At times, the tower seemed to resemble the miserable grandeur of mad King Ludwig's Neuschwanstein Castle; at others it reminded them of a Teutonic fortress, or Heinrich Himmler's SS 'Order Castle' at Wewelsburg.

Inside the Yumbu Lagang was a womb-red chapel and gleaming gold and silver images of the Buddha, Sakyamuni (Prince Gautama) and the Tibetan king Srongtsan Gampo. Tibetans believed that the royal lineage had first become manifest on Lhabab Ri, the mountain that lay across the valley from Yumbu Lagang. The first king, so the story went, had descended from heaven on a silk rope and was discovered and enthroned by local chieftains. He and his successors returned on their silk ropes to heaven whenever their time on the throne was considered to be at an end. Then one king severed his rope at the climax of a bitter duel with his court magician, and Tibetan kings were earthbound and mortal ever after.

This kind of legend fascinated Heinrich Himmler, who had informed Schäfer at their first meeting that 'Aryans came from heaven'. Now freed from his obligations as a 'medicine man', Beger was able to pursue these obsessions of the Reichsführer.

As they travelled south, he sought fresh subjects for his anthropometric work. He measured, photographed and cast face masks at every opportunity, assisted either by Kaiser or Möndro, who became intrigued by what Beger was doing with his callipers and eye charts and asked him to explain what he was up to. He was unimpressed by Beger's explanation, but 'luckily, Möndro had got to know the character and thinking of Europeans more than almost any other Tibetan. It was in his power to prohibit my research. He had figured out that we weren't interested solely in Buddhist philosophy and religion a long time ago.'

Karl Wienert, for his part, was now freed from the daily surveillance that had crippled his work in Lhasa. He, too, could also resume work; he would set up fifteen magnetic stations between Lhasa and Shigatse. Schäfer's own experience was mixed. He was still using the rubber catapults to collect more avian specimens, but on one occasion he returned to camp in a filthy mood having torn the elastic. Geer good-naturedly repaired it for his fuming leader, who returned to the hunt. Möndro occasionally let him or Geer use their rifles, as Schäfer's diary makes clear. 'I can't believe my eyes. Krause and I have just been enjoying the spring: ten wonderful blue pheasants [*Ohrfasanen*] with white ears. We wait. Eventually Möndro comes . . . We have a lengthy debate. Shall we or shall we not? Then he allows us ONE bullet . . .' They bagged a beautiful pheasant with that single shot. On another occasion Schäfer returned from a hunt in an agitated state. He had been pursued by a group of Tibetans, one wielding a long sword, and had been forced to take refuge in a mill, where he had terrified the miller and his family. It turned out that Schäfer had abandoned his two servants, who made their way back much later having hidden in a ditch. Möndro calmed everyone down and made sure no-one reported the incident to Lhasa.

Without the distractions of Lhasa, the old tensions surfaced between Schäfer and the rest of the expedition, and they would worsen as Schäfer sensed new pressure from his imperial hosts. Although he had trounced Richardson in Lhasa, Schäfer became increasingly anxious about British intentions and began to fear that troops were being sent from Gyantse to 'arrest him, shoot him or send him down to India'. When members of his caravan, including Rabden Kazi, the aristocratic translator he so mistrusted, told him unexpectedly that they had to return to Sikkim, he suspected another British plot to rob him of his best men. Then he heard from someone in Lhasa that he was now suspected of prospecting for oil and gold which he planned to steal from the Tibetans. Schäfer was also preoccupied with plans to take his assistant Kaiser Thapa back to Berlin. Apart from Beger's diaries, the only other source describing Schäfer's state of mind is the British secret reports by Richardson and Sir Basil Gould. Their accounts, while hardly objective, are consistent, even sympathetic. One report says, 'Dr. Schäfer is clearly a man of a highly emotional nature and he seems to have allowed the atmosphere of international tension to inspire him with a sort of persecution mania, so that he got the idea – which was quite unfounded – that every man's hand was against him . . .'

Although the British had indeed made no such plans – Richardson must simply have made good use of Lhasa's rumour mill – after Hitler's occupation of Czechoslovakia fortune was turning against the German Tibet Expedition. Schäfer had made skilful use of the spirit of appeasement; his expedition was the gift of Munich. Now, in the British Parliament, questions were being asked that implied that the Government of India had been a little too sympathetic to this 'SS Expedition', and in *Punch* Giles the cartoonist showed the SS 'Secret Agents' standing next to a yak with a swastika burnt into its hide. From the Viceroy down, a new strategy was hammered out. The upshot was summed up as follows:

> We may not have heard the last of [Schäfer] . . . The conclusion that seems clear from this account is that his excitable nature, his tactlessness . . . his methods of dealing with his servants, and his ardent Nazi-ism do not make him the kind of person whose presence in this part of the world is to be encouraged . . . It may be . . . that Dr Schäfer's chief trouble is that he is unbalanced mentally but it must be noted that he is described as an ardent Nazi who is apt to let himself go when he gets on to politics. In addition he has taken no thought to respect local prejudices in the matter of taking life etc. For all these reasons, it seems highly desirable to get him back to Germany as soon as may be possible, and to see that he is granted no further facilities in India . . .[1]

Schäfer's fears, then, were not entirely groundless. The British wanted him out, but there was little they could do while he travelled on with the Kashag's permit. Schäfer rode as far as Podrang, the oldest inhabited village in Tibet, before turning back towards the Tsang Po. Many of the *dzongpons* in the area seem to have been casualties of the struggles in Lhasa, and few of them, if we are to believe Beger's diary, had any liking for the British. One he identifies as the Kalön Lama, a monk official in the Kashag who Beger says was 'in charge of restoring the Potala Palace but had fallen out of favour and been exiled'. This sounds more like Kumbela, the Dalai Lama's favourite, who had indeed renovated the eastern part of the Potala and the Dalai Lama's Summer Palace at Norbulinka. His downfall had been engineered after the Dalai Lama's death by Lungshar and he had been exiled to the Kongpo region not far from the Yarlung Valley.

There was another interesting encounter at Tseringjong in the Chongye Valley. Beger described it as follows:

> I travelled ahead of the others [and] was greeted by a friendly elderly man. I quickly realized that he was our host. Once he must have been a strong and powerful man in Lhasa. He was 76 and marked by age and experience. After his downfall, to which the British had contributed, he had initially dealt with building works in Samye for four years before starting his current post two years ago. His family was living on a large farm nearby. We were having a long conversation about many things. He loathed the British . . . When we left he gave us some fabric and a sack of peas and asked us to greet Hitler.

Beger does not name this individual, but it may well be Trimön Shapé, who had accompanied the Regent to Lake Lhamolatso and who believed he was the incarnation of the builder of the Blue Stupa at Samye. In the early 1930s he was the most important power broker in the Kashag, but the Regent had engineered his fall after their visit to the lake. As to his 'loathing' of the British, Trimön was a plenipotentiary at the Simla Conference in 1914 and this experience might have left him embittered. He was certainly very conservative. At any rate, their dinner in Tseringjong provided more evidence of just how shallow goodwill was for the British in Tibet.

Once they had returned to Tsetang, the expedition headed west along the Tsang Po back to Chusul, where they had crossed in December and Schäfer had been so optimistic about the reception he would receive in Lhasa. Now he led his men away from the Holy City and back over the Karo La Pass to the turquoise waters of Lake Yamdrok Tso. At Pede Dzong a crisis over the mail erupted. They had been expecting letters but it now turned out they had not been sent on from Gyantse. The

Nepali postmaster had been afraid that, after Czechoslovakia, he would be penalized by the British. A letter had been forwarded to Kaiser, however, and it contained more unsettling news: Rabden had not returned to Sikkim to look after a sick parent, he had simply been too frightened to stay on with the German expedition. Schäfer's mood darkened. On 20 April he sent Beger and Kaiser south to Gyantse with the bulk of the caravan to prepare for departure and to retrieve the mail while he took the road to Shigatse with the others. Beger was very happy to travel alone with the congenial Kaiser. 'We had been on expedition for a year and I thought back over a year full of great experiences, but also a year of the school of hard knocks and a certain bitterness . . . We had sworn to stick together no matter what and to return home together. Barasahib [Schäfer] made this difficult for us at times, yet we reminded ourselves of the tragic fate that he had suffered with the death of his wife, which he still struggled with emotionally.'[2]

When the German Tibet Expedition arrived in Shigatse, thousands came out to greet them. This was the second city in Tibet and close to the Tashilunpo Monastery, the seat of the Panchen Lamas. Beger left Kaiser in Gyantse and rode with a single Tibetan guide to join Schäfer. The American vice consul and Major Mackenzie had been in Gyantse but neither had taken the time to greet Beger. The atmosphere had been distinctly frosty. In Shigatse, the Tibetan response was very different – at first. Beger was once more inundated with the sick, some of whom had been referred by Möndro. He measured whenever he had the opportunity and began to catalogue the enormous number of artefacts the expedition had accumulated. Schäfer was now using his rifles to hunt, as well as the catapults, and earned a stiff rebuke from the Abbot of Tashilunpo.[3] One morning he found a corpse washed up on the edge of a river. He ordered Beger to remove the skull and add it to their collection. Although the idea turned his stomach, Beger returned to the river but found the skull was too crushed to be of any use.

There was another postal disaster. Schäfer had arranged for presents to be despatched from Berlin to Lhasa for distribution to their friends, but at the beginning of May they discovered that the packages had been impounded in India. When Schäfer discussed the problem with Möndro, this time their friend was unhelpful and 'evasive'. He suggested they travel to Gyantse to see if anything could be done there, so on 20 May Schäfer left Shigatse and took his small caravan south for the last time. As they travelled back across the flat, treeless Tibetan plateau, Beger took as many measurements and photographs as he could, sometimes getting through as many as ten subjects in a day.

Schäfer received more bad news in Gyantse: Kaiser's application for a passport had been turned down by the Maharajah of Sikkim. The reason given was that Kaiser had been very expensively educated and if he left for Germany all that investment would be thrown away. The truth, as the secret British files show, was that the British feared that Kaiser would be converted to Nazism and would return to Sikkim to spread propaganda. They made sure that the Maharaja was under no illusions about their strong desire that Kaiser should be prevented from leaving with Schäfer.[4] It will come as no surprise that Schäfer believed he could change their minds. Indeed, the rejection of Kaiser's application seemed to heighten Schäfer's feelings for this young man. He wrote desperately to Gould:

> I am much thinking of Kaiser these days, he is now absolutely alone, he wrote me a pitiful letter today. It would be utterly immoral now, if I would leave him. I have the greatest hope that

> he can come with me. You do not know how I like this boy, my friends – as I heard yesterday – have already found us a flat in Berlin. I have lost my wife, I also have nobody, I might even adopt him as my son and he has a good heart and is graceful I know. Even if I got married again K. would stay with us. I have had so many disappointments in life already but I am sure that K. does not disappoint me and I will not disappoint him. I know from [Joseph] Rock[5] what harmony and success I can expect; it is far from an experiment with human characters, it is a piece of my life. K. makes me happy because I again have somebody to care for . . .

To the public-school-educated British 'men on the spot', Schäfer's thwarted passion for a young Nepali man must have looked decidedly queer. Rock, like Hedin, was homosexual.

In Gyantse there were more tense encounters with Captain Clifford, whose opinion of Germans had not improved. Nor had he lost his thirst for strong drink. The evening began innocuously enough with card games and what Beger called 'throwing small sharp arrows at round plates' (German lacks a word for darts), but as the alcohol flowed the arguments erupted, Clifford saying he would have shot Schäfer and Geer had he been given the chance. Beger commented, 'Richardson was surely of the same opinion, which we had been suspecting for some time. Only as a diplomat, he did not express his views out loud. Instead he preferred intrigue.' But the British captain, even in his cups, was no fool: 'Clifford compared Schaefer's actions with the politics of the German Reich. When he [Schäfer] had arrived in Gyantse he had said that we could only stay in Lhasa two weeks, yet we had remained for two months.' The Germans argued back: 'The original invitation of the Tibetan government had been for a fortnight. That the government had extended this period repeatedly demonstrated its independence.' As Schäfer could have predicted, his conversation with the Regent was no longer a secret: 'Clifford alleged that we had tried to sell 200 guns to the Tibetans, which provoked our strongest possible denial as we had refused the Regent's request most strongly. It became dawn before we stopped arguing . . .'

What Schäfer did not know until a few days later was that the newspaper article he had written months before in Sikkim had now been published in *Frankfurter Zeitung*. In London, it had been picked up by both the *Evening Standard* and *The Times*, and as a result a hurried translation had been sent to the Foreign Office. In the office of Secretary of State for India Lord Zetland there was an explosion of rage. Here is what Schäfer was reported to have said:

> East of Shigatse, April 19th: We do not know whether our reports are now getting through, for the British have stopped our post. The post may not get through, but we shall penetrate south over the Himalayas somehow. It is very regrettable that the British act this way, almost as if the Empire might crack up at any moment . . . The friendship shown us here [in Tashilunpo] is a pleasant contrast to the unfriendly voices reaching us from British India . . . The political conditions, chiefly the unintelligible attitude of the British, who met us only a few months ago in a friendly manner, induce us to terminate the expedition in the autumn.

All the evidence suggests that this was indeed the authentic voice of Ernst Schäfer *in extremis*. Furious telegrams were sent to Linlithgow and Gould and a plan was hatched to haul Schäfer over the coals and make him explain his ingratitude. The Viceroy replied in a most revealing telegram: 'I hope that Schaeffer [*sic*] will not be a nuisance . . . while I have no disposition whatever to adopt a rabidly anti-German attitude, I suspect that we are reaching a stage at which, unless international relations improve, good nature on our part may be taken for weakness by the Germans and pro-German sympathizers; and may be entirely misunderstood by the Indian public.' It was no time for the Raj to look weak and to be made a fool of by a foreigner.

Schäfer was summoned to the headmaster's study on 24 June.

Gould travelled from Gangtok to Dochen, where he set up camp. From Gyantse, Schäfer rode ahead of his comrades with Kaiser because he sensed something was very wrong and did not want to lose face. He thought it probably had something to do with his 'sneaking over the border' escapade to Doptra or his frustrated plans for Kaiser, and with respect to that he was determined to exploit this opportunity to get Gould's support. It is typical of Schäfer that he still fervently believed he could get whatever he wanted.[6] Gould had pitched his tents next to Dochen Lake, whose limpid blue surface stretched away towards the Bhutanese Himalayas. As he cantered down towards the tents, Schäfer could see the massive spire of Chomolhari on the edge of Bhutan. Memories flooded back of their triumphant ride up the Chumbi Valley – so long ago, it seemed.

Gould had for some time been sick with a duodenal ulcer, and frequent hiccoughs compromised his dignity. With him at Dochen were Captain James Guthrie and a missionary, both of them keen to make a study of this 'priest of Nazism'. As soon as Schäfer had dismounted and sat down, Gould came quickly to the point and spread out in front of Schäfer the offending newspapers. This seems to have given Schäfer something of a shock; he was expecting quite a different discussion. He blustered, 'This is the first time I see. I should not myself have wished publication. An entirely private letter. Most regrettable. These are things I do not like. It was written at the worst of our times. It was very nervous. I was sleeping very badly and was expecting that troops would move to arrest us . . .' The argument went on for some time and Gould must eventually have been satisfied that Schäfer had got the message. Unlike Richardson, he had some affection for this odd German. They moved on to the Kaiser issue. According to Gould, Schäfer became extremely emotional and talked for at least an hour. He offered to repay the Maharajah for Kaiser's education, as well as his medical training in Berlin. In another rush of feeling, he spoke about a new expedition to Tibet through the Chungtang and 'he wanted someone as staunch as Kaiser, who would stand by him even if, as on a former occasion, all his staff mutinied; had not an American colleague on an earlier expedition said meet you at X (their objective) or in hell and the man had ratted and their next meeting had been at a hotel bar in Shanghai . . .' Despite his dollars, Dolan had never been forgiven.

By now it was lunchtime, and Gould served a 'steaming hot ham' that pleased Schäfer no end. Gould observed that 'small things' often produced a 'large response' in him. He also understood that whenever Schäfer felt he had done something wrong he would talk about it at length. Given the opportunity to observe the Nazi scientist and his comrades, the other guests were not impressed. Schäfer spoke, they noticed, in a blustering tone, especially to Kaiser. They concluded, 'we are all inclined to think that the gentle Kaiser has some sort of special appeal for the dominant Schäfer'. After lunch, the British toasted Schäfer and the expedition, and Schäfer made a short, appreciative speech, even managing to find words of praise for Captain Clifford. Not long afterwards, Beger overheard him discussing independence for Sikkim with a fervent nationalist in Gangtok.

Beger and the other Germans were, of course, witnesses to this meeting at Dochen, and Beger's diary gives us a rare glimpse of what Schäfer's colleagues thought about his plans for Kaiser. Gould had argued that he thought it inappropriate to remove someone from their native culture and, naturally, Schäfer had vehemently disagreed. But when they returned to Gyantse, Beger turned against Schäfer and said he agreed completely with Gould. He liked Kaiser a great deal but he thought it was foolish and wrong-headed to think of taking him to Germany. The passage opens a small window on what the Germans argued about among themselves and goes some way towards explaining the nature of the table-banging debates Akeh witnessed on many occasions without knowing what they were about. It shows too that Schäfer was a more sensitive and enlightened man than reports and some events might suggest. It is very unlikely that his feelings for Kaiser went beyond paternalistic affection; his grief for Hertha made him emotionally not sexually vulnerable. The English thought there was something fishy going on, but they were all products of public schools where homoeroticism was a social norm. Gould also possessed all the prejudices of the imperial Englishman concerning the proper place of the native.

In Gangtok in 2002, another much more interesting interpretation of Schäfer's behaviour was suggested to me by K. C. Pradhan, whose father had known Schäfer. The Thapas were by origin Gurkhas, the fierce Himalayan tribe the British had absorbed into the forces of the Raj. According to Mr Pradhan's well-connected father, Schäfer was planning to send Kaiser Thapa back to India where he would enlist in one of the Gurkha regiments and poison its loyalty to king and country. This is, of course, hearsay, but Schäfer's diary adds some weight to the allegation, and to the complexity of this perplexing friendship. Here is an entry from June: 'Kaiser got into serious emotional conflicts when he saw his future as a British subject, that lay in the hands of that "gang" [presumably the British], destroyed – and he collapsed completely. Now the time had come to get him completely on my side . . .'[7] But Kaiser now told Schäfer that his responsibility lay with his family, his mother and his sisters, so Germany was out of the question. Schäfer reacted with brutal aggression: 'I became very angry. I called him a characterless liar – told him that hardly anyone I had put my hopes in had ever disappointed me as much as he did. I sacked him immediately, wrote him a cheque and threw him out. Half an hour later he came back to apologize. Whatever happened he would stay with me . . .'[8] For Schäfer, a very great deal was at stake.

In the weeks that followed their meeting Schäfer sent letter after letter pleading with Gould, but Kaiser would never leave Sikkim. Gould sensed Schäfer's misery and presented him with the dead body of an eagle he had found on a driveway. Schäfer thanked him, noting that it was a *Haliaetus leurcororyphus* Pallas; 'once in Northern Sikkim I shot one, tied it up to the saddle, then the horse got afraid and galloped away with the bird. We got the horse back but not the bird . . . Well Mr Gould . . . I have been longer in Tibet than I anticipated and also killed a few more birds than I was allowed to, but my line, my great line was always straight and straight forward . . . Now it became very late . . . It's still raining outside.'

There was a harder rain falling in Europe, and the expedition continued to receive telegrams and letters imploring them to return to Germany. Beger wrote: 'One of the letters for Schäfer was from his father . . . Its contents affected [him] so much that he disappeared for an hour. Then we heard what he had written: [Hans] Schäfer had strongly hinted that it would be good if we returned to Genoa by mid-August. We sat around the fireplace and discussed it. Suddenly we realized: the letter and transmission from [Berlin] had the same message; my wife had been hinting too. Wienert's fiancée had written that in informed circles it was believed it would start after the harvest.' Soon afterwards, Gould unexpectedly offered them two more months in Sikkim. They realized with a shock that the wily old man was hoping that he could detain them until the war began, as everyone now knew it would. They refused his offer and made plans to leave as soon as possible.

It was all over. Kaiser and Akeh organized the transport to Siliguri and then by train to Calcutta of the riches Schäfer and his men had accumulated in Sikkim and Tibet. There were live animals, thousands of rare skins, and of course the shapi. After he had completed this monumental task, Kaiser moped about; he missed his German companions and wrote plaintively to Schäfer. Beger made a last, diversionary dash to Phari Dzong, where he made some final measurements and saw his last patients. Schäfer paid another visit to Lord Linlithgow and apologized all over again, promising to speak his mind to Herr Hitler and stop the war. Wienert re-calibrated his findings at the British Survey in Dehra Dun, the small town where the British would later build a POW camp and imprison, among other German nationals, SS officer and hero of the White Spider Heinrich Harrer. In Calcutta, the expedition was met by Wilhelm Filchner, who had been in west Nepal carrying out a geomagnetic survey in appalling conditions. He was very sick and would spend the entire war in Kathmandu and then, voluntarily interned, in India, where he would be very well looked after by the British. He eventually settled in Poona.

In Berlin, Heinrich Himmler had no desire to see his precious Tibet expedition interned by the British, so he organized their escape – his last and most important contribution to Schäfer's expedition. In Calcutta, the Germans boarded a British Indian Airways Sunderland flying boat. As it lifted off from the Hoogli, they looked back for the last time at Asia. From the Bay of Bengal they flew to Baghdad, where they found a Junkers U90 waiting to fly them on to Vienna. From there, a U52 took them to Munich, where they were greeted by the Reichsführer himself. After a celebratory cup of coffee, Himmler and the German Tibet Expedition flew on to Berlin and a huge reception. Beger remembers that they had all eaten so much in the aircraft that no-one was hungry when they touched down at Tegel Airport. It was 4 August 1939.

In Calcutta, Akeh and Kaiser wondered what had happened to their German friends. A file in the Sikkim archives reveals something of what transpired. First there is an enquiry about Kaiser's whereabouts, addressed to the Commissioner of Police in Calcutta:

> You have probably heard of Dr. E. Schafer, a German who spent midsummer 1938 to July 1939 in Sikkim and Tibet. We allowed him to employ as interpreter a Sikkim subject of Nepalese extraction, Kaiser Bahadur Thapa, who was a junior clerk . . . Schaefer professed a passionate affection for the young man and made great efforts to obtain permission for him to proceed to Germany at the expense of the German government . . . In my letter of 14 July 1939 Kaiser was told that he should report to duty to the Assistant Engineer, Sikkim as soon as his duty with Dr. S terminated. He failed to do so, and we are glad not to have him back in Sikkim . . . I suggested that the Calcutta Police should be asked to keep an eye on him.

Another report soon revealed Kaiser's sorry fate:

> He has been closely watched while in Calcutta and I have had him up for official examination. He appears to have lost his head completely at the prospect of going to Europe and had

> developed a kind of hero worship for Dr. S. Shortly after he came down here the German consulate secured a job for him in a German motor firm, so that he has now lost his job and is looking for work elsewhere. If you like, I will send him straight back to Sikkim, but having once tasted life in Calcutta where he was earning Rs 70 per month as salary, I very much doubt that he will stay with you . . .

Beger later summarized the achievements, as he saw them, of the expedition. As well as collecting enormous numbers of plants and butterflies, Krause took eighteen thousand metres of 16mm black and white film and coloured film and forty thousand photographs. Beger collected two thousand ethnographic artefacts documenting Tibetan and regional culture, and recorded the measurements of 376 people, mainly Tibetans but also from other ethnic groups. He also took two thousand photographs, made casts of the heads, faces, hands and ears of seventeen people and took the finger and hand prints of another 350. He added: 'Notes on the health of the Tibetans were derived from my work as a "medicine man".' It was an odd and rather muted end to a most unusual episode in the history of Central Asia. Ernst Schäfer's Expedition simply vanished, leaving behind baffled Englishmen, diplomatic queries and enigmas. For the real climax to the Ernst Schäfer Tibet Expedition would *not* take place in Lhasa in 1939, but four years after the five SS officers' return to Germany – in 1943, at a place called Auschwitz.

On the evening of 21 August, a message was sent from Moscow to Hitler's retreat at the Berghof. Its wording was simple and devastating: the Soviet dictator Josef Stalin and his new premier Vyacheslav Molotov had agreed to sign a non-aggression pact with Nazi Germany and expected Joachim von Ribbentrop, the architect of the agreement, to be in Moscow to finalize the agreement on the 23rd. Hitler was ecstatic. 'That will really land them in the soup,' he said, referring to Britain and France. In London, Paris and even in Rome the news fell on appalled ears like a blitzkrieg. The British had made a feeble attempt to prevent the pact by sending Admiral Sir Reginald Aylmer Ranfurly Plunket-Ernle-Erle Drax to Moscow to shore up the Soviet side, but he'd failed miserably. In Germany, too, there was confusion, but many simply accepted the word of the Führer that Germany's eastern border was now secure. *Pravda* called it an 'act of peace'. Now Hitler could turn to 'Case White' and the annihilation of Poland without distraction. The generals were summoned to the Berghof and harangued about the demands that would now be placed on the Wehrmacht, which was at least two years away from preparedness for war. This time, last-minute negotiations with Sir Nevile Henderson did nothing to alter Britain's commitment to Poland.

Stalin had remarked to von Ribbentrop that it was ridiculous for 'a few hundred Englishmen to dominate India'. In secret, Hitler declared, 'Russia will be our India.'[9]

PART THREE

VALLEYS

CHAPTER THIRTEEN

THE DEVIL'S SCIENTIST

Schäfer: . . . You know that the Viceroy of India asked me to talk to Hitler about peace. One thought in democratic ways and believed one could use one's influence. I really thought of that as a mission. I thought I could change things.
Q: You lived in that delusion.
A: Yes, but it wasn't a Nazi delusion.
Q: It was a national socialist delusion.
A: Then many people, who suffered under the national socialist regime, are also deluded . . .

– interrogation of Ernst Schäfer, 1947[1]

On the evening of 23 June 1942, Dr Walter Hauck boarded the SD25 Munich to Berlin *Luxuszüge* night express.[2] As the train, the pride of the German Mitropa rail network, roared out of Munich Bahnoff, Hauck and his wife shared a meal in the dining car before they retired. Through the windows the last light faded over the Bavarian Alps, and Hauck enjoyed a small cigar. Soon, they knew, the enemy bombers would begin their runs over the battered city.

At nine, the Haucks retired to their adjoining sleeping compartments. In Hauck's *Schlafwagen*, the upper bunk already had an occupant, a young man who glanced up briefly from a folder of papers. A rather jaunty suit had been hung on the wall of the narrow compartment. After a perfunctory exchange of 'Heil Hitlers', both men introduced themselves. Hauck enjoyed teasing out information from people he met – a habit of his profession. He discovered that his companion was a Herr Schäfer. He had an important appointment the following morning in Berlin and said he was an expert on Asian affairs, but despite Hauck's best efforts his fellow traveller volunteered nothing more and rather pointedly returned to his files. Hauck readied himself for bed, and as the train roared on through the night he quickly fell asleep.

At two in the morning, the express halted briefly at Saalfeld where the engine was changed for the steeper gradients that lay ahead. As the switch was being made, the *Schlafwagen* attendant stepped down from the train to stretch his legs and smoke a cigarette. He could hear the new engine hissing in the dark, and watched moonlit phantoms of steam drifting across the fields by the station. He threw his cigarette away and walked back towards the train. Overhead, he could hear the low throb of American or British bombers. Like many Germans, he suspected that the war was going badly, whatever Herr Goebbels said.

As he reached up to pull himself back on board, the attendant was astonished to hear loud cries for help from inside the train. Inside the carriage, he sprinted down the narrow corridor as the new engine lurched forward. Its wheels screamed on the tracks. By now, a small crowd of passengers had gathered outside the last but one compartment. A tearful woman shouted at him that her husband was being attacked by a maniac inside his compartment. The attendant elbowed the passengers aside and leant against the door. A ferocious struggle was taking place, so he pushed his way, with difficulty, inside.

The narrow compartment was a scene of mayhem. Dr Hauck and another man appeared to be engaged in mortal combat. The attacker, his face contorted, had his hands around the throat of the doctor, who was bellowing hoarsely and turning purple. The attendant seized the attacker's wrists and wrenched them from his victim's neck. The attacker struggled for a moment but then quite suddenly relaxed and looked aghast at the man he had assaulted, then at the attendant and back again. Then he buried his head in his hands. The doctor's wife peered tearfully round the door. What had happened? Why had her husband been attacked? It was not, it seemed, a question the attacker could readily answer. He looked as stunned as his victim.

Dr Hauck, bruised and scratched though he was, recovered sufficiently to demand an explanation himself, but Herr Schäfer had none to offer. He had been having a nightmare, he said, and apologized abjectly. Somehow – the attendant's report is not at all clear on this point – the two passengers were reconciled. Although he was in pain, Dr Hauck consoled his wife and both men settled down for the rest of the journey. Both slept fitfully until the express pulled into Anhalter Bahnhof in Berlin the following morning. Herr Schäfer was now feeling even more contrite; he apologized again to the Haucks and left the train hurriedly. They watched him sprint down the platform into the station concourse where he was met by a tall, fair-haired man wearing the uniform of an SS officer. The two men talked briefly and looked back at the Haucks. Then they walked out of the station.

Dr Hauck was busy during his stay in Berlin and had only a few moments in which to reflect on his very odd experience, but on his way back to Munich with his wife he became increasingly angry. A few days later, he sat down at his desk and began to write a letter. He addressed it directly to the SS Reichsführer Heinrich Himmler himself. He informed him that he had been 'violently pulled from his bed' by a Herr Schäfer, a high-ranking SS officer, who had tried to strangle him with 'immense violence'. He could remember only his family name which was, of course, a very common one, but he understood that his attacker had at some time travelled in Asia, which must surely be an important clue to the man's identity. Would it not be appropriate that this unfortunate individual receive proper treatment? Herr Schäfer was apparently using the Munich–Berlin train every week and other people could be in danger.

Hauck's letter, written on 24 July, soon whipped up a blizzard of paperwork that swept from desk to desk through Himmler's empire. The situation was complicated because it turned out that *two* 'Herr Schäfers' had been travelling on the Munich–Berlin express that night, and both were SS officers. So for a brief time the finger pointed to one Willy Schäfer, who was pulled in for questioning. He was quickly eliminated from inquiries. He had never been anywhere near central Asia and had for some reason on the night of 23/24 June been wearing his uniform. Inevitably the investigators put two and two together and came up with SS Hauptsturmführer Ernst Schäfer, Tibet explorer. Letters were now urgently sent to Schäfer himself in Munich. The matter had been referred to Dr Leonardo Conti, the Reich Health Leader, and Schäfer was ordered to arrange a medical examination. Did he suffer from epilepsy?

Schäfer hunkered down in Munich and dragged his heels. Another letter was sent from SS headquarters requesting that Schäfer prepare a defence so that they could respond to Hauck, who had continued to make complaints. By now it was

September, and the Reichsführer himself decided to intervene. He took immediate and decisive action. Dr Hauck was informed that the matter was being taken care of by the Reichsführer personally so he need have no further concern that the matter would not be resolved to his satisfaction. Himmler issued further instructions to the SS officers who had been harrying his favourite. Dr Schäfer had been 'overworking' and from now on his workload would be reduced. He would also be required to travel first class, where he would be more relaxed. The case was closed. Dr Hauck was never heard from again. Himmler had made very sure that the strange incident on the Munich–Berlin express was swept under a very thickly woven carpet.

The task of understanding the inner lives of the men who participated in the Nazi dictatorship, at whatever level, presents almost intractable difficulties. Only in very rare cases is there a record of motive or feelings, and then they are invariably 'through a glass, darkly'. Ernst Schäfer was a most unusual man, and his case is just as perplexing as any other. The records show that he argued with Himmler and was disciplined at least twice, but until 1945 he took what he was offered by his friend the Reichsführer. The incident on the Munich–Berlin express has the effect of an arc light turned on in a darkened theatre. For a brief moment there is action; we hear fragments of dialogue, but all too quickly the scene is plunged into darkness once more. But in that short time of illumination, we can see a different Ernst Schäfer – a divided, tormented man, barely able to suppress a pent-up violence. It is possible to recognize the same difficult, grieving man who marched his comrades to Lhasa and back to Berlin. During his interrogation after the war, he said that he felt increasingly trapped – 'in a spider's web'. Schäfer was no longer the stalker and hunter; he had been ensnared by the second most powerful man in Germany. It was more than five years since his first encounter with Heinrich Himmler at Prinz-Albrecht-Strasse. He could not have known then, when he chuckled with his friends about the Reichsführer's ridiculous ideas about Aryans from heaven, that he would become involved with a dictatorship that would spill so much blood. Schäfer reflected on his time in Philadelphia when he might have had a choice, to stay in the United States with Brooke Dolan or return to Germany. And yet, on the surface, in 1942 Schäfer was a dazzling success. Since his return to Germany from Tibet he had been honoured and celebrated. But the nightmares had not stopped.

By the summer of 1942, Schäfer could no longer pretend that he knew little or nothing about the savagery of the regime he served. He had by then seen it at first hand. But in his waking life, Schäfer must have learnt to repress his queasiness and to discover ways to believe that he, unlike his fellow SS officers, was unsullied. His hands were clean. A seasoned hunter and explorer, Schäfer was accustomed to acting alone: it was he and he alone who faced the wilderness, with its furies and dangers, pulled the trigger and brought back nature's bounty. Now he imagined himself untrammelled by the catastrophe that was unfolding across Europe. And above all, he must have calculated that his friendship with the Reichsführer would still offer him more. There was talk of a new and even more ambitious expedition, to the 'Mountain of Tongues', the Caucasus. His new Sven Hedin Institute was growing in power and influence and he had a splendid new headquarters in a castle near Salzburg.

Schäfer had also remarried. His new wife was Ursula von Gartzen, and Schäfer had needed to work very hard to persuade her aristocratic parents that he was an appropriate husband. In a letter to Himmler, he had referred to their 'tremendous opposition'. By 1942, however, the couple had two young daughters. It is impossible to know whether he had exorcised the stunning grief he'd experienced after Hertha's death or whether it was merely dulled, but marriage meant that he became a supplicant again. In the same letter to Himmler he requested a loan to tide him over the first year of marriage. His excuse was that he had 'not realized there was going to be a war' and had splashed out on a new car. Himmler was happy to make the loan. After all, it was essential for his SS men to breed. But Schäfer was by now accustomed to rewards from the Reichsführer.

The Schäfer Expedition had been flown out of India on Himmler's flying boats in August 1939. Schäfer, who had made sure he had a stranglehold on any publications resulting from the expedition, became an instant celebrity. Himmler presented him with an SS death's-head ring and the SS ceremonial sword, the *Ehrendegen*, which was inscribed with a runic double lighning bolt. In the files of the Bundesarchiv is a letter from Hermann Göring thanking Schäfer for the gift of a Tibetan mastiff; the ones intended for Hitler appear to have died en route to Calcutta – a sad end to a sorry tale. Schäfer was not yet thirty and he was one of the most celebrated men in Hitler's Reich. But for Schäfer and his colleagues the European world was shifting, fracturing and shattering; they didn't know it yet, but 'the devil's potion' they had drunk when they signed up with the SS would soon poison their lives for ever, as science was enlisted for racial murder. None of the five Germans could have imagined this possibility when they crossed the Natu La Pass and entered Tibet.

In the same month that the German Tibet Expedition returned, Hitler had made a strategic alliance with Stalin, the Nazi–Soviet Pact, which he called 'a pact with Satan to cast out the devil'.[3] Then, with his eastern front safe and risking almost certain war with Britain and France, Hitler ordered the invasion of Poland, a good three years before his generals thought Germany would be ready. The onslaught on Poland needed a provocation, so convicts disguised as Polish soldiers – code-named 'Tin Cans' – were ordered to storm a German radio station near the Polish border and start broadcasting Polish nationalist music. Once they had successfully carried out the plan, the Tin Cans were shot by their SS minders and the Nazi news service announced that the Polish Army had attacked the Reich. At 4.30 a.m. on the morning of 1 September 1939 the first shots were fired near Dirschau, and a battleship, the *Schleswig-Holstein*, began firing on Polish positions in Danzig. Then fifty-two divisions with fifteen hundred aircraft roared across the border from the north, the west and the south, banshee Stuka dive-bombers smashing transportation links and the desperate refugees using them. For the first time, SS Einsatzgruppen waded in behind the Wehrmacht divisions, 'mopping up' Jews and other 'undesirables'. The Soviet Red Army invaded on the 17th, and Warsaw fell at the end of the month. Poland had effectively ceased to exist.

Appeasement had long been a busted flush, as Schäfer knew very well. Britain, which had guaranteed Poland's sovereignty, declared war on Germany on 3 September. In the Reich Chancellery that morning Hitler is reported to have turned angrily to Joachim von Ribbentrop – who had always told him that Britain would never go to war – and asked him, 'What now?' In the German Foreign Office Ernst von Weizsäcker realized that the wagon had begun to roll towards the abyss: 'Hitler could hardly have turned the carriage around without being thrown off himself.'[4] It was a metaphor that must have occurred to many as Nazi Germany went to war.

The historian Ian Kershaw has observed that 'In war, Nazism came into its own.' Nazism was born from the trauma of defeat in 1918, and preparations for war dominated policy in the

1930s. More profoundly, war concentrated then spat out all the savage poison of Nazi ideology. It was no accident that as Hitler made preparations for war he surrounded himself with the elite of Himmler's SS. And as the Polish armies were swept aside by the Wehrmacht, the SS moved in to turn Poland into a laboratory of ideological horror. Goebbels reported Hitler's comments on the Poles: 'More like animals than human beings, completely primitive and amorphous. And a ruling class that is an unsatisfactory result of a mingling between the lower orders and an Aryan master-race . . . Now we know the laws of racial heredity and can handle things accordingly.'[5] In these extraordinary words, Hitler and his acolytes made clear their debt to race science. The language could have come straight from the lectures and books of Professor Hans 'Rassen' Günther. Reichsführer Heinrich Himmler was determined that such words become deeds.

In the last week of September Himmler and Hitler relaxed at the Polish resort of Zoppot. Himmler seized the opportunity to persuade Hitler to allow him, as Reichsführer-SS, to take on the 'resettlement tasks' in the conquered Polish territories. This meant moving in ethnic Germans and moving out or 'evacuating' non-Germans, meaning Poles and Jews. As a birthday present on 7 October, Himmler was secretly appointed 'Settlement Commissar for the East' with responsibility for 'a solution of the Polish problem'. It could be said that at this moment the Nazi genocide began.[6]

With shocking speed, the Schäfer Expedition members became combatants in a world war. Beger, Krause and Wienert were dragooned into Waffen-SS units and were not to work together again for more than two years. Himmler had a different purpose in mind for Schäfer, and it led to one of the oddest secret military plots of the Second World War.[7] The facts are well documented, yet remain perplexing, and they inevitably prompt questions about Schäfer's activities after he arrived in Lhasa in 1939. States often exploit people with expert knowledge for their own ends, but Schäfer's strange plan is hard to explain away and implies that he was never just interested in science alone.

After September 1939, no-one in the German High Command could predict the outcome of a war with England, but if it went badly, the pact with Stalin offered an unexpected means of assaulting the heart of the British empire – or so Schäfer believed. What he was now contemplating, with the connivance of Himmler, was a return to Tibet in order to incite rebellion against the Raj. Lord Curzon would have immediately understood the Soviet Union's interest in such a plan; it was, after all, his fear of Russian ambition that made him send Younghusband and his 'escort' to Lhasa in 1903. Germany, too, had an historic interest in playing the Great Game, and Schäfer's plot would be one of the last hands to be played.

It might seem obvious or even trite to say that a *German* expedition to Tibet, sponsored by *Heinrich Himmler*, might be interested in plotting against the enemies of the Reich. But Schäfer always insisted that he was doing pure science (or what passed for pure science), and Beger is adamant to this day that the German Tibet Expedition had no other motive. I believe the evidence implies less high-minded intentions. This analysis reflects the complexity of both Schäfer's personality and the changing international situation during the period he was in Tibet. From the outset he'd exploited British appeasement of Nazi Germany to get what he wanted. Whenever he was frustrated, he went behind British backs, for example by illegally crossing into Tibet and negotiating with the Tering Raja, who had good reason to dislike the British. After he arrived in Lhasa in 1939, he waged a daily battle with Hugh Richardson who had fought to stop the German Tibet

Expedition from the start. As war became increasingly certain Schäfer realized that his friendships with the Tibetan regent and the Lhasa nobility could be of strategic value. As Beger's diaries show, the expedition became aware that some Tibetans were very hostile to the British; the Regent had even asked Schäfer for rifles, a request he had spurned. But compare that rejection with this extract from a letter written on 12 January 1940; he is talking about leading a 'military' and a 'political' group to Tibet: 'The political group has to be equipped with machinery, guns and 200 military fire arms *that I promised to the regent of Tibet.*' So either Schäfer dissembled even to his colleagues – Beger professed to be shocked by the idea of supplying weapons – or he contacted the Regent again after September. Either way, it's a damning statement that Richardson would have found very interesting indeed.

There is also circumstantial evidence. As soon as Schäfer arrived in Lhasa, scientific activities were largely neglected as he set about charming the Tibetan nobility and the Regent with impressive success. At first this was to try to extend his stay in Lhasa, but that alone does not explain the length of the expedition's sojourn in the city. We know that he took every opportunity to extol German culture and technology, and even pressed the Regent to correspond with Hitler – with the somewhat comic results uncovered by Dr Engelhardt. Schäfer must have known, as Richardson himself admitted in his report to London, that the Kashag was not always well disposed towards the British and some in Lhasa resented the fact that the British had been so parsimonious about supplying arms to the Tibetan Army.

It is very unlikely that Schäfer entertained any thoughts of espionage until the end of 1938. A great deal changed after the New Year, and Schäfer might even have been impressed by the violent response of the Buddhist monks when he and

Krause had been filming in Lhasa. As well as the coming conflict, there might have been another, more private reason for a change of plans. Although he frequently professed his gratitude to Sir Basil Gould, his relationship with Hugh Richardson was from the start chilly and at the end downright hostile. Schäfer would never forget his humiliation when he arrived in Lhasa. As with Dolan's betrayal in 1936, this very personal hostility could have tipped Schäfer towards a powerful dislike of the British which he kept to himself until he left India in August 1939. After all, he did not want to be interned, so keeping Gould and the Viceroy on his side while aggravating their 'man on the spot' Richardson was a small price to pay. When he was leaving India, he seemed to 'protest too much': he offered Wienert's data to the Survey of India and promised to try to persuade Herr Hitler to make peace.

In the Public Record Office in Kew, I discovered a most interesting report from Nordhu Dondup, who had temporarily taken over from Richardson in Lhasa. He told the Indian government that when he had discussed the European war with the Kashag, he had found that they 'did not mention explicitly that they wished an early victory in our [i.e. British] favour'. Then he says, 'It is quite possible that remembering the recent visit of Dr Schaefer [*sic*] and party, they considered it inadvisable to commit themselves in any way.'[8] This is not quite the smoking gun, but it's very telling. Some parties in Lhasa were rooting for the German side.

Schäfer was aware that the idea of inspiring indigenous people to topple the hated British empire – in Kaiser Wilhelm's paraphrase, 'that hated, lying and unscrupulous nation of shopkeepers' – had a long tradition in German geopolitical thought.[9] The German government had frequently used 'scientific expeditions' as a cover for espionage. Schäfer called the plot he hatched with Himmler the 'Lawrence Expedition', and this is an important clue to the origins of the idea. He was not referring *directly* to T. E. Lawrence, 'Lawrence of Arabia', who had very successfully masterminded an Arab revolt against the Turks during the First World War; Schäfer would have known that there was a *German* Lawrence called Wilhelm Wassmuss (1880–1931), whose exploits had inspired John Buchan's *Greenmantle* and had in 1937 been told at length in a book by English author Christopher Sykes that had been translated into German the following year. Briefly, here is the story, more fully told in Peter Hopkirk's *On Secret Service East of Constantinople*.

Even before the First World War, Germany had been conspiring to throw the British out of India, and were aided and abetted in this by a group of Persian exiles who wished to free their own country from both British and Russian control. In 1913, Wassmuss, a 'manly, blond Saxon', arrived in Persia, where he began meeting local tribal leaders. His plan was to incite holy war against the British and pave the way for a German empire in the east. Like T. E. Lawrence, Wassmuss was both a scholar – he spoke fluent Persian and Arabic – and a tough adventurer who had a great deal of experience of the region and its people. His accomplices included men who would play a part in Schäfer's scheme decades later, among them the geologist Oskar von Niedermayer, who had followed Wassmuss to Persia with a battalion of handpicked men disguised as a travelling circus. The mission was something of a fiasco, but Wassmuss, who split off from the main party, had some success persuading Tangistani, Dashtistanu and Dastiti tribes to attack the British.[10] His British biographer wrote that Wassmuss believed that 'The flame of war against the infidel power of the British would then have reached the gates of India. Then would the conflagration be at its height and every available man sent from France to the rescue of the Empire.'[11]

Schäfer's plot must have been inspired by the Wassmuss

campaign, but just what was he planning? As historian Michael Kater has admitted, it is not easy to decipher from the records. The idea was to proceed to Moscow where, with Soviet help, Schäfer would begin preparing a guerrilla campaign enlisting the tribes of Tibet, Kashmir and Afghanistan in a many-pronged assault on India. But it is difficult to understand precisely what he hoped to accomplish with his tribal guerrillas. He appears to have imagined that the Tibetan government or the Regent would agree to an attack on the British, but this was harebrained: both the Kashag and the Regent would certainly have been interested in acquiring arms to deter the Chinese, but to rise against the British would have been suicidal and pointless, and the Tibetans knew it.

Schäfer's letters provide a few more clues. They refer to leading twenty or so 'commandos', including Geer and Wienert, into Tibet from the north, following Sven Hedin's trail across the Takla Makan. It would be a small party equipped above all with a great deal of money. He discussed the need to pay heavy bribes in Chinese Turkestan and also to match 'the British bribe' – in other words, paying the Regent as much as the British had been doing to secure his goodwill. It is possible that Schäfer was thinking about recruiting the warlike Ngoloks, whom he had encountered in eastern Tibet in 1935 and then again in Lhasa during the New Year celebrations in 1939. In the 1950s, the CIA sponsored attacks on the Chinese by tribes in the east. Later, perhaps in 1941, Schäfer would coordinate a bigger military force of two hundred or so that would advance into Sikkim; Wienert's hard-won data would surely prove very useful, as would Filchner's from the northern regions of Tibet. Another of Schäfer's letters contains a very cryptic reference to seeking Soviet 'assurances' about territory in Tibet and Sikkim, presumably to make sure they would not become part of the Soviet empire. Kashmir was, of course, always a hot spot in the Great Game and it is noteworthy that while Schäfer was in Tibet the British discovered that he was seeking permission to travel on to Kashmir, and were relieved when this was denied by the Kashmiri government.

From the start, very little went right. Schäfer soon discovered that he was not the only aspiring 'Lawrence'. There was already acrimonious competition between different schemes. A former member of the Sven Hedin central Asian expedition, a Major Zimmerman, had also concocted a proposal long-windedly called 'The Encirclement and Submission of World Enemy England by Germany, Italy, Russia, Iran and Japan'.[12] Inside the German Foreign Office was a cadre of 'Afghanistan Experts', including Wassmuss's old comrade in arms von Niedermayer, who even before the war was feverishly hatching a plot to unleash ferocious Afghanis on the British through the Khyber Pass. There was also the 'Amanullah Plan', designed to restore the deposed King Amanullah to the Afghan throne (he was living rather well in Rome and knew very little about what was being plotted in his name) and then to use him to undermine the British. The plan was energetically promoted by the treacherous Afghan minister in Berlin, Ghulam Siddiq Khan. Khan wanted to gather a group of two thousand armed tribesmen in Soviet Turkestan on the Afghan border; they would then cross over and establish a base at Mazar-i-Sharif in northern Afghanistan. After the invasion of Poland, von Ribbentrop, the architect of the Nazi–Soviet Pact, embraced these fantastical schemes with enthusiasm. It is almost certain that Himmler resented this, and asked Schäfer to come up with his SS plan. So it is not at all surprising that von Ribbentrop disparaged Schäfer's scheme: the cost, which Schäfer had estimated at 'silver coins and gold bars to the value of 2–3 million marks', was astronomical and the idea was unworkable. As Isrun Engelhardt put it, 'This story is not so much a story of

ES, it is much more a typical story of the polycracy and chaos of power of Nazism between Rosenberg's "Aussenpolitisches Amt" and the Foreign Office and even internal rivalries *in* the Foreign Office.'[13]

There was also dissent between Schäfer and Himmler. Himmler demanded that Schäfer's commandos train together in Prague with the Leibstandarte Adolf Hitler, the most elite corps of the SS, in the use of 'grenade-guns and heavy machine guns'. This was not a welcome idea to Schäfer and his comrades; surely with their unique experience they knew better than any strutting SS brigade commander with a loud voice? Secretly, Schäfer had also become concerned that Himmler had little idea of the practical issues. The Reichsführer's grasp of geography was decidedly wobbly. He was fond of unfurling large maps and gesturing expansively. And with one of those odd half smiles that all his colleagues recalled, Himmler proposed that when Schäfer's commando group finally left Germany for Asia an announcement should be made that the famous explorer had 'died suddenly'. This, quite naturally, made Schäfer extremely nervous.

As his anxieties multiplied, Schäfer made his first serious mistake: he turned to Admiral Wilhelm Canaris, who had had some contact with Hans Schäfer, Ernst's father, and headed the Abwehr, the military intelligence office. Canaris remains something of an enigma, and has been described by one historian as a Hamlet-like figure, indecisive and ambivalent. He was, says Peter Padfield, 'small, white haired, rather round shouldered and even shabby looking'.[14] After a war spent in U-boats and naval intelligence, he had after 1918 become aggressively anti-communist and thrown in his lot with extreme right groups. By 1935, Canaris was a powerful man, but he had become increasingly disillusioned with Hitler. Or had he? Canaris appeared to maintain a close personal relationship with his and Himmler's protégé and rival Heydrich, and later, during the war, Himmler deflected any inquiry into Canaris's affairs. He might have been a Trojan horse. Nevertheless, under his protection, the leading opponent of the Hitler regime Hans Oster liaised with and organized opposition groups from within the Abwehr itself. Both Oster and Canaris were executed in 1944 after the failure of the Bomb Plot.

Whatever the truth about Canaris, Schäfer had picked the wrong man at the wrong time. As the Wehrmacht swept across Poland, Himmler's killing units the Einsatzkommandos began murdering aristocratic Poles and intellectuals, priests and Jews wherever they found them. Although the Wehrmacht generals were keen to crush Poland, they were frequently disgusted by the brutish activities of the SS, which they thought were underhand and unsoldierly. Canaris asked his agents to submit detailed reports on Einsatzkommando activities, and when he discovered what was happening he was shattered. He made a timid complaint to Hitler, much to Himmler's great annoyance.

When Schäfer met Canaris, almost certainly unaware of these developments, he pleaded with the Abwehr head for a more realistic approach to his mission. He argued that it would be better to fly into Tibet rather than cross the Takla Makan Desert and the Kunlun Mountains, and complained that the training exercise in Prague would be a waste of time. Canaris was also aware of the Amanullah Plan and did not need much convincing that some co-ordination was needed. Soon after his meeting with Schäfer, Canaris raised these matters with Himmler, who exploded with rage. On 7 September 1939 he wrote a scalding letter to Schäfer from his train the *Sonderzug Heinrich*, which was stopped near the Polish border.

> Today I learned from Admiral Canaris that you visited him, that you discussed this task with him and that you mentioned

> that the route via Russia would be too long-drawn-out. Further that the military training in Prague would not be necessary. I understand that you wish to get on with your mission as soon as possible; I have to demand though exact and strictest obedience. You have to make decisions at a time when you, as unaided commander, find yourself alone. As long as this is not the case you have to obey – the same way you had to demand from your team during the expedition. If YOU HAVE TO SOLVE a military order, you first have to be trained and educated as a soldier. A little bit of sabotage and *Herumspringen* [literally, 'leaping and gambolling about'] does not work. During these two months you only have to think about your training according to the instructions of my letter. Further I forbid you to talk to any office about your mission, except with me personally . . . I think that it is possible that . . . your mission has been already sentenced to death. We do not want to forget that we deal with counter espionage . . . there is only one solution – to keep your mouth shut, not to tell anybody more than one has to know in order to execute one's task. Discretion regarding number, time and range of information: these principles were totally forgotten during your discussion – also with this military office. I am convinced that you now behave according to my orders – and that you proceed with the requested task and, last but not least, accomplish your task. (With the unruly will that lies within you) . . .[15]

When they met face to face, Schäfer was screamed at 'as he had never been screamed at in his life before'. The chastened hero had little choice but to spend the next eight weeks marching up and down with the Leibstandarte Adolf Hitler. On 3 November he wrote to Himmler, 'May I inform you that the training . . . is about to end: I am very grateful for these eight weeks.' Schäfer had talked to Heydrich, who had given him 'lots

Auschwitz: Beger came here to pursue his anthropological investigations.

Himmler with Adolf Hitler. By the time Schäfer returned to Germany in 1939 his patron, Hitler's 'true Heinrich', was close to the height of his power.

ABOVE

Himmler at Quedlinburg Cathedral in 1938. While Schäfer was in Tibet the Reichsführer was disinterring the remains of king 'Henry the Fowler' from the cathedral crypt: he believed he was the Fowler's reincarnation.

BELOW LEFT

Karl Maria Wiligut, or 'Weisthor', Himmler's 'Rasputin', who asked Bruno Beger to see if Tibetan women carried sacred stones in their vaginas.

BELOW RIGHT

Schäfer and Krause at work on Geheimnis Tibet, *the film they would make about their experience.*

TOP
SS Untersturmführer Sigmund Rascher conducting a 'freezing' experiment on a camp inmate in Dachau. Schäfer did his best to extricate himself from any involvement with Rascher's deadly experiments – or so he claimed.

MIDDLE
The concentration camp at Natzweiler-Struthof, where the prisoners worked on by Beger in Auschwitz were murdered in 1943.

BOTTOM
Himmler visiting Dachau – the first concentration camp, completed in 1933 and often used as a showpiece for visiting Nazi sympathizers. Schäfer was asked to photograph deadly medical experiments here in 1942.

ABOVE
A rare photograph of Beger's professor Ludwig Ferdinand Clauss. Both men protected Clauss's Jewish assistant.

BELOW
Josef Kramer, the Natzweiler camp commandant.

ABOVE

Brooke Dolan (left) got to Lhasa with Ilia Tolstoy (right) at the end of 1942. Standing between them is Tsarong Dzasa; behind is Frank Ludlow, one of the British 'Tibet cadre'.

BELOW

Bruno Beger in 2001.

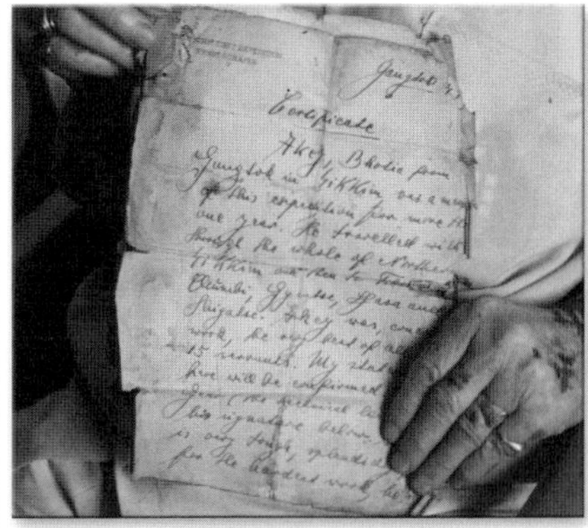

Certificate

Akey Bhotia from
Gangtok in Sikkim was a member
of this expedition for more th
one year. He travelled with
through the whole of Norther
Sikkim and then to Tibet
Chumbi, Gyantse, Lhasa and
Shigatse.

ABOVE LEFT
'German' Akeh Bhutia in 2002.

ABOVE RIGHT
Akeh's certificate proving he had worked for Schäfer.

RIGHT
Kelsang Gyatso, who remembered the Germans arriving in Sikkim as a schoolboy, in 2002.

BELOW

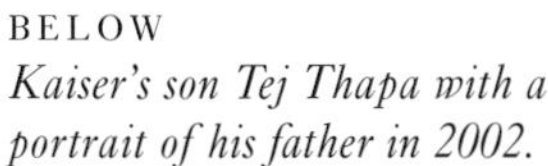

Kaiser's son Tej Thapa with a portrait of his father in 2002.

The last picture taken of Ernst Schäfer before he died in 1992.

of tips'. From the evidence of this letter, Schäfer's enthusiasm to become a new Wassmuss appears undimmed. He also raises the question of getting time off to start work on the documentary film about his expedition. He has been assured that the rushes were 'better than Sven Hedin and Wilhelm Filchner' by the head of Tobis, the film company that was producing what would become *Geheimnis Tibet*. Himmler responded immediately: *nothing* was to be done with the film yet. It would not be completed until 1942 and its making was dogged by acrimonious argument between the two men.

Both the Amanullah Plan and Schäfer's 'Lawrence of Arabia' mission were, in any case, doomed. Himmler's rival Alfred Rosenberg had gone to Hitler and poured scorn on the idea of using Afghanistan or Tibet as staging posts to attack the British empire. Hitler, always ambivalent about England, thoroughly admired the Raj's subjugation of native peoples and instinctively disliked the idea of destabilizing it or making common cause with dark-skinned peoples. According to Sven Hedin, who was in Berlin in December 1939 and was no friend of the English,[16] Hitler informed him that preserving the British Empire was entirely in Germany's interest. With the collapse of the plans for Afghanistan, Schäfer's too were gradually mothballed. It all depended on Moscow, and no-one in Berlin was certain how much support the Russians would provide. The 'Lawrence Plan' seems to have made only halting progress, and in any case, Operation Barbarossa soon demolished any idea of working with the Soviets.

For Schäfer, the experience was frustrating and often humiliating. In one letter he complained that he had been told of a meeting in Berlin he was not required to attend. 'I feel I am being treated like a slave,' he went on. 'I was not even consulted on matters I have knowledge of . . . Instead of being able to continue with *Feuer und Flamme* [enthusiastically] I am very upset. Financial matters are even worse. I am not interested in fame. I want simply to serve the Fatherland with my mind and heart.' And far from distancing himself from the Ahnenerbe, Schäfer obsequiously discussed new scientific plans that he hoped he would not be excluded from.

Himmler soon forgave Schäfer his indiscretion. As in a love affair, rejection seemed to make Schäfer's heart grow fonder, while the possibility of his loss prompted Himmler to bring his troublesome adventurer back into the fold. By January 1940 the Reichsführer was spending much of his time overseeing resettlement tasks in Poland with his customary zeal and ardour. New scholarship about the Final Solution has shown that there was more of a piecemeal development of exterminatory policies than a pre-existing master plan, despite the extremism of Hitler's speeches, but there is no doubt that murder in the service of German ethnic 'purity' began to take place very soon after the panzers had roared across the Polish border.

The task Hitler had set his 'true Heinrich' was the annihilation of the Polish aristocracy and the Jews. Both would be ruthlessly cleansed in mopping-up operations behind the front line.[17] Himmler incited and managed these murderous policies from his luxurious mobile headquarters on the *Sonderzug Heinrich*. Poland was the first great bureaucratic challenge of the war. As the new territory was savagely cleansed of Slavs, Jews and gypsies, millions of ethnic Germans had to be moved in to 'Germanize' the conquered lands. In a speech to the Gauleiters, Himmler said, 'the new provinces must really be a Germanic blood wall, must be a wall within which there is no blood question . . .' In other words, there should be no ambiguity about ethnic identity, no mixing; everything would be directed to a cleansing of the blood stock: 'I believe that our blood, Nordic blood, is actually the best blood on this earth . . .'[18] The Nazis transformed Poland. Enormous tracts of territory had been absorbed into west and east Prussia and Silesia. A new administrative area called the Warthegau had been created around Posen, and the rest was turned into a German-administered rump called the 'General Government'. Here, Hitler said, 'they could offload all their rubbish', meaning 'the Jews, the sick, the slackers'. This was Himmler's new laboratory of blood management, and Ernst Schäfer would now see at first hand what his friend was planning.

At the end of January, Himmler invited the contrite Schäfer to join him on the *Heinrich*. It was a tantalizing invitation. It meant that he had been forgiven, and he accepted without question. As Schäfer boarded the Reichsführer's impatiently hissing train in Berlin, we can be certain that he had very little idea about the nature of the journey he was about to take. His companions on the *Heinrich* included Himmler's chief of staff Karl Wolff, his office manager Rudolf Brandt, his bodyguard and adjutant, and a sycophantic poet, Hanns Johst,[19] celebrated for the phrase usually attributed to Hermann Göring: '*Wenn ich Kultur höre, entsichere ich meinen Browning*' ('When I hear the word "culture", I cock my Browning'). Schäfer was not just along for the ride; he had been asked to design new cold-weather coats for the German forces, drawing on his experience in the Himalayas.[20]

Their first destination would be Przemyśl. During his interrogation, Schäfer squirmed as he recounted the events of this journey and what he claimed he was seeing for the first time. The *Sonderzug Heinrich* was the nerve centre of Himmler's murderous plans, in Schellenberg's words, 'the control panel of a great war machine operating at full speed'. He knew very well it was a killing machine. On board, couriers dashed from one high-ranking SS officer to the next, and then on to Himmler's opulent cabin, clutching fluttering sheaves of paper. Telephones rang from every direction. There was an incessant and deafening clatter of typewriters, all churning out the memoranda of destruction. As the train steamed into the new Reich, Schäfer joined Himmler's adjutant Joachim 'Jochen' Peiper. Peiper was fiercely loyal to Himmler. His father was a veteran of Germany's Africa wars and Jochen himself was a proud graduate of the Leibstandarte Adolf Hitler. Through the bulletproof glass windows, they both studied the wide, flat Polish plains blanketed by a pristine layer of snow. They passed villages, churches and farmhouses. All were deathly quiet. There was little sign of the carnage of war until the *Heinrich* sped alongside a road crammed with the blaring traffic of conquest: tanks, lorries and armoured cars in an endless river of steel heading east.

Peiper was proud of his intimate knowledge of Himmler's great plans, and was pleased to tell Schäfer all he knew. Hitler himself had ordered the destruction of the Polish intelligentsia – 'they had to go' – so that any resurgent nationalism would be still-born. Peiper said that Himmler had personally assisted at a series of executions and had been silent for days afterwards. He thought his boss was squeamish. He relished one tale especially. One of Himmler's staff, Oberführer Ludolf von Alvensleben, had been particularly punctilious in carrying out the necessary executions, even when he encountered a relative, the Count von Alvensleben-Schöneborn, who owned an estate in Poland and had married a Polish woman. The count had nationalist sympathies and knew many of the Polish leaders; he was also on excellent terms with many Jews. But for Oberführer von Alvensleben, the Count von Alvensleben-Schöneborn was a traitor, the betrayer of his nation and race. So he shot the count and every member of his family one by one. Peiper believed that this showed impressive dedication to the Master Race.

On these eastern journeys, Himmler enjoyed stopping the train and scrambling onto the fields beside the track. Here he would take a pinch of earth and hold it up to his nose, 'sniff it thoughtfully', then 'gaze out over the wide, wide expanse . . . now all German earth'.[21] On one occasion, when Himmler's train stopped to meet Hitler's, the Reichsführer stepped from the carriage onto a hastily positioned crate. It collapsed and he crashed head first to the ground, his pince-nez, gloves and peaked hat flying in all directions.[22] The officer who had positioned the crate was never seen again.

For Ernst Schäfer, the journey was an education in what the euphemism 'resettlement' really meant. At Przemyśl, Himmler's destination, his policies were reaching a climax. Already seven hundred Jews had been killed. When Himmler and his entourage entered the town, thousands of 'Volhynian Germans' were arriving by train and by farm wagon from a region in the east that had been handed over to the Russians. In the 1930s, linguists and anthropologists had paid special attention to the German villages in the Volhynian region. Although the farmers there were often illiterate and spoke Polish, they were thought to be ethnically pure and biologically superior, and thus prime material for assimilation. In the 1920s scholars like Walter Kuhn, dressed in a Wandervogel costume, had tramped through the western Ukraine enthusiastically listening to the tales of old Volhynian peasants and trying to instil in their offspring a sense of ethnic nationalism,[23] even if the farmers themselves preferred to talk about rent levels. It was Kuhn who, in 1939–40, became responsible for resettlement policy, exchanging his Wandervogel outfit for SS black. They were mainly farmers, superbly fit, Brandt recalled, with fine horses. These were people of 'blood and soil', and Himmler had been especially enthusiastic about their arrival in his new order. This outing to Przemyśl was made specially to welcome them into the Reich. It can hardly have escaped Schäfer's notice that there were no longer any Jews living in Przemyśl, and he admitted that Peiper told him all about the murders of Polish aristocrats and intellectuals.

From Przemyśl, the *Heinrich*, with Schäfer still on board, steamed on to Cracow. We know that there he and the rest of Himmler's entourage breakfasted with some of Himmler's most savage SS henchmen. The conversation must have been instructive. Sitting at Himmler's table, in place of honour, was Lublin SS and Police Leader Odilo Globocnik – 'Globus' was Himmler's affectionate name for him – an Austrian Croat who would soon be given responsibility for 'Operation Reinhard' which would rid Poland of its Jews. Globocnik was violently anti-Semitic, and he was also a greedy speculator who made money by preying on his victims, seizing their property and even their gold teeth.[24] As he now reported with satisfaction to Himmler, he had recently murdered all the inmates of a Polish mental hospital at Hordyszcze.[25]

Schäfer's American interrogators were very interested to find out how much Schäfer had learnt on his excursion on the *Heinrich*. It is reasonable to conclude from his answers that he did not close his ears and eyes. In his own defence, Schäfer told his interrogators that he had contacted a professor at Hanover University, a botanist called Tuex, who was friendly with the city's Regierungspräsident, Rudolf Diels. Diels had been the first Gestapo head but had been dismissed; later in the war he was sacked from his position in Hanover when he refused to arrest Jews in the city. So it makes sense that Schäfer might have thought Diels would be sympathetic if he wanted to make a protest about what he had seen and learnt in Poland. 'I expressed my revulsion and my indignation,' Schäfer claimed, 'and I asked him . . . and talked to him about what could be done so that HIMMLER would stop these things or that these things would be stopped in general.' 'These things', as far as we can tell, referred to the killing of the Polish intelligentsia rather than Jews.

But Diels betrayed Schäfer. The result was another summons to Berlin, another shouting match and another banishment, this time to Finland to serve time on the front. It was not an especially arduous punishment, however, and Schäfer spent most of his time there bird-watching.

In 1945, Schäfer also had a witness who testified on his behalf. He was a German called Gerd Heinrich who had lived just twelve miles from the Polish border and, like Count von Alvensleben-Schöneborn, was known to have Polish sympathies and friends. Fearing what would happen as Himmler's resettlement programme intensified, and knowing that thousands of Poles were being executed, he looked around for help. Somehow he had heard of Schäfer, and he sent his sister, a 'Mrs Lukowicz', to Berlin to see what he could do for them. In his testimonial for Schäfer in 1945 he wrote, '. . . without considering the danger to himself [Schäfer] immediately tried to help and succeeded in saving Heinrich's life by intervening with the highest SS HQ in Berlin . . .'[26] The story is supported in the interrogation files by Heinrich's signed deposition.

What compromises Schäfer is not the absence of a few good deeds but knowledge and involvement. If he *knew* what was happening in Poland, and it is clear that he did, and continued to work under Himmler, the architect of genocide, it makes it almost impossible to build a convincing case in his defence. Even after that journey into hell on the *Heinrich*, Schäfer continued to deepen his involvement with Himmler's savage world. The question can also be asked another way: what did *Himmler* gain from Schäfer's presence on board the *Heinrich*? The answer was something very precious: complicity. Throughout the war and the enactment of the 'Final Solution of the Jewish problem' Himmler would seek to act in secret, but he would also make sure that his subordinates knew they were in as deep as he was. This was one of the purposes of the notorious speech made to his Gruppenführers at Posen later in the war when he concluded by saying, 'Now you know your way about [i.e. the elimination of the Jews] and you will keep it to yourselves. Perhaps at some much later date one will be able to consider whether one should say something more about it to the German *Volk*. I believe it better that we – all of us – have borne it for our *Volk*, have taken the responsibility on ourselves – the responsibility for a deed not only for an idea – and that we take the secret with us to the grave.'[27] This was another lesson learnt from Genghis Khan. According to historians, the Mongolian leader had practised what Germans called *Blutkitt*, or 'blood cement'. Shedding the blood of others bonded warriors and clans to the cause. The SS shared not only a blood line but the ties of spilling blood together. Every SS Gruppenführer present in that room in Posen was therefore made responsible along with Himmler. Murder became a matter of shared duty, not of 'following orders'. Himmler liked and admired Schäfer; he viewed him as something of a curmudgeon but he did not want to lose him or the status he conferred on the SS. By inviting him on to the train he was practising the profoundest of all seductions: the sharing of a guilty secret.[28]

We can get some insight into Schäfer's position from an independent source. Sven Hedin was in Germany in the early 1940s, and he kept a 'German Diary'.[29] Like the British members of 'Ribbentrop's kindergarten'[30] who assisted Schäfer in London, Hedin was sympathetic to the Nazi New Order while making the odd protest or three. Most of the time, though, he was a sycophant. '[Hitler] received me at the Reichs Chancellery as though we had been old friends,' he noted. 'He was tall and manly, a powerful harmonious figure who held his head high, walked erect and moved with assurance and control.' The Nazi leader passed on important dietary information to Hedin: 'Yes, yoghourt [*sic*], sour milk is the best of all foods and good to eat. Anyone who has made yoghourt his staple diet for twenty years will be as strong as a bear and live longer than other people.'[31] One intriguing insight comes from Reich Minister Dr Kerrl's presentation to Hedin of Michael Pradin's 'masterworks': *Genghis Khan: the Storm out of Asia* and *The Heritage of Genghis Khan*. Pradin was the pen-name for a Russian called Michael Charol who combined facts with a great deal of imaginative licence.[32] Both Hitler and his Reichsführer admired the conqueror from the East. They revered his ruthlessness and the tribal loyalty of his generals. Himmler liked the books so much that he had a one-volume version prepared as an SS training manual: wisdom from the East.

Hedin met Himmler in March 1940, just months after Schäfer's excursion to Poland. Like so many others, he begins his report with a description of the Reichsführer's unpleasant physiognomy: 'He had none of the appearance of a cruel and ruthless despot and might just as well have been an elementary school teacher from some provincial town. One felt a lack of character and pregnancy [*sic*] in his face, of the strongly moulded lines that tell of will and energy. It bore not a trace of the classical beauty of Greece and Rome, not a suspicion of race or culture . . .'[33] Hedin obviously did not think Himmler Aryan enough! Himmler opened the conversation, Hedin recalled, by talking about Ernst Schäfer, who had led 'an able and successful expedition into Southern Tibet'. Hedin knew of Schäfer's earlier expeditions but recorded his surprise when he discovered that his last had been made under Himmler's patronage. The Reichsführer, he now realized, must have a 'keen and enlightened interest in the snow-lands north of the Himalayas'. Schäfer had successfully evaded 'British prohibitions', Himmler told Hedin, perhaps aware of the Swede's antipathy to England, and had made a film Himmler wanted Hedin to see as soon as possible. Most revealingly, Himmler 'asked me to show as much interest in his young protégé as I felt he deserved . . .'[34] This is very much discussion about a favourite, not a recalcitrant rebel.

Later that year, in November, Hedin returned to Germany to prepare an 'objective' study of the Third Reich. Hedin's gullibility is frequently astonishing. Despite wartime privations, he and his entourage were promised a car and as much fuel as they needed 'so that we should be independent' as they toured the Reich. Invited by the Deutsche Akademie to visit Munich, Hedin 'dashed' out of Berlin, through Potsdam, Wittenberg, Leipzig and Halle, and then onto one of Hitler's celebrated autobahns 'that vanished like a white ribbon ahead of us'. Wooden poles had been erected every thirty yards to prevent enemy aircraft landing on the gleaming surface.

In Munich, Hedin was invited to lunch at the Akademie, where he met a distinguished gathering of German intellectuals. There were 'a number of Generals', the rector of Munich University SS Hauptsturmführer Walther Wüst, Professor Karl Haushofer – the geopolitican who had invented the idea of *Lebensraum* but by now was disillusioned with the Nazi ideology he had inspired – Princess Elizabeth Fugger of Wellenburg and Ernst Schäfer. During the meal, when Hedin toasted Schäfer's success, the room became very quiet. Schäfer himself shifted uneasily as he accepted the great explorer's compliment. What Hedin couldn't know was that by singling out Schäfer he had infuriated Wüst, his superior. After lunch, Schäfer took Hedin to his 'Research Institute' where he showed off his collection of Tibetan ritual objects and ran what must have been unedited highlights of his film: footage of Tashilunpo, processions and ceremonies with drums, trumpets and flutes, and of course Lhasa itself and the New Year ceremonies. Hedin, it seems, was jealous of his young admirer. He had been prevented from reaching Lhasa, and he wrote that

Haushofer made a 'far too flattering speech' about Schäfer's accomplishments. Once again, Hedin's memoir highlighted the peculiar fascination with the East among the Nazi intellectual elite. Haushofer, who had lived in Japan, compared a Germany 'toiling, seething and fighting for her life' with 'the snow-capped mountains and golden temple-courts of his youth'.[35] All in all, Hedin's fawning book provides a corrective to Schäfer's own accounts.

At the beginning of this book I suggested a simple metaphor, that joining Himmler's SS was like boarding a train that promised glory somewhere down the line. At some moment in the journey, you make a horrifying discovery: academic glory is merely a branch line; the real destination is very different. You are no longer comfortable. But the train is not slowing down and things seem much too interesting to disembark yet. This was the position Schäfer found himself in at the beginning of the 1940s. He was repelled, that is believable, but he was still capable of being flattered by Himmler's attention. His ambition as a scientist was very far from being sated. And Himmler still had plenty to offer him.

CHAPTER FOURTEEN

THE CASTLE

'Ich dachte ich werde meinen Vaterland damit einen Deinst erwisen.'
('I thought I was doing a service for the Fatherland.')

– Rudolf Höss, Auschwitz commandant

It stands on a ridge overlooking the Pinzgau Valley near Salzberg. Schäfer first saw it when he drove from Munich, thinking of ways to escape the Allied bombing. From the valley, a long drive snakes upwards between trees that stand like green sentinels. A last turn, and straight ahead is a gatehouse and the towering pink torso of the keep. When Heinrich Harrer came here he noticed a yak skull nailed to the wall and wondered how it had come to be in Austria. Behind the gatehouse, a whitewashed wall hugs the contours of the hill. There is a turret at the far corner. Today, Schloss Mittersill is a Christian retreat. When Schäfer first saw the castle it was home to a sports and shooting club with an absentee owner. It resembled an Austrian Yumbu Lagang, the mysterious tower Schäfer had studied in Tibet. From the castle's high windows Schäfer could see the luminous green of the Alpine pastures and hear, across the tangy air, the sound of hundreds of tiny bells. Beyond shimmered the snowy peaks of the Alps. Schloss Mittersill was just what he was looking for to house his new Institute for Central Asian Research. The castle would be his fortress and a potent symbol of power.

In late 1940, when Hedin met him in Munich, Schäfer was struggling to find his way upwards within the labyrinthine scientific institutions of the Reich. In January he had finally accepted a position in the Ahnenerbe and been rewarded with the gift of the Institute for Central Asian Research. It was housed to begin with in Munich on the third floor of the Ahnenerbe House at 35 Widmayerstrasse. This was where Hedin had been taken in 1940. Schäfer's boss was Professor Wüst, who was the president of the Ahnenerbe as well as the rector of Munich University. Neither man trusted the other, as Hedin's toast had inadvertently revealed. Schäfer thought Wüst a crank; Wüst did not trust Schäfer.

Why had Schäfer capitulated to an organization he correctly perceived as cranky and unscientific and whose 'business manager', that malevolent 'Bluebeard' Wolfram Sievers, he hated? The decision appears even more remarkable when we recall that he had only recently seen the results of Himmler's 'resettlement policies' in Poland and had had a row with the Reichsführer about the slaughter of the Polish intelligentsia.[1] The answer is provided by Michael Kater:[2] Schäfer had been rebuffed by a number of universities and the Ahnenerbe had begun to seem the only way he could get an academic post – of sorts – and, he hoped, prestige. It was not enough for Schäfer, as it had been for Brooke Dolan, to be a gung-ho explorer and hunter. He wanted respectability, and Wüst, as rector, had the power to grant him the professorship he coveted. More than that, embracing the Ahnenerbe had given him directorship of an institution – real power – and now he vigorously sought to expand its role and somehow, if possible, slowly distance himself from the Ahnenerbe and Sievers.

The new institute also allowed Schäfer to extract his old Tibet comrades from the clutches of the Waffen-SS, and he was eventually joined at Widmayerstrasse by Beger (on a temporary basis), Geer, Krause and Wienert. It would offer them all new opportunities and, finally, shame. In the first year, all went well. To begin untangling the bonds that tied him to the Ahnenerbe, Schäfer needed to get his institute accepted in its own right as a 'Reichinstitut', and to do that he needed the approval of Bernhard Rust, the Reich Minister of Education, who had engineered the Aryanization of the universities in the 1930s and was a suspected paedophile. It was Sven Hedin, who was revered by the Nazi elite, who provided the key. If Schäfer could get Hedin's blessing, it would give him the status to break away from Wüst and the Ahnenerbe. With Princess Elizabeth Fugger's backing, Schäfer flew to Sweden to secure Hedin's permission to play midwife to his Institute for Inner Asian Research. Records of Schäfer's expenses show that he lavished hundreds of Reichsmarks on gifts and bouquets of flowers to tempt the grand old man to give his blessing. According to Schäfer, his courtship was very successful and Hedin agreed to donate his name to the new institute.

In his diary, Hedin recalled these events rather differently. On 10 June 1942 he was in Berlin and received a 'strange deputation' in his sitting room at the Kaiserhof Hotel. It was led by Professor Wüst and included the 'energetic' Ernst Schäfer as well as 'various doctors'. Wüst read to Hedin a 'deed of foundation' which proposed the creation of a 'Reich Institute for the Exploration of Central Asia' which he hoped would bear Hedin's illustrious name. Hedin says that he protested that it would be more appropriate to commemorate a great German explorer like von Humboldt or Carl Ritter, but Wüst told him that approval from Rust and Himmler depended on his acceptance, which he duly gave. It is certain that Schäfer visited Hedin in Stockholm, but it is possible that he was economical with the truth about later events. Hedin might have needed extra persuading and Wüst might, in reality, have been a useful ally rather than a rival. In other words, Schäfer later tried to present himself at a greater remove from the Ahnenerbe than he really was or wished to be.

So the 'Sven Hedin Institute for Inner Asian Research' was born. Schäfer moved out of the Ahnenerbe House in Munich – Allied bombing raids were becoming increasingly frequent – and took his staff, collections and papers lock, stock and barrel to Salzburg. The Schloss Mittersill was a fifteenth-century castle, his own version of Wewelsburg or Hitler's own nearby Eagle's Nest at Berchtesgaden. In the 1930s the castle had been the haunt of diplomats and film stars. A fire had ruined part of the structure and the owner had fled to New York. Schäfer set about renovating the castle and filling it with artefacts and treasures from Tibet. He was backed in this by the regional leader of Salzburg, Gauleiter Scheel, who had been promised his own quarters in the castle. With Scheel standing beside him, Schäfer opened the Sven Hedin Institute with due ceremony on 16 January 1943.

Although he had escaped Ahnenerbe House and was now director of a Reichinstitut, Schäfer was not completely independent. Kater describes the Sven Hedin Institute as a hybrid 'creature with three legs' – one in the Ahnenerbe, the second in the university of Munich and the third in the Reich Education Ministry. It was a confusing state of affairs that Schäfer exploited after the war – although he could hardly have anticipated needing to – denying any connection with the Ahnenerbe which he denounced as a 'stronghold for failures'.[3]

In reality, the Sven Hedin Institute became the biggest institute *in* the Ahnenerbe.

I found a letter in Washington's National Archives that is most revealing about Schäfer's motives:

> To all comrades in Munich and the other gentlemen of the different departments. During the last days I was able to have long and thorough talks with Gauleiter . . . Scheel. By the way, the Gauleiter promised me his complete support. He views our project as important for the war. I therefore wish that the individual departments would be transferred to Mittersill as soon as possible. Work should start as soon as possible. After reorganization Gauleiter Scheel will pay us a visit. It is quite clear to me that in the near future I have to request a number of sacrifices from each and every one, but I am convinced that everybody will understand this. I expect from each and every one that he does his utmost so that Mittersill soon will be *the* place of Science in Gau Salzburg.

Schäfer was determined to be a leading German scientist, but he also wanted to play his part in the war effort and would use any contact to get to the top.

But if Schäfer harboured any delusions about personal or academic freedom, they would be brutally dashed. In 1942, not long before he boarded the train in Munich with Dr Hauck, Schäfer had been summoned to see Wolfram Sievers, the most powerful man in the Ahnenerbe. He had a special task for the great Tibet explorer: he was to take Krause and his camera equipment to record some medical experiments that were of vital importance in the war effort. The experimenter's name was Dr Sigmund Rascher. Their destination was a place called Dachau, not far from Munich.

Dachau had its origins in the first repressive actions taken by the Nazis after 1933. Communists, social democrats, journalists and Jews were rounded up and dumped in prisons all over Germany. When these were full, 'wild' concentration camps were constructed to take the overflow. The first of these was Dachau, improvised in early 1933 from a derelict munitions factory on the edge of Munich.[4] It was soon notorious, at least outside Germany; in 'Journey to a War' (1938), W. H. Auden refers to places 'where life is evil now / Nanking, Dachau . . .' For Himmler, its function was summarized in a slogan painted across one of its barracks: 'There is one way to freedom. Its milestones are: obedience, zeal, honesty, order, cleanliness, temperance, truth, sense of sacrifice and love for the Fatherland.'[5] He might have added to these perverse Victorian values 'submission to the whims of doctors', for after 1939 Himmler began to use Dachau's inmates in medical experiments. Blocks were isolated and used to test homoeopathic drugs in the treatment of TB.[6] He allowed Klaus Schilling to conduct malarial experiments by infecting captured Polish priests. In the kingdom of death, the Hippocratic oath was void; inmates were expendable, medicine would profit from death.

The man they were to assist was one of the most dishonourable of all the Nazi medical experimenters. Sigmund Rascher was a pioneer, the first of the Nazi doctors to assume his experiments could be terminal – in other words, it was permissible for them to end with the death of the test persons (TPs).[7] In this he was fully supported by Himmler. Violence intimately linked the two men; Himmler would later commit suicide by biting on a cyanide capsule patented by Rascher. They also shared sexual partners.

Himmler had first met Rascher in 1939 when they were introduced by the Munich concert singer Karoline 'Nini' Diehl, who was by 1942 Frau Rascher. Diehl and Himmler were intimate friends, probably former lovers. He had long abandoned Marga Himmler, in private at any rate, and would soon make Hedwig Potthast his mistress. Nini was, according to Peter Padfield, a 'shameless scrounger, asking [Himmler] for more money, reduction of taxes, extra fruit allowances, servant girls from the east – in all of which he indulged her . . .'[8] She was remembered as 'a typical, overdressed, ageing mistress'. Urged on by Nini, Himmler made Rascher an Untersturmführer in the Ahnenerbe and channelled funds that allowed him to carry out private cancer research on cancer-prone rats.[9]

When the war began, Rascher joined the Luftwaffe as a junior doctor and was introduced to the deadly consequences of high-altitude depressurization. Some experiments had already been carried out using monkeys, but there had been frustration with the results. Because of his acquaintance with Himmler, Rascher believed there was an opportunity to use human subjects, despite the extreme danger they would face and the moral doubts of the Luftwaffe top brass. In a bizarre letter to Himmler dated 15 May 1941, Rascher began by thanking the Reichsführer for his help 'in making [our] marriage possible . . . I thank you with all my heart'. Then he goes on to make a suggestion: 'I therefore ask this question in all seriousness. Cannot two or three professional criminals be made available for these experiments . . . The experiments during which, of course, the test persons may die will proceed with my collaboration . . . I have talked about this matter in strict confidence with the deputy air surgeon . . . and he shares my view that the problems in question can be clarified only by way of experiments on human beings . . .'[10] Himmler agreed, readily. 'The prisoners will of course gladly be made available,' Brandt told Rascher, and he arranged for a 'pressure chamber' from the German Experimental Institute for Aviation (DVL) to be delivered to Dachau, whose inmates would be handed over to Rascher. Only some of them were criminals; one survivor of Rascher's work was Father Leo Miechalowski, a Catholic priest. The pressure chamber was a cabinet constructed from wood and metal three feet by six feet whose internal pressure could be controlled by exhausting air to simulate conditions at high altitudes. A small window allowed the test person to be observed and photographed.[11]

There then followed a delay while Luftwaffe researchers squared what was going to happen with their consciences – or, as Padfield suggests, succumbed to Himmler's blackmail. The Luftwaffe made an attempt to exclude Rascher, but the ferocious Nini was quickly on the telephone to Berlin and her husband was reinstated. The experiments finally began in March 1942. Rascher reported eagerly to Himmler again on 5 April: 'SS [Obersturmbannführer] Sievers took a full day to watch some of the more interesting standard experiments . . . I believe these experiments would hold extraordinary interest for you, dear Reichsführer . . .'[12]

Sievers now brought Rascher to meet Schäfer at his Munich apartment in Widmayerstrasse. He explained that he wanted Krause, who was on the institute staff, to make a record of the experiments. Apparently, no reference was made to the fate of the test persons. To get a sense of what was required, Schäfer was asked to visit the camp. A few days later, a long black Mercedes arrived at his home to take him out of Munich through the dull northern suburbs with their blank, unseeing windows to Dachau. It was a journey of just nine miles. At the end of Dachaustrasse, the Mercedes turned into the long, straight approach road to the camp. A railway line ran parallel to the road. Every day, trains brought thousands of new prisoners to this 'model camp' which had so impressed Admiral Sir Barry Domville, Schäfer's admirer in London four years earlier. After a few minutes, they began to pass the stylish villas of the SS families. This was another world altogether, where SS wives and families led ordinary lives in *faux* peasant homes. Behind a gate topped by a huge Nazi eagle clutching a swastika in its talons were sports and recreational facilities that would not have been out of place in a luxury hotel. There were immense factories too, where prisoners churned out porcelain, bicycles and electrical goods – a profit machine for the SS.

Schäfer's car slowed and stopped in front of Dachau's rusticated neo-classical gatehouse. Spelt out in wrought iron was the slogan of the camps: *ARBEIT MACHT FREI*. On either side Schäfer could see stretching for more than a mile electrified barbed-wire fences punctuated at intervals by guard towers. As Schäfer exchanged Heil Hitlers with an SS guard and was admitted into the camp, he claimed he felt increasingly anxious. Carrying out tests on the effects of high-altitude depressurization was a worthy cause, but he distrusted Sievers – and there could be only one reason why the work had been transferred from a Luftwaffe research institute in Munich to Dachau. But so far, he had not walked away.

As he was escorted to Rascher's laboratory, Schäfer must have looked up at the crematoria chimney which belched smoke night and day. Dachau was not an extermination camp, it had even been shown off to foreign visitors, but its gruelling work regime and deadly punishments meant that life here led to death. Prisoners said that the colour of the smoke signalled how long the dead had been in the camp: new arrivals produced yellow smoke; old survivors sent a thin green pall over the camp and the town.

Inside Dachau, Rascher had been busy. He had created a quick and efficient experimental factory. The test person would be brought from a barracks and wired up to instruments that recorded vital functions, and in many cases their termination.

Then they would be locked inside the chamber, from which the air would be sucked out to simulate an ascent of over three thousand feet per minute. The TP could breathe oxygen until the test altitude was reached. Rascher frequently sent his subjects to the full altitude permitted by the apparatus, some thirteen miles. When the required altitude was reached, the TP would be ordered, often suffering severe pain, to perform 'five knee bends each, with and without oxygen', which replicated the effort of leaving the cockpit of an aircraft.[13] Then Rascher would begin raising the pressure again at different rates to mimic the effects of either a parachute bail-out or a free-fall descent. The pain would have been unspeakable. The prisoners suffered convulsions, blindness, even paralysis. They contorted their faces, foamed at the mouth or bit off their tongues. Some tore at their heads and faces before losing consciousness. We know this because they were photographed and filmed. Of the 150 or more prisoners Rascher used, *half* died.[14]

In his records, Rascher marked terminal experiments with an 'X' and, according to letters from Nini to Himmler, her husband carried them out alone. Himmler continued to protect Rascher from his 'squeamish' colleagues who made several attempts to remove his equipment. 'My husband is very lucky', she wrote to her powerful friend, 'that you take so much interest in the experiments; just now over Easter he has carried out single handed only those experiments for which [Luftwaffe] Dr Romberg would have had scruples and shown compassion'.[15] One such experiment was conducted on a '37 year old Jew in good general condition'[16] who was taken to an altitude of 29,400 feet without oxygen. After five minutes spasms occurred, followed by unconsciousness and slowed respiration. Intense cyanosis (bluish discoloration of the skin) was observed, and frothing at the mouth. Breathing then heart action ceased after half an hour. The experiment was over. A life was ended.

Other experiments, equally brutal, were carried out to determine the effects of sustained low temperatures – in only one or two cases was Rascher forced by appalled colleagues to use anaesthetics – and 'warming of chilled persons by animal heat'. That there was a peculiar mix of violence and pornography in Rascher's experimental work is evident in the reports on the warming experiments: 'the test persons were placed between two naked women on a wide bed . . . Once the test persons regained consciousness, they never lost it again, quickly grasping their situation and nestling close to the naked bodies of the women . . .'[17] Rascher's data showed that a single female was most effective since the subjects became more intimate.

When Schäfer was ushered into Rascher's laboratory that morning in 1942, there was at first little evidence of what had been taking place there. With brutal naivety – no-one regarded him as especially bright – Rascher unlocked a cabinet and carefully removed a prized exhibit. It was a brain extracted during an autopsy of one of the prisoners. For Schäfer, this was a shocking revelation. Next, Rascher summoned one of the prisoners and locked him inside the pressure chamber. On this occasion, sensing Schäfer's disquiet, he was somewhat less crude in his methods and slowly evacuated the pressure, taking the test person to a lower than normal altitude. When he was released, the man, obviously disorientated, was ordered to walk along a white line painted on the floor. 'Look at the disturbance of equilibrium, that has to be filmed!' said Rascher. But Schäfer had seen enough. His acceptance of the assignment in one of Nazi Germany's most notorious concentration camps was compromising enough. But there is genuine revulsion in the story he told his Nuremberg interrogators:

A: . . . I tried to pick up information and I heard from SCHNITZLER in Munich, who was an adjutant of Himmler, that he also called RASCHER a murderer. He was a stupid but decent man. I visited him to get more information. I heard about the low temperature experiments ... At that point we had decided that KRAUSE had to fall ill immediately. There were several phone calls from SIEVERS. We also said that the camera wasn't working. The plan was then abandoned.

Q: Why did they want KRAUSE?

A: That's the point. The only reason I can think of is that they wanted to make us confidants and accomplices. That was obvious to me. The same evening I told my wife about these things. We decided that if the Nazis won the war I wouldn't [want to] be a German anymore.

Q: Now many people don't want that.

A: Yes, perhaps I don't want it now. It was the most dreadful experience of my life. I hadn't imagined these things could be possible. [. . .] In any case that had been the crucial incident. I immediately left for a business trip and went to see my father.

Q: Did you tell him about it?

A: Of course.

Q: What did he say?

A: That it was horrible. I didn't know if I should go to Switzerland, Sweden or if I should stay. From that time on I constantly discussed with my father what should be done. He gave me the following advice: 'Keep your institute as clean as possible. See that you keep out of everything. You can be completely sure that the war will not be won.' My father knew that since Dunkirk. I then informed my father of everything that had happened. I said to him: 'Look, I'm a member of the SS.' My father said: 'As far as I know the English, nothing can happen to you.'

I have quoted this at length because it is testimony to Schäfer's state of mind. At first reading there is something a little unconvincing about Schäfer's escape: the claim that Krause was ill and that their filming gear wasn't functioning. *Someone* filmed Rascher's experiments; the hard evidence is in the film archive. Was Schäfer hoping that the results of his work with Krause would not come to light? Was he covering for Krause? Further investigation shows that Schäfer was telling the truth – at least in part. The filming was carried out *not* by Krause but by a 'specialist', SS Hauptsturmführer Helmut Bousset, and the results were shown to Himmler in Berlin. But in the Bundesarchiv I found a letter from Krause to Beger that adds yet more ambiguity to the story. It begins by explaining that he was asked first of all to film some vultures in Salzburg:

> When I was in Berlin the time before last time, Wolf told me that the Obersturmbannführer wanted to speak to me on the phone regarding the vulture shots. I then called Sievers who told me that I should get [. . .] directly into contact with Stubaf. Bousset. This way I found out that Bousset, who had filmed the resettlement works [presumably in Poland] for Sievers, should also film the vultures on Sievers' command (with standard film equipment), while I should only do the detail shots with the 'substandard' film camera following Bousset's instructions. Although I know from experience that it is best to work alone when filming animals, I didn't object. First of all because an order is an order [*Befehl ist Befehl*] and secondly because I didn't want to give the impression that I wanted to be competitive. After our adventures in the Himalayas, filming vultures near

> Salzburg can only be a sort of education for me and from this perspective would be highly valuable for us. I had asked Schäfer to talk about this with Sievers. But obviously this has been understood in the wrong way, as Obersturmbannführer Sievers' behaviour showed. I was then ordered to film scientific experiments (highly confidential) here in Dachau. Schäfer said that this could only be done with a standard film camera. We told Sievers this and also asked him (and the Ahnenerbe) to provide us with such an Arriflex hand camera [...] that would be absolutely necessary for this [Dachau], the vulture shots and other training tasks. As an answer we received a telegram from Sievers saying that Bousset would arrive in Munich soon to do the shots in Dachau. But now E. has told me that Bousset has called the Institute in the meantime and asked again if we could maybe do the filming in Dachau. All this back and forth seems very strange to me, so that I don't know what to think about all this. I only let you know about this to keep you informed. Please regard it as highly confidential.

Krause's letter muddies the waters. Rivalry and a rather fastidious concern with using exactly the right equipment appears to have been much more important than the moral disgust Schäfer alleges he experienced. Would not Krause, in his confidential letter, have confirmed Schäfer's story that they planned to tell Sievers that the camera wasn't working and that *he* was ill? At the beginning of the same letter Krause tells Beger that he had indeed been ill as a result of catching a chill in Berlin, but he does not connect this with any attempt to trick Sievers. It does look as if Schäfer was much less scrupulous than he claimed he had been in 1945. Krause's strange letter casts some light on this tense moment during Schäfer's post-war interrogation:

> Q: Let's come back to the experiment in Dachau. You said that you would contact your father, whom you had told about it. This is not mentioned in the copy of the letter you sent me. You told me that you had informed your father, filled with horror.
>
> A: Yes, of course I did do that. That must be a misunderstanding. I'm terribly sorry about that. You must excuse that.
>
> Q: Also, this letter [from Hans] doesn't satisfy me at all.
>
> A: Me neither. That is the industrialist, who doesn't care.
>
> Q: [...] Write to your father and tell him that his statement is insufficient ... He should confirm that you told him about the incident in Dachau and that you had explained the reasons to him why they tried to make you an accomplice.
>
> A: I will do that.

There is no evidence that this happened.

Rascher's career came to a sordid end. His wife had been unable to have children, and to acquire the perfect Aryan family this odd couple had abducted children. For this, Rascher was hanged on the gallows at Dachau, alongside Nini, in 1944. Whatever the truth of Schäfer's involvement with this nasty little doctor, he was often tripped up during his interrogation. His biggest problem was trying to explain away his membership of Himmler's 'Circle of Friends', the Freundeskreis RFSS.[18] There was a damning paper trail linking Schäfer to this club for big-business sycophants, and the men questioning Schäfer had done their homework.

The Freundekreis was founded by Wilhelm Keppler, an industrialist friend of Himmler, and his protégé Fritz Kranefus. Many of Germany's businessmen had seen in the NSDAP an anti-socialist mass movement that could serve their needs well as they struggled to recover from the Depression. Himmler's elite SS, with its considerable upper-middle-class and aristocratic recruitment programme, was the ideal instrument for big-business interests inside the Nazi machine. Both parties would benefit. The SS would suck in new revenue – it was always greedy – and the businessmen and industrialists would have a powerful lobby. SS salaries were low, and Himmler used Freundeskreis funds to gild the lives and buy the loyalty of his men. There were exclusive SS clubs and resorts, tailors and shoemakers, as well as automobiles available to this elite by the truckload.[19]

During his interrogation, Schäfer twisted and turned around the truth. He was forced to join; he disliked the other *Freunde* and distrusted them; yes, he did hear Himmler making some very disturbing speeches, but what could he do? He suspected that one 'wing' of the Freundeskreis, led by the devious Kranefus, was spying on the 'scientists' and lubricating their talk with alcohol. He went very infrequently; he was threatened if he didn't attend. Only the Allied raids on Munich gave him a good enough excuse not to turn up.

The reality was that he was trapped in a tangled web. Unless he left Germany – and there is no hard evidence that this was an option he ever seriously considered – there was no safe position where compromises did not have to be made. It was a dirty pool. But however compromised he was, Schäfer still had that 'unruly will'. Where he could, he fought his tight corner, just as he had with the Tibet expedition. He battled Himmler over *Geheimnis Tibet*, although the end result was very much a film of its time. There was often tension between the two men. On one occasion when Schäfer misbehaved, Himmler refused to let him make a lecture tour and insisted that he declare he was ill. Himmler's office wrote later to Schäfer asking exactly *which* disease he had chosen to suffer from.[20] Schäfer reported back, appropriately enough, that he had a nervous complaint – *nervenleiden*. Throughout 1943, Schäfer had to make one excuse after another. Although in February 1943 he wrote 'next month it is probably possible [to come to Norway] . . . I'd like to fly with my wife because she has not been in a foreign country', by July his health had apparently worsened. Then he had 'most important special tasks', and finally a 'long business trip'.[21]

Whatever differences Schäfer had with the Reichsführer, Himmler had one final and tantalizing bait to lure back his troublesome explorer. In June 1941 Hitler betrayed his pact with the Russians and launched a crusade against Bolshevism, just as he had always planned. He threw 3 million troops, 3,600 tanks, 600,000 motorized vehicles, 7,000 artillery pieces, 2,500 aircraft and 625,000 horses east against Stalin's Red Army. In the first year of Barbarossa the Wehrmacht's success was spectacular as Stalin's armies, crippled by a murderous purge of their generals, reeled back. But a year later there were ominous signs that Hitler's brutal success was about to be reversed, and through his own megalomaniac misjudgement. In July 1942 he split his army into two, sending Army Group B against Stalingrad and a much more powerful A Group rampaging towards the oil fields of Maykop, Grozny and Baku, and the high peaks and mountain passes of the Caucasus. Himmler's SS Einsatzgruppen had as usual been expanding their murderous empire behind the lines, the Reichsführer had loftier ambitions. As the Wehrmacht pushed towards the Caucasus, he turned to Schäfer once more to garner, if he could, science from slaughter and conquest. In August 1942 Himmler proposed a combined scientific and military expedition, led by Schäfer, that would travel deep into the Caucasus. It was an audacious plan.

Himmler had, as ever, the measure of his fretful adventurer.

For Schäfer, a Caucasus expedition must have been highly seductive. He had always wanted to explore the Caucasus, the 'Mountain of Tongues' whose flora and fauna he believed were a bridge between Europe and Asia. Here were the highest mountains in Europe and highly diverse peoples who would provide rich opportunities for anthropometric analysis. Schäfer threw himself into his new mission. As his plans for this 'Sonderkommando Kaucasus' developed, the scale of the enterprise became recklessly ambitious, even when reports of German military reverses began to filter back from the faraway, overstretched front lines. 'They promised me anything I wanted,' Schäfer confessed in 1947.

His detailed plans are on record, and they reveal a scheme much more ambitious than his 1938 Lhasa expedition. Nearly twenty scientists covering a bewildering range of disciplines were invited, Dr Beger being appointed the '*Leiter und gleichzeitiger Führer des Anthropologen Trupps*'.[22] Wienert, again, would be in charge of geophysical work, but the entomologist this time was not Krause but a Dr Sick. There were in addition experts on farming, botany, archaeology, geophysics and religion. There was as well, of course, a large (forty-seven men) and heavily armed SS escort, and there was no doubt that they would need them: like the Russians today, the Wehrmacht was making little progress subduing the remote mountain valleys. At least forty PKW type Volkswagens were ordered, seventeen lorries and even a Kondor aircraft, as well as a huge quantity of scientific equipment.

But unknown to Schäfer, Himmler had other plans – after all, the expedition motto stated that this was 'Social Science Applied to War'. It was, in reality, war applied to social science. One of the names referred to in correspondence is Otto Ohlendorf,[23] who was Heydrich's chief business manager. Ohlendorf was a highly intelligent, high-minded and outspoken economist who had joined the NSDAP in 1925. Himmler called him *Gralshüter* – guardian of the Holy Grail. After the beginning of the onslaught on Russia, Heydrich made sure Ohlendorf proved his worth during the SS-organized genocide behind the front line. SS Gruppenführer Ohlendorf was put in charge of Einsatzgruppen D attached to the southern Army Group. In September 1941 Ohlendorf's D group massacred 22,467 Jews and communists in the Nikolayev area near Odessa. He returned in triumph to his desk in Berlin, his loyalty proven in blood. Ohlendorf's involvement in the 'Sonderkommando Kaucasus' strongly implies that science would be combined with mass murder. According to Kater, Beger's interest was in the Jews of the region – the Cagh Chafut, or 'mountain Jews', and the Hebraile Jews of Georgia – and it is certain that their discovery would have led to extinction.

Schäfer appears to have sensed he was being used, for he complained to Brandt that he was being 'treated like a sherpa'. In a letter written months later, Brandt discussed with a colleague how he could break the news to Schäfer that the scientific objectives of this new expedition were increasingly to be downgraded in favour of military ones. But before these subterfuges and conflicts exploded into open acrimony, Barbarossa began to go disastrously wrong. Army Group A found that the Maykop oil fields had been expertly destroyed by the Red Army, and their advance through even the wooded terrain of the foothills of the Caucasus ranges was frequently bogged down. Hitler was infuriated when he heard that his mountain troops had climbed and planted a flag on Elbrus, the highest peak in the Caucasus – a gesture Schäfer would have admired. As Hitler's military fortunes were being reversed, this seemed a foolish gesture. In the following months Army Group A was driven slowly back by the Red Army. After the catastrophe at Stalingrad, Army Group B surrendered on 29 January 1943.

Himmler postponed the Caucasus Expedition that same month, but the project was completely cancelled only at the end of the year. By then the Sven Hedin Institute had become involved in an even more deadly scheme that involved Bruno Beger – described in the next chapter. It would make Schäfer and his institute complicit in the Nazi holocaust itself.

The Caucasus fiasco was to be Schäfer's last humiliation. He was left with only a few absurd experiments, breeding Tibetan dogs and horses for Himmler and trying to cultivate the seeds he had brought back from Tibet. As the Thousand Year Reich began to shrink and collapse, Himmler had one last request: he wanted Schäfer to discover a red horse with a white mane that he had read about in an old Nordic fairy tale. Schäfer had never heard of such a thing, and pursued the mission less than half-heartedly. Likewise, Karl Wienert, the geophysicist, was ordered to investigate other equally chimerical fantasies of the Reichsführer. One was the search for gold in the Isar River that runs through Munich.[24] Himmler was obsessive about gold. He had even incarcerated a man called Tausend who had claimed to have alchemical powers, and tried to force him to make gold from base metals. Wienert knew that there was no gold in the Isar but he spun out the investigation to humour Sievers. When Wienert finally reported back empty-handed, Himmler drafted in a Dr Josef Rimmer, a geologist with 'divining' skills. Rimmer was much more optimistic. Impressed, Himmler proposed to compel *all* geologists to take divining courses and then to form brigades of geologist-diviners. But no gold was ever found.

As the Allied armies swept across Europe in 1945, Schäfer realized the game was up. Like Speer, he realized that the best strategy was surrender, then confession. In Tibet, Gould had noticed 'the curious way [Schäfer] has of seeking to condone what he has done by talking about it'.[25] Schäfer was in a perilous position after the defeat of the Nazis. He had been an SS officer since 1933, a friend of Heinrich Himmler, and he ran all but three of the SS Ahnenerbe's labyrinth of departments. After sending Ursula and his three daughters to safety, Schäfer returned one last time to his stronghold, the Schloss Mittersill. Then, with no fuel to be had anywhere near Salzburg, he found a bicycle, pedalled down to the US front line and surrendered. He had, of course, no difficulty making himself understood.

Schäfer offered to make the Sven Hedin Institute available to the Philadelphia Academy of Natural Sciences, but it did him no good. 'I was grossly mistaken,' he wrote later. 'I lost everything.' Schloss Mittersill was ransacked, its priceless treasures scattered. Schäfer listed every searing loss: 'Sixty thousand Tibetan photographs, forty thousand metres of moving picture films, my library, all my personal belongings, including my wife's property, my collection of paintings, my furniture, my clothes, everything was taken away. I do not even own a bed for my three little children. Then I was interned . . .'[26] The castle was left to rot. When Heinrich Harrer visited Schäfer's stronghold a few years after the war, the only sign of the Sven Hedin Institute was that battered yak skull hanging forlornly over the main entrance.

Schäfer's home for the next few years was Camp Moosburg, formerly POW Camp Stalag VII and now Civil Internment Camp 6. He was one of twelve thousand Germans accused of actively supporting the Nazi dictatorship or being members, as Schäfer was, of a 'criminal organization'. In 1947 he was transferred to Cell 264 in Nuremberg. One day in May, he requested a typewriter. When it arrived, he placed it on a narrow table and sat down, closely scrutinized by an American military policeman. Then he began to pound out a desperate plea addressed to Telford Taylor, the US Army's 'Judge Advocate General' and prosecutor of the Nazi war criminals. What he came up with showed that he had not lost his touch for highly emotional plea bargaining.

'During the longer time of the Hitler regime,' he wrote, 'the aims of which were not known to me, I therefore was abroad working for the benefit of an American scientific institution and risking my life for it . . . After my name had been promulgated in the European press I was out of obvious reasons [*sic*] called back to Germany and simultaneously appointed an honorary leader in the SS. This constituted one of those notorious machinisations [*sic*] of the Nazi-leaders to bind young and able scientists to their system and it was affectet [*sic*] without my own free will . . .' Schäfer says that he was a completely unpolitical man who waged a never-ending struggle which brought him 'to the very brink of destruction and to the gates of the KZs [concentration camps]'. It was a struggle, he claims, 'directed against the Nazi system', in the course of which he protected Jews, Poles, Russians and German 'persecutes' 'within the realm of my institute'. He makes no mention, of course, of the Freundeskreis, the proposed guerrilla incursion into Tibet or the Caucasus Expedition, organized in the bloody wake of Barbarossa. Schäfer says he faced a choice between emigration and devoting his 'exercions [*sic*] to the common cause of humanity . . . I chose the last, or rather there was no other choice without seriously endangering the lives of my co-workers, the lives of my wife and my children and last not least my work'. Not least at all; work and ambition were always the key to Schäfer's decisions. Probably with good reason, he reserves his venom for colleagues who were a few years after the war happily teaching in universities, and for fellow former internees – 'scores of Nazis' – who had been quickly released, 'given back the bliss of freedom', while he remained incarcerated. One of these men was Bruno Beger, who, as we will see in the next chapters, would have good reason to be grateful for the uneven application of 'de-nazification'.

Basil Gould would have recognized the writer of that extraordinary begging letter. And Schäfer was, even now, persuasive. He received the most exemplary of all certificates of exoneration, a Category V, which required merely payment of a twenty-five-mark fee. His interrogators had concluded that, on balance, Schäfer had done more good than bad. In their interrogations, both Wienert and Krause were completely exonerated; only Geer, who had been a Nazi Party member since the 1920s, was given a more damning Category IV. Both Wienert and Krause slipped back into academic life. Not long after his release Schäfer was offered a job creating a new wildlife park in Venezuela, and he took his family there in 1949. Ursula Schäfer informed Isrun Engelhardt that it was only then that she felt 'completely married'; until then, her husband had been too busy. In 1954, Schäfer brought his family back to Germany. According to friends, he was never completely reconciled with his past involvement in Himmler's deadly world. He died in 1992.

Back in the 1940s, as Schäfer was being sucked deeper into the moral quagmire of wartime Germany, his old friend Brooky was on his way back to Tibet on behalf of the OSS – the fledgling CIA. The American military brass under President Roosevelt – working from his 'Shangri-La Retreat', later renamed Camp David – was desperately trying to sustain the Chinese Army of Chiang Kai-shek in the war with Japan. The OSS came up with the idea of a supply route from India to China through Tibet. Someone needed to persuade the Tibetans. Dolan got the job.

He embarked on this high-risk mission with Major Ilia Tolstoy, a grandson of the Russian novelist, who had come to America in the 1920s to pursue his work as an explorer in the Canadian Arctic. In India they were assisted by Sir Basil Gould, who had of course once listened to the hysterical lamentations of Ernst Schäfer. Dolan reached Lhasa in 1942, three years after his German friend. His account and Tolstoy's beautiful photographs and film are among the most vivid records of this once Forbidden City. Dolan impressed the Tibetans with his knowledge of their language and culture, so much so that the daughter of a noble Tibetan was carrying his child when he left Lhasa after a sojourn of many weeks. A few years later, mother and child drowned in a river near Gyantse. Both Dolan and Tolstoy became fervent advocates of Tibetan independence, but their plans came to very little amid the labyrinthine intrigues of the nationalist Chinese and the American intelligence agencies.

A washed-up alcoholic, Brooke Dolan killed himself in China on 19 August 1945.[27] He wouldn't be there to defend his old friend as he faced his interrogators. Perhaps he might have chosen not to do this favour for 'Junge' anyway.

CHAPTER FIFTEEN

RACE WARRIOR

'Schwarze Milch der Frühe wir trinken dich nachts
wir trinken dich mittags der Tod ist ein Meister aus Deutschland
wir trinken dich abends und morgens wir trinken und trinken
der Tod ist ein Meister aus Deutschland sein Auge ist blau
er trifft dich mit bleierner Kugel er trifft dich genau'

'Black milk of daybreak we drink you at night
we drink you at noon death is a master from Germany
we drink you at sundown and in the morning we drink and we drink you
death is a master from Germany his eyes are blue
he strikes you with leaden bullets his aim is true'

– Paul Celan, 'Todesfugue', 1945, trans. Michael Hamburger

'Struthof is a favourite resort in both winter and summer. In summer, it is notable for its views and promenades. In winter, it attracts skiers from every part of Europe. In summer, it recalls the words of Goethe when he lived in Strasbourg: "Über allen Gipfeln ist Ruh" ["above every mountaintop is silence"].'

– a guidebook, quoted in *Hitler's Death Camps: The Sanity of Madness*, Konnilyn G. Feig

When the mist comes down, temperatures fall towards the bone-chilling. The wind blows hard from the cloud-covered peaks and cuts like a knife. Tongues of snow lick across steep, twisting roads between black trees. This could be the roof of the world. Until you see the barbed wire. Follow the wire, which shrieks in the wind, and you come to a wooden gate. Beyond that rise flat, snow-shrouded terraces cut from a bare hillside. On the lower levels are the unmistakable relics of barrack blocks. Only foundations remain on the levels above. When the mist clears there is a fine view of the Vosges Mountains. You can see forests and small villages.

This is Natzweiler/Struthof, the only concentration camp built by the Nazis in France. The nearest big city is Strasbourg, which has a famous university and medical school. A printed request attached to a tree reads 'Struthof, Zone of Silence. Be Silent in Memory of our Martyred Dead'. A few miles from the camp is a luxury hotel called Le Struthof. Here, the wealthy citizens of Strasbourg celebrate their weddings. Just ten yards away is a building that was once an extension to the hotel, containing extra showers and washrooms. On its door is another sign: CHAMBRE À GAZ. Its presence seems never to have dimmed a smile or spoilt a reception.

In August 1943, Bruno Beger travelled to Natzweiler from Berlin on a secret mission. Soon afterwards, a lorry delivered 115 dead bodies to the anatomy department at Strasbourg University. They had been gassed and were still warm. In Nazi Germany, anthropology led to mass murder. How did the road from Lhasa lead to a cadaver-filled anatomy theatre in Strasbourg? The route is not an easy one to follow, but there is no avoiding the journey. It began with Beger's return to Germany.

As an SS officer, he immediately found himself ordered on active service with Himmler's military wing, the Waffen-SS. At the end of June 1941, Beger and the Nordland Regiment of the Waffen-SS Viking Division swept across the Ukraine towards the Dnieper River in the greatest land invasion in modern history, Operation Barbarossa. Alongside them was a horde of more than three million German soldiers, as well as some six hundred thousand Croats, Finns, Romanians, Hungarians, Italians, Slovaks and Spaniards.[1] The Nordland itself could boast volunteers from Scandinavia and France; it even had six serving men from England. They were all united by a searing hatred of Bolshevism. Near Kiev, the Nordland threw itself against the retreating Red Army and, in Hitler's words, 'stormed the heavens'. Beger's experiences were very different from Ernst Schäfer's in Finland. While his colleague went bird-watching, Beger was fighting hard in a bitter race war.

Hitler said that Russia would be Germany's Raj. Like the English in India, he planned to rule its immense spaces, once they had been conquered, with a mere handful of administrators. And he had an ulterior motive: Barbarossa was a race war; he said so explicitly, and so did Göring and Himmler. The Nazis would rid Russia's tremendous expanse of its Jews, gypsies, Slavs and other unworthy lives. German, Scandinavian, Dutch and Norwegian settlers would follow in their millions. As Hitler's armies swept through the Ukraine, Byelorussia, Lithuania, Latvia and Estonia, hundreds of thousands of Jews were rooted out and shot by the SS Einsatzgruppen units as well as by ordinary soldiers.

Hitler had predicted that Russia would prove to be a pig's bladder: 'Prick it,' he had ranted, 'and it will burst.' By July it seemed that the Axis was indeed winning its race war, but as the Wehrmacht pushed across the endless plains they had to fight other battles. They faced unrelenting heat and torturing swarms of stinging insects. In the autumn came rain and viscous, sucking mud. The winter brought freezing blizzards.

Barbarossa slowed and faltered as its soldiers sweltered or froze. Fighting was tough, exhausting and bloody. One soldier called Russia 'thrice damned'.

Later that year, however, Schäfer's machinations with the Institute for Central Asian Research led to Beger's recall to Germany. Now he could find other ways in which to serve the Reich. At first, Beger spent a great deal of time trying to get his Altmärkische paper completed so that he could receive his *Doktortitel* and complete his interrupted education. He also wanted to get it published, presumably to earn some money. In the files of the Sven Hedin Institute there is a great deal of correspondence between Beger, his mentor Professor Hans Günther and various academic publishing houses. Indeed, Beger became so preoccupied with the Altmärkische that Schäfer had to apologize to Himmler's assistant Brandt that his colleague had been tardy in working up the anthropological material from Tibet.[2]

There were other tensions, too. When the expedition returned to Germany, Schäfer made sure that he alone would receive the lion's share of celebrity. Only he, for example, would be able to publish any 'belles lettres' or popular accounts of the Schäfer Expedition. He would bask in the limelight while his colleagues took on the hard slog behind the scenes. Beger chafed at these restrictions, and his disgruntlement seems to have led him to seek allegiances outside Schäfer's circle – in particular with the hated Ahnenerbe chief Wolfram Sievers. It was, of course, Sievers who had introduced Schäfer to Rascher and chauffeured him to the experimental laboratory in Dachau. Schäfer, in that case, pulled back from the brink; Bruno Beger would not make the same choice.

When he was in Berlin, Beger also began to establish himself as the Ahnenerbe's race expert. He was, of course, already part of Himmler's *Persönlicher Stab* (personal staff) and his work in the mid 1930s for the RuSHA (the Race and Settlement Office) had shown how usefully he could serve Himmler's often peculiar interests. According to Michael Kater, Beger had been involved with the study of the newly excavated skeleton of King Heinrich I, or 'Henry the Fowler', at Quedlinburg Cathedral. Himmler, of course, believed himself to be his re-incarnation. The royal remains were measured and studied and then solemnly reinterred beneath the cathedral floor in a ceremony lit by the torches of SS officers.

Now Beger became involved with another pet project of Himmler's. For many years he had been intrigued by pre-historic Venus figurines. The most celebrated had been found in Willendorf in Austria just after the turn of the century, but since then thousands more had been unearthed at sites all over Europe. The Venus figurines are small carved stones representing generously proportioned females with large breasts, swollen stomachs and distended thighs. Himmler was especially fascinated by their prominent rears, and following his own peculiar logic had begun asking his Ahnenerbe colleagues to discover whether there might be an ancestral bond with similarly well-endowed African 'Hottentot'. Might the Venus figurines represent an older people who had been expelled from Europe when the superior, presumably more modestly proportioned Aryans had come on the scene? Himmler had another thought, too. He had observed on many occasions that Jewish women had comparable endowments. Were Jews *and* Hottentots living representatives of the prehistoric people who created the Venus figurines? Was this proof positive that Jews were the primitive relatives of Hottentots?[3]

Beger seems to have enthusiastically endorsed Himmler's ideas. He wrote, 'The racial similarities between the Hottentots, the North Africans, and the Near Eastern peoples are unmistakable. Among the Jewesses it is noticeable that they have very well-developed bottoms which could be linked to the fat bottomed lineage seen amongst Hottentots and bushmen.'[4]

With the precedent before them of the German anthropologists who had exploited the bloody Namibian war to acquire the skeletal trophies they coveted, Beger and his colleagues in the SS realized that the camps and ghettos created by resettlement were an outstanding opportunity for science. Beger enthusiastically recommended that 'The RuSHA, when they assemble foreigners and the women are mustered together and undressed, might pay special attention to how fat the women's bottoms are – and perhaps some photographs could be taken.' Warming to his theme, he added, 'It would be possible for the RuSHA to examine a line-up of Jewish women from the Polish ghettos with strong evidence of highly developed fat content in their rears. This would allow us to establish that this fat development comes from the same inherited factors as can be seen in Hottentots and Bushmen – allowing us to prove that this race existed in Europe as well.'

Beger's involvement in Himmler's Venus project was a turning point. As so often with these hobby-horse assignments of the Reichsführer, little more was done, but Beger had accepted that as an anthropologist he could go much further than simply endorsing the race theories of the Reich. As a scientist, he could exploit the human booty of conquest. At the time, Beger also travelled to Norway, which Hitler had conquered in 1940. Here, for the first time, he used a new technique to get metrical data. X-rays, radiography, could see beneath the skin as anthropologists had always wanted to do. When he saw the results, Beger reported enthusiastically to Himmler himself and proposed an ambitious plan using X-rays to produce a directory of Nordic types. 'Very good,' was Himmler's response. These were profitable times for anthropologists.

Historians continue to contest the chronology of the

Holocaust. When was it decided to use mass killing to solve 'the Jewish problem'? There is fierce debate, too, about intent and authority. Who issued the orders for genocide? Was it Hitler himself, or were critical decisions made by his subordinates? There is more controversy about who knew what was taking place and when. There is little disagreement, however, that the 'road to Auschwitz' was a 'twisted one'. No-one doubts, except perhaps the controversial historian David Irving, that Hitler and his circle were aggressively anti-Semitic and that after 1933 Nazi domestic policy was above all an expression of their Judeophobia. In a speech to the Reichstag at the end of January 1939, Hitler had made this prophecy: 'If the Jews . . . should succeed once more in plunging the nations into a world war, then the consequence will be . . . the annihilation of the Jewish race in Europe.' With the invasion of Poland, Jews and others were slaughtered in enormous numbers, but as far as historians can tell there was no agreed Final Solution to deal with the Jewish problem. Instead there was debate and argument about the means of removing all Jews from the new Reich territories, linked to plans to move in ethnic Germans. This led to the so-called Madagascar Plan as well as fierce arguments about how to use the newly conquered lands to the east. These had at first seemed to offer a solution. Adolf Eichmann began to evacuate Czech Jews to a 'reservation' in the swampy Lublin district. It was winter. Hundreds died in the trains, and it is very likely that discussions of resettlement and population transfer were secretly genocidal.

Outside Germany, a few journalists saw that this was indeed the real intent of Nazi policy. *The Times* called the Lublin plan 'political cynicism'. In the *Spectator* an American warned that the final act of Hitler's brutal and cruel treatment of Jews 'is now going on'. Eichmann's resettlement was mass migration in the dead of winter to 'a habitation of death'. These observers were right. It is now known that this was precisely the Nazis' intention. Nazi administrators had indeed begun to use the word 'evacuation' to mean 'annihilation'. With the invasion of Russia came mass shootings on an unprecedented scale and a paroxysm of violence. Hitler had demanded the killing of 'Jewish-Bolshevik Commissars' and 'everyone who even looks oddly'. Himmler ordered, 'All Jews must be shot. Jewish women to be driven into the marshes.'[5] Soldiers and Einsatzgruppen enthusiastically obeyed. Germany was told that 'the Jewish problem is being solved with imposing thoroughness'.

At the beginning of 1942 any radicalization of this policy depended on victory in the east, but with the Wehrmacht still engaged in savage fighting, Hitler ordered that all Jews in the Greater German Reich be deported to the ghettos of eastern Europe. It was a response to Stalin's deportation of six hundred thousand Volga Germans and, as Ian Kershaw has written, it brought the Final Solution a massive step closer. New policies and initiatives 'tumbled out' of the Nazi race cupboard.[6]

When mass shootings proved inefficient, and even psychologically damaging, a more sophisticated technology was demanded. Hitler's T4 euthanasia programme had already used gas to kill the mentally handicapped. In the summer of 1941, trucks used by the T4 technicians had been sent to a village called Chelmno and the local SS and police leader Wilhelm Koppe had begun to murder Jews in 'batches' of up to 150 at a time. In December 1941, Rudolf Höss, the commandant at Auschwitz–Birkenau, had killed six hundred Soviet prisoners and two hundred sick prisoners in Block 11 using, for the first time, Zyklon-B. Within months the gas would be in regular use as Auschwitz was transformed by the diligent Höss into a factory of death. Now, as the sparse and fragmented documents reveal, *Ausmerzung* ('eradication') and *Vernichtung* ('annihilation') became the means to achieve the '*endgültige*

Lösung' to the Jewish problem. Nazi leaders openly discussed the 'biological eradication of all of European Jewry'. For German bureaucrats desperate to rid their new territories of Jews, gas was the way ahead.

In the meantime, Heinrich Himmler fought to seize control of resettlement and the Jewish problem. Like Beger's professor Hans Günther, he believed that Aryan blood must be made safe from contamination. If removing Jews and other undesirables from the Reich became his special responsibility then he and the SS would have enormous power. Himmler's blood utopia depended on getting rid of Jews, but other Nazis viewed them as a resource: Germany needed slave workers, and Himmler knew that slave workers meant big profits. There was also squabbling among local district leaders, the Gauleiters, about Jews in their domains and why they had not been removed. To resolve these arguments, Himmler asked Reinhard Heydrich, his 'twin dark angel', to organize a conference. It took place at the beginning of 1942 at the Berlin Interpol Office at 56 Am Grossen Wannsee, and what happened inside this elegant lakeside villa decided the fate of millions of Jews. Much time was spent haggling over the fate of 'half- and quarter-Jews', the *Mischlinge* with ties to Aryans. 'Mixing' was a topic that had frequently perplexed Günther and his friends, and Heydrich and his experts had no solution either. The fate of the *Mischlinge* was postponed until victory; as for Jewry itself, it would be 'appropriately dealt with'. Himmler had his Final Solution. Debórah Dwork and Robert Jan Van Pelt expertly summarized Himmler's accomplishment: 'No more local initiatives. The murder-machine would run with the assembly line efficiency he was so proud of. Many arms of the Nazi state participated in this process – and it led to a new entity in the history of the western world: the extermination camp.'[7]

In the Sportpalast on the ninth anniversary of the takeover of power, Hitler made a speech to a packed, baying crowd: 'For the first time the old Jewish law will now be applied: an eye for an eye, a tooth for a tooth . . . And the hour will come when the most evil world-enemy of all time will have played out its role, at least for a thousand years.'[8]

It was inside this infernal system, as Primo Levi described the Holocaust, that Dr Bruno Beger would now pursue his science.

At the end of the war, Beger was a prisoner of war in Italy. He was returned to Germany in 1948 and faced a much less strenuous 'de-nazification' than Schäfer had endured in Camp Moosburg; and Beger, too, received the coveted Category V exoneration and duly paid his twenty-five marks. No-one seemed to have connected him with the 'Bruno Beger' who had been referred to during the Doctors Trial in connection with a 'collection of Jewish skulls'. His name came up again in 1961 during the trial of Adolf Eichmann in Jerusalem, and this time Germany's lethargic prosecutors took note. According to the investigators who called on him in 1961, Beger was implicated in the murder, in a 'cruel and malicious manner', of 115 people who had been gassed at Natzweiler. During this *Vorontersuchung*, or pre-investigation, he denied any involvement at all. When confronted with his name on letters and documents, he said that he had made studies of these 115 men and women but knew nothing of their fate. Over the course of the next ten years, a steady accumulation of evidence stripped away his defence. In 1971, the Beger Trial began in Frankfurt. Author Michael Kater, the historian of the Ahnenerbe, provided evidence for the prosecution; Ernst Schäfer, Professor Ferdinand Clauss, Edmund Geer and Beger's wife Hildegart were witnesses for his defence. The trial judges faced a daunting mass of paper evidence and testimony which was ambiguous and often contradictory. Beger had been involved, but was he a murderer?

The complete truth can be told only by Beger himself, and for now and perhaps for ever he is silent. After two interviews, he finally agreed to answer my questions by letter. In the course of this very difficult correspondence Beger filled in many details, but he continued to deny that he knew about the fate of the people he had been accused of killing. The evidence implies that his denial cannot be believed, but there are, however, ambiguities and puzzles, and they deserve to be properly explored.

A story can have many beginnings. Here is one: a letter dated 2 February 1942 from Wolfram Sievers to Dr Rudolf Brandt.[9] It refers to a Professor Dr Hirt who has written a report 'concerning the acquisition of skulls of Jewish-Bolshevik Commissars'. 'Jewish-Bolshevik' has a precise meaning in Nazi ideology. In *Mein Kempf*, Hitler represented Bolshevism as a poisonous concoction of Jewish origin. According to him, the Russian Revolution was in reality a Jewish revolution inspired by a Jew, Karl Marx, and a warning that Germans must act against a 'Judeo-Bolshevik conspiracy'. During the onslaught on Russia this chimerical figure of the 'Jewish-Bolshevik Commissar' was used to sanction the genocidal slaughter of Jews wherever they were discovered.

Professor Dr Hirt, Sievers wrote, was 'stricken with pulmonary haemorrhages' but hoped to be able to resume work on two important tasks as soon as he recovered: one concerned a new research microscope; the second was the 'securing' of the Jewish-Bolshevik skulls. Hirt was sick, we now know, because he had been carrying out human experiments with mustard gas. He had contaminated himself as well as his subjects. When Himmler discovered that Hirt was ill, he had ordered Sievers to send fruit to the stricken doctor.

Sievers enclosed with his letter a now notorious document. It was a scientific research proposal that depended on murder, and it might have been written by Beger himself. This is unproven and denied by him. This is what it says: 'There exist extensive collections of skulls of almost all races and peoples. Of the Jewish race, however, only so very few specimens of skulls are at the disposal of science that a study of them does not permit precise conclusions. The war in the east now presents us with the opportunity to remedy this shortage. By procuring the skulls of the Jewish-Bolshevik Commissars, who personify a repulsive yet characteristic sub-humanity, we have the opportunity of obtaining tangible scientific evidence . . .' How was this to be done? A directive would be issued to the Wehrmacht to turn over alive all captured commissars, then a 'junior physician' would 'take a prescribed series of photographs and anthropological measurements' and record 'origin, date of birth, and other personal data of the prisoner'.

Read no further, and the scheme seems to be little different from the research carried out by Rudolf Virchow and his colleagues during the Herero war in the first decade of the twentieth century. These anthropologists, too, demanded that German Army officers procure native skulls from battlefields, though they stopped short of killing anyone. But in the next paragraph Hirt – or Beger – throws aside any vestige of scientific ethics: 'Following the subsequently induced death of the Jew, whose head must not be damaged, he [the junior physician] will separate the head from the torso and will forward it to its point of destination in a preserving fluid in a well-sealed tin container especially made for this purpose.' This eerily mimics Felix von Luschan's request that overseas volunteers use appropriate 'packaging' for anthropological specimens, making it more likely that this was written by Beger, who was educated as an anthropologist in Berlin, rather than

Hirt, who was an anatomist.[10] The skull, 'repulsive and subhuman' as it was, possessed great value for research on racial classification. Speculating about who wrote the notorious enclosure is really academic; both Hirt and Beger must at least have read the proposal and understood what was required.

SS Hauptsturmführer Professor Dr August Hirt was a cut above Dr Sigmund Rascher, who was despised by everyone except Himmler and his own wife. Hirt was a professor at Strasbourg University's medical school. Like Joseph Mengele, he had an impressive curriculum vitae: he was able to list twenty-seven research publications and chapters on micro-anatomy and fluorescence microscopy published between 1921 and 1940.[11] But he used his academic position to seize power and status within the SS, and thus to gain access to concentration camps. What had led Hirt to abandon medical ethics and tear up the Hippocratic doctrine?

Hirt was born in Mannheim, the son of an alcohol manufacturer and salesman. He volunteered for military service in the First World War and received injuries to his upper and lower jaws, which were so severely damaged that it was said he 'presented a terrifying appearance' for the rest of his life. This trauma might have led Hirt to take up medicine, and he did well at the Medical School in Heidelberg. He remained there, marrying and becoming an assistant professor in 1931. He was described as 'a good teacher . . . very charming . . . a great friend of the female gender . . .' Beger was also in Heidelberg at this time and might well have met Hirt then.

There is now a surprising twist in the story. Hirt began a close and productive association with Dr Philipp Ellinger, a much admired researcher and a Jew. Both men shared a passion for urinary function and the delicate internal world of the kidneys. Ellinger and Hirt were innovative and productive collaborators and together they took out an international patent on a new type of fluorescence microscope. For its time, their invention was a small miracle. Made by Zeiss/Jena, it used dyes to track the flow of blood inside organs like the kidneys and liver, and it was widely used in the 1930s. In 1932, Ellinger was promoted to director of the Pharmacology Institute in Dusseldorf. But it was a position he did not enjoy for very long.

In 1933, everything changed. Hirt, like many other 'Aryan' medical professionals, joined the SS (#100414), alienating one friend who said that Hirt 'suddenly decided to be a Nazi and wear a Brown Shirt! This ended my relationship with him . . . He had been always quite compulsive and a little erratic in his ideas, but from that moment on one could not discuss politics with him anymore . . .'[12] It is evident that Hirt was an enthusiast: he had also joined the NSDAP itself (#4012784) and, more surprisingly, was an SA stormtrooper adjutant. There was no possibility that he could continue working with a Jew, and he callously made sure that his friend Ellinger lost his job. Now Hirt seized the chance to claim all credit for the microscope and turned Ellinger, who had fled to England, into a non-person.

Around this time he must have shifted his allegiances from brown to black, from the SA to Himmler's SS. Like many doctors, Hirt soon benefited. In 1936 he became Director of Anatomy at Greifswald University, an appointment supported by a reference dated 16 July 1936 and signed 'A. Hitler and Hermann Göring, Berchtesgaden'. In 1938 he moved on to the Frankfurt University Medical School, despite spending many hours every week on manoeuvres with the Army Medical Corps. According to Michael Kater, doctors with military experience generally found it much easier to contemplate medical experiments with living subjects.[13] It's likely that in 1937 he encountered Bruno Beger again, who was then working with the SS RuSHA; both had some involvement with the study of the remains of Heinrich I in Quedlinburg Cathedral.

After the onslaught on Poland in 1939 Hirt became a military physician in a panzer unit. In Frankfurt, his assistant Josef Wimmer worked long, solitary hours doing fresh experiments with the celebrated microscope. Articles were published, as if written by Hirt and Wimmer together. Then in 1941 Hirt was appointed to a new job at Strasbourg University. At the date of its foundation, Strasbourg was French, but it had become a German university in 1872 after the Franco-Prussian War. In 1919 it was French again, then German once more after 1939, when its French faculty fled to Clermont-Ferrand. Now Strasbourg was the Reichsuniversität Strassburg, reorganized along SS lines. At the formal opening of the new university in November 1941, Hirt was introduced to Sievers by Bernhard Rust, the education minister. Both Sievers and Himmler's assistant Brandt became Hirt admirers. They reported back to Himmler, who requested copies of research papers and, naturally, a full Hirt genealogy. He liked everything about this ambitious doctor.

Hirt, predictably, grabbed every opportunity offered by Himmler's patronage. He transferred his military activities to the Waffen-SS and joined Himmler's personal staff, thus becoming one of the most powerful researchers in the German scientific establishment. At Strasbourg, Hirt's Section H had a unique advantage: it had access through the SS to the nearby Natzweiler/Struthof concentration camp. Medical experiments were already taking place there under Professors Eugen Haagen and Otto Bickenbach. Hirt used his SS clout to take over. Now he had power, a big budget and a large staff, all thanks to the Reichsführer.

Over dinner at the opening of the university in November, it is likely that Hirt discussed with Sievers the desirability of having a collection of skeletal materials. There is no doubt that both men would have had Natzweiler and its resources in mind.

Just after the New Year in 1942, Sievers sent a letter marked SECRET to Hirt: 'With regard to your anthropological research work, I can already today inform you that the Reichsführer-SS would then give you an opportunity to conduct experiments of any kind and which might aid you in your research work, on prisoners and real criminals who would never be released anyhow and on persons scheduled for execution.' It was this letter that provoked someone to write the research proposal about the 'Jewish-Bolshevik Commissars'.

But who? Beger's case in Frankfurt rested on denying knowledge of the fate of the prisoners after he had measured them. If he wrote the proposal to procure the skulls of 'Jewish-Bolshevik Commissars', or co-authored it with Hirt, then he has no case at all: he was involved with a murderous plot from the start. The two men had known each other since university, and both were on Himmler's personal staff. Both, too, were involved with the Ahnenerbe. It is difficult to believe that Hirt, conspiring with Sievers, kept Beger ignorant of the details of the plan. Would Beger, as a friend of Hirt and a subordinate of Sievers, not have heard what his friend was up to? Besides, Beger was an anthropologist and Hirt an anatomist, and Sievers' letter refers to 'your anthropological research work'. The phrase suggests that Beger was already involved. The enclosure itself is full of the language of metrical analysis, suggesting his hand.

In July 1942 Himmler appears to have developed his plans further. A memo from Brandt to Sievers authorized the creation of the Institut für Wehrissenschaftliche Zweckforschung (Institute for Practical Military Scientific Research). This would be based in Dachau and at Strasbourg and would be devoted to research on humans. A few months later, we have the first hard evidence of Beger's involvement. Sievers wrote to Beger and, according to court records, discussed an *anthropological* collection. Even if Beger had not written the 'Jewish-Bolshevik Commissars' document, it should have been obvious that Dr August Hirt was not interested in face masks and numbers. He wanted bodies.

CHAPTER SIXTEEN

THE SAVAGE MIND

'The trouble with Eichmann was precisely that so many were like him, and that the many were neither perverted nor sadistic, that they were, and still are, terribly and terrifyingly normal . . . this new type of criminal . . . commits his crimes under circumstances that make it well nigh impossible for him to know or to feel that he is doing wrong . . .'

– Hannah Arendt, *Eichmann in Jerusalem*

Auschwitz was the axis of the Nazi empire of killing. It was an immense factory of death, an archipelago of thirty-nine separate camps grouped into four main blocks. Auschwitz I was the administrative centre; Auschwitz II was the extermination camp and boasted four crematoria with eight gas chambers and forty-six ovens which could accommodate more than four thousand corpses a day; Auschwitz III was also known as Buna-Monovitz, referring to its 'Buna' rubber plant (never completed); Auschwitz IV supplied Buna-Monovitz's insatiable appetite for slaves. It was a place of exploitation and death and contained a diverse population of inmates dominated by up to twelve thousand Jews. Work itself was exterminatory. According to Rudolf Vrba, who escaped in 1944 to tell the world what was happening, this was the 'most isolated spot in Europe'.[1]

Himmler visited the camp on a hot day in July 1942. He was greeted by the camp orchestra playing the 'Triumphal March' from Verdi's *Aida*, then he strolled about chatting with Rudolf Höss, the camp commandant, with, in Vrba's words, 'grace and easy charm'. He smiled and laughed as if he were at an English garden party. Then he 'very carefully observed the whole process of annihilation . . . He did not complain about anything.' On that hot day in July, Himmler ordered that 'Eichmann's programme will continue and will be accelerated every month from now on. See to it that you move ahead with the completion of Birkenau. The gypsies are to be exterminated. You will exterminate the Jews who are unable to work.'[2] On 26 September Höss was told that from that day on the property of people arriving at the camp was to be shipped to SS headquarters. Shoes and clothes would be sent to the Ethnic German Liaison Office for distribution to resettled Germans; any German money would be deposited in an SS bank account. Prior to this date property had been labelled and stored; now it was explicitly acknowledged that it would never be reclaimed.[3]

As Himmler was strolling around his camp, Sievers and Hirt were making plans to send Bruno Beger there to begin selecting suitable subjects for their collection. Sievers and Hirt both understood that this would involve killing the selected individuals – this is explicit in the notorious 'enclosure' – but how much did Beger know about his colleagues' intentions?

Beger was now splitting his time between Schäfer's institute in Munich and the Ahnenerbe headquarters in Dahlem, the Berlin suburb whose leafy streets and academic buildings were said to resemble Bloomsbury or Hampstead. One day that summer Wolfram Sievers ordered him to contact Dr Hirt in Strasbourg and arrange to visit him at the university to start making practical arrangements. All parties clearly expected the project to be completed that year. Beger appears to have hesitated. In September, Hirt wrote to Beger with some impatience saying that he was 'expecting you here in Strasbourg'. Beger did not receive the letter before the proposed meeting time – he was discussing Tibetan stones with a geologist called Putzer – so he telephoned Hirt instead. During this conversation he agreed to carry out the examinations. In a memo to Sievers, Hirt said this: 'I spoke [to Beger] about our other [*anderen*] plan . . . and *it should be fine* [my italics].' He could have been referring to a plan other than the skull-collecting – namely, the second proposal in the original Sievers letter – *or* it could mean that Beger now knew that more than measurement and analysis would be involved. Certainly by now Hirt and Sievers were referring to their murderous scheme as '*Auftrag Beger*' – Project Beger. Was Beger completely in the know, or were his less than scrupulous colleagues setting up a patsy?

On 3 October 1942 Beger discovered that there was a typhus epidemic raging at Auschwitz and immediately got in touch with Sievers. Not only would Beger and his family be at risk, but there was a serious danger of bringing the disease back into Germany. *Auftrag Beger* was postponed until November 1943. In his correspondence, Beger refers only to an 'investigation' – *Untersuchung*. A week later there was another flurry of correspondence, this time between Sievers and Himmler's assistant Brandt. Sievers reminded Brandt of the agreement to support Hirt's research and said that he and Hirt in Strasbourg were ready to receive *150 skeletons* of Jews from Auschwitz. He complained that the camp authorities were not being co-operative and asked Brandt to intervene. Brandt obliged. On

6 November he wrote to Adolf Eichmann, who was chief of the Jewish Office of the Gestapo, and Obergruppenführer Oswald Pohl, who was in charge of the economic management of the camps.[4] Brandt informed Eichmann that Hirt must be 'furnished with everything he needs for his research work. By order of the Reichsführer-SS, therefore, I ask you to make possible the establishment of the planned collection . . .' This was no 'investigation'.

Typhus epidemics were in fact frequent occurrences at Auschwitz; the camp was overcrowded, hygiene was non-existent, and inmates were ill fed and ill treated. Was Beger therefore using the news he had received about the epidemic to delay *Auftrag Beger*? Was he having second thoughts? The evidence for this comes from testimony given at the 1971 trial by Ludwig Ferdinand Clauss, who had been Beger's professor in the 1930s. According to Clauss, Beger came to him in early 1943 and revealed that he was increasingly unhappy about his task. Clauss was, of course, appearing on Beger's behalf and would naturally want to mitigate his friend's guilt, but there is other evidence that adds weight to Clauss's story.

Clauss was an unusual man.[5] Christened Götz Brandeck, he had been a childhood friend of Hans Günther and a student of the philosopher Edmund Husserl in Freiburg, where he changed his name. During the war Clauss had been a navy cadet but was discharged for being 'inclined to contradictions'. It was an apt description. Like his friend Günther, he had a passion for all things Nordic, and both men shared an ardent belief in Nordic pre-eminence, but for Clauss superiority was embodied in the 'Race Soul', not in the measurable body. Both men, however, agreed that an unbridgeable chasm divided Aryans from lesser races, whether the differences were defined by inner or outer qualities. But Clauss's convictions about race barriers were challenged in his private life. After his wife deserted him for a close friend, Husserl introduced the stricken Clauss to another of his students, Margarete Landé. The Landé family were Jewish converts but Margarete would become indispensable to Clauss.

In the mid-1920s Clauss left Germany and went in search of the Race Soul. Instead of heading north, he travelled to Palestine and rented a house in Jerusalem. The culture and people of the Middle East would fascinate Clauss all his life. He began by learning Arabic and studying the farmers and settled Bedouin in the area around Hebron, where Jews and Arabs worshipped uneasily together at the Tomb of Abraham, the ancestral father of both peoples. Clauss's plan was to cross into Jordan and spend time studying the great desert tribes, but although he was heavily disguised he was repeatedly turned back. He made many friends among the Arabs in Jerusalem and became known as the 'German Sheikh'. As a result, he was eventually given permission to cross the desert to Amman, where he was able to settle down in the camp of a powerful Bedouin tribe. But Clauss faced another seemingly intractable difficulty: the harem was closed, and without access to the women of the camp his work would be incomplete. It was Margarete Landé who gave Clauss a solution to this problem.

Landé was by now a committed Zionist and wanted to join one of the new Jewish settlements in Palestine to test her beliefs. When Clauss discovered this, he made a proposal: he would support her trip if she could help him win over the Arab women. So Landé arrived, with just a three-month tourist visa, and went underground. She opened a kindergarten for Jewish children but whenever possible joined Clauss in the desert. She spent long periods inside the women's tents, talking, learning and earning Clauss's lifelong gratitude. It is ironic that as Landé deepened her friendships in the desert camps, her passion for Zionism declined. Clauss himself became a Muslim.

In April 1931, their work in the desert completed, they returned to Germany, together.

For the next five years Clauss and Landé laboured on the material they had gathered in the Middle East. It was an increasingly warm partnership, but it did not stop Clauss joining the Nazi Party in 1933 and declaring, 'Any foreign blood line disrupts our world-form. We can respect the other, as any creation of the Almighty – but they can never be a part of us. The other is foreign to us . . .' Clauss would try to explain away his party membership after the war by saying that he wanted to prevent race theory being misused. But he was as devoted as Günther was to the cause of Nazi race theory. In a letter sent directly to Hitler, he'd pleaded for a better salary on the grounds that his academic work was vital to the Third Reich.

In 1936, Beger became Clauss's student, and in the months before his departure for Tibet he spent many days at Clauss's country home in Rüthnick. A warm friendship developed between the young man and his new professor. As Beger was getting to know him, Clauss was sparring acrimoniously with Günther, and Beger has said that he began to abandon Günther's ideas and methods at this time.[6] Perhaps, but his work when he travelled to Tibet shortly afterwards was, of course, anthropometric in technique and designed to prove Günther's theories about the expansion of Nordic peoples into central Asia. After his return from Tibet he would meet Clauss again in very different circumstances.

While Beger was in Tibet, Clauss had married again. His new wife was Mechthilde von Wuchnow, and their relationship turned as sour as his first had been. There was a difference in temperament and careers, and Clauss's continuing and intense relationship with Margarete Landé caused bitter arguments. Worse was to come. Frau Clauss knew all about Landé's family tree, and after the pogroms of November 1938 she realized that the risks for both Clauss and Landé were very high indeed. Their relationship was intimate and professional, and secret. In 1939 Mechthilde sued for divorce, and she used what she had discovered about Landé to blackmail and harass Clauss. In 1940 a new law was passed that forbade contacts between Aryan Germans and Jews, and Mechthilde reported her husband to an academic rival, Professor Walther Gross. This was bad news. Gross, yet another doctor, was head of the RPA, the Nazi Party Office for Racial Purity (Rassenpolitisches Amt der NSDAP). He was a fanatical anti-Semite and was disgusted by Clauss's association with Landé. Gross publicly accused Clauss of betraying the NSDAP. In his defence, Clauss used all the twisted logic of Nazi race theory: 'I am interested in Jewry as a physician is interested in disease. I set an anti-bacillus against a bacillus. Only by being part of Jewry can one track down every last Jew. I cannot live with Jews – that is too much to expect of me . . . Miss Landé finds it difficult but she can do it . . . If I give her up I will need someone else and I will be in the same situation as before. I must ask the Party, therefore, to allow me to continue to employ her under these conditions . . .' This didn't convince Gross, who remained a formidable and tenacious enemy.

Mechthilde, in the meantime, continued to barrage the Nazi police with poison letters. She addressed some to a student of her husband's who she knew was an officer in the SS, Bruno Beger. She even telephoned him to deliver one venomous tirade. Beger was confused and decided to visit Clauss in Rüthnick. Clauss realized this was an important opportunity. If he could get Beger on his side, he might stand a chance of being reinstated in the party. He believed Beger was an ardent and loyal SS officer, but he also hoped that his former student would honour the qualities of courage, honour and camaraderie that both believed were the unique attributes of the Nordic race.

So Clauss took Beger for a long walk in the forest that surrounded his house and appealed to the nobility of friendship. Beger was, he hoped, a friend, and he described the special comradeship that he and Margarete had forged during their desert adventures. Beger admired Clauss and Landé's work; he despised 'table anthropologists' who never got out into the field. Clauss told him, 'The desert expects it of a man to protect anyone who seeks his help, irrespective of any danger this might involve him in . . .'

All this won Beger over, and he agreed to help Clauss and to protect Landé. He turned to a man called Egon Landling who was an officer in the SD (Sicherheitsdienst), the Nazi intelligence and security body. Beger knew that he had read and admired Clauss's books. It is now known that Landling was in the German resistance, warning conspirators of planned arrests and reporting on conditions in prisons, but Beger seems not to have known this. Between them they hatched up a scheme to get Clauss inside the SS itself.

Events now moved rapidly. In 1941, Landé was arrested for the first time and held in Potsdam, where she was interrogated about her relationship with Clauss. Clauss himself was in Rome, but he returned as soon as he heard that Landé was in prison. With Beger's and Landling's help, he concocted a story that Margarete's mother had confessed on her death bed that she had been having an affair with a Prussian officer and that this man was Margarete's father, which made her a 'half-Jew'. Beger himself travelled to Potsdam, met the prison governor – who turned out to be yet another enthusiast for Clauss's work – and procured Landé's release. This incensed Gross, and the RPA brought in Clauss, Landé and Beger for questioning. Then, in 1942, Clauss's teaching permit was withdrawn and he was summoned before a party court (*Oberstes Parteigericht*) in the Brown House in Munich. For having had 'intimate relations' with a Jew, Clauss was expelled from the NSDAP. Both he and Landé were now in a very vulnerable position indeed.

Beger now made a radical proposal to the SS, no doubt relying on his own high standing as an officer in Himmler's personal staff. In a letter addressed to the Reichsführer, he praised Clauss's work and urged that 'the war experience should also be made available for race studies', and that Clauss should be involved in a study of 'races in conflict'. Beger's adroit appeal to Himmler's intellectual snobbery worked perfectly, and Clauss was soon recruited by the Waffen-SS.

But for Margarete Landé there was only danger and acute insecurity. Although she had a brother in the United States, by 1942 emigration was no longer possible: Germany's borders were closed and the United States had filled its quotas. So Clauss decided to send his research assistant underground – literally. One moonless night, he emerged from the back door of his house and checked to make sure he was not being watched. He found a spade and walked into the woods behind his home. Then he began to dig, stopping only when it became light. He returned again the following night, and the night after that. When he had excavated deep enough, he brought a hammer, nails and planks and built a primitive shelter. He cut steps down to a hidden door, then piled branches and shrubs over the roof. This would be Margarete's secret home for the next three years.

Beger remembers that in the autumn of 1942 he arrived late at Rüthnick Station and was forced to walk the five miles to Clauss's home. As he approached, he noticed a light in the trees. He told Clauss, who became very alarmed. He took Beger into the woods and showed him the shelter. They went downstairs. A window was open, and a lamp was close by, which Clauss turned down. For furniture there was only a bed – and it had just been used. 'So this was where Landé sometimes slept,' Beger commented. 'I realized she had gone out for some fresh air behind the house. I pretended to know nothing. This was surely the most agreeable way to behave with my host, especially since there were new searches for her again and again.'[7]

When Beger, that same year, had told Clauss about his planned visit to Auschwitz, Clauss had made an astonishing suggestion. Could Beger find out more about the conditions in the camp? Perhaps Landé would be safer there, interned freely of her own accord, while there was a war on? Clauss's ignorance is astounding, and Beger must have made it clear that Margarete would certainly not be safe. It might have been at this moment that Beger confided in Clauss that he felt uneasy about his work.

I have told this story at some length not because it in any way exonerates Beger. Quite the contrary: knowing that Beger assisted these two individuals reinforces the horror of what he was about to do for the Ahnenerbe and for his other friend Dr Hirt. It resembles the psychological splitting that American psychologist Robert Jay Lifton saw as the definitive psychic state of the Nazi doctors he investigated. The group, the race, is easier to hold in contempt than the individual. A Jew can be a friend, but Jews must be annihilated.

Whatever he said to his friend that evening in Rüthnick, by the spring of 1943 *Auftrag Beger* was once more moving forward. On 5 April Sievers wrote to Beger telling him that the typhus epidemic had been contained and Auschwitz was now accessible, and that Eichmann had informed him that there was 'suitable material' available in the camp. By this he must have meant prisoners from the Russian front. Beger requested that his colleagues SS anthropologists Dr Hans Fleischacker[8] and Dr Rübel be released so that they could assist him when they arrived in the camp. He also arranged for Willi Gabel, who was making heads from the casts Beger had taken in Tibet, to join the team.

In documents written before the end of June 1943, Hirt and Sievers continue to refer to a '*Skelletssammlung*' – a skeletal collection – although Beger is still using the word '*Untersuchung*' – investigation. A person cannot give up his skeleton for research and still remain alive; Dr Hirt's plan depended on murder. It is very hard to believe that Beger was still not aware of this – unless his colleagues had planned a particularly elaborate deception. Or in his mind, did he split his research from their need for a skeletal collection? Another important point also emerges. By including Gabel, Beger made it clear that Schäfer's Sven Hedin Institute was also involved. As will become clear, the Institute hoped to benefit from Beger's 'special anthropological mission' to Auschwitz.

While Clauss had been building his underground hideout, Josef Kramer, the Natzweiler camp commandant, had also been busy with construction work. He had discovered that there was an airtight storage building in the camp, and after a discussion with Dr Hirt he had converted it into a gas chamber. He was ready to play his part in 'Project Beger'. He revealed at his trial, 'When I went to . . . where Hirt was working, he told me that he had been informed of a convoy of Auschwitz prisoners bound for Struthof. He made it clear to me that these people were to be executed in the Struthof gas chamber by means of asphyxiating gases, and that their corpses were to be taken to the Institute of Anatomy and put at his disposal . . . The professor indicated to me the approximate dose I should use to personally asphyxiate the prisoners . . .'

On 12 March 1943, a transport of nearly a thousand Jews began a one-way journey from Berlin, locked in cattle trucks with neither food nor water. Their destination was Auschwitz. Their names can still be read in the record '36. Osttransport', and we know that one of them was forty-two-year-old Menachem Taffel who had lived at 9 Elsässerstrasse in Berlin.

As well as Menachem, there were 620 women and children and 343 men in the trucks that pulled out of Putlitzstrasse Station north of Berlin. For hours, the train rolled on eastwards. Some tried to fathom where they were being taken by peering through gaps in the wagons. They steamed through the Spree Forest, on past Lausitz, Reichenbach and Breslau. The train stopped frequently, and rumours spread that everyone was going to be killed during one of these halts. The atmosphere inside the cattle truck was suffocating and pestilential. There was no privacy. Pails splashed and spilt over and the floor was awash with piss and shit. Then it grew dark outside. Hours later, the train shuddered and squealed to a halt for the last time. The doors were pulled open with a crash and men barked orders in German. When Menachem staggered out, he was blinded by spotlights and giant reflectors. There were many soldiers wearing the double thunderbolt insignia, and he realized he was in the claws of the SS. Under the blazing lamps, 147 women were selected for labour and the others were immediately led away and gassed. Out of 343 men, 218 were selected for work, identified by numbers 107772 to 107989. Some of them would soon be meeting Dr Bruno Beger.

On 6 June, Beger began his own more comfortable journey from Berlin–Dahlem to Auschwitz. From Berlin, he took a train to Breslau-Kattowitz, where he changed onto the Auschwitz line itself, although not the one used for transports. An hour later Beger disembarked at Auschwitz Station. He registered with the 'Haus der Waffen-SS', an attractive establishment on the east side of the station square, where he met Fleischacker and Rübel. That evening they tucked into the hotel's celebrated Wiener Schnitzel, and after coffee and brandy dropped by the casino for off-duty SS men. The following morning, the three SS officers left their lodgings and were driven to the back entrance of the camp, which was next to Crematorium 1. After a meeting with Rudolf Höss, the commandant, to smooth out last-minute details, Beger and his colleagues proceeded to Block 28 and began work.

There is convincing evidence that Beger was shocked by conditions in the camp. As Robert Jan Van Pelt and Debórah Dwork have documented,[9] the design of the camp was race theory as architecture. To sleep, sit and store possessions, each prisoner was provided with a space the size of a coffin. Tadeusz Borowski was in Auschwitz in 1943. He survived, and remembered that 'one of the ugliest sights to a man is that of another man sleeping on his tiny portion of the bunk, of the space which he must occupy, because he has a body – a body that has been exploited to the utmost: with a number tattooed on it to save on dog tags, with just enough sleep at night to work during the day, and just enough time to eat. And just enough food so it will not die wastefully . . .' The latrines were an 'excremental assault', stripping away any last scrap of self-worth. 'There was one latrine for thirty to thirty-two thousand women,' Gisella Perl recalled; 'we could rarely wait until our turn came, and soiled our ragged clothes, which never came off our bodies, thus adding to the horror of our existence by the terrible smell that surrounded us like a cloud'. This was Beger's human laboratory. The bodies here possessed a unique advantage: there was no fat to get in the way of a pair of callipers.

Willi Gabel remembered walking through the camp with Beger looking for appropriate subjects. Did both men know that as their gaze alighted on this man or that woman they were sentencing him or her to death? This 'scientific selection' was as much about death as the 'selections' being made when the trains pulled in and discharged their human cargo. In Munich, Gabel had been making full-size 'Tibetans' for Schäfer's Institute for Central Asian Research, and a splendid new bust of Mozart; Beger had said it would be good for him to see some 'real

Asians' after spending so much time with his face masks. Gabel had understood that their mission was indeed to find people from central Asia – 'Mongoloids', in race terminology. Auschwitz had many prisoners from every region of the Soviet Union, but as they walked through the seething mass of inmates, Gabel later recalled being surprised that Beger chose so many Jews. Beger claimed later that he had been disappointed to find so few central Asian specimens, only six or eight Asiatic types, and had been forced to choose from what was available.

After the selections had been made, the prisoners were brought to an improvised laboratory where their heads were measured and photographed. Apparently, Beger was developing a new data collection method for the Caucasus Expedition. In a letter he later sent to Rudolf Höss, he thanked our 'especially skilful' prisoners who had assisted the team, among them Adolf Laatsch #112118 and Josef Weber #15386, a Polish medical student. The fact that only cranial measurements were taken must have reflected the original proposal to acquire the 'skulls of Jewish-Bolshevik Commissars'.

The scientists' visit was remembered by a camp survivor called Hermann Reineck. He described seeing up to 150 prisoners gathered in front of Block 28. Then Beger's party arrived accompanied by several SS officers in uniform. They began measuring heads with circular instruments. Reineck said that 'he could not imagine why this was done'. He noticed a prisoner assisting by taking the names of the prisoners being measured.

Beger stayed working in Auschwitz for another eight days, then he left for Berlin alone, leaving his colleagues behind to complete the work. On 21 June Sievers sent a letter to Eichmann marked TOP SECRET to inform him that 'the co-worker in this office [Ahnenerbe, Institute for Military

Scientific Research] who was charged with the execution of the above mentioned special task, SS Hauptsturmführer Dr. Bruno Beger, ended his work in the Auschwitz concentration camp on 15 June 1943 because of the existing danger of infectious diseases'. Why, then, did Beger leave Fleischacker and Rübel at Auschwitz? Surely they were no less at risk from typhus? It seems a very callous calculation. Beger wrote to Schäfer in Munich soon afterwards. He began by telling his friend that he would not describe his experiences in a letter but would telephone instead. There is, of course, no record of what Beger said, but Schäfer replied on 24 June: 'it would be good if you could finish your work as fast as possible . . . I was happy about your letter from the beginning of June because I have thought a lot about you, especially because the assignment was not pleasant . . .' 'Not pleasant'! It was much less 'pleasant' for the camp inmates, and perhaps for Beger's colleagues who were still in the camp. Schäfer's concern is ameliorated by the good news, however: 'It's good that you have acquired a Mongoloid type for us.' This is a quite remarkable statement from Schäfer, completely in line with his interest in acquiring skulls in Tibet; it implies that Beger would have some macabre gifts to deliver to Schloss Mittersill.

And just *how* 'unpleasant' is made abundantly clear in Sievers' next letter. The subject is now unambiguous: 'Assembling of a Skeleton Collection'. It is copied to Hirt and to Beger, who, even if he had so far ignored every other indication that the prisoners would be murdered, could not now have mistaken the implications. 'A total of 115 persons were worked on,' Sievers wrote, '79 of them were Jews, 2 Poles, 4 Asiatics, and 30 Jewesses. At present these prisoners . . . are in quarantine. For further processing of the selected persons an immediate transfer to Natzweiler concentration camp is now imperative; this must be accelerated in view of the danger of infectious diseases in Auschwitz …' Sievers then reveals the real fate of the 'persons': 'one must provide for the accommodation of the 30 women in the Natzweiler camp for a short period'. Beger could not have misunderstood the import of that chilling phrase 'for a short period'. We can now be certain that from the moment he received Sievers' letter, Beger knew what was going to happen to the prisoners he had selected. He eventually confessed during his trial that he had indeed discovered the fate of the prisoners, but only when it was too late to do anything about it. Why, then, did he not cease his involvement?

As he measured their heads, did he meet their eyes?

Despite the urgency of Sievers' letter to Eichmann, the prisoners left Auschwitz for Natzweiler on 30 July. Himmler's second in command, Obergruppenführer Karl Wolff, sent telegrams to Hirt and Beger (who was again in Rüthnick with Clauss) informing them that the transport was on its way. Hirt was already busy expanding the facilities at the Anatomical Institute.

The prisoners arrived on 2 August. Another inmate, Jean Lemberger, watched them come in. They wore patched 'zebra' clothing with yellow stars and were very pale. They were taken first to Hut 10. Lemberger discovered that they were not assigned to any of the work gangs and asked a kapo (a prisoner coerced into assisting the SS guards) whether he could be transferred. The kapo told him that this would be 'sheer folly'. One morning, Lemberger recalled, all the people in Block 10 had disappeared.

During his trial in July 1945, camp commandant Josef Kramer straightforwardly told his interrogator Major Jadin what happened next:

> So at the beginning of August 1943, I received the 80 prisoners to be killed by means of the gases given to me by Hirt, and I

> started with a first group of about fifteen women, taken to the gas chamber one evening, at about 9 o'clock, in a delivery van [the gas chamber was a few kilometres from the camp]. I told these women that they were going into a disinfection room, without letting them know that they were going to be asphyxiated. Assisted by several SS men I had them take off all their clothes and pushed them into the gas chamber once they were completely nude. As soon as I locked the door they started to scream. Once the door was closed, I placed a fixed quantity of the salts in a funnel attached below and to the right of the peep-hole . . . I noted that the women continued to breathe for about half a minute, and then fell to the ground . . .[10]

Apparently one of the men resisted and was shot. His body was rejected and burnt in the camp crematorium. Kramer added: 'I do not know what Hirt was going to do with the corpses of these prisoners . . . I did not think it appropriate to ask him . . . I felt no emotion while accomplishing these tasks because I had received an order to execute the 80 internees . . . That is simply how I was brought up.'

According to a witness at the Anatomical Institute, Pierre Henripierre, the bodies were brought to Hirt in three trucks in the early morning. They were still warm. The men were castrated and the bodies injected with a preservative and then placed in six vats containing diluted ethanol. Henripierre secretly copied the numbers on their arms onto a piece of paper, which he hid. Hirt had said to him, 'Pierre, if you can't keep your trap shut, you'll be one of them . . .'

Hirt never made use of the bodies. It is not known why.[11]

At the beginning of August, as Kramer was carrying out his task, there was a flurry of telegrams requesting Beger to proceed to Natzweiler. 'Beger has not arrived yet,' Hirt telegramed Wolff on the 5th, then Wolff sent a message to Beger saying that Hirt expected to see him 'very soon'. On 7 August, at 8.45 a.m., Beger caught a train at Rüthnick Station and travelled first to Berlin–Dahlem and then across Germany to Alsace. En route he stopped in Erfurt to visit his brother Horst, who was then in a Wehrmacht prison. We know that Beger travelled to Natzweiler, and why, because he submitted *eine Reisekostenabrechnung*, a travel expense report, for the journey. In this banal document he explained the purpose of the journey as a *Sonderauftrag*, or 'special task', at Natzweiler involving making X-rays and analysing blood groups. Writing to the SS in Berlin from the Schloss Mittersill in October, he complained that he had not yet been compensated for '*meine Reise nach Natzweiler*' – my journey to Natzweiler. Although he now denies this, there is evidence that Beger X-rayed and blood-typed the prisoners sent from Auschwitz and killed at Natzweiler.

Since the end of the war there have been persistent rumours that 'heads' from Auschwitz prisoners found their way to Schäfer's institute. So many documents have been destroyed that discovering the truth is extremely difficult, but there are disturbing scraps of evidence that implicate Schäfer and his institute. In May 1943 an SS officer wrote to Beger, 'What exactly is happening with the Jewish heads? They are lying around and taking up valuable space . . . In my opinion, the most reasonable course of action is to send them to Strasbourg . . .' This vile complaint makes it clear that there were body parts somewhere other than in Hirt's anatomy department. Later a secretary at the castle remembered 'two collections'; she recalled 'administrative goings on' about a collection of skeletons and a collection of heads.[12] So it seems very likely that Beger made two collections at Auschwitz, one for Dr Hirt and another for the Sven Hedin Institute. We know that he described one of his subjects to Schäfer: 'A tall healthy child of nature who could have been a Tibetan. His manner of speaking, his movements and the way he introduced himself were simply ravishing, in a word: from the Asian heartland.' Beger's catch must have sounded eminently collectible – and, it seems, he was.

After the war there were persistent rumours that the Red Army had uncovered the dead bodies of Tibetans in the rubble of Berlin. In one version of the story, they were found in Hitler's bunker. The fate of Beger's 'ravishing' child of nature is the infinitely more shocking truth.

CHAPTER SEVENTEEN

RETRIBUTION

'Even today I find it hard to understand the Germans. Is This A Man? *had the echo in Germany I had hoped for, but I do believe it came from the very Germans who least needed to read it. The innocent, not the guilty, repent . . .'*

– Primo Levi, in a letter written in November 1966

The Schloss Mittersill was a bustling hive of activity throughout 1943 and until the end of the war. Schäfer hunted down a large staff of Tibet experts, gave lectures and put on exhibitions featuring Beger's Tibetan face masks and a giant model of the Potala Palace. Some time after his return from Auschwitz, Bruno Beger finally delivered a paper on the races of Tibet at the institute. Read today, it is barely comprehensible. He makes only a half-hearted attempt to link some Tibetan groups to an older 'Europid' group – he always avoided using terms like 'Aryan' or 'Nordic' even though this is precisely what he meant. This feeble paper was the last anyone would ever hear of Beger's quest to find traces of the Nordic race in the Himalayas.

As this imaginary Reich contracted, so too did Hitler's. The Russian campaign was a catastrophe, and the Wehrmacht reeled back as Stalin's forces recovered and sought revenge. British and American armies swept through North Africa and then across the Mediterranean. Allied bombing of German cities was relentless. At the beginning of 1943, Josef Goebbels had invited a representative German audience to the Sportspalast; it included, according to Michael Burleigh, workers, intellectuals and scientists, the blind, the halt and the lame. Goebbels screamed for total war and the applause lasted for twenty minutes after he sat down. At the climax of his harangue he had bellowed, 'Germany has no intention of bowing to this threat [of the Jews], but means to counter it in time and if necessary with the most complete and radical exter— (corrects himself) elimination of Jewry.'[1]

As the Thousand Year Reich collapsed, Goebbels' request was heeded and the SS was unrelenting in its prosecution of Himmler's race war. Impending military defeat spurred on the destruction of life and there were vicious spasms of killing. In Operation Harvest Festival in November 1943, forty-three thousand Jews were shot in specially constructed zigzag trenches. In 1944, Hungary's Jews were exterminated. And as the edges of the Reich frayed and collapsed, hundreds of thousands of Jews died on 'death marches' as the SS moved them hither and thither from camp to camp. Still more were killed, their remains clumsily obliterated as the Germans struggled to conceal the enormity of what they had done. Himmler remarked, 'All in all . . . we can say that we have carried out this most difficult of tasks in a spirit of love for our people.' For Bruno Beger, and for his mentor Ludwig Ferdinand Clauss, defeat did not mean they had to give up scientific enquiry. They now began investigating how different races behaved in war. And the disintegrating Reich offered yet another richly endowed human laboratory: the Waffen-SS itself.

In the autumn of 1944 Clauss and Beger were drafted into the Waffen-SS regiment the 13th Handschar.[2] Their destination was Yugoslavia. Like the other regiments the two anthropologists had fought with, the Handschar was made up almost entirely of non-Germans; one of their comrades-in-arms was the future leader of Bosnia-Herzegovina, Alija Izetbegovic.[3] Beger and Clauss now found themselves in one of the dirtiest corners of the disintegrating Reich, a hellish combustion of overlapping conflicts and tribal blood feuds. The Nazis had installed the fascist Ante Pavelic as Croatian dictator in 1941, and over the next four years his repellent regime killed hundreds of thousands of Jews, Roma and Serbs. In this Balkan cauldron of hate, Croatian fascists and chetniks butchered Bosnian Muslims. At the same time, Pavelic rallied Islamic fundamentalists to his side, including Hajj Amin al-Husseini, the Mufti of Jerusalem, who spent the war spreading anti-Semitic poison from his luxury suite in the Hotel Adlon in Berlin.[4] Some twenty thousand Muslims fought with the Handschar; Himmler had relaxed many of the usual SS regulations to encourage recruitment. The regiment has been linked to some of the worst atrocities of the war, although it is fair to emphasize that most of these took place when German officers were not present. By 1944, however, Beger and Clauss realized that the Handschar was disintegrating. There were mass desertions to Tito's partisans and the Reich itself was now in military free-fall.

In September 1944, the Allies launched Operation Ratweek. Wave after wave of bombers was sent to crush railways and transportation hubs in Yugoslavia. Beger recalled:

> Here I lived through the most terrible hours of my life. At night American bomber units destroyed the marshalling-yard at

> Winkowzi. At the station, thousands of refugees from Siebenbürgen, Banat and Batschka were crowded together. Thirty-five trains were at the platforms, five of them ambulance trains and some wagons with ammunition. The inferno was indescribable! The deaths uncountable! Dr Clauss was injured in the face. The next morning there was a raid by British Lightnings. I took refuge in the fields north of the station. In three approaches they didn't bomb the station itself – but the field I was hiding in! One bomb fell next to me and tore a deep crater – I was buried under earth at its edge. Before the next two bomb raids I took refuge in the crater. Fate was with me![5]

But it was the end for the Handschar.

In March 1945, Beger, without Clauss, was sent to Upper Italy, this time with the Osturkische Division. This, too, was one of the most ethnically diverse of all Waffen-SS regiments, but Beger had little time to play the anthropologist. The division eventually surrendered to an American tank unit. 'The Americans', Beger told me, 'delivered the East-Turks, Krimtartars, Uraltartars, Kazakhs, Uzbeks, Tajiks and Azerbaijanis to the Soviets, who killed them.'[6]

Beger was transported to the POW camp in Pisa, and then to an American-run camp at Livorno, where the SS men were deliberately starved. By now the Allies had seen the camps. At the end of the summer, Beger and his compatriots were loaded into cattle wagons and returned to Germany. At a camp in Bad Aidling, the Waffen-SS officers were singled out and taken to a special camp near Dachau. In the spring of 1946 Beger was taken to yet another camp near Nuremberg, and finally to Darmstadt, where he was interrogated. Beger then contacted Clauss, who sent Margarete Landé to testify on his behalf. She knew nothing of his work with Dr Hirt, and as a result of her testimony he was released in February 1948. He joined his family in Frankfurt. Both he and Clauss worked briefly in the Kompass publishing house, which was owned by the Landé family.

Neither Clauss nor Beger sought academic positions. Today, Beger explains this by saying that the salaries were too low. It is more likely that he was keeping his head below the parapet: when Wolfram Sievers was put on trial in 1946, his prosecutors learnt all about the Strasbourg skeleton collection and Beger's name was mentioned. In the 1950s Beger and Clauss organized two anthropological expeditions to the Middle East and to North Africa; they were still in search of the Race Soul. When the Landé family informed Yad Vashem about Clauss's wartime activities they awarded him status as a Righteous Gentile and planted a tree for him in Jerusalem, but it did not prosper. Clauss was no Schindler. A researcher unearthed his Nazi Party papers and his record of service with the SS, which Beger had fought so hard to arrange in 1943, and the tree was uprooted.

The end for Dr Hirt was more brutal. In August 1944, with Alsace declared a war zone, thousands of prisoners from Natzweiler were transported to Dachau. The US Army was close to Strasbourg, so Hirt appealed to Sievers: what should he do with the specimens from Auschwitz which had lain undisturbed in his vault for more than a year? Sievers wrote immediately to Brandt. He reminded him of the directives from the Reichsführer that had permitted Hirt to assemble a skeleton collection, then confessed that 'the job of reducing the corpses to skeletons had not yet been completed . . .' Now, as Nazi Germany collapsed and dragged down their little empires, everyone involved in Hirt's *Sonderauftrag* sensed the approaching chill of retribution. They were murderers, or accomplices to murder – in the name of science, to be sure, but murderers all the same. Sievers went on: 'The collection can be de-fleshed and thereby rendered unidentifiable. This however would mean that at least part of the whole work had been done for nothing and that this singular collection would be lost to science, since it would be impossible to make plaster casts afterwards . . .' Sievers then remembered the history of the university: 'The flesh parts could be declared as having been left by the French . . .'

In October, the Reichsführer's office telephoned Sievers and ordered him to 'completely dissolve' the collection, but Hirt couldn't let go of his booty. Only a perfunctory and macabre effort was made by his assistants; one of them, Otto Bong, said that 'we couldn't cut up all the bodies, it was too much work'. Like all murderers, the Strasbourg scientists found out that the biggest problem is always disposal of the body. Hirt made sure, though, that he was given all the gold fillings extracted from the teeth.

Strasbourg was liberated by the French Second Armoured Division on 23 November 1944. Sixteen entire corpses and body parts from seventy others were discovered in the Anatomical Institute, but of Hirt there was no sign. For many years after the war no-one was certain what had happened to him. Secret service agents from France, the United States and Israel searched in vain for any traces. There were rumours that he had fled to Switzerland. Then, in 1980, medical historian Frederick Kasten discovered what had happened. Hirt, he found out, had been dead for many years.

As the Allies approached Strasbourg, Hirt had fled. He had gone first to Tübingen, where Beger's colleague Fleischacker worked at the Institute of Racial Research, and had even begun to set up a new laboratory. But after the discovery of the corpses in his Strasbourg mortuary, the news filtered through to the Foreign Office in Berlin. Already anxious about war crime trials, the German authorities turned against Hirt. Inside the SS it was realized that Hirt had lied when he'd claimed that the evidence had been destroyed. Hirt denied everything – it was all a fairy story, he claimed – but in February 1945 he fled with three other SS officers to the Black Forest, where they buried food rations and set up a camp. Whenever he could, Hirt walked to a nearby farmhouse where he listened to the radio. As he sat with the farmer's family in the kitchen, news came through of the appalling discoveries being made in places like Dachau, Belsen and Auschwitz. Hirt told the farmer, 'This is not true . . .' But it seems he became increasingly depressed. He told the farmer that his wife and daughter had been killed in Strasbourg; he said that his research was 'senseless'.

Hirt persuaded the farmer to give him a gun. At eleven a.m. on 2 June 1945, Hirt left the farm, saying, 'I depart for Mannheim [his birthplace] and remain a decent person.' He walked into the forest for about twenty minutes, then shot himself. Hirt had requested the farmer to hide his body, but instead he reported what had happened to the authorities, who came and buried Hirt where he lay. Twenty years later, following a request from the Israelis, the local German authorities exhumed the body and made a positive identification. Professor Dr Hirt was at last officially dead.

Heinrich Himmler's Order Castle at Wewelsburg was discovered at the end of March 1945 when the US Third Division stumbled on its smouldering remains.[7] The Third US Armoured Division spearhead had advanced from the Remagen bridgehead intending to capture Paderborn, which was close to the 'Ruhr cauldron' and had been heavily bombed. Hearing news of their advance, on 30 March Himmler ordered the castle to be blown up and demolished. The Americans ran into stiff opposition from the SS Panzerbrigade 'Westfalen' and from scattered groups of Hitler Youth; General Maurice Rose was killed in the fighting and SS men were shot in reprisal. By the time they arrived on the Alme, the castle was in ruins.

The people of Wewelsburg had already begun plundering the castle, and the Americans joined in. The Allied 'Monuments, Fine Arts and Archives Group' under Captain S. F. Markham arrived in May, but the castle contained only a fraction of the treasures – antique weapons, paintings, objects excavated from archaeological digs in the region, treasures from Tibet – Himmler had accumulated. It still held thirty thousand volumes, much the worse for wear, on subjects ranging from archaeology and the history of 'Indo-Germanic' peoples to bizarre cosmological theories and speculations about the lost city of Atlantis.

As Markham walked through the wrecked labyrinth of Wewelsburg, Himmler was on the run with two adjutants including Werner Grothman, who had led the demolition squad. The three men were captured on 21 May near Hamburg. Himmler was travelling with false papers and was wearing an eye patch, but he was recognized by a British officer. As he was searched, the former Reichsführer, 'a small, miserable-looking and shabbily dressed man', crushed a cyanide phial between his teeth. He was dead within seconds. Chaim Herzog, who saw him moments before he died, said he could have passed for a small, anonymous clerk – although his eyes were 'steely and bereft of all expression'.[8] On 25 May Himmler's body was buried on Lunenburg Heath in an unmarked grave.

Rudolf Brandt and Wolfram Sievers were both hanged in 1946. The oleaginous Sievers had claimed he was in the German resistance, but his case collapsed under cross-examination.

Bruno Beger was brought to trial in the Kleiner Auschwitz Prozess in 1971, accused of murdering 115 prisoners at Natzweiler. He was found guilty of being an 'accomplice to murder' and sentenced to three years, suspended because of the time he had already spent in custody. The court concluded that he had acted voluntarily, but they could not decide whether or not he had originated what Hirt and Sievers both referred to as *Auftrag Beger*. The court noted that he had called Auschwitz a 'dreadful place' and concluded that he had no personal commitment to the Final Solution.

According to Kasten,[9] a French medical student in a post-war class at Strasbourg University was given the opportunity to dissect corpses left over from the Hirt era. He remembers that at least one of them had unmistakably 'Asiatic' characteristics. The student could have had no idea that this unfortunate individual had played an unwilling part in a story whose greatest moment had come on a winter's day in Tibet nearly a decade earlier when a group of triumphant German scientists had ridden on the backs of horses into the Holy City of Lhasa. Thus, the Nazi quest to find a lost Nordic race on the roof of the world ended in a cadaver-filled laboratory.

Searching for lost Aryans or the Holy Grail or Atlantis may seem harmless enough, but German occultism was founded on a racial vision of history. It validated German national identity by conjuring up a bogus yet seductive ancestral past. By taking this chimerical past literally, men like Heinrich Himmler were able to infuse policies of racial purification with an irresistible potency. As a result, occultism facilitated murder. The rich ground loam of pseudo-Darwinian theory, improbably mixed with deluded yearnings for a lost Aryan civilization, led the 'scientists' of the SS to the killing fields of the concentration camps.

CHAPTER EIGHTEEN

AFTERMATHS

GANGTOK, SIKKIM, OCTOBER 2002

In October 2002, I followed in the footsteps of the Schäfer Expedition to Calcutta. One evening I walked into the humid and thronging Sealdah Station. I easily found the Darjeeling Mail and bought some water. Precisely on time, the train pulled out of Calcutta and headed north across the Plain of Bengal. The following morning we arrived in Siliguri. In 1938, Schäfer had travelled on to Darjeeling to meet Hugh Richardson for the first time, but I was heading straight for Gangtok with Vanu, a Sikkimese guide.

Siliguri town was a hot and teeming place, and as I left the station I felt for the first time the warm hands of begging children persistently brushing my arm. We drove out of town, fighting for road space with hundreds of rickshaws, squadrons of big colourful lorries and knotted crowds of people. The road ran flat through a forest until we reached the Tista River. Here we took a sharp right and crossed a green box-girder bridge. Ahead lay the foothills of the Himalayas. We climbed rapidly and the Tista was soon far below the road in a green, densely wooded trough. Monkeys swarmed along the roadside. We were still in Bengal, and the Sikkimese border lay ahead.

Then we hit an unexpected snag. As we turned into one village, Vanu braked suddenly. The road was blocked by crowds of angry young men who insistently waved us down. It turned out that Chandra Kumar Pradhan, the charismatic leader of the Gorkha National Liberation Front, had been assassinated in Kalimpong the day before. No-one was being allowed to travel any further or to cross the border into Sikkim. My companions were all for giving up and returning to Siliguri, where we could get a flight to Gangtok, but when I informed the young men that I was a British journalist they agreed to let us drive on and try our luck at the next check point. Remarkably, we got through every time, and within an hour we were crossing a narrow bridge over the turbulent, white-flecked waters of the Tista into Sikkim.

After the border, where we presented passports to a guard, the road plunged down towards the river then rose again. There is no flat land anywhere in Sikkim. Far below us, the river roared. Three bumpy and twisting hours later we spiralled upwards towards Gangtok, and I could just make out the prayer flags of the Rumtek Monastery on the other side of the valley.

Today, Gangtok sprawls across its high jade-green hills whose slopes are laced with cardamom fields and sinuous rice paddies. In 1938, Gangtok was a city of three peaks and three competing powers. Crowning one was the palace of the Chogyal, the ruler of this tiny Himalayan kingdom. A little higher was the residence of the chief minister, the Dewan. On a third, much higher peak was the British Residency that John Claude White had built to assert the power of the Raj over the unfortunate hare-lipped Chogyal Thutob Namygal, who cowered below in his palace and no doubt envied his half brother, Schäfer's 'King of Tharing', who was safely ensconced in Tibet. White's residency is today the home of the Indian governor of Sikkim. The Chogyal's palace is empty, its gates securely bolted and guarded. Sikkim was annexed by India in 1975, the royal family stripped of their powers, but I met many Sikkimese who remained fiercely loyal. In their houses, a big portrait of the last Chogyal, Palden Thondup, who had married the American debutante Hope Cook, hung in a place of honour festooned with silk scarves.

The hotel promised a view of Kangchendzonga but, although the sky produced exquisite variations on pink and mauve until it grew dark, thick cloud covered the granite face of the god and would do so for many days. Gods, it has to be remembered, can never be too transparent. That evening I met Anna Balikci, an expert on shamanism, and her husband Jigme Dorje Denjongpa, who had written to tell me that they knew someone who had been with Schäfer. He was called 'German' Akeh, and I recognized his name from Schäfer's diaries. He had been quite a character.

Akeh lives a short if precipitous walk below the palace in a green, wooden bungalow that seems rather precariously clamped to the steep side of the hill. Beger's 'strong man who sometimes caused trouble', who loved women and beer, was surprisingly frail and delicate with oddly pigmented skin. His sons and grandsons had all turned up to hear him talk about his time with Ernst Schäfer long ago. Jigme had heard Akeh talking about the 'German Expedition' when he was a child. Akeh showed me the postcard he had received from Dr Beger and told us that this was the first time in more than sixty years that he had heard from any of his German friends.

At the end of July 1939 he and Kaiser had been in Calcutta looking after Schäfer's animals. It was expensive: Akeh was shelling out hundreds of rupees a day. One morning, Akeh was astonished to discover that all five Germans had vanished from their hotel. There had been no goodbyes, no thanks, and worst of all no payment for the animals. Soon British policemen – the CID, Akeh calls them – picked up Akeh and Kaiser and began to question them about their association with 'Nazis'. Akeh proudly showed me his certificate allowing him to work with Schäfer, handwritten on paper headed DEUTSCHE TIBET EXPEDITION ERNST SCHÄFER. Akeh vividly recalled his first meeting with Schäfer in the gardens of the British Residency when he had been handed a rifle and asked to try to hit a cigarette packet on a tree stump. He suddenly leant forward and showed me his gold tooth – a memento of that fight in Lhasa. He told me about Schäfer buying skulls from the *ragyapa* and insisted that he too was supposed to go to Berlin with the Germans. I sensed that he envied Kaiser. Akeh's name Bhutia means that he was of Tibetan origin; Kaiser was a Gurkha.

The side streets of Gangtok are unlit and inky black when the sun has gone down. This is where the city's elite resides, including Tej Thapa, Kaiser's son and now lawyer for the surviving members of the royal family. There is the usual portrait of the last Chogyal in his study. Tej is a youthful, energetic man and fiercely protective of his late father. Kaiser had four sons, and even together, Tej said, they could not 'fill his shoes'. Although we talked for more than two hours, he was very suspicious. He was frightened that his father would be associated with Nazis; even worse, it seemed, he feared that there was an improper relationship with Schäfer.

Tej leapt up and said, 'I have something to show you.' Ten minutes later he returned with a blue, battered file. Tej had taken it from the Sikkim State Archives and had no intention of returning it – 'I am a lawyer.' He permitted me a brief examination before snatching it back. It was the 'File on Kaiser Bahadur Thapa' Nr. 723, and a visit to the state archives the following day confirmed that the file was indeed 'missing' and that there was no copy. What Tej didn't know is that Jacqueline Hiltz, a friend of Hope Cook who is writing a history of Sikkim, had made detailed notes on this file and sent them to me just weeks before I arrived in India. I knew exactly what it said.

In other ways, Tej was compulsively revealing. He told me about the Thapa family's Gurkha origins and said that his father was 'poorly looked after' by his family. Kaiser's father had deserted his wife and he eventually became the only breadwinner, as Schäfer discovered. He must have been very vulnerable to the appeal of this dynamic, paternalist German who took him under his wing and promised him so much. The file that Tej is so frightened of refers to Kaiser 'moping about' Calcutta with a bad case of 'hero worship'. During the war, Kaiser worked in an RAF ground crew and loyally maintained Allied fighters and bombers all over Asia, ending up in Japan. When he returned to Gangtok, he set up a transport company and made a fortune. Kaiser corresponded with Schäfer and Ursula and saw his old friend one more time as Schäfer lay dying in a German hospital. He had been sent to give Schäfer news of his precious shapis.

In Gangtok, I discovered that Schäfer is remembered as the man who found the shapi. Keshab Pradhan, who is head of the Sikkim Development Foundation, showed me his father's diary entry for 20 June 1938 where he recorded giving Schäfer permission to hunt in the Tista Valley. Schäfer had presented Keshab's father with a copy of Ernst Krause's book on Alpine flowers, and Keshab showed me Salim Aki's glowing account of Schäfer's achievements as an ornithologist in his *The Birds of Sikkim*. Schäfer, it seemed, had wanted to return to Sikkim in the 1970s to set up a shapi conservation project but had been denied a visa by the Indian government. His wartime activities had not been forgotten, long after the departure of the British. There are still shapis roaming a valley in the north controlled by the Indian Army. In Lachen, on the road to Thanggu, I met a retired headmaster, Mr Kelsang Gyatso, who vividly recalled meeting the German expedition as a schoolboy. He remembered seeing Timothy, the young man from the Finnish Mission who told Schäfer about the legendary animal and led him to its secret realm. Villagers there still refer to a 'German Cave' high above their village where Schäfer read Goethe to his friend Edmund Geer as they waited for the shapi.

In Sikkim, only the secretive Tej Thapa seemed to be concerned about the darker side of Schäfer's expedition, fearful of revelation. Mr Pradhan was certain that Schäfer wanted to take Kaiser to Berlin so that he could later be used as a 'Trojan Horse' in a Gurkha regiment. When I returned to London, I searched through the files of the British intelligence service, the CIC.[1] There was one reference to the 'notorious Schäfer expedition' but nothing more about Kaiser. But it was very clear what the British were frightened about. There were a number of German academics in India and educational organizations like the Deutsche Orient Verein that seemed to be grooming upper-caste Indians for some kind of service. At least one Indian intellectual began broadcasting propaganda from Nazi Germany. The man Beger admits to meeting in Calcutta and again in Berlin, Subhas Chandra Bose, was a persistent thorn in the side of the declining British empire. The files provided another intriguing insight: Wilhelm Filchner had somehow ended up in Nepal, and his presence there, along with his daughter who was an enthusiastic Nazi, caused great concern. Schäfer had planned to visit Nepal and was very friendly with the Nepali representative in Lhasa, Major Bista. There were, of course, German delegations to Kathmandu and presents of Mercedes for the royal family. At the end of 1939, one agent reported that 'The expeditions of Dr Schaefer . . . are . . . indications of the directions in which German interest lies.' Taken together, there was a complex mosaic of evidence that supported the suggestion that for Ernst Schäfer politics was as important as science. Still, in Sikkim, Schäfer is remembered as he himself would have liked, as a dedicated ornithologist and the man who gave his name to a rather special goat.[2]

When the five young German men returned to their homeland they were almost immediately overwhelmed by Hitler's war, their reputations contaminated. Although Schäfer made his film and published at least three accounts of his time in Lhasa, the scientific results of his expedition were fragmented and many of the treasures brought back from the roof of the world lost and destroyed. Today, it is not surprising that there is little interest in bringing together what remains, since it is tainted by the Nazi period. The SS expedition to Tibet has also gathered a thick crust of myth and misunderstanding that has obscured its remarkable significance.

Schäfer was not looking for Atlantis, nor did he bring Tibetan monks back to Germany to die in the ruins of Hitler's bunker, but his activities were not purely scientific either, however much he protested that they were. It is very likely, as I have argued, that by the beginning of 1939 Schäfer was already thinking ahead to the absurd 'Lawrence Expedition' that would come to obsess both him and Heinrich Himmler. Poor Kaiser, who served the RAF with such dedication after Schäfer deserted him in Calcutta, was a pawn in a game he would never understand.

Of Krause's botany and Wienert's magnetic measurements – the latter could have been invaluable had Schäfer ever become a 'German Lawrence' and returned to Tibet to incite a rebellion against the Raj – there is little to be said. Their work belongs in the museum. So, too, in a different way, does the anthropometric work of Bruno Beger. Even in 1938, the measuring of native peoples to determine their racial identity and kinship was falling into disrepute. It had never been especially important for British anthropologists, and in the United States, where Native American crania had been obsessively collected and measured since the middle of the nineteenth century, the powerful impact of Franz Boas had eroded the talismanic power of anthropometric calculations. As early as 1912, Boas had demolished the link between skull shape and race. After the Second World War, the simultaneous revelation of the death camps and the Nazi enthusiasm for race science founded on measurements smashed the power of the calliper for ever.

Beger's own attempts to make sense of his Tibetan data were inconclusive and fragmentary. They did not tell the story of Nordic expansion that he wanted to bring back to his professors and the expedition's patron. Much of what he reported simply showed what any visitor to the market in Gangtok would have seen – that the people of India and Tibet were highly diverse. His 'Europid traits', too, have a simple explanation that has nothing to do with a wandering Aryan Master Race, an idea that so fascinated Heinrich Himmler that he murdered millions of Jews, Slavs and gypsies in order to ringfence the purity of Aryan blood.

After the seventh century, the Tibetan kings extended the boundaries of the empire north, south, east and west. Tibetan merchants and soldiers were violently, profitably and intimately in contact with other empires and states: Persians in the west, Indians to the south, Chinese and Mongolians to the east. To the north, a quite remarkable multitude of peoples travelled back and forth along the Silk Road – actually an interlaced network of tracks – whose caravans traded in jade, spices, wool, musk, ivory, gems and precious metals. The cast changed as empires rose and fell, but they included Greeks, Scythians, Persians, Turks, Indians, Arabs, Chinese, Sogdians and Mongolians, and they were Buddhists, Manichaeans, Nestorian

Christians and Muslims. Some of the first Buddhist monks in Tibet came from the Tarim region along the Silk Road. From the seventh century, when King Srongtsan Gampo began to build his empire, Tibetan soldiers, merchants and administrators would have been part of this thronging world. There would have been frequent and tumultuous gene flow in the cities and caravanserai. History is shaped by sex.

In 1994, an astonishing discovery was announced by the London newspaper the *Mail on Sunday*. A cache of mummies had been discovered in Ürümchi in China's Xinjiang province. They were spectacularly preserved in the dry desert sands, but what caught the attention of the world was the fact that these people were tall and light-skinned and dressed in tartans. The discovery of the Ürümchi mummies confirmed the almost limitless variety of the people of the Silk Road. The tall, fair-skinned people were not supermen or women but ordinary people who had joined the ceaseless ripple of trade and migration in central Asia. The ancient people of Tibet and their descendants were simply part of history. Their genes, the shapes of their heads and the colours of their eyes, were bound to show traces of that complex past. If Bruno Beger discovered anything it was simply that, not the fingerprints of the Aryan Master Race.

The ideas that obsessed the Nazi elite have reappeared on the fringes of European culture. At the beginning of the 1960s two French writers, Louis Pauwels and Jacques Bergier, reheated many of the occultist, 'lost civilization' ideas that had so consumed Himmler. In a book called *The Morning of the Magicians*, they argued that the Nazis possessed occult powers and secret extraterrestrial technologies. In the 1980s these fantasies took on a more sinister significance. Ernst Zundel, whose name became notorious during the Irving libel trial in London in 2000, is the founder and owner of the neo-Nazi Samizdat

Publishers based in Toronto. He is best known as the virulent 'holocaust denier' who commissioned the notorious 'Leuchter Report' which alleged that the gas chambers at Auschwitz had not been used for killing – a claim that has now been thoroughly discredited. Zundel combines holocaust denial with attempts to glorify the Third Reich and to publish 'evidence' for German secret weapons and post-war Nazi bases in Antarctica (which seems to have replaced the Arctic or Tibet as an Aryan homeland). Zundel has worked hard – he appears to have considerable resources – to promote a cult interest in Nazism and ancient mysteries. He re-published the repellent books of Savitri Devi (Maximiani Portas), a Nazi fellow traveller who was fascinated by Indian philosophy and the Vedic texts and became a leading figure in the neo-Nazi movement. Her ideas combined Aryan supremacy with Hinduism, social Darwinism and animal rights. Madame Blavatsky had, it seemed, returned, holding aloft a swastika.

The ideas of Austrian hotelier Erich von Däniken appeared at first sight foolish rather than sinister, but von Däniken too had links to the far right and his money-spinning notion that ancient civilizations flourished as a result of the mating of human races and superior aliens (read Aryans) was dangerously xenophobic. It is noteworthy that some of von Däniken's favourite evidence came from the ancient site of Tiwanaku in Bolivia, which he had discovered after reading long-forgotten books on ancient America by an Austrian adventurer called Arthur Posnansky. Posnansky, of course, had collaborated with Edmund Kiss, the SS 'scientist' Ernst Schäfer had refused to include in his expedition.

A new development came in the 1990s. There was a popular upsurge in what has come to be called 'alternative history', and books like *Fingerprints of the Gods* revived a fascination with ancient lost civilizations. No-one is talking about Aryans, of course, but the idea remains the same. Long ago, at the end of the last ice age, there existed a superior godlike people. Their destruction by flood led to the scattering of their culture across the globe and the seeding of the great civilizations from the Nile Valley to the Andes. Like the occultists of the nineteenth century, this revival seems to be driven by disillusionment with the modern and a longing for long-lost spiritual values.

The authors who have propagated this revival of nineteenth-century occultism are not, as far as anyone can tell, racists and certainly have no means at their disposal to act upon their elitist views of the past as Himmler and his followers did in the 1930s. But, incontestably, the early twenty-first century is a period of intense national chauvinism and ethnic exclusivity. In this context, the persistence of these bogus visions of the past cannot be treated as foolish diversions or harmless fantasy; they emerge from a long and dangerous history, and in different circumstances might turn into a slippery slope, descending into darkness.

NOTES

PRELUDE

1 Goethe, *Faust, Part Two*, translated by David Luke (Oxford University Press, 1994), from p.218.

INTRODUCTION

1 See Kater, *Das Ahnenerbe*; Goodrick-Clark, *Black Sun*; and Isrun Engelhardt in Alex McKay (ed.), *Tibetan History.*

2 See Engelhardt, ibid.

3 Quoted in Padfield, *Himmler*, p.167.

4 See Heiber, *Reichsführer*, pp.71–2.

5 There was at first some pretence that the Ahnenerbe was independent of the SS.

6 Quoted in Petropoulos, *The Faustian Bargain*, p.168.

7 L/P&S/12/4343 (OIOC).

8 *Julius Caesar*, act 2, scene 1, lines 22 and 24.

9 Bruno Beger denies *any* interest in 'Aryans'. German anthropologists tended to use either 'Nordic' or 'Indo-German' as terms when they discussed the ancestral origins of Germans. In the Third Reich, 'Aryan' was used in both everyday and legal discourse as a benchmark of racial purity. If the original German race was 'Nordic' or 'Indo-German', it followed that 'Aryan' blood defined its genetic inheritance. In a paper on his findings in Tibet, Beger used none of these words; instead he referred to his discovery of 'Europid' traits in the Tibetan nobility. What he meant by that was traits shared by some Tibetans and Europeans, and thus what

everyone else called Indo-Germans, Nordics or Aryans. To all intents and purposes, therefore, the four terms are interchangeable.

10 Quoted in Lochner, *What About Germany?*, p.260.

11 Tudor Parfitt's superb *The Lost Tribes of Israel* (London: Weidenfeld & Nicolson, 2002) is a magisterial study of how Europeans have alchemized non-European 'others' and turned them into fodder for myths.

12 Referring to Canada, but the reference is equally apposite to Tibet.

13 All quotations from the narration for *Geheimnis Tibet* (Tobis Films/Germany, 1942).

14 Lopez, *Prisoners of Shangri-La*, p.31ff.

15 See the *Oxford English Dictionary*; quoted in Lopez.

16 Lopez, *Prisoners of Shangri-La*, p.31ff.

17 Strunk, *Zu Juda und Rom-Tibet*, referenced in Lopez. I was able to find a microfilmed copy of Strunk's work in the New York Public Library.

18 And other Nazi thinkers, too: Alfred Rosenberg, in his book *Myth of the 20th Century* (*Mythos des 20. Jahrhunderts*), discussed dangerous influences from central Asia; devilish sexual cults had been introduced to Europe and had led to cultural degeneration. Rosenberg had acquired his theory from the writings of Tibetologist Albert Grünwedel, a Catholic who had been appalled by Tibetan Buddhist writings and cave art. In his scientific publications he unmasked the 'devilish and blasphemous contents' of Tibetan art, as well as the European movements Expressionism, Surrealism and Dadaism. See 'The Tibet-Image of the National Socialists' by Reinhard Greve in Dodin and Räther, *Mythos Tibet*.

19 The title of an essay by Donald S. Lopez in Dodin and Räther, *Imagining Tibet*, p.183ff.

20 There are many descriptions of Shambhala. This one borrows from Lopez, *Prisoners of Shangri-La*, p.182.

21 The story is superbly told by Karl Meyer and Shareen Brysac in *Tournament of Shadows*, p.448ff.

22 It pervades the so-called 'alternative history' churned out by writers like Erich von Däniken and, more recently, Graham Hancock. An elite race of aliens or the spiritual masters from a

twelve-thousand-year-old lost civilization is their recycled version of Shambhala.

23 There is substantial and serious scholarship on Blavatsky, much of it brilliantly brought together in Meyer and Brysac's *Tournament of Shadows.* There are biographies by Marion Meade (1980) and Sylvia Cranston (1993); there are two controversial but detailed and scholarly investigations by K. Paul Johnson which present new accounts of Blavatsky's 'Masters'; and Blavatsky's connections with the Russian secret service are discussed by Maria Carlson, whose work is cited in Meyer and Brysac, p.247. For an acerbic overview of theosophy there is no better account than Peter Washington's *Madame Blavatsky's Baboon.*

24 Meade, *Madame Blavatsky*, p.31.

25 Ibid., p.188.

26 From Carlson, *No Religion Higher than Truth*, p.216.

27 Johnson, *Initiates of the Theosophical Masters*, p.24.

28 See Johnson, *The Masters Revealed*, p.198ff.

29 From Hopkirk, *Trespassers on the Roof of the World*, p.55.

30 I am indebted to Marion Meade's summary.

31 See Goodrick-Clark, *The Occult Roots of Nazism*, p.22ff.

32 Goodrick-Clark's three books (see bibliography) are definitive accounts of this strain in European thinking. Other sources include Poliakov, *The Aryan Myth*, and Mosse, *The Crisis of German Ideology*.

33 One of the best recent accounts of this can be found in Allen, *The Buddha and the Sahibs*.

CHAPTER ONE

1 The Final Interrogation Report is held in the National Archives in Washington (RG338 OI-FIR No. 32, 12 February 1946).

2 NS19 Files, Personal Staff of Heinrich Himmler (BA).

3 Or, to give it its German title, *Sturm über Asien* (see bibliography).

4 See Kershaw, *Hubris*, p.322.

5 From a letter to General Taylor, American Military Tribunal in Nuremberg, 8 May 1947. Many thanks to Dr Isrun Engelhardt for showing me her copy of this remarkable document.

6 This account of the Schäfer and Dolan expeditions is based on, and quotes freely from, Schäfer's series of books, none of them available in English, published before and after the Second World War (see bibliography). I am very grateful to Diana Böhmer for her invaluable assistance with these voluminous texts. An account of the expeditions can be found in Meyer and Brysac, *Tournament of Shadows*, and I would like to thank both authors for their guidance.
7 References to Dolan are based on documents held by the Academy of Natural Sciences in Philadelphia.
8 This is in Schäfer's SS files (RG 242 SS 138803, NARA).
9 See Meyer and Brysac, *Tournament of Shadows*, p.334ff.
10 Ibid., p.311.
11 Hedin, *Transhimalaya*.
12 For more on this, see Kuhl, *The Nazi Connection*; Stephen Jay Gould, *The Mismeasure of Man* (New York and London: W. W. Norton, 1996); and David Hurst Thomas, *Skull Wars: Kennewick Man, Archaeology, and the Battle for Native American Identity* (Basic Books, 2000).
13 Bowles, p.317.
14 Speer, *Diaries*, pp.109 and 286.
15 From J. Spence and A. Chin, *The Chinese Century*, p.82ff.
16 From Sergeant, *Shanghai*, p.53.
17 I have taken these facts from Simon Winchester's *The River at the Centre of the World*, which was inspirational research for this chapter.
18 See Meyer and Brysac, *Tournament of Shadows*, p.342.
19 From *The Schellenberg Memoirs*, pp.20–2.
20 See Kater, *Doctors under Hitler*, pp.70–1.

CHAPTER TWO

1 *The Yangtze and the Yak* (Alexandria, Virginia, 1952), on pp.163, 169 and 171.
2 Duncan's letters are in Collection 64b in the archives of the Academy of Natural Sciences, Philadelphia.
3 From 'Road to the Edge of the World' by Brooke Dolan II (*Frontiers*, October 1936, pp.5–9).

4 Academy of Natural Sciences, Philadelphia.
5 Duncan, *The Yangtze and the Yak*, p.165.
6 Ibid., p.171.
7 Ibid., p.208.
8 Ibid., p.246.

CHAPTER THREE

1 B.F. Smith and A.F. Petersen (eds), *Heinrich Himmler: Geheimreden, 1933–1945* (Berlin: Propyläen, 1974), quoted in Padfield, *Himmler*.
2 See Breitman, *The Architect of Genocide*, p.5. The source is a British intelligence document and is unattributed, but Breitman is certain that the author is Kersten.
3 Engelhardt in McKay (ed.), *Tibetan History*.
4 Quoted in Höhne, *The Order of the Death's Head*.
5 This is widely quoted – here from Fest, *Speer*, p.185.
6 Quoted in Cook and Russell, *Heinrich Himmler's Camelot*.
7 See Brebeck and Hüser, *Wewelsburg 1933–1945*.
8 According to Michael Kater, 'a dependable, scholarly biography of Himmler has yet to be written'. I have used Breitman's *The Architect of Genocide*; Höhne's *The Order of the Death's Head*; Padfield's *Himmler*; Koehl's *The SS: A History*; Smelser and Zitelmann's *The Nazi Elite*; and Peter Loewenberg's article 'The Unsuccessful Adolescence of Heinrich Himmler' in *American Historical Review 76*, 1971, pp.616–18.
9 Fischer, *Nazi Germany*, p.213.
10 From Alfred Andersch, *The Father of a Murderer* (1961), quoted in Ackermann, *Heinrich Himmler*, p.99.
11 See Ackermann, *Heinrich Himmler*, p.100.
12 From Padfield, *Himmler*, p.20.
13 From Albert Krebs, *Tendenzen und Gestalten der NSDAP; Errinerungen* (Stuttgart: Deutsche Verlag Anstalt, 1959), p.210, quoted in Padfield, *Himmler*, p.93.
14 See Kershaw, *Hubris*, pp.99–100.
15 From Ackermann, *Heinrich Himmler*, p.103.
16 See Goodrick-Clark's *The Occult Roots of Nazism* for a superb

account of this and other occult groups in Germany. Goodrick-Clark's book remains the only serious and scholarly account of a field otherwise dominated by trash literature.

17 Hesse was banned after 1933, however.

18 Quoted in Ziegler, *Nazi Germany's New Aristocracy*, p.176.

19 From Fischer, *Nazi Germany*, p.328.

20 Quoted in Padfield, *Himmler*, p.143.

21 Quoted in Cohn, *Warrant for Genocide*, p.51.

CHAPTER FOUR

1 Quoted in Muller-Hill, *Murderous Science*, p.20, from the *Deutsche Allgemeine Zeitung* (Verlag Dieter Schwarz, Taubenweg 3, Wiesbaden).

2 See Smith, *The Ideological Origins of Nazi Imperialism*, and Peter Hopkirk's racier *Like Hidden Fire* (New York: Kodansha International, 1994), published first in the UK as *On Secret Service East of Constantinople* (see bibliography).

3 I am grateful to Andrew Zimmerman for discussing with me the history of German anthropology. His *Anthropology and Antihumanism* was an invaluable and unique resource.

4 Quoted in Zimmerman, Adventures in the Skin Trade (forthcoming).

5 Quoted in Bridgman, *The Revolt of the Hereros*, p.131.

6 Quoted in Kershaw, *Hubris*, p.86.

7 In John Keegan's *The First World War*, p.31.

8 Hitler admired Grimm's novel and did what he could when the NSDAP came to power to keep it in the bestseller lists. At the 1936 Chicago World Exhibition, Grimm's novel was the only literary work chosen to represent Nazi Germany. Grimm was a Nazi sympathizer, although he never joined the NSDAP and sometimes spoke out against its policies. He continued to defend Hitler even after the end of the Second World War, calling him a 'martyr' to British warmongers and the 'greatest statesman Europe has ever known'.

9 This fascinating argument is made in Dwork and Jan Van Pelt's *The Holocaust: A History*; see pp.32–3.

10 Quoted in Kershaw, *Hubris*, p.319.
11 See Weindling, *Health, Race and German Politics*, pp.309–11.
12 From Padfield, *Himmler*, p.69.
13 See Mosse, *The Crisis of German Ideology*, pp.208–9.
14 Paul Weindling's *Health, Race and German Politics* gives an outstanding account of these events.
15 Günther, *The Racial Elements of European History*, p.26ff. As far as I can discover this is the only Günther book that has been translated into English; it was logical to make use of this more accessible text.
16 Ibid., p.78.
17 Ibid., p.207.
18 Ibid., p.140.
19 Quoted in Padfield, *Himmler*, p.101.

CHAPTER FIVE

1 Records of the DFG, BA R73/14198, quoted in Deichmann, *Biologists under Hitler*, p.131ff.
2 Academy of Natural Sciences, Collection 64b.
3 SS files (NARA).
4 Schäfer, lecture for the Himalayan Club, July 1939. It was never given, of course.
5 Engelhardt in McKay (ed.), *Tibetan History*.
6 Quoted by Goodrick-Clark in *Black Sun*, p.129.
7 See ibid., pp.131–3.
8 Readers of the latest 'alternative histories' will recognize many of Kiss's ideas in books such as Graham Hancock's *Fingerprints of the Gods* (1995) and R. and R. Flem Ath's *The Atlantis Blueprint* (2001). Kiss tried to organize another SS expedition to South America in 1939. During the war he fought with the Waffen-SS and also proposed leading a group of commandos to Tibet. Captured in 1945 and incarcerated in a POW camp, Kiss met another prisoner, Rudolf Mund, who spread Kiss's ideas after the war. They re-emerged first in Erich von Däniken's fantasies about alien civilizers building Tiwanaku and the Pyramids, and then in the works of Hancock and others.

9 See Engelhardt in McKay (ed.), *Tibetan History*.
10 Ibid.
11 Proctor, *The Nazi War on Cancer*, p.152.
12 Quoted in Szöllösi-Janze, *Science in the Third Reich*, p.6.
13 See Filchner, *A Scientist in Tartary*, p.45ff.
14 Alexander von Humboldt was the first to discover the dependency of magnetic intensity on latitude based upon measurements he took during his voyages through the Americas between 1799 and 1805. Afterwards, he organized the first simultaneous observations of the geomagnetic field at various locations throughout the world. He, Wilhelm Weber and Carl Gauss organized the Göttingen Magnetic Union, and from 1836 to 1841 simultaneous observations of the Earth's magnetic field were made in non-magnetic huts at fifty different locations, marking the beginning of a magnetic observatory system.
15 Schäfer, *Geheimnis Tibet*, pp.8–9.
16 See Remy, *The Heidelberg Myth*, p.53ff.
17 See Gallenkamp, *Dragon Hunter*, p.26.
18 Foreword by Henry Fairfield Osborn to Roy Chapman Andrews' *On the Trail of Ancient Man* (1926).
19 From Karl Sabbagh, *A Rum Affair* (London: Penguin Books, 1999), p.8.
20 See 'The Tibet-Image of the National Socialists' by Reinhard Greve in Dodin and Räther, *Mythos Tibet*.
21 Schäfer to Himmler, 5 June 1938, Zentrales Staatsarchiv (Bundesarchiv Abt.), Potsdam, ZM 1457 A5.
22 From 'Goals and Plans of the Tibet Expedition of the Society "Das Ahnenerbe" under the leadership of SS-Obersturmführer Dr Schäfer' (1938, no date), R 73/12198 (BA).
23 After the invasion of Russia in 1941, Göring planned to appropriate immense tracts of Poland and the Ukraine as game reserves. They would be repopulated with extinct animals like the auroch, using selective breeding methods in order to recreate the great forests of German antiquity.

CHAPTER SIX

1 The July 1939 lecture, which was, of course, cancelled.

2 Sutton's *In China's Border Provinces* is an excellent account of Rock's life from which I have borrowed the phrase 'life-de-luxe'. Rock's own account is 'Seeking the Mountain of Mystery: An Expedition on the China–Tibet Frontier to the Unexplored Amnyi Machen Range, One of Whose Peaks Rivals Everest' in *National Geographic* LVII, 1930, pp.131–85. Rock would make outlandish claims for the height of the Minya Konka Range as late as 1930.

3 Lecture in the records of the Sven Hedin Institute (BA).

4 Nor would anyone else for some time. A Chinese climbing team claimed they had made the ascent in 1949 and reported that Amne Machin reached 23,491 feet; thirty years later they were forced to admit they had climbed the wrong mountain and had then exaggerated its height. In 1980, the Chinese permitted an American team to make the first successful attempt.

5 This analogy is taken from Lamb, *British India and Tibet*, p.289.

6 L/P&S/12/4286 (OIOC).

7 Quoted in McKay, *Tibet and the British Raj*, p.75.

8 Ibid., p.73.

9 Even after the war, by which time Tucci had lost his chair at Rome University, Richardson continued to support his travels in Tibet. See McKay, *Tibet and the British Raj*, p.174.

10 From Hauner, *India in Axis Strategy*, p.70ff.

11 See Lamb, *British India and Tibet*, p.418ff.

12 Quoted in ibid., p.427.

13 L/P&S/12/4343 (OIOC).

14 Domville and other appeasers are discussed at length in Griffiths, *Fellow Travellers of the Right*, p.179ff.

15 Ibid.

16 Quoted in French, *Younghusband*, p.369.

17 See Meyer and Brysac, *Tournament of Shadows*, p.320.

18 Younghusband, *India and Tibet*, p.78.

19 See French, *Younghusband*, pp.264–5.

CHAPTER SEVEN

1 My sources for the account of the 1938–9 German Tibet Expedition are the books Schäfer wrote between 1943 and 1961 (see bibliography); Bruno Beger's account *Mit der deutschen Tibetexpedition Ernst Schäfer*; the records of the India Office; and interviews and correspondence with Beger. Dr Isrun Engelhardt very generously permitted me to make use of extracts from her decipherment of Ernst Schäfer's expedition diaries.

2 From L/P&J/12/633 (OIOC).

3 From 'The Heart of Nature', quoted in French, *Younghusband*, p.162.

4 Gould, *The Jewel in the Lotus*, p.137.

5 F. Spencer Chapman, in *Lhasa, the Holy City*, p.52.

6 Gould, *The Jewel in the Lotus*, p.168.

7 Claude White, *Sikkim and Bhutan*, p.75.

8 Maraini, *Secret Tibet*, p.46.

9 Confusingly, 'sherpas' is often used as a catch-all term for native peoples who assisted explorers in this part of Asia. As Schäfer said, sherpas are a Nepali aboriginal tribe from close to Mount Everest. Some of Schäfer's men were sherpas, others were not.

10 The words are those of Lord Curzon, quoted in Meyer and Brysac, *Tournament of Shadows*, p.310.

11 Quoted in Rossler, *Science in the Third Reich*, p.65.

12 Even before 1933, geographers were the facilitators of German colonial aspirations. One of the most celebrated, Carl Troll, carried out pioneering aerial survey work, financed by the Kaiser Wilhelm Institute, in East Africa. This was territory which many in Germany craved as a new colonial empire. Much later, Troll was also the botanist-geographer on the Nanga Parbat Expedition in 1935, and his work was front-page news in the Nazi paper, the *Völkischer Beobachter*. The scientific conquest of highland and lowland was as well rewarded in the New Germany as the subjugation of the great peaks by men like Heinrich Harrer, and Wienert must have had a keen sense of how much he stood to gain. In the field, though, it was never an easy task.

13 See also Matthiessen, *The Snow Leopard*. During the autumn of

1973 Matthiessen accompanied the naturalist George Schaller on a two-month expedition into the high mountain country of Nepal and Tibet. Schaller's aim was to study the mating behaviour of the blue sheep, or bharal, and to solve the puzzle of its identity.

14 Bruno Beger, personal communication.

15 According to Schäfer, he also referred to himself as a Lachenese.

16 Schäfer's spelling.

17 Goethe, *Faust, Part One*, 24, Walpurgis Night, translated by David Luke (Oxford University Press, 1987).

CHAPTER EIGHT

1 *Dzongpons* came in five 'grades', were usually armed, and controlled local taxation and trade along their section of a road.

2 See Singh, *Himalayan Triangle*, pp.231–2, and Taring, *Daughter of Tibet*, pp.105–7.

3 See L/P&S/12/4343 (OIOC).

4 Quoted in Padfield, *Himmler*, p.241.

5 In his post-war account, Schäfer describes only the bonfire and the walk to the lake.

CHAPTER NINE

1 French, *Younghusband*, pp.199–201.

2 Candler, *The Unveiling of Lhasa*, p.203 – one of a number of vivid accounts of Younghusband's invasion of Tibet, and well known to Schäfer.

3 See accounts of the build-up to the invasion in Hopkirk, *The Great Game*; Meyer and Brysac, *Tournament of Shadows*; and Lamb, *Tibet, China & India*. Hopkirk's spelling is Aguan Dorjieff.

4 Filchner, *Sturm über Asien*, p.62ff.

5 See Goldstein, *A History of Modern Tibet*; Hopkirk, *Trespassers on the Roof of the World*; McKay, *Tibet and the British Raj*.

6 Wienert, 'Preliminary Report', p.5.

7 For an explanation, see Goldstein, *A History of Modern Tibet*, p.4.

8 Gordon Bowles, the anthropologist on the 1931 expedition, called it 'Ulag' in his Harvard dissertation.

9 For a more detailed discussion, see Maraini, *Secret Tibet*, p.61.

10 Alternatively, Phari was said to have the 'highest post office in the world'.
11 Not Warren Hastings himself, as Schäfer believed.
12 'Rimpoche' is an honorific title given to incarnate Buddhist teachers whose incarnate line is recognized to extend across a series of lifetimes, such as the Dalai Lamas and the Panchen Lamas. It is therefore equivalent to the Tibetan word *tulku* (Sanskrit: *nirmanakaya*; Mongolian: *qutuqtu*; Chinese: *ho fu*). 'Lama' (Sanskrit: *guru*) refers to a spiritual teacher who is able to transmit a lineage of Buddhist teachings from one generation to the next. Some lamas are also rimpoches, and some monks (Tibetan: *gelong*; Sanskrit: *bhiksu*) will be lamas, but there are also lamas and rimpoches who are married and therefore not monks. Personal communication, Gyurme Dorje.
13 Quoted in Fleming, *Bayonets to Lhasa*, p.132.
14 Detailed accounts of this clash can be found in French, *Younghusband*; Meyer and Brysac, *Tournament of Shadows*; and Fleming, *Bayonets to Lhasa*. French reproduces reports from Tibetan witnesses that describe considerable brutality and looting.
15 There are many discussions of the swastika's place in Tibetan culture. An excellent summary can be found in Allen, *The Search for Shangri-La*, pp.88–9.
16 See McKay, *Tibet and the British Raj*, p.90.
17 Ludlow discovered that parents were paying stand-ins to attend the school instead of their own children, and that some fourteen- and fifteen-year-olds were suffering from venereal disease.
18 Bruno Beger, *Mit der deutschen Tibetexpedition Ernst Schäfer*, pp.135–6.
19 According to the Gould mission diary.
20 See Chapman, *Lhasa, the Holy City*, pp.70–1.

CHAPTER TEN

1 This account is indebted to Goldstein, *A History of Modern Tibet*, p.139ff, and Smith, *Tibetan Nation*, from Chapter Seven onwards.
2 In Maraini, *Secret Tibet*, p.342.
3 Isabel Hilton in *The Search for the Panchen Lama* gives an

illuminating account of Buddhist reincarnation, and I have made extensive use of it here.

4 From Goldstein, p.53.

5 Quoted in Goldstein, p.79.

6 The other three young aristocrats sent to Rugby were Sonam Gombo Gorkhawa, Rinzin Dorje Ringang and Wangdu Norbu Kyibu.

7 According to Sikkim political officer F. W. Williamson, quoted in Goldstein, *A History of Modern Tibet*, p.151.

8 Derrick Williamson, quoted in McKay, *Tibet and the British Raj*, p.141.

9 The *ragyapa* also worked as butchers at the slaughterhouse which lay just outside Lhasa, and were charged with dismembering corpses for sky burials.

10 Shakabpa, *Tibet*, p.132ff.

11 See also Schäfer's account on p.29 of *Fest der weissen Schleier* (*Festival of the White Scarves*), which adds other details based on a conversation with the Regent in 1939.

CHAPTER ELEVEN

1 L/P&S/12/4193 (OIOC).

2 L/P&S/12/4197 (OIOC).

3 See McKay on prestige in *Tibet and the British Raj*, p.146ff.

4 Beger, *Mit der deutschen Tibetexpedition Ernst Schäfer*, p.161.

5 See Goldstein, *A History of Modern Tibet*, p.330ff.

6 Beger, *Mit der deutschen Tibetexpedition Ernst Schäfer*, pp.161–2.

7 See ibid., p.182, and Alex McKay's 'Swastikas, Medicine and Tibet' in *Wellcome History* issue no. 20, June 2002, pp.10–12.

8 And, according to McKay (*Tibet and the British Raj*, p.163), made his fortune there. One official visitor noted, 'No means of extracting money from impoverished subjects is neglected by this avaricious *dzongpon*.'

9 See ibid., p.68.

10 Schäfer, *Fest der weissen Schleier*, p.164.

11 This account uses information from Engelhardt *The Ernst Schaefer Tibet Expedition (1938–1939): New Light on the Political History of*

Tibet in the First Half of the 20th Century pp. 187–95, in McKay *Tibet and her Neighbours*. Dr Engelhardt is not responsible for any of the opinions expressed in this chapter.

12 Engelhardt, p.193: her translation.

13 See, for example, Victor and Victoria Trimondi: *Der Schatten des Dalai Lama* (1999) and *Hitler, Buddha, Krishna* (2003).

14 Engelhardt, p.194.

15 This account is based on the Hugh Richardson papers, Oriental Collections, Bodleian Library.

CHAPTER TWELVE

1 L/P&S/12/4343 (OIOC).

2 Beger, *Mit der deutschen Tibetexpedition Ernst Schäfer*, p.221.

3 According to the British files, 'Professor Tucci in a letter dated 30th June writes that on the 29th June he arrived in Shigatse "where my impression is that the Germans made the Europeans rather unpopular: people here seem to have been shocked by the great shouting [*sic*] which they did".' In the margin someone has queried: *shouting or shooting?*

4 Metcalfe to Peel, 12 June 1939: 'His Excellency assumes that in view of the attitude which Dr Schaefer has taken up in the German press and also his behaviour in Sikkim and Tibet, His Majesty's Govt. will not desire that any special favour should be shown to him against the wishes of the Sikkim Darbar . . . No pressure should be brought on the Sikkim Darbar to allow Dr Schaefer to remain in Sikkim for further investigations . . . they should be given a definite hint not to ask for a passport for Kaiser. We feel strongly that it would be a mistake to allow Kaiser to go to Germany and there to be trained as a Nazi agent for propaganda in Sikkim and Tibet.'

5 The explorer.

6 Gould: 'What struck me most forcibly was Schäfer's utter surprise at the bare idea of anybody interfering with his plans.'

7 R 135/40.

8 Ibid.

9 Sources for this account of the pact are Kershaw, *Nemesis* and Shirer, *This is Berlin*.

CHAPTER THIRTEEN

1 Interrogation #1018-b, 2 April 1947 (NARA).
2 I have reconstructed this incident from correspondence in Ernst Schäfer's SS files (NARA).
3 Quoted in Kershaw, *Nemesis*, p.217.
4 From von Weizsäcker, *Erinnerungen* (1950), quoted in Kershaw, *Nemesis*, p.228.
5 Quoted in Davies, *Europe: a History*, p.1,002.
6 But see Longerich for a discussion of the origins of the *Endlösung*, or Final Solution, itself in *The Unwritten Order*.
7 Sources for Schäfer's wartime ambitions and activities are the Himmler files (NS21), the voluminous records of the Sven Hedin Institute (R135) in the Bundesarchiv, and his own self-serving and evasive post-war interrogations held by the National Archives in Washington (German Captured Documents, RG238).
8 FO 371/24693 File 272 (PRO).
9 See Peter Hopkirk's revelatory *Like Hidden Fire: the Plot to Bring Down the British Empire* (New York: Kodansha International, 1994), published in the UK as *On Secret Service East of Constantinople*.
10 See Sykes, *Wassmuss*, p.38.
11 Ibid., p.46.
12 See Hauner, *India in Axis Strategy*, p.160ff.
13 In an email to author, 10 February 2003.
14 Padfield, *Himmler*, p.274.
15 NS19 (BA).
16 See Meyer and Brysac, *Tournament of Shadows*, p.340ff.
17 It should be pointed out that the Soviet treatment of Poles on its side of the agreed demarcation line was even more brutal, at least during the first few months of the war. The level of collaboration between the Soviet NKVD and the SS during the period of the Nazi–Soviet Pact has yet to be established conclusively. For a discussion of this, see Mazower, *Dark Continent*, p.164ff.
18 Quoted in Padfield, *Himmler*, p.289.

19 Poet and playwright; he became the 'Nazi laureate'.

20 Q: When were you sent on that *Kälteauftrag* [cold mission], which is described in your statement?
A: *Kälteauftrag*? May I say something: that was a journey to Poland, where I should design uniforms, because I was a Tibet specialist, a high-mountain expert. That was the hard winter of 1939/1940. Winter uniforms were required. I should advise them on that matter (NARA).

21 According to the poet Hanns Johst.

22 The incident is described in Schellenberg, *Memoirs*, p.74.

23 See Burleigh, *Germany Turns Eastwards*, p.158ff.

24 Globocnik later claimed to have acquired 180 million marks for the Reich – without doubt an 'underdeclaration'.

25 In the autumn of 1939, not long after the beginning of the war, Hitler had ordered, in writing, 'mercy deaths' for the incurably ill. Killings were carried out by 'specified doctors' using carbon monoxide gas or by SS squads. The euthanasia programme was administered from a confiscated Jewish villa at Tiergartenstrasse 4 in Berlin, and was given the code name 'T4'. The T4 doctors and their killers, like 'Globus', claimed at least ninety thousand 'lives not worth living' by the time the programme was wound up in August 1941.

26 Interrogations (NARA).

27 Quoted extensively; see, for example, Padfield, *Himmler*, p.470.

28 Both Padfield (*Himmler*) and Kershaw (*Nemesis*) make this point about the Posen speech.

29 Published in 1951 – see bibliography.

30 From Hedin, *German Diary*, p.152. Hedin records a meeting with Lord Londonderry, a leading German sympathizer and author of *Ourselves and Germany* (1938).

31 Hedin, *German Diary*, p.74.

32 See Fischer, *The History of an Obsession*.

33 Hedin, *German Diary*, p.121.

34 Ibid., p.122.

35 Ibid., pp.144–5.

CHAPTER FOURTEEN

1 Hedin also recalled another interview with Himmler when the Reichsführer enlisted his assistance in making sure Schäfer did not go gallivanting off on another expedition. Hedin agreed that it was essential for him to work on his collections and seems to have urged Schäfer not to neglect his academic work. This suggests that Himmler was frightened that Schäfer might escape his clutches. Himmler said to Hedin, too, that he did not want Schäfer's book and film to be released 'until the end of the war'. They would suffer inevitable neglect, he said – but what Himmler wanted was control, of course.

2 In *Das Ahnenerbe*, p.213.

3 Q: How was Mittersill linked to the SS?
A: Not at all.
Q: But that is not true.
A: I build up Mittersill to get away from the SS. Formally there was a connection to the SS, of course. All the members of the expedition were members of the SS.
(NARA Interrogation #1018-c, 16 April 1947)

4 See Padfield, *Himmler*, p.127.

5 See Berben, *Dachau*, p.4.

6 Support for alternative healing rose during the Nazi period, but medical journals continued to publish significant criticism from doctors, insurance companies and the pharmaceutical industry. Some well-known medical figures warned that alternative methods threatened scientific thinking and were dangerous doctrines. During the war, labour leader Robert Ley established an Office for the Occult (Hauptstelle Okkultismus) to combat a wartime 'flight into the occult'. See Proctor, *Racial Hygiene*, pp.244–8.

7 My account of Rascher's activities is based on Mitscherlich and Mielke's *Doctors of Infamy*, Padfield's *Himmler* (p.374ff), Kater's *Das Ahnenerbe* (p.262ff), and Robert Jay Lifton's *The Nazi Doctors* (London: Macmillan, 1986), which is now rather dated.

8 Padfield, *Himmler*, p.377.

9 See Proctor, *The Nazi War on Cancer*, p.121.

10 Quoted in Mitscherlich and Mielke, *Doctors of Infamy*, pp.4–6.

11 Dimensions are from Padfield, *Himmler*, p.374.
12 Quoted in Mitscherlich and Mielke, *Doctors of Infamy*, p.7.
13 Ibid., p.8.
14 Ibid., p.19. According to a witness, Walter Neff, 180 to 200 TPs were used and 70 to 80 died.
15 Quoted in Padfield, *Himmler*, p.377.
16 Mitscherlich and Mielke, *Doctors of Infamy*, p.9.
17 Ibid., p.28.
18 For more on the 'Circle of Friends', see Vogelsang, *Der Freundeskreis Himmler*.
19 From Padfield, *Himmler*, p.194.
20 The letters are in Schäfer's SS files (NARA).
21 Records of the Sven Hedin Institute in BA, R135.
22 'The goal was to do scientific research on the many tribes of the Caucasus and at the same time form friendly relationships with the tribe leaders. Schäfer constructed the research team in the manner that had proved to work well: Earth: Wienert, animal: Schäfer, man: I. My sector had the largest staff, approximately ten scientists including myself. After the defeat at Stalingrad in January 1943 this Sonderkommando K, which was supposed to be accompanied by a guard unit, was reduced to a few people. Optimistic about a positive change of the state of war and the reoccupation of the Caucasus, the expedition was postponed.' Personal communication, Bruno Beger.
23 The Einsatzgruppen Trial of late 1945 was 'United States of America v. Otto Ohlendorf et al'.
24 See Kater, *Das Ahnenerbe*, p.221ff.
25 L/P&S/12/4343 (OIOC).
26 From the letter to General Taylor, Nuremberg, 8 May 1947.
27 According to Meyer and Brysac in *Tournament of Shadows*, p.550.

CHAPTER FIFTEEN

1 Statistics given in Burleigh, *The Third Reich*, p.489.
2 NS19 (BA).
3 It need hardly be said that this was nonsense. The Venus figurines have been found all over Europe. They were made between twenty

thousand and twenty-seven thousand years ago and there are numerous interpretations of their significance – as fertility symbols, shamanistic tools, individual portraits of women or even portable pornography. Whatever they represent, the Venus figurines do not depict racial types.

4 Quoted in Kater, *Das Ahnenerbe*, p.207ff.

5 Quoted in Longerich, *The Unwritten Order*, p.70.

6 Kershaw, *Hubris*, p.479.

7 Dwork and Jan Van Pelt, *The Holocaust*, p.287.

8 Quoted in Kershaw, *Hubris*, p.494.

9 Quoted in Pressac, *The Struthof Album*, p.32.

10 See Zimmerman, *Anthropology and Antihumanism*, p.161.

11 Hirt's career is documented in Frederick H. Kasten's 'Unethical Nazi Medicine in Annexed Alsace-Lorraine', in Kent, *Historians and Archivists*.

12 Quoted in ibid., pp.177–8.

13 See Kater, *Doctors under Hitler*, p.72.

CHAPTER SIXTEEN

1 Vrba, *I Cannot Forgive*, p.25.

2 According to Höss, 'Death Dealer', p.290.

3 From Dwork and Jan Van Pelt, *Auschwitz*, pp.322–3.

4 Pohl was also a member of the Freundeskreis.

5 See Peter Weingart, *Doppel-Leben: Ludwig Ferdinand Clauss*.

6 Personal communication, Bruno Beger.

7 Ibid.

8 The unfortunately named Hans Fleischacker was a co-defendant of Beger's in 1971. He was born in 1912 and educated like Beger at Jena University. He joined the SS in 1937 after being appointed to the Institute of Racial Research in Tübingen. He joined the NSDAP in 1940 and worked for the RuSHA.

9 In *Auschwitz*, p.268.

10 Kramer's interrogation is quoted at length in Pressac, *The Struthof Album*.

11 Many Nazi medical experiments were carelessly and erratically carried out. As a result of Allied bombing, Hirt might not have

received the maceration equipment needed to deflesh the bodies.

12 Quoted in Edouard Conté, 'Au Terme de L'Horreur: La "Collection de Squelettes Juifs" de l'Université du Reich de Strasbourg', in Conté, *La Quête de la Race*.

CHAPTER SEVENTEEN

1 Burleigh, *The Third Reich*, p.767.

2 Or Handjar, meaning 'sword'.

3 There were close to five thousand Germans in the division, including 279 officers, a number which comprised about a fifth of the Handschar's fighting strength.

4 The Catholic Church has an equally poor record. Fanatical priests actively participated in the creation of Europe's third largest death camp at Jasenovac.

5 Personal communication, Bruno Beger.

6 Ibid.

7 This account is based on Cook and Russell, *Heinrich Himmler's Camelot*.

8 Quoted in Padfield, *Himmler*, p.610.

9 Kasten, 'Unethical Nazi Medicine in Annexed Alsace-Lorraine', in Kent, *Historians and Archivists*, p.189.

CHAPTER EIGHTEEN

1 L/P&J/12/633 (OIOC).

2 Schäfer's claim that he had discovered an animal unknown to science has been disputed, as pointed out at the end of Chapter Seven. The fact is that no-one can be certain whether he was right or wrong. There has been no genetic study of the animal and no attempt to trace its ancestral lineage. The shapi remains a mystery, and Schäfer remains for most Sikkimese an obscure German who gave his name to a rare kind of goat.

SELECT BIBLIOGRAPHY

This listing is necessarily selective, especially with the literature on Hitler, Nazism and the Holocaust, which in both English and German is vast (my emphasis in the 'Germany' list is on English-language sources). Multiple entries under an author have been arranged in order of date of publication.

DOCUMENTARY SOURCES

Academy of Natural Sciences, Philadelphia (PAS)
Federal Archives, Berlin-Lichterfelde (BA)
Federal Archives, Koblenz (BK)
Institut für Zeitgeschichte, Munich (IZ)
National Archives, Washington DC (NARA)
Oriental and India Office Collections (OIOC), British Library
Public Record Office, Kew (PRO)

ORIGINAL EXPEDITION ACCOUNTS

Beger, Bruno, *Mit der deutschen Tibetexpedition Ernst Schäfer, 1938/9 nach Lhasa* (Wiesbaden: Verlag Dieter Schwarz, 1998)

Dolan, Brooke, 'To the Edge of the World' (Philadelphia: Proceedings of the Academy of Natural Sciences, 1937)

Duncan, Marion, *The Yangtze and the Yak: Adventurous Trails in and out of Tibet* (Alexandria, Virginia, 1952)

Schäfer, Ernst:

THE DOLAN EXPEDITIONS

Berge,Buddhas und Bären: Forschnung und Jagd in Geheimnisvollem Tibet (Berlin: Verlag Paul Parey, 1933)

Unbekanntes Tibet: Durch die Wildnisse Osttibets zum Dach der Erde Tibetexpedition 1934/36 (Berlin: Verlag Paul Parey, 1937)

Dach der Erde: Durch das Wunderland Hochtibet Tibetexpedition 1934/6 (Berlin: Verlag Paul Parey, 1938)

Tibet ruft: Forschung und Jagd in den Hochgebirgen Osttibets: Tibetexpedition 1931–1932 (Berlin: Verlag Paul Parey, 1942)

TIBET EXPEDITION 1938–9

Geheimnis Tibet, erster Bericht der deutschen Tibet-Expedition, Ernst Schäfer, 1938/39 (Munich: F. Bruckmann, 1943)

Fest der weissen Schleier; eine Forscherfahrt durch Tibet nach Lhasa, der heiligen Stadt des Gottkönigtums (Braunschweig: Vieweg-Verlag, 1949, 1961)

Unter Räubern in Tibet; Gefahren und Freuden eines Forscherlebens (Braunschweig: Vieweg-Verlag 1952)

Über den Himalaja ins Land der Götter: auf Forscherfahrt von Indien nach Tibet (Braunschweig: Vieweg-Verlag, 1959)

Auf einsamen Wechseln und Wegen: Jagd und Forschung in drei Erdteilen (Hamburg: Verlag Paul Parey, 1961)

Wienert, Karl: 'Preliminary Report of the Magnetic Results of a Journey to Sikkim and Southern Tibet' (London: *Journal of Terrestrial Magnetism*, December 1947)

TIBET AND CENTRAL ASIA

Allen, Charles, *A Mountain in Tibet: the Search for Mount Kailas and the Sources of the Great Rivers of India* (London: Deutsch, 1982)

—— *The Search for Shangri-La* (London: Little, Brown & Co., 1999)

—— *The Buddha and the Sahibs* (London: John Murray, 2002)
Bechert, Heinz and Gombrich, Richard, *The World of Buddhism* (London: Thames & Hudson, 1984)
Bell, Charles, *Tibet, Past and Present* (Oxford: 1924, 1968)
—— *Portrait of the Dalai Lama* (London: Collins, 1946)
Beckwith, Christopher, *The Tibetan Empire in Central Asia* (Princeton University Press, 1987)
Bishop, Peter, *The Myth of Shangri-La: Tibet, Travel Writing and the Western Creation of Sacred Landscape* (London: Athlone, 1989)
Bjerken, Zeff, *Tibetan Nativism and the Quest for Indigenous Bön* (forthcoming)
Candler, Edmund, *The Unveiling of Lhasa* (London: E. Arnold, 1905)
Chapman, F. Spencer, *Lhasa, the Holy City* (London: Chatto & Windus, 1938)
Claude White, John, *Sikkim and Bhutan: Twenty-One Years of the North East Frontier 1887–1908* (London: Edward Arnold, 1909)
Das, Sarat Chandra (ed. W. W. Rockhill), *Journey to Lhasa and Central Tibet* (New Delhi: Manjusri Publishers, 1970)
David-Neel, Alexandra, *My Journey to Lhasa: the Personal Story of the Only White Woman Who Succeeded in Entering the Forbidden City* (London, New York: Harper, 1927)
Desmond, Ray, *Sir Joseph Hooker: Traveller and Plant Collector* (Woodbridge: Antique Collectors' Club with the Royal Botanic Garden, Kew, 1999)
Dodin, Thierry and Räther, Heinz (eds), *Mythos Tibet: Wahrnehmungen, Projektionen, Phantasienherausgegeben von der Kunst und Austellungshalle der Bundesrepublik Deutschland in Zusammenarbeit* (Cologne: Dumont, 1997)
—— *Imagining Tibet: Perceptions, Projections, Fantasies* (Boston: Wisdom Publications, 2001)
Dorje, Gyurme, *Tibet Handbook* (Bath: Footprint Handbooks, 1999)
Filchner, Wilhelm, *Sturm über Asien, Erlebnisse diplomatischen Geheimagenten, mit vielen Abbildungen, Karten und Vollbildern nach Skizzen des Verfassers* (Berlin: Neufeld & Henius, 1924)
—— *A Scientist in Tartary: from the Hoang-ho to the Indus* (London: Faber & Faber Ltd, 1939)

French, Patrick, *Younghusband: the Last Imperial Adventurer* (London: HarperCollins, 1994)

Gallenkamp, Charles, *Dragon Hunter: Roy Chapman Andrews and the Central Asiatic Expeditions* (New York: Viking Penguin, 2001)

Goldstein, Melvyn, *A History of Modern Tibet 1913–1951: The Demise of the Lamaist State* (Berkeley: 1989)

—— *The Snow Lion and the Dragon: China, Tibet and the Dalai Lama* (Berkeley: 1997)

Gould, Sir Basil, *The Jewel in the Lotus: Recollections of an Indian Political* (London: Chatto & Windus, 1957)

Goullart, Peter, *Land of the Lamas: Adventures in Secret Tibet* (New York: Dutton, 1959)

Harrer, Heinrich, *Lost Lhasa: Heinrich Harrer's Tibet* (New York: H. N. Abrams, 1992)

Hedin, Sven, *Adventures in Tibet* (London: Hurst and Blackett Ltd, 1904)

—— *Transhimalaya, Discoveries and Adventures in Tibet* (London: Macmillan and Co. Ltd, 1909–13)

—— *A Conquest of Tibet* (New York: E. P. Dutton, 1934)

—— *German Diary, 1935–1942*, translated by Joan Bulman (Dublin: Euphorian, 1951)

—— *My Life as an Explorer: Sven Hedin*, illustrated by the author, translated by Alfhild Huebsch, with a new prologue and epilogue by Peter Hopkirk (New York: Kodansha International, 1996)

Hilton, Isabel, *The Search for the Panchen Lama* (London: Viking, 1999)

Hoffmann, Heinrich, *The Religions of Tibet* (London: Allen & Unwin, 1961)

Hopkirk, Peter, *Foreign Devils on the Silk Road: The Search for the Lost Cities and Treasures of Chinese Central Asia* (London: John Murray, 1980)

—— *Trespassers on the Roof of the World: The Race for Lhasa* (London: John Murray, 1982)

—— *The Great Game: On Secret Service in High Asia* (London: John Murray, 1990)

—— *On Secret Service East of Constantinople: The Plot to Bring Down*

the British Empire (London: John Murray, 1994)
Kimura, Hisao, *Japanese Agent in Tibet: My Ten Years of Travel in Disguise* (London: Serindia, 1990)
Kvaerne, Per, *The Bön Religion of Tibet* (London: Serindia, 1995)
Lamb, Alistair, *Britain and Chinese Central Asia: The Road to Lhasa 1767–1905* (London: Routledge and Paul, 1960)
—— *British India and Tibet, 1766–1910* (London and New York: Routledge and Kegan Paul, 1986)
—— *Tibet, China & India 1914–1950: A History of Imperial Diplomacy* (Hertingfordbury (Britain): Roxford Books, 1989)
Larsen, Knud and Sinding-Larsen, Amund, *The Lhasa Atlas: Traditional Tibetan Architecture and Townscape* (Boston: Shambhala, 2001)
Lopez, Donald Jr, *Curators of the Buddha: The Study of Buddhism under Colonialism* (University of Chicago Press, 1995)
—— *Prisoners of Shangri-La* (University of Chicago Press, 1998)
—— (ed.) *Asian Religions in Practice: an introduction* (Princeton University Press, 1999)
McGovern, William Montgomery, *To Lhasa in Disguise, a Secret Expedition Through Mysterious Tibet* (New York, London: Century, 1924)
MacGregor, John, *Tibet: A Chronicle of Exploration* (London: Routledge and Kegan Paul, 1970)
McKay, Alex, *Tibet and the British Raj: The Frontier Cadre, 1904–1947* (Richmond: Curzon Press, 1997)
—— *Tibetan History: Tibet and its Neighbours* (London: Hans Jorgemeyer, 2003)
Maraini, Fosco, *Secret Tibet* (London: Hutchinson, 1952)
Matthiesen, Peter, *The Snow Leopard* (London: Penguin, 1978)
Meyer, Karl and Brysac, Shareen, *Tournament of Shadows* (Washington: Counterpoint, 1999)
Millington, Powell, *To Lhassa* [*sic*] *At Last*, New York Public Library microfilm (London: Smith, Elder, 1905)
Pallis, Marco, *Peaks and Lamas* (London: Woburn Press, 1974)
Richardson, Hugh, *Tibet and its History* (Oxford University Press, 1962)

—— *Ceremonies of the Lhasa Year*, ed. Michael Aris (London: Serindia, 1993)

—— *High Peaks, Pure Earth: Collected Writings on Tibetan History and Culture* (London: Serindia, 1997)

Sergeant, Harriet, *Shanghai* (London: John Murray, 1991)

Shakabpa, Tsepon, *Tibet: A Political History* (Newhaven and London: Yale University Press, 1967)

Singh, Amar Kaur Jasbir, *Himalayan Triangle* (London: the British Library, 1982)

Smith, Warren W., *Tibetan Nation* (Boulder, Colorado: Westview Press, 1996)

Snellgrove, David, *Himalayan Pilgrimage* (Oxford: 1961)

—— *Nine Ways of Bön* (London: 1967)

Stein, R.A., *Tibetan Civilization* (London: Faber & Faber Ltd, 1972)

Sutton, S. B., *In China's Border Provinces: the Turbulent Career of Joseph Rock, Botanist-explorer* (New York: Hastings House, 1974)

Taring, Rinchen Dolma, *Daughter of Tibet* (London: John Murray, 1970)

Tucci, Giuseppe, *Secrets of Tibet: The Chronicle of the Tucci Scientific Expedition to Western Tibet (1933)* (London and Glasgow: Blackie & Son Ltd, 1935)

—— *The Religions of Tibet* (London: Routledge, 1970)

—— *Indo-Tibetica* (New Delhi: Aditya Prakashan, 1988)

Waddell, L. A., *Lhasa and its Mysteries, with a Record of the Expedition of 1903–1904* (London: John Murray, 1910)

Whitfield, Susan, *Life Along the Silk Road* (London: John Murray, 1999)

Williamson, Margaret, *Memoirs of a Political Officer's Wife in Tibet, Sikkim, and Bhutan* (London: Wisdom, 1987)

Winchester, Simon, *The River at the Centre of the World: A Journey up the Yangtze and back in Chinese Time* (London: Viking, 1997)

Wynn, Antony, *Persia in the Great Game: Sir Percy Sykes Explorer, Consul, Soldier, Spy* (London: John Murray, 2003)

Younghusband, Sir Francis Edward, *India and Tibet: a history of the relations which have subsisted between the two countries from the time of Warren Hastings to 1910; with a particular account of the mission to Lhasa of 1904* (London: John Murray, 1910)

HISTORY OF THE OCCULT

Blavatsky, Helena Petrovna, *Posthumous memoirs of Helena Petrovna Blavatsky. Dictated from the spirit-world, upon the typewriter, independent of all human contact, under the supervision of G. W. N. Yost, to bring to light the things of truth, and affirm the continuity of life and the eternal activity of the soul immortal* (Boston: J. M. Wade, 1896)

—— *Isis Unveiled: A Master Key to the Mysteries of Ancient and Modern Science and Theology* (Point Loma, California: Aryan Theosophical Press, 1919 – NB: there are modern abridgements available)

—— *The Secret Doctrine: The Synthesis of Science, Religion, and Philosophy* (Los Angeles, California: Theosophical University Press, 1963)

Carlson, Maria, *No Religion Higher than Truth: A History of the Theosophical Movement in Russia* (Princeton University Press, 1993)

Cranston, Sylvia, HPB: *The Extraordinary Life and Influence of Helena Blavatsky, Founder of the Modern Theosophical Movement* (New York: Putnam, 1993)

Goodrick-Clark, Nicholas, *The Occult Roots of Nazism* (New York and London: New York University Press, 1985)

—— *Hitler's Priestess: Savitri Devi, the Hindu-Aryan Myth and Neo-Nazism* (New York and London: New York University Press, 1998)

—— *Black Sun: Aryan Cults, Esoteric Nazism and the Politics of Identity* (New York and London: New York University Press, 2002)

Hancock, Graham, *Underworld: Flooded Kingdoms of the Ice Age* (London: Michael Joseph, 2002)

Johnson, K Paul, *The Masters Revealed: Madame Blavatsky and the Myth of the Great White Lodge* (State University of New York Press, 1994)

—— *Initiates of the Theosophical Masters* (State University of New

York Press, 1995)
Meade, Marion, *Madame Blavatsky: The Woman Behind the Myth* (New York: Putnam, *c.* 1980)
Poliakov, Leon, *The Aryan Myth* (New York: Barnes and Noble Books, 1971, 1974)
Strunk, Joseph, *Zu Juda und Rom–Tibet: ihr Ringenum die Weltherrschaft* (Munich: 1938 – microfilmed copy available in the New York Public Library)
Washington, Peter, *Madame Blavatsky's Baboon: Theosophy and the Emergence of the Western Guru* (London: Secker & Warburg, 1993).

GERMANY

Ackermann, Joseph, *Heinrich Himmler als Ideologe* (Göttingen: Musterschidt, 1970)
Aly, Gotz, Chroust, Peter and Pross, Christian, *Cleansing the Fatherland: Nazi Medicine and Racial Hygiene* (Baltimore, Maryland: Johns Hopkins University Press, 1994)
Arendt, Hannah, *Eichmann in Jerusalem: A Report on the Banality of Evil* (New York: Viking, 1963)
Berben, P., *Dachau, 1933–1945* (London: Norfolk Press, 1975)
Berenbaum, Michael and Gutman, Yisrael (eds), *Anatomy of the Auschwitz Death Camp* (published in association with the United States Holocaust Memorial Museum, Washington DC, by Indiana University Press, 1994)
Bloch, Michael, *Ribbentrop* (London, New York: Bantam, 1992)
Brebeck, Wulff and Hüser, Karl, *Wewelsburg 1933–1945: A Cult and Terror Centre of the SS* (Landschaftsverband Westfalen-Lippe, 2000)
Breitman, Richard, *The Architect of Genocide: Heinrich Himmler and the Final Solution* (Hanover: University Press of New England, 1992)
Bridgman, Jon M., *The Revolt of the Hereros* (Berkeley: University of California Press, 1981)

Browning, Christopher, *Ordinary Men: Reserve Police Battalion 101 and the Final Solution in Poland* (New York: Aaron Asher Books, 1992)

Burleigh, Michael, *Germany Turns Eastwards: A Study of Ostforschung in the Third Reich* (Cambridge University Press, 1988)

—— (with Wolfgang Wippermann) *The Racial State: Germany, 1933–1945* (Cambridge University Press, 1991)

—— *The Third Reich: a New History* (London: Macmillan, 2000)

Clauss, Ludwig Ferdinand, *Rasse und Seel: Eine Einfuhrung in die Gegenwart* (Munich: Lehmanns Verlag, 1926)

Cohn, Norman, *Warrant for Genocide* (London: Eyre and Spottiswoode, 1967)

Conté, Edouard (ed.), *La Quête de la Race: Une Anthropologie du Nazisme* (Paris: Hachette, 1995)

Cook, Stephen and Russell, Stuart, *Heinrich Himmler's Camelot* (Kressmann-Backmayer Publishing, 1999)

Davies, Norman, *Europe: A History* (Oxford University Press, 1996)

Deichmann, Ute, *Biologists under Hitler* (*Biologen unter Hitler*), translated by Thomas Dunlap (Cambridge, Massachusetts: Harvard University Press, 1996)

Dwork, Debórah and Jan Van Pelt, Robert, *Auschwitz, 1270 to the Present* (New York: W. W. Norton, 1996)

—— *The Holocaust: a History* (New York: W. W. Norton, 2002)

Feig, Konnilyn G., *Hitler's Death Camps: The Sanity of Madness* (New York: Holmes and Meier Publishers, 1981)

Fest, Joachim C., *Speer: The Final Verdict* (London: Weidenfeld & Nicolson, 2001)

Fischer, Klaus, *Nazi Germany: A New History* (New York: Continuum, 1995)

—— *The History of an Obsession: German Judeophobia and the Holocaust* (New York: Continuum, 1998)

Friedlander, Saul, *Nazi Germany and the Jews: The Years of Persecution* (London: HarperCollins, 1998)

Gasman, Daniel, *The Scientific Origins of National Socialism: Social Darwinism in Ernst Haeckel and the German Monist League* (London: Macdonald and Co., 1971)

—— *Haeckel's Monism and the Birth of Fascist Ideology* (New York: P. Lang, 1998)

Griffiths, Richard M., *Fellow Travellers of the Right: British Enthusiasts for Nazi Germany 1933–9* (London: Constable, 1980)

Günther, Hans F. K., *Kleine Rassenkund Europas* (Munich: Lehmanns Verlag, 1925)

—— *The Racial Elements of European History*, translated from the second German edition by G. C. Wheeler (London: Methuen, 1927)

—— *Rassenkunde des deutschen Volkes* (Lehmanns Verlag, 1930)

—— *Rassenkunde des jüdischen Volkes* (Lehmanns Verlag, 1930)

—— *Die nordische Rasse bei den Indogermanen Asiens: zugleich ein Beitrag zur Frage nach der Urheimat und Rassenherkunft der Indogermanen* (Munich: Lehmanns Verlag, 1934)

—— *Ritter, Tod und Teufel: der heldische Gedanke* (Munich: J. F. Lehmann, 1937, new edition)

Hauner, Milan, *India in Axis Stategy: Germany, Japan and Indian Nationalists in the Second World War* (Stuttgart: Klett-Cotta, 1981)

Heiber, Helmut, *Reichsführer! Briefe an und von Himmler* (Stuttgart: Deutsche Verlags-Anstalt, 1968)

Höhne, Heinz, *The Order of the Death's Head: The Story of Hitler's S.S.*, translated from the German by Richard Barry (New York: Coward-McCann, 1970)

—— *Der Orden unter dem Totenkopf: die Geschichte der SS* (Augsburg: Weltbild Verlag, 1994)

Höss, Rudolf, *Commandant of Auschwitz: The Autobiography of Rudolf Hoess* (Cleveland: World Publishing Co., 1959)

International Auschwitz Committee, *Nazi Medicine: Doctors, Victims and Medicine* (New York: Howard Fertig, 1986)

Kater, Michael, *Das Ahnenerbe der SS, 1935–1945: ein Beitrag zur Kulturpolitik des Dritten Reiches* (Stuttgart: Deutsche Verlags-Anstalt, 1974)

—— *The Nazi Party: A Social Profile of Members and Leaders, 1919–1945* (Cambridge, Massachusetts: Harvard University Press, 1983)

—— *Doctors under Hitler* (Chapel Hill: University of North Carolina

Press, 1989)

Kent, George O., *Historians and Archivists: Essays in Modern German History* (Fairfax, Virginia: George Mason University Press, 1991)

Kershaw, Ian, *Hitler, 1889–1936: Hubris* (London: Allen Lane, 1998)

—— *Hitler, 1936–45: Nemesis* (London: Allen Lane, 2000)

—— *The Nazi Dictatorship: Problems and Perspectives of Interpretation* (London: Arnold, 2000)

Klemperer, Victor, *I Shall Bear Witness: The Diaries of Victor Klemperer* (London: 1998–9)

Koehl, Robert Lewis, *The SS: A History* (Tempus, 1989, 2000)

Kuhl, Stefan, *The Nazi Connection* (New York and Oxford: Oxford University Press, 1994)

Lerner, Richard, *Final Solutions: Biology, Prejudice and Genocide* (University Park, Pennsylvania: Pennsylvania State University, 1992)

Lochner, Louis P., *What about Germany?* (New York: Dodd, Mead & Co., 1942)

Longerich, Peter, *The Unwritten Order* (Stroud: Tempus, 2002)

Mazower, Mark, *Dark Continent: Europe's Twentieth Century* (London: Allen Lane, 1998)

Mitscherlich, A. and Mielke, F., *Doctors of Infamy: The Story of the Nazi Medical Crimes*, translated by Heinz Norden, with statements by Andrew C. Ivy, Telford Taylor and Leo Alexander, and a note on medical ethics by Albert Deutsch including the new Hippocratic oath of the World Medical Association (New York: H. Schuman, 1949)

Mosse, George, *The Crisis of German Ideology: Intellectual Origins of the Third Reich* (New York: Grosset & Dunlap, 1964)

—— *Toward the Final Solution: A History of European Racism* (Madison, Wisconsin: University of Wisconsin Press, 1985)

Nyiszli, Miklós, *Auschwitz: A Doctor's Eyewitness Account* (New York: Fell, 1960)

Padfield, Peter, *Himmler: Reichsführer-SS* (London: Macmillan, 1990)

Petropoulos, Jonathan, *The Faustian Bargain* (Penguin Books, 2000)

Pressac, Jean-Claude, *The Struthof Album* (New York: Beate Klarsfeld Foundation, 1985)

Proctor, Robert N., *Racial Hygiene: Medicine under the Nazis* (Cambridge, Massachusetts: Harvard University Press, 1988)
—— *The Nazi War on Cancer* (Princeton University Press, 1999)
Remy, Steven, *The Heidelberg Myth: The Nazification and Denazification of a German University* (Cambridge, Massachusetts: Harvard University Press, 2002)
Schellenberg, Walter, *The Schellenberg Memoirs* (London: Andre Deutsch, 1956)
Schleunes, Karl, *Schooling and Society: The Politics of Education in Prussia and Bavaria, 1750–1900* (Oxford University Press, 1989)
—— *The Twisted Road to Auschwitz: Nazi Policy towards German Jews 1933–1939* (Urbana: University of Illinois Press, 1990)
Sereny, Gitta, *Albert Speer: His Battle with Truth* (London: Macmillan, 1995)
Shirer, William, *This is Berlin* (London: Hutchinson, 1999)
Smelser, Ronald and Zitelmann, Rainer, *The Nazi Elite* (London: Macmillan, 1993)
Smith, Bradley F., *Heinrich Himmler: A Nazi in the Making 1900–1926* (Stanford, California: Hoover Institution Press, 1971)
Smith, Woodruff D., *The Ideological Origins of Nazi Imperialism* (New York and Oxford: Oxford University Press, 1986)
Speer, Albert, *Inside the Third Reich* (London: Cardinal, 1975)
—— *The Slave State: Heinrich Himmler's Masterplan for SS Supremacy* (London: Weidenfeld & Nicolson, *c.* 1981)
Sykes, Christopher, *Wassmuss, the 'German Lawrence': His Adventures in Persia during and after the War* (London: Longmans, 1936)
Szöllösi-Janze, Margit (ed.), *Science in the Third Reich* (Oxford University Press, 2001)
Thomson, Ian, *Primo Levi* (London: Hutchinson, 2002)
Van der Vat, Dan, *The Good Nazi: The Life and Lies of Albert Speer* (London: Weidenfeld & Nicolson, 1997)
Vogelsang, Reinhard, *Der Freundeskreis Himmler* (Göttingen, Zurich: Musterschidt, 1972)
Vrba, Rudolf, *I Cannot Forgive* (New York: Grove Press, *c.* 1964)
Weindling, Paul, *Health, Race and German Politics between National Unification and Nazism 1870–1945* (Cambridge University Press,

1989)

Weingart, Peter, *Doppel-Leben: Ludwig Ferdinand Clauss: zwischen Rassenforschung und Widerstand* (Frankfurt and New York: Campus, 1995)

Weitz, John, *Hitler's Diplomat: The Life and Times of Joachim von Ribbentrop* (New York: Ticknow and Fields, 1992)

Ziegler, Herbert, *Nazi Germany's New Aristocracy: The SS Leadership 1925–1939* (Princeton University Press, 1989)

Zimmerman, Andrew, *Anthropology and Antihumanism in Imperial Germany* (Chicago: University of Chicago Press, 2001)

—— 'Adventures in the Skin Trade: Physical Anthropology and the Colonial Encounter', in Matti Bunzl and Glenn Penny (eds), *Worldly Provincialism: German Anthropology in the Age of Empire* (Ann Arbor: University of Michigan Press, forthcoming)

INDEX

NOTE: the English articles 'A', 'An', 'The' are ignored in alphabetization; e.g. *The Link* journal is listed under L.

Academy of Natural Sciences (Philadelphia) 113, 121, 174
Aeluropus melanolueca see pandas
Afghanistan 216–17, 445, 449
Ahnenerbe 31, 33, 40, 138
  and Berger 502
  and Kiss 185
  and Schäfer 179, 182, 185, 450, 461, 463–4, 480
Akeh *see* Bhutia, Akeh
al-Husseini, Hajj Amin 522
'Albrecht the Bear', Prince 170
Allen, Charles 323
Altan Khan 344
Altiplano (South America) 183
altitude sickness 264
Altmärkische Wische region 170, 242
Alvensleben, Ludolf von 452
Amanullah Plan (Afghanistan) 445, 447, 449
Amdo province (China) 362
Amery, Leo 214
Amne Machin mountain (Tibet) 115, 208–10, 548*n*
Amt Rosenberg 180
ancestor-worship *see* Ahnenerbe
Anglo-German Review 222
anthropology 64, 80–1, 90, 144–9, 244
  influencing Himmler 169–70
  result of war and defeat 161–2
  Schäfer's angle 196–7
  sexual mores of native people 257, 278, 348, 374
  use of corpses 148, 149–50
  use of skulls 495–6
  see also face masks; Günther, F K. ('Rassen'); measuring people
anthropometry *see* measuring people
anti-Semitism 76, 101, 132, 134, 139
  at Jena and Heidelberg 159, 165–6
  in Austria 226
  during and post-World War I 153, 154, 158

anti-Semitism (*cont.*)
Holocaust controversy 489–90
in Poland 453–6
purge of academia 162
Reichskristallnacht 295
repression under Hitler 178
see also Astor, Lord and Lady (Nancy) Waldorf; Domville, Admiral Sir Barry; genocide; Jews; Lehmann, Julius; *The Link* journal
Apollo student fraternity 133
appeasement before war 214, 220, 287–8, 295, 406, 438
advantage to Schäfer 410, 440
archaeology 188
argali (wolves) 265
Arminius (Cherusci leader) 151
Artamanen League/Society 65, 133
Aryan race theory 32, 37, 40, 43, 139
'Aryan physics' 187
literature 164
'master race' idea 60–6, 81, 143, 169, 197
in Tibet 370, 520, 528, 537
'mixing' problem 492
post-World War I 161–3
traced to Asian roots 167–8, 191–2, 211, 410
see also Ahnenerbe; anti-Semitism; genocide; Günther, F. K.
Astor, Lord and Lady (Nancy) Waldorf 220
Atlantis myth 59, 65, 139, 184
Auf gut Deutsch newspaper 134
Aufschnaiter, Peter 383
August (cook on Dolan Expedition) 87
Auschwitz concentration camp 44, 133, 141, 491
design and structure 501–2, 513
Sievers and Beger 502–4
transport of 1000 Jews 511–12
typhus outbreak 503–4, 510
Austria 207, 225–6
Avalokiteśvara (Chenresig) 411
Aymara people (South America) 183

Bailey, F. M. 325
Balikci, Anna 531
Balkan massacres 522
bandits 69–71, 86–7, 110
Barbarossa, Friedrich 150–1, 188
Barbarossa, Operation 476, 478, 481, 486–7
Bastian, Adolf 147
Batang (Tibet) 113, 114
Bauer, Paul 265
Bauze (Chinese orphan boy) 92, 93
Bavaria 154
Beger, Bruno 39, 41, 43–4, 61, 72, 74, 540*n*
appearance and character 156–7
at Natzweiler camp 518
background and family 150–6, 168–9
death camp involvement 485–9, 493–4, 499, 502–4, 509–10, 511
in Auschwitz 512–15
describes lunar eclipse 290–1
exoneration (1948) 493–4
and genocide 141–3
influence of F. K. Günther 161–2, 164, 167–8
joins expedition 188, 228, 229–30
joins Schäfer's Institute 462
joins SS 168–9, 170
and Ludwig Clauss 506–8

measuring people 170–1, 242–3, 251–2, 314–15, 410, 412–13
in Auschwitz 514–16
as 'medicine man' 243, 256–7, 264, 289–90, 389
dzongpon's wife 326–7, 549*n*
in Shigatse 417–18
Tredilinka as dispensary 384–5
meets Tering Raja's minister 276
Möndro's obsession with 387
in Norway 489
in Operation Babarossa 486–7
in Phari *dzong* 313–14
and Reting Rimpoche (Regent) 380
summarizes Expedition achievements 427
trial (1971) 493–4, 527–8
university studies 158–60, 161, 162, 164, 168–9
in Upper Italy (1945) 523
in Waffen-SS regiment 522
Beger, Friedrich (father of BB) 150–2
Beger, Gertrud (mother of BB) 150, 153, 155–6, 159
Beger, Karl (uncle of BB) 153
Bell, Charles 213, 218, 305, 350, 351, 389
attack by monks 393–4
Tibetan boys to Rugby 354
Berchtold, Joseph 136
Bergier, Jacques 537
Berlin 25–34
Olympic Games (1936) 28, 80, 177–8
Schäfer in 178–9
Best, Dr Werner 101
Bhagavadgītā 122, 134
bharal ('blue sheep') 264–5, 306
Bhutan 301
Bhutia, Akeh 143, 186, 248, 256, 296, 297, 377, 531–2
Bhutia people (Sikkim) 244, 247, 256
Bible and origins of man 60
Bickenbach, Otto 498
Bismarck, Otto von 63, 145
Black Hat Magician (New Year) 391–2
Black Knights *see* SS
Blaumen, Käthe 228, 230
Blavatsky, Helena ('H.P.B.') 51, 52–9, 64, 132, 161, 542*n*
Blumenbach, J. F. 99
Boden, Margarete *see* Himmler, Margarete
Bogle, George 319, 322
Bolshevism 486, 494
Bose, Subhas Chandra 236, 534
Bousset, Helmut 472–3
Bowles, Gordon 77, 80–1, 90–1
Brahmaputra River 332
Brandt, Rudolf 451, 494, 503–4, 527
Britain and Tibet 349–52, 358–60, 364–5
British East India Company 241
British Himalayan Club 179–80, 210
British Library India Office 210
British Mission in Lhasa 205
British Mount Everest Expedition (1938) 262
Buddhism 47, 90, 94–5, 322, 333–5
black magic tradition 374
and Bön religion 375, 391–2
Dalai Lamas' reincarnation 411
and race 167
Schäfer's knowledge of 282–3, 285
in Tibet 341–2, 343–9, 377, 380–1
Yumbu Lagang fortress 412

INDEX

Bulwer-Lytton, Edward 55
Buna-Monovitz *see* Auschwitz concentration camp
Burleigh, Michael 521

Cadwallader, Charles 175
Calcutta 234–7, 239, 295, 425–6
Camp David (USA) 482
Camp Moosburg (formerly Stalag VII) 32, 480
Canaris, Admiral Wilhelm 446–7
cancer research 187
Candler, Edmund 302, 308, 321
Caroe, Olaf 212
'Case Green' *see* Czechoslovakia
'Case White' *see* Poland
Caucasus campaign plans 476–9, 514
Celan, Paul 26, 484
Chaksam 332–3
Chamberlain, Houston Stewart 63, 133
Chamberlain, Neville 214, 222, 232, 287, 406
Champithang rest house (Chumbi Valley) 302
Chang Wei-pei 358
Changu lake 297
Chapman, F. Spencer 359, 389
Charol, Michael 457
Chengdu (China) 89, 90, 108
Chiang Kai-shek 70, 84, 94, 105, 353, 357
  and Regent Reting 362
  and Roosevelt 482
China 78, 83–9
  and Tibet 301, 305, 343, 346, 349–51, 353–4, 357–8; since Cultural Revolution 370
Chinghis Khan 342, 344
Chogyal Thutob Namygal 284, 530–1
Chokyi Nyima 282
Chomolhari, Mount 301
Chongqing (China) 87
chortens 309
Christianity 135
Christmas in Yatung 305–8
Chumbi area of Tibet 301–5, 309
Chungtang 253
Churchill, Winston 211, 288
CIA (formerly OSS) 444, 482
Ciana, Signora 137
Claude White, John 246, 284, 302, 530
Clauss, Ludwig Ferdinand 260, 504–11, 521–3
Clauss, Mechthilde (née von Wuchnow) 506–7
Clifford, Captain 324–5, 419–20
Cliveden Set (Astors) 220
Cold War 26
colonialism and anthropology 144–50
Communism 353
concentration camps 29, 39, 137, 149
  see also Beger, Bruno, concentration camp involvement; *individual camps* e.g. Auschwitz
Conti, Dr Leonardo 434
Cooper, Duff 214, 288
cosmogony *see* World Ice Theory
cosmology 181–2
Crookes, William 55
Crowley, Aleister 265
Csoma de Köros, Alexander 52
culture and race 63–4
Cunningham family (missionaries) 91
Curzon, Lord 223–4, 275, 440

Czechoslovakia 231, 287–8, 318
invasion 403–4, 490–1

Dachau concentration camp 222, 464–74, 499
Dagg, S. G. 359
Daladier, Edouard 288
Dalai Lama 37–8, 44–5, 84, 94, 204–6, 303, 325
13th Dalai Lama 339–40, 349–53
function and power 341–2, 344–8
Taktse Boy discovered in Kumbum 328, 362–4, 380
d'Alquen, Gunter 101
Däniken, Erich von 538
Darjeeling and Himalayan Railway 240–1
Darré, Walther 133, 136
Darwin, Charles 56, 63
Das Innere Reich (Nazi magazine) 161
Das, Sarat Chandra 57–8
de-nazification tribunal 74, 176
death camps *see* concentration camps
Dêgê (Tibet) 115
Dekyilinka 359, 366–7
Demo Rimpoche 340
Der Bolschewismus von Moses bis Lenin (Eckart) 134
Der Schwarze Korps (SS journal) 77, 136, 194
Deshohdunpa tribe (Tibet) 113
Deutsche Forschungsgemeinschaft 186
Devil Dance (New Year) 391
Die Nordische Rasse bei den Indogermanen Aliens (Günther) 167
Diehl, 'Nini' (later Frau Rascher) 465–6, 467, 474
Diels, Rudolf 454
Dochen meeting with Gould 421–3
doctors, Nazi 510
Doctors' Trial 493
Dohr family (Chongqing) 87
Dolan, Brooke 69, 71, 77–82, 173, 483
first Tibet expedition 81–5, 87–97
goes berserk in Philadelphia 103–5
second Tibet expedition 108–20
preparation 103–9
reconciled with Schäfer 120
slips away to Sining 117–18, 176
Dolan, Emilie (née Gerhard) 103, 105, 106, 107, 108
Dolan-Philadelphia Academy of Natural Sciences 81
Domville, Admiral Sir Barry 220–2, 467
Donnelly, Ignatius 52
Doptra 279, 280, 284
Dorje Phagmo (Tibetan incarnation) 331
Dorje Tsegyal *see* Lungshar, Tsipön
Dorzhiev, Agvan 303, 331
Doyle, Sir Arthur Conan (quotation) 51
Drax, Sir Reginald Plunket-Ernle-Erle 428
Dubois, Eugene 79
duelling 133
Duncan, Marion 69–71, 104–5, 107, 113–14, 119, 308
Dürer, Albrecht 163
Dwork, Debórah 492, 513

INDEX

Eckart, Dietrich 134–5
economy, German 155–6, 318
Eden, Anthony 214
Eichmann, Adolf 226, 490, 493, 504, 514
Einsatzgruppen SS group 476
Einsatzkommandos killing units 447
Einstein, Albert 182
Ellinger, Dr Philipp 496, 497
empires collapse 154
Engelhardt, Isrun 43, 199, 445–6
English Society for Psychical Research 60
eschatology and race 182
Essay on the Inequality of Human Races (Gobineau) 63
'ethnic cleansing' in Poland 450
Ethnic German Liaison Office 502
euthanasia programme (T4) 491
Evans, Professor Cornell 220
Evening Standard (London) 420
extermination camp *see* concentration camps
Exsternsteine rocks 125

face masks 143, 147–8, 171, 251–3, 262, 277–8, 413
Ferdinand, Archduke 151
Fest Der Weissen Schleier (Schäfer) 222
Filchner, Wilhelm 75, 189–90, 258–9, 303, 425
Final Solution *see* concentration camps; genocide
finance in post-World War I Germany 155–6
Finnish Missionary Station (Lachen) 262, 267–8
First World War *see* World War I
Fischer, Eugen 141, 164, 169
Fischer, Klaus 127
'Flamme Empor' military song 297–9
Fleischacker, Dr Hans 510, 515, 525
flora and fauna in general 239, 243–4, 255, 289, 297, 308
Unknown Tibet (Schäfer) 177
Foreign Office, British 207, 233, 239, 242, 420
Foreign Office, German 234, 438
Fox, Reginald ('Reggie') 219, 360
Frankfurt University Medical School 497
Frankfurter Zeitung newspaper 315, 420
Freemasons 134, 139
Freikorps Landshut 131
French, Patrick 302
Freundeskreis RFSS ('Circle of Friends') 138, 474–5
Frick, Wilhelm 162
Fugger of Wellenburg, Princess Elizabeth 458, 462

Gabel, Willi 510, 513–14
Galton, Francis 144–5
Gangtok (Sikkim) 245, 251, 295, 354
  author's visit (2002) 529–37
Gartzen, Ursula von *see* Schäfer, Ursula
Gauss, Carl Friedrich 99, 259
Gayokang 266
Geer, Edmund 188, 196, 227, 251, 252, 253
  as aide to Beger 387, 413
  joins Schäfer's Institute 462
Geheimnis Tibet film 46–51, 103, 190, 247, 251, 277, 285, 341, 449
Gelukpa sect ('Yellow Hats') 344

Genesis 60
Genghis Khan *see* Chinghis Khan
Genoa 229–30
genocide 142, 486, 490–2, 495–500, 521–2
'Gentlemen of the Swastika' 155, 162
geography and *Lebensraum* 260, 549*n*
geophysics 258–9
George II, King of England/ Elector of Hanover 99
Gerhard, Emilie *see* Dolan, Emilie
German Embassy (London) 218
German Experimental Institute for Aviation (DVL, Munich) 466–7, 468
German Physics Society 187–8
German Research Association (DFG) 175
German Tibet Expedition (1938)
  affected by impending World War II 414–15, 534–5
  aims and motives 36–42, 44–6, 440–2, 534–7
  arrival in Tibet 310–12
  attacked by Lhasa monks 398–9
  Christmas in Yatung 305–8
  complaints about behaviour 329–30
  disappointing reception in Lhasa 336–7
  en route for Lhasa 253–6, 295–6
  extension of time 385–6, 387–9, 399–400, 409
  film of trip 46–51
  Genoa to Calcutta 228–35
  goods carried from Tibet 409, 425
  Gyantse 323–7
  illnesses 283
  investigations forbidden 329
  leaves Tibet (August 1939) 424–7
  mail from Germany 384, 416–17
  medical factor 243
  members plunged into war (1939) 439–40
  new caravan and porters 308
    see also individual names
  remaining puzzle 397
  report from Richardson to Gould 367
  as representatives of modern Germany 383
  Schäfer's efforts in London 214–27
  split at Doptra 280
  taking on porters 248–50
  Tuna and Guru villages 320–2
  see also Schäfer, Ernst; Sikkim
German Workers Party 154
Gestapo 137
Gibb, Philip 220
Gillet, M. C. 189
Gleichschaltung (unity) 191, 192
Globocnik, Odilo 454
SS Gneisenau 228, 229, 230, 231, 233–4
Gneiser, Otto 81, 90–1
Gobineau, Arthur de 63
Gobshi 327–8
Goebbels, Josef 45, 521
Goethe 33, 99
Goodrick-Clark, Nicholas 139
Göring, Hermann 41, 98, 197–8
Göring, Carin (née von Fock) 197
Gorkha National Liberation Front 530
Gösling, Hans 235
Göttingen University 75–6, 99

Gould, Sir Basil 206, 216, 219, 233, 245
  assists Dolan (1942) 482
  and Kaiser 418
  mission to Lhasa (August 1936) 359
  and Schäfer 247–8, 267, 286, 288–9, 292–3, 336, 414
    argument over newspaper articles and Kaiser 418–22
Graf, Reinhold 200
'Grant' (American in Yatung) 305
Grant, Madison 163
'The Great Memorandum' 152
Great Prayer *see* Mönlam Chenmo
Great White Brotherhood myth (Blavatsky) 59
Greibel, General Walther 174–5
Grimm, Hans 157–8, 545*n*
Gross, Professor Walther 507
Grynszpan, Sindel and Herschel 294
guns, Tibetan request for 400–1
Günther, Hans F.K. ('Rassen') 134, 161–8, 260, 439, 487, 504
Gurkhas 241, 423, 533, 534
Guthrie, Captain James 421
Gyantse (Tibet) 316, 317, 322, 323–7, 417–21

Haagen, Professor Eugen 498
Habibullah, Amir 216
Hácha, Dr Emil 403–4
Haeckel, Ernst 63, 160
Hahn, Peter and Helena von 53
Hambro, Charles 220
Hangzhou (China) 106
Hankow (China) 86
Harrer, Heinrich 383, 425, 460
Harvest Festival, Operation 521
Hauck, Dr Walter 431–5
Hauner, Milan 217
Haushofer, Professor Karl 145, 161, 458
Hedin, Sven 33, 44, 75, 78, 79–80, 556*n*
  at Berlin Olympic Games 178
  'German Diary' 456–9
  launching of Schäfer's Institute 462, 463
  and Younghusband 225
Hegel 48
Heinrich, Gerd 455
Heinrich, Prince of Wittelsbach 127, 128, 129–30
Henderson, Philip 57
Henderson, Sir Nevile 220, 428
Henripierre, Pierre 517
Hentig, Dr Werner Otto von 216
Herder, Johann Gottfried 48, 60–1
Herero tribe (Namibia) 149, 161, 495
Herzog, Chaim 527
Hess, Rudolf 66, 100, 145, 169
Hesse, Herman 134
Heydrich, Reinhard 130
Hilton, James 338
Himalayan Club (London) 209
Himalayan range 310, 316–17
Himmler, Ernst (brother of HH) 128
Himmler, Gebhard (brother of HH) 127, 128
Himmler, Gebhard (father of HH) 127, 128
Himmler, Gudrun (daughter of HH) 136
Himmler, Heinrich 27, 100
  appearance 122–3, 130, 457
  attack on German academia 101–2
  attitude to religion 134–5

background and childhood 127–31
broadcast from Sudetenland 299
character 130–1
'Circle of Friends' club 474
and 'Final Solution' 455–6, 492, 499–500, 521
as Gestapo chief 137
letter to Schäfer on Tibet plot 447–8
military service 130–1
money-raising schemes 138
obsession with gold 479
occultism 137, 140
organizes Expedition's escape (1939) 425–6
passions and fantasies 137
patron of expedition 123, 232–3
as farmer 131, 132–3, 135–6
in Poland 450–4, 455–6
political career begins 134–7
(quotation) 122, 203
racial beliefs 38–40, 132, 133–4, 140
as student 132–3
suicide 527
use of Schäfer 31–3, 72–3, 175–81, 455, 476, 479–80
Venus project 488–9
visits Auschwitz 502
Wewelsburg 124–7, 526–7
Himmler, Margarete (née Boden) 135–6, 466
Hindenburg, President von 99, 100, 154
Hindu Kush 217
Hinduism and caste 167
Hirt, Dr August 44, 169, 494, 496–500, 523–6
and Beger 502–3, 518–19
history
German-speaking people 129
Sikkim 245–7, 284
Tibet 50, 305–6
Hitler, Adolf 25, 28, 76, 100
in Austria 226
and Eckart 134
gift to King of Nepal 382
and Hedin 456–7
letter from Reting Rimpoche 401–2
method of ruling 177–8
and Nazi Party rise 162
Nazi-Soviet Pact 437, 476
New Order 177, 186, 260, 285
on Poles 439
post-World War I 154
putsch (1923) 155, 162
quotation 172
return to Reich Chancellery 410
speeches to Wehrmacht 318
see also Austria; Czechoslovakia; Memelland; Poland; Sudetenland
Höhn, Reinhard 101
Höhne, Rolf 195–6
Holdich, Colonel Sir Thomas H. (quotation) 338
Holocaust controversy 489–91, 538
Hooker, Sir Joseph Dalton 275
Hooton, Dr Ernest A. 81
Hopkirk, Peter 443
Hörbiger, Hanns 181–2
Horizon series (BBC) 65
Höss, Rudolf 133, 460, 491, 513
'Hottentots' (Nama tribe, Namibia) 149, 488–9
House of Parliament (London) 214
Huang Mu-sung, General 357–9
Hugenberg, Alfred 157
Humboldt, Alexander von 547*n*
Husserl, Edmund 504

SS *Ichang* (steamer) 85, 87, 107
IG Farben 75, 87, 186
imperialism 64
incarnation 345, 348, 353, 360, 361–2
  mice 373
India 55–7, 62, 65, 98
  Assam 217–18
  British India security problems 216–18
  political geography 211–13
  search for 'German India' 145, 191–2
India Office (London) 210, 213, 215, 217–18, 232
  file on Schäfer 210, 219, 293, 329–30
Institute for Central Asian Research *see* Sven Hedin Institute
Institute for Practical Military Scientific Research 499
Isis Unveiled (Blavatsky) 55, 56, 58

Jachow (Szechuan) 120
Jacolliot, Louis 55
Jampey Yeshe (abbot of Reting) *see* Reting Rimpoche (Tibetan Regent)
Japan 209, 368
'Java Man' 79
Jena University 159–62
Jerusalem 505
Jesuits (Society of Jesus) 125, 128, 134, 346
Jews 28–9, 44, 63, 129, 319
  linked with Bolshevism 153
  threat to Nordic culture 165
  see also anti-Semitism; genocide
Jigme Dorje Denjongpa 531
Jigme Tering (son of Tering Raja) 284, 355, 382
Johst, Hanns 451
Jokhang Temple (Lhasa) 373–4, 394–5
Jones, Sir William 61
Jyekundo (Tibet) 115–17

Kaiser Bahadur Thapa 248–50, 251, 252, 266, 279
  attacked by dog 383
  in Khampa Dzong 281–4
  and Rabden Kazi 306, 308
  Schäfer's attachment to 315–16, 414, 418–19, 422–3
  sorry end to his story 424–7, 531–3
Kalmyck people (Tibet) 53
Kangchendzonga, Mt. 241, 247, 254–5, 266, 279, 531
Kangra La Pass 280
Kant, Immanuel 61
Karo La Pass 330–1, 416
Karshag (government) *see* Tibet, Karshag (government)
Kastell-Rüdenhausen, Wulf Dietrich zu 191
Kasten, Frederick 525, 528
katas see scarves, white
Kater, Michael 191, 444, 461, 463, 493, 497
Kelsang Gyatso (of Lachen) 265, 534
Keppler, Wilhelm 474
Kerrl, Reich Minister Dr 457
Kershaw, Ian 231, 438, 491
Kersten, Felix 122, 134
Keshab Pradhan 533
Ketsang Rimpoche 362–5
Khampa Dzong 254, 281
kiang, wild 265, 322
'King of Tharing' *see* Tering Raja
Kingdon Ward, Francis 218

Kipling, Rudyard (quotation) 46, 69, 228
Kirchiesen, Inge 217
Kiss, Edmund 183–5, 538, 546*n*
Klemperer, Victor (quotation) 25
Kompass publishing house 524
Koppe, Wilhelm 491
Kramer, Josef 511, 516–17
Kranefus, Fritz 474
Krause, Ernst 41, 46, 188, 196, 227
  at Dachau with Schäfer 464, 467, 471–3
  complete exoneration (1947) 482
  injured in rock fall 262
  joins Schäfer's Institute 462
  in Lhasa 369
  New Year celebrations 390, 394–5, 397–8
  problems in Khampa Dzong 281
  puzzle over photos of Regent Rimpoche 381
  in Sikkim 244, 264–5, 277
  summary of achievements 427, 535
Krebs, Albert 128–9, 137
Reichskristallnacht 295
Krupp arms manufacturers 157
Kühn, Alfred 174
Kuhn, Walter 453
Kulturvölker and *Naturvölker* ideas 146
Kumbela (Dechen Chödrön/ Thubten Kumbela) 354–5, 415
Kumbum Monastery 328, 363–4
Kyffhauser Castle archaeological dig 188
Kyi Chu Valley 333, 394, 397, 408

Laatsch, Adolf (#112118) 514
Lachen 261–2
Laithwaite, J. G. 238
Lamaism 47, 90, 95
Lamb, Alistair 350
Land of Lipp (Westphalia) 125
Landé, Margarete 505–10, 523–4
Landling, Egon 508
Landon, Perceval 311
League of Nations 178
Lebensraum 82, 145, 157, 161, 458
leeches 254
Lehmann, Julius 162–4
Lemberger, Jean 516
Lepcha people of Sikkim (Rongpa) 244, 247, 253, 256
Levi, Primo 493
Lezor (cook) 250
Lhamolatso Lake 360
Lhasa (Tibet) 33, 35–7, 106, 204
  1938 Expedition enters 334–7
  Austin cars 353
  beggars' feast 393
  British mission and wireless station 358–60
  condition of the city (1939) 369–77
  Jokhang temple 370, 373–41, 394–5
  Lingkor (sacred way) 374–7
  National Assembly (1936) 361, 395
  Potala Palace 334–5, 337, 341–2, 375–6, 379
    Germans visit 377–82
  Schäfer's secret objective 211
  State Oracle (Nechung) 335, 339, 395–6
  tombs of God-kings 376
  trade goods 371
  untouchables (*ragyapa*) 377
  variety of races 370–2
  Younghusband in 224
  see also Richardson, Hugh

Lichtenecker, Hans 156, 159
Lifton, Robert Jay 510
Lightfoot, Captain G. S. 218
Lingkharshee people (Tibet) 114
Lingkor (sacred way in Lhasa) 374–7
Lingma Thang 309
The Link journal 222
Linlithgow, Victor Hope, Lord 224, 232, 238, 425
(quotation) 408
Schäfer's newspaper article 420
List, Guido von 132
Litang (Tibet) 111
Liu Hsiang (Chinese warlord) 109
Liu Wen-hui, General 84, 357
Lloyd, Peter (British Everest Expedition) 262
Lobsang Drakpa 343–4
Loibl, Anton 138, 185
Lombroso, Cesare 81
London 207–8, 214–16
Long March (1934) 105, 110
Lopez, Donald 338
Ludendorff, General 153
Ludlow, Frank 326
Lufthansa airline 217
lunar eclipse 290–1
Lungshar, Tsipön (Dorje Tsegyal) 354–7
Luschan, Felix von 146, 148, 149–50
Lysenko, Trofim 193

Ma Pu-fang, General 84, 113, 117, 328, 357, 363–4
MacDonald, Brigadier James 312–13
Mackenzie, Major 324
Madagascar Plan 490
Mail on Sunday 537
Manchuria 105
Mandoy (taxidermist) 250
Mann, Thomas 154
Manning (traveller with Younghusband) 369
Mao Tse-tung 70, 94, 353
maps *see* geography
Maraini, Fosco 235, 246, 317, 343
marginal people 377
Markham, Captain S. F. 527
'master race' theory *see* Aryan race
May, Karl 73, 74, 76
measuring people 144–7, 161, 164–5, 170–1
Altiplano 183
Auschwitz 513–16
Schäfer's expedition 227, 242, 412
Tibet 314–15
medical experiments in camps 465–70
skull and skeleton collection 511–19
medicine on 1938 Expedition 243, 256–7, 262, 264, 289–90
Mein Kampf (Hitler) 82, 89, 135, 151, 160, 206
Memelland 406
Miechalowski, Fr Leo 467
military collapse in Germany 153–4
Mingma (Krause's assistant) 279
Mittersill, Schloss 460, 463, 480, 520
Molotov, Vyacheslav 427
monasteries 347–9, 351–2, 357, 360, 371
New Year celebrations 389–90, 393–6
Möndro (Khenrab Künsang Möndrong) 352–3, 382, 386–9, 398–9, 410

Mongolians 342–3, 346
Monist League 64
Mönlam Chenmo (New Year Great Prayer) 389, 393, 394, 395–7
monsoon conditions 108–10, 239–40, 255–6
Monumenta Germaniae Historica 129
Morning of the Magicians (Pauwels and Bergier) 537
Morton, Samuel 144
Moscow 81–2
mountain-climbing ambitions 209–10
Mountains, Buddhas and Bears (Schäfer) 29, 82, 98, 177
Muli (Tibet) 97
mummies discovered in Ürümchi (China) 537
Munich 132–3, 288, 317, 463, 508
Museum of Natural History (New York) 191
Muslims in Waffen-SS 522
Mussolini, Benito 288

Namibia 149, 157, 489
Nanga Parbat 210
Nangartse 328
Nanking (China) 85
National Archives (Washington) 464
National Geographic 78, 88
National Socialist Association of Teachers 196
nationalism
  German 160–1
  and race 63–4
Nationalpreis 189
Natu La Pass 296, 299, 300–3, 304
Natural History Museum (London) 207
Naturvölker and *Kulturvölker* ideas 146–7
Natzweiler/Struthof concentration camp 485, 493, 498, 511
  prisoners from Auschwitz 515–19
  prisoners sent to Dachau 524
Nazi Party 76, 99–100, 134–5
  formation and rise 154, 160, 162
  and German businessmen 474–5
Office for Racial Purity 507
Nazi-Soviet Pact 437, 476
Nazism 438–9
Neame, Brigadier Philip 359
Nehru, Jawaharlal 238
Nepean, Lieutenant E. Y. 359
Nethang 334
New Order 177, 186, 260
New Year in Tibet 389–99
Ngoloks 106, 108, 115, 116, 208, 399, 444
Nicholas II, Tsar 303
Nichols, Captain (SS *Ichang*) 85, 86
Niederhagen Forest concentration camp 126
Niederkirchnerstrasse (Berlin) 26–34
Niedermayer, Dr Oskar von 216
Niemüller, Pastor 214
'Night of the Long Knives' 137
Nobel Prize 189
Nomoto, Jinzo 368
Nordhu Dondup 359, 442
Nordic race *see* Aryan race theory
Norway 489
NSDAP *see* Nazi Party
Nuremberg trials 74, 137
Nyang Chu valley 322, 328

occultism 137, 140, 143, 373, 528
Ohlendorf, Otto 101, 477–8

Olcott, Henry Steel 54, 60
Olympic Games (Berlin) 28, 80, 178
O'Malley, Captain (medical officer) 326
On Secret Service East of Constantinople (Hopkirk) 443
opium 91, 108, 116
Oriental and India Office *see* India Office
OSS *see* CIA
Ossietzky, Carl von 189
Oster, Hans 447

Padfield, Peter 130, 446, 466, 467
paganism and ritual 126–7, 132, 135, 297–9, 373
Pallas, Peter Simon 48
Pan German culture 63, 65
Pan Germans 63
Panchen Lama 57–8, 84, 106–7, 282, 357–8
  and Ketsang Rimpoche 362–3
pandas 90, 92–4, 175
Pänsy (Schäfer's servant) 250, 277–8
Papen, Franz von 99, 100
Passang (sherpa) 251–2
The Passing of the Great Race (Grant) 163
Pauwels, Louis 537
Pavelic, Ante 522
Pede 331
Peiper, Joachim 'Jochen' 452
Perl, Gisella 513
Phari (Chumbi Valley) 310–16
physiognomy and racial types 164–6
  see also measuring people
Pius XII, Pope (Eugenio Pacelli) 318–19
plant breeding 193
Plessen, von (German consul-general, Calcutta) 234
plots against British Empire 444–6
Pohl, Oswald 504
Poland 36, 406, 428, 438–9, 447–8, 450–4
  Danzig 207, 318, 406, 438
Polte (member of Himmler's staff) 182
polyandry 371
Posnansky, Arthur 183, 538
Potthast, Hedwig 466
Pottinger, Sir Henry 86
Pradhan, Keshab 251, 423
Pradin, Michael *see* Charol, Michael
Prinz-Albrecht-Strasse 8 (Berlin) 27–34
Proctor, Robert 187
prostitution 372
The Protocols of the Elders of Zion 134, 180
Przemyśl (Poland) 451–4
Pu Yi Hsüan-t'ung, last Emperor of China 350, 353
Public Record Office (Kew) 442
'Pyrmont Protocol' 184
Quedlinburg Cathedral 195–6

Rabden Kazi (interpreter) 296, 306, 312, 414, 417
The Racial Elements of European History (Günther) 164
Racial Lore of the German Volk (Fischer) 164
racism *see* Aryan race
Rascher, Dr Sigmund 464, 465–74
Rasmussen, Knud 139
Rath, Ernst vom 294
Ratweek, Operation 522

rearmament 318
Red Idol Gorge 322
Reichskriegsflagge organization 135
reincarnation *see* incarnation
Reineck, Hermann 514
Reinhardt Plan 177
religion and power 343
  see also Buddhism
reparation in post-war Germany 155–6
'resettlement' policy 453, 455, 461, 489, 492
Reting Rimpoche, Regent (Jampey Yeshe) 355, 360–3, 379–83
  request for guns 401
  Schäfer's final interview 400–3
Rhineland 178
Ribbentrop, Joachim von 108, 427–8, 438, 445
Richardson, Hugh 41, 71, 203–6, 213–14, 219–20, 293–5
  Darjeeling meeting with Schäfer 241–2
  extension of Expedition's time 389
  Gyantse meeting with Schäfer 325
  in Lhasa 335–6, 359–60
  mail as source of dispute 384
  outmanoeuvred 382–3
  'rearguard action' against expedition 330
  relationship with Tibetans 383
  report on Schäfer 366–8, 414
Rimmer, Dr Josef 479
Rinzin Dorje Ringang 359, 382
The Rise of Mankind (Wirth) 138
Rite of Strict Observance society 53–4
Ritter, Tod und Teufel (Günther) 134, 163
ritual and myth 39–41
rivers of Asia 310, 332
Rock, Joseph 78, 88, 91, 97–8, 209, 548*n*
Roerich, Nicholas 52
Röhm, Ernst 136, 137
Roof of the World (Schäfer) 177
Roosevelt, President Franklin D. 482
Rosenberg, Alfred 180, 217, 449, 541*n*
Royal Asiatic Society 61
Rübel, Dr 510, 515
Rubens Hotel (London) 208
'Rugby Boys' 354, 386, 388, 552*n*
A Rum Affair (Sabbagh) 193
RuSHA (Race and Settlement Office) 169, 188, 197, 489, 497
Russian Revolution (1917) 153–4, 494
Rust, Bernhard 462

Saarland 178
Sabbagh, Karl 193
Sachsenhausen concentration camp 126
Sakya-pas sect ('Red Hats') 344
Sanskrit 61, 62
Sarajevo (Bosnia-Herzegovina) 151
Savitri Devi 538
scarves, white (*katas*) 378, 392
Schäfer, Ernst 27–34, 41–3, 44–6
  ambush in earlier expedition 69–71
  attachment to Kaiser 315–16, 414, 418–19, 422–3
  attacks Dr Hauck on train (1942) 431–5
  background and early life 74–6
  and Beger 196–7

Schäfer, Ernst (*cont.*)
behaviour
on 1938 Expedition 233–4, 236–7, 263, 266, 291, 414
divided personality 435–6
believed to be spy 234–5
celebrity on return from Expedition 437
complaints about companions 256
complicity destroys his defence 455–6
disagreements with Himmler 446, 475–6
Dolan's first expedition 77–97
Dolan's second expedition 108–21
film of Tibet *see Geheimnis Tibet*
funding of expedition 185–7
and Hedin in Munich 458–9, 461–2
with Himmler in Poland 450–5
illness on 1938 Expedition 283
India Office file 210, 219, 329–30
joins SS 100–1, 102
in Khampa Dzong 281–2
in London 214–16, 218–25, 227
meets Tering Raja's minister 276–8
passion for hunting 74–5, 92–4, 96, 97–9, 118
burns animal skins 120
fatal accident 197–200
shapi hunt 268–72
in Sikkim 250–1, 264–6, 275
Tibet 313, 413
plot to invite rebellion in Tibet (1939) 439–50
political motivation 194–5
prisoner in Nuremberg 431, 435–6, 454, 470–2, 473–4, 475, 480–2
remarriage 436–7
remembered in Tibet 531–4
return to Germany (1936) 177
as scientist 188, 190–1
in Shanghai 172–5
in Sikkim 241–89
surrender to Allies 479–80
Venezuela (1949–54) 482
wooed by Himmler 175–6, 179–81, 182–3, 184–7
writings 71–2
see also Caucasus Expedition; German Tibet Expedition (1938); Gould, Sir Basil; Kaiser; Lhasa; Sven Hedin Institute; Tering Raja
Schäfer Expedition *see* German Tibet Expedition
Schäfer, Hertha (née Volz) 178–9, 198–200, 236, 266, 423, 437
Schäfer, Ursula (née von Gartzen) 436, 480
Scheel, Gauleiter of Salzburg 463, 464
Schellenberg, Walter 100–1, 124
Schilling, Klaus 465
Schinkel, Karl Friedrich 27
Schirmer, Erwin 188
Schlagintweit, Hermann von 147
Schlegel, Friedrich 61–2
Schlieffen, Alfred von 152
Schorfheide 197–200
Schröder, Kurt von 100
Schuschnigg, Kurt 207, 225–6
Schweibus district (German-Polish border) 200
science
as cover for espionage 442–3; for

evil 40–5, 64, 143–50, 164, 260–1
see also anthropology; geophysics
Himmler's absurd experiments 479
'racial' 169–70
and totalitarian regime 187–90
Sea of Tethys (ancient) 309, 317
Second World War *see* World War II
The Secret Doctrine (Blavatzky) 58, 60, 64, 192
Seekt, General Hans von 105
Seven Tribes (Tibet) 113–14
sexual practices 257, 278–9, 348, 374, 381
Shakabpa, Tsepon 360–1
Shambhala myth 51–2, 59
Shanghai 83, 97, 105, 106, 118, 172–4
shapi hunt 268–72, 533–4
Shigatse (second city in Tibet) 417–18
Shirer, William 226, 288
Sievers, Wolfram 137–8, 185, 461–2, 464, 467, 472–3
and Brandt 503
hanged (1946) 527
racial murder plans 487, 494–5, 498–9, 502
reports to Himmler 515–16
skeleton collection 524–5
Sikkim 35, 47, 233–4, 235, 241–53, 255–6
file on Tibet Expedition 426–7
politics 245–7, 284, 349
Schäfer's diaries 275
see also Gangtok (Sikkim)
Siliguri (Plain of Bengal) 239–40, 529–30
Simla 236–9
Sining (Tibet) 117–18, 176
Sino-Japanese War 105
Sippenbuch (SS clan book) 189
Six, Franz 101
skeleton collection for research 511, 524–5
skulls
Auschwitz experiments 494–6, 510–11, 518
one stolen in Tibet 95
sky burial in Tibet 110–11, 346, 377
Society of Jesus *see* Jesuits
Solomon Islanders 161
Sönam Gyatso 344–5
Sonderzug Heinrich train journey 450–4
Soviet Russia 438, 476
see also Barbarossa, Operation; Nazi-Soviet Pact
Spain 318
Spectator 490
Speer, Albert 25, 73–4, 83, 178
spiritualism 54–5
SS 26–7, 100–1, 136–7
Einsatzgruppen 439, 486
expeditions department 180
lifestyle near Munich 468
membership 39–40, 41–42, 100–2
science 37–8, 195
as security empire 39
as state within state 136–7
Waffen-SS (Handschar) 485–6, 522–3
Wewelsburg Castle 124–6, 526
Stalin, Josef 427–8, 491
The Stanzas of Dzyan (Blavatsky) 58
Stark, Johannes 187
State Oracle (Ta Lama Rimpoche, Nechung) 335, 339, 395–6

Stölze, Paula 128
Strasbourg 485, 498, 499, 525
Strasser, Gregor 135
Strunk, Joseph 48
Struthof *see* Natzweiler/Struthof
Sudetenland 207, 231, 287
Sven Hedin Institute for Inner Asian Research 44, 73, 436, 458–64, 479–80, 511, 518
swastika symbol 96, 124, 127, 132
  in Tibet 322–3, 325, 383
Sykes, Christopher 443
Szechuan (China) 87

Ta Lama Rimpoche *see* State Oracle
Table Talk (Hitler) 182, 187
Tachienlu (Tibet) 90, 96
Taffel, Menachem 511–12
Tang La Pass 316–17, 319
Tashi Namygal 246
Tawang area (near Tibet) 218
taxidermy 84–5, 250
Tej Thapa (son of Kaiser) 532–3
Tering Raja 246, 276, 279, 284–5
  history of family 284
  second visit 327
Teutoberger Forest (Westphalia) 125, 151
Thanggu base camp 262–4
Thapa *see* Kaiser Bahadur Thapa; Tej Thapa
Theosophical Movement 55, 64–5
Third Reich 26
Thubten Gyatso *see* Dalai Lama, 13th Dalai Lama
Thule Society and myth 132, 134, 184
Thutob Namygal 246
Tibet 29, 32, 46–51, 69–71, 79–80
  and Britain 349–52, 358–60, 364–5
  and China 342–4, 346, 349–51, 353–4, 357–9
  borderland 78, 90–1, 94, 301–2
  Chumbi area 301, 304–5, 309
  exhibitions and lectures at Schloss Mittersill (1943) 520
  feudalism 340–2
  geology and geography 309–11
  history 50, 305, 340–4, 536–7
  industrialization 353
  Kashag (government) 216, 219–20, 227, 234–5, 285–6
    apology to Schäfer 400
    first established 347
    and Lungshar 355–6
    permission granted 292–3
    and Younghusband 320–1
  monasteries 347–9, 351–2, 357, 360
  New Year celebrations 389–99, 393–6
  political geography 212–13
  regency *see* Jampey Yeshe (abbot of Reting)
  sky burial 110–11
  transportation corvée system 308
  in Western mythology 52, 56–9
  see also Blavatsky, Helena; China, relationship with Tibet; Dalai Lama; German Tibet Expedition; *individual places* e.g. Lhasa; Shigatse
Tibet ruft (Schäfer) 94
The Times 420, 490
Timothy (Christian Tibetan servant) 267–8, 534
'Tin Cans' 438
Tista Valley 254–6
Tiwanaku (South American Altiplano) 183
Tolstoy, Major Ilia 482–3

trade in Lhasa 371
Trapchi Lotrü Laygung (Electrical Machine Office) 353
Treaty of Versailles *see* Versailles Treaty
Tredilinka residence (Lhasa) 337, 368, 372–3, 378–9
Trimön Shapé 359–61, 416
Tringleh (sherpa) 70–1, 114
Trongdra Regiment 354–5
Trotha, General Lothar von 149
Tsarong Dzasa (Shapé) 205–6, 351–3, 378, 382
Tucci, Giuseppe 376
Tucci, Professor Giuseppe 216
Tuex, Professor (botanist) 454
Tulku, Sengchen 57–8

Urchs, Dr Oswald 236

Van Pelt, Robert Jan 492, 513
Vavilov, Nikolai Ivanovic 193
The Veda 167
venereal disease 289–90, 385
Venus project 488–9, 557–8*n*
Versailles Treaty (1919) 82, 131, 155, 178
Virchow, Rudolf 148, 495
Volk ohne Raum (People without Space) (Grimm) 157
Völkischer Beobachter newspaper 180, 187
Volz, Hertha *see* Schäfer, Hertha
Vrba, Rudolf 502
Waffen-SS *see* SS, Waffen-SS
Wagner, Richard 63
Wallace, Alfred Russel 55
Walton, Sir John 215–16, 219, 227
Wandervogel movement 83
Wang (expedition member) 92, 95
Washi tribe (Tibet) 111–12
Wassmuss, Wilhelm 443
Weber, Josef (#15386) 514
Wegener, Alfred 138
Weigold, Hugo 77, 81, 97
Weimar Republic 76, 157, 177
Weizsäcker, Ernst von 438
Wewelsburg Castle and village (Westphalia) 39, 124–6
White, John Claude *see* Claude White, John
Wienert, Karl 41, 188–9, 257–61, 266, 289, 535
- complete exoneration (1947) 482
- devoted to taking sightings 306, 307, 314, 315, 317, 413, 425
- Himmler's search for gold 479
- joins Schäfer's Institute 462

Wilhelm, Kaiser 154, 155
Wiligut, Karl Maria 139–40, 229
Wimmer, Josef 498
wireless station in Lhasa 358–60, 383, 384
Wirth, Hermann 138–9
Wisleceny, SS Captain Dieter 137
Wolff, Karl 451, 516–18
World Ice Theory 181–3, 184, 259
World War I 130–1, 151–6, 160–1
World War II 36, 214
- Caucasus campaign 476–9
- gathering storm 287–8, 317–19, 382
- non-aggression pact with Soviets 427–8, 476
- *see also* Barbarossa, Operation

Wuchnow, Mechthilde von *see* Clauss, Mechthilde
Wüst, Professor Walther 458, 461–3

Yad Vashem and Clauss 524
yaks 79, 88–9, 175, 330

Yangtze river 85–8, 97, 107–8, 119–20
Yarlung Valley 411–12
Yatung (Tibet) 306–8
Yeshe Dolma 246
yeti fears 263
Yigtsang Office (religious authority) 333
Younghusband, Sir Francis 213, 223–5, 234, 302–4, 350
  in Chumbi Valley 306
  in Karo La 331
  massacre in Tuna and Guru 320–1
  in Phari 312
  (quotation) 300
  Schäfer follows his plan 275, 280, 302–3
  on Sikkim 241, 244
Yugoslavia 522–3
Yumbu Lagang fortress 412

Zemu Glacier (Kangchendzonga) 265
Zerempil (Russian arms dealer) 303
Zetland, Lord (Secretary of State for India) 215
Zhenjiang (China) 85
Zimmerman, Major (anti-British plot) 445
Zundel, Ernst 537–8
Zweig, Stefan 152
Zyklon-B gas 491, 516–17